THE LATIN AMERICA READERS
Series edited by Robin Kirk and Orin Starn

THE ARGENTINA READER
Edited by Gabriela Nouzeilles and Graciela Montaldo

THE BRAZIL READER
Edited by Robert M. Levine and John J. Crocitti

THE COSTA RICA READER
Edited by Steven Palmer and Iván Molina

THE CUBA READER
Edited by Aviva Chomsky, Barry Carr, and Pamela Maria Smorkaloff

THE ECUADOR READER
Edited by Carlos de la Torre and Steve Striffler

THE GUATEMALA READER
Edited by Greg Grandin, Deborah T. Levenson, and Elizabeth Oglesby

THE MEXICO READER
Edited by Gilbert M. Joseph and Timothy J. Henderson

THE PERU READER, 2ND EDITION
Edited by Orin Starn, Iván Degregori, and Robin Kirk

THE WORLD READERS
Series edited by Robin Kirk and Orin Starn

THE ALASKA NATIVE READER
Edited by Maria *Shaa Tláa* Williams

THE CZECH READER
Edited by Jan Bažant, Nina Bažantová, and Frances Starn

THE INDONESIA READER
Edited by Tineke Hellwig and Eric Tagliacozzo

THE RUSSIA READER
Edited by Adele Barker and Bruce Grant

THE SRI LANKA READER

The Guatemala Reader

THE

GUATEMALA

READER

HISTORY, CULTURE, POLITICS

Greg Grandin, Deborah T. Levenson, and Elizabeth Oglesby, eds.

DUKE UNIVERSITY PRESS   *Durham and London*   2011

Printed in the United States of America on acid-free paper ∞
Typeset in Monotype Dante by BW&A Books, Inc.
Library of Congress Cataloging-in-Publication Data appear
on the last printed page of this book.

To the memory of Quetzaly Angélica Tzita Mejía
Joyabaj, October 28, 1999–July 29, 2010

And to the friendship of Clara Arenas, José García
Noval, and Arturo Taracena—clear minds, strong
hearts, and raised fists.

Cuando despertó, el dinosaurio todavía estaba allí.

(Upon awakening, the dinosaur was still there.)

—The story "El dinosaurio," shown here in its entirety,
was written by the Guatemalan author Augusto
Monterroso in 1959.

Contents

Illustrations

Acknowledgments

Over the long course of writing this *Reader* the editors incurred so many debts that it would take a registry as long as the book to list them all. In addition to all the writers, artists, photographers, scholars, editors, activists, and publishers who generously granted permission to publish their work, we would like to thank Clara Arenas, Ximena Morales of Prohibido Olvidar, Derrill Bazzy, John Womack, Federico Velásquez, Leslye Rivera Juárez, Sonia Alvarez, Mary Jo McConahay, Liza Grandia, Tom Melville, Dina Bursztyn, Jessica Lagunas, Anastasia Mejía, José Manuel Mayorga, Jessica Masaya, Yolanda Colom, Tani Adams, Moisés Barrios, Isabel Ruiz, Edwin Rabinales, Daniela Triadan, Carol Smith, José García Noval, Arturo Taracena, Gustavo Palma, Helen Mack, Carlos Sánchez, Carlos Beristain, Ana Estrada Levenson, Jasmin Estrada Levenson, Isabel Recinos, Anabella Acevedo, Julia González, Diane Nelson, Richard Adams, Linda Green, Martha Few, Brinton Lykes, Matt Creelman, Emma Maasch, Michelle Switzer, Amy Ross, Kile Smith (the curator of the Fleisher Collection of Orchestral Music), Gary Galván (who helped identify the Castillo music composition), Luis Pedro Taracena, Kate Doyle, George Lovell, Karen Dakin, Jean-Marie Simon, Nancy McGirr, Juan Antonio Martinez Mateo and the Centro Cultural de España in Guatemala City, James Robertson, and Ketillonia Publishing.

The editors wish to mention in particular the work of Luis Solano. Luis's keen understanding of Guatemalan politics and economics runs through this *Reader* in the many selections he suggested and the generous advice he gave to the editors. We are inspired by the friendship and commitment of Marcie Mersky and Paula Worby. Timothy Smith and Robert Scott insightfully contributed to putting together parts 1 and 2. Chris Lutz kindly read part 2, offering very useful suggestions. Ginny Burnett suggested a wonderful text and helped find a great image. Kirsten Weld helped with the translation, skillfully capturing subtle nuances and meanings. Michelle Chase doggedly tracked down many an obstinate permission. Ashley McLaren provided excellent research assistance. The Centro de Investigaciones Regionales de Mesoamérica (CIRMA) is a national treasure in Guatemala, and we thank Lucía Pellecer and Anaís García, from CIRMA's *fototeca,* for many of the book's images. Thelma

Porres, CIRMA's archivist, provided key assistance, helping to nail down elusive references. We also thank J. T. Way and Claudia Alonzo for helping to track down sources. Valia Garzón, art historian par excellence, is responsible for the (re)discovery of Julio Zadik and graciously communicated with the Zadik estate for permission to use his photographs. Two rounds of anonymous reviewers made excellent suggestions. The Center for Latin American Studies at the University of Arizona and Boston College provided generous financial assistance during the final stage of manuscript preparation. Duke University Press's editorial interns, especially Rebecca Mormino and Mitch Fraas, performed heroic work, especially in securing rights. Beth Maudlin, Duke's art editor, helped us enormously in putting together the volume's illustrations. And, of course, we need to thank our editors, Valerie Millholland and Miriam Angress, who waited patiently—even when we were less than patient ourselves—for us to finally finish.

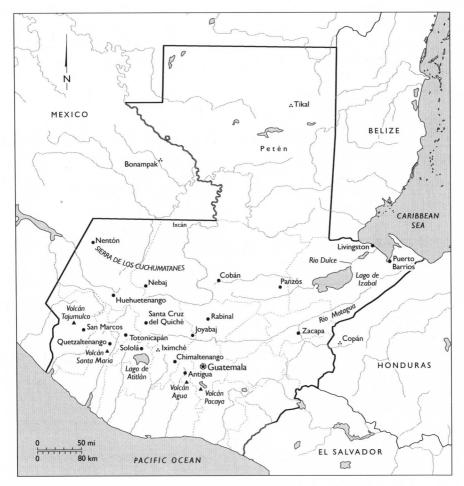

Map of Guatemala. Drawn by Bill Nelson for this volume.

Introduction

Most people in the United States likely know Guatemala for two things: tourism and terrorism. Almost two million people visit Guatemala every year. They take in the country's many Maya and colonial ruins, stunning landscapes, and mountain lakes, and they visit its picturesque towns and verdant lowland rainforests. At the same time, over the last thirty years the country has become practically synonymous with government-backed political repression. The CIA's 1954 orchestration of a coup that overthrew a democratic government is so well documented that it has become the example of choice by teachers, historians, reporters, and politicians when they want to illustrate the misuse of United States power in Latin America. In turn, this coup precipitated an appallingly violent civil war that lasted nearly four decades. By the time the war ended, government agents had killed hundreds of thousands of Guatemalans, committed more than six hundred massacres in indigenous communities, and completely razed hundreds of Maya villages in a campaign the United Nations ruled to be genocidal.

Tourism and terrorism have been intertwined since Guatemala's founding in 1821, when the country, roiled by war, began to attract the attention of amateur archaeologists, ethnographers, and naturalists, mostly from the United States and Great Britain. In their dispatches home, published widely in magazines, broadsheets, and travel books, these travelers depicted Guatemala as a beautiful but strife-ridden land. One of them, John Stephens, entered Guatemala from the Caribbean along the lush, green Rio Dulce in 1839. In his subsequent best-selling book, *Incidents of Travel*, Stephens speaks of the river when he asks: "Could this be the portal to a land of volcanoes and earthquakes, torn and distracted by civil war?" He had come to survey Maya ruins, and he landed in the country at the tail end of a massive insurrection led by Rafael Carrera, an illiterate peasant swineherd. Stephens's book tacks between celebrating the wonders of half-buried, vine-wrapped acropolises and luridly relating the atrocities of the "tumultuous mass" of the "half-naked savages" who supported Carrera. In one widely excerpted passage, Stephens writes that when he had "asked the Indians" who had made one particularly intricate set of stone carvings, "their dull answer was

'Quién sabe?' 'Who knows?'" Stephens didn't know either, but he was sure it wasn't the Guatemalans he met on his journey. "Architecture, sculpture and painting, all the arts which embellish life, had flourished in this overgrown forest; beauty, ambition and glory had lived and passed away, none knew that such things had been, or could tell of their past existence," he wrote. "No remnant of this race hangs around the ruins."[1]

The romance of a lost civilization capable of sublime achievements, and the tragedy of a lost country—lost not to the mists of time but to an inability to overcome its culture of violence: these twin genres continue to define the way foreigners write and think about Guatemala. The persistence of these themes has as much to do with a tendency to "orientalize" the Maya as it does with Cold War politics. In 1954, Washington's nearly year-long campaign to destabilize the government of president Jacobo Arbenz led to a rapid decline in foreign visitors. But after the overthrow of Arbenz and the installation of a pliant government, the United States began to invest heavily in tourism. Major chains built hotels; Washington funded the construction of roads and the modernization of the country's airport so it could handle jets; and the Guatemalan government relaxed its visa and currency-exchange requirements. While Arbenz was president, the US press had relentlessly depicted him as a threat and his country as a shambles; now it touted Guatemala as the "Land of the Quetzal" and of "Eternal Spring," the "Switzerland of the Tropics." The New York Times played an enthusiastic role in painting Guatemala in the worst possible terms in 1954. Three years later, it was encouraging people to come and see what the Eisenhower administration was calling a "showcase for democracy": the "volcano-rimmed capital has undergone a great change since the last months of the Communist-infiltrated regime of Jacobo Arbenz," the Times wrote. "The streets are lively with tourists, a big new hotel has opened, others are planned and official figures confirm that more vacationists are coming here to relax."[2]

Over the next three decades, tourism and terrorism grew in tandem; the infrastructures of both were built with US aid. The national treasury needed the revenue, but the Guatemalan government also promoted tourism to counter the bad publicity that its mass murders of unionists, students, politicians, intellectuals, and peasant activists had generated. In May 1980, just a few months after security forces firebombed the Spanish embassy and burned scores of people alive (including the father of future Nobel laureate Rigoberta Menchú), the minister of tourism, Alvaro Arzú—who would go on to be president—told reporters that "violence is no obstacle for the growth of tourism." Arzú was then in the middle of carrying out a major renovation of the country's most famous archaeological site, Tikal, to make it more accessible to travelers. Officials like Arzú did their best to keep the war away from the "Maya Trail," even as soldiers were reducing Maya villages to ashes. But sometimes the conflict couldn't be kept from intruding, as this *Washington Post* story describes:

> In Antigua, the center of the tourist route and Guatemala's magnificent colonial capital partially destroyed by earthquakes, a group of French tourists recently strolled around the town hall. They started taking pictures of a woman dressed in native embroideries. Some took close-ups of the two children she carried, one in a shawl on her back. Suddenly the woman starting crying and shouting and the bewildered French group turned away. Via an interpreter, the woman later explained in her native Quiche language what was on her mind. "The soldiers came and took away my husband. He is the father of my children and never been dishonest in his life. Until they give him back to me I cannot go away."[3]

More than 160 years have passed since the publication of *Incidents of Travel*, and much has subsequently been written about Guatemala by foreigners and Guatemalans alike, now including this *Reader*. Similar to other volumes in this series, this book is meant to be a broad introduction to the country. The editors of the anthology have struggled to avoid the facile equation of Guatemala's history, culture, and politics with its long experience of conflict, racism, and violence. Guatemalan history pulls together in one story compelling issues of colonialism, imperialism, and brutality carried out in the name of corporate rapacity. Yet it does so almost too neatly, in a way that has allowed much of the voluminous writing on the country over the last two decades to reduce its inhabitants to stock characters in a one-dimensional morality play. Guatemala as a real place—one with joys, creativities, social solidarities, and routine sorrows that can't be reduced to a litany of resistance and repression—often gets effaced in this narrative. Thus, in what follows we have included the opinions of politicians, activists, and scholars, as well as poems, songs, plays, jokes, fiction, recipes, art, photographs, and an opera score—selections that capture the diversity of Guatemala life. We mean "diverse" not just in the obvious sense of ethnicity or social class but also in terms of breaking free, however fleetingly, from historical oppressions and cruel routines, small liberations that are captured in snapshots of everyday life.

Yet Guatemala is not just any country. For a small nation, it has a weighty history, paralleling and often driving broader Latin American conflicts. In October 1944, Guatemalans overthrew a thirteen-year dictatorship. For one full decade thereafter, two democratically elected presidents—Juan José Arévalo and Jacobo Arbenz—presided over a series of impressive political and social reforms, including an expansion of voting rights, abolition of forced labor, ratification of a social-democratic constitution, adoption of a labor code, creation of a national health system and social security, extension of public education, and, most famously, the implementation of an ambitious agrarian reform. Guatemala's "October Revolution" was the vanguard of a continental wave of social-democratic reform that would wash over the hemisphere during the two years following the end of the Second World War. As conservatives elsewhere in Latin America leveraged the dawning Cold War to regroup and push back, democracy in Guatemala deepened. The country became one of the few bright spots—as illustrated by Pablo Neruda's selection in this volume—in an otherwise bleak hemispheric landscape.

The CIA's June 1954 overthrow of Arbenz was one of the most consequential events in Latin American history. It was a full-spectrum coup, distinguished from previous US interventions in Latin America and elsewhere because it drew on every aspect of US power, using politics, economics, diplomacy, psychology, and mass media to destabilize Arbenz's government. This campaign to unseat Arbenz was itself a vanguard action, not of democracy but of three decades of political polarization and escalating government terror on the continent. Well before the Cuban revolution, this event radicalized a generation of Latin American reformers. For instance, a young Argentine doctor, after completing a motorcycle trip through Chile and the Andes, found himself in Guatemala, where he became close to the Partido Guatemalteco del Trabajo—the small but active Communist Party responsible for many of the October Revolution's most ambitious democratic reforms—and watched the CIA's destabilization campaign unfold. "This is a country in which one can open up one's lungs and fill them with democracy," Ernesto "Che" Guevara wrote his aunt in Argentina; "there are newspapers supported by United Fruit that, if I were Arbenz, I would have closed down in five minutes, because they are shameful and yet they say what they like and contribute to the atmosphere that the USA likes." After the coup, when Guevara was about to seek asylum in the Argentine embassy, he wrote that the effort to build a more just society "has all gone by like a beautiful dream that one is bent upon continuing after one has woken up"—which of course he would seek to do, in Cuba and elsewhere.[4] (The coup also helped shape the anti-imperialist politics of author Gore Vidal, who considered himself a "Tory" and who lived in Antigua at the time; he had many pro-Arbenz politicians and artists as friends.)[5]

After 1954, Latin American reformers and nationalists increasingly viewed the United States not as a model to emulate, as they had done during the 1930s and 1940s, but a threat to be confronted. After Guevara fled to Mexico and joined Fidel Castro's revolutionary movement, he would explain the militancy of the Cuban revolution in these words: "Cuba will not be Guatemala." For its part, the United States would model its disastrous 1961 Bay of Pigs invasion of Cuba on its 1954 Guatemalan operation, a serious miscalculation that not only failed to topple Castro but further polarized hemispheric politics.

Back in Guatemala, the building of a counterinsurgent death-squad state quickly eroded whatever compromise-seeking center had survived 1954, thus leading to the start in 1960 of what is generally described as a thirty-six-year civil war. The conflict—more of an extended period of crisis politics than a recognizable civil war between two clearly defined opposing camps—was driven by, on the one side, diverse and increasingly militant peasant, worker, indigenous, and political movements and episodic armed insurgencies; on the other, murderous military and paramilitary forces financed by domestic economic elites and the United States. The conflict officially ended in 1996, but its climax took place between 1981 and 1983. During those years the military government launched a scorched-earth campaign against Maya communities, the savagery of which was matched only by historical memories of the Conquest. All told, the state killed two hundred thousand people, tortured tens of thousands more, drove hundreds of thousands into exile, and committed more than six hundred massacres. In some parts of the highlands, as much as eighty percent of the population was forced to leave their homes for a period of time. A subsequent investigation by the United Nations Comisión para el Esclarecimiento Histórico, a truth commission, called this genocide and said it was rooted in a long history of racial domination and subjugation of the Maya dating back to the sixteenth-century Spanish conquest.

To avoid a direct engagement with this violent history would in fact lead to a naturalization of violence. Consider how strange it would be for a comparable anthology on Germany to relegate Nazism, the Second World War, and the Holocaust to a few scattered entries alongside selections highlighting German beer or Bauhaus architecture. This would be unacceptable because political violence in Europe is considered a historical problem, something that needs to be explained, while episodes of repression in Latin America are often taken as a given, a fact of life, if not nature. We hope this volume, by fully considering Guatemala's half century of upheaval, is a small corrective to that tendency. In addition, a lack of attention to these issues would deny readers an opportunity to hear Guatemalans' views of their country. Nearly all of the revival in Guatemalan scholarship, literature, and art that has occurred since the war ended in 1996 has consisted of efforts to come to terms with either Guatemala's history of violence or the enduring inequalities and dislocations of its present, which are inevitably traced to that history. This is true both of those who lived through and survived the war and, showing a tenaciousness that is typically Guatemalan, of a new generation of writers and artists. As literary critic Anabella Acevedo writes in a piece included in this anthology, although there are generational disagreements over politics and interpretations of the past, there has been no postbellum retreat into aesthetics or alienated irony, which, in other places at other times, has commonly followed periods of mobilization and defeat.

History is palpable in Guatemala, and no analysis is possible without the *coyuntura*—or conjuncture—being set in its context. The three editors of this volume, and undoubtedly many of the readers of this volume, have attended presentations describing particular popular struggles in which the speaker will start with the Conquest, work her or his way through the foundation of the 1871 coffee state, the 1944 October Revolution and its 1954 demise, the massacres of the 1980s, and the 1996 peace accord before turning to the topic at hand. One of us even heard a similar narrative arc in Morganton, North Carolina, in the basement of a Catholic church, offered by Q'anjob'al Maya immigrants involved in a union campaign in a local chicken-processing plant. Guatemala has had two Nobel laureates, one for literature and the other for peace, but they both might as well have been for history, because their work shared a confrontation with socially determined structures of violence. "Our books do not search for a sensationalist or horrifying effect in order to secure a place for us in the republic of letters," said Miguel Angel Asturias, considered by many to be the originator of magical realism, in his 1967 Nobel lecture. "We are human beings linked by blood, geography and life to those hundreds, thousands, millions of Latin Americans who suffer misery in our opulent and rich American continent. Our novels attempt to mobilize across the world the moral forces that have to help us defend those people." Twenty-five years later, upon accepting her prize, Rigoberta Menchú said "it is known throughout the world" that Guatemala in 1944 began a "period of democracy" when institutional protections and human rights reigned. "At that time," she said, Guatemala "was an exception in the American continent, because of its struggle for complete national sovereignty. However, in 1954, a conspiracy led by the traditional national power centers, inheritors of colonialism, and powerful foreign interests overthrew the democratic regime

. . . reimposing the old system of oppression which has characterized the history of my country."

This *Reader* is organized roughly chronologically, beginning with the pre-Conquest Maya. It ends with a part we have titled "The Sixth Century," which fitfully tries to take the measure of contemporary, neoliberal, multicultural, and—considering the ways in which national and ethnic identities have been maintained in the midst of significant migration to the United States—transnational Guatemala. The one exception to this chronological ordering is the penultimate chapter, "Maya Movements." In choosing this chapter title and its selections, we do not intend to ghettoize indigenous issues. Nor do we endorse a position that abstracts indigenous identity, politics, or culture from the forces that have shaped the Guatemalan state. Throughout the process of assembling this *Reader*, we have been informed by an understanding of history in which culture and power are mutually interdependent, and we have selected contributions that emphasize the role of popular and marginalized groups, including indigenous communities and activists, in the making of the modern Guatemalan nation (much of the material found in other chapters could easily be included in "Maya Movements," and vice versa). But in the wake of a war in which the military and the landed class emerged triumphant, what can broadly be called a Maya cultural and civil rights movement proved to be particularly consequential in its partial success—incomplete, no doubt, but real—in contesting racism. It is, in a way, an instance of what the nineteenth-century British socialist William Morris meant when he wrote that sometimes people "fight and lose the battle, and the thing that they fought for comes about in spite of the defeat, and when it comes turns out not to be what they meant, and other [people] have to fight for what they meant under another name."

Throughout the early 1990s, as peace talks between the military and the Unidad Revolucionaria Nacional Guatemalteca (the united front made up of four armed groups) progressed, most traditional left unions, reformist political parties, and popular organizations found themselves decimated and disoriented, unable to gain traction in a quickly shifting national landscape. For their part, the guerrillas, after years of siege and paralyzed by infighting, found it impossible to make the transition to a successful peacetime political party (as, for instance, the Frente Farabundo Martí para la Liberación Nacional was able to do in El Salvador). But what had come to be called the "Pan-Mayan Movement"—defined here inclusively, to mean both urbanized cultural-rights activists and rural popular organizations self-identified as Maya—was growing in visibility, with its intellectuals and spokespeople shaping the way the war and state repression were understood and influencing

the terms of the peace process. With the oligarchy and the military committed to making sure the peace process didn't get out of hand, and many on
the Ladino Left trapped in debates over what had gone wrong, Mayans—
long referenced in official nationalist discourse as remnants from a past that
had to be overcome if Guatemala was to become a modern nation—at times
seemed to have the most vibrant vision for the future.

It became widely accepted that "postwar Guatemala," whatever else it
would be, should be officially multicultural, which would include recognizing
not just the more than 20 Maya language groups—among the most prominent being the K'iche', Mam, Poqomam, Kaqchikel, Ixil, Q'eqchi', Tz'utujil,
and Jakaltek—but the non-Maya Xinca, who live in the departments of Santa
Rosa and Jutiapa bordering El Salvador, and the Garifuna on the Atlantic
coast as well. Cultural-rights activists pushed for bilingual education, a judicial system that could incorporate community mechanisms of justice, and
an active commitment to include Mayans in the institutions that govern national life. Beyond this self-conscious political work, there also has been what
sociologist Santiago Bastos calls a diffuse "Mayanization of everyday life,"
which includes a resurgence of commonplace indigenous religious practices,
language use, and an ability to retain one's ability to consider oneself Maya
even if separated or uprooted from a home community.

In this sixth century since the creation of what came to be called Latin
America, Guatemalans face some old obstacles—poverty, lack of land, unemployment, poor housing, disease, illiteracy—and many new ones. At home,
they live under a government eviscerated by neoliberal austerity and military
gangsterism, which have fostered escalating gang violence, rising crime, and
drug addiction. Daily life in a sprawling, polluted, poorly administered capital city is hard for most of its inhabitants, and in some rural areas, environmental degradation is reaching a crisis point. Abroad, in the United States,
undocumented workers face heightened jingoism and a resurgent national
security state, which in recent years have made the lives of migrants, difficult
in the best of circumstances, even more painful. It is of course impossible
to say what the future holds for Guatemala and for Guatemalans. Throughout the first half of the twentieth century, Guatemalan writing, including
the early work of Miguel Angel Asturias, catalogued the supposed "fatal-
ism" of Maya culture, a resignation often blamed for what was identified as
a generalized subservient malaise that infected national life. But what comes
through the selections in the nine chapters presented here are an almost biblical resilience and unrelenting refusal to accept a condition that centuries of
hardship have not yet been able to inscribe as destined.

Notes

1. John Lloyd Stephens, *Incidents of Travel in Central America, Chiapas, and Yucatan*, 12th ed. (New York: Harper & Brothers, 1858), 1:105.

2. "Guatemala Economic Program Aired," *New York Times*, November 9, 1955; "Americas Speed Highway Links," *New York Times*, November 27, 1956; "Selling Central America," *New York Times*, November 22, 1959; "Guatemala City Aerial Hub Streamlined by New Jetport," *Christian Science Monitor*, August 5, 1969; "What's Doing in Guatemala City," *New York Times*, May 21, 1978; "Everything Is Fun in Guatemala," *Christian Science Monitor,* November 19, 1979; and "Guatemala Is Gay Despite Tragedy," *New York Times*, August 4, 1957. For the *Times*'s role in the campaign against Arbenz, see Harrison Salisbury, *Without Fear or Favor: The New York Times and Its Times* (New York: Times Books, 1980), 486; Homer Bigart, "How to Cover a War in Guatemala: It's Best Done from a Bar in Honduras," *New York Herald Tribune*, June 26, 1954; and Stephen Streeter, *Managing the Counterrevolution: The United States and Guatemala, 1954–1961* (Athens: Ohio University Press, 2000), 30, which cites a memo from the *New York Times*'s archive on the CIA's relationship with the paper.

3. Marlise Simons, "Tourism, Terror Coexist in Guatemala," *Washington Post*, May 27, 1980.

4. Ernesto Guevara Lynch, *Young Che: Memories of Che Guevara by His Father* (New York: Vintage, 2008), 206, 231.

5. Gore Vidal, "In the Lair of the Octopus," *The Nation*, June 5, 1995. In this essay Vidal recounts a conversation with his good friend Mario Monteforte Toledo, a writer and Arbenz's vice president, who told him as early as 1946 that the United States would soon intervene. Based on this conversation, Vidal wrote the 1950 novel *Dark Green, Bright Red* about the return of a Jorge Ubico–like dictator who leads an uprising in an effort to take Guatemala back for the United Fruit Company. Vidal says he considers the novel "prophetic."

I

The Maya: Before the Europeans

Before the Spanish invasion in 1524 and independence from Spain in 1821, no nation called Guatemala existed. Today's Guatemala is part of what was once a far-flung Maya civilization that developed along a backbone of volcanoes in Chiapas, Mexico, extending down into what are now Honduras and El Salvador, and into the lowlands along the limestone shelf that forms the Yucatán Peninsula and the Petén. Since at least 15,000 BC, people in these areas had been planting maize, beans, squashes, and chili peppers, crops that remain central to the Guatemalan diet. Maya city-states appeared in what is now the Valley of Guatemala around 250 BC. The best-known of these ancient settlements is a large, barely excavated site called Kaminaljuyu. Most of this site of hundreds of temples has been lost to bulldozers, brickyards, and expanding neighborhoods; today, fragments of it lay buried under Guatemala City's Zone Seven (Guatemala City is administratively divided into an ever-expanding number of "zones").

The center of this Maya world moved into the lowlands of the northern Petén jungle and what is now Belize. Here, great city-states such as Tikal, Aguateca, Uaxactún, Copán, Caracol, and Naranjo arose in the AD 200s and then declined precipitously after about AD 800 for many interwoven reasons, including land overuse, drought, and endemic internecine war. Scholars still vigorously debate the causes of the Maya city-states' decline as new evidence continues to be gathered through tree-ring data, historical climate modeling, and new archaeological discoveries. Archaeologists and anthropologists once imagined the Maya to be peace-loving folk, but information supplied by newly found murals and the recently acquired ability to read Maya writing reveal that Maya society was wracked by conflict. The Maya had a complex intellectual and spiritual culture about which we know only a fraction. We know that the Maya had the concept of zero and calculated the movements of Venus, the moon, and the sun almost perfectly. The Maya used base-twenty (vigesimal) numeral systems, and Maya languages contain words for vigesimal multiples. The complexities of the

Maya calendar reflect its many purposes, which ranged from agriculture to divination. It is believed that within the Maya worldview, time was not linear but rather consisted of cycles of creation and destruction, and it was conceptualized as sacred. What would have been the trajectories of Maya elites and commoners, and of their local and regional cultures, if the Spanish *conquistadores*, guided by conquered Mexicans, had not arrived in 1524?

In the centuries before the Conquest—which archaeologists divide into a Classic Period (AD 250 to 900) and a Postclassic Period (the tenth through the early sixteenth centuries)—the Maya world became increasingly dispersed. Groups of Mexican origin ruled the Maya Yucatán, and confederations of the K'iche', the Kaqchikel, and (to a lesser extent) the Tz'utujil and Poqomam dominated millions of commoners, farmers, artisans, and hunters in the highlands of Guatemala. The linguistic cohesion of the different groups in this widespread area consisted of closely related but often mutually unintelligible languages, such as the two oldest, Cholan and Yucatec. Their many gods embodied material forces, such as Chak, the god of rain; Aha K'in, the sun god; Itzamná, god of maize; and Chak Chel, old moon goddess and goddess of medicine.

Our knowledge about the pre-Conquest Maya is mediated by scholars interpreting scant primary sources. Only a handful of Maya texts survived the Conquest because the Spaniards destroyed thousands of scroll books full of histories, sciences, songs, and prophecies. As archaeologist Michael Coe says: "It's as if all that posterity knew about us [in the United States] were based on three prayer books and *Pilgrim's Progress*." Archaeologists deciphered Maya writing only recently (see "Breaking the Maya Code" in this volume) and are now able to read ancient Maya inscriptions set on vertical stone slabs called stelae. Other sources include texts written in the Roman alphabet after the 1524 conquest, such as the *Popol Vuh*, the *Título de Totonicapán*, *Annals of the Kaqchikel*, and the *Books of Chilam Balam*. Most of these sources provide information about elite politics and cultures; only glimpses of commoners' lives appear, even though strands of their culture survived the trauma of European invasion and remained in everyday spiritualism, household life, agriculture, art, and community values.

Popol Vuh

Unknown K'iche' authors

In the mid-1500s, decades after the Spanish invasion, anonymous K'iche' scribes in the town of Santa Cruz (built of stones from the conquered Maya city of Utatlán) wrote down the Popol Vuh, *or* Council book. *The* Popol Vuh, *often called the "K'iche' Bible," is a creation story believed to be the single most important source documenting Maya culture. The book was written in K'iche' using the Roman alphabet. It was passed down secretly from generation to generation until one of the manuscript's guardians showed it to the Spanish Dominican priest Francisco Ximénez in 1702. Ximénez copied it and translated it into Spanish. The manuscript remained with the Dominicans until the region achieved independence from Spain, and thereafter it traveled. First it was sent to the University of San Carlos, but it was stolen and taken to France by a French abbot at mid-century. It was sold in the 1890s to a US business magnate who deposited it in the Newberry Library in Chicago. It was not until 1941 that a Guatemalan scholar, Adrián Recinos, rescued it from obscurity.*

The Popol Vuh *tells how the many gods residing in the sky/earth (the K'iche' way of saying "world") in the "prior world"—that is, before the Christians came—went about making human beings. On their first try, the gods made creatures that could only shriek and had no arms. On their second try, the mud the gods were using wouldn't retain a shape. Before making a third attempt, they decided to consult an elderly couple: Xpiyacoc, divine matchmaker, and Xmucané, divine midwife. The couple told the gods to use wood. This worked, but the humans were emotionless, and they were soon destroyed by a hurricane. The deities then used corn, which worked because corn-humans—"men of corn"—grew in the rain. But before they completed their task, the gods became involved in the complex adventures of Xmucané's twin sons, who embarked on a mission to defeat the underworld—Xibalbá, or Place of Fear—in order to make the world safe for the yet-to-be-invented corn-humans. The twins traveled to Xibalbá, where they were captured by the lord Blood Gatherer, who turned one of them into a calabash hanging on a tree made of bones. Blood Gatherer's daughter, Blood Moon, found the calabash tree one day. Her intervention saved the first generation of twins and allowed a second genera-*

tion of twins, her children, to defeat the Place of Fear. The following excerpt from the manuscript tells how Blood Moon finds the tree and later makes her way out of Xibalbá to join her new mother-in-law, Xmucané.

And here is the account of a maiden, the daughter of a lord named Blood Gatherer.

And this is when a maiden heard of it, the daughter of a lord. Blood Gatherer is the name of her father, and Blood Moon is the name of the maiden.

And when he heard the account of the fruit of the tree, her father retold it. And she was amazed at the account:

"I'm not acquainted with that tree they talk about. Its fruit is truly sweet, they say, I hear," she said.

Next, she went all alone and arrived where the tree stood. It stood at the place of Ball Game Sacrifice:

"What? Well! What's the fruit of this tree? Shouldn't this tree bear something sweet? They shouldn't die, they shouldn't be wasted. Should I pick one?" said the maiden.

And then the bone spoke; it was here in the fork of the tree:

"Why do you want a mere bone, a round thing in the branches of a tree?" said the head of One Hunahpú when it spoke to the maiden. "You don't want it," she was told.

"I do want it," said the maiden.

"Very well. Stretch out your right hand here, so I can see it," said the bone.

And then the bone spit out its saliva, which landed squarely in the hand of the maiden.

And then she looked in her hand, she inspected it right away, but the bone's saliva wasn't in her hand.

"It is just a sign I have given you, my saliva, my spittle. This, my head, has nothing on it—just bone, nothing of meat. It's just the same with the head of a great lord: it's just the flesh that makes his face look good. And when he dies, people get frightened by his bones. After that, his son is like his saliva, his spittle, in his being, whether it be the son of a lord or the son of a craftsman, an orator. The father does not disappear, but goes on being fulfilled. Neither dimmed nor destroyed is the face of a lord, a warrior, craftsman, orator. Rather, he will leave his daughters and sons. So it is that I have done likewise through you. Now go up there on the face of the earth; you will not die. Keep the word. So be it," said the head of One and Seven Hunahpú—they were of one mind when they did it.

This was the word Hurricane, Newborn Thunderbolt, Sudden Thunderbolt had given them. In the same way, by the time the maiden returned to her home, she had been given many instructions. Right away something was generated in her belly, from the saliva alone, and this was the generation of Hunahpú and Xbalanque.

And when the maiden got home and six months had passed, she was found out by her father. Blood Gatherer is the name of her father.

And after the maiden was noticed by her father, when he saw that she was now with child, all the lords then shared their thoughts—One and Seven Death, along with Blood Gatherer:

"This daughter of mine is with child, lords. It's just a bastard," Blood Gatherer said when he joined the lords.

"Very well. Get her to open her mouth. If she doesn't tell, then sacrifice her. Go far away and sacrifice her."

"Very well, your lordships," he replied. After that, he questioned his daughter:

"Who is responsible for the child in your belly, my daughter?" he said.

"There is no child, my father, sir; there is no man whose face I've known," she replied.

"Very well. It really is a bastard you carry! Take her away for sacrifice, you Military Keepers of the Mat. Bring back her heart in a bowl, so the lords can take it in their hands this very day," the owls were told, the four of them.

Then they left, carrying the bowl. When they left they took the maiden by the hand, bringing along the White Dagger, the instrument of sacrifice.

"It would not turn out well if you sacrificed me, messengers, because it is not a bastard that's in my belly. What's in my belly generated all by itself when I went to marvel at the head of One Hunahpú, which is there at the Place of Ball Game Sacrifice. So please stop: don't do your sacrifice, messengers," said the maiden. Then they talked:

"What are we going to use in place of her heart? We were told by her father: 'Bring back her heart. The lords will take it in their hands, they will satisfy themselves, they will make themselves familiar with its composition. Hurry, bring it back in a bowl, put her heart in the bowl.' Isn't that what we've been told? What shall we deliver in the bowl? What we want above all is that you should not die," said the messengers.

"Very well. My heart must not be theirs, nor will your homes be here. Nor will you simply force people to die, but hereafter, what will truly be yours will be the true bearers of bastards. And hereafter, as for One and Seven Death, only blood, only nodules of sap, will be theirs. So be it that these things are presented before them, and not that hearts are burned before them. So be it: use the fruit of a tree," said the maiden. And it was red tree sap she went out to gather in the bowl.

After it congealed, the substitute for her heart became round. When the sap of the croton tree was tapped, tree sap like blood, it became the substitute for her blood. When she rolled the blood around inside there, the sap of the croton tree, it formed a surface like blood, glistening red now, round inside the bowl. When the tree was cut open by the maiden, the so-called cochineal croton, the sap is what she called blood, and so there is talk of "nodules of blood."

"So you have been blessed with the face of the earth. It shall be yours," she told the owls.

"Very well, maiden. We'll show you the way up there. You just walk on ahead; we have yet to deliver this apparent duplicate of your heart before the lords," said the messengers.

And when they came before the lords, they were all watching closely:

"Hasn't it turned out well?" said One Death.

"It has turned out well, your lordships, and this is her heart. It's in the bowl."

"Very well. So I'll look," said One Death, and when he lifted it up with his fingers, its surface was soaked with gore, its surface glistened red with blood.

"Good. Stir up the fire, put it over the fire," said One Death.

After that they dried it over the fire, and the Xibalbans savored the aroma. They all ended up standing here, they leaned over it intently. They found the smoke of the blood to be truly sweet!

And while they stayed at their cooking, the owls went to show the maiden the way out. They sent her up through a hole onto the earth, and then the guides returned below.

In this way the lords of Xibalbá were defeated by a maiden; all of them were blinded. And here, where the mother of One Monkey and One Artisan lived, was where the woman named Blood Moon arrived.

And when Blood Moon came to the mother of One Monkey and One Artisan, her children were still in her belly, but it wasn't very long before the birth of Hunahpú and Xbalanque, as they are called.

And when the woman came to the grandmother, the woman said to the grandmother:

"I've come, my lady. I'm your daughter-in-law and I'm your child, my lady," she said when she came here to the grandmother.

"Where do you come from? As for my little babies, didn't they die in

A phallic-nosed, masked figure dressed as Ek Chuah, god of merchants and patron of cacao, interpreting the impregnation of Blood Moon. Vase painting. Northern El Petén, AD 600–800. Photograph K1549 © Justin Kerr. Used by permission of Mayavase.

Xibalbá? And these two remain as their sign and their word: One Monkey and One artisan are their names. So if you've come to see my children, get out of here!" the maiden was told by the grandmother.

"Even so, I really am your daughter-in-law. I am already his, I belong to One Hunahpú. What I carry is his. One Hunahpú and Seven Hunahpú are alive, they are not dead. They have merely made a way for the light to show itself, my mother-in-law, as you will see when you look at the faces of what I carry," the grandmother was told.

And One Monkey and One Artisan have been keeping their grandmother entertained: all they do is play and sing, all they work at is writing and carving, every day, and this cheers the heart of their grandmother.

And then the grandmother said:

"I don't want you, no thanks, my daughter-in-law. It's just a bastard in your belly, you trickster! These children of mine who are named by you are dead," said the grandmother.

"Truly, what I say to you is so!"

"Very well, my daughter-in-law, I hear you. So get going, get their food so they can eat. Go pick a big netful of ripe corn ears, then come back, since you are already my daughter-in-law, as I understand it," the maiden was told.

"Very well," she replied.

After that, she went to the garden; One Monkey and One Artisan had a garden. The maiden followed the path they had cleared and arrived there in the garden, but there was only one clump, there was no other plant, no second or third. That one clump had borne its ears. So then the maiden's heart stopped:

"It looks like I'm a sinner, a debtor! Where will I get the netful of food she asked for?" she said. And then the guardians of food were called upon by her:

"Come on out, rise up now, come on out, stand up now:
Thunder Woman, Yellow Woman,
Cacao Woman and Cornmeal Woman,
thou guardian of the food of One Monkey, One Artisan,"

said the maiden.

And then she took hold of the silk, the bunch of silk at the top of the ear. She pulled it straight out, she didn't pick the ear, and the ear reproduced itself to make food for the net. It filled the big net.

And then the maiden came back, but animals carried her net. When she got back she went to put the pack frame in the corner of the house, so it would look to the grandmother as if she had arrived with a load.

And then, when the grandmother saw the food, a big netful:

"Where did that food of yours come from? You've leveled the place! I'm going to see if you've brought back our whole garden!" said the grandmother.

And then she went off, she went to look at the garden, but the one clump was still there, and the place where the net had been put at the foot of it was still obvious.

And the grandmother came back in a hurry, and she got back home, and she said to the maiden:

"The sign is still there. You really are my daughter-in-law! I'll have to keep watching what you do. These grandchildren of mine are already showing genius," the maiden was told.

Now this is where we shall speak of the birth of Hunahpú and Xbalanque.

Breaking the Maya Code

Michael D. Coe

Ancient Maya hieroglyphic writing is visually striking and intricate, with hundreds of unique signs, or glyphs, in the forms of humans, animals, supernaturals, objects, and abstract designs. The meanings of Maya hieroglyphs eluded scholars for centuries. Conventional interpretations viewed the stone-carved glyphs as primitive drawings. We now know, however, that they represent a complex writing system. The archaeologist Michael D. Coe recounts how the Maya code was cracked in a breakthrough achieved by the late Soviet linguist Yuri Knorosov. Cold War politics, which so tragically marked modern Guatemalan history, intruded on this story of cultural discovery. Knorosov traveled from Russia to Guatemala in 1990, where he received a medal from Vinicio Cerezo, Guatemala's first civilian president since the 1960s. Shortly afterward, however, Knorosov received a death threat and had to leave Guatemala in haste. Despite academic and political tensions, breaking the Maya hieroglyphic code opened the door to a world of new discoveries about ancient Maya politics, ceremonies, and everyday life.

The story of the Russian scholar Yuri Valentinovich Knorosov is a study in the triumph of spirit and intellect over almost insuperable odds. This great epigrapher, who until recently had never been permitted to leave the Soviet Union to visit a Mesoamerican site, who had never seen first-hand any of the great Maya inscriptions, cracked the phonetic code of Maya hieroglyphic writing in the confines of his Leningrad study.

I first visited Knorosov with my Russian-speaking wife Sophie in 1969, during the grim, gray "years of stagnation" under Brezhnev. It was January, and it was bitterly cold in Leningrad. Knorosov's office was, and still is, located in the blue-and-white Kunstkammer, the baroque building on the Neva built to house Peter the Great's "cabinet of curiosities" (including the skeleton of his giant manservant). Here, Knorosov shared his modest office with four colleagues at the Ethnographic Institute—privacy of any kind is in short supply in the Soviet Union. In this crowded scene, our friend occupied a desk in the corner near a window, while the ever-present samovar bubbled away, the source of the tea without which Russian intellectual life would be unthinkable. I gazed in awe at the view from the window: beyond the frozen river, the feeble rays of the low-lying winter sun were picking out the golden Admiralty spire celebrated in Pushkin's poetry. It was a very far cry from the hot and humid forests in which the Maya cities had risen and died.

Knorosov is a striking man, with iron-gray hair brushed back severely, and sapphire-blue eyes almost hidden behind his bushy eyebrows. A formal dresser never to be seen on Leningrad's streets without brown beret, white shirt, and necktie, he wears his World War II battle medals, though he now omits the one bearing Stalin's portrait, proudly pinned to his double-breasted suit. A chain-smoker, Knorosov has a wonderfully ironic sense of humor, like many Russians who have survived the terrible events of this century. He is a mine of information on his beloved city, especially on its history under Peter the Great and his corrupt henchman Menshikov.

Thanks to Knorosov's breakthrough in Maya epigraphy, we can now hear ancient Maya glyphs as the scribes wrote them, and not merely interpret them as soundless visual patterns. Knorosov's great achievement lay in demonstrating that the Maya scribes could and often did write syllabically, each glyph standing for a consonant followed by a vowel. Most Maya words are single syllables made up of a consonant-vowel-consonant combination. They were generally written with two glyphs, but the vowel of the second glyph was not pronounced. Basic to Knorosov's approach was his "Principle of Synharmony," according to which the silent second vowel in these combinations often repeats the vowel of the first glyphs. Hence, the word for the quetzal bird—a beautiful tropical species highly prized by the Maya for its ornate feathers—is the monosyllabic *kuk*, but was written with two *ku* glyphs, the second *u* sound being suppressed.

This approach is universally accepted today by all serious Mayanists, but it was initially rejected by the scholarly establishment here in the West. Indeed, all of Knorosov's work on Maya glyphs came under heated attack for many years from the dean of Maya studies, J. Eric Thompson, whose formidably influential views of the Maya held sway in the Americas for more than a generation. Thompson launched his relentless and often unfair rebuttal in Cold War terms in the Mexican journal "Yan" in 1953. Indeed, until his death in 1975, Thompson rejected all of Knorosov's work, both in general and in detail. The very vehemence of his attack suggests that he might have had something to fear from Knorosov's quarter.

The critical point in Knorosov's career occurred in 1947, when his teacher, the orientalist and archaeologist Sergei Tokarev, came to him with a pro-

Excavation of Tikal, El Petén, 1892. Photo by Alfred P.
Maudslay. From the collections of the Centro de Investigaciones Regionales de Mesoamérica, Guatemala.

posal. Two years before, the respected German Mayanist Paul Schellhas,
then near the end of his long life, had published a very pessimistic article
stating that the decipherment of Maya glyphs was an unsolvable problem.
Tokarev's challenge to his student was this: "If you believe that any writing system produced by humans can be read by humans, the[n] why don't
you try to read the Maya hieroglyphs?" Knorosov took up the challenge
and turned it into his doctoral research, which would lead to his degree in
historical sciences (magna cum laude) in 1955.

The subject of Knorosov's groundbreaking study was the work of Fray
Diego de Landa, the fanatical and cruel Spanish Franciscan missionary.
Landa, who eventually became Provincial (ruling prelate) in Yucatán, both
persecuted the Maya and recorded their customs and history. Famed for his
complete mastery of the Maya tongue, he combated what he perceived to be

widespread idolatry among his charges in 1552 by conducting an auto-da-fé. In the process, he did massive and irreparable damage to the Maya's written legacy by burning a large number of native Maya texts or codices "because they contained nothing but superstition and the Devil's falsehoods."

Landa was recalled to Spain in 1564 to face charges that he had over-stepped his authority in the investigation and torture of native lords and commoners. During his years of exile, he wrote an "Account of the Affairs of Yucatan," which, ironically, is our single most important Colonial-period source on the lowland Maya. The original has been lost, but a seventeenth-century abridgement was discovered in 1862 in Madrid by the Abbe Brasseur de Bourbourg. This precious document not only provided detailed information on all aspects of Maya life on the eve of the conquest, it also—more important in this context—outlined the workings of the Maya calendar and gave the glyphs for the days and the months.

Landa gave us something else that would prove decisive to Knorosov's breakthrough—a description of the Maya writing system itself, albeit one containing a crucial error. From material he had elicited from his informants, Landa pictured 27 signs that, to his mind, formed part of the Maya "alphabet," as well as three additional signs drawn from examples of how signs were strung together in written words and sentences. Early efforts at translating Maya glyphs based on Landa's interpretations ranged from the bad to the ridiculous.

The phonetic approach remained in eclipse for almost a century, until Knorosov published his bombshell in the form of an article written in 1952. The article appeared in *Sovietskaya Etnografia,* a journal in those days otherwise given over to praise of Marx, Engels, and, above all, Stalin. In this article, Knorosov rejected several basic conclusions to which Mayanists had adhered. To begin with, he refuted the evolutionary approach of the development of languages, a position embraced by important Maya scholars like Sylvanus Morley. This approach argues that writing had passed through various stages, beginning with the pictographic, then proceeding through the "ideographic" (in which an idea or object is given by a sign having little or no pictorial reference), and finally moving to the phonetic (in which a sign stands only for a sound). Wrong, said Knorosov. These supposed stages coexist in all early scripts, including Egyptian, Mesopotamian, and Chinese, all of which, like the Maya system, are authentically hieroglyphic; they are typical of state societies in which they are maintained as a monopoly by a class of priestly scribes. In such systems, one finds "ideograms" that have both conceptual and phonetic value; phonetic signs; and "key signs" or de-terminatives, classificatory signs with conceptual value only that remain

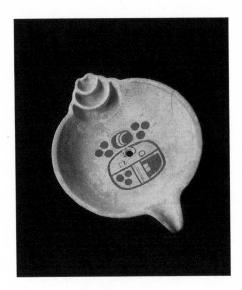

Ceramic vessel shaped as the side of a conch shell and used as a paint well. Scribes were considered artists. The glyph literally reads *kuch sabac,* "a container for ink." Burial 116 Tikal, AD 200–600. Photograph K6580 © Justin Kerr. Used by permission of Mayavase.

unpronounced. Knorosov then zeroed in on the Landa "alphabet," which he argued was not an alphabet at all but a syllabary—a list of signs standing for consonant-vowel combinations and not individual letters. (Landa himself recorded five of his "letters" as consonant-vowel combinations.) Knorosov claimed, for instance, that the sign given by Landa as the letter *l* actually represents the syllable *lu*.

In this and a spate of other articles, Knorosov closely compared the texts with the pictures they accompany in the few surviving Maya codices, especially a manuscript known as the Dresden Codex; and he applied the Landa "alphabet" in light of his theoretical system.

Despite the early attacks on his discoveries, Knorosov's logic proved compelling. Linguists and younger colleagues in the United States had a considerably less hostile reaction to Knorosov's work than people like Thompson, and in 1962 the important American epigrapher David Kelley published a paper accepting many, but not all, of Knorosov's readings. Kelley took the Russian's methodology one step further into the inscriptions, and read the syllabically written name of a great leader at Chichen Itza as *ka-ku-pa-ca-l* or Kakupacal, "Fiery Shield." It was a first for Maya studies, and the tide has never turned back. . . .

[T]wo new approaches, phoneticism and the historical approach, coalesced in 1973 at the groundbreaking first Mesa Redonda of Palenque. For the first time since the collapse of Classic Maya civilization in the ninth century AD, the kings of Palenque, including Pacal the Great and his son Chan Bahlum, became real people with real histories.

Bonampak Mural

Unknown artists

Dating to AD 750, Bonampak was a Maya site located in the Lacandon jungle in the present-day Mexican state of Chiapas, close to the Guatemalan border. Unknown to academic scholars until Lacandon Maya guides took two US backpackers there in 1946, the Bonampak murals record the history of one battle and its aftermath. Remarkably preserved images of Maya nobles in beautifully pigmented robes, tortured prisoners of war, and rituals of bloodletting illuminate Maya militarism and the ability of Maya artists to paint figures alive with movement and subtle emotions.

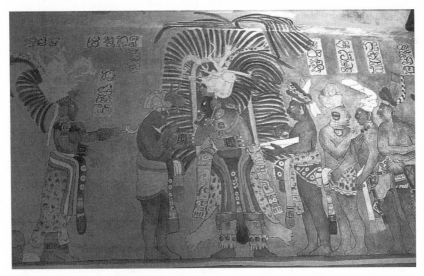

(*top*) Parade of musicians.
(*bottom*) Attendants applying yellow paint to the body of a Bonampak lord. Artist renditions of the Bonampak mural, Museum of Maya Culture, Chetumal. Photograph used by permission of Ruud van Akkeren.

Gendered Nobility

Rosemary A. Joyce

As an ornate, spiritually rich, ritual-bound polity, the Maya assigned moral value and cultural meaning to the relations that bound women and men together. They held sets of ideas and expectations about women and men that differed according to one's place in the status hierarchy. In the selection below, the archaeologist Rosemary A. Joyce examines the traces of gender in Maya art and artifacts, and she posits tentative answers to questions surrounding how noble women and men lived and interacted. She argues that the Maya understood gender to be more ambiguous and variable than simply a male-female binary and that both everyday activities and ceremonial rituals were important to the performance of Maya gendered identities.

Beautiful Bodies, Sexual Performances

In idealized performances of gender recorded in paintings on Classic Maya pottery, young men engaged in dancing and playing ball display their bodies in front of audiences of older men and women. Pots made for serving food and drink, painted or carved with pictorial scenes like these, were among the most widely admired objects produced in the courts of Classic Maya rulers and nobles. Many of the intact pots found in museums and illustrated in art books were recovered in illegal excavations and exported against the laws of their countries of origin, destroying clues that might otherwise have been used in their interpretation. Some have been excavated by archaeologists, as have vast amounts of fragments from broken pots. Residues of chocolate drinks have been identified in many pots, supporting the captions painted or carved on them that identify the foods they were made to contain. It is clear that each court used many of these pots for feasts and for everyday meals. They were also often placed in the tombs of the highest-ranking families. The imagery they carry would have been pervasive in the lives of the ruling social group. What was selected for representation incorporated the values of this group.

What was represented also served as a model against which individual living action was interpreted. This is a familiar experience for us today. Contemporary controversies swirl around the influence photographs of dangerously thin fashion models can have on girls and women. These images present idealizations of the body that serve as models against which women evaluate themselves, and that they strive to approximate, sometimes at great cost. Similarly, the visual media that circulated in Classic Maya courts provided precedents recreated by living people in their own performances of gender, models against which they must have measured themselves. I decided to study how images like these, circulating in Classic Maya cities, provide evidence for the ways in which Maya men and women formulated and indeed reformulated gender identities.

I began with an attempt to move beyond the correspondence model of sex and gender, because it was clear from even a cursory review of sixteenth-century texts that indigenous people in Mexico and Central America understood gender to be more variable than could be captured by two dichotomous sexes. Texts talked about supernatural beings who encompassed male and female aspects, or who were male and female at different points in time. This kind of variability, part of what the art historian Cecilia Klein has characterized as gender ambiguity, was routinely associated with positions of political power. Some male officials in Classic Maya and sixteenth-century Mexica societies appeared to cross-dress, wearing items of clothing understood to be normal for women.

I wondered if the imagery used in Classic Maya art could show how indigenous people could take on multiple gender identities in the same way that these later texts did. Initially, I assumed that sex was a biological reality, and gender was a social construct through which sex was interpreted. This was the idea of sex and gender current in archaeology in the early 1990s, but it soon became clear that this approach led to results that simply did not match the way that the ancient Maya led their lives. Why force the lives of these people into a straitjacket of notions invented by late-twentieth-century societies? Once I began to try to understand the gender identities of the Maya on their own terms, I realized that visual media could be considered as active, part of the way concepts of gender were given a sense of naturalness, rather than as passive reflections of something that simply existed. Gender was a work in progress, it was something people did, not something people were. Representations were part of the material that people employed as they performed their own gender and as they shaped gendered experiences of others.

I now see my first attempts at gender analysis as compromised by the two-sex model. Separating sex out as "real" makes it easy for critics to suggest that gender is "unreal," that it does not come to terms with the realities of people's lives, let alone the "given" of biological sex. But even with this initial flaw, adopting a concept of gender that was not predetermined as dual and that did not automatically group all males together and separate them from a second category of females proved to be a useful way to start my analysis, as it was for many other researchers.

Steps to Sex in Classic Maya Archaeology

Initially, I examined Classic Maya stereotyped images in monumental sculpture and painting as precedents for the actions of women, men, and persons of alternate genders. I compared what was being represented in these media with painted and carved pots and fired clay figurines, produced in molds or modeled by hand, recovered from house compounds. I quickly realized that I needed to specify that the kind of womanhood and manhood I was disentangling was specific to the noble sector of society. Very little archaeological exploration had been carried out in the houses of rural farmers or the more modest residences in cities. Where such work had happened, visual images of any kind were quite rare, suggesting that the way gendered personhood was shaped in these parts of the society was different.

I also quickly realized that the most common imagery of womanhood and manhood depicted young or middle-aged adults. Imagery of children and of elderly adults was either uncommon or absent, depending on the medium. In ceramic figurines, elderly men and women, infants held in arms, and children appear. In carved stone monuments, even people described in accompanying texts as young children were depicted as if they were smaller-scale adults, while other people whose advanced age was recorded in the texts were represented as in the prime of life. Why would monumental art insist on showing everyone as if they were young adults? If we remember that images serve as patterns against which we measure ourselves, then this makes sense: not unlike modern fashion ads, the patrons and artists of these Classic Maya images wanted to project an ideal to which the population could compare themselves. Modern fashion ads are shaped by companies to persuade consumers to continually buy new products that promise to help them achieve an impossible look. Classic Maya monuments were patronized by Classic Maya rulers and nobles. Their interests were in persuading people that the rulers were the ideal against which everyone else should be measured.

The figures depicted in monuments offered a clear image of heterosexual adult gender performance that was simultaneously a precedent for the

Noblewomen watch costumed dancers with rattles. Vase painting. Highland Guatemala AD 600–800. Photograph K6888 © Justin Kerr. Used by permission of Mayavase.

enactment of noble status and public formality. That sex mattered in formal public performances by the nobility was suggested by the frequency with which female images were paired with male images. Tatiana Proskouriakoff's research had originally called attention to the presence of female figures standing at ground level gazing up at the enthroned males in "ascension scenes" from Piedras Negras. Female figures also were juxtaposed with male figures through the creation of paired monuments that stood facing each other in many Classic Maya sites.

Following from a suggestion by the influential feminist theorist Judith Butler that gender is a kind of "incessant action," I paid as much attention to what different figures were doing as I did to the visual clues in clothing that, following Proskouriakoff, I used to recognize female and male figures. In monumental images, what I found was that most actions were common to men and women. Men and women both held the most important symbols of royal power, a bar with heads of a serpent on both ends, or an axe with a handle in the form of an image of a Maya deity. Both men and women stood on the backs of defeated warriors. Even the display of shields and weapons by male figures was echoed by the female figures. These actions together formed what Joyce Marcus called an "iconography of power," the kinds of actions expected of ruling factions. Rather than discriminate between the sexes, these images presented both men and women as members of the ruling faction. . . .

Looking at Bodies

The way women's robes were carved on monuments was curiously unrelated to the contours of the bodies they covered. The same monuments lovingly detailed the arms, torso, and legs of noble men. While both men and women were presented in idealized youth, their bodies made beautiful by rich jewelry and elaborate clothing, I began to think that I needed to examine more closely how Classic Maya visual imagery portrayed bodily experience itself.

Whether in monuments or the multi-figure compositions painted or carved on pottery vessels, the young, active male body was the object of the gaze of both older males and adult women. On painted pottery depicting court scenes, older seated males glanced toward groups of warriors, athletes, and dancers. On monuments, women gazed upward at seated or standing men. The profusion of male images in Maya visual media provided ample evidence of the idealization of young, active male bodies as objects of contemplation by both men and women. I suggested that in this sector of Classic Maya society, the young male exemplified beauty, and admiration of male youths by both men and women was modeled as normal.

If the beauty of young males was admired in Maya society, could this suggest that such admiration led to same-sex relationships between males? This is a controversial argument, one not easily accepted, given the basic homophobia of modern archaeology. When heterosexual activity is considered the norm, same-sex relationships can be recognized only as abnormal or transgressive, not as accepted or idealized. Contemporary archaeologists share wider cultural orientations that merge a fascination with sex with a tendency to see sex as private and potentially a source of public shame. Archaeology can provide powerful reminders that this is a modern attitude, one with a history that is very well known but whose effects on our reading of clues to the past needs to be more clearly acknowledged.

Space and Sex

Sex was not always as closely policed or separated into a sphere of privacy in past societies. . . . My initial exploration of the way all-male groups of youths were depicted as beautiful subjects in Classic Maya art led me to ask whether there was evidence for accepted practices of same-sex sociability that might have included sexuality. Sixteenth-century text describing descendants of the Classic Maya described young men as moving into common houses together, where they developed their skills at athletic contests and dances. Spanish sources accused the residents of such young men's houses of sexual crimes against young women, while asserting that sexual relations between males were not practiced. At the same time, contemporary dictionaries included entries for words describing male-male sex acts, casting some doubt on the categorical claim that no same-sex activity was practiced among the Yucatec Maya. Manuscripts written in the Yucatec Maya language in the centuries following the Spanish invasion contain many mentions of male-male sexual activity ascribed to poltical enemies. Because Spanish missionaries had branded such activity as sinful, we cannot assume Maya informants were open and complete in reporting who participated in same-sex encounters. Nor can these later sources be used on their own as clues to practices centuries earlier. . . .

Actual scenes of sexual activity of any kind are extremely rare in Classic Maya sites, and none are yet known in residential contexts. Naj Tunich cave has produced several images of sexual acts. Here, the art historian Andrea Stone has identified scenes of male masturbation in close proximity to an image of two nude standing figures shown in profile, locked in an embrace. One figure has an erect penis, and the other was originally interpreted as his female consort. Subsequently, Stone called attention to details of the second figure more likely to be seen on a Classic Maya male, suggesting the embracing pair were two males.

The proposal that there were special places in some Classic Maya cities where young men socialized together, and perhaps resided, is fairly uncontroversial. Taking the next step and suggesting that the young men in these sites experienced same-sex desire and acted on it, however, has literally created a backlash among some scholars. One of the interesting aspects of this backlash has been the clear assumption that same-sex desire and practice would be incompatible with the social value placed on male-female sex by social groups like those of the Postclassic Maya and Mexica, among whom reproduction of the social group was represented as a duty to family and the state. The heteronormative perspective demands that people have one naturally given sexual orientation, and allows for same-sex desire only if it is an exception that literally proves the rule. Long gazes focused on young male bodies, whether from men or women, are pervasive in Classic Maya visual culture, which presents young male bodies as objects of desire while simultaneously recognizing male-female parents and their children as important subjects.

How a regime of bodily presentation for the sexuality of men and women, like Classic Maya images, was related to sexual lives and understandings of reproduction should be an open topic for research. The assumption that male-female sex was the dominant norm in ancient societies, incompatible with other forms of sexual experience, supplies a pre-existing answer before the question of other forms of sexual activity has been asked.

Rabinal Achí

Anonymous

Rabinal Achí (Man of Rabinal) *is a Maya dance-drama also known as* Dance of the Trumpets. *Once remembered orally and performed without a script,* Rabinal achí *dramatizes a time before the arrival of Europeans, when the two great highland kingdoms of Rabinal and K'iche' were at war. The first* Rabinal Achí *script was written after the Spanish invasion in the sixteenth century, when missionaries introduced the vernacular theater tradition of medieval Europe.* Rabinal Achí *tells how the K'iche' renegade, Cawek of the Forest People, disrupts Rabinal territory, located in what is now the Baja Verapaz region in north-central Guatemala. Cawek is captured and beheaded, but only after his dignity as a K'iche' noble is duly acknowledged. Below are the final words of Cawek of the Forest People.*

CAWEK OF THE FOREST PEOPLE speaks alone.
Little EAGLE, little JAGUAR:
Just now you were saying, "He left!"
        But I didn't leave.
I simply said farewell from here
            to the face of my mountain
                the face of my valley. . . .
        Alas, O Sky!
        Alas, O Earth!
Can it be true
        that I'm dead here
            I'm lost
here at the navel of the sky
        navel of the earth?
You then!
        My golden metal
            my silver metal
and you, strength of my weapon
        strength of my shield

my upraised ax handle
        my upraised ax blade
and likewise you
        all my clothes
                along with my sandals.
You then!

While speaking the next five lines, he turns toward the west and extends his ax in that direction.

        Go to our mountain
                go to our valley
Then tell our story
        before our lord
                our liege
talk this way
        to our lord, our liege:
"The road is closed
        for my courage
                my manhood
searching
        striving
        for our meals, our morsels."
Say this
        to our lord
                to our liege.
Isn't that what you'll say
        if my fate is simply
                to die
                        to disappear
here at the navel of the sky
        navel of the earth?
Alas, then, Sky!
        Alas, then, Earth!
If I am truly dead
        if I am lost
at the navel of the sky
        navel of the earth
then I shall resemble
        that squirrel
                that bird

that died on the branch of a tree
    in the flower of a tree
while searching
    for his meals
        his morsels
here at the navel of the sky
    here at the navel of the earth.
You then, Eagle
    you then, Jaguar:
Come now!
    Do your duty
        do your work.
Do it now with your teeth
    your claws.
But you certainly won't stand my hair on end
    in the blink of an eye
because
I am truly brave
    coming as I do
        from my mountain
           my valley.
May Sky and Earth be with you too
    little Eagle, little Jaguar.

Fanfare. All walk a counterclockwise circle around the stage, with CAWEK falling in behind EAGLE and JAGUAR bringing up the rear. When CAWEK has almost finished his circle, approaching west center, he begins to spiral inward toward the very center of the stage with the others following. He reaches the center at the same moment his spiral brings him into position to face west. As the music begins he kneels with his head bowed; the others shift to dancing and form a tight counterclockwise circle around him. As they progress around the circle they move inward toward CAWEK with each left step and farther away with each right. With each left step the right arm moves toward CAWEK; those who bear axes make a chopping motion (but without touching him), aimed at the back of his neck if they happen to be in the right position at the moment.

As RABINAL completes a full circuit of CAWEK, which finds him facing west, CAWEK rises with a fanfare and steps into place behind him. Everyone breaks into a walk, spiraling counterclockwise and outward until CAWEK reaches the middle of the east side. Then they dance the square, breaking

Capture of the K'iche' lord Cawek of the Forest People, during a performance of the
Rabinal Achí dance drama in Rabinal, Baja Verapaz, 2002. Prominent in the photograph is a refrigerator full of Gallo, the domestically produced beer ubiquitous in Guatemala. Photo by Bert Jensen. From the collections of the Centro de Investigaciones
Regionales de Mesoamérica, Guatemala.

into the usual groups to turn circles at each corner. When EAGLE comes back around the east side of the stage he continues to the northeast corner and stays there; the rest fall in behind him, forming a line across the east side with JAGUAR at the south end. They all turn to face east and continue to dance in place for a few measures, keeping the left foot forward and shifting their weight back and forth between left and right; on the left shift they swing the right arm forward. Next comes a fanfare with a standstill.

When the music resumes, they do an about-face, dancing westward while staying in line. On the way, CAWEK turns with RABINAL while LORD turns with QUETZAL, SLAVE and LADY; EAGLE and JAGUAR turn independently. All arrive at the west side with a fanfare and stand still. ROAD GUIDE rises and moves to a position in front of the others, facing west, and when the fanfare stops the musicians also face west. Everyone prays to the ancestors at the same time, but independently; only murmurs can be heard.

Apocalypto

Bruno Waterfield, The Telegraph (London)

As with most scholarly disciplines, a good deal of quackery can be found in the origins of what eventually became Mayanist archaeology. At different moments, the Maya have been thought to be descendants of Phoenicians, Mormons, the lost tribe of Israel, or even survivors of Atlantis. The professionalization of archaeology marginalized such assertions, but similar speculation lives on in New Age musings, and the Maya continue to be the subject of stories the West tells about itself. In particular, a number of best-selling books—and at least one Hollywood movie—argued that the long-count calendar, which expires in 2012, predicts the end of the world. This newspaper report discusses this belief in Holland and suggests that many Europeans deal with the economic and ecological uncertainty of modern times by displacing their anxiety onto the Maya, who actually did suffer a real apocalypse as a result of European colonialism.

Dutch Prepare for Maya Apocalypse

By Bruno Waterfield, *The Telegraph* (London), June 25, 2008

Thousands of Dutch people are buying boats and rations and building bunkers to await an apocalypse predicted by the Maya of South America.

The calendar of the Maya civilisation, celebrated for its advanced writing, mathematics and astronomy, resets on December 21, 2012.

On December 21, 2012, the "Long Count" calendar of the Maya people clicks over to year zero, marking the end of a 5,000-year era.

Belying their country's rational and laid-back image, thousands of Dutch people are convinced the date coincides with a world catastrophe, the *Volkskrant* newspaper reports.

Petra Faile and her husband have bought a life raft and other survival equipment in preparation for Armageddon.

"In another four years it will all be over," she said.

"You know maybe it's really not that bad that the Netherlands will be destroyed. I don't like it here any more."

Mrs. Faile said she was concerned that immigration was pushing the Netherlands, a low lying country protected by dikes and sea walls, beneath the waves.

"They keep letting people in. And then we have to build more houses, which makes the Netherlands even heavier. The country will sink even lower, which will make the flooding worse," she said.

The ancient Maya civilisation, celebrated for its advanced writing, mathematics and astronomy, flourished in Mesoamerica for six centuries from AD 300.

Its calendar, which fell out of use after the Spanish conquest, covers 5,126 years and then resets at year zero on December 21, 2012.

Popular books, such as *Apocalypse 2012: A Scientific Investigation Into Civilization's End* or *2012: The Return of Quetzalcoatl*, have spawned a global movement.

As the clock ticks on the date, the Mayan calendar has assumed new significance for people who believe humanity is creating ecological disasters and needs to learn from ancient wisdom.

II

Invasion and Colonialism

When the Spanish conquistador Pedro de Alvarado marched south from the newly conquered México capital of Tenochtitlán with 250 Spanish soldiers and a larger number of Nahuatl-speaking México troops, no unified Maya opposition awaited him. Rather, the indigenous populations who lived in what is now Guatemala were divided among various confederations of K'iche', Kaqchikel, Mam, Tz'utujil, and others, who ruled over different regions of the highlands and the Pacific coast plains. Some indigenous confederations were of relatively recent origin; the Kaqchikel formed their capital in Iximché in 1478. These separate fiefdoms warred with one another over territory. Each had its own internal conflicts, just as feudal estates did in Europe at this time. Through political manipulation of these preexisting conflicts, the Spaniards achieved military victory.

Alvarado made a short-lived alliance with the Kaqchikels, who had been battling against the more powerful K'iche' for decades, and this enabled the defeat of the K'iche' in their highland capital of Utatlán or Gumarcaaj (present-day Santa Cruz del Quiché) and of the Tz'utujiles at Lake Atitlán. When the Kaqchikels realized that the Spaniards aimed to virtually enslave all native peoples, they rebelled and fought for six more years. Guatemala was still not completely conquered; Alvarado's brother Jorge had to bring more than five thousand México soldiers in order to finally establish Spanish dominance. The Spanish built their new capital in 1527 in the Valley of Almolonga on the slopes of the Volcán de Agua volcano. When this city was destroyed by a mudslide in 1541, the seat of Spanish rule moved to what is now Antigua, which was called Santiago de los Caballeros de Guatemala in the colonial era.

Spain governed through various means. In order to facilitate colonial control, Spanish authorities forced the newly baptized "indios" to first construct, and then relocate into, new communities called pueblos de indios away from ancestral lands and under Spanish administrative rule. In the name of the Spanish king, colonial officials parceled out land to every com-

munity so that each could provide its own subsistence and pay tribute to
the Crown in the form of textiles, cacao, and other items. These communities had to supply a *reparto*, which involved one-third of their male residents laboring on Spanish-owned plantations and haciendas in nine-month
shifts. These laborers carried goods and built whatever the Spaniards commanded, from streets and fountains to churches. The labor drafts were duly
counted and recorded by colonial officials, and punishment could be severe
for those who did not comply. Under tremendous duress, *los indios* built the
colonial landscape, fed the colonists, and supplied them with export crops
such as indigo. Colonialism disrupted or distorted the rhythms of agrarian
life by appropriating native land, labor, space, and time, and by driving underground the pre-Conquest *cosmovision* (the word commonly used in Guatemala to describe Maya spirituality or worldview) that gave life meaning.

Christianity was the culture of Spanish colonialism. The Spaniards drew
ethical legitimacy and authority from Catholicism, and missionaries saw
this "new world" as a canvas on which to paint a utopia of new converts.
The missionaries' attempts to spread their truths met with uneven results.
Maya communities remained hostile to priests as late as the close of the
colonial period, despite mass baptisms, even while fusing many Christian
figures and concepts with their own. During three centuries of colonialism, Maya learned how to defend themselves by utilizing imperial culture,
including its new trinitarian God and its saints.

Spanish edicts on race sought to create an idealized social hierarchy and
separation, but the colonial reality was far more complex. Children born in
the colonies to mixed-descent parents—Maya, Spaniards, and the Africans
the Spaniards brought to supplement indigenous labor—belonged to many
worlds at once. The Spaniards, however, ranked them into a racialized caste
system that started with *blancos* (whites) at the top of the hierarchy and traveled through various combinations to *los indios* and *los negros* at the bottom.
Meanwhile, the *pueblos de indios* lived within the confines of Spanish rule
while maintaining their own cultural and religious traditions. The Maya
majority spoke no Spanish during the colonial period. The Maya who did
learn Spanish were called Ladinos, and they often served as intermediaries
between the *pueblos de indios* and Spanish officials. The Spanish invoked
purity of bloodline when bestowing social status, even though "Spanish
blood" emanating from the Iberian peninsula was itself the result of a mixture of different cultures. By the end of the colonial period, Guatemala included peoples far more complex than the categories *indio*, *español*, *negro*,
and Ladino suggest. Indigenous flight from forced labor, tribute, and Christianization gave rise to a rural population that lived outside the classifica-

tion of *indio*. A growing number of people of mixed Maya, European, and African descent became part of the colonial system of *"castas"* and were not subject to the demands placed upon the indigenous population. Although Guatemala was not a major slave importer like Brazil or the Caribbean countries, African slaves were concentrated in particular areas, such as the sugar plantations in the eastern part of the country. There were transient communities of escaped slaves in various parts of the country, while free blacks and *mulatos* played an important role in everyday life in the colonial capital of Santiago de Guatemala.

The Spaniards changed the human and natural environment forever by bringing with them new animals and plants and—fatally—European diseases. Even before 1524, pandemics of measles, smallpox, and other illnesses to which the indigenous population had no immunity had traveled south from Mexico. These strange and inexplicable sicknesses demoralized and weakened the Maya confederations before the Spaniards set foot in their territories. What was a new world for the Spaniards became a holocaust for the indigenous population. By the end of the colonial period, at the close of the eighteenth century, Maya populations still had not recovered demographically from the impact of the Spanish invasion. The Spaniards needed to keep indigenous populations intact as a source of labor and taxes, so they granted limited political and economic autonomy to Maya communities. Indigenous communities learned how to use the colonial system to gain a modicum of concessions from Spanish authorities, and village leaders often derived clout from their ability to negotiate with representatives of the church and the Crown, which over time gained a degree of legitimacy. After three hundred years, the Maya were neither Europeanized nor destroyed. They survived, in transformation, to become political forces in the centuries to come.

Invading Guatemala

Various authors

Pedro de Alvarado was about thirty-eight years old when he invaded Guatemala in
1524. He had arrived in the New World with his brothers more than ten years earlier, participating with Cortés in the conquest of Cuba and Mexico and perfecting
the art of "divide and conquer." Alongside about 250 Spanish soldiers, his invading
army included numerous Nahua warriors from Mexico, as well as African slaves
and freemen. Alvarado took advantage of historic rivalries between Guatemala's
warring indigenous kingdoms and forged a temporary alliance with the Kaqchikels
to defeat the K'iche' kingdom. Not long after, Alvarado's troops brutally crushed
a Kaqchikel revolt before moving on to present-day El Salvador and defeating the
Tz'utujil and Pipil south of Lake Atitlán and along the Pacific coast.

    The story of the invasion of Guatemala is usually told from the perspective of
the conquerors. In this selection, the historian Matthew Restall and the archaeologist Florine Asselbergs present two different accounts of the Spanish invasion. The
first comes from a letter written by Pedro de Alvarado to Cortés in 1524, narrating
victory over the K'iche's. Alvarado evidently hoped news of his exploits would reach
the king of Spain and translate into royal favors for him and his men. He writes of
a landscape of war and "punishment" for the "infidels" who resisted his advance.
The second account is from a later document called the Annals of the Kaqchikels,
written in the late sixteenth century. This document was written in Kaqchikel and
discovered in the Convent of San Francisco in Guatemala City in 1844. Part of a
community archive maintained by the elders of Sololá, a town high above Lake
Atitlán, this document chronicles the bloody conquest wars between 1524 and 1530
and tells the story of the Kaqchikel revolt against the Spanish and the abandonment
of the Kaqchikel capital of Iximché by 1526. It also describes forced labor and the
onerous tribute system of early Spanish rule.

Account Made by Pedro de Alvarado to Hernando Cortés, April 11, 1524

After having sent my messengers to this country, informing them of how I
was coming there to conquer and pacify the provinces within His Majesty's

dominion . . . I [asked them for] passage through their country; that if they did this, they would be good and loyal vassals of His Majesty and would be greatly favored . . . but if not, I threatened to make war on them as on rebellious traitors and as such I would treat them, and I would also treat as slaves those taken alive in the war. . . .

And after arriving at this town, I found all the roads open and very wide, the highway as well as the roads that crossed it, but the roads that ran to the principal streets were obstructed; then I understood their evil plan and that those [barricades] were made for battle. And indeed there came few of them sent to me, and from far away they told me I should enter into the town to lodge, so they could more conveniently fight us, as it had been arranged. . . . When I was informed of this, I sent some of the men on horseback to reconnoiter the countryside, and they found many warriors with whom they fought, and that afternoon some horses were wounded.

Next day I went to see the road that we had to take and also saw warriors, and the country was so hilly and thickly wooded with cacao plantations and trees that it was more suited to them and not to us, so I returned to camp. The following day I left with all the men to enter the town. In the road was a river, difficult to cross, at which the Indians were positioned, and there we fought and defeated them. . . . And after entering the houses we struck the people down, and continued the chase as far as the marketplace and half a league beyond; afterward we returned to the marketplace to make camp. Here we spent two days reconnoitering the country.

And at the end of that time I left for another town called [Quetzaltenango]. That day I crossed two terrible rivers with sheer, rocky banks, which we crossed over with much difficulty, and began to climb a mountain pass that was six leagues in length. . . . The pass was so rough that the horses could scarcely climb. Next morning, I continued on, and above a gully, I found a woman and a dog sacrificed, which, according to the interpreter, was a challenge. . . . We had just gotten through the pass with crossbowmen and foot soldiers in front of me, as the horses had not been able to keep up the lead owing to the roughness of the road, when about three or four thousand warriors came over a ravine and struck at the troops of our allies, forcing them back, but then we defeated them. While on the high ground, collecting the troops to rally them, I saw more than thirty thousand men coming towards us. I thanked God that there we found some plains, and although the horses were tired and fatigued from the pass, we waited until they came close enough to shoot their arrows, and then we smashed into them; as they had never seen horses, they grew very fearful, and we made a very good advance and scattered them and many of them died. . . .

[W]e collected ourselves and went to make camp a league away near some spring. . . . While dismounted and drinking, we saw many warriors approaching us, and we allowed them to approach us as they came over very large plains; and we broke them. Here we made a very big advance to where we found people waiting, one of them to two horsemen. We continued the advance for a good league, and they brought us to a sierra, where they faced us. I put myself in flight with some of the horsemen, to draw them into the open, and they followed us. . . . I turned on them, and here was made a very great charge and punishment. In this [battle] one of the four chiefs of [Utatlán] was killed, who came as the Captain General of the whole country. . . .[1]

I returned to the spring and that night made camp there; we were greatly fatigued, and there were Spaniards and horses wounded. The following morning I left for the town of Quetzaltenango, which was a league away, but after the punishment of the day before, I found it deserted; there was not a single person there. There I camped and reformed, reconnoitering the country, which is as greatly populated as Tascalteque [Tlaxcala, Mexico] and more or less as cultivated, and excessively cold. . . .

At the end of the six days that I was there, one Thursday at noon, a great multitude of people appeared on many sides; and according to they themselves, twelve thousand were from within this city and surrounding towns, and the others they said could not be counted. As soon as I saw them, I put my men in order and went out with ninety horsemen to give them battle in the middle of a plain . . . and at no more than a gunshot from the camp, we began to crush them and scattered them in all directions. . . . Our allies and the foot soldiers wrought destruction, the greatest in the world, at a brook, and they surrounded a bare sierra where they had taken refuge, and pursued them up to the top, and took all that had gone up there. That day we killed and imprisoned many people, many of whom were captains and lords and distinguished people. . . .

[Alvarado relates how the K'iche' lords tried to lure him back to the impregnable city of Utatlán in order to ambush him there. He describes mountain gorges eleven hundred feet deep leading up to Utatlán, "on account of which one cannot pursue the war and punish these people as they deserve." Alvarado writes of capturing a group of K'iche' lords and burning them alive; he then orders the city of Utatlán to be razed, calling on the help of warriors from the rival Kaqchikel kingdom. *Eds.*]

And seeing the damages which they had suffered, they sent me their messengers to explain how they now wished to be good, and that if they had erred, it had been at the order of their lords, and that while their lords

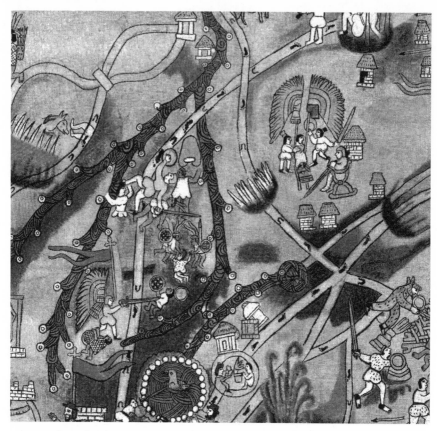

A scene from the *Lienzo de Quauhquechollan* (ca. 1530), a firsthand indigenous account of the conquest of Guatemala. Painted on cotton cloth by the Quauhquecholteca of central Mexico. It shows how the Quauhquecholteca invaded Guatemala in alliance with the Spanish. From the San Pedro Museo del Arte, Puebla, Mexico. Digital restoration, Universidad Francisco Marroquín, Guatemala City, 2007. © 2007 Universidad Francisco Marroquín. Used by permission.

were alive they dared not do otherwise, but as now their lords were dead they begged me to pardon them. And I spared their lives, and ordered them to return to their houses and inhabit the land as before; and this they did, and presently I have them in the same condition as they were before, at the service of His Majesty. And to better secure the land, I released two sons of the lords, whom I placed in their fathers' positions, and I believe that they will carry out well all that pertains to the service of His Majesty and to the good of this land.

And as far as touches the war, there is nothing more to say at present, save that all those who were captured in the war were branded and made slaves, of whom I gave His Majesty's fifth part to the treasurer, Baltasar de Mendoza, which he sold by public auction, so as to make more secure His Majesty's revenue. . . .

May it please Our Lord to give me victory over these infidels, so that I may bring them to His service or that of His Majesty. . . . The Spaniards in my company, both on foot and on horse, have done so well in the war that I have offered them—and they are worthy of—much gratitude. At present I have nothing more of importance to say, except that we are placed in the wildest country of people that has ever been seen. . . . Also may Your Grace take care to let His Majesty know that we have served him with our persons and our properties at our own cost . . . so that His Majesty may grant us favors. May Our Lord protect the very magnificent person of Your Grace for as long a time as you desire. From the city of Uclatan [Utatlán], on the 11th of April. . . .

I kiss the hands of Your Grace.

Pedro de Alvarado.

A Kaqchikel Maya Account

THE ARRIVAL OF THE CASTILIANS AT XE TULUL

This was truly the year when the Castilians arrived at Xe Pit, Xe Tulul [Zapotitlán]. . . . Tonatiuh was the name of their lord; truly, he defeated the whole nation. Until then, their faces were unknown; homage was still given to wood and stone.

Then they came to Xelajub' [Quetzaltenango], and there too the K'iche' men were dissolved and died; then all the K'iche's were routed, all of them who opposed the Castilians; then the K'iche's were dissolved before Xelajub'.

When he came to the town of Q'umarka'j, he was immediately received by the lords, the Ajpop and Ajpop K'amajay [the king or ruler and his deputy]. Immediately, the K'iche's paid them tribute, for at that moment the lords were put in irons by Tonatiuh. . . .

The lords, Ajpop and Ajpop K'amajay, were burned by Tonatiuh. Tonatiuh's heart had not been satisfied by war. A messenger from Tonatiuh soon came to the [Kaqchikel] lords, an order for warriors: "Let the warriors of the Ajpop Sotz'il [and] Ajpo Xajil come here to kill the K'iche' men!" Thus spoke Tonatiuh's messenger to the lords. As soon as Tonatiuh's orders were fulfilled, four hundred warriors went to kill the K'iche's. But only those of the town went; he did not ask all the warriors to appear before the lords. When the warriors went for the third time, the K'iche's began to pay tribute. We also went forth to receive Tonatiuh here, you, my sons!

THEN TRULY HE ARRIVED HERE IN IXIMCHE'

On 1 Junajpu' [of the Maya calendar], the Castilians arrived here in the town of Iximche'. Tonatiuh was the name of their lord. Immediately, Tonatiuh was greeted by the lords B'eleje K'at and Kaji' Imox. Tonatiuh's heart was good toward the lords when truly he arrived in town. There was no war; Tonatiuh was happy when truly he entered Iximche'. This was how it was when the Castilians arrived long ago, you, my sons! Truly it was frightening when they arrived; their faces were not known. The lords wondered if they were godlike beings. We, your fathers, wondered about them, we who truly saw their arrival at Iximche'. . . .

Soon after, Tonatiuh asked the lords about enemies. The lords said then, "I have two enemies; the Tz'utujil and those of Atakat, you, godlike lord!" he was told by the lords. Five days later, Tonatiuh left the town to do this: the Tz'utujils then died because of the Castilians. On 7 Kamey, the Tz'utujils were killed by Tonatiuh.

Just twenty-five days later, he passed from the town to do this: then Tonatiuh went to Kuskatan [Cuzcatlán, present-day El Salvador], killing the Atakat as he passed through. . . .

On 10 Junajpu' he came back, he returned from Cuzcatlán, just forty days he was gone campaigning in Cuzcatlán, then he returned to town. Then Tonatiuh asked for one of the daughters of the lords; she was given to Tonatiuh by the lords.

HERE WAS THE DEMAND FOR PRECIOUS METAL

Then the lords' precious metal was demanded by Tonatiuh. Although he wanted to be given precious metal that was collected, truly, only in gourds, and crowns, they brought nothing. Tonatiuh soon became angry with the lords, saying, "Why won't you give me precious metal? Has the precious metal of the whole kingdom not arrived here with you? Do you want me to burn you, to hang you?" he said to the lords.

The Tonatiuh demanded 1,200 pesos in yellow gold. The lords tried to have it reduced; the lords cried before him. But Tonatiuh did not want to do it. He just said, "Deliver the precious metal! You have five days to give it up. If you do not deliver it then, you will know my heart!" the lords were told. . . . Then the lords collected their precious metal; all the grandsons of the lords and the sons of the lords gave their precious metal; the people did as much as possible for the lords.

In the middle of delivering the precious metal to Tonatiuh, a demon warrior appeared: "I am thunder; I will kill the Castilians!" he said to the lords. "They will be drowned in fire! Let me strike the town! Let the lords leave across the river!" . . . said the demon warrior to the lords. The lords believed this was the truth; the man's words were obeyed by them. In truth, half of the precious metal had been delivered when we dispersed.

HERE TRULY WE DISPERSED FROM THE TOWN

On 7 Ajmaq the dispersal occurred. Then the town of Iximche' was abandoned; because of the demon-warrior the lords then left. "Now, truly, Tonatiuh will die!" they said. There was no war in Tonatiuh's heart; he was happy because precious metal was being given. But, because of the demon-warrior, the town was left abandoned on 7 Ajmaq, you, my sons!

However, Tonatiuh missed the lords. So ten days after we dispersed from the town, the war was begun by Tonatiuh. On 4 Kamey began our being killed by the Castilians. Then our suffering began; we dispersed beneath the trees, beneath the vines, you, my sons! The whole kingdom was in a fight to the death with Tonatiuh. At the peak of it, the Castilians went elsewhere. They left the town; they abandoned it. Then the Castilians were opposed by the Kaqchikels. Trenches were dug, pits for horses were made, with stakes to kill them. Truly war was waged again by the people. Many Castilians died, and also many horses died in the horse pits. The K'iche's and the Tz'utujils were dissolved; all the kingdoms were thus dissolved by the Kaqchikels. The Castilians distinguished themselves, but the whole [Kaqchikel] kingdom also distinguished itself. . . .

[The chronicle goes on to describe how the Kaqchikels held out against Alvarado and his troops for nearly six years. Even while Alvarado laid waste to several towns, "no one bowed down before him," and "nobody paid tribute in the whole land." On 6 Tz'I' in the Maya calendar, tribute was resumed. *Eds.*]

Then the tribute began again. It brought new sufferings. But we had had enough with war; for twice, truly, we had made great wars, much death. . . .

ON 3 AJ ELAPSED THIRTY-THREE YEARS [JULY 10, 1529]

In this year the lords Ajpop Sotz'il and Ajpop Xajil appeared again before Tonatiuh. Five years and four months the lords were beneath the trees, beneath the vines. The lords did not wish to go; their deaths were threatened by Tonatiuh. They appeared and spoke before Tonatiuh. On 7 Ajmaq the lords were forced to leave. They arrived at Ruya'al Chay [Izapa]. Many lords assembled; all of the lords' grandsons, all of the lords' sons. Many people went accompanying the lords. . . . At that moment Tonatiuh was happy with the lords when he saw them before him again.

ON 13 AJ ELAPSED THIRTY-FOUR YEARS SINCE THE REVOLT
[AUGUST 14, 1530]

In this year it is frightful how much tribute was paid. Tribute in precious metal was given again to Tonatiuh. Tribute was made by four hundred men, four hundred women, who went to wash metal [pan for gold]; all the people dug for metal. Another four hundred men and four hundred women were given as tribute. They were used by Tonatiuh to build Pan Q'än [a town on the slopes of the Agua volcano]. He became the lord of the land. We all saw all of this, you, my sons!

Note

1. This defeat of K'iche' Maya forces has come to be known as the Battle of El Pinar. Alvarado never names the Maya rulers whom he defeats and kills, but late colonial sources name Tecún Umán as the heroic K'iche' leader. Utatlán was the Nahua name for the K'iche' urban and religious center of Gumarcaah. Its ruins are an archaeological site about two miles outside the town of Santa Cruz del Quiché.

Tecún Umán and the Conquest Dance

Irma Otzoy

*Tecún Umán is a legendary Maya-K'iche' warrior king believed to have died at
the hands of the Spanish conquistador Pedro de Alvarado. Tecún Umán's image
is commonplace in Guatemala. He appears on the country's currency, called the
quetzal after another famous symbol, the iridescent, long-tailed quetzal bird. According to legend, Tecún Umán is said to have transformed himself into an eagle
or a quetzal while defending his people against Alvarado. Around the country,
the battle between Alvarado and Tecún Umán is memorialized in school pageants
and in a colonial-era folkloric dance called* el Baile de la Conquista, *the* Dance
of the Conquest, *still enacted in indigenous communities today. In 1960, at the
height of the Cold War, the military government of General Ydígoras Fuentes declared Tecún Umán a national hero—Guatemala's "first soldier"—linking ethnic
imagery to patriotism as a cornerstone of anticommunist nation-building. Yet, as
Maya-Kaqchikel anthropologist Irma Otzoy explains, Tecún Umán is an ambiguous emblem of military nationalism. For many, Tecún Umán and the* Dance of
the Conquest *symbolize resistance. For others, Tecún Umán represents a fractured Guatemalan nation that exalts historically remote Maya figures while marginalizing the living Maya.*

Today is the four hundred seventy-second anniversary of the death of the K'iche'
chief. According to legend, the quetzal fell on his chest, symbolizing our race's
defeat. Historically, he has no profile . . . Tecún Umán of the green, green, green
feathers.

[Today is] a festive day, of Tecún Umán and the marimba. Day of our nationality.
Guatemala is multiracial. . . . We feel happy today because Guatemala is so beautiful! Let's not ruin her.—Radio announcements on "Tecún Umán Day," February
20, 1996

In the school where I studied in Guatemala City, on February 20 at seven
o'clock AM we would set out to the Tecún Umán monument five kilometers
away. The program would begin with a series of civic acts: a salute to the

flag, the national anthem, government and army speeches, schoolchildren's poems, and songs to Tecún Umán. We would be accompanied by government officials, uniformed soldiers, and Indian brotherhoods from around the country. Even so, I never heard my classmates say that February 20 had any major significance, beyond being an especially tiring day for us.

After nearly three decades, on February 20th, 1996, I found myself in front of the Tecún Umán monument once again. Several things had changed. The monument is now half hidden by roads and bridges. It looks like a recently excavated archaeological site, not an emblem of Guatemalan nationalism. Pedro de Alvarado has had better luck, however. A portrait of Alvarado hangs prominently in the city hall building in Guatemala City. (Before he became president, [the light-haired] Alvaro Arzú [1996–2000] was the mayor of Guatemala City, and he liked to pose in front of Pedro de Alvarado's portrait. Perhaps this habit and his physical similarity to Alvarado is why some Guatemalans nicknamed Arzú "Tonatiuh," after the name that the Indians called Pedro de Alvarado.)

The different meanings associated with Tecún Umán can be seen in the Conquest Dance that people in many parts of rural Guatemala perform during their patron saint festivals. The Conquest Dance was performed historically (in Guatemala and other areas of colonial Latin America) at the urging of Catholic friars as part of their efforts to convert the population to Catholicism. Its structure is based on the Spanish *baile de los moros*, a dance commemorating the fifteenth-century expulsion of the Moors from Spain. The dance's contemporary performance in Maya communities, however, is not just a naïve reaffirmation or acceptance of the "conquest." Nor is it merely local entertainment. Through the re-enactment of the Conquest Dance in these communities, the Maya people demonstrate their cultural resistance on a local level. At the same time, the dance is also performed by non-Maya, and it may re-affirm oral traditions regarding the ethnic conflicts between Maya and non-Maya. The figure of Tecún Umán is central to the dance-drama.

Tecún Umán on Stage

Ciudad Vieja. Founded in 1527, Ciudad Vieja (Valley of Almolonga) has been an important town in the history of Guatemala. Since its inception, Ciudad Vieja was inhabited by Spanish people and Indian families, primarily Tlaxcalans, who accompanied the Spaniards from Mexico. The city is located only five kilometers from the famous colonial and tourist town of Antigua.

The dancers of the Conquest Dance in Ciudad Vieja are mainly adults.

They are farmers, carpenters, drivers, accountants, tailors and workers. Most of them have finished grammar school, and some have attended junior high school. Their participation in the Conquest Dance is entirely voluntary; no government or non-governmental agency funds are used. Ciudad Vieja has many visitors during its fiestas, including people from neighboring communities, the central highlands, and national and international tourists.

The local dancers' understandings of Tecún Umán seem to come primarily from their relationship with the Conquest Dance rather than from grammar school. As one actor/dancer described: "Tecún Umán wanted to defeat Pedro de Alvarado. But, since the Christians [Spaniards] had God's power, they had the faith to defeat them. . . ." The actors maintain an oral and local historical understanding, in which Tecún Umán's death is consonant with the transition to Catholicism and the superiority of the Catholic religion and Spanish culture.

In Ciudad Vieja, the emergence of Tecún Umán as a national hero has not been difficult for Ladinos [non-Indians] to accept. One of the actors remarked: "Tecún Umán is a hero because he was defending the nation's soil. As commander of the troops, he defended Guatemalans." Another actor, referring to the ethnic identity of the town's inhabitants, said, "We call ourselves Ladinos because of our dress and all that. But, we are all Indians because we are all descended from King Tecún."

Santa María de Jesús: Tradition as Resistance. Santa María is a K'iche' town in the municipality of Zunil, six miles from the important highland city of Quetzaltenango. Santa María is also an "historically" important place: the Santa María volcano lies within its borders, to which the Spanish chroniclers of the sixteenth century referred in their writings, and it is near this site that the battle between Tecún Umán and Pedro de Alvarado is said to have taken place.

On the day of its patron fiesta, the town "takes out" its Conquest Dance after Mass, from about eight in the morning until about five in the afternoon. Not all of the dancers have attended grammar school. Some have finished third grade. There are illiterate dancers; in these cases, all of the learning of the scripts is done through memorization. In the "Conquest Dance," the majority of the nineteen dancers are men. The dancers' preparation includes Maya-Christian religious and philosophical elements that must be rehearsed for ten months. Before the first rehearsal, the men must go to the church with candles and flowers. They all go together to choose, rent and bring home the costumes. They also must go together to bless them and pray, with the help of the catechist the day before the presentation. One dancer recalls how the night before they "burned" (a Maya religious act of praying and burning, among other things, candles, honey, lemon and natural incense as an offering to divine beings and the ancestors). The dance is rehearsed every Sunday in the town plaza, and this is where the dance is eventually performed. One dancer comments, " . . . the dance takes place in the plaza because it is a good place. Each corner has a short wall in the ground. There are four, which makes it nice and square." The four little "walls" are oriented to the four cardinal points often associated with Maya cosmovision.

When talking about the events surrounding the "conquest," one dancer remarked, "Tecún Umán was courageous for keeping his head raised when facing the invader Pedro de Alvarado. He fought for his rights." For the dancers, the Conquest Dance not only situates Tecún Umán as an important historical agent, it also fulfills cultural expectations regarding continuity. They claim the Conquest Dance "is a commitment to remember our ancestors, the ancient customs and a devotion to the Virgin."

"We make a memory of Tecún Umán. Or rather, of our ancestors. We no longer have the others who participated [referring to previous generations of dancers]. So now we young adults are participating [in the dancing], right? We want to participate as they participated . . . to represent how the conquest was when the Spaniards came."

The memory of Tecún Umán in the Conquest Dance may include several contemporary Indian cultural elements. When it is time for the scene where Tecún Umán dies, someone goes to sound the church bells. Although Tecún Umán is only a memory, this is a practice done when someone actually dies in the community. The performance of the Conquest Dance in this community is a conscious act to remember and sustain resistance.

Palín: A Counter-Official Attempt. Palín is the only Indian community located in the municipality of Escuintla, 40 kilometers from Guatemala City. The majority of the inhabitants are Poqomam Indians. They are subsistence farmers, but they spend most of their time as laborers harvesting coffee and tropical fruits. The young Poqomam adults are important participants in the Maya movement.

The "Invasion Dance" was first performed in Palín on December 25, 1992. This new version of the dance-drama exhibits a deliberate Maya questioning of the popular discourse concerning the "conquest" and the figure of Tecún Umán. One dancer explains the altered performance script: "For example, instead of 'gentlemen' [referring to the Spaniards], we put 'foreigners.'" Many terms in the Invasion Dance were rewritten using the official alphabet of the Academy of Maya Languages.

Traditionally, the Conquest Dance in Palín was run by Ladinos. Beginning several decades ago, the Indian people in Palín have presented their own Conquest Dance. Since the 1970s, there has been competition between the Conquest Dance performed by Indians and Ladinos; Indians present the Conquest Dance one year, and the Ladinos do so the next year. The "Invasion Dance" this group of intellectual youth presented in 1992 is different from the Conquest Dance that another group of Indians presented, which in turn competed with the Ladino people of Palín.

One organizer summarized the Maya questioning of colonial history through the dance:

> They call it the "Invasion Dance." . . . Tecún Umán gets stabbed in the back, as a symbol of treachery. They elaborate a series of masks. Not from the *morerías* [traditional masks] because those seem almost blond. The dancers' clothing is not made of corduroy and silk, but of colorful weavings, like present day Maya dress with real fabric, adorned with many feathers. . . . The dress is not destroyed but later used as everyday clothing.

Through the dances, we can see that Tecún Umán is a contested symbol of nationalism and resistance in Guatemala. There are also debates over the historical authenticity of Tecún Umán. Rather than a national hero, Tecún Umán is sometimes seen as a national myth.

Tecún Umán between Myth and History

Pedro de Alvarado himself was laconic in his tales and sometimes careless about the names of rivers and other geographical details. Alvarado never mentions Tecún Umán by name. Instead, he records that after a military maneuver in which the Spaniards ran the Indians off to the plains, ". . . there was a great achievement and punishment: one of four men of this city who was a captain general of all the land died. . . ."

Criollo [Creole, a European born in the Americas] author Francisco Antonio Fuentes y Guzmán, writing in the late seventeenth century, relates that during the confrontation between Tecún Umán and Pedro de Alvarado, Tecún Umán, possessed by the devil, transformed himself into an "eagle" or "quetzal" and attacked the Spanish army:

> . . . that eagle, which was dressed in beautiful and enlarged feathers, decorated with shiny jewels, gold and precious stones, flew with singular force over the army . . . against the heroic *caudillo* [leader] D. Pedro de Alvarado, and this illustrious *caudillo*, without hesitating and not even slowing down, took a sword into hand, and, without dismounting, hurt her [the bird], with such skill, that she landed dead. . . . and the quetzal having died, he also found the King Tecún dead in his tent, with the very same blow the bird received. It seems from the Indian manuscripts that the name of this prince was Tecún Umán. . . .

An anonymous Dominican friar, writing in the early eighteenth century, described Tecún Umán as "a great warlock [who] flew over all the armies in the form of a bird they call Quetzal. . . . It is known that [some Indians] still preserve that cursed pact with the demon. So it is not unbelievable that this King Tecum Umán was a warlock and that he turned into a Quetzal."

Nineteenth-century writer José Milla relates the confrontation between Tecún Umán and Pedro de Alvarado, in which legend has added "the appearance of a marvelous eagle or quetzal of gigantic proportions, and it was the prince's *nahual*, which ferociously attacked the Spanish warrior. . . ." A *nahual* is an animal spirit that accompanies each person throughout his or her life. (*Nahual* has two meanings. *Nahual* is a synonym for sorcerer, magician, or soothsayer. It may also mean individual totemism, alter ego, or guardian angel. A person has a *nahual* from birth. The *nahual* depends on the person's birth date according to the Maya calendar; this determines the name of the animal that will be their *nahual*. The *nahual* will accompany and protect the person while they are alive.) Twentieth-century historian Ernesto Chinchilla gives Tecún Umán a symbolic patriotic meaning: "In the sacrifice of this Indian lord, posterity has witnessed the symbol of the man who would lose his life before losing his freedom, in defense of his country." Chinchilla notes that little is known about the life of Tecún Umán, concluding, "it might be [that] no one particular Indian group in Guatemala may appropriate his cradle." The nebula that surrounds this historical character thus fulfills a sublime nationalist sentiment. Shorn of any "Indian particularity," Tecún Umán can be appropriated by the Guatemalan nation-state.

The *Historia General de Guatemala* is one of the most serious contemporary sources on Guatemalan history. In the section relating to the "conquest" of Guatemala, the historians Jorge Luján and Horacio Cabezas ar-

Tecún Umán on the back of a truck, Izabal. Photo by Eny Roland Hernández Javier. Used by permission of the photographer.

gue that Tecún Umán did not exist. According to these authors, no Indian or Spanish source close to the conquest mentions his existence. Luján and Cabezas propose that the name Tecún Umán might have come from the conquest dance introduced by the Spanish during the colonial era. The storyline of the dance-drama required a confrontation between Alvarado and the K'iche' chief, and the K'iche' leader needed a name. In other words, Tecún Umán was invented by the Spaniards through the Conquest Dance.

Indian documents from the colonial period give interpretations of Tecún Umán that differ from these Spanish, Criollo, and Ladino authors. Three Maya documents, or Indian Titles, mention Tecún Umán: *Títulos de la Casa Ixquin-Nehaib Señora del Territorio de Otzoya*, *Título de Ajpop Hutzitzil Tzunun* and *Título de los Señores Coyoy*. These three *títulos* are colonial documents written in the mid-sixteenth century. Their authors were K'iche' leaders who described themselves as the descendants of K'iche' chiefs who participated directly in the conquest wars. The documents were written in K'iche' using the Latin alphabet. The three titles were written as legal documents to establish property rights and legitimacy for the principal families in the K'iche' region.

The three Maya documents make specific mention of the quetzal feathers that adorned Tecún Umán. Bird feathers undoubtedly were very precious to the pre-Hispanic cultures; they were used frequently by politico-military elites, as represented in many Maya estelas, in the Bonampak murals and even in the Tlaxcala canvasses painted during the colonial period. Yet, only the Tzunun Title refers to Tecún Umán as a bird, stating: "Don Tecún flew three times up to the sky, in the form of a very gallant bird." Neither of the other two documents refer to Tecún Umán's transformation into a quetzal. The Nehaib Title, like the Tzunun Title, says, "Captain Tecúm flew up, as an eagle, full of feathers that sprouted from . . . himself. They were not artificial. He carried wings that also grew from his body. . . ." Even in this Title, the description is one of a human, "from whom feathers grew" from the human body. It does not state that he actually transformed into a bird. The Coyoy Title reads: ". . . in a second attempt . . . King Tecún came from the sky to surrender . . . and the captain fell into the hands of the Castilian people . . . his blood mixed with the Quetzal feathers which stemmed from the center of his body. . . ."

The quetzal feathers, the "flights," and even the "gallant bird" figure imply that Tecún Umán never really shed his human form. Nahualism, that is, the ability of certain people to turn themselves into an animal or supernatural being, is a belief that has always existed in the Maya cosmovision and mythology. Where Tecún Umán is concerned, the Titles' authors use a more figurative style of nahualism to emphasize beauty, physical dexterity, and the high politico-military rank exercised by Tecún Umán during his combat with the Spaniards.

The creation of an official story about Tecún Umán has turned into a confrontational game between what is "historical" and what is "mythological." The story is grounded in a Spanish document that is incomplete. In order to make it complete, it has become necessary to turn to a series of Maya documents. But the Maya documents are considered to be mythological. The end result is a confusing story of a character who is nonetheless a "national hero."

Tecún Umán and Nation-Building

For most people in Guatemala, Tecún Umán is perhaps the only Indian name that carries any meaning, as vague as it may be. On the other hand, Tecún Umán has had a curious career in this Guatemalan desire for nation-building.

An army pamphlet from the 1990s gives a military view of the significance of Tecún Umán:

For all Guatemalans, the figure of our courageous warrior TECÚN UMÁN should represent a) a lesson in patriotism; b) an example of authentic nationalism; c) a symbol of national identity; d) an example of the defense of freedom, foundation for national unity; e) champion of sovereignty; f) the honor and courage of the Guatemalan soldier; g) principle of dignity for the Guatemalan army.

The insurgent struggle also inspired poetic renditions of Tecún Umán. In a series of leftist poems, Tecún Umán's Indian characteristics are subsumed by an image that harkens to the popularized portrait of Che Guevara:

If on this night Tecún does not arrive
we shall all die . . .
If on this night Tecún does not appear
dawn's companion
companion of he who guards the ravine
the companion who makes the field grow through his gaze alone
the companion who with saliva heals wounds
the companion who knows the word for freedom in all languages . . .
the companion who incarnates the names of all the heroes
If on this night Tecún does not show
what awaits us, we all know.
Ten seconds later Tecún appears, donning a beard and black beret
offering a cigarette he smiles at us
and we all understand that nation and life . . . we shall overcome.

The Maya questioning of Tecún Umán includes both rejection and reinterpretation. Ironically, much of this questioning emerges after many Maya learned about the official story of Tecún Umán in school. A well-known leader of the Maya movement reflects: "What do the social studies textbooks say? It is history, but mixed with fable, with storytelling, right? And, instead of elaborating upon the political fact of the invasion, it stops right there with distractions."

The official history barely makes reference to other Indian figures. According to the Maya leader quoted above:

They say we should know about Tecún Umán, but what about the Tecún Umáns? For example, there is a book called *One Hundred Famous People in Guatemalan History*, and there are only two or three Indians. . . . And on February 20 [Tecún Umán Day], the army would pass out leaflets . . . presenting Tecún Umán as the first anticommunist(!!). . . .

That is, the Spaniards were Communists [he laughs] . . . and poor Tecún Umán was combating them.

Another Maya activist expresses:

Tecún Umán is a hero, but it depends on who says so. The thing is that there has been a type of usurpation. He *is* a national Maya hero. But the irony is that it is the Ladino society here, through the state, which proclaims him a "national" hero. . . . So, it is as if they compliment the resistance of the first Mayas, but not the present-day Maya resistance. . . . and, also, the [purpose of the Ladinos] is sort of to go on building a supposed nationality, because, ultimately, what are they going to hang on to?

  Ultimately, [Ladinos] realize they are mestizos [mixed race]. So, who are they going to identify with? With their father who raped their mother? Or, with their raped mother? Up to a certain point, consciously or unconsciously this is their dilemma. So, when they talk about Tecún Umán it is as if they are taking a hero away from us as well. Since Tecún Umán is one of them, the Maya reaction, at least for some people, is to say "no." Tecún Umán is a Ladino hero, nothing to do with us. When it really isn't like that.

A Maya intellectual elaborates:

Tecún Umán is a Maya hero. He is not a Guatemalan hero. . . . The thing is that Guatemala lacks symbols; it lacks personalities, it lacks heroes. . . . I have asked [Ladinos], "Who are the personalities who make the mestizo or Ladino proud?" So . . . lacking symbols, lacking reasons to be proud, they grab [that which is] Maya. . . .

Tecún Umán as a national hero is a problematic symbol for a multicultural nation. Some Guatemalans can embrace the idea of a national hero, but for others, this is unconvincing. Some consider Tecún Umán a governmental excuse for ignoring the present-day Indians' socioeconomic needs. Others view him as an act of cultural appropriation. And still others do not even believe that the character ever existed. Besides Ladinos, other populations have protested the official story of Tecún Umán. As one Guatemalan Garífuna notes: "Instead of making us memorize about Tecún Umán and the quetzal, they should teach us about what is ours; they should teach the Garífunas [Afro-Caribbean communities on the Atlantic Coast] and any other ethnic group about their own culture, their own race."

The Maya movement has a dilemma: to forget about Tecún Umán or re-appropriate him? Once in a while an individual or a Maya organization will do something special in his name. But Tecún Umán is criticized more than he is used as a call to struggle. With Tecún Umán, Mayas are presented in a petrified way, in the form of death, without any real political inclusion. As one Maya activist comments, Tecún Umán is "tainted" by the official story. So they silently choose to leave him alone. Some Mayas argue that Tecún Umán is K'iche', and as such does not represent all Mayas. Others believe that Tecún Umán should be rescued from the official blur; his story should be rewritten, and everything taught about him in school should be unlearned.

If we want to give a new timbre to history and to the country, we should begin by de-officializing Tecún Umán. A re-appropriation of Tecún Umán, albeit difficult, would allow Maya intellectuals to learn from the rural Mayas. As evidenced by the Conquest Dance, neither they nor their history have been totally conquered.

Great Was the Stench of the Dead

W. George Lovell

Epidemics preceded the Europeans into Guatemala in the early 1500s. Old World diseases, such as smallpox, had already ravaged indigenous populations on the Caribbean islands and in Mexico. In the densely populated Guatemalan highlands, disease and high mortality created panic and social disorder in Maya communities and helped the Spanish take control. An indigenous account written during the early colonial period describes the outbreak of disease: "First they became ill of a cough. They suffered from nosebleeds and illness of the bladder. . . . Little by little heavy shadows and black night enveloped our fathers and grandfathers. . . . Great was the stench of the dead." [1]

In this selection, the geographer W. George Lovell studies demographic trends in Guatemala's northwestern Cuchumatán mountains, where population levels plummeted by 90 percent during the Spanish invasion and early colonial period.

It is now generally recognized that the New World was densely settled on the eve of its "discovery" by Renaissance Europe, and that native American populations declined drastically in size following contact with Old World intruders. Catastrophic depopulation among Amerindians whose lands and islands were conquered by imperial Spain has traditionally been attributed to unmitigated carnage, ruthless enslavement, and harsh exploitation by Spanish colonists, the thesis of the infamous *Leyenda Negra*, or Black Legend. It is not difficult to find references in the literature that support the thesis of the Black Legend. According to Bartolomé de las Casas, for example, five million Indian lives were lost in Guatemala alone because of the tyranny of the conquistador Pedro de Alvarado. In his *Brevísima relación de la destrucción de las Indias*, Las Casas singled out Alvarado as being among the most rapacious conquistadors of all, stating bluntly that "the enormities perpetrated by himself especially . . . are enough to fill a particular volume, so many were the slaughters, violences, injuries, butcheries, and beastly desolations." Writing to King Charles V in the mid-sixteenth century, Las Casas declared that "Your Highness can be sure that of all the parts of the

Indies where there have been the most excesses and disorder in committing injustices and iniquities . . . there are, and have been, so many and such grave and evil vexations . . . made against the Indians . . . of the province of Guatemala . . . one cannot imagine the ways and cunning manner . . . used to secure them."

While the criticism of Las Casas and the moral position he and others represented must always be taken into consideration, the principal cause of native depopulation was not massacre and mistreatment at the hands of bloodthirsty Spaniards, but the introduction by the invaders of Old World diseases against which Amerindians were immunologically defenseless.

The inhabitants of the New World lived in virtual isolation from those of the Old. This long period of isolation weakened considerably the resistance of Amerindians to most of the major diseases of mankind. Whatever the reasons, the inhabitants of the New World developed tolerances for only a limited number of indigenous American diseases. During pre-Columbian times, Amerindians appear to have suffered primarily from gastro-intestinal disturbances and respiratory disorders. Prior to the arrival of Europeans, therefore, Amerindians enjoyed an existence relatively free of infectious diseases. Maladies such as measles, mumps, smallpox, and plague—all of which were endemic to the Old World—were apparently unknown. When these diseases were inadvertently brought to the New World by Spanish conquerors and colonists, their impact on hitherto isolated human communities may well have caused, in the words of one scholar, "the greatest destruction of lives in history."

[Alfred] Crosby thinks the first disease to arrive in America was smallpox. [Murdo] MacLeod reckons that the impact of smallpox on the native population of the New World was at least as cataclysmic as the impact of the Black Death of 1346–50 on late medieval European society; that is, one-third to one-half of the people who came in contact with the disease would have perished. From the testimony of Toribio de Benavente, a sixteenth-century Franciscan better known by his adopted name Motolinía, we know that smallpox swept through central Mexico with horrendous human devastation. It continued its lethal passage south toward Guatemala, accompanied perhaps by pulmonary plague or typhus. By the end of 1520, four years before the *entrada* of Pedro de Alvarado, the Indians of highland Guatemala were reeling from their initial encounter with what MacLeod has appropriately called "the shock troops of the conquest." The chroniclers of the Cakchiquel lamented that it was "in truth terrible, the number of dead among the people . . . in that period . . . when the plague raged." This first bout of pestilence was followed about twelve years later by a pandemic of measles.

Thereafter, chronic outbreaks of Old World sickness were a common feature of Indian life in colonial Guatemala and resulted repeatedly in high
mortality among a native population that was ill equipped physiologically
to fight off infection. As well as being struck periodically by diseases of
pandemic proportion, the Indian peoples of the Cuchumatanes also had to
contend with more localized outbreaks of pestilence.

The demographic collapse of the Cuchumatán population is therefore
most critically linked to the ravages of Old World disease on vulnerable native inhabitants. Subjugation by imperial Spain was certainly not achieved
and maintained without brutality and exploitation, but Old World microbes
consumed more Indian lives than did Hispanic depravity and greed. From
the 1520s until the end of Spanish rule in 1821, Cuchumatán Indians were
subjected to unrelenting waves of pestilence. Mortality rates varied but were
consistently high. Between 1520 and about 1680, native population declined
by more than 90 percent, falling from perhaps 260,000 to a nadir of about
16,000. The collapse seems to have abated by the end of the seventeenth
century, when the first signs of demographic recovery are manifest. Several
fluctuations in the course of the eighteenth century, however, indicate that
the Indians had still not built up effective immunities to diseases such as
smallpox and typhus. Only at the very end of the colonial period are there
signs of a sustained increase in native numbers across the region as a whole.

Note

1. Adrián Recinos, Delia Goetz, and Dionisio José Chonay, eds. and trans., *Annals of the
Cakchiquels* (Norman: University of Oklahoma Press, 1974).

Good Government

Bishop Francisco Marroquín

Shortly after the Spanish military conquest of Guatemala, the Spanish clergyman Francisco Marroquín was appointed the region's first Catholic bishop. Launching what he called a "spiritual conquest" of the countryside, he learned K'iche' and led the church's efforts to extend its reach and authority. Bishop Marroquín was also one of Guatemala's first governors, and his collected writings, from the 1530s to the 1560s, show a preoccupation with building political stability in the colony.

A similar concern led the Spanish Crown, in 1542, to pass a set of decrees called the "New Laws," designed to restrict the power of Spanish colonists. Indians were declared to be vassals of the Crown, not slaves of individual Spaniards, and new legal protections and limited autonomy were granted to indigenous communities. The New Laws proved difficult to enforce, however, and in his writings, Bishop Marroquín criticized the ongoing abuses of Spanish conquistadors. Marroquín advocated for the reducciones de indios, that is, the "reduction" of indigenous populations into concentrated, controllable settlements patterned on the urbanized grid of Spanish towns. The reducciones were supposed to "civilize" Indians through exposure to Christian doctrine. They are the origins of the municipal and parish structure that today still characterizes much of rural Guatemala. The reducciones also had the effect of crowding indigenous populations into unsanitary living conditions that worsened the horrific death toll from Old World diseases (see "Great Was the Stench of the Dead," this volume). Finally, Bishop Marroquín warns that unregulated female sexuality threatens the formalized separation of the races inscribed in Spanish colonial edicts.

Maxims of Good Government. . . .

It's very necessary that there not be [Indian] slaves, whether these are slaves of *rescate* [Indians who had been slaves under their own people] or slaves of war.

Children under the age of fourteen should not be submitted to forced labor for any reason; they should receive the doctrine as children.

The kingdom of Guatemala, as Your Majesty knows, is divided into two parts: mountain and coast. The coast is very hot, and the mountains are very cold. It is very important that Your Majesty orders that those who live in one part of the kingdom not be sent to work in the other part of the kingdom, since out of ten who are sent, not even five will return to their houses.

Your Majesty knows that in the province of Guatemala, the largest part is all mountains, a very rough and rugged land, and with houses set at large distances from each other. If the Indians are not brought together, it will be impossible to indoctrinate them. The *servicio ordinario* they provide to their masters will also be eased by bringing them together. [The historian Christopher Lutz notes that *servicio ordinario* was a system of ongoing labor duties for former indigenous slaves who had been emancipated by the late 1540s in or near the colonial capital of Santiago, under which men and women performed tasks that included street cleaning and household labor for the Spanish. *Eds.*]

This gathering together of the Indian towns is the most important thing for these parts; since they are men, it's only right that they should live together and in company, which will have a positive effect on their spirits and bodies: we must get to know them, and they must get to know us.

The Indians should not perform any kind of service in the towns or villas, except for turning in their tribute at harvest time.

The Indians must not be made to excavate gold except in the dry season, in November, December, January, February, and March. In April the rains begin, and the Indians begin their planting; it is a very convenient time for them to be in their houses, so they can recuperate and procreate.

The Indians should not be used to carry cargo in any way, on any route, since this offends God . . . there are plenty of horses, oxen and carts for hire.

No one, not even the bishop, the president, a visitor, or another private person, should be so bold as to take anything from the Indians, not even a feather.

It is necessary to recalculate the rate of tribute, because [the Indians] would never be able to make the target all at once, or even over many tries, since they are so poor.

Two royal judges should always travel through the land and help mitigate conflicts; [the Indians] are such poor and fearful people that it is necessary to go directly to them or else nothing is gained.

Few see or understand the labyrinth of these Indians with the simplicity that is required; over there [in Spain] it is impossible to understand. Here, most lack this necessary simplicity, and those who have it and speak the truth are mostly ignored.

Pasos (Steps). Photo by Moisés Castillo. Used by permission of the photographer.

The clerics have to be very serious to come to these parts. A bad cleric does more damage than twenty good clerics. I beseech Your Majesty not to send any more; and since those who are here have endured their burdens and have helped me, I ask that they be rewarded in some measure, even if I am left with nothing.

Likewise, I wrote to Your Majesty about the abundance of young girls, daughters of Spaniards, in these parts; some have a father, and some don't, and all of them are anxious not to have one. So much danger is expected that it would be a great charity to gather these girls up in a monastery.

With the above, everyone wins: God first, then Your Majesty, the naturals [Indians], conquistadors and settlers, and with this I am silent and I ask for forgiveness if I have not told the truth.

Translated by Elizabeth Oglesby

For the Eyes of Our King

Various authors

The Guatemalan countryside felt the impact of Spanish colonialism in different ways. Many areas remained relatively untouched by Spanish occupation; but in the mining regions of the western highlands and in the central Valley of Guatemala, forced labor and tribute demands were onerous. Beginning in the 1550s, indigenous communities began to petition Spanish authorities for relief, usually addressing their pleas to a high-ranking Spaniard, sometimes the viceroy or the king. The language was reverential, with the petitioners describing themselves in humble language emphasizing their poverty and distress. The document presented below is part of a series of petitions presented in 1572 by Kaqchikel communities near the colonial capital city of Santiago de Guatemala. These early letters were written in Nahuatl using the Latin alphabet. Nahuatl, a language originating in central Mexico, was a lingua franca among many communities in pre-Conquest and early colonial Mesoamerica.

A second round of petitions was written in Spanish in 1576, complaining that indigenous commoners—known as macehuales—*were subjected to harsh treatment and crushing labor demands. They also protested that the indigenous aristocracy faced similar servitude. Indeed, political subordination and downward social mobility among elites produced what some historians call "macehualization," or erosion in noble lineages, in many Maya communities in the sixteenth century. In other Maya communities, however, precolonial indigenous social and political hierarchies survived to become the foundation of Spanish colonial rule. The below petition is from Jocotenango, an indigenous community contiguous to Santiago, the colonial capital, today known as Antigua.*

For the Eyes of Our King and Emperor of Castile, don Felipe

Jocotenango, April 3, 1572

We, the *caciques* [chiefs], are the mayors Pedro Gómez and Diego Pérez, and the councilmen Alonso Pérez, Juan Pérez, Diego Pérez, Juan Pérez,

Alonso Pérez, Gaspar Arias, Francisco Pérez, and Diego Velasco. We are all Guatemalateco [in this context, "Guatemalteco" means Kaqchikel speakers of Jocotenango, as opposed to Utatecas or K'iche' speakers of Jocotenango, mentioned below] mayors and councilmen. All the chiefs were slaves of don Pedro de Alvarado, conqueror, and of His Holiness don Francisco Marroquín, bishop from here, of the lands of don Pedro de Alvarado. We were all slaves and children of slaves from Jocotenango, all the chiefs and natives. It distressed us that the *licenciado* [Valdés] sold the girls, that he sold the boys and girls. This began three years ago. President Valdés, the king's prosecutor, Argueta, the treasurer, and Gabriel Mejía, the judge, made all the *macehuales* suffer. . . . The Spanish enslaved the *macehuales*; they beat them in the Spanish *fincas* [haciendas]. They exhausted them, making widows, single men, sick people, children, and dead people give tribute. They raised the tribute. Everything is sold. Corn is sold in the houses of the Spanish every week. . . . All the inhabitants of the *milpas* [a word that usually means corn-fields but which here refers to small rural settlements or villages] of Guatemala are upset. Three times [a year] a person makes tribute and [gives] corn and a chicken, so that for the past nine years every person has given four *tostones* and three *reales* [coins] in tribute to the King . . . the *macehuales* suffered. *Licenciado* Valdés, the president, Argueta, the king's prosecutor, *Licenciado* Aguirre, the treasurer, and the judge exhausted everybody. The poor men, the widows, the young people and the dead people gave tribute. The president and the judges brought so many troubles to the *macehuales*; they made them suffer. Every day they jailed the mayors.

This is how we live in servitude. Help us, Your Highness, our King don Felipe, King of Castile. Here, in Guatemala, we call upon the king to help all of us, to give us a dispensation from the emperor king. The *macehuales* live naked. The people suffer greatly. They only raise tributes on them. The tributes are very large. The president judge asks much tribute from us, the Indians. The witnesses know this: friar Diego de la Cruz, friar Sebastián, friar Domingo Azcona, friar Juan de Castro, provincial, friar Tomás de Cárdenas, who are faithful witnesses, and [also] friar Benito is a witness to all this. . . . No one has rested from the servitude. . . . Everyone suffers greatly. All the Indian people, all the people, as don Felipe [King] of Castile will see in all the reports and processes. Every day [they demand] that we give partridges, bulrushes, and plank-beds. All the mayors of the city's villages were imprisoned because of the dances and [the music of] the drums. The *macehuales* serve without any pay . . . every week they ask for eggs, hens, and fodder. They abuse our children. Every week, thirty *macehuales* work as slaves in the Spaniards' houses. Fifty *macehuales* are sold every week to work for a week as slaves. . . . *Licenciado* Valdés, president, and the judges asked for 410 [*macehuales*] without any pay. They made six hundred *macehuales* serve without any pay. They asked for corn grinders for the house of the president. All the *macehuales* carry water to irrigate the president's farms. These are all the difficulties, all the evils the *macehuales* face. Each week, the *macehuales* who are in prison are sold to the Spanish houses. Some of our children do not have loincloths or shirts. The weeding hoe was lost. The *macehual* women cry because of all this. In your lands live the slaves of don Pedro de Alvarado and don Francisco Marroquín. There are no longer any lands of the king in which to live. Everyone who lives here in Jocotenango are slaves of don Pedro and the bishop, although we are sons of don Jorge Sechul, sons of don Juan Cortés de Tecpan Utatán [respective references to the leading Kaqchikel leader and the K'iche' ruler of Utatlán, today the city of Santa Cruz del Quiché] who are chiefs, nobles, principals, and elders from here, Jocotenango, Guatemala, under the tutelage of [the Dominican order]. . . . Now, help us, King don Felipe of Castile, give us a dispensation here in the lands of don Pedro and Bishop don Francisco Marroquín, help us with our difficulties, help the sons of the King of Castile, Emperor.

Pedro Gómez, mayor
Diego Pérez, mayor

Principals and chiefs: Juan Juárez, Gaspar Arias, Diego Pérez, Juan de Chávez, Alonso Pérez, Alonso Gutiérrez, Alonso Pérez, Pedro Gómez, Domingo Marroquín, Diego Hernández, Andrés García, Juan Pérez and Juan Pérez, Fracisco López, scribe, Diego Velasco, scribe.

Guatemalans, Utatecans, chiefs of Jocotenango

Translated by Elizabeth Oglesby

Colonial Cartographies

Various authors

Beginning in 1575, King Philip II of Spain ordered a massive project to map Span-
ish colonial territories in the New World. By this time, the Crown's concern was
shifting from war and pacification to administration of its vast empire. To learn
about its territories and codify the new imperial boundaries, Spain commissioned
a survey of colonial officials, asking for local maps as well as descriptions of local
resources, history, and geography. The fifty-question survey was addressed to colo-
nial officials, but those officials often summoned indigenous elders and community
leaders for help in answering the survey. The resulting reports, called "Relaciones
geográficas," are a heterogeneous collection of print and graphic renderings of the
colonial landscape, illuminating conflicting Spanish and indigenous traditions of
imagining and inhabiting space.

The selection presented here is from the Relación geográfica *of Santiago Ati-*
tlán, on the southern shore of Lake Atitlán between the highlands and the Pacific
coast piedmont. The district governor, two "prominent [Spanish] citizens," and
three elder "Indian chiefs" provided information to complete the survey, which was
penned by a town scribe in 1585. The accompanying map was commissioned to a lo-
cal painter. Both text and map illustrate the imposition of a Spanish colonial order
through the renaming of places and the political hierarchy of Spanish urban settle-
ments. Because these documents were produced for the Crown, they often portray
an overly harmonious vision of Spanish administration. Yet the visual and textual
representations of the Relaciónes geográficas *also give evidence of the enduring*
indigenous presence in the early colonial period.

This village and district of Atitlán has one thousand and five tribute-paying
married Indians at the present time. In the time of their infidelity [before
the Spanish], the old Indians who, as has already been mentioned, are the
oldest it was possible to find, say that at that time there were more than
twelve thousand Indians, and that the cause for their number being greatly
diminished has been that when don Pedro de Alvarado arrived at this said
village of Atitlán, he took Indian men, sometimes as many as six hundred,

to serve as soldiers at different times after the land was won, to war against the Indians of the village and district of Tecpán Guauhtemala, a separate kingdom, as well as against other rebellious provinces that did not wish to make peace. In the already mentioned wars that occurred, many Indians from this village were killed. Many others died in the mines, mining gold. The Indians that went to the mines were taken by the *encomenderos* [Spanish colonists] who at that time held this village.

According to the Indian chiefs, the number of Indians taken for the mines every ten days was two hundred and forty. Others died of smallpox, measles, typhoid fever, blood flux that caused the blood to run from their noses, and other epidemics and ailments that befell them. When the aforementioned two hundred and forty Indians went to the mines to mine gold, they took their wives with them to prepare their food and to render other personal services, which could be needed in the mines. Because of this and the hard work they endured, their number has suffered so great a decrease. And also because at that time the Spaniards used them as carriers for their trade and commerce, which they had in various places, and the Indians underwent great suffering. Because of these hardships, the wars, and the said ailments, many Indians are no more, and there remains only the small number left at present.

This village of Santiago Atitlán, thus called because of the name of the church located here, is a settled village with well-laid-out streets and squares, the same as is done in Spanish villages, with a square plaza in the middle, although not too big. Toward the west is located the monastery and church of the village, and there reside five religious of the order of St. Francis. One of them is the guardian, who, along with the others, looks after the conversion of the natives. They say Mass, preach the Holy Gospel to the natives in their own tongue, marry them, baptize the children, and administer the other sacraments. On the northern side of the plaza is the house of Justice, where the *corregidor* [Spanish royal official] has his home and residence. To the south of the main plaza are the houses of the city council, where the Indian governor and *alcaldes* [mayors] hold their audiences. This village is the best governed in the district. The language of its natives, which is the principal language used for communication among them, is the native tongue of the founders of the village, and is called Cotohil [Tz'utujil], but they understand other languages different from theirs. . . . Some of them even understand a corrupted version of the Mexican language, but they do not speak it with as much eloquence as the native Indians of Mexico.

The natives of this village are intelligent, docile, and favorably inclined to understand and learn all that they are taught. This is particularly true of those connected with the church, such as the singers, who know how to read, write, and sing. They have learned to sing the *canto organo* and the Gregorian chant very well. They sing it at Muse, at Vespers, and other divine offices. They play the organ, trumpets, flutes, oboes and other instruments. . . . There is a school where the village children gather to learn the Spanish doctrine in the native tongue, and to learn to read and write. . . . They have, with the authority of the Royal Audencia [a combination of high court and governing body in Spanish Central America], chosen and named an Indian who is very well fitted for the purpose and who is a prominent citizen of the town, to be the teacher of the children. He is paid a salary out of the goods of the community. . . .

To the ninth question, as already said, this town is called Atitlán in the Mexican language, which means, in the tongue of Castille [Spanish], "village near the river." It is called thus because in the time of their infidelity the Indians were settled around the banks of the lake, and it is located on [the lake's] edge today. . . . After this land was conquered and pacified and placed under the Royal dominion of His Majesty, Padre Fray Francisco de la Parra and Fray Pedro de Betancour . . . seeing that the road to visit them was troublesome and that because of the manner and form in which they lived it was difficult to reach them and influence them better . . . [various officials] issued a decree in the name of the king, ordering the aforementioned commissary general and the [church] by virtue of the said royal command to take the natives from the banks of the lake, where they were living, and settle them in a comfortable and convenient location in a formal village. . . .

To the fourteenth question, the old Indians, principal chiefs of this village, named individually at the beginning of this report, who have been assembled here to comply with what His Majesty in His Instruction commanded, having been questioned on what is said in the article fourteen of the said Instruction jointly and individually in their native tongue, by Fray Pedro de Arboleda, the guardian, and by the said *señor corregidor,* and by myself, the aforementioned Scribe, in the Mexican tongue, which they understand, they replied that in the time of their infidelity the village and its people were always subject to the hereditary lords and chiefs of this district, as was the case with Atecpan Tototl. This was the name in the Mexican language of the chief and natural lord of this village and its subjects. In the language of the mother tongue he was called Ahgtiquinehay, which, literally speaking, meant "lord of the house." The Indians knew and respected this lord and all his descendants as their hereditary rulers. All other [rulers] descended from him in a direct line had a right to the lordship and chiefship. They paid tribute to them and rendered them other personal services, repaired and built their houses, answered to their calls, and followed their orders . . . they also paid them tribute of cloth, honey, and cacao, as well as quetzal feathers. . . .

To the eighteenth question, they responded thusly: The village is hemmed in and surrounded by high mountains, which on the east side begin almost at the edge of the village itself. There is a mountain, which rises to a height of two thousand paces more or less, and between it and another peak a little further on, there is a plain. The further on, begins the other mountain, which is twice as high as the first. On this mountain there is a volcano on the east side. And going south there is another one next to it, located in such a way that they are the two highest and largest mountains. Of one, it is said that in years past, some eighty years ago, more or less, it erupted and poured forth much molten rock and fire. Even now, evidence of this may be seen around what is called the mouth of the volcano where there is a burned bare space. Like a boiler, this volcano burst a second time in the year 1541, which was when the volcano of the old city of Guatemala erupted and drowned several citizens living there. . . . The volcano of Atitlán threw out fire about three years ago, but it was very little. It still throws up smoke from time to time in the mornings, and sometimes in the evenings, although it is not much. This volcano is called *kungat* in the native tongue, which means "a thing that burns within itself." The other volcano, which is next to it in a northerly direction has never erupted and never has been seen to smoke. In the maternal tongue, the natives call it *oicjakil*, which means "the three young men." The mountain is heavily forested, covered from top to bottom with pines and evergreen oaks, dark oaks, and alders. . . .

To the twentieth question they replied that next to the village is a large lake, which must be, it seems, twenty-five leagues in circumference because of the many bays and inlets it has. It is of striking depth, and the water is dark and cold. The Indian chiefs already mentioned by name, who were the oldest to be found in the village, declared for this report that don Francisco Marroquín, the first bishop who came to this land, while at the village . . . wishing to determine the depth of the said lake, took soundings. They threw in a long cord one thousand two hundred fathoms in length with a large lead weight, and having thrown it in, they found no bottom. . . .

To the twenty-fourth question it was answered that the grain and other products grown in this land are derived from native seeds, such as corn, chile peppers, beans, and squash from which the seeds are taken, sweet potatoes, sweet cassava, tomatoes, and sage. This is a seed that when ground and roasted and mixed with ground corn makes a good brew to drink. The

Indigenous map of Santiago Atitlán, 1585. Used by permission of the Nettie Lee Benson Latin American Collection, University of Texas Libraries, The University of Texas at Austin.

natives drink it and they hold it to be a thing cool and healthful. Indians of this village subsist upon these things. . . .

To the twenty-sixth question, they answered that . . . the trade which the natives and Spaniards have in this land is in cacao, which they obtain by barter, or by harvesting it, as many of the natives have plantations in their lands located six leagues from this village. They make a good profit from cacao, either by selling it for money, or exchanging it for clothing of all kinds. With cacao they buy what they need for their dress, and also for their wives and children, for cacao to them is money with which to buy. With it they pay their tribute in kind, according to the assessment assigned to them. They also use it as a drink. They have packhorses for the trade and transport of their goods and supply of corn. Everything has to be brought from outside. . . .

After answering the aforementioned questions and having made an examination of the said persons in the presence of the said Señores Alonso Páez de Betancour, His Majesty's *corregidor* [mayor] of the aforementioned village, and Padre Fray Pedro de Arboleda, guardian of this convent, they signed their names here and ordered me, the said clerk, that in regard to the painting which is to be made of the location and plan of this village, and nearby lake, as well as the volcanoes of the vicinity, which have been mentioned, I should contact personally those who are to make it, and once it is made and finished, that I place it together with this report in order that it may serve better to understand this report, and that I should, of course, put thereon whatever is seemed advisable that everything may be made clearer for His Majesty. This, together with the other reports, which are to be made, is to be sent to the Illustrious Señor *Licenciado* García de Valverde of His Majesty's Council, and President of the Royal Audiencia, who resides in the city of Santiago [colonial capital of Central America], and is the governor and captain general of this district. Made in this royal village of Atitlán in the lands given in *encomienda* to Sancho Barahona on the ninth day of the month of February of the year fifteen hundred and eighty-five.

Translated by Ray F. Broussard

All Sorts and Colors

Thomas Gage

Since precolonial times, the three-hundred-mile-long Motagua River Valley, flanked by the Sierra de Santa Cruz to its north and the Sierra de las Minas to the south, has been the main transport route connecting Guatemala's populous highlands to the Bay of Honduras and the Atlantic. The violence of the Conquest, followed by heavy tribute and forced labor demands, decimated the valley's indigenous population. As a result, African slavery became a more established component of the colonial economy here than elsewhere in Guatemala. Africans, both slaves and freemen, worked the mines and the cattle and indigo haciendas (also called estancias). They were used as muleteers, and they harvested commercial crops such as cacao, achiote (used as both a spice and a dye), and "apothecary drugs," or medicinal herbs such as the diuretic zarzaparrilla (sarsaparrilla) and the purgative canafistula. Large numbers of African slaves were likewise put to work on the Dominican sugar plantations of Amatitlán, Palencia, and San Gerónimo.

In this selection, the seventeenth-century English priest Thomas Gage describes slavery in Guatemala's colonial society. Gage spent over a decade ministering in Central America, and his 1648 account of his experiences was one of the earliest and most comprehensive surveys of the region available in English. Gage had a keen eye for colonial politics and economics, and he discusses the conditions of African slaves ("blackamoors") in three different settings: a community of runaway slaves that harassed trade routes and that local authorities couldn't pacify; a wealthy ex-slave who had purchased his freedom and who enjoyed a degree of grudging respect from colonial authorities; and one hundred slaves, including women and children, who suffered horrendous violence at the hands of their owner, a prosperous mule driver.

Great plenty and wealth hath made the inhabitants as proud and vicious as are those of Mexico. Here is not only idolatry, but fornication and uncleanness as public as in any place of the Indies. The mulattoes, blackamoors, mestizos, Indians, and all common sort of people are much made on by the greater and richer sort, and go as gallantly appareled as do those of Mexico, fearing neither a volcano or mountain of water on the one side, which they confess hath once poured out a flood and river executing God's wrath against sin there committed; neither a volcano of fire or mouth of hell on the other side, roaring within and threatening to rain upon them Sodom's ruin and destruction. . . .

The way from this gulf [on the Pacific] to Guatemala is not so bad as some report and conceive, especially after Michaelmas until May, when the winter and rain is past and gone and the winds begin to dry up the ways. For in the worst of the year mules laden with four hundred weight at least go easily through the steepest, deepest, and most dangerous passages of the mountains that lie about this gulf. And though the ways are that time of the year bad, yet they are so beaten with the mules, and so wide and open, that one bad step and passage may be avoided for a better, and the worst of the way continues but fifteen leagues, there being *ranchos,* or lodges in the way, cattle and mules also among the woods and mountains, for relief and comfort to a weary traveler. What the Spaniards most fear until they come out of these mountains are some two or three hundred blackamoors, *simarrones,* who for too much hard usage have fled away from Guatemala and other parts from their masters unto these woods, and there live and bring up their children and increase daily, so that all the power of Guatemala, nay all the country about them . . . is not able to bring them under subjection. These often come out to the roadway, and set upon the . . . mules and take of wine, iron, clothing, and weapons from them as much as they need, without doing any harm unto the people, or slaves that go with the mules; but rather these rejoice with them, being of one color, and subject to slavery and misery which the others have shaken off; by whose example and encouragement many of these also shake off their misery, and join with them to enjoy liberty, though be but in the woods and mountains. Their weapons are bows and arrows which they use and carry about them only to defend themselves if the Spaniard set upon them; else they use them not against the Spaniards. . . .

About Acacabastlán, there are many *estancias* of cattle and mules, much cacao, *achiote,* and drugs for chocolate. There is also apothecary drugs, as *zarzaparrilla,* and *canafistula,* and in the town as much variety of fruits and gardens as in any one Indian town in the country. . . . Among these mountains there have been discovered some mines of metal, which the Spaniards have begun to dig, and finding that they have been some of copper, and some of iron, they have let them alone. . . . But greater profit have the Spaniards lost, than of iron and copper, for using the poor Indians too hardly, and that in this way, from Acacabastlán to Guatemala, especially about a place called El Agua Caliente, The Hot Water, where is a river, out of which in some places formerly the Indians found such store of gold that they were charged by the Spaniards with a yearly tribute of gold. But the Spaniards being . . . too greedy after it, murdering the Indians for not discovering unto them where about this treasure lay, have lost both treasure and Indians also. Yet unto this day search is made about the mountains, the river, and the sands for the hidden treasure, which peradventure by God's order and appointment doth and shall lie hid, and kept for a people better knowing and honoring their God.

At this place called El Agua Caliente liveth a blackamoor in an *estancia* of his own, who is held to be very rich, and gives good entertainment to the travelers that pass that way; he is rich in cattle, sheep, and goats, and from his farm stores Guatemala and the people thereabout with the best cheese of all that country. But his riches are thought not so much to increase from his farm and cheeses, but from his hidden treasure, which credibly is reported to be known unto him. He hath been questioned about it in the chancery of Guatemala, but hath denied often any such treasure to be known unto him. The jealousy and suspicion of him is, for that formerly having been a slave, he bought his freedom with great sums of money, and since he hath been free, hath bought that farm and much land lying to it, and hath exceedingly increased his stoke; to which he answereth, that when he was young and a slave, he had a good master, who let him get for himself what he could, and that he playing the good husband, gathered as much as would buy his liberty, and at first a little house to live in, to which God hath since given a blessing with a greater increase of stock. . . . .

It is called the Valley of Mixco and Pinola from two towns of Indians, so called, standing opposite the one to the other. . . . Here do live many rich farmers, but yet country and clownish people, who know more of breaking clods of earth than of managing arms offensive or defensive.

But among them I must not forget one friend of mine, called Juan Palomeque, whom I should have more esteemed of than I did if I could have prevailed with him to have made him live more like a man than a beast, more like a free man than a bond slave to his gold and silver. This man had in my time three hundred lusty mules. . . . And for them he kept above a hundred blackamoor slaves, men, women, and children, who lived near Mixco, in several thatched cottages. The house he lived in himself was but a poor thatched house, wherein he took more delight to live than in other houses which he had in Guatemala. . . . But the miser knew well which was the best way to save, and so chose a field for a city, a cottage for a house, company of blackamoors for citizens, and yet he was thought

Thomas Gage receiving gifts from his parishioners. From *A New Survey of the West Indies* by Thomas Gage (1648), frontispiece of the first German edition (Leipzig, 1693). From the collections of the Centro de Investigaciones Regionales de Mesoamérica, Guatemala.

to be worth six hundred thousand ducats. He was the undoer of all others who dealt with mules for bringing and carrying commodities to the gulf for the merchants; for he having lusty mules, lusty slaves, would set the price or rate for the hundredweight so, as he might get, but others at that rate hiring Indians and servants to go with their mules might lose. He was so cruel to his blackamoors that if any were untoward, he would torment them almost to death; amongst whom he had one slave called Macaco . . . whom he would often hang up by the arms and whip him till the blood ran about his back, and when his flesh being torn, mangled, and all in a gore blood, he would for last cure pour boiling grease upon it; he had marked him for a slave with burning irons upon his face, his hands, his arms, his back, his belly, his thighs, his legs, that the poor slave was weary of life, and I think would two or three times have hanged himself, if I had not counseled him to the contrary. He was so sensual and carnal that he would use his own slaves' wives to his pleasure; nay when he met in the city of that kind handsome and to his liking, if she would not yield to his desire, he would go to her master or mistress, and buy her, offering far more than she was worth, boasting that he would pull down her proud and haughty looks, with one year's slavery under him. He killed in my time two Indians in the way to the gulf, and with his money came off, as if he had killed but a dog. He would never marry, because his slaves supplied the bed of a wife, and none of his neighbors durst say him nay; whereby he hasted to fill that valley with bastards of all sorts and colors, by whom, when that rich miser dieth, all his wealth and treasure is like to be consumed.

A Creole Landscape

Francisco Antonio Fuentes y Guzmán

Francisco Antonio Fuentes y Guzmán was born in Guatemala in 1643. As the great-grandson of Bernal Díaz del Castillo, the famed Spanish chronicler of the conquest of Mexico, Fuentes y Guzmán was considered a "man of lineage," and he held many political and military posts throughout his life. He is also remembered as the first Creole—that is, a Spaniard born in the Americas—to write about Guatemala as his patria *(fatherland). By the time Fuentes y Guzmán wrote* Recordación florida, *the conquest wars were a memory, and his landscape is not one of conquest and violence but of emerging agricultural wealth and an encyclopedic account of the countryside. The selection presented here describes the colonial-era region of Cazabastlán in eastern Guatemala, south of the Motagua River (the present-day municipality of San Juan Acasaguastlán). Its language is idyllic and chauvinistic, as Fuentes y Guzmán compares Guatemala's economic potential to other areas of Spanish America. Creoles, by now a distinct social class, appear poised to exploit the land's promise. Standing in the way of Creole progress, however, are "unproductive" indigenous communities, still in possession of much of the emerging country's land.*

Of the Precious Fruits Produced and Harvested in
This District of the Province of Cazabastlán

This countryside is formed by plains and hemmed in by a great mountain ridge. It becomes even more fertile than its natural state because in wintertime water cascades down the slopes of the Sierra de Chiquimula, and with it the best topsoil from those hills flows down into the plains, filling up the rivers, and the bells would ring for miles around [i.e., it would be miraculous] if only the cultures [people] of this great land would put more effort into their crops . . . not to mention everything that's produced in the rural haciendas: cheeses, meats, tallow, lard, and leather for the provision of the *navíos de registro* [licensed ships that sailed from Guatemala's eastern port]. The corn that is harvested once a year in this excellent bit of land provides not a bad livelihood for the *vecinos* [local elite]; some of it is consumed within the haciendas and the rest is sold on the canoes that pass up and down the river.

But the most precious is cacao, a common treasure of the *indios*, which is valued even more by the *indios* here for the excellence and goodness of the bean; since it is sweet and very juicy, it is also very large, and very heavy, and the ones that are harvested in Zacapa weigh more than 80 pounds a load. They are prized for their excellence and qualities and fetch a good price all year round. The *achiote* [a shrub whose fruit produces a red dye] is undeveloped here, [but] is of a very good quality and purity, unadulterated, untainted and clean. This fruit, just like the cacao, could be harvested in abundance . . . if planted in excess of the quantities that satisfy the limited acquisitiveness, the great idleness, of the *vecinos* around here. . . . Mostly it is the *indios* who exhibit this uselessness and neglect, against all good judgement, toward anything that's proposed to them and that they imagine to involve work, even if it would bring them great benefit. The only thing that's certain is that even for their basic provisions it is necessary to apply violence [toward the *indios*]. It is notorious that since the year 1674, when the *jueces de milpas* [colonial officials who ensured that Indians produced surplus corn to feed urban populations] were eliminated, corn harvests are down, [the *indios*] cannot pay their tribute, which explains the stagnation of the Royal Treasury, and [instead of growing corn] the *indios* have to purchase it from elsewhere, leading to their humiliation and ruin.

And among other things that are produced in this great expanse of land are the *corozo* palms, which produce a kind of nut that in its size and shape is similar to a hen's egg. The flesh of this nut has a copious, sweet, and delicious oil and, when tender and supple, yields a liquid similar to cow's milk, and it can be used to make a very good rice and other dishes. Everyone around here knows how to use this sort of coconut, its shell is commonly called *cachimbo* and it is passed around by all the men, to be carved into pipes for smoking tobacco or used as snuffboxes and other curious things that are crafted. . . . Much tobacco is planted and harvested in these parts, and there is great distinction in the quality and kind of the Cazabastlán tobacco; the tobacco here is the best because the seeds came to this kingdom from Havana, and its production here is very similar, and so is the texture, color, smell, and strength of the leaf, and the gains from its production.

And just like in other lowland parts of this kingdom, here in Cazabastlán are found gourds of all kinds, and a little bit of cotton. Cotton is not planted very much, even though it would grow well here and would be very useful and a great income for the poor families. The cotton here in Cazabastlán is

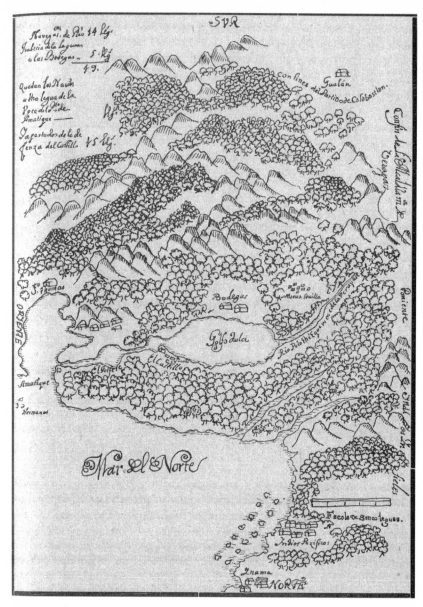

Drawing of an orderly agricultural landscape, by Francisco Antonio Fuentes y Guzmán, 1695. From the collections of the Centro de Investigaciones Regionales de Mesoamérica, Guatemala.

very white, very loose and with smooth seeds. [Elsewhere in this volume] with God's favor, in what we will say about the province of Suchitepéquez, we will write about the utility [of cotton] and the very excellent properties of this beneficent plant.

And among the precious things that nature produces for the benefit of man, to be put to good use assisted by knowledge and art, one of these is the *piedra imán* [lodestone, a naturally occurring magnet], so useful and necessary for navigation, as we know, and since this is so well known I have no need to expound on its virtues. Between the jurisdictions of Cazabas- tlán and Amatique, and the Golfo Dulce, there is a hill where you can walk to a fault trench with an open vein, or veins, of this metal, from which large quantities are taken, and I have a large rock of this mineral, and other smaller rocks. . . .

This countryside of Cazabastlán is abundantly productive and vigor- ously fertile. Its fruits are recognized to be superior and very large, and in its large expanse there is hardly any spot that is not capable of producing copious benefits and profitability for man; even the little forests that spill out from the plains are covered with agave and coconuts, and *corozo* and *coyol* palm trees. The areas where great care has been taken in cultivation can expect to yield fruits as ripe and vigorous as what is produced in Chile and other fertile and profitable areas; the melons here are evidence of this: the size of a regular melon is half a *vara* in length [about 15 inches] and the *sapotes* [an apple-shaped fruit] and the plantains are very large and of an excellent flavor and consistency. The pineapples are also very large, and very sweet, very tender and with an admirable transparency. In spite of this excellence, the land could yield even more opportunities, as we have been saying, if it were cultivated to better advantage, but the negligence and lazi- ness of its inhabitants doesn't allow for achievements on the scale of other countries that are so profitable, healthy, and pleasant; there is so much to think and reflect upon regarding the more excellent and privileged lands in the known world.

Translated by Elizabeth Oglesby

Chocolate, Sex and Disorderly Women

Martha Few

Europeans and their African slaves discovered chocolate in Mesoamerica. Mayas had long used cacao beans as currency and to produce a bitter drink that they believed held sacred meanings. During the European colonization of Guatemala, sweetened chocolate became an increasingly popular drink by the late seventeenth century. Historian Martha Few studied the Catholic Church's Inquisition records in Santiago de Guatemala (today's Antigua), the colonial capital of Central America. She found chocolate repeatedly mentioned as an ingredient used by women from all social groups in colonial Guatemala, as well as a potent weapon in women's everyday struggles. Chocolate came to be associated with female sorcery and other threatening behavior, real or imagined.

Europeans writing about their experiences during the Spanish conquest and its aftermath often included descriptions of cacao trees and commented on native practices of chocolate drink preparation and consumption. . . . [One] European observer, Gonzalo Fernández de Oviedo, commented that when he saw Indians drinking chocolate mixed with *achiote* (annatto), the drink turned their mouths, lips, and whiskers red, as if they were drinking blood. Initially, Spaniards for the most part spurned chocolate beverages. . . .

The earliest descriptions of chocolate as an aphrodisiac date from the Spanish conquest of Mexico. Bernal Díaz del Castillo, writing about his experiences as a foot soldier in the defeat of the Aztecs at Tenochtitlán in the 1520s, described a banquet he attended held by the emperor Moctezuma. He noted that Moctezuma was served gold cups filled with chocolate "that they say was for success with women." Native women continued to be responsible for chocolate beverage preparation after the Spanish conquest. Díaz noted that at Moctezuma's banquet women prepared chocolate by first grinding the cacao on a stone and then mixing it into a frothy drink.

Starting in the 1590s, Spaniards overcame their aversion to chocolate. Unlike native peoples, Spaniards often mixed in vanilla, cinnamon, and sugar. By the seventeenth century, Guatemalans from all social and ethnic groups had access to chocolate in cities such as Santiago de Guatemala, and they drank it in a wide range of contexts in daily life. The transformation of chocolate drinks into a basic staple that could be consumed daily by not only Mayas but also Spaniards and *castas* (mixed-race peoples) probably occurred, in part, through native women working as servants in colonial kitchens. Not everyone could afford servants, however, which meant that less-wealthy Spanish, *casta*, and Afro-Guatemalan women most likely learned to prepare chocolate from their Indian neighbors and served it to their families. . . .

Chocolate had properties associated with healing, as well. A free *mulata* [mixed African descendant] servant described how a female Indian curer of magical sickness administered a healing chocolate beverage to heal the *mulata*'s Indian husband of *locura* (insanity). Hospitals in the capital city of Santiago budgeted money for chocolate among their food expenditures for their patients. . . .

Women continued to prepare chocolate for their families and neighbors as part of their social roles in food procurement and preparation. Female market sellers also sold chocolate drinks in stalls in the capital's outdoor markets. Only in extreme cases did men prepare chocolate, as seen in Juan de Fuente's complaint to Inquisition authorities that his wife bewitched him with sorcery. Juan, a thirty-three-year-old *mulato* construction worker in Santiago, denounced his *mulata* wife Cecilia to the Inquisition, accusing her of acting as a sorcerer-witch (*hechizera-bruja*). He charged that Cecilia used spells and curses "so that he could not be a man on all the occasions that he desired to have intercourse with his wife." Ultimately, Juan's evidence that Cecilia had used sorcery to bewitch him centered on what he perceived to be their inverted household gender roles, shown by his inability to control his "unnatural" behavior of preparing the morning chocolate while his wife slept in. The Inquisition gave the following summary of his testimony:

> His wife treats him not as a husband but as a servant. He lights the fire in the kitchen, he boils the water, he mixes the chocolate and heats the food . . . and he gets up very early every morning to do this while his wife stays in bed and sleeps until very late. And when his wife wakes, he brings her chocolate so she can drink it after she dresses. And even though it is very late [in the morning], he has the water ready, [and] he drinks chocolate with his wife . . . in this way his wife has turned him into a coward, and all this cannot be a natural thing.

Cecilia was eventually convicted by the Inquisition in Santiago for sorcery, and officials sent her overland under guard to the central Inquisition jail in Mexico City. Cecilia brought a number of items along with her to ease her stay in jail, including clothing, bedding, and an image of the Virgin of Guadalupe. She also brought with her four cakes of chocolate and a gourd cup called a *jícara*, specifically used to drink chocolate.

By the late seventeenth century, as inhabitants from all social and ethnic groups in colonial Guatemala drank chocolate in large quantities in many contexts in daily life, the cultural meanings of chocolate had expanded from ancient Maya ritual and economic meanings and became refashioned and transformed to include associations with female social disorder. In accounts of women who acted "disorderly" in a variety of public contexts, colonial authorities and inhabitants of the capital often included descriptions of women's illicit sexual activity and practices of sexual witchcraft, where women took advantage of their roles in food preparation to assert power over the men in their lives.

Because of its dark color and grainy texture, chocolate provided an ideal cover for items associated with sexual witchcraft. These included various powers and herbs, as well as female body parts or fluids, which women then mixed into a chocolate beverage and fed to men to control their sexuality. Manuela Gutiérrez, a twenty-year-old girl [and a] single *mulata* servant, consulted a *mulata* sorcerer named Gerónima de Varaona for sexual witchcraft. Gutiérrez described how she was having problems with her lover and wanted something to attract him. De Varaona gave her some powders and told Manuela to wash her *partes naturales* (genitals) with water, then beat the powders and the water into a hot chocolate drink and give it to the man she desired. Nicolasa de Torres, a single, free *mulata* servant, wanted to sexually attract her employer. She consulted an Indian woman named Petrona Mungia, who told her to take her pubic hairs and a small worm found under a certain type of stone, and then mix everything together and put it in her employer's chocolate. . . .

Not only poor, mixed-race, and Indian women consulted female sorcerers for sexual witchcraft using chocolate; elite Spanish women did as well. Women often asked their neighbors and friends for recommendations on whom to consult for sorcery, and they also used them as go-betweens to acquire the necessary ritual items. Gerónima de Varaona, herself a well-known sorcerer in late-seventeenth-century Santiago, acted as a go-between for doña Luisa de Gálvez. Doña Luisa gave Varaona half a loaf of bread and four bread rolls and asked her to take them to the house of an Indian woman named María de Zumagra and trade them for some ritual powders for sexual witchcraft. De Varaona went and returned with three packets of powders, one for doña Luisa to place in the clothes of the man she desired and the other two to put in his chocolate and food. Doña Luisa then washed her armpits and genitals with water, and another woman mixed the powders and this water for her into a chocolate drink. Despite doña Luisa's elite status, she had a violent reputation as shown by her nickname, La Machete. De Varaona explained that everyone called doña Luisa "La Machete" "because she can cut out a tongue with a machete." . . .

Women also used bewitched chocolate drinks to take revenge against sexual competitors. Doña Catarina Delgado, a twenty-eight-year-old Spanish woman, accused a woman named Agustina of doing just that. Doña Catarina's husband, Sargento Nicolás Callejos, also a Spaniard, had been conducting an illicit affair with Agustina, a *mulata* servant who lived next to the University of San Carlos, in the house of her employer. According to doña Catarina, one day Agustina came to their home and fought "with much brazenness" in public with her husband Nicolás. A few days passed and Agustina and a female friend brought them over some chocolate as a peace offering. Doña Catarina, her husband, and their female Indian servant all drank the chocolate. Doña Catarina soon fell ill, describing her sickness as *"echando el curso negro o amarillo"* (expelling the black or yellow flow), where she alternately vomited yellow, green, and blood-colored water-like substances through her mouth. The female Indian servant fell ill with the same sickness and died, while the husband apparently remained healthy.

Men were well aware that women used chocolate as vehicles for sexual witchcraft, and they sometimes took advantage of the association between hot chocolate drinks and sexual witchcraft in their pursuit of female lovers. Rosa de Arrevillaga was a twenty-eight-year-old *mulata* slave of a nun and lived cloistered in the convent of Santa Catalina Martir in Santiago. Despite her slave status, Inquisition authorities listed de Arrevillaga as *doncella*, or virgin. She had received an education in the convent, as evidenced by the letter she wrote to Inquisition authorities denouncing her confessor for solicitation in the confessional. In the letter, Rosa described how she had gone to confess during the Easter holidays. As she waited, she served the priest, Padre Francisco de Castellanos, a cup of chocolate in front of the other priests "as it was the fashion and kindness that one does in the convent for the confessors." When she entered the confessional, Padre Francisco attempted to seduce her, calling her "his soul, and his life, and his Rose of Jericho." As Rosa fended off his advances, Padre Francisco told her that he knew that she had put powders in the chocolate she served him so "to gain his love."

Because of the close association between chocolate drinks and sorcery in colonial Guatemala, those who were served chocolate by women with

The city of Antigua as seen from Cerro de la Cruz, with Volcán de Agua in the background. Photo by Jean-Christophe Surateau. Used by permission of the photographer.

whom they had ongoing conflicts treated the drinks with suspicion. In 1730, Manuel Antonio Calderón, a twenty-one-year-old free mulatto weaver, described his marriage to his seventeen-year-old wife Magdalena as contentious. According to the Inquisition's summary of his testimony, "there has not been one day that they [Manuel and Magdalena] have not fought, because she mistreated him in word and deed." Manuel suspected that his wife had cast a spell on him, putting demons in his body that caused him to suffer from an "affliction of reason." He recounted how six months before, Magdalena, his mother-in-law, and his sister-in-law offered him a cup of chocolate. When Manuel took the cup, he noticed that it weighed more than usual and became suspicious, thinking that the women had perhaps added something nefarious to the drink. Manuel decided not to drink the chocolate and placed the cup in the corner of the room. He put next to the chocolate a sprig of rosemary, an herb associated with ritual cleansing and protection from evil in Spanish culture. When Manuel returned, his wife and her mother and sister "laugh[ed] at [him], taking [him] for an idiot." The next morning when Manuel checked the cup, he "found the cup of chocolate filled with such a large quantity of white worms that the cup of chocolate appeared to move on its own, which horrified [him]." Manuel pointed to the bewitched chocolate as the first in a series of incidents which led him to believe that his wife cast a supernatural illness on him that caused symptoms of "confusion" and "insanity." He eventually underwent a series of exorcisms conducted by the local priest to cleanse his body of the sorcery. . . .

The association between chocolate and disorderly women extended to elite women, as well, especially their unruly behavior in public settings. Thomas Gage, an Englishman traveling in Central America in the mid-seventeenth century, described a public confrontation between the bishop of Chiapas, located on the far northwestern edge of colonial Guatemala, and his elite female parishioners over the consumption of hot chocolate during mass. According to Gage, Bishop Bernardino de Salazar complained that the women insisted on drinking hot chocolate in church, disrupting the mass. The bishop became so angry that he posted signs on the cathedral declaring that he would excommunicate those women who continued to drink chocolate in church. The women unsuccessfully tried to change the bishop's mind, and Gage wrote:

> That women, seeing [the bishop] so hard to be entreated, began to stomacke him the more and to sleight him with scornfull and reproachfull words; others sleighted his excommunication, drinking in iniquity in the Church, as the fish doth water, which caused one day such

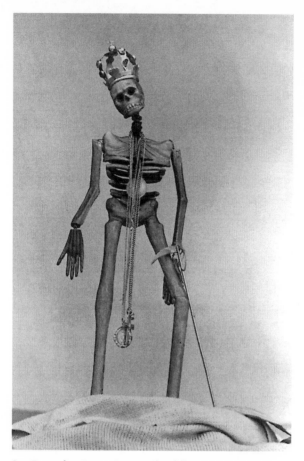

San Pascualito Rey, a Guatemalan folk saint associated with
the curing of disease, also called "King of the Graveyard."
Photo by Mitchell Denburg. From the collections of the
Centro de Investigaciones Regionales de Mesoamérica,
Guatemala.

> an uproar in the Cathedral, that many swords were drawne against
> the Priests and Prebends, who attempted to take away from the maids
> the cups of chocolate, which they brought unto their mistresses.

The conflict between the bishop and the women escalated, with both
sides refusing to compromise, or, as Gage put it, "the women would not
obey." The women proceeded to boycott cathedral services to protest the
bishop's prohibition of chocolate during mass. When the bishop became ill
during the boycott, rumors spread through the city that one of the women

had poisoned his chocolate. The bishop's head and face became greatly swollen, and any touch "caused his skin to break and cast out white matter, which had corrupted and overflowne all his body." Physicians called to the bishop's sickbed agreed that someone had poisoned him, and he died from his illness a week later. Gage claimed that from the incident emerged the warning, "Beware of the Chocolate of Chiapa[s]." . . .

In colonial Santiago de Guatemala, as chocolate became widely available to men and women of all ethnic groups and social statuses, the cultural meanings associated with chocolate began to transform. Colonial authorities, as well as ordinary men and women, increasingly associated chocolate with female social disorder, which cut across racial and status boundaries. Mixed-race, indigenous, and African women in particular were described as using chocolate as the basis for a wide variety of sorcery activities, sexual witchcraft, casting supernatural illness, and extracting revenge. Potions were infused with power from the ritual ingredients mixed into the chocolate, including herbs, powders, and body fluids and hairs. While elite women availed themselves of chocolate-based potions, they also defended their rights to consume chocolate beverages in public settings, such as during church services, refusing to obey edicts against the practice. Women in late-seventeenth-century and early-eighteenth-century Santiago who prepared and consumed chocolate ran the risk of being accused of sorcery and other types of disorderly and illegal behavior. Despite discourses that linked chocolate with female social disorder, however, especially in sexual contexts, women often took advantage of those associations by serving, or threatening to serve, doctored chocolate beverages in the day-to-day conflicts and confrontations between men and women.

Fugitive Indians

Archbishop Pedro Cortés y Larraz

From the Crown's perspective, the ideal colony functioned in the following man-
ner: Christianized pueblos de indios fed themselves and supplied labor and goods
to the Spanish towns, haciendas (large holdings with diverse economic, agrar-
ian, and artisanal activities), and plantations, all of which in turn sent fees to
the Crown. In the 1760s, King Charles III sent Archbishop Pedro Cortés y Larraz to
investigate whether all was well in the diocese of Guatemala. It was not. As Cortés
y Larraz traveled from parish to parish, he was dismayed by the harsh demands of
forced labor, the violence with which priests and colonial officials routinely treated
Indians, and the refusal of indigenous communities to assimilate Christian Eu-
ropean culture. The following excerpt from his account of his trip, Descripción
geográfico-moral de la diócesis de Goathemala, *suggests a territory occupied*
by foreigners rather than one settled by them for 250 years. Indigenous resistance
only rarely flared into open rebellion, however; Indians engaged in work stoppages
and in limited protests against specific abusive officials. The archbishop was horri-
fied to learn of the widespread flight by Indians out of towns and parishes and into
the mountains, river gorges, and salt pans outside of the reach of colonial authority.
Up to half of Guatemala's population lived itinerantly in these ungoverned places
not subject to the king or the church.

Los Esclavos Parish

Even when Christian doctrine is taught in all the pueblos, there are still
many people in the parish who are not taught, and these are the ones who
live in the haciendas, huts, and encampments, where ignorance and all
kinds of vices dominate, since what is sought after and found in these places
is liberty and escape from all kinds of laws. The result is nothing more than
cohabitations, robberies, and the breaking of all Christian laws. . . .

Santa Cruz el Chol Parish

The valleys, as has been said before, contain a collection of disorderly, unsubdued people, without justice officials, without a priest, without a temple and therefore without any brake to contain them, and so they abandon themselves at will. People who are fugitives from their pueblos gather in these valleys, no one ascertains or even inquires who they are; and even when inquiries are made, in order not to be discovered they frequently change their names, deny their places of origin, and claim to be from somewhere else; they lie and hide their status; they come and go as they please, and this produces all kinds of disorder and even marrying as many times as they want. . . . In the valleys of this jurisdiction . . . there are a mix of Spaniards, promiscuous Indians, and Ladinos [people of mixed European and Maya descent], so that in the same spot all these species live together, the supremely insolent Spaniards, the equally frightful Indians, the deceitful and cunning Ladinos, all naked and together at all hours of the day and night, without God, without the Church, without the King, without shame or honor, such that I must abstain from any further reflection. . . .

Espíritu Santo La Zacualpa Parish

In several pueblos, many people are always missing, few or none are left . . . has something noteworthy happened here? And where do they all end up, since they don't return? Everyone replies that they flee to the coast of San Antonio [Suchitepéquez], where they live more abundantly, and that's why they settle there.

Hearing this, I must surely be persuaded that said coast of San Antonio is a very large place, yet even so, it wouldn't be able to support so many people taking refuge there. Well, the truth is that the area is very small, it's ten leagues long and about the same, or less, in width . . . so from this I infer that the fugitives take shelter in the haciendas and valleys, or they hide in the mountains, or they drown in the rivers and many perish that way, or another way.

The safe and advisable course of action would be to take measures to extinguish or moderate all this flight, whether that be going after them when they flee, severely prohibiting flight into the haciendas or other pueblos without a license, turning the valleys into pueblos, not allowing them to live out in the scrub under the pretext of farming the land, not marrying them so easily, because the next instant they regret it, and other means to keep such considerable damage in check. . . .

Salamá Parish

The haciendas use *repartos de indios* [forced labor of indigenous workers] for their harvest labor. The landowners order these *repartos* during planting time, weeding time, and any time they need labor to work the land, and this labor schedule overlaps with the time when the Indians need to be tending their own land, so their own plots are neglected because they are forced to work on the haciendas.

The forced labor is carried out with brute force, without respect for the fields and lands of the Indians, much less for their health and lives; as an example, I relate an incident in the parish of Chimaltenango, where a group of wretched [Indians] brought me some money and tried to leave it on the table so that I would give it to the landowners, so that they could be released from the labor draft because they were too sick to go, and it pained me that I could not console them. . . .

San Jacinto Parish

The Indians often see in us a kind of avarice, believing that we are not satisfied with anything, not with their goods, their labor, their services; and that we are so rigid that if our every whim is not fulfilled, we respond with scorn, jailing and whipping. The Indians contribute much to the priests, giving them many coins, serving them for free, and feeding them with hens, eggs, fish, spices, milk, water, and even hay for the mules; with this the Indians don't pay, or pay only a little, for services such as baptisms and burials. . . .

With respect to whether the Indians are religious, when one speaks with them about the mysteries of our Holy Faith, they never respond affirmatively, but add "maybe." This happens constantly, so if the Indians are asked, "Is it true that there are three persons in one Godhead?" they answer, "Maybe it's true, Father." "Who knows if Jesus Christ is in the Holy Sacrament?" But it's worth noting that in my experience they respond the same way no matter what question they're asked. Are the roads good? Are the rivers wide? Is one pueblo far from the other? They always respond, "Who knows if the road is good?" "Maybe the river is wide." "It could be that the pueblo is far." . . .

Santa María Xoyavah [Joyabaj] Parish

Without a doubt, as I have said many times, there are not, nor have there ever been, creatures more deserving of compassion than the Indians, but toward whom such compassion has so little effect. I don't know how to explain what I mean, except by giving an example. The Indians send to the archbishop, to the president, to the Royal Audiencia [a high court and ruling body] a petition against the priest, or against the mayor or the lieutenant. And I suppose that many times the petition contains lies, but other times it may be the truth; in any case, it has to be investigated. But as soon as the accused get wind of it, they threaten the Indians with skinning them alive; the Indians are so fearful that it's enough just to confront them with an air of authority, demanding to know, "What have you accused me of?" Later, they respond, no, Father, and they come back with other petitions, denying the first petition as a thousand lies; that the *principales* [elders, often considered members of the lower indigenous nobility] didn't know anything about it, that two or three *maceguales* [indigenous commoners] had sent the petition, that these later fled the pueblo to avoid being punished; that really they are very content with their priest, with their mayor, and they view them with much love and affection.

Some of these proceedings relate to atrocious crimes, such as failure to administer the sacraments, unjust *repartos* and beatings, whippings so cruel that some people die. So it's necessary for the accused to respond. The priests respond that it's all fabricated, that they comply with their obligations, and since the Indians don't want to comply with their duties as Christians they make up lies to discredit the priest. The mayors respond that it's the only way to subdue them, since otherwise they lose respect and become unruly. And so, while the Indians are called on to ratify the petition, the priests threaten them, the mayors imprison and beat them, everyone tells them they'll be treated worse later, and since the Indians have the proof of experience, in the ratification the priests and the mayors end up vindicated, and not only vindicated, but conceited and arrogant. . . .

Zumpango [Sumpango] Parish

I have said many times that it would be better not to do these confessions and communions, since they are evidently sacrilegious. But it's no use speaking to these people or to these priests hardened by being among such monsters and abominations. In this parish, during Lent the priest makes the mayors round up seventy or eighty people every day to bring them to confession. What kind of confessions are these except something clearly sacrilegious? The world would be horrified to learn how these confessions are carried out, since to increase the number, Indians are dragged in against their will, without even knowing what's happening, and shoved violently into the church. . . .

San Christoval Totonicapam [Totonicapán] Parish

The weak adherence to the sacraments is seen in the small number of people who are confirmed. After several attempts to get people to show up for confirmation, the Indians justify their refusal by claiming that the fever had come since the last attempt at confirmation. . . . They won't confirm their children because they say that children become weak in the head and are then no use for carrying cargo, and because the fever enters them with the sacrament of confirmation.

During another visit the priest showed me various idolatries, and it was difficult to get him to show them to me, because he claimed he could be killed. Among other things, he claimed that on certain days the Indians would perform Mass with a portable altar in the middle of the church, with the bells ringing, and then at midnight they would go in procession with many lights to a certain hill outside of town to burn resin [hold a Maya ceremony] and that he himself saw this. . . .[1]

Zamayac [Samayac] Parish

The Indians of this parish are well-behaved because of the way the priest treats them, repressing their excesses prudently and helping them generously with their needs, acting soft or severe with them depending on what's called for; but with all that, they keep on being Indians. I went out for a walk one afternoon and I came across an old man who spoke Castilian [Spanish] and had with him a large troop of his little grandchildren. I stopped to talk with him, and I asked him to give me one of the many children as a servant, offering to take care of him, and after I kept insisting, he answered flatly that no way would he give up the child. Since he responded with such resolve, I toned down the conversation, and I asked him why he was walking barefoot. Well, he said it was because he was an Indian. But the Indians are Spanish just like us, I said to him; he replied that he wasn't Spanish, but Indian. I asked again if he wanted to be Spanish. He said no, and when I asked him repeatedly, he insisted on saying outright that he didn't want to be Spanish. . . . You can clearly see the ideas these wretched Indians have about the Spanish. . . .

San Miguel Totonicapam [Totonicapán] Parish

In the plaza of this pueblo, instead of a whipping post there is a black man who holds the Indians by the hands when they are being whipped. This invention came from the royal magistrate, and its purpose is to make the Indians feel even more subjugated, since a black man is holding them down. The magistrate told me this as if it were a great feat, but I think it is a sign of how downtrodden these wretched Indians are. It's not only devoid of charity and compassion but it also has the drawback of deepening the horror, tedium, and aversion that they feel toward the Spanish, as they see the Spanish trying to inflict more and more punishments and humiliation on them. . . .

San Antonio Suchitepeques Parish

The Indians are whipped for any little thing that goes wrong. To give an idea of the cruelty: I often hear their shouts and cries from my chambers, even when the whippings are far away, and I don't know how to contain my emotions. I say to myself: these wretched Indians are fools to work so hard to bring supplies to Goathemala, they should leave us to our own devices and surely we would perish if daily they were not bringing us everything we need to live. Who cares if once in a while some bananas or fruit go missing? Who cares if they are not always punctual? Or that fear makes them lie sometimes? It's true the Indians drink too much *aguardiente*. But why don't they lash to the whipping post the Ladinos who sell it to them? . . .

San Juan Zacatepeques [Sacatepéquez] Parish

This territory is the center of the *pajuides* [informal settlements]. . . . There are countless people living here from various parishes, and some without a parish. They don't think about Mass at all, or about the Christian doctrine or the sacraments, or about life or death; their main thought is to hide from the priests and get away from all civilization and religion, so that no one will know where they live, or when they die, or when they're baptized, or when they marry, or who they are, because they're from all around; some claim to be Spanish, others Indians, and others Ladinos. . . .

Since the inclination of the Indians is to live by themselves in the hinterlands, there are *pajuides* in all of the pueblos, but the ones here are the most famous, surely because they are the largest; my understanding is that a great many people in this kingdom live in the hinterlands, and I don't know if it's the majority, or one-third, but I fear it is not less than one-third and may even be much greater than half, certainly if you add in those who live in the salt pans, haciendas, and valleys, which are all very similar places in terms of how they live. . . .

Certainly, I cannot cease to admire the priests who, seeing such a monstrous disorder in their parishes, refuse to say anything to the prelate to seek a remedy. . . . They dedicate all of their wits to lying in order to hide everything. . . .

Translated by Elizabeth Oglesby

Note

1. As the historian Martha Few notes in a personal communication with the editors, another common occurrence involved Indians going into parish churches at night to conduct their own ceremonies, which often extended outside of the church into the surrounding countryside. "These always happened at night, they were associated with sorcery, and they often occurred unnoticed, while the priest slept. Copal was always involved, as a semiotic sign of Indianness and also as the actual object that was used to denote religious activities, purification, and medicinal rituals by colonial Maya groups." Thomas Melville, in part 5 of this volume, recounts how mid-twentieth-century Catholic clergy reacted to the persistence of Maya religious rituals.

An Indian King on the Eve of Independence

Aaron Pollack

By the beginning of the eighteenth century, with the ascension of the Bourbon
dynasty to the Spanish throne, the frequency and intensity of revolts increased
from the Central American provinces to northern Mexico. The Bourbons tried to
strengthen colonial administration, regulating nearly every aspect of social life, including alcohol, cockfighting, religion, education, and disease control. They also
demanded more and more taxes and tribute in order to fund the Crown's wars
with other European empires. Yet Spain's colonial control actually grew weaker. Regional commerce picked up during the eighteenth century, strengthening the power
and wealth of local Creole elites. As Creoles became more aggressive in extracting labor, revenue, and land from indigenous communities, indigenous reactions became
increasingly aggressive, as well. In what is now Guatemala, at least fifty serious
indigenous riots took place between 1710 and 1821, when independence from Spain
was achieved. News of the French and Haitian Revolutions, and their principles of
rights, liberty, and equality, also increased conflict.

   Starting in 1810, Spanish jurists, along with delegates from the Americas and the
Philippines, took advantage of Napoleon's occupation of Madrid to convene a constitutional assembly, adopting a charter two years later that abolished tribute, established equality before the law, and proclaimed anyone born in a Spanish possession (save those of African ancestry) to be citizens. King Ferdinand VII was forced
to accept the constitution, but two years later, after being restored to the throne
following the fall of Napoleon, he repealed it. Then, six years later, a military revolt forced him to reinstate the charter. Weakened royal sovereignty, emboldened
Creoles, indigenous communities that had been pushed to their limits, and new
ideas concerning equality and freedom combined to create a combustible situation
throughout Mesoamerica.

   The beginning of the end of Spanish rule in Mesoamerica came in 1819, with
a massive uprising in Mexico's central valley led by a Spanish priest, Miguel Hi-
dalgo. In Guatemala, the pace and intensity of indigenous protests picked up, with
riots or uprisings taking place in Santiago Sacatepéquez (1811), Patzicía (1811 and
1821), Momostenango (1812), Comalapa (1812), Sololá (1813), Chichicastenango (1813),

Santa Ana Malacatán (1814), San Juan Ostuncalco (1815), Quetzaltenango (1815), San Martín Jilotepeque (1815), Santa María Chiquimula (1814 and 1818), San Andrés Sajcabajá (1819), Santo Domingo (1821), and San Francisco El Alto (1821). The most serious uprising was in the K'iche' region of Totonicapán in 1820, recounted below by the historical geographer Aaron Pollack. This uprising spread quickly through highland towns. For nearly half a year, on the eve of Mexico's and Central America's final break with Spain, indigenous rebels held colonial troops at bay and crowned the revolt's leader, Atanasio Tzul, as an Indian king. Guatemala gained its independence a year later.

The mail carrier must have been happily surprised by the reception he received, a cup of traditional chocolate ceremoniously served in the home of Juan Monrroy, a leader of the anti-tribute movement in the provincial capital, San Miguel Totonicapán. After two days on the road from the capital, Nueva Guatemala, and the tiring hike across the mountains from Sololá, Mariano Asturias was escorted into town by a large group of Indians—led by Atanasio Tzul and Lucas Aguilar—who had long awaited the copies of the Constitution that, according to them at least, ended Indian tribute payment.

A few days later, on 9 July 1820, as people in the capital and elsewhere in the Kingdom of Guatemala celebrated the reinstatement of the 1812 Constitution, the Indians of Totonicapán rejoiced with bullfights, music, and fireworks over the changes in their status that the document legislated. The K'iche's acted in accordance with orders sent by the colonial authorities, but in the absence of the *alcalde mayor* (district magistrate), José Manuel Lara, who fled the town two days later, fearing for his life. The festivities, and the flight of the *alcalde mayor*, initiated twenty days of K'iche' rule in Totonicapán District, the largest Indian uprising during the colonial period in what is now Guatemala.

The Indians organized the 1820 celebration along the lines of the ceremony held in 1812 that marked the initial promulgation of the Constitution. In the earlier event, Narciso Mallol, then *alcalde mayor*, spared nothing to show his admiration for the document and its liberal pronouncements that he would do his utmost to promote and enforce in the following year.

The 1812 Spanish Constitution came into being as a result of the Napoleonic invasion of Spain that drove Carlos IV and his son Ferdinand VII from the crown, placing in their stead Bonaparte's brother, Joseph. The document was written by representatives from the Spanish mainland and colonies meeting in the Cadiz Courts who, though they wielded little power on the peninsula, did retain the allegiance of Spanish colonial authorities, most of whom were struggling against powerful independence movements throughout the Americas. The Constitution reflected the political context in which it was conceived, and in that logic, the attempts by its authors to reduce the pressures from below on the colonial officials were reflected in the abolition of tribute payments and ecclesiastical taxes provided by the Indians.

The *alcalde mayor* of Totonicapán, Mallol, attempted to enforce the abolition of rations and personal services, and his efforts—in combination with a number of other factors, including his opposition to the attempts by Ladinos [people of mixed European and Maya descent] and Spaniards in Quetzaltenango to extend their regional power—would end with his ouster. The *alcalde mayor* did not act alone, but in close coordination with the Indian leaders of the town of San Miguel Totonicapán, many of whom, including Atanasio Tzul, took on leadership roles in 1820.

The conflict became palpable as the majority of the Indian leadership of Totonicapán allied with Mallol in 1813 against the civil and religious colonial authorities, the Spanish and Ladino leaders of Totonicapán and nearby Quetzaltenango, and also the *caciques* of Totonicapán, the latter a relatively large group with historically derived privileges that set them apart from the remainder of the Indians in town. As tensions mounted, the colonial authorities opened a judicial case against Mallol and exiled him provisionally from his capital. A few weeks later, in late October 1813, some 4,000 Indians—and seemingly a few Ladinos as well—from Totonicapán and the surrounding towns accompanied the *alcalde mayor* in his return to Totonicapán, in the process running off Spanish and Ladino leaders and colonial authorities while violently protesting the actions of those Indian authorities who had worked with them.

In 1814, Ferdinand VII, upon his return to the throne, abolished the Constitution, and the following year he called for Indian tribute to be reinstated beginning in 1816; and the K'iche's in Totonicapán immediately began to resist the newly reestablished charges. In Totonicapán District, with a very large and very dense Indian population, opposition began immediately upon the renewal of tribute, in part related to the human and material suffering caused by a severe smallpox epidemic in 1815 and an earthquake in 1816. San Cristobal Totonicapán, San Francisco El Alto, and Momostenango fought legal battles and dragged their feet, but Santa María Chiquimula and the provincial capital of San Miguel Totonicapán simply refused payment.

Between 1818 and 1820 the K'iche' towns became increasingly recalcitrant toward tribute charges, and in part because the colonial authorities' refusal to use violence as a means to force acquiescence strengthened the resolve of the Indians, they became ever more hostile toward other demands imposed by the colonial authorities. In separate events in early 1820 the people of Santa María Chiquimula and nearby Sacapulas rose up and frightened off authorities who had attempted to demand payment.

Between April and June 1820, however, as the K'iche' rebels consolidated their position in San Miguel Totonicapán, the commander of the regional militias and longtime power broker in the area, Prudencio Cozar, maintained consistent communication with the town councils and *principales* [elders] of the three largest towns, Momostenango, Santa María Chiquimula, and San Miguel Totonicapán. Cozar threatened, cajoled, negotiated, and arrested, choosing his means according to his personal experiences with the towns and his reading of the anti-tribute movement in each of them. These counterinsurgency efforts would be crucial in setting the stage for the repression of the movement and the retaking of Totonicapán in early August.

In early May, news arrived in Nueva Guatemala that Spanish army officers in Madrid had forced King Ferdinand to reestablish the Constitution, and it seems that the Indian leaders in Totonicapán had received warning of this radical shift, a fact that points to communication with individuals who had access to privileged knowledge in the capital or elsewhere. The news reinforced the already ample powers that the Indians held in Totonicapán and most certainly put them at the ready for the moment when the Constitution would be officially declared the law of the land.

When they finally received official announcement of the reinstatement of the Constitution, and duly celebrated it, as described above, the K'iche's publicly declared their control over the town of San Miguel Totonicapán even as they took power, with the support of local allies, in the nearby towns of San Francisco El Alto, San Cristóbal Totonicapán, and San Andrés Xecul, while also making inroads into Momostenango. The K'iche's publicly recognized Atanasio Tzul and Lucas Aguilar as governmental leaders, and those who had collaborated with them in the preceding months and years acquired new responsibilities in the administration of the town and in the consolidation of the movement.

As an Indian *principal*, Tzul had been involved in town government for many years, most recently serving as First Mayor in 1816, and in that capacity he refused to collect tribute. Even prior to his formal investment as the Indian town Governor (King, according to some) in 1820 during the celebration in which the Constitution was proclaimed, Tzul was already the most important Indian leader in his role as *primer principal*, representative of the powerful Lincaj *parcialidad* [clan], and had clearly used that position to unite the town through the unofficial governmental system organized through the *parcialidades*. Once officially proclaimed by the townspeople, he began to hold court in a freshly decorated town hall beneath a painting of Ferdinand VII, meting out justice and receiving petitioners from San Miguel Totonicapán and the neighboring towns.

It seems that though Tzul was held in greater esteem and hence provided more legitimacy to the movement, Lucas Aguilar, a *macehual*, or commoner, wielded as much or more power than his colleague; in fact, on several occasions people from the surrounding towns referred to Aguilar, rather than Tzul, as "King." As the *alcalde* of the powerful Santísimo Sacramento brotherhood, Aguilar had organized the religious brotherhoods (*cofradías*) in support of the movement, thereby ensuring that the two most significant sources of Indian power in Totonicapán, the *cofradías* and the *parcialidades*, would promote the anti-tribute struggle. Aguilar, also a more violent man that Tzul, on a few occasions ordered the beatings of town officials who refused to return tribute that had previously been collected (and most probably already turned over to the colonial officials).

As of July, the new self-declared government collected funds, punished its opponents, posted sentinels on the borders, maintained correspondence, and continued to proselytize, rapidly gaining adherents among the *macehuales* of San Cristóbal Totonicapán, San Andrés Xecul, and San Francisco El Alto. At the same time it was rejected by the *principales* of both San Cristóbal Totonicapán and San Andrés Xecul, violently so in the former, where divisions among the Indians, and in particular the divided loyalties of the *principales*, became strikingly visible.

After months of preparation, on 3 August 1820, one thousand Spanish and Ladino militiamen from Quetzaltenango, Salcajá, San Carlos Sija, Momostenango, and Santa Cruz del Quiché traveled by four different routes to the central plaza of San Miguel Totonicapán. On the way forty of them were injured in an ambush by Indians from San Francisco El Alto and San Cristóbal Totonicapán, in which one of their assailants was killed. That, and a shower of rocks that they suffered on the edge of town, were the only attacks that the militias faced. Once inside Totonicapán, the troops publicly whipped a number of men and raised a gallows to frighten any who may have considered further resistance. Naked and tied, the movement leadership was transferred to prison in Quetzaltenango.

From jail, however, the prisoners began to write to the colonial authorities, complaining of mistreatment by the militiamen, and in January of 1821 they requested a pardon. They were supported in that effort by family members who organized a large protest in Nueva Guatemala, which seems to have supplied enough pressure for a pardon to be granted on March 1.

Even so, the prisoners from San Cristóbal Totonicapán and San Francisco El Alto did not obtain their freedom, and the movement leadership traveled to Quetzaltenango on March 30 to demand their release.

The 1820 uprising and attempt at regional government, heavily influenced by the events of 1813, would have an important impact. While it failed to create a regional Indian government, the movement reinforced Indian power at the municipal level, helping to guarantee its continued function as a bulwark against Creole and Ladino incursions in the years following independence in 1821.

III

A Caffeinated Modernism

On the eve of independence in 1821, Guatemala remained an economic backwater. Unlike more vital centers of Spanish colonialism, Central America could claim little economic importance. It had some mines of gold, silver, and lead, and African slaves or *mestizo* peons worked cochineal, indigo, sugar, and cattle haciendas west of Guatemala City. But Guatemala produced nothing like the wealth of Mexico or Peru. Because of the country's relative lack of importance to the Spanish Crown, when the indigenous population of the western highlands recovered from the demographic catastrophe that followed the Spanish invasion, it did so largely rooted in specific communities with claims to common land. These communities were structured by local political and religious institutions, particularly *cofradías* (saint cults), and divided by distinct dress and language. During the colonial period, the foundations were laid for the alliance between indigenous communities and the Catholic Church because the mendicant orders were able to protect their indigenous charges from heavy labor-tribute demands levied by *encomenderos* (colonists) and royal officials. This alliance would play a decisive role in Guatemalan politics in the half century after its break from Spain.

Nearly two decades of constant conflict between Liberals and Conservatives plagued Guatemalan politics after independence. (The division between "Liberals" and "Conservatives" ran through all of Latin America during the nineteenth century, at times referring to specific political parties but more broadly to political persuasions.) At times, little separated the two groups; but in general, the former mostly comprised middle-class urban and provincial elites, while the later came mostly from Guatemala City's old colonial merchant and governmental aristocracy. Liberals tended to understand themselves as modernizers and, as part of their drive to limit the power of the Catholic Church, anticlerical. Conservatives, on the other hand, while accepting the fact of independence, fought to protect the hierarchies of colonial society and the church's power. Following a two-year annexation to Mexico, the Central American countries—Guatemala, El Salvador, Honduras, Costa Rica, and Nicaragua—formed a sovereign nation called the United Provinces of Central America (later known as the Federal Republic of Central America), with its capital in Guatemala City. Yet in 1826 civil war broke out in the new nation, with Liberals, under the leadership of the Honduran Francisco Morazán, triumphing in 1829 and ruling Central America until 1839.

At first, indigenous communities stayed out of these elite conflicts; but because many Liberal reforms weakened indigenous power and autonomy, they were increasingly drawn into playing a decisive role. During the initial decade of Liberal rule, the government in Guatemala City pushed through a series of aggressive initiatives to dismantle what it felt were archaic Spanish institutions. This new and fragile Liberal nation-state attempted to privatize lands held by the Catholic Church and indigenous communities. Education was placed under secular government control, divorce was legalized, marriage was made civil, and, in the interest of disease prevention, burials were prohibited within church buildings. The Liberals enacted free-trade policies, invited foreign capital to invest and immigrants to settle, and substituted the old colonial tithes with an array of "modern" taxes on income, land, commerce, as well as on village treasuries. The government abolished corporal punishment, established the right to trial by one's peers, declared Spanish the national language, and took steps to "extinguish aboriginal tongues" and promote cultural assimilation through education.

By 1837 the countryside was in revolt, spurred on by a widespread anger against these Liberal reforms and sparked by a raging cholera epidemic. Indigenous communities, conservative elites, and Catholic clergy united behind the illiterate *mestizo* swineherd Rafael Carrera, who was instrumental in the young nation's dissolution in 1839. He then ruled Guatemala either directly or de facto until his death in 1865. His long reign is best described as a neocolonial Catholic restoration. Church authority was restored, and the erosion of indigenous autonomy was stemmed. Nevertheless, the secularization of society and the privatization of land continued at a diminished yet steady pace. Urban elites and mixed-race Ladinos began to spread out into the indigenous countryside, slowly usurping control of local politics and markets.

Starting in the 1860s, an emerging planter class began to sow a new crop: coffee. In 1871, Liberal insurgents from the western highlands, representing these planters, toppled Carrera's successor. This new political class, led by Justo Rufino Barrios, enacted land and labor reforms intended to promote coffee cultivation and exportation. These reforms included laws that, while not abolishing communal property, encouraged its division and transfer to private title. Highland communities in zones too high to grow coffee were better able to hold onto their land, but towns in the lower fertile volcanic ridge were stripped of their lands nearly overnight. Forced labor, which had been gradually declining through the early nineteenth century, was resurrected through a variety of mechanisms. The infamous 1877 *mandamiento* decree, for example, obligated communities to send work gangs to work on plantations during the harvest, as did assorted vagrancy and debt peonage laws. After this method was applied to coffee agriculture, the cultivation of other crops such as sugar, bananas, and cotton followed this plantation model.

Scholars have distinguished the nationalism that developed in Guatemala in the late nineteenth century from expressions of national identity in Mexico and other Central American countries by its rejection of *mestizaje*, which celebrates, at least rhetorically, the genetic and cultural hybrid that supposedly manifests the best of both European and American "races." In Guatemala, by contrast, "Ladino"—a term used in the western highlands since the late 1700s to identify non-Indians, which spread nationwide when planters from that region took over the state in 1871—refers to an exclusively European identity. One conceit of this nationalism was that Indians could become Ladinos by giving up the cultural traits that marked them as Indians. Many mid-twentieth-century writers, anthropologists, and policymakers, including many self-identified progressive democrats, advocated for the active promotion of this process, both for the good of Indians and the health of the nation. This advocacy has been condemned for some time now as a form of cultural genocide; both its defenders and its detractors tend to miss how the "Liberal" promotion of assimilation masked more rigid, unbending forms of segregation. As Guatemalan historian Arturo Taracena points out, for all the talk of promoting "Ladinoization," the Guatemalan state in fact put into place legal mechanisms that institutionalized inequalities between Indians and Ladinos. This system of segregation was reinforced by a highly exploitative, militarized plantation economy dependent on the ongoing existence of indigenous communities, which served both as a ready, easily controllable source of cheap labor and a way to reproduce a seasonal workforce that planters only needed for part of the year. In other words, republican Guatemala was a society founded on apartheid-like institutions lacquered with a Liberal glaze.

Furthermore, researchers have recently begun to contest the long-held notion that the Guatemalan nation and nationalism comprised two groups, Indians and Ladinos. They have documented the long-unacknowledged importance of African slavery in colonial Guatemala, as well as the multiple divisions and subdivisions that have constituted nonindigenous identity, which were often subsumed under the category of Ladino within the expanding bureaucracy and legal system of the liberal state. The Guatemalan anthropologist Ramón González Ponciano has described how these divisions—which reveal the cross-ethnic class stratification that the Indian–Ladino divide tends to obscure—range from the degenerate *mucos, shumos,* and *choleros* to the esteemed *fresas, caqueros,* and *normales.* The combination of a state that talked about assimilation but enforced segregation and an imagined national category—Ladino—that assumed common interests among non-Indians but in fact obscured deep class divisions was a formula for illegitimacy, which contributed to the quickening cycles of mobilization and repression that would plague Guatemala in the twentieth century.

The fortification of a highly militarized state was one response to this illegitimacy, the energies of which were oriented toward the control of a plantation workforce. This militarization became the signal feature of Guatemala's political life, as a series of "Liberal" dictators—Justo Rufino Barrios (1871–1885), Manuel José Estrada Cabrera (1898–1920), and Jorge Ubico (1931–1944)—ruled the country until 1944. It was also during this time that the lineaments of Guatemala's national urban life began to take shape. After the First World War, the "Generation of the 1920s," cultural modernists and political democrats, joined with a small working class and emerging middle class to begin to challenge this oppressive system, prefiguring much of the activism and optimism that would burst forth in 1944.

Travels amongst Indians

Lindesay Brine

After independence in 1821, foreigners, mostly from the United States and Great Britain, began to arrive in Guatemala on a regular basis, traveling through the indigenous highlands, surveying archaeological sites, and writing up their adventures in travel books or serialized magazine articles. The explorer and diplomat John L. Stephens, for example, toured Guatemala during the convulsive 1830s and 1840s, and his ethnocentric writings portrayed a land of untamed passions and constant political strife, governed by obscurantist indigenous and Catholic superstitions. Below is an excerpt from a later writer, Lindesay Brine, who visited Guatemala in the late 1860s. Compared to Stephens, Brine paints an almost idyllic image of rural life. Brine appreciates what might be called the pax Carrera *during the last years of Rafael Carrera's reign. His account offers a tranquil picture of highland indigenous communities. Unbeknown to Brine, the coming turmoil of the coffee revolution was but a few years away.*

On our way to Jacaltenango we had to cross the Sierra Madre, a range of mountains which traverses the centre of Guatemala. The mule tack led us over some steep and rugged ascents, and through a long and deep *barranco* [gully] filled with a cold damp mist. During the greater part of the day we were enveloped in clouds which covered the summits of the hills. We finally reached the hamlet of Todos Santos, and obtained shelter at an Indian *rancho*.

Towards night-fall we heard the distant bell of the chapel ringing for evening prayer. The Indians stood in front of their huts, and looking in the direction of the sound of the bell, recited the Ave Maria. This is one of the religious customs taught by the Spanish friars that retains its influence upon the inhabitants of these remote highlands.

Darkness rapidly succeeds daylight in tropical latitudes, and upon my return to the *rancho* I observed that the hut was lighted by a method mentioned by the early historians of the conquest as having been in universal use amongst the Mexican Indians. In the centre of the room was a rude wooden stand, upon which was placed crosswise, a lighted piece of resinous pinewood. The flame gave a sufficient light for all practical purposes. After turning into my hammock, I watched by the fitful glare of the firebrand, the domestic habits of the Indians. The first thing done, was to put the child to bed, and this was managed in the following manner: The mother wrapped the child tightly in swaddling clothes, until it looked like a mummy. The head was left exposed. It was then fastened upon a flat board about three feet high and eighteen inches wide. This board was put upright against an angle of the wall. The child remained throughout the night perfectly quiet. The bed upon which the father and mother slept, was a low wide frame resting on four legs, and raised a few inches above the ground. Everything was of the rudest simplicity. The smoke from the fire rose directly upwards and escaped through the roof. . . .

After leaving the hamlet, we passed by the little church whose bell we had heard upon the previous night. The door was closed, and I noticed that it was charred by burning and blackened by smoke. I was told that this remote church was frequently closed during the time that the priest was away in other parts of the district, and when the Indians came here, they stuck lighted candles upon the door as nearly as possible in the direction of the image to which they wished to make their offerings. The church door was consequently deeply marked by the flames. Here, as also before the closed doors of other chapels in the mountains, the Indians have the custom of raising a temporary altar outside, before which they place offerings, and sit patiently in silence for many hours. They then fill a brazier with chips of resinous wood, and light their candles and the brazier and go away to their huts, leaving the incense burning. This is possibly a survival of the ancient usage of burning copal incense before their idols.

During the forenoon we went over several steep ranges of hills, and down very abrupt descents until we arrived at the village of St. Martin, when we stopped at a deserted shed, and Carlos proposed that he should get ready the breakfast. It was always a pleasure to watch an Indian lighting a fire. His materials are usually a few dry sticks, some leaves, a flint, a steel, and a roll of prepared cotton, which, when slightly burnt, easily catches fire from the sparks of the flint. There was often, however, a difficulty in getting the fuel to burst into a flame, and the steady persistent patience of Indians in doing this is extraordinary. It was a great comfort in riding amongst the sierras, to have always the power of making a fire. It was of still greater importance to carry your own bed.

Each morning when starting upon a journey over an unknown country with much uncertainty as to where quarters would be found for the night, there was a sense of satisfaction in seeing placed upon the pommel of the saddle the hammock in which you intended to sleep. It gave freedom from all anxiety with regard to the future. There was no cause to feel any doubts respecting the beds at a Spanish *posada*, or the rough interior of an Indian hut, and there was always the prospect of obtaining, after the fatigues of the day, a good night's rest. In thus traveling and having at hand sufficient provisions and fuel to guard against being by any accident in want amongst these mountainous regions, there was a feeling of independence which was very exhilarating. This kind of gypsy, Bohemian life was singularly attractive, and the small element of risk from the possibility of meeting hostile Indians was too slight to have any influence upon the mind. There was a certain degree of solitude in thus riding without a companion, as the guide ran several hundred yards ahead, but this was not much felt, for there was a never ending change of scene, and every hour brought something new and unexpected.

In the evening as we descended the slopes of the valleys, we met numbers of Indians carrying heavy loads on their backs. I had noticed when riding amongst the higher parts of these hills that crosses were placed upon all remarkable positions, and at the corners where paths branched off towards the hamlets. When passing these crosses the men invariably took off their broad straw hats, and showed by their manner great respect.

I was surprised at observing in the valleys that the Indians suffered much from goitre. This unsightly growth seemed chiefly to affect the women. It was the same in size and appearance as that which exists amongst the inhabitants of several of the secluded valleys in Switzerland.

At intervals during the afternoon we heard the distant sound of the beating of a drum calling the attention of the Indians for some purpose which we did not then understand. When we drew near to Jacaltenango we became aware that something was occurring which caused considerable excitement amongst the people. We passed an open space at the entrance of the pueblo, upon which had been built, temporarily, a *"santo"* house. It was a small round hut, within which was an image, which had been removed from the church and placed there, in order that it should receive special honour and devotion. Before this shrine a dance was taking place. It represented incidents of the wars between the Spanish Christians and the Moors during the period when the latter were finally driven out of Spain. A little beyond the *"santo"* house was the church where an Indian festival was in progress, and an orchestra was busily engaged within, performing a musical service. I stopped for a few minutes to look at the strange and fantastical scene, and the groups of swarthy, wild looking Indians, and then rode on to the convent, where we were welcomed by Padre Juan Chrysostemos Robles. My guide Carlos went away to join in the festivities of his tribe.

In the morning an Indian passed rapidly through the village beating a small drum, and later in the day, a large crowd of Indians assembled in the square in front of the church. It thus became known that an important meeting was to be held in order to bring about a settlement of some difficulty or disagreement between two hamlets, with respect to the buying and selling of lands. About three hundred of the men, chiefly interested, gathered together. The speaking began in tones so harsh that it was almost inconceivable that human language could have developed into such rough and grating sounds.

These Mams were men of strong and muscular frames, compact and well made, but they were all short in stature. Their general appearance was wild and they had a restless manner. They came from the adjacent hills, and it was noticeable with them as with other Indians I had seen in the mountains, that they were darker than those living on the plains. The meeting lasted for about an hour, and as soon as the business was ended they immediately left Jacaltenango and returned to their homes. I was told that the matter in dispute had been settled to the satisfaction of all present, and that there was no longer any fear of local disturbances.

Meanwhile the numerous orchestral services within the church were still proceeding. It was a curious scene. The chief instrument was a large wooden marimba made on the principle of short and long sounding boards, the upper notes of which were played by the leading performers, whilst three other men kept up a continuous accompaniment on the bass. It was evidently an improvement upon the African marimba which had probably been introduced into America by the negro slaves. There were also violins and several rudely constructed guitars. The musical ceremonies were performed before the altars, the Indian congregation maintaining a complete silence. Not the least strange part of the function was the fact that Padre Robles was an unconcerned spectator, although it was his church that was occupied by the Indians and his *"santos"* that were being carried about and worshiped, and to whom the offerings were made.

Although the music was noisy and monotonous, the players seemed to have a correct knowledge of harmony. The Padre explained how this happened. He said that this comparative knowledge of music was obtained in consequence of the teaching of the friars before the dissolution of the monasteries. These friars devoted much of their time to the education of a certain number of Indian lads in orchestral music, in order to train them to take part in the church services, and he supposed that the instruction then given was kept up in some way which he did not understand, and that young Indians were taught in their villages for this work. He thought that the preparations for the church festivals and for the dances were also arranged in a similar manner.

In the afternoon we went to the entrance of one of the valleys, as the Padre wished to show me the position of an Indian *"adoratorio"* situated on the side of a steep mountain. He said he had not seen it, but had been told by his Indians what occurred there. An idol, held in much reverence by the Mams, had its shrine inside, and the *alcaldes* charged with the duties of the religious rites and other ceremonies relating to Indian sacerdotalism, visited it at certain seasons of the year and offered sacrifices to it. The idol had also days for the performances of penances, and there was one special day when there was a solemn feast, and turkeys were killed and eaten with peculiar observances, and the blood of the turkeys was sprinkled and offered in a manner unknown to him.

After passing through the place where the *"santo"* house was erected, and before which dances and other ceremonies were still going on, we returned to the convent.

Soon after sunset an event occurred which proved that a disturbance had taken place in the interior of the earth. We were sitting inside the precincts when we were alarmed by, what was to me, a quite unknown rumbling sound amongst the adjacent mountains. At first I thought that it was caused by distant thunder reverberating amongst the valleys, but it was soon evident that the sounds were of an entirely different character.

The Padre, who was listening attentively to the noise, said, after a few moments' pause, that it was a "Temblor" or trembling of the earth below, and that it was quite different from a "Terra Moto" or earthquake, as it never caused any harm, although it was considered to be a warning. According to my map, the nearest crater was the Volcán de Tacara [Tacaná], fourteen leagues away in a south-easterly direction. The deep sounds rolled like thunder beneath the massive ranges of the Sierra Madre.

When living amongst these mountains, and hearing these intimations of great volcanic movements below the surface of the ground, it can be understood how it came to pass that the superstitious and fanatical Indians living in these regions believed that the earth beneath them was peopled by evil demons capable of doing injury, who required to be propitiated, and that when seeing the expression of their anger in the fire, smoke, and ashes issuing from the craters, thought it necessary to appease them by offering them their daughters. It is probable that the sacrifices known to have taken place to the volcanoes near Atitlán and Quetzaltenango were also customary throughout the long range of volcanoes in this part of Central America.

When talking about the present customs of the Indians living in these sierras, the Padre said that the ancient rule of young men serving for a certain time the parents of the girl they wished to marry had ceased, and that now it was usual for an Indian to make up his mind on the subject, and then to begin his courtship by giving presents of maize, fowls, or clothing to the parents. Finally he proposes to take the girl in marriage, and if they consent, he pays for her according to his means, generally about two dollars, but sometimes as much as eight dollars. . . .

By this time Carlos had filled his pack, fitted the head band over his forehead, and was waiting to start: so I said goodbye to the kind Padre, and as I turned round in the saddle to get a last glimpse of Jacaltenango, the most beautifully situated village that I had seen in Guatemala, I observed him watching us from the top of the convent steps.

Land, Labor, and Community

David McCreery

In the decades after independence in 1821, the first generation of Liberal elites en-
couraged the export of cacao and the red dye cochineal, but with little success. Then
came coffee. Starting in the 1860s, regional Ladino elites, many of them based in the
provincial cities of San Marcos and Quetzaltenango, began to plant coffee along
the Pacific piedmont, mostly on land rented from local municipalities. As demand
for coffee increased, at first from Germany, the need for both land and labor grew
insatiable. Indigenous communities had both in ample supply, but they had little
economic reason to make them available for coffee production. Following the Liberal
Revolution of 1871, which was largely led by the first generation of coffee planters
from the western highlands, the government passed a series of laws aimed at break-
ing the autonomy of indigenous communities. In particular, it passed a forced-labor
law in 1877, called the mandamiento, *which resurrected the colonial-era forced-*
labor regime and obligated communities to provide laborers to coffee plantations.
Because many communities did not have official title to their commons, wealthy
planters with access to legal resources took advantage of the new legal regime to ex-
tend their holdings. Although the forced-labor law was abolished officially in 1894,
forced labor persisted through a variety of means until well into the twentieth cen-
tury (see parts 4 and 5 of this volume).

This extension of capitalist agriculture took place along clearly defined ethnic
lines, deepening the country's divide between indigenous and Ladino. At the same
time, continued access to subsistence production meshed well with the seasonal cul-
tivation of coffee. Growers could maintain a part-time workforce, and indigenous
seasonal workers received some cash, which allowed them to keep alive certain ritu-
als and institutions that defined indigenous identity, especially saints' festivals as-
sociated with cofradías *(religious brotherhoods). In the following selection, histo-*
rian David McCreery discusses the foundations of coffee capitalism in Guatemala.

From the 1850s, and at an increasing rate in the 1860s, the new export crop
of coffee revolutionized the countryside of Guatemala. Planters, made increasingly desperate by the declining situation and prospects of the cochi-

neal industry, and then merchants after the mid-1850s, experimented with a variety of new export possibilities. None proved as promising as coffee: by 1871 it amounted to half of the republic's overseas sales. Although coffee eventually would engage the resources of the Guatemalan countryside as no commodity had ever done before, production expanded erratically, in a rhythm driven by the ups and downs of the world market and conditioned by peculiar regional circumstances and patterns of acceptance or resistance among the rural population. Coffee made its way in different regions of Guatemala at different times and in different forms; each part of the country had its own coffee history. . . .

The history of early efforts to establish coffee cultivation in Guatemala demonstrated the difficulty of putting together the proper combination of land, labor, and transport to make the crop a profitable enterprise. . . .

At the root of many of the planters' difficulties, or so it seemed to a growing number of them, was the conservative attitude toward the Indian, captured well in the sentiment, "Those poor Indians are better off the way they are." The role of the government, the *Gaceta de Guatemala* admonished in 1865, was to protect the Indians and to improve their spiritual and material situation; they should be "moralized" with "kindness and prudence." . . .

Guatemala's lack of a central title registry and up-to-date regulations for land measurement and titling made it almost impossible to develop any system of credit based on land. To many among the burgeoning coffee elites it seemed that the Conservative regime was holding the country back. More active measures were needed, as one observer explained:

> Neither the mildness of the climate nor the excellence of the soil nor its aptitude for one or another sort of production nor the advantageous position of our country for maritime commerce nor the many other gifts a generous God has heaped upon our country have been enough to overcome the obstacles that to date have blocked the development of agriculture. It is a principle of political economy that the state ought to limit its involvement to removing hindrances to individual action. This, like many other doctrines, necessarily must be modified in the case of new countries such as ours, where shortages of capital, of institutions of credit, of foreign immigration, of the spirit of enterprise and other obstacles require that the government more actively assist the interests of the individual. . . .

In 1871 a new generation of Liberals under the leadership of Miguel García Granados and Justo Rufino Barrios brought down the Conservatives and initiated a reformist regime. . . .

The object of the Liberal regime was "development," which they equated with their own prosperity and with the introduction into Guatemala of many of the readily apparent material and cultural characteristics of North Atlantic civilization, be these railroads or an opera house, or modern weapons and training for the army. Infatuation with "progress" and the material evidence of progress had two important results. On the one hand, these Liberals assumed that progress and "development" were politically neutral—that is, they expected to import technology and the products of technology without in any way threatening their hold on political, social, or economic power. In the short run they were correct. More accurately, new technologies such as the railroad and the repeating rifle actually reinforced and extended their control, allowing them to build a state of unprecedented power. On the other hand, they constantly were tempted to substitute appearance for reality. But they were not stupid. The erecting of, for example, a modern capital in a country blighted by miserable roads and endemic disease had a purpose beyond simply providing a more pleasant city for the privileged to live in. It was an important part of elite Guatemala's presentation of self to representatives of the developed world as a country and a government worthy of credit and investment. If subsidizing an opera company while closing an agricultural school seems foolish, President Estrada Cabrera's program of building temples to Minerva instead of schools was perfectly logical within the perspective of the economic and political interests of the planters. Liberal development was a class project that defined itself in terms of class well-being, and by that measure it was enormously successful. . . .

Coffee provided the motive and the means for the Guatemalan state to penetrate the indigenous community to an unprecedented degree, and it destroyed much of what remained of values shared between the elites and the mass of the population. The Liberals did little to seek a popular consensus. Despite much rhetoric about schools, education, and the uplifting of the masses, most of which, in any event, was the work of Liberal intellectuals and not of the average planter, what is striking about this new generation of Liberals is the absence of any serious attempt to indoctrinate the peasantry in its vision of development or of modern society. Whereas the Enlightenment Liberals [an earlier generation of Liberal reformers] had seen the Indian as a block to national development that should and could be overcome by means of education and integration, the Neo-Liberals [after the 1870s] looked upon the Indian as probably essentially, and certainly in the short run unalterably, inferior:

The Indian is a pariah, stretched out in his hammock and drunk on *chicha,* his natural beverage. His house is a pig sty; a ragged wife and six or more naked children live beneath a ceiling grimy with the smoke of a fire that burns day and night in the middle of the floor; some images of saints with the faces of demons, four chickens and a rooster and two or three skinny dogs [etc.]. Yet in this state the Indian is happy.

. . . Most planters and would-be elites agreed that the Indians would have to be made to work, and to work hard, under the close supervision of Ladinos: "In the past he was not civilized but 'utilized' and now cannot be civilized because he opposes it, so there is no alternative but to continue to utilize him." The labor of the Indian, unless and until he could be replaced by a superior immigrant population, was an all-important ingredient for export agriculture and elite prosperity. What the Indians thought mattered far less, if it mattered at all, than that they should be readily and cheaply available for work in the coffee groves; the growers wanted their bodies more than their minds. . . .

An alternative to "civilizing" the Indian was what was sometimes referred to as the "North American" solution. This involved either physically eliminating the inferior race or "bleaching it out" with superior white immigration. The first was hardly feasible for Guatemala given the overwhelming predominance of the indigenous population, and the second met with little success. . . .

The Instruments of Control *

Control of the countryside after 1871 rested on the army and the militia, mobilized when needed in the diverse geography of Guatemala by the telegraph. The Conservatives had flirted with the new technology, but the Liberals installed the first telegraph line in 1873, between the Pacific port of San José and Guatemala City. The events of their own successful revolt had made them acutely aware of the importance of rapid communication for political intelligence and control, and they spread the telegraph quickly to the rest of the country. . . . Government telegrams increased from an average of less than 1,000 a month in the early 1870s to 15,000 a month in 1898, and rose to more than 20,000 in the peak labor mobilization month of August; by the end of the century the system handled more than 180,000 official messages a year. The telegraph played the vital role, too, in repressing disturbances. . . . As the judge remarks in Miguel Angel Asturias's *El señor presidente*: "What was the telephone invented for? To see that orders were carried out! To arrest the enemies of the government!" . . .

Armies and militias had existed from the colonial period, but usually they were no better than ad hoc, ragtag affairs based in the towns and commanded mostly by amateurs. In times of conflict the state filled out the ranks with press-ganged, poorly trained and armed Ladino and Indian peasants. . . .

The regime also moved to put the militia on a more or less regular footing. After 1871 it becomes possible to differentiate the regular army, which in peacetime rarely numbered more than 2,000–4,000 men, garrisoned in the urban centers and on the frontiers, from the militia. In theory the latter included all Ladino males between the ages of eighteen and fifty who were not otherwise exempt. Whereas the army's principal task was national defense, the militia, although it acted as a reserve for the army and might be called up in time of war, served in the absence of a regular rural police force as the state's chief instrument of control and repression in the countryside. By the turn of the country there were 173 militia detachments based throughout the country in Ladino-controlled towns and settlements. . . .

Land

. . . Although the Liberals did not issue a revised general land law until the 1890s, the regime moved almost immediately to make public land more easily available to those who would produce for export. . . . The towns had claim to much of the best area, and growers sought land close to whatever roads and resident labor supply a region offered. Under the Liberals this leasing of land for coffee and other export crops accelerated, as did the protests of the communities. Where the towns resisted, the new government was more likely than the Conservatives had been to intervene on the side of coffee. In January 1874, for example, when the Indians of Cobán refused to give more land [for rent] for coffee, the departmental governor made his choice clear:

> To put an end to the obstacles being placed in the way of growers who wish to use land possessed by Indians . . . and keeping in mind the difficulties the Municipality of Cobán has encountered in providing land to those who wish to plant coffee because of the illegal possession of much of it by Indians: 1. The only concessions will be for the planting of coffee or sugar cane and this includes all land that from remote times has been considered to be *ejidos*, even if not yet measured.

Increasingly, too, it became the practice to shift from the fixed scale of rents set in the 1830s to competitive bidding. This tended to push rental prices beyond the reach of local Indians and subsistence food producers and concentrate the best land in the coffee areas in the hands of large users. . . . Without ready access to credit, local Indians could neither afford the rising prices for land in the coffee areas nor compete at auction with the superior resources of the Ladinos. More and more, they found themselves priced out of the market for land they had always imagined was theirs.

Labor

As coffee production expanded, a more pressing problem for growers than land was labor. Because coffee must be picked when it is ripe or the harvest is quickly lost, the success of the new crop depended on the availability of workers when and where needed.

In April of [1877] the Liberals issued their first general agricultural labor law. In contrast to most laws of the time, and perhaps because the need and justification for it seemed self-evident, Decree 177 carried no prologue or explanation. All rural laborers were required to carry a workbook, or *libreta*, that was to include a copy of their contract and a record of debts and credits and days worked. Decree 177 further specified that *jefes políticos* and village authorities, not the regular court system, were to handle employer-worker disputes and to help employers when needed to round up contracted workers.

Articles 31–37 of Decree 177 systematized *mandamientos*. The governors of the departments were now to grant planter requests for agricultural labor drafts from the Indian communities. The law provided that they could dispatch groups of up to sixty workers at a time, for fifteen days if the property was in the same department or thirty if outside it. . . .

The coffee growers welcomed the new regulations enthusiastically: "Now the employers will not lack labor; they will not lose crops for want of workers when they need them." Such expectations died aborning, however, for the problem of *brazos* ("arms," i.e., workers) proved much more intractable than the signers of the above letter anticipated. One result was that the Liberal state continued over the next decades to issue and reissue labor-related laws, regulations, and directives—"so many that only the books of the municipal secretaries know for certain." In 1881, for example, a circular reminded state officials that to ensure that Indians complied with their labor obligations, local authorities or the *jefes* could jail them "until they reached an agreement with their employer." . . .

In 1875, the San Francisco–based photographer Eadweard Muybridge was hired by the Pacific Mail Steamship Company to produce promotional images of Central America to stimulate investment and travel. Ignoring the deep social convulsions of the emerging coffee economy, he depicted Guatemala as a rural idyll. (*top*) Lake Atitlán from the east. (*bottom*) Coffee harvesters at the Las Nubes Plantation. From the collections of the Centro de Investigaciones Regionales de Mesoamérica, Guatemala.

Coffee cultivation did not implant capitalism in rural Guatemala, but it did transmit the secondary effects of an expanding world capitalist economy to large areas of the countryside and to much of the indigenous population that before had had little or no part in cash or export agriculture. It absorbed enormous amounts of land and labor that formerly had been devoted to subsistence activities or had been left isolated in the wake of past booms; it paid for the construction of railroads and ports to export the new crop and bring in imports. In part these effects were the result of the ecology of coffee, for the new crop found its best conditions in areas such as the *boca costa* and the upper Verapaz that until then had been little exploited commercially. Even more, they were the result of the scale of coffee. Both Guatemalan and world coffee production increased dramatically after mid-century while the price held firm and even moved up, at least until the 1898 crisis. The enormous and expanding market was a product of European and North American urbanization as those economies shifted from a dominance of mercantile to industrial capital. Coffee was the classic example of an "industrial" food product, or, better put, food substitute. Not only did it benefit from the improvements in transportation and the mechanization of processing that came after 1859, but it quickly became an important element in the capitalist dynamic of raising profits by cheapening the costs of maintaining and reproducing the work force.

The Saddest Day in Cantel

Anonymous

Cantel, a Maya-K'iche' town in the western highlands, is famous for two incidents that gained it a reputation as a combative community. The first occurred in 1884, when a number of its leaders, angry that the government was allowing an industrial textile factory to be established on communal land, joined a regional conspiracy to overthrow President Justo Rufino Barrios, who supported the factory owners. When the conspiracy was uncovered, Barrios had six Cantelenses executed. The second took place nearly one hundred years later, in 1983, when leaders of the community prevented the imposition of a civil patrol, the forced conscription used to fight the guerrilla insurgency (see part 6 of this volume). Cantel was the only town that refused to participate in the military's program from the start—at the cost of dozens of lives.

Written by an anonymous author and kept in the municipal office in the town of Cantel, the selection below recounts the events leading up to the 1884 execution. In many indigenous towns throughout Guatemala, there exists a tradition of popular history, either written, like the case of the account presented here, or passed down orally through the generations. Such stories often recount tales of violence associated with the coming of coffee capitalism or with the consolidation of a centralized state, both of which often led to a loss of political autonomy, expropriation of land, and an increase in forced labor. Though at times contradictory and exaggerated, they often capture the texture of local memories of dispossession. Historical documents confirm that Barrios did indeed levy a fine on Cantel, as the account below alleges. Though the fine was considerably lower than reported in this history (fifteen thousand pesos as opposed to 1,200 pounds of silver), it was enough to force some Cantelenses who had land—and who thus had no need to seek out wage labor—to find work on coffee plantations, to help the municipality raise money to pay the fine.

The fateful year of 1884 arrived in Cantel after countless other dispossessions and humiliations before it, including the imposition of slavery. [President General Justo Rufino] Barrios knew perfectly well that the people of the town—or, better said, of the entire Nation—only respected him out of fear. But deep inside they detested his arbitrary rule. He decided that in order to establish who his true enemies were, he would avail himself of the help of a loyal servant . . . who from Chiapas would fake an armed invasion. This supposed enemy of Barrios sent messages inciting the people to rebellion. Because the Municipality had already protested a number of injustices, and because Cantel residents maintained a vibrant commercial relationship at that time with the town of Comitán, whose traders came and went with their mules laden with market goods and had befriended certain of Cantel's own merchants, the fake insurrectionary movement sent letters of incitement directly to the Municipality of Cantel via these traders. Cantel's authorities never suspected that these missives were false incitements; instead, in response, they confessed the problems they suffered due to Barrios's abuses, and they promised that in the case of an invasion they would assist the invaders with money and provisions.

Finally, a delegate from the invented Anti-Barrios Revolution came to Cantel, supposedly to learn about the town's problems and promising help and restitution for all the land seizures Cantel had suffered. He obtained a signed document outlining the secret agreement [to help in the insurrection], signed and sealed by the Municipality. The emissary then showed the document to Barrios who, without further ado, traveled to Quetzaltenango and immediately ordered General Manuel Lisandro Barillas, the Military-Political Chief of the region, to arrange a meeting with the Cantel town council on September 3, 1884. . . . Barrios berated the members of the council and beat them, ordering them to be locked up in the [nearby] army base until the next day, when he ordered a military escort under the command of Colonel Florencio Calderón (alias Lenchón) to bring them back to Cantel, while he simultaneously ordered all the townspeople to assemble for a firing squad.

At about three o'clock in the afternoon, the council members were escorted to the Public Plaza, and the school's students and its neighbors were ordered to form a square, and at four in the afternoon, the military escort executed six men who had defended and endured the dictatorship, and without any due cause the population had to witness their execution, under orders that if they did not, they themselves would be shot. Meanwhile, three artillery pieces were stationed around the town, two on the Quiac Hill and one on Puík'ajk'ik, and they named a new mayor, don José Unaldo Ruíz, and a new town council, in order to, the very next day, announce that the townsfolk had twenty days in which to pay a type of ransom fee, of one hundred and twenty *quintales* [one *quintal* equals one hundred pounds] of silver. If they did not comply, under pain of punishment, the town would be destroyed piece by piece and all of Cantel's territory would be transferred to the municipality of Salcajá.

In light of this urgent situation, they set about collecting from each resident the pounds of silver each had to give; the silver was piled up in the passage of the parish convent, with Domingo García and Miguel Colop serving as secretaries. When the hundred and twenty *quintales* had been weighed out, the secretaries sent for mules to transport it to the Dictator in person, and when he saw that the price had been paid, he said: "No, I will never again return to disturb the town of Cantel while my attentions are devoted to the unification of Central America; afterwards, we shall see. For now, you are excused." At the same time, he gave the order for the troops and artillery to be withdrawn, which had been readily awaiting their command to "fire."

The hardship of the ransom caused the town to sell the lands on the Urbina plains to the neighboring towns, and many of the people who had lived there fled to different parts of the Republic, changed their names, and established themselves with the aim of never returning to their Beloved Land.

The assassinated martyrs were:

FRANCISCO CHOJOLÁN

FELIX SACALXOT

ANTONIO SALANIC

VENTURA ORDOÑEZ

NICÓLAS SAM (Municipal Secretary)

Along with two mayors, executed in the Capital:

Don ANTONIO SALANIC and CRUZ SACALXOT.

. . . It would prove one of destiny's cruel ironies that the Tyrant would enjoy only 210 further days on this earth. And what would the slain say, when they saw the man responsible for hastening their own journey to the next life arrive there himself?

It is said that doña Francisca Aparicio, Barrios's widow who fled the country and traveled to France in order to better enjoy her deceased husband's wealth, said to those who gathered to bid her farewell: "Let it be known that I will take not even the dust from this land; I will cast off its vestments." (She did not take the dust, but SHE DID TAKE CANTEL'S MONEY.)

. . .

As for the bodies, they were taken to a common grave and buried immediately, to the pain and emotion of all of the victims' family members.

Unfortunately, the authorities—for fear of themselves being executed—did not mark the location of the grave. Though the Municipality erected a monument to the fallen martyrs in 1959, it was not placed at the precise site of their burial.

In similar circumstances, and also for the supposed crime of having stood up to one of our beloved Guatemala's most feared dictators, fell the Municipalities of Retalhuleu and Mazatenango, where a pregnant woman was among those executed; the same transpired in San Pedro Sacatepéquez, where both the mayor and a town official were killed. In Retalhuleu, a young lawyer was named to the position of judge—one Manuel Estrada Cabrera—and he was tasked with bringing a case against the Municipality, which ended with shootings ten days later. The reader can imagine why this occurred, and how it might even have involved forced confessions to nonexistent crimes. Cabrera, who as a youth had been corrupted by Barrios in the very earliest days of his career, later became the Dictator par excellence, keeping a humiliated military wrapped around his finger and becoming the model for General Ubico. . . .

Today, thanks to Divine Providence, everything has changed.

Translated by Kirsten Weld

The Ladino

Severo Martínez Peláez

The term Ladino *is commonly used to refer to Guatemalans who are not Maya. First utilized in Guatemala in the 1500s to refer to Mayas who spoke Spanish, its meanings have changed over time. In the 1800s and early 1900s, Ladino sometimes referred to all lower-class people in the city and countryside who did not use Maya clothes or languages but also did not belong to the Creole elite. The concept evolved to mean "non-Maya," a claim that disguises the reality that many Ladinos are descendants of Mayas and Europeans and are thus "mixed" by definition. In many parts of the country, small groups of town-based Ladinos have more wealth and authority than the predominantly Maya population living in surrounding villages. Even so, most Ladinos are poor people. Guatemala's dominant culture of racism historically has kept poor Ladinos and Mayas apart. In this selection, Severo Martínez Peláez, Guatemala's great historian of the colonial period and author of the magisterial* La patria del criollo, *discusses the etymology of the word and the concept* Ladino.*

Like all concepts, that of Ladino is associated with a word. In this case, the word came into being and evolved in Spain in the same way that it arose and developed in relationship to the Maya. This word is old, but not ancient: it originated in the Castilian-speaking part of fifteenth-century Spain before the sixteenth century of discovery and conquest. Its oldest and best-known use had to do with Jews who spoke Castilian [Spanish]. Initially, Ladino was the name of the Castilian language of the Jews. Its second connotation was with ability. A Ladino was a Jew with a knack for business dealings. To speak of a "Ladino Jew" referred to someone good at business, a man tolerated yet marked by ultra-Catholic Spain. Already in [Don] *Quijote* we have Ladino as an adjective to mean crafty, very crafty. In fifteenth-century Spain, this word was used, but it is not yet found in Mesoamerica. I cannot recall Bernal Díaz using it. In 1492, the expulsion of the Arabs from Europe was completed, and the invasion and colonization started. But no one [in Spanish America] is called Ladino in its substantive sense.

As mixed-race *mestizos* appeared and became an important labor force,

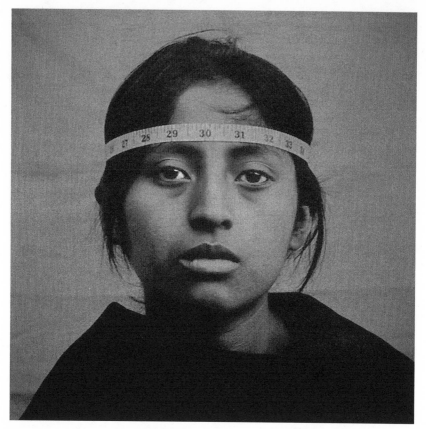

Critical Gaze by Luís González Palma (b. 1957). Used by permission of the artist.

they eventually came to be called Ladinos. Why? What does this have to do with Jews? What happened in Spain also happened here. In Spain there was a shift from using Ladino to mean the Castilian that Jews spoke, to eventually calling the Jews themselves Ladinos. That process repeated itself here. Before the actual renaming of *mestizos* as Ladinos, the historical documents began to include phrases such as "so and so is an Indian who is very Ladino." And this is how the word started to appear in Mesoamerica.

Mestizos appeared after the Conquest, yet it took the Spanish conquerors a while to create a term for the children of Spanish men and Indian women. Insofar as these children of "mischief" (rape) spoke Castilian, they were called Indians who were very Ladino. As the numbers of *mestizos* grew so did the "very Ladino Indians," and the word Ladino started to appear in official documents more than *mestizo.* . . . The configuration of Ladino as an objective category began. The noun Ladino was born with a negative connotation. It is important to emphasize this because it is commonly as-

López, *f* instrumento con el que.se realiza un trabajo manual o mecánico: *las herramientas de un fontanero.* ‖ *Fig; y fam. Cornamenta de; tc.*

López by Aníbal López (b. 1964), ca. 1996, from a series offering mock dictionary definitions of common Guatemalan surnames. This one defines the artist's own name as an "instrument with which one performs mechanical or manual labor." Another in the series, titled *Ladino*, defines "Pérez Sanik" as "*f.* right of inheritance; goods that are passed down by succession. // *Biol.* transmission of normal or pathological characteristics from one generation to another." Used by permission of the artist.

sumed that there is a world of Ladinos and a world of Indians, that everyone is a Ladino who is not an Indian. But that was not the case. The Spaniards were not Ladinos; anyone who might have said "señor Ladino" to a Creole [a well-to-do descendant of a Spaniard born in the Americas] would have suffered a blow to the head. "What Ladino? I am a Spaniard, and you are abusive. Ladino, your mother!" Yes, that was the Creole language: Ladino, your mother!

Today, sometimes when I speak with my indigenous brothers, they speak of "Ladinos" as a global enemy. So it is important to know that Ladi-

nos faced discrimination. To be a Ladino was to be half Indian. In the colonial period, Ladinos were in the middle: above them were the Spaniards,
the maximum authority, and with the Spaniards the Creoles. During the
colonial era, legislation was passed that prohibited Indians from entering
artisan trades controlled by the Spanish. Ladinos were not subject to this
legislation, and many Ladinos became artisans. The Indians were obliged
to work on the Spaniards' properties, but the Ladinos were not, and this
gave the Ladinos a way to collaborate in the control of Indians. *Mestizos*
appeared on the haciendas as trusted workers who wished to remain on
good terms with the Spaniards. A Ladino would hit an Indian to look good
in the eyes of the Spaniards. . . . The *mestizos* developed within this colonial
context, and they struggled to gain privileges. They had access to positions
of power within colonial rule. . . . *Mestizos* came to be managers, who controlled the work force. . . . They fit within the colonial matrix by serving
colonial rule. This Ladino constituted, globally speaking, an enemy of Indians. Indians took up the word Ladino, one invented by colonial power
to name *mestizos*. For the Indians, the term Ladino has the connotation of
someone not to be trusted. . . .

When did the idea begin that a Ladino was anyone not Indian? This
came from the legislation of [Justo Rufino] Barrios after the wealthy coffee
planters took power [in the 1870s]. The new elites wanted to increase this
distinction between Ladino and Indian. They legislated only two categories [of Guatemalans]: Ladino and Indian; this benefited Ladinos because
it meant that they were not subject to the forced-labor laws passed at that
time. And the door was open to what developed in this period . . . the new
military, the new police force, the new civil servants, all became a terrain
for Ladinos. . . . [late-nineteenth-century president Justo Rufino] Barrios
was the man who said "these are Ladinos and those are Indians," and he
legislated favorably for the former and unfavorably for the latter.

These days we all recognize that there are different social classes and
groups within the Indian community, even though it is thought to be homogeneous. And in the interior of what is called Ladino, there are also different classes and social groups. After all is said and done, there exist today
a minority of exploiters and a majority of those exploited, Indian and Ladino. It is important to study the complexity of social classes. If one starts
thinking that all that is Indian is good and all that is Ladino is bad, or the
reverse, one is falling into a mental trap, an ideology that does not permit
us to see the real nature of the struggle within Guatemalan society.

Translated by Deborah T. Levenson

Accustomed to Be Obedient

Richard N. Adams

The creation of a professional military was crucial to the consolidation of the Liberal state, allowing it to effectively respond to domestic unrest. But in a country divided by racism and devoid of other potentially unifying traditions, the military also became one of the few national institutions. The anthropologist Richard N. Adams discusses the debates that led to the integration of Mayas into its ranks.

Liberal Party president Justo Rufino Barrios (1873–1885) had a vision of a well-trained and educated Ladino army, loyal to the central government, under the command of professionally trained officers; but this vision proved unrealistic. It was part of the strategy of developing a country that lacked effective interior communication and was segmented into private domains and indigenous communities, and had its share of regional *caudillos* whose interests were not always one with those of the people who controlled the central government. . . . Given the need to use force to control Indian labor, it was not logical to build the army out of people who might be the target of army action. Indians were, after all, an object of the army, not the subject. . . . The Liberals were very serious about this. They erred, however, on a number of counts: (1) in thinking that educated Ladinos would flock to the service; (2) in allowing people to purchase their way out of the service; (3) in thinking that rural Ladinos would make better soldiers than Indians; (4) in thinking that Indians could not be trusted to control other Indians; and (5) in trying to do so much with so little available manpower.

By 1894, the Barrios experiment had gone far enough to have shown some of its weaknesses. Also, some newspapers and intellectuals in the country were showing concern about the condition of the Indian and what should be done about it. The harsh and oppressive forced labor decreed by Barrios in 1877 was not compatible with a world where republicanism, liberty, justice, and equality were increasingly touted as touchstones of the future.

In 1893, President Reina Barrios issued Decree 471, in which he argued that (1) the government was responsible for the liberty, equality, security, and respect of the individual and his property, but the forced labor on the *fincas* (plantations)—especially of the Indian who constituted the majority of the inhabitants of the Republic—contradicted these principles; therefore (2) he abolished the forced labor that had been established in 1877; but (3) because it was the obligation of all citizens to give personal service to the nation, he also (4) decreed that "the persons who had been obligated to provide the forced labor of the *mandamientos*, would now become incorporated into the *compañías de zapadores* [military work corps]" to be established. Exemptions to promote export agriculture were made for Indians from specific municipalities designated by the government, and for day laborers and *colonos* (resident farm labor) over twenty years old who contracted for more than thirty pesos (fifteen for *colonos*), provable by written contracts and certified by the respective *patrones*, to work on *fincas* of coffee, sugar, cacao, and bananas.

In January 1894, the *zapadores* were established. . . . The municipalities were to provide annual lists of all Indians between sixteen and fifty years of age, forming a pool from which a drawing would be made. As with the other sectors of the military service, there were exemptions: one could be excused by paying ten pesos a year or by presenting a workbook that showed a commitment to work at least three months in a *finca* of coffee, sugar, cacao, or bananas.

Reina Barrios's efforts, however, changed little. The *zapadores* exemption for working on farms was abolished four months later, presumably reverting to the earlier system. In 1897 and 1898 the *mandamientos* were reestablished, and, according to one source, the *zapadores* were eliminated. By the turn of the century, the problems of a clearly defective system were being discussed openly in the military press. In 1899, the army's *Revista militar* observed that while public law required all children between six and fourteen years of age to be in national schools, in fact some "were not able to enjoy this privilege due to their extreme poverty, or to living in remote areas, or for some other reasons. Because of this, more or less half of our army is composed of illiterate men whom the officers and instructors find very difficult to train." The army also had to compete with the Liberal government's insatiable need for labor to develop roads, telegraph lines, ports, public buildings, and above all to supply the labor for the expanding export agriculture. The papers of the *jefe político* of San Marcos from the first decade of the century contain much material, often conflicting, requesting men for one or another of these efforts. The policy that farms had priority over the army for these purposes made it constantly difficult for the military to keep itself well staffed. . . .

But nothing seemed to work. The universal, obligatory military service did not work, agricultural labor was still short in many regions, and justice and equality existed only in print. . . .

The failed strategy to create a literate Ladino army led to discussions reinterpreting the nature of the Indian and what that, in turn, might mean to the military service. One element of this discourse rationalized that the ancient Maya had been notable warriors and that this ancestry was an important component in the contemporary soldier. An anonymous romantic waxed enthusiastic in 1904:

> Easily aroused by noble ideas, and tenacious to defend them are Guatemalan soldiers, as in them are combined the contrary ethnic conditions that permit a combination of all that was good in their ancestors. . . . Valiant and inured to war were the Indian tribes that populated ancient Guatemala; on the other side, the Spaniards came preceded by great fame as the vanguard of the Roman legions, now having fought for centuries against the Arabs, then for having shaken Europe through victorious campaigns in Flanders and Italy. The Guatemalan soldier, heir to both, has glorious antecedents. . . .

The enthusiasm for the heroic contribution that the Indian component lent the army did not reflect an unalloyed ardor for the Indians as such. The *Revista militar* provided a more common view in an essay titled "The Indian," in a section called "Advice for a Child." While too long to quote in its entirety, a few selections may suffice:

> There he comes, hunchbacked, a bundle on his shoulders, sweating, panting, half naked, filthy . . . apparently forever condemned to look downwards, to focus on the things small; always looking at the earth. Has he once seen the majestic flight of the eagles? smiled with the dawn? felt God in his soul when watching the stars? . . . Should we leave him, forever bound to the routine, wasting his virility that with some help from others could allow him to work more easily and to gain better and more plentiful benefits?

In contrast, a more pragmatic and balanced assessment of the utility of the Indian for the military was proposed in 1915 by Guillermo Kuhsiek: "Although he is extremely self-denying, malnourished, and badly clothed, he works with the same endurance in the heat of the coast as in the cold of the mountains, in the summer sun and the winter rains." He then proposes that the army can take advantage of the Indian in two ways: first as a soldier, integral to the army, and second as an auxiliary component, a sapper or a carrier:

These corps have shown the military strengths and weaknesses of the pure Indian, indeed. . . . He can be a good soldier if he receives sufficiently intense instruction. Although the Ladino will be superior in intelligence, the Indian is superior to him in some military qualities. The Ladino is superior in active qualities, i.e., initiative, quickness of comprehension and judgment, but is inferior in passive attributes such as subordination, loyalty, and attention. The Indian, accustomed to be obedient to and recognize the superiority of the Ladino, brings an innate sense of subservience and obedience. Moreover, the simplicity of his life leaves him unaware of anything beyond his personal concerns, immune to fluctuations in the political process. The Indian blindly obeys his chief, he enters the struggle, fights, and dies without questioning the reasons or objectives of the campaign. . . . They fight for a cause that is unknown, and probably totally foreign, to them, and they die for a fatherland of whom they are the most despised sons, sacrificed on altars of blind obedience. . . . The Indian knows no patriotism of the kind known to the Ladino; he fights for his chief, not for the fatherland. The materiality of the Indian life, the lack of intellectual activity, and the narrow radius within which he moves has made him provincial, but not a patriot. It is obedience that pushes the Indian soldier to confront death, not the enthusiasm borne of conviction and patriotism. But this is not without value. Although the individual Ladino is more fearless, fighting in a group [the Indian] displays great tenacity.

However, Kuhsiek rejects the idea that Indians will make good officers; their initiative and decision-making ability is inferior to the rank and file of Ladinos. "As an auxiliary, be it as a sapper or as a carrier, the Indian provides the army with services of incalculable importance. Accustomed as a *mozo* [laborer] to the heavy work in the fields, as a sapper he is extremely useful for his endurance, even though his passive spirit makes him no more than a work machine that has to be directed, even down to the least details in the execution of a task." . . .

The Emergence of Indian Soldiers

Militarily, this era was full of wars, or threats thereof, with neighboring Central American countries and Mexico. Besides the 1885 conflict in which Barrios lost his life, General Barrillas declared war on El Salvador in 1889, and there were invasions of Guatemala—principally by Guatemalan exiles in combination with Salvadoran and or Honduran troops—in 1898, 1899,

1903, 1906, 1915, and 1916. During the entire era the army did include Indians, but we are far from knowing just how many, relatively or absolutely. Moreover, regardless of opinions about the use of Indians in the army, it is clear that in time of war, obligatory service was often employed, both formally and informally. In the 1889 war against El Salvador, Barrillas issued an official decree of universal military service. Apropos of the 1906 war, Arévalo Martinez quotes Gamboa as saying that Cabrera "daily sent heavy contingents of troops to the slaughterhouse, troops composed of 'volunteers'"— laborers who worked on the coffee farms. . . .

In the half century that followed the Liberal decrees to create a Ladino professional army, the army that emerged was far from what was wanted. The officer corps, increasingly a product of the elite Escuela Politécnica, wanted the army to both represent the country and to be of high quality. The two goals were not readily coherent. Those who could afford it purchased their way out of the service, such that only the poorer Ladinos, of whom there were not enough, became soldiers. So it was necessary to recruit Indians as well, in spite of the ideological and legal obstacles that stood in the way. Precisely because of this, however, we find that Indians were being used in some instances, and a literature began to put forth arguments, both practical and ideological, for why more Indians needed to be incorporated into the military service. . . . In short, from the perspective of a service that needed them, the Indians looked very good indeed. The fact that many Ladinos were indistinguishable from Indians physically would have materially eased the decision to opt for more Indians.

Guatemala Facing the Lens

Images from CIRMA's photographic archive

In the 1860s, foreign visitors started to use the new technology of photography to document Guatemalan society and geography. The German photographer Emilio Herbruger used photographs as an ethnographic tool to record the physical and cultural traits of Guatemalan Mayas. In 1875, the famous British "motion" photographer Eadweard Muybridge toured Guatemala and took a series of photographs that captured nearly every aspect of social life, from German coffee planters to indigenous communities, from urban scenes to the bustle of the Pacific port of San José. Two years later, Kohei Yasu arrived from Japan, changed his name to Juan José de Jesús Yas, and set up a studio in Antigua, where he photographed Guatemalans of all classes and races. At the end of the nineteenth century, the Mexican-Italian immigrant Tomás Zanotti settled in Quetzaltenango and apprenticed with the Englishman James Piggott, who then opened the city's first portrait studio. Zanotti soon took over the business and actively cultivated a large K'iche' clientele, whom he portrayed not as ethnographic specimens but as full bourgeois subjects.

These photographs come from the photographic archive of the Centro de Investigaciones Regionales de Mesoamérica (CIRMA), which holds the largest collection of images in Central America. They portray a Guatemala far more diverse than the Maya–Ladino dichotomy would suggest.

All photographs, pages 139–143, from the collections of the Centro de Investigaciones Regionales de Mesoamérica, Guatemala.

Maya-K'iche' man dressed for the Dance of the Conquest. Photo by Tomás Zanotti.

(below) Maya-Kaqchikeles from Comalapa. Photo by José Domingo Noriega.

Maya Poqomam woman from Mixco, 1895. Photo by Alberto Valdeavellano.

Photo by Ramiro Díaz Pinot, from the Rodí Studio collection, ca. 1910.

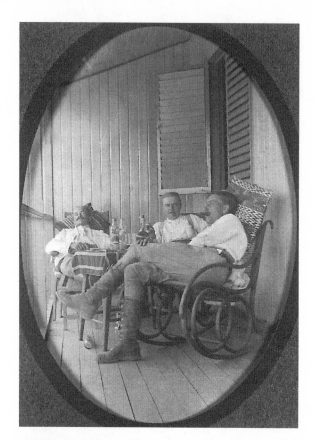

European men in Quetzal-
tenango, ca. 1897. Photo
by Piggott and Zanotti
Studio.

(below) Auto mechan-
ics in workshop, Quet-
zaltenango, 1920. Anony-
mous photographer.

Family of Chinese immigrants, ca. 1910. Photo by Tomás Zanotti.

(below) Garífuna family from Livingston, Izabal, ca. 1980. Photo by Mitchell Denburg.

Conquest of the Tropics

Frederick U. Adams

The banana was the first mass-marketed fruit, introduced to US consumers in the late nineteenth century by an elaborate advertising campaign that included songs, picture postcards, and doctors hired to tout the nutritional value of the "wonder fruit." Foreign corporations, mostly based in the United States, dominated banana production and trade in Guatemala and throughout Latin America. The United Fruit Company was founded at the end of the nineteenth century through a merger of shipping lines, railroads, plantations, and distribution networks; by the 1950s, this company controlled one-third of the world's banana trade. United Fruit was the prototype of the modern transnational corporation, vertically integrated and both a financial enterprise and a political force. In exchange for building railroads and promising to provide jobs, United Fruit secured lucrative concessions that granted it control over large swaths of land, where it effectively set up sovereign states. It paid little or no taxes, used violence to suppress union movements, and throughout the early twentieth century was complicit in overthrowing uncooperative governments (in 1954, United Fruit played a key role in the ousting of Guatemalan president Jacobo Arbenz; see part 4 of this volume).

Many Latin Americans criticized the company. The Chilean poet Pablo Neruda wrote that "United Fruit Inc. reserved for itself the central seaboard of my land, America's sweet waist [Central America]. It re-baptized its lands 'Banana Republics.'" The company also had defenders. Frederick Upham Adams, United Fruit Company's official historian, praised the company's hospitals and high wages, and he highlighted United Fruit's funding of the archaeological restoration of the Maya ruins of Quiriguá, which today is a UNESCO *World Heritage site. In this 1915 piece, Adams draws an implicit link between the "civilizational" works of the company and the great civilization of the ancient Maya, in effect inoculating the company against nationalists' charges that it was a foreign exploiter.*

Cruising up the shores of Central America we will make no stop until we reach Puerto Barrios, Guatemala. About ten years ago Minor C. Keith began operations to provide Guatemala and Salvador with railroad communication to the Atlantic coast. This was in furtherance of his plan to connect the United States by rail with the Panama Canal Zone. He had completed the main lines of the railroad system in Costa Rica, and now assumed, with his accustomed energy, the task of opening two more nations to the commerce of the world. . . .

On the great plateau of Guatemala are scores of towns and cities, including Guatemala City with a population of 100,000 or more, the largest city in Central America. It was for the purpose of giving these populous and productive districts an outlet to the Atlantic and communication with the trade of the world that Mr. Keith planned a railroad which would connect Puerto Barrios with Guatemala City, capital of the Republic of Guatemala, and San Salvador, capital of the Republic of Salvador, with branches touching various ports on the Pacific.

It seems strange, does it not, that the Guatemalan railroad was not constructed years and years ago? It seems such an obvious thing to do, yet our American tropics are filled with obvious opportunities and with political problems for which there are obvious remedies. We of the United States spend tens of millions of dollars on huge engineering plants intended to bring our deserts to cultivation, but our statesmanship declines to glance south of the Rio Grande and of Tehuantepec, where uninhabited empires of rich soil are already provided with water and with the climate which must have existed in the Garden of Eden.

When Mr. Keith and his associates decided to build a railroad from the Caribbean through these neglected countries the United Fruit Company agreed to undertake the banana development of sections of the uninhabited eastern lowlands. The Motagua River empties into the sea on the border line between Guatemala and Honduras, and is the longest and most important river in Central America. It has a broad and very fertile valley reaching more than two hundred miles toward the Pacific, and scores of branches are also natural centers of cultivation.

For seventy miles or more back of its mouth the Motagua flows between lands well suited to banana cultivation, and in 1906 the United Fruit Company acquired by purchase tracts with a total acreage of 50,000. There was at once developed an experimental plantation of 1,250 acres. The test was successful, and an additional 747 acres were planted in 1907. In the following year the banana plantings were increased to 5,080 acres. . . . It was not until 1910 . . . that the United Fruit Company increased its holdings by the purchase of an additional 30,549 acres, and since that year it has gradually acquired other tracts which gave it in 1913 a total of 126,189 acres, of which 27,122 were devoted to banana cultivation. . . .

Puerto Barrios has deep water and an excellent natural harbor, lying well within the shelter of an island which forms the Gulf of Amatique, but at the present time Puerto Barrios is the least attractive and sanitary of all the ports largely used by the United Fruit Company. Work is now in rapid progress which will change all this. The low site of the native town of Barrios will be raised and protected with a sea wall. The squalid huts which line the beach will disappear, and in their place will rise a fine hotel and office structures for the company. All of the adjacent swamps and lowlands have been reclaimed and made sanitary, and the reconstruction of the small native town will solve the only remaining sanitary problem which has harassed the company. . . .

Leaving Barrios by train, we plunge almost immediately into the most perfect jungle I have ever seen in the tropics. On both sides of the track for miles is a tropical display of trees, plants, flowers, ferns, vines, and shrubs, all woven into an impenetrable network of a thousand hues so delicately blended that it would seem that some horticultural genius had spent a lifetime in arriving at this perfection. A Newport millionaire would give a fortune for an acre of this splendid but worse than useless jungle. For miles it crashes its pulsating beauty in the face of the beholder. Orchids which would drive a connoisseur to frenzy flame their delicate colors from thousands on thousands of trees. Other towering trees are veritable masses of huge flowers, some of them purple, others tantalizing shades of red, blue, orange, and violet. Why has no artist ever painted such a jungle? He could not do it justice, but he might try. I have never seen on canvas any creation which even pretended to depict in form and color the representation of this native tropical jungle.

We leave the jungle and strike the Motagua River and the banana country. For fifty miles or more we run west and fairly parallel with the Motagua, with bananas on both sides of us most of the time. . . . For fifty miles we stop at town after town which had no existence prior to the advent of the banana industry. Some of them betray their newness and their American origin by their names, for instance the town of Dartmouth and the thriving town of Virginia. The latter is in the heart of the banana district, and is modern in every respect. It is a railroad division point. Here are well-equipped railroad shops, an electric lighting and power plant, an ice plant, steam laundry, and up-to-date stores with supplies fresh from the United States and abroad. The residential district contains streets and dwellings which would be a credit to any community, yet all this was a wilderness only a few short years ago. The same is true of Dartmouth and of Quiriguá. In the latter is located the wonderful new hospital erected by the United Fruit Company, which will be described elsewhere.

The Guatemala Division of the United Fruit Company is in the charge of a manager who maintains headquarters in Puerto Barrios and branch offices in Virginia and Guatemala City. The Guatemala Division is divided into three districts, El Pilar, Quiriguá, and Los Andes, each under a superintendent, and each district divided into plantations of about 1,000 acres each. These plantations are conducted by *"mandadores,"* or foremen, who are assisted by two timekeepers. All of these officials are white, and most of them are Americans. It is the duty of the *mandador* to give out and supervise the execution of the contracts with the workmen.

In this district, as in all others conducted by the United Fruit Company, the labor of clearing new lands, keeping plantations in order, cutting bananas, etc., is done by contract. . . . Only a theorist would dream of employing Jamaican negroes and Central American Indians to work on banana or other plantations by day wages. To quote a current phrase: "It can't be done." These toilers lack that altruism which impels some men to work when they are not watched, and you cannot watch negroes and Indians scattered in a wilderness of banana plants which extends for miles in all directions. Hence a contract system which is absolutely fair to all concerned, and which operates to the complete satisfaction of the men, who make a good living from it.

William Joseph Showalter, in the *National Geographic Magazine* of February, 1913, writes entertainingly of "The Countries of the Caribbean," and has this to say concerning the United Fruit Company:

> It is in Guatemala that one begins properly to appreciate the great civilizing influence of the United Fruit Company. That corporation has many thousands of acres of banana plantations along the lowlands of the Motagua River and extending to the Caribbean Sea. It pays its laborers a dollar a day, eleven times as much as the laws of Guatemala say shall constitute a day's wage. One can readily imagine what a boon this is to poor Indians who have formerly been paid only nine cents. Yet the United Fruit Company voluntarily pays this wage, and is able to give work to every Guatemalan Indian who applies for a job.
>
> It is the advent of such organizations as these—powerful enough to protect their own interests when disputes arise with local governments—that spells the economic salvation of these countries and promises an honest wage to the laboring classes. I hold no brief for the United Fruit Company, but it must be said that that great corporation has done more for Central America than all other agencies combined.

There is every likelihood that the payment of good wages, coupled with sanitary surroundings and civilizing influences, will breed in Guatemala and in all of Central America strong, self-reliant, and progressive races of people, and with these traits will come that sense of responsibility and real patriotism which ever serves as the foundation for orderly government and national advancement. Men who are forced to work for nine cents a day or any small multiple of that wage have no interest in government and nothing to arouse a sentiment of national patriotism. Having nothing to lose and all to gain—they naturally turn to revolutions and anarchy. This is the secret of the sad conditions which inevitably lead to political lawlessness in many sections south of the Rio Grande. Central America needs an influx of more corporations that are able and willing to "exploit" her natives by paying them eleven or more times the prevailing legal rates of wages, and whose productive operations will pour a flood of revenue into impoverished national treasuries. There is no other peaceful solution of this problem, and most unbiased critics agree with Mr. Showalter that the United Fruit Company "has done more for Central America than all other agencies combined."

The view from the hospital in Quiriguá is the most impressive in Central America from a banana standpoint. The hospital is on a hill, with the railroad at its base. Beyond the tracks is the front rank of a row of bananas which extends as far as the eye can reach to the east and west. Miles away to the south is the Motagua River, swinging in a curve almost to the Honduras line, but it is buried in a forest of bananas which extends to our south in an unbroken mass a distance of ten miles or more. Beneath the rays of a tropical sun this vast reach of vivid green banana fronds is an impressive sight. Here and there a spiral of steam or smoke indicates the location of a railway train on tracks which place all parts of this plantation within easy access of the workers.

Centuries ago a mighty race of people lived in the valleys of the Motagua and for hundreds of miles along the now deserted coast lands of Guatemala and Honduras which the United Fruit Company is quickening to step with the new civilization. There are no legends, no traditions, and no understandable records of this people, but within the tangle of the jungle and partly buried beneath its dead fecundity are the ruins of cities, temples, and monuments which declare more vividly than printed words the tale of their progress and achievements.

The lowlands, which now hold such terrors for the ignorant and physically deficient Indian tribes of Guatemala, did not deter their worthy predecessors of centuries ago from mastering the sanitary problems of these valleys. They knew that these fertile lands were perfectly fitted to support in comfort and luxury large masses of people, and it was here that they lived and wrought, and finally faded from memory and history, without leaving behind any translated sign of what caused their disappearance.

In a jungle belonging to the United Fruit Company are the famous ruins of Quiriguá, only a few miles from the town of that name. In the extension of its banana development the United Fruit Company acquired the tract on which the center of the ancient metropolis was located, and the company has extended substantial financial aid to archaeologists who have performed the work of exploration and excavation under the direction of the School of American Archaeology.

It is the aim of the United Fruit Company to clear all of seventy-five acres which contain the wonderful ruins of temples and the scores of huge and superbly carved monoliths which rise out of the encroaching jungle. This will result in the creation of a tropical park district. . . .

There is every reason to believe that the enterprises set on foot by Minor C. Keith and his associates in cooperation with the United Fruit Company will pave the way for the lifting of Guatemala and Salvador to the plane made possible by their varied natural resources.

Marimba

Arturo Taracena Arriola

In a highly polarized society, the marimba is a symbol of Guatemalan national unity, played during urban and rural social gatherings of all kinds. The first written mention of the Guatemalan marimba was in 1680, when it was played in front of the cathedral in what is now the town of Antigua. Yet its origin is uncertain. Although the marimba in Guatemala is often associated with Mesoamerican indigenous cultures, some scholars argue that West African slaves brought it to Central America and that the word "marimba" is derived from Bantú. Traditional marimbas are made of resonating gourds of differing sizes, each lined with pork tripe to produce distinct pitches. Similar to a xylophone, the gourds are suspended below wooden bars that are struck with mallets to make a note. Single-row gourd marimbas can still be found in many places in the indigenous highlands, but starting in the late nineteenth century, a second row of bars, designed to add a contrasting scale of notes, was incorporated into the design. This innovation and the replacement of gourds by wooden boxes helped make the marimba compatible with a wide range of ensemble instruments. Some of Guatemala's most revered musicians were marimba players, including Paco Pérez (1917–1951), whose waltz "Luna de Xelajú" remains one of Guatemala's most beloved songs. In this selection, historian Arturo Taracena Arriola analyzes the marimba as an instrument of national identity in Guatemala.

The Quetzaltenango-based maestro Sebastián Hurtado revolutionized the marimba in 1894, adapting it to play the chromatic scale [twelve notes, each half a step apart], thus creating the double marimba. There is, of course, a history behind this innovation: the history of a cultural change, the result of class struggle in Guatemala following the Liberal Revolution of 1871. Previously, possibly dating back as far as the colonial era, the first improvement made by Indians to the gourd-resonator marimba was to expand the note range to five, then six, and then eight octaves. . . . During the last four decades of the nineteenth century, poor Ladinos made another modification to the gourd-resonator marimba. They substituted box-like resonators for the traditional gourds—or *tecomates*, the dry, hollow fruit of the *Legenaria vulgaris* plant—in order to achieve better resonance. But the instrument still lacked the ability to play semitones. In order to play semitones—necessary for the waltzes, mazurkas, and ballads of the era—marimba players placed wads of beeswax inside the gourds or boxes or, sometimes, at the ends of the keys, which is still done in certain indigenous communities. This is the origin of the Guatemalan expression, "the marimba needs wax" (*faltarle cera a la marimba*), said when the mood of a celebration is suffering due to a lack of liquor or interesting musical repertoire. . . .

In the late nineteenth century, the marimba began to be used at official functions, but not at the celebrations of the Guatemalan upper class, where pianos and string instruments continued to dominate musical taste. The dictator Manuel Estrada Cabrera (1898–1920) helped institutionalize the marimba as an instrument of state. Cabrera hailed from Quetzaltenango and came from a middle-class family, similar to the many maestros who at that time were revolutionizing the marimba. In other words, the successive innovations that transformed the marimba were part of the same dynamic that propelled regional coffee growers [from around the city of Quetzaltenango] into the national bourgeoisie. So, at the end of the nineteenth century, the maestro Germán Alcántara composed the waltz "La flor del café," which became the hymn of the Guatemalan bourgeoisie and a classic piece of Ladino marimba music.

The number of marimba groups and of Ladino marimba compositions began to multiply. . . . But because it was difficult and costly to build a double marimba, its geographic distribution increased only slowly. In 1905, the first marimba arrived in San Marcos from Quetzaltenango. The maestro Benigno Mejía remembers that even by 1920, there were but a few double marimbas in the capital.

This cultural movement emanating from the grassroots—marimba players and bandleaders tended to belong to the popular and middle classes—was strengthened by the intellectual defense of Guatemala's indigenous peoples offered by musicologists Julián Paniagua and Jesús Castillo. Castillo, who began his studies of autochthonous music in 1885, aimed to valorize the soul of marimba music. In 1909 he composed a waltz called "Fiesta de pájaros" (which ends with birdsong), adding considerable sophistication to Ladino marimba music. Castillo had become convinced that a strain of indigenous music was based largely on birdsongs (ornithophony), which he arbitrarily called "Maya-K'iche' musical art" and believed to be the inspirational font of authentic Guatemalan music.

Castillo's attempt to identify and codify a national musical tradition fit into the context of the Guatemalan intelligentsia's *indigenista* ideas of the

Playing the marimba, Las Viñas, Santa Rosa, ca. 1878. Photo by Agostino Somelliani.
From the collections of the Centro de Investigaciones Regionales de Mesoamérica,
Guatemala.

period. In 1894, Antonio Batres Jáuregui won a prize for his essay "The Indians: Their History and Civilization" in a competition about indigenous civilization sponsored by President Reina Barrios. Batres Jáuregui also directed
a study of Guatemalan provincialisms, an etymology published in 1892. It
built on Santiago Barberena's earlier analysis of "Quichéisms." In the visual
arts, Carlos Mérida in the early twentieth century incorporated the colors
and patterns of Indian weavings into his paintings. . . .

Succinctly put, the Ladino community understood the importance and
value of indigenous culture but had very little awareness of those who produced it. In fact, the Ladino bourgeoisie understood well how the Maya
civilization enriched its overall project of strengthening Ladino dominant
ideology, but it would never think to incorporate the actual indigenous
majority into Guatemalan national identity. At the musical level, and concretely with regard to the marimba, this contradiction is resolved in the
terrible expression: "'We're the musicians,' said the Indian who carried the
marimba." . . .

In the cultural sphere, North American films saturated Guatemala's few
city cinemas, gramophones played Victor-label records, newspapers regu-

Workers at the Coca-Cola bottling plant in Guatemala City playing the marimba at a union event. Photo by Deborah T. Levenson.

larly published articles about daily life in North America, and so forth. As a result, marimba players began to be influenced by jazz, using the bass, saxophone, and snare drum as accompaniments instead of such indigenous instruments as the *pito* (wooden flute) and the *tun* (wood block). . . .

The 1920s in Guatemala cannot be understood without grasping the meaning of the insurrectionary triumph that ended the twenty-year Estrada Cabrera dictatorship. . . . Between 1920 and 1932, Guatemala experienced a political and ideological effervescence, poorly studied even today. The labor movement grew, politicized by disputes between Communists and anarchists (the Communist Party was founded in 1922, and the Union Action Committee was founded in 1926), as well as by labor struggles against the government and dominant classes. This provoked a broad intellectual movement now known as the "Generation of the 1920s," in which nationalism—particularly Ladino legends and Maya myths—played an important role in the presentation of Guatemala to the outside world. In literature, Miguel Angel Asturias was this generation's principal exponent; in music, José Castañeda wrote "La chalana," the university's anthem, which forever secured the place of the marimba in Guatemalan university student life. . . .

With the introduction of radio stations in 1932—the year in which the TGW, the state broadcasting station, was established—the country was invaded by Mexican *bolero* songs, in vogue at the time, and by North American dance tunes. "At night there was a marimba set up in the patio of the Hotel Aurora [in Antigua]," wrote a North American traveler in 1936, "and everyone danced to a fantastic mix of North American and Mexican dance numbers." Guatemalan marimbists felt obliged to play "Somos diferentes" [a *bolero* rhythm] along with "Yankee Doodle," "Smoke Gets in Your Eyes," and "The Music Goes Round and Round." At the same time, the spread of radio stations increased the popularity of the marimba, which by now was truly a national instrument. . . . In 1933, President Jorge Ubico had the group Los Chatos play in the Presidential Palace, the German Club, the Military Casino, and on the radio stations Liberal Progresista, Fomento, and TGW. The marimba came to be so closely linked to the conduct of official functions that in 1934, Ubico personally sponsored the creation of the group Maderas de mi Tierra, the official marimba ensemble of the National Police. Later, each of the country's military barracks would have its own marimba group. . . .

The double marimba's golden period was from 1940 to 1955. The Quetzalteco composer Paco Pérez became famous with his waltz "Luna de Xelajú," which won a national competition in 1942. Higinio Ovalle's "Turismo guatemalteco" and Salomón Argueta's "Llegarás a quererme" were smash hits. In "Tristezas quetzaltecas," the composer Wosvelí Aguilar created a 6/8 time variant that came to be known as *guarimba*. . . . And during the presidency of Jacobo Arbenz—who was born in Quetzaltenango—the marimba took a truly national-popular character. For example, from 1951 to 1953, national holidays were marked with a ten-marimba concert in the National Palace. At these events, workers and peasants could celebrate alongside government functionaries, intellectuals, diplomats, and certain members of the national bourgeoisie. . . .

The French researcher Raymond Pilet, having traveled through Guatemala from 1879 to 1882, wrote that the marimbas he heard in Quetzaltenango had thirty notes and a resonator, whether made of *tecomate* gourds or of wood. But his most interesting observation pertained to the melodies he recorded. "The two melodies that I will have you listen to," Pilet writes, "were performed on the marimba by Indians from Quetzaltenango. . . . The harmonies were perfect. The second of these pieces is a dance called the *barreño*, notable for its Spanish lyrics. But these lyrics were obviously adopted after the fact by Ladinos or *mestizos*, which I deduced from the following two pieces of evidence: first, only Ladinos sang along with the verses; second, the words themselves demonstrate that this was a dance that had recently become popular. . . ." Pilet was unaware that the *barreño* originated

in San Marcos, which is why it was new to the residents of Quetzaltenango.
. . . If what Pilet heard performed in 1882 in Quetzaltenango were indigenous songs, despite being sung in Spanish, they would confirm a character-
istically Guatemalan trait of marimba music: the fusion, at a popular level,
of indigenous and Ladino melodies. Many "traditional" songs are examples
of this phenomenon.

Translated by Kirsten Weld

¿Vos sos de Guatemala?

Proyecto Lingüístico Quetzalteco de Español

Students in the United States learn, correctly, that the Spanish language is highly formal. Students are taught two standard second-person singular pronouns, the informal tú and the more respectful usted. But the Spanish spoken in Guatemala, along with that in the rest of Central America and in Chiapas (but not in the rest of Mexico, nor in the Caribbean) uses a third form, known as voseo, or vos. It is easily conjugated by removing the r of any regular verb and adding an accent on the last vowel and an s at the end of the word, as in vos tenés. In the nineteenth century, its use marked status and power. Indians who spoke Spanish used voseo among themselves and reserved usted to address Ladinos. Ladinos used voseo as an indication of their social superiority over Mayas, and they also regularly employed usted among themselves. In the twentieth century these rules broke down, particularly among those who consciously tried to democratize Guatemalan culture. Vos could still be used to establish or acknowledge hierarchy, yet increasingly it was also deployed as a sign of solidarity, particularly among individuals associated with the left.

Some grammarians have identified voseo as an indication of the inferiority of American Spanish (it is also used in Argentina, Uruguay, and Chile). "The proportion of the use of vos" in any country, wrote one Spain-based linguist, "is directly proportional to the lack of culture of its inhabitants." But today many Guatemalans affectionately embrace vos—combined with somebody's name in a way that isn't done with tú or usted, as in vos Federico, vos Carlos, or vos Sonia—as a joyous part of national identity. The following description of the proper use of voseo is from a textbook published by a Spanish-language school in Quetzaltenango, Guatemala, Proyecto Lingüístico Quetzalteco de Español.

Many Latin American countries use the *voseo* as an alternative to the *tuteo*. Though many people believe that the *voseo* is used in only a few countries, in fact, people use it in more Spanish-speaking countries than not. *Vos* is the second-person singular pronoun used between friends as an alternative to *tú*. Sometimes people confuse the pronoun *vos* with the pronoun *vosotras/vosotros*, which is used commonly in Spain. However, *vosotras/vosotros* is a plural pronoun, not a singular one. Therefore, *vosotras/vosotros* is the plural of *vos*, although, ironically, there is no country that popularly uses the *vos–vosotros* combination. In Spain, the singular of *vosotras/vosotros* is *tú*, whereas in Latin America, the plural of *vos* is *ustedes*.

Unfortunately, *voseo* is not often included in educational curricula, except in the *voseo*-using countries. As a result the *voseo* has taken on some negative connotations, including a belief that *voseo* is grammatically incorrect, and there is a lack of knowledge of how to conjugate verbs using the *voseo*.

In the nineteenth century, Andrés Bello [an influential Venezuelan writer, poet, and grammarian] resisted the *voseo*, which was scorned by the more educated classes. But during the second half of the twentieth century, the *voseo* reappeared, particularly on university campuses; thus, it ceased to be considered a vulgarism and is now used colloquially. As [the Argentine writer] Ernesto Sabato points out: "Language is the blood of the spirit, it is a way unto itself of seeing the world, a highly personalized form through which human beings feel, understand, and use the universe in which they live; and so, in America, it isn't that people speak Spanish poorly—rather, the people simply speak an 'other' Spanish, which is distinct." . . .

Thanks in part to contemporary Latin American literature, artists, and radio and television programming, the use of *vos* has achieved greater recognition, and it has become understood that far from being an incorrect manner of speaking, *vos* is a characteristic element of Spanish that was invented by Latin Americans themselves. . . .

Different forms of the *voseo* exist, depending on the cultural region and social class of the speaker. There is a distinction between the pronominal *voseo*, which is the use of *vos* as a pronoun, and the verbal *voseo*, which is the use of verb conjugations corresponding to *vos*. Some people use the verbal *voseo* together with the pronominal *voseo*, especially in Argentina, Bolivia, and Central America: *vos caminás* (you walk), *vos querés* (you like), *vos vivís* (you live). At the same time, though it is slightly less common, the pronominal *voseo* can be used without the verbal *voseo*: *vos caminas*, *vos quieres*, *vos vives*.

When vos is used as a substitute for *tú*, the conjugation of the verb is modified somewhat.

Tú necesitas *leer la historia de Guatemala* (You need to read Guatemalan history): *Vos* necesitás *leer la historia de Guatemala. Tú* tienes *que decir la verdad* (You must tell the truth): *Vos* tenés *que decir la verdad*. . . . . .

Con vos can be substituted for *contigo*. *No pienses que voy a caminar* contigo (Don't think I'm going to walk with you): *No pensés que voy a caminar con* vos. . . .

We can identify two basic meanings in the use of the *voseo*. First, in its *familiar usage*, voseo has come to mean a close form of address; that is, it is frequently used between siblings, friends, companions, et cetera, at nearly all levels of society. Here is an example from Virgilio Rodríguez Macal's "Guayacán":

"Vos me querés embolar, Samuel . . . ¿para qué querés embolarme?" decía el infeliz herido empuñando el vaso que le ofrecían, rebosante de líquido hasta los bordes. "Tomá, hombre! Es por tu herida. Te hace bien y te sentís mejor!"

("You're trying to get me drunk, Samuel . . . why do you want to get me drunk?" asked the unhappy wounded man, holding the glass he was being offered, which brimmed to the very top with liquid. "Drink, man! It's for your wound. It's good for you, it'll make you feel better!")

Here are some other examples:

Guillermo, hermano, necesito que vengás pronto.
(Guillermo, brother, I need you to come soon.)

and:

Vos, que decís que sos mi hermano, podés ayudarme.
(Hey, you say you're my brother, can you help me?)

The second meaning of *voseo* is its hierarchical usage. The personal pronoun *vos* is frequently used by those in positions of authority to address people of inferior status, in contexts in which those of inferior status must use the personal pronoun *usted* to demonstrate respect. Here is an example from Miguel Angel Asturias's *El señor presidente*:

"No tengás cuidado, hijito; la ley es severa con los criminales empedernidos, pero tratándose de un muchachote! Perdé cuidado, decime la verdad!"
—"Ay, no me vaya a hacer nada, vea que tengo miedo."

("Stop being so cautious, son; the law is harsh for hardened criminals who pretend to be big boys! Let your guard down, tell me the truth!"
"Don't do anything to me, you can see that I'm scared.")

And here is an example from the story "El cadejo," in Francisco Bamoya Gálvez's *Cuentos y leyendas de Guatemala*:

"¿A esa pieza, patron?" me dijo el Chus, más asustado que si lo hubiera picado la cazampulga. "Usted está loco! No sabe, pues, que en ella se murió el finado patron viejo, el tata de don Nacho, y que cuando alguno se va a dormir allí le aparece el cadejo? Meterse allí, patron, es lo mismo que puyar el hormiguero."
"El Cadejo? Qué patrañas son esas, vos Chus? le respondí."

("To this room, boss?" Chus asked me, as frightened as if he had been bitten by a poisonous spider. "You're crazy! You don't know that this is the room where the deceased boss, the elderly father of Don Nacho, died, and that whenever anyone goes to sleep there, they see a spirit? Entering that room, boss, is the same as stepping on an anthill."

"The Spirit? What tall tales are these, *vos* Chus?" I answered.) . . .

Many people use the personal pronoun *tú* in a context of familiarity or trust between two people of equal social standing, but will switch from *tú* to *vos* when they are in a position of authority or superiority over others. In certain countries, the pronoun *tú* is not used between people of the male sex, because this is considered a usage distinct to the female sex: *Miguel, vos tenés que participar en la marcha!* (Miguel, you have to participate in the march!) *Miguel, vos no podés dormir aquí.* (Miguel, you can't sleep here.)

Yet, the use of the *voseo* between women, or between people of the opposite sex, is very common, although often the pronoun *vos* will be replaced by *tú* [while retaining the *voseo* form of the conjugated verb]. *Patricia, tú sos importante en este trabajo.* (Patricia, you're important for this task.) *Claudia, ¿Tú querés ir a la reunion?* (Claudia, do you want to go to the meeting?)

For practical, effective study of the second-person singular pronoun *vos*, we suggest that you learn its verb conjugations in the present, imperative, present subjunctive, and present perfect tenses (the other verb forms are the same as those corresponding to the personal pronoun *tú*), derived from the infinitive of the verb.

Present Tense

Regular Verbs
    Ayudar: Ayudás (to help)
    Tener: Tenés (to hold)
    Salir: Salís (to leave) . . .

Irregular Verbs
    The following verbs do not conform to the above norms:
        ser (to be), *ir* (to go), and *haber* (to have)
    Ser: Sos
    Ir: Vas
    Haber: Has
Examples: *¿Vos sos de Guatemala?* (Are you from Guatemala?)
¿Vos a dónde vas este fin de semana? (Where are you going this weekend?)

Translated by Kirsten Weld

A Taste of History

Popular Guatemalan recipes

Guatemalans have long combined ingredients and dishes of Maya, Spanish, and African origins into a transcultural cuisine. The first of the following recipes is for pepián, the classic Guatemalan national dish based on pre-Conquest moles, sweet-spicy sauces made of seeds, chiles, and cacao. They also utilize small amounts of spices such as cinnamon, a commodity of European trade with Asia. The second recipe is for atol de maize, a nourishing pre-Conquest Maya corn drink. Sold in open markets and on the streets and routinely prepared in homes, atol has been a staple of the poor for centuries. Pan de coco (coconut bread), the third recipe, is from the nineteenth-century town of Livingston, on Guatemala's Caribbean coast. Livingston's unique culture has been shaped by the presence of Garífunas, people of Caribbean indigenous (Carib and Arawak) and West African descent.

Pepián

(This recipe is adapted from Creole Guatemalan historian Antonio Batres Jáuregui's *Vicio del lenguaje*, published in 1892. Batres Jáuregui's knowledge of this recipe comes from his household cook. He suggested adding wine to taste, but this damages the delicate flavors of the dish.)

- 12 chiles guajillo and 2 chile pasillos seared to almost burnt on a hot grill, peeled and seeded
- 2 roasted tomatoes
- 20 roasted tomatillos
- 6 black pepper seeds
- 4 almonds
- 1–2 cinnamon sticks, broken into pieces
- 1 oz. of Mexican chocolate (chocolate with vanilla and cinnamon)
- 3 tablespoons of toasted sesame seeds
- 3–4 tablespoons of toasted pumpkin seeds
- A few drops of annatto

A little flour

1 lump of sugar

1 chicken, hen, or turkey boiled to just done (take care not to overcook)

Broth from the above pot

Salt to taste

Blend the chiles, tomatoes, tomatillos, almonds, pepper, and annatto in a blender. Pour this mixture into a pan; cook and stir. Slowly add the pumpkin and sesame seeds, some of the broth from the pot, the chocolate, and the flour to the pan. Stir as this mixture thickens. Finally, add the chicken, turkey, or hen, cut into pieces, and serve immediately.

Atol

2 cups of freshly scraped corn kernels

4½ cups cold water

1 cup sugar

½ teaspoon of salt

Blend the kernels and ¾ cup of water for a few minutes before adding the rest of the water, the sugar, and the salt. Pour this liquid into a pot and boil it on a low flame, stirring constantly, for about ten minutes. Serve warm.

Pan de Coco

1 cup vegetable oil

2 cups white sugar

4 eggs

3 cups all-purpose flour

1/2 teaspoon salt

1/2 teaspoon baking powder

1/2 teaspoon baking soda

1 cup coconut milk

1 cup fresh shredded coconut

Preheat oven to 375° F. Lightly grease a 9 × 5 inch loaf pan. In a large bowl, beat together sugar and vegetable oil. Beat in eggs. Sift together flour, salt, baking powder, and baking soda in a separate bowl. Alternately stir flour mixture, coconut milk, and coconut into egg mixture. Bake in preheated oven for 35 to 40 minutes.

Magical Modernism

Catherine Rendón

*In the early 1900s, in face of the Liberal Party's failures to promote public education
and develop a nation that was "civilized" by its standard of France or Belgium,
President Manuel Estrada Cabrera—who took as his official title "The Protector of
Studious Youth"—ordered the building of Roman temples to the goddess Minerva
in Guatemala City and the capital towns of each of the country's twenty-two departments. For the next fifteen years, the government held an elaborate "Festival of
Minerva" at the close of every school year in late October. This week-long festival
consisted of flowery speakers and exhibitions displaying modernist national and
international themes and goods. Children throughout the country dressed up in
school uniforms, finery, or a fantasized, stereotypical US or European style, such
as a Swiss Miss, a cowboy of the Old West, or in Greek/Roman togas. Thus at-
tired, the children paraded past large cardboard pavilions representing European
countries or modern agriculture, industry, and commerce until they reached the
Temple of Minerva. It was a pasting of "civilization" onto Guatemala's rough rural
landscape. In the essay below, scholar Catherine Rendón discusses the importance
of the festivals, which came to be called* Minervalías. *As export agriculture came
to dominate Guatemala's economy (and repression its politics), and as public education actually shrank in size, costumes, prints, and paints heralded Guatemala's
faux modernity.*

In 1934, Aldous Huxley took a side trip from a Caribbean cruise to visit Guatemala. He boarded a train in the Atlantic port of Puerto Barrios, traveling
along the banana plantations that flanked the railroad line most of the way
to the Guatemalan capital. Along the way he spotted some unusual structures, not Maya ruins as one might expect, but something Huxley described
as more akin to the silhouette of a Greek temple. He was baffled by these
and thought them coarse imitations of the originals.

What were these pseudo-classical structures doing in tropical America?
Huxley probably never discovered the answer and had he done so he would
have been surprised. Thirty-five years before, in 1899, Rafael Spinola, advi-

sor to the new president of the Guatemalan republic, Manuel Estrada Cabrera, conceived of the idea. The president, only in power for a year, wished to be recognized by some distinctive feature. . . . Spinola suggested that a big celebration be held at the end of every school year to recognize the academic achievement of every schoolchild in the republic and work "well done" by their teachers. In addition to this, the academic year, which ended in October, was also a good excuse to lead into a salute to *el señor presidente,* whose own birthday was on November 21. Spinola recognized the beneficial effects of flattery on an able politician, and Estrada Cabrera made Spinola's idea completely his own. It was useful in convincing other governments, especially nations like Great Britain and the United States, that in Central America an enlightened despot could at last be found.

As Estrada Cabrera's regime took root, the republic began to fill up (like a Monopoly board game) with Greco-Roman temples—from the Guatemalan capital to the remotest provincial town. Quetzaltenango, Guatemala's second-largest city, and Estrada Cabrera's birthplace, was home to the second-most-important temple in the country. These civic temples became essential symbols of fealty to the new president. As the years passed, the *Minervalías,* as the annual celebrations held at these monuments were called, grew more elaborate and became the hallmark of the regime. *Jefes políticos,* or local political chiefs, were often forced to tax citizens and recruit the poorest Guatemalans to build the structures. . . .

The *Minervalías* combined all the magnificence of the processions of Holy Week with the allure of classical mythology in fin-de-siècle style. Pupils were easily recognized by their uniforms and school flags. In the capital, great floral arches, trompe l'oeil backdrops, and large floats with *tableaux vivants* made their way down past the race track to the capital's Temple of Minerva, not far from the old cathedral. Period photographs show nubile young girls dressed in white flowing gowns, personifying virtue, knowledge, and nobility. The crowning glory came once all the schools were congregated around the great temple to the strains of local bands. Here, they would be organized in order of scholastic rank, engendering pride, competition, and other elements worthy of the ethos of ancient Rome and Greece. . . .

Since the late nineteenth century, Guatemala had a tradition of welcoming writers to its shores. With the appearance of the *Minervalías,* many writers voluntarily, and sometimes less willingly, added Guatemala to their itineraries. Guest speakers, often well-known literary figures, would recite poetry or deliver speeches on the benefits of an educated society of the philanthropy of *el Benemérito.* In 1901, the Latin American Oscar Wilde and

Minervalía festival in Antigua, Guatemala. Photo by José Domingo Noriega. From the collections of the Centro de Investigaciones Regionales de Mesoamérica, Guatemala.

Guatemala's most illustrious man of letters, Enrique Gómez Carrillo, spoke at the *Minervalía* in the capital. In 1909, the Peruvian poet José Santos Chocano, considered the Walt Whitman of Spanish America, spoke on behalf of Central America's fledgling newspaper corps. The popular Guatemalan poet Máximo Soto Hall spoke to cheering *Minervalía* crowds on numerous occasions. The *Minervalías* brought culture and glamour to the masses and a taste of Paris, New York, or Buenos Aires to a tiny nation. . . .

No expense was spared, particularly when it came to exporting the idea of educational renaissance. This was done with the publication of fine albums, known as the *Albums of Minerva*, which commemorated the events of each year. Most souvenir books contained poems and musical scores by local composers, as well as several photographs of local scenes, *Minervalía* parades, and allegorical tableaux vivants of Ladino girls dressed in white gowns. Poems and quotes from well-known writers, statesmen, and public figures from around the world also appeared. . . . A typical souvenir of the day might show a photo-collage of the president, in white tie, surrounded by beatific-looking children under the colonnades of a classical temple with a large globe of the world before him.

The largest and best-known Temple of Minerva was in the capital, at the end of the Avenida del Hipódromo. It was of considerable size, spanning a space comparable to that of the Smithsonian Castle in Washington, DC, and served to showcase all October events, and on occasion to impress visiting foreign dignitaries. . . . In March 1912, the US secretary of state Philander C. Knox traveled to Guatemala as part of his goodwill tour to the continent, representing President William H. Taft. Even though it was not October, Estrada Cabrera thought it appropriate to present a *Minervalia* of sorts to show his best side to the American envoy. By 1912 Estrada Cabrera had been in power for fourteen years, and many of the more repressive aspects of his regime were now firmly in place. These involved espionage, a legal system that permitted him to be reelected (even though this was unconstitutional), and a crippled army.

On the first evening of Knox's visit in the capital, a parade of ten thousand indigenous citizens is said to have marched before him in their most elaborate woven attire. Schools, too, prepared to receive him. For weeks before Knox's visit, teachers rehearsed songs in English with their students, and the red, white, and blue flag was carried alongside Guatemala's blue and white when he finally appeared. The great boulevard of La Reforma was lined with waving children as the US envoy made his way downtown. The jacaranda trees were in bloom and created a canopy of purple, adding a rich dappled effect to those early spring days.

Everything was in place with the exception of the star pupils, the students of the Instituto Nacional Central de Varones, Central National Institute of Boys (INCV), who refused to participate in this extravagant welcome. The INCV brought the brightest and most talented youths of the nation together. Their refusal came as a surprise. When the president heard of this digression, he ordered the *jefe politico* of the capital to deal with the boys. He had no success in convincing them, nor did the minister of education. . . . The boys remained firm and announced that they would not take part in the fanfare. Nevertheless, four hundred of them went to the Temple of Minerva to watch events unfold. The general rejoicing was drowned out by a constant and mounting mantra of "No, no Knox! No, no Knox!" emanating from the bleachers. This had not been choreographed. As their clamor drowned out all other sound, many participants grew afraid that there would be terrible consequences. It was well known that the president had no qualms about squelching opposition.

For some reason, Estrada Cabrera overlooked the rude behavior on Knox's visit, and there was no retaliation. Some historians have speculated that Estrada Cabrera might have secretly approved of the students' protest (or even set it in motion) to show the US envoy how "free" his country was and how, in spite of the heartfelt admiration for the United States, there was also a healthy dose of antipathy.

After Knox's visit, Guatemala returned to its old rhythms. These end-of-the-year festivities were now part of the yearly calendar and came and went with little more change than the appearance of a different writer. As the years passed, and Estrada Cabrera grew more reclusive and suspicious of conspiracies, he did not always participate in these highly orchestrated massive celebrations. . . .

Despite the celebratory nature of the *Minervalías* and their lighter side, a great deal of collective control and complicity was involved, and it was easy to gauge if anyone or any group was reluctant to play along. Their preparation and participation put everyone on the same level—adults and children alike, rich and poor—all came down to the level of sycophants if they wished to be left in peace. Perhaps the younger set was at first oblivious to the tribute to be paid to *el Benefactor de la Juventud Estudiosa,* but as time passed, and petitions of adulation had to be signed, some citizens grew restless and resentful. Still, the idea of broader horizons spurred them on to jump through the hoops even if, at times, they felt as if the president were holding a whip to them. . . .

Estrada Cabrera managed to keep the republic in his grip until the end of 1917, when a series of powerful earthquakes nearly destroyed the capital and shook the country to its core. This marked the beginning of the end for his regime. After 1920, as a weakened Estrada Cabrera steadily lost control of the presidency, the *Minervalías,* too, became a thing of the past. The temples fell into disrepair and became dilapidated, much as Huxley saw them. They continued to be a favorite haunt for schoolchildren and parades were still held there, but with less frequency as the years passed. Like the many volcanoes that fill the republic, the temples' distinctive outlines weathered storms and further earthquakes. Then one day in the early 1950s during Jacobo Arbenz's presidency, a minor public official secured permission to dynamite the temple in Guatemala City in order to make way for a baseball diamond. The space was thus transformed to another center of entertainment. Francisco Vela's great relief map still stands there, but many of the youths who play in the park or visit the map know nothing of the temple that once stood nearby. Only in Quetzaltenango does a vestige remain of an era's tributes to the goddess Minerva and a president called Estrada Cabrera.

El señor presidente

Miguel Angel Asturias

The diplomat and novelist Miguel Angel Asturias, who won the Nobel Prize for Literature in 1967, is one of the best-known Guatemalans in the world. In his youth, he wrote a thesis in sociology titled "Qué es el indio," in which he advocated for the cultural disappearance of indigenous identity. Yet Asturias was proud of his own Maya descent, defended indigenous rights, and went on to fill his novels with lavishly wrought indigenous protagonists and richly detailed indigenous villages, similar to those he had known as a child. Many consider Asturias the unacknowledged originator of magic realism, a technique often credited to Latin America's later "boom" generation of writers, on whom Asturias was a great influence. He deployed the technique most famously in his 1946 novel El señor presidente, *about the dictator Manuel Estrada Cabrera (1898–1920). Estrada Cabrera's long, violent, and increasingly absurd and senile rule provided ample material for a literary style that fused social critique with phantasmagorical happenings. The below selection is the opening chapter of* El señor presidente, *titled "In the Cathedral Porch." It provides a window into a world far removed from the imaginary one celebrated by Estrada Cabrera's Cult of Minerva (see "Magical Modernism" in part 3 of this volume).*

"Boom, bloom, alum-bright, Lucifer of alunite!" The sound of the church bells summoning people to prayer lingered on, like a humming in the ears, an uneasy transition from brightness to gloom, from gloom to brightness. "Boom, bloom, alum-bright, Lucifer of alunite, over the somber tomb! Bloom, alum-bright, over the tomb, Lucifer of alunite! Boom, boom, alum-bright . . . bloom . . . alum-bright . . . bloom, alum-bright . . . bloom, boom."

In the frozen shadow of the cathedral, the beggars were shuffling past the market eating-houses as they made their way through the ocean-wide streets to the Plaza de Armas, leaving the deserted city behind them.

Nightfall assembled them, as it did the stars. With nothing in common but their destitution, they mustered to sleep together in the Porch of Our Lord, cursing, insulting and jostling each other, picking quarrels with old enemies, or throwing earth and rubbish, even rolling on the ground and spitting and biting with rage. This confraternity of the dunghill had never known pillows or mutual trust. They lay down in all their clothes at a distance from one another, and slept like thieves, with their heads on the bags containing their worldly goods: leftover scraps of meat, worn-out shoes, candle-ends, handfuls of cooked rice wrapped in old newspapers, oranges, and rotten bananas.

They could be seen sitting on the steps of the Cathedral Porch with their faces to the wall, counting their money, biting the nickel coins to see if they were false, talking to themselves, inspecting their stores of food and ammunition (for they went out into the streets fully armed with stones and scapularies) and stuffing themselves secretly on crusts of dry bread. They had never been known to help each other; like all beggars they were miserly with their scraps, and would rather give them to the dogs than to their companions in misfortune.

Having satisfied their hunger and tied up their money with seven knots in handkerchiefs fastened to their belts, they threw themselves on the ground and sank into sad, agitated dreams—nightmares in which they saw famished pigs, thin women, maimed dogs and carriage wheels passing before their eyes, or a funeral procession of phantom monks going into the cathedral preceded by a sliver of moon carried on a cross made of frozen shin-bones. Sometimes they would be woken from their deepest dreams by the cries of an idiot who had lost his way in the Plaza de Armas; or sometimes by the sobs of a blind woman dreaming that she was covered in flies and suspended from a hook like a piece of meat in a butcher's shop. Or sometimes by the tramp of a patrol, belaboring a political prisoner as they dragged him along, while women followed wiping away the blood-stain with handkerchiefs soaked in tears. Sometimes by the snores of a scabby valetudinarian, or the heavy breathing of a pregnant deaf-mute, weeping with fear of the child she felt in her womb. But the idiot's cry was the saddest of all. It rent the sky. It was a long-drawn-out inhuman wail.

On Sundays this strange fraternity used to be joined by a drunk man who called for his mother and wept like a child in his sleep. Hearing the word "mother" fall more like an oath than a prayer from the drunkard's lips, the idiot would sit up, search every corner of the Porch with his eyes and—having woken himself and his companions with his cries—burst into tears of fright, joining his sobs to those of the drunkard.

Dogs barked, shouts were heard, and the more irritable beggars got up and increased the hubbub by calling for silence. If they didn't shut their jaws the police would come. But the police wanted nothing to do with the beggars. None of them had enough money to pay a fine. "Long live France!" Flatfoot would shout, amidst the cries and antics of the idiot, who became the laughing-stock of the other beggars in the end, simply because this scoundrelly, foul-mouthed cripple liked to pretend to be drunk several nights every week. So Flatfoot would pretend to be drunk, while the Zany (as they called the idiot), who looked like a corpse when he was asleep, became more lively with every shriek, ignoring the huddled forms lying under the rags on the ground, who jeered and cackled shrilly at his crazy behavior. With his eyes far away from the hideous faces of his companions, he saw nothing, heard nothing and felt nothing, and fell asleep at last, worn out with weeping. But it was the same every night—no sooner had he dropped off than Flatfoot's voice woke him again:

"Mother!"

The Zany opened his eyes with a start like someone who dreams he is falling into space; he shrank back with enormously dilated pupils as if mortally wounded and the tears began to flow once more; then sleep gradually overcame him, his body became flaccid, and anxious fears reverberated through his deranged mind. But no sooner was he thoroughly asleep than another voice would wake him:

"Mother!"

It was the voice of a degenerate mulatto known as the Widower, snivelling like an old woman, amidst bursts of laughter:

" . . . mother of mercy, our hope and salvation, may God preserve you, listen to us poor down-and-outs and idiots . . ."

The idiot used to wake up laughing; it seemed that he too found his misery and hunger so amusing that he laughed till he cried, while the beggars snatched bu-bu-bursts of la-la-laughter from the air, from the air . . . la-la-laughter; a fat man with his moustaches dripping with stew lost his breath from laughing; and a one-eyed man laughed till he urinated and beat his head against the wall like a goat; while the blind men complained that they couldn't sleep with such a row going on, and the Mosquito, who was legless as well as blind, cried out that only sodomites could amuse themselves in such a fashion.

No one paid any attention to the blind men's protests and the Mosquito's remark was not even heard. Why should anyone listen to his jabber? "Oh yes, I spent my childhood in the artillery barracks, and the mules and officers kicked me into shape and made a man of me—a man who could work like a horse, which was useful when I had to pull a barrel-organ through the streets! Oh yes, and I lost my sight when I was on the booze, the devil knows how, and my right leg on another booze-up, the devil knows when, and the other in another booze-up, knocked down by a car the devil knows where!"

The beggars spread a rumor among the people of the town that the Zany went mad whenever anyone mentioned his mother. The poor wretch used to run through the streets, squares, courtyards and markets, trying to get away from people shouting "Mother!" at him from every side and at any hour of the day, like a malediction from the sky. He tried to take refuge in houses, but was chased out again by dogs or servants. They drove him out of churches, shops and everywhere else, indifferent to his utter exhaustion and the plea for pity in his uncomprehending eyes.

The town that his exhaustion had made so large—so immensely large—seemed to shrink in the face of his despair. Nights of terror were followed by days of persecution, during which he was hounded by people who were not content to shout: "On Sunday you'll marry your Mother, my little Zany —your old woman!" but beat him and tore his clothes as well. Pursued by children, he would take refuge in the poorer quarters, but there his fate was even worse; there everyone lived on the verge of destitution, and in-sults were not enough—they threw stones, dead rats and empty tins at him as he ran away in terror.

One day he came to the Cathedral Porch from the suburbs just as the angelus was ringing, without his hat, with a wound in his forehead, and trailing the tail of a kite which had been fastened to him as a joke. Every-thing frightened him: the shadows of the walls, dogs trotting by, leaves falling from the trees, and the irregular rumbling of wheels. When he ar-rived at the Porch it was almost dark and the beggars were sitting with their faces to the wall counting their earnings. Flatfoot was quarreling with the Mosquito, the deaf-mute was feeling her inexplicably swollen belly, and the blind woman was hanging from a hook in her dreams, covered in flies, like a piece of meat at the butcher's.

The idiot fell on the ground as if dead; he had not closed his eyes for nights, he had not been able to rest his feet for days. The beggars were silently scratching their fleabites but could not sleep; they listened for the footsteps of the police going to and fro in the dimly lit square and the click of the sentinels presenting arms, as they stood at attention like ghosts in their striped *ponchos* at the windows of the neighboring barracks, keeping their nightly watch over the President of the Republic. No one knew where he was, for he occupied several houses in the outskirts of the town; nor how he slept—some said beside the telephone with a whip in his hand; nor when—his friends declared he never slept at all.

A figure advanced towards the Porch of Our Lord. The beggars curled themselves up like worms. The creak of military boots was answered by the sinister hoot of a bird from the dark, navigable, bottomless night. Flat-foot opened his eyes (a menacing threat as of the end of the world weighed upon the air) and said to the owl:

"Hoo-hoo! Do your worst! I wish you neither good nor ill, but the devil take you all the same!"

The Mosquito groped for his face with his hands. The air was tense as though an earthquake were brewing. The Widower crossed himself as he sat among the blind men. Only the Zany slept like a log, snoring for once.

The new arrival stopped; his face lit up with a smile. Going up to the idiot on tiptoe he shouted jeeringly at him: "Mother!"

That was all. Torn from the ground by the cry, the Zany flung himself upon his tormentor, and, without giving him time to get at his weapons, thrust his fingers into his eyes, tore at his nose with his teeth and jabbed his private parts with his knees, till he fell to the ground motionless.

The beggars shut their eyes in horror, the owl flew by once more and the Zany fled away down the shadowy streets in a paroxysm of mad terror.

Some blind force had put an end to the life of Colonel José Parrales Son-riente, known as "the man with the little mule."

It was nearly dawn.

"La chalana"

Miguel Angel Asturias, Alfredo Valle Calvo, David Vela, and José Luis Barcárcel

Guatemalans are known for their humor and sarcasm, often using wordplay, puns, and double entendres. Such is the case with the Huelga de Dolores, *or Strike of Sorrows. For over a hundred years, from the authoritarian liberalism of the first half of the twentieth century to the anticommunist and counterinsurgent terror of the second half of the century (except for a hiatus in the early 1980s at the height of the repression), the* Huelga de Dolores *has lambasted the nation's political, military, religious, and economic elites.*

The Huelga, *a fool's parade, began in 1898 as a strike by students from the public University of San Carlos, directed against the dictator Manuel Estrada Cabrera. It takes place on the Friday before Palm Sunday, known throughout Latin America as the Friday of Sorrows. Crude, risqué, and often wickedly obscene, the parade consists of hooded or masked students manning satiric floats, singing parodies, reciting poems, and carrying placards that ridicule the country's dominant institutions, particularly the military, the Catholic Church, oligarchy, politicians, and, after 1954, the* US *embassy and* US *corporations. Nothing is off limits as participants lampoon current events, scandals, and, inevitably, military repression (see the YouTube video titled* "Reseña histórica de la Huelga de Dolores," *at http:// www.youtube.com/watch?v=KIP_ClQu-3Q). Over the years, some of Guatemala's most renowned writers have participated in the* Huelga *as university students, often writing its biting broadsheet,* No nos tientes *(Don't tempt us). Since the war ended in 1996, the Strike of Sorrows has contributed to the revival of satirical and popular theater in Guatemala. Below are the lyrics of* "La chalana," *the farcical hymn of the* Huelga de Dolores, *written in 1922 (la chalana literally means "horse trader" and in this context denotes venality).*

Chorus:
Matasanos practicantes, del emplasto fabricantes
güizachines del lugar, estudiantes, en sonora carcajada prorrumpid, ja,
ja.
(Practitioners killing the healthy [reference to medical students], makers
of poultices [pharmacy students], insects of this place [law students], students, in sonorous loud laughter: beat them down, ha, ha.)

Sobre los hediondos males de la patria arrojad flores,
ya que no sois liberales ni menos conservadores,
malos bichos sin conciencia que la apresan en sus dientes
y le chupan inclementes la fuerza de su existencia.
(Toss flowers over the heinous wrongs of the country, now we are not
Liberals, much less Conservatives, evil insects without conscience, who
grab you by their teeth and mercilessly suck your vitality.)

Chorus: Matasanos practicantes . . .

Reíd de los liberales y de los conservadores (bis)
Nuestro quetzal espantado por un ideal que no existe
se puso las del hule al prado, más mudo, pelado y triste
y en su lugar erigieron cinco extinguidos volcanes . . .
(Laugh at the Liberals and at the Conservatives. Our quetzal [national
bird, currency] frightened by an exhausted ideal, has fled, mute, bald, and
sad; in its place they have raised up five extinguished volcanoes [symbols of
the five Central American countries] . . .)

Chorus: Matasanos practicantes . . .

Reíd de los volcancitos y del choteado quetzal (bis)
Contemplad los militares que en la paz carrera hicieron
vuestros jueces a millares que la justicia vendieron,
vuestros curas monigotes que comercian con el credo
y patrioteros con brotes de farsa, interés y miedo.
(Laugh at the little volcanos and the abused quetzal; think about the military officers who profit from peace, judges who sell justice for a few thousand, and little puppet priests who trade in faith and jingoism, festooned
with farce, self-interest, and fear.)

Chorus: Matasanos practicantes . . .

Huelga de Dolores, Guatemala City, ca. 1928. Unknown photographer. From the collections of the Centro de Investigaciones Regionales de Mesoamérica, Guatemala.

Reíd de la clerigalia, reíd de los chafarotes (bis)
Patria palabrota añeja, por los largos explotada
hoy la patria es una vieja que está desacreditada,
no vale ni cuatro reales en este país de traidores
la venden los liberales como los conservadores.

(Laugh at the clergy, laugh at the military pigs, homeland, ancient word, so long exploited, today our homeland is an old woman, discredited, not worth fifty cents in this country of traitors, betrayed by both Liberals and Conservatives.)

Chorus:

Practitioners killing the healthy,
Makers of poultices,
Insects of this place,
Youths of the exhausted country:
We laugh. Ha. Ha.

Translated by Greg Grandin

Indigenismo and "The Generation of the 1920s"

Image by Carlos Mérida

A famous aphorism of essayist and poet Luís Cardoza y Aragón (1901–1992)—"I remind myself that I am mestizo, my reality is founded on two myths: Coatlicue and Apollo"—reflects the centrality that the "Generation of the 1920s" gave the so-called "Indian Question," which they approached from all directions.

This young generation, concerned with the social imaginary of the nation and the presence or absence of the indigenous population therein, sat between two dictatorships, both of which many helped overthrow, and two world wars, and it had anxieties and hopes about the national meaning of modernity. Urban, educated mestizo intellectuals and artists promoted indigenismo, an often romanticized or outright racist picture of the Maya people that was intended to be sympathetic and nationalistic. In addition, they unknowingly became translators of "Indianness" to an art world eager to consume the exotic, whether from Africa or the Americas. Cardoza y Aragón translated the Rabinal Achí into French; at age twenty-eight, the Quetzalteco painter Humberto Garavito (1897–1970) won praise in Paris for his modernist paintings of serene Guatemalan Indians, while his friend Alfredo Galvez Suarez (1899–1946) covered the National Palace walls with murals, including La nacionalidad guatemalteca, *consisting of stereotyped but positive depictions of the ancient Maya and present-day "indios."*

Perhaps the most famous twentieth-century Guatemalan painter, Carlos Mérida, was a member of the Generation of the 1920s. Born in 1891, Mérida lived in Quetzaltenango and studied art there before continuing to paint in Paris, where he moved in the company of modernists such as Pablo Picasso. After returning to Guatemala, he went on to Mexico and worked with the famous Mexican muralists. An innovator and abstractionist who was proud of his K'iche' and Spanish heritage, Mérida took beautiful aesthetic leaps with Maya imagery. The image reproduced here is one of ten lithographs Mérida did in the 1950s, when his style became increasingly geometric. The piece is from the series Trajes indígenas de Guatemala, *portraying the distinct clothing of different highland towns. This image depicts San Martín Chile Verde, located near Quetzaltenango, the city where Mérida was raised.*

One of a series of lithographs by Carlos Mérida of the clothing worn in different indigenous villages in the highlands. Image used by permission of Arte Maya Tz'utujíl.

A Mexican Bolshevik in Central America

Jorge Fernández Anaya, interviewed

by Carlos Figueroa Ibarra

For decades after 1910, Central America lived in the shadow of the great Mexican Revolution, the effects of which reverberated beyond Guatemala, through Central and South America. A death blow against nineteenth-century authoritarian liberalism, it made land reform and labor rights central demands of the democratic agenda. It exported agrarian and labor organizers, anarchists, and Communists, such as Jorge Fernández Anaya, to neighboring countries, where they worked alongside local activists.

Throughout his life (1906–1990), Fernández Anaya was active not only in Mexico, as a labor organizer, member of the Mexican Communist Party, and secretary general of the Young Communist Federation of Mexico, but in international politics, helping to run the Comintern's Caribbean Bureau and risking his life rescuing German Communists from the Nazis during the Second World War (his daughter died in the siege of Leningrad). In this interview, Fernández Anaya talks with the Guatemalan sociologist Carlos Figueroa Ibarra about his activities in Central America starting in 1929, a moment of relative political openness in Guatemala and El Salvador. Of Maya descent, he was short, dark-skinned, and able to speak Nahuatl, and thus was able to travel in the countryside without attracting official suspicion. In this interview, Fernández Anaya discusses differences in the levels of economic development of El Salvador and Guatemala and talks about the difficulties of organizing rural workers.

CARLOS FIGUEROA IBARRA (CFI): Don Jorge, I understand that you have been a Communist militant since the 1920s. Can you tell me about your experiences during that early decade?

JORGE FERNÁNDEZ ANAYA (JFA): I joined the Communist Youth in August 1923. It was a very small organization. One of the problems it faced was that during the 1920s, there was no revolutionary literature. Still today, if you seek out the works of Marx and Engels, you can only find those published by the Fondo de Cultura Económica [i.e., *Capital* and *Theories of Surplus Value*]—nothing more. And in those years there was nothing, absolutely nothing, besides a few articles about socialist revolution in the Soviet Union. Nothing else. . . .

CFI: How was it that you came to hear of the situation in Central America and developed an interest in traveling there?

JFA: After I was named secretary general, in January 1929 I was named secretary of the Caribbean Bureau of the Young Communist International. Letters would arrive at the Caribbean Bureau. Among the people writing to us was Miguel Angel Vásquez, who wrote from Guatemala City. Miguel Angel wrote to ask if we would help them, but as one can imagine, it was very difficult.

CFI: Did the Mexican Communist Party [PCM] assist in the founding of other Communist parties in Latin America?

JFA: Yes. The PCM was involved in the forming of four parties: those of Cuba, Guatemala, El Salvador, and Ecuador. . . . I was a member of the Youth but we knew nothing of the travels or the activities of the party leadership. To the contrary, we were ignorant of everything to do with the international relations of the Party. . . .

CFI: When did you first travel to Guatemala and Central America?

JFA: November 1929 was the first time that I traveled to Guatemala. . . . Several comrades came to wish me farewell. I remember that one of them, a Venezuelan named Salvador de la Plaza, told me: "Be very careful, because they'll kill you there." . . . In order to reach El Salvador I passed through Guatemala, where I met up with an organization of artisans, because the members of the Party were artisans. All of these men were very self-sacrificing! This was because any of the Party's ideas and propaganda, and especially membership in the Party itself, were met with vicious and extremely violent persecution. When I arrived in Guatemala, I met Miguel Angel Vásquez. He was an important Guatemalan notary. He was a notary public and lawyer, and he defended the workers for free, without charging them a single cent. He also worked on ways to make it easier for workers to obtain collective-bargaining agreements. Vásquez was the one who had written us asking for help. He was linked to the leadership of the Guatemalan Communist Party [PCG]. I had the impression that he was a very humble man who was responding to the tremendously difficult situation in those years. It was very tough, there was incredible persecution then. . . . Vásquez was considered the patriarch of Central American communism, and he was greatly respected even though he was quite young. . . .

CFI: You mentioned that you were imprisoned during your time in Guatemala.

JFA: Yes, but that was afterwards, in 1931. . . . As I was telling you, disgracefully in Mexico and Latin America there was the very grave problem of a lack of revolutionary literature. Only people who had traveled, like Peru's Mariátegui, for example, had any real understanding of what Marxism was, and this formed the basis for his writings. . . . So the problem was discussed. Miguel Angel Vásquez intervened to support the idea of transforming the Central American Communist Party into a Guatemalan Communist Party. To form a national party that would truly perceive Guatemala's issues. But there was one difficulty: Guatemala was a very backward country. The only important workers were the railway workers, those from International Railways of Central America [IRCA], and those workers didn't want to have anything to do with the Communist Party. They were terrified of it, they would run away—literally, they would physically run away from us, it was primitive and infantile. And we couldn't do anything about it. There was a tiny union of the electrical company's workers, but it was the same situation. All we had were the artisans.

CFI: In those years, did the PCG already have a goodly number of members?

JFA: No. There were about three hundred members of the Party. But what I mean is that there were no factory workers in the Party, just artisans. They were all very brave people. . . . People were recruited in all of these [indigenous and peasant] communities for the formation of Communist Party cells, and we began to collaborate with the IRCA workers; we could organize there, as well as in a few factories. There were two such factories, not very large, dedicated to textile production, where unions formed. A union was also organized at the electrical company. We also organized the small artisans' workshops. This was all organizing work. And thus, as the result of all this organizing, the federation was formed, in which both reformist and anarchist sectors converged. . . .

These sectors provided certain contrarian voices, but we had always believed in the importance of openly discussing any disagreements, and this proved very beneficial. For this reason, at a moment when we were dominating the discussion, the people started to ask us: "Who are you? Why are you here? What is it you seek to accomplish?" And we replied that we wanted to form the Communist Party of El Salvador. . . . Guatemala was much less advanced than El Salvador. It hardly had any factories at all. The cement factory was one of a very few. In El Salvador, we worked in many different areas. In Ahuachapán, Raúl Equizábal helped us. In Santa Ana, there were other comrades who we ended up bringing with us so that they could see how things were done.

CFI: And you worked principally with peasant farmers?

JFA: Yes, with agricultural workers.

CFI: Was the work with Salvadoran farmers easier than the work with the Guatemalans?

JFA: Yes. Once, I worked in Totonicapán, and how difficult it was! Because Guatemala is a multinational country, and the agricultural workers are of different nationalities. For this reason, going on strike with translators trying to convince the Indians to fight to be paid in money, and for them to actually learn what they were being paid and to be able to purchase what they wanted with that money, was a wonderful achievement despite the many problems and challenges.

CFI: Was the strike on one hacienda, or various haciendas?

JFA: There were many haciendas, it was the entire area, and I believe the workers were K'iche' Mayas. In El Salvador it was easier. . . . .

CFI: Was it easier to enter the haciendas in El Salvador?

JFA: Yes, absolutely, it was very easy to enter the haciendas there and speak with the workers, to have them listen to what you had to say. In Guatemala, no, that possibility did not exist. . . .

CFI: Where were you during the 1932 Salvadoran insurrection?

JFA: I had already arrived in Moscow by January 1932. . . . I had learned of the insurrection from the newspapers. And I said to myself, "What I predicted has indeed come to pass." I was among those most opposed to the uprising. We had tremendous mass support. . . .

CFI: I understand that in early 1931, you returned to Guatemala when you were en route to Mexico. How much time did you spend in Guatemala on that visit?

JFA: Two or three months.

CFI: Did you engage in political activity during that time?

JFA: Yes. When I returned to Guatemala in 1931, I learned of a large company, a very large cement producer. And we organized a cell there, and began to prepare for a strike. Many members of the union organizing committee were taken prisoner. In the end, we won, but many comrades were taken prisoner. . . . The police, they were beasts. During the time I was in Guatemala, I also went to an area of Totonicapán, and a comrade there took me to a hacienda, an enormous hacienda where different sectors of the population worked [K'iche's]. And using translations that were quite primitive, we succeeded in carrying out the strike for workers to be paid in money, all throughout Totonicapán. There, the peons were paid only in vouchers. I already spoke of how I was able to go to Totonicapán, because a comrade knew a fellow there who spoke various of the regional languages, and he was looking for people to assist in bringing this struggle to different nuclei in other haciendas, there were apparently a number of other haciendas. And so they spoke, and they told the peasants what we would have wanted them to be told. It took me a month to prepare the strike in Totonicapán. I entered the hacienda, and once inside, I could not exit easily, because leaving also represented a great risk. So I spent the entire month hidden in a hut.

CFI: What were the demands of these striking agricultural workers?

JFA: The first demand they presented was to be paid in money, and no other demand could reasonably be presented, because these people had never acted politically in such a manner before. Afterward I realized that what the people wanted was to find some form of salvation or liberation from their bosses, and they saw that in the possibility of being paid in cash. Their consciousness did not extend beyond that. In contrast, in El Salvador the peons were much more aware. Because they had the consciousness to be able to act, and so it had less to do with our brilliance than with our having taken good advantage of their existing awareness in order to explain things to them. And at a certain point they asked us, "Who is organizing us? Why are we being organized?" And we replied, "The Communist Party, which fights for precisely these concerns." And this sort of thing could absolutely not be spoken of in rural Guatemala. The level of culture was much lower; logically they were much further behind. On top of the issue of linguistic difference, they were less culturally advanced. Even in the cities, the artisans were loath to accept the presence of the Communist Party. . . .

CFI: In 1931, had the PCG already done much organizing in the countryside?

JFA: Yes. At least, there were other comrades that I knew who were working in El Petén, although I was not able to go there myself. There was organizing in the countryside. . . .

CFI: Were people taken prisoner during the Totonicapán strike?

JFA: There were many prisoners. Indians. As I was saying, the organizing was very difficult in Guatemala. I remember that they rounded up many peons on that occasion, I don't remember how many exactly, but they took many of them off to jail. It was Miguel Angel Vásquez who went to defend them in the prison. And Vásquez was no ordinary person. He wasn't a braggart, he didn't act like a hero, but he was a very responsible man. Many people were taken prisoner, and the lawyer who went to defend them was Vásquez. And because he was a respected notary who was very well known for his honesty and his ability, he was invulnerable. Everyone respected him. But we won the strike, and we achieved our demand that the peons be paid in *quetzales*. And by that time, the PCG had indeed grown. . . .

CFI: Did the Totonicapán strike take place before they captured you in the city? Please tell me about when you were captured.

JFA: As I told you before, anti-Communist persecution was vicious in Guatemala. There were many people who, unfortunately, were assassinated by the police. In March 1931 they caught four of us—it was perverse! We were in the street, and at that time no more than two or three people could congregate publicly in the streets, because the police would arrest you. We were in the street with two young people and the police came down upon our heads. And all four of us went to jail! . . .

CFI: Did the police know that in Guatemala there was a "Mexican Bolshevik?"

JFA: Yes. In the Salvadoran newspapers they also spoke of a "Mexican Bolshevik." [Antonio] Cumes [shoemaker and founder of the PCG] knew who I was and he was the first one to receive a beating. They kicked him, punched him. . . . And he didn't talk. They went after the other two youngsters as well. There were three or four of these pathetic characters who were beating us. You can imagine that this was horrifying.

CFI: And did they beat you as well?

JFA: Yes. In my case, I told myself, "If I speak here, these bastards will kill me."

CFI: How is it that they didn't notice your Mexican accent?

JFA: I had learned how to speak, what to say. In Guatemala, at that time, they would ask you where you were from, and I would tell them that I was from a border town, I don't remember its name now. They asked us where the people were from, if they were from the city, from La Parroquia. It was a very complicated problem. Afterwards, they hung us from our fingers; you felt like they were tearing you into pieces. They lashed us with whips. We were held prisoner for a week. Then they threw us into a well of cold water at the police station; they stood us up by the edge, tied us around the waist, and then they plunged us in. There was nothing left to do but to try and stave off death. One day, in the middle of the night, a police wagon came to take us out. There were several police officers inside. On the road, they asked us where we lived, and then they started throwing us out of the wagon. They threw the first young man out; he was already dead. Then they pushed the second young man out, then myself, and then Cumes. I don't know the names of those young men. I have forgotten them completely. The one who died was not able to withstand the tremendous blows they dealt us.

Translated by Kirsten Weld

Anthropology Discovers the Maya

Carol A. Smith

Guatemala was the subject of some of the earliest ethnographies written by scholars from Europe and the United States, and the country became a popular "field site" during anthropology's early years. As the discipline professionalized and universities established anthropology departments, the amateur ethnography of earlier travelers (see "Travels amongst Indians" in this volume) gave way to observations that were purportedly more "scientific." Throughout the twentieth century, the study of the Maya remained bound up in the politics of US economic and cultural expansion. In the 1950s, for example, two anthropologists associated with the University of Chicago, Manning Nash and Sol Tax, wrote ethnographies that sought to prove that there was nothing incompatible between Maya culture and modern capitalism. Their work was predicated upon an understanding of the individual that would serve as the foundational premise of what was later called "modernization theory" and "rational choice theory." Nash's Machine-Age Maya *examined how the inhabitants of the town of Cantel meshed the coming of a textile factory with preexisting communal relations, and Tax's* Penny Capitalism *studied the tourist town of Panajachel to argue for the existence of a transcultural and universally competitive "economic man." Such arguments were an advance from the scientific racism of the nineteenth and early twentieth centuries, yet they ignored the violence required to force peasants into the wage economy and the ways that Guatemala's brutal plantation economy generated race-based exploitation and reproduced inequality. While the discipline as a whole would come to reject hard-edged racism, a denial of "race" as a category of analysis often paradoxically reinforced the power of racism as an instrument of rule, as suggested by the selection below, a reflection on the history of twentieth-century anthropology in Guatemala by one of its most prominent practitioners, Carol A. Smith.*

Anthropologists since Franz Boas (1858–1942) have contended that race and culture are *entirely separate* phenomena and that culture explains more about human differences than race. But the discipline of anthropology could not change entire ways of envisioning the world or make racism disappear by insisting on that separation. . . . Anthropologists had various explanations for Western "dynamism" (values, capitalism, religion), but almost all of them believed that the more dynamic Western culture would invasively transform the less dynamic non-Western cultures to the point that the latter would disappear. Only now do most of us recognize that all cultures constantly shift and change through both internal dynamics (which operate in "simpler" societies as well as "complex" ones) and external influences (which operate in "complex" societies as well as "simpler" ones) over historical time. Some anthropologists who worked in Guatemala wanted to capture the distinctive nature of "traditional" Maya culture before it was swallowed up by Western (Ladino) culture; others wanted to study the nature of change or "modernization" in Maya or Ladino cultures. But almost everyone assumed that "traditional" Maya cultures would be enveloped by more Western cultural forms rather than create their *own* "modern" forms. In consequence, they assumed that most of the cultural variability and change they saw among Maya was the result of either cultural loss or Ladinoization (Westernization).

[This generation] paid very little attention to historical political events (such as revolutions) or ideological processes (how nation-states defined Indians or ethnic groups). . . . Basically they saw themselves analyzing two "cultures," Spanish and Maya (on which anthropologists rather than historians were experts), in a "contact" situation in which political economy and ideology were insignificant. Perhaps the most consequential position, from the perspective of the issues treated here, was that change and modernity were associated with urban and *mestizo* (Ladino) cultures, whereas stasis and tradition were linked to Maya cultures—conveying the notion that modernization would come to indigenous Latin Americans only with *mestizaje* or Ladinoization. . . . People modernized and became historical subjects only to the extent that they participated in "Western" culture. By creating a culture continuum from most to least European, and equating cultures on that continuum with more or less potential for cultural transformation, anthropologists not only essentialized the culture concept, but also (one could argue) partially biologized it.

Initially, there were two basic schools of anthropology working in Guatemala: the Boasian school, trained by Franz Boas at Columbia University, and the Robert Redfield school, trained at the University of Chicago. The two groups differed mainly in methodology and focus rather than in their understanding of race or culture. The group doing "salvage" ethnography in the Boasian manner sought traditional communities in remote areas (such as Huehuetenango), where "modern" intrusions into indigenous life seemed minimal, in order to mine the "essence" of Maya culture before it disappeared. The Chicago-influenced anthropologists worked mainly in the midwestern highlands. They chose small, nucleated settlements, where a particular "problem focus" could be selected. Sol Tax, of the Redfield school, especially recommended the villages around Lake Atitlán because they were compact, traditional, and relatively homogeneous within themselves, and hence good choices for functional analysis. Very little work was done in communities that held a significant number of both Indians and Ladinos. No anthropologist worked in the plantation zones, where most Maya were wage laborers; few noted and none studied the large numbers of Maya who worked several months each year on lowland plantations; and no anthropologists worked with urban Indians in places like Quetzaltenango or Totonicapán, where most Maya made a living as large-scale *comerciantes*, artisans who hired workers, or artisanal workers, rather than as subsistence-oriented corn farmers. The indigenous communities that met the Boasian and Redfieldian criteria for selection were, in fact, rather unusual indigenous communities.

The basic fieldwork method used by the Boasian anthropologists was to rely heavily on key informants for information about beliefs and traditions ("culture"), covering many domains but gathering relatively little data in a practical context. Probably the best and most complete ethnography of this type was written by Charles Wagley, who had more data than usual on actual individuals and behavior. Redfield's students, in contrast, tended mostly to focus on some specific topic; Sol Tax, for example, focused on economy, and Benjamin Paul focused on the life cycle. They examined both the social (practical) and cultural (worldview) aspects of the topic. Both kinds of anthropologists concentrated on those aspects of Indian lives and communities most independent of Ladinos and the state. Even when dealing with the economy, which had always linked Indians and Ladinos in Guatemala on a regional and national scale, they treated the phenomenon mainly as it operated within the confines of small communities.

Though no anthropologist specialized in social relations between Indians and Ladinos, a general position had been taken on the subject in the early 1940s that no anthropologist in the first generation challenged. To quote Tax:

> The distinction between Indian and Ladino as it is commonly recognized in Guatemala is not difficult to define. . . . If a person's mother tongue is Indian, and his Spanish (if any) obviously a second language; if he wears an Indian costume rather than European-type clothing; if

he participates in the politico-religious life of an Indian community—if any or all of these things can be said of him, he is certainly to be counted Indian by Indians and Ladino alike. . . . The difference between an Indian and a Ladino is not biological, but cultural.

Ladinos are equally a cultural product, according to Tax, and are publicly seen to be such:

A person whose parents are in every sense Indians but who himself fits all criteria by which Ladinos are distinguished may very well be known as a Ladino not only by his Ladino neighbors, but by his Indian relatives themselves! Once it is clearly understood that the difference between an Indian and a Ladino is not biological, but cultural, it need not seem strange that one of two brothers can be an Indian and the other, perhaps living in the same town, a Ladino.

Tax argued that there was "a danger of bestowing upon Guatemala a race problem that does not exist."

Many of the first generation of anthropologists, probably encouraged by Redfield, fully supported the Instituto Indigenista in Guatemala, established in 1945 (under the reform government of Arévalo) with the aim of implementing a policy of indigenous assimilation like Mexico's. Redfield and Tax had trained a number of Guatemalans at the University of Chicago, and two of them (Antonio Goubaud Carrera and Flavio Rojas Lima) became directors of Guatemala's Instituto Indigenista. Sol Tax, among others, assisted the institute in its early programs to integrate (Ladinoize) indigenous Guatemalans. In this way US anthropology came to have a major influence on Guatemalan policy toward the Maya.

As Tax noted, one Indian brother could remain Indian while the other could choose to become Ladino, and no Guatemalan would think anything of it. To integrate Guatemalans into a single national identity, then, all that was needed was encouragement for the Maya to choose the preferred status. After all, most existing Indian traits were basically negative: Indians were those who "lacked health, sanitation, education, capital, food- and wealth-producing capacity." . . . By anthropological authority, the real barrier to Maya assimilation was community insularity. Few people, whether anthropologists or Guatemalan citizens, observed that the community insularity of the Maya was a social and political construct of both Maya and Ladino, manipulated for centuries by both groups and capable of continued resilience as well as change. Nor did they consider that the Maya had been fully integrated into Guatemalan national life—as producers of much of the food supply, as labor on the plantations, and as the standard against which Ladinos could define themselves as an ethnic group and national elite—for at least one hundred years.

Most people working in Guatemala in the late 1950s and 1960s continued working in the Redfield/Tax tradition with respect to ethnic relations. . . . The main difference in the second generation of scholars was a greater concern with historical change and political economy. Another difference is that the second generation read more of the work produced by Guatemalan and Mexican scholars than the first generation did. And here history and political-economy concerns were dominant. . . .

Rodolfo Stavenhagen, a Mexican sociologist influenced by Marxist and dependency theory, published a study of ethnic and class relations in Chiapas and Guatemala in 1969. This work may have had a greater impact on the second generation of anthropologists working in Guatemala than anything else that was new. Stavenhagen, unlike the others, directly critiqued the "culturalist" assumptions of the first generation of anthropologists and placed the issue of race and culture within a historical analysis of Mexican and Guatemalan political economies. . . .

The interest in political economy was widespread in the US during the 1970s because of the impact of the Vietnam war on academic sensibilities and the growing influence of Marxist theory among younger scholars. But political economy was not the only "school" represented in Guatemala's second generation. About one third of the generation remained interested primarily in cultural issues concerning the Maya, though with different emphases from the first generation. Members of both groups, however, read some of the literature produced by Latin Americans, especially works by Guatemalans: for example, Severo Martínez Peláez and Carlos Guzmán Böckler. . . .

Those of us interested in political economy conducted studies about the mechanisms by which Ladinos exploited Indians in the contemporary period, most emphasizing monopolization of land and the plantation economy. I concentrated on commercial monopolies—how throughout the western highlands Ladinos controlled the wholesaling and transport infrastructure, while Indians mainly worked as market *comerciantes* or small-scale artisans. . . . We made much of the fact that Indian labor was crucial to the operation of Guatemala's coffee economy and that it had been coercively obtained from indigenous communities since the 1880s. . . .

The smaller group of scholars who concentrated on Maya culture in the second generation also paid more attention to the historical particularity of Guatemala than the first generation of scholars. Two of this group, Rob-

ert Carmack and his student Barbara Tedlock, sought continuities in Maya
culture between the past and the present, without denying the historicity
of what remained "essentially" Maya. Like those concentrating on issues
of political economy, everyone retained the use of the term "ethnic group"
to describe relations between Indians and Ladino. And virtually all of us
reiterated the common belief among North Americans that racism did not
really exist in Guatemala because Indians could "become" Ladino. More
of us noted that it was not easy to become a Ladino—that one had to leave
one's community to do so, and it took several generations for one to be accepted as a Ladino. Several in the political-economy school argued that the
Ladinoization process was in fact a proletarianization process because the
people becoming Ladino lost access to resources in their communities.

It would be too simple to say that the second generation avoided the issue of race and racism in Guatemala because we were all convinced that
discriminatory behavior in Guatemala could be explained in terms of
class—though many of us certainly were class-reductionist. But *all* North
Americans avoided discussion of race and racism, even those who were not
entranced with political-economy paradigms. . . . One reason for this is that
"race" had been almost entirely discredited as a concept in anthropology.
. . . Most of us lost sight of the fact that social constructions of difference
(whatever their bases) ramify along multiple dimensions (culture, language,
class, biology) to explain, defend, and reproduce power-laden forms of social exclusion. Even when culture *is* the primary basis for making ethnic
distinctions, if the distinction forbids (or highly constrains) marriage and reproduction between the groups who are distinguished, different groups can
be (and will be) distinguished by more than one criterion (language, class,
biology, as well as culture), and exclusionary practices will also be based on
multiple criteria. As criteria multiply, groups will be distinguished by more
than one "inherited" trait because distinct mechanisms of inheritance are
not easily distinguished from each other. . . . Thus, marriage and reproduction practices, even though they are clearly cultural phenomena, ultimately
can and do have biological (racial) effects. Whenever distinctions acquire
multiple signifiers and array themselves in a hierarchy of power, regardless
of their original basis, ethnocentrism becomes indistinguishable from racism. Anthropologists appear to have been more comfortable with the idea
of ethnocentrism (which implies mutual exclusion rather than hierarchical
discrimination) because it was a less evaluative term. But . . . erasing discussion of race and racism from the US academy was not a progressive move
but rather a move toward avoiding a contentious political issue. . . .

One can also blame us for not asking the Maya with whom we worked whether they experienced racism—or what they experienced and how they would depict it. In the last decade a significant Maya movement has developed whose intellectual spokespersons (Demetrio Cojtí, Demetrio Rodríguez Guaján, Victor Montejo, Enrique Sam Colop, Irma Otzoy) have all vividly recounted their experiences with racism in Guatemala. . . .

Hymn to the Sun

Jesús Castillo

*The composer and ethnomusicologist Jesús Castillo (1877–1946) was another artist
who drew inspiration from real and imagined Maya culture. Born in the Mam
town of San Juan Ostuncalco, near the K'iche' city of Quetzaltenango, Castillo
can in a way be considered a homologue of someone like the more famous John
Lomax, who traveled rural byways in the United States, preserving traditional
music. Castillo did his fieldwork mostly in the K'iche' and Mam regions, and he
came to believe that Maya music was composed of six scales that closely simulated
what he called the "exceptionally beautiful" songs of the* pito real *and the cen-
zontle, Guatemalan mockingbirds.*[1] *Castillo also received classical music training in Paris. Urban Guatemala had cultivated an active classical music culture
since independence; beginning in the mid-nineteenth century, Italian opera companies toured Guatemala; Guatemala City boasted a number of theaters; and a
National Conservatory of Music was established in 1875. Drawing from these two
traditions—Maya and European—Castillo composed a number of operas, ballets,
minuets, and chamber pieces, including* Quiché vinak, *which Castillo worked on
between 1919 and 1924.*

*Quiché vinak, the first opera to be composed by a Guatemalan, was based on
the* Rabinal Achí *dance (see part 1). It was first performed, with an orchestra of
sixty, in Guatemala City's Teatro Abril in 1924. Like other indigenista intellectuals
of his time, Castillo sought to rescue what he imagined to be a disappearing Maya
culture, and he strove to fashion it into what he hoped would be a modern national
identity. It is perhaps emblematic of Guatemalan modernism that much of his sheet
music has been lost. Below are three nonconsecutive pages from* Quiché vinak's
"Prelude and Hymn to the Sun"*—which, according to Castillo, seeks to capture
the feel of "dawn in the tropics"—as it was transcribed in the 1930s by a New Deal
Works Project Administration music program.*

Note

1. See Castillo's *La música Maya-Quiché* (Quetzaltenango, Guatemala: Tip. Cifuentes, 1941).

Andante (♩. = 60)
Piccolo
Flute I-II
Oboe I-II
English Horn
Bassoon I-II
Andante (♩. = 60)
Horns in F I-II III-IV
Trumpet in C I-II
Trombone I-II
Tuba III
Andante (♩. = 60)
Timpany
Chinchines
Indian Drum
Bass Drum
Cymbals
Andante (♩. = 60)
Violins I II
La cascada
Viola
Violoncello
Controbass

IV

Ten Years of Spring and Beyond

In October 1944, a movement spearheaded by students, teachers, military reformers, and an emerging middle class overthrew the thirteen-year dictatorship of Jorge Ubico. The October Revolution was one of the most ambitious social-democratic experiments in Latin America after the Second World War. It produced two elected governments, the first headed by the pedagogue Juan José Arévalo and the second by the nationalist military officer Jacobo Arbenz Guzmán. Over the course of a decade, these reformers consolidated constitutional rule; extended the franchise to women, the poor, and Mayas; established state-run social security and health care; enacted a labor code; ended forced labor on coffee plantations; and implemented far-reaching agrarian reform. At the same time, Guatemala's cultural and intellectual life blossomed. Members of the "Generation of the 1920s" matured and joined with a younger cohort of writers, poets, and artists, many of them affiliated with an experimental artistic group called Saker-Ti, to work toward creating a democratic political culture—no mean task in a society as unjust as Guatemala at that time.

The October Revolution lasted exactly ten years, until it was overthrown by the CIA's first extensive Latin American coup of the Cold War. The United States had tolerated Arévalo, mostly because he had refused to legalize a small Communist Party, which operated under the name Partido Guatemalteco del Trabajo (PGT), but they distrusted his nationalism, particularly his labor reforms. After Arbenz legalized the PGT and implemented a land reform, the CIA moved against him in late 1953. Until recently, scholars attempting to explain why the United States overthrew Arbenz have focused on the threat the land reform posed to US economic interests, particularly to the United Fruit Company, which had close connections with many members of President Dwight Eisenhower's administration. The law firm of Eisenhower's secretary of state, the implacable anticommunist John Foster Dulles, had the company as a client and prepared its contracts with

Guatemala. The secretary of state's brother, CIA director Allen Dulles, had worked for United Fruit's law firm; and the assistant secretary of state for inter-American affairs, John Moors Cabot, had a brother who was a former United Fruit Company president. Lately, however, historians have stressed the growing influence of the PGT over Guatemalan society and over Arbenz. According to this perspective, Washington's actions in Guatemala were motivated above all by anticommunism rather than contempt for Arbenz's nationalism or the defense of private economic interests.

Yet interpretations that highlight the anticommunism of the Cold War miss a key point: the Communists were responsible for a significant expansion of democracy in Guatemala. Arbenz, though not a Communist himself, looked to the PGT because it had the clearest analysis of how to break the feudal power of the landed class, which all reformers across the political spectrum understood as the chief obstacle to democracy. Membership in the PGT remained small, but the most dedicated agrarian organizers came from its ranks. At the same time, the PGT was just one part of a larger democratic universe. Every viable political party called itself "social-democratic," had some design for an agrarian reform, and competed for organized labor's suddenly vital support. Every newspaper liberally used terms such as "proletariat," "feudal landlords," and "reactionaries"; had sections devoted to the peasantry and the working class; and supported, at least nominally, the modernizing goals of the October Revolution.

In Guatemala, the 1952 agrarian reform law did more than just distribute uncultivated land to peasants; it created a parallel system of rural power meant to dilute planter authority. Key to the agrarian reform law were local agrarian committees called CALS (for the Spanish acronym), described by political analyst Gustavo Porras Castejón as the most democratic institutions that had ever existed in Guatemala. These committees were an institutional front line in the struggle against the power of the landed elite and an important arena of consciousness-raising. Controlled by peasants, local-level CALS were responsible for inspecting land disputed in the agrarian reform and passing the decision up to departmental and national committees. In its short life, the agrarian reform law spurred a rapid growth of rural peasant organization among both poor Ladinos and Maya communities in various parts of the country. This provoked a backlash not only from the landed oligarchy but also from some local elites, who saw the agrarian reform process as a direct challenge to their political, economic, and racial dominance in the countryside. Every revolutionary process has these sorts of currents and cross-currents; but given the lack of organized domestic resistance to Arbenz, it is unlikely that Guatemala's October Revolution would have terminated in a coup without Washington's direction.

The October Revolution and the CIA coup that ended it are two of the most momentous events in Latin America's Cold War history. Throughout Latin America, the coup radicalized a generation of activists, confirming their suspicions that Washington promoted not democracy but US corporate control in Latin America. The expectations raised and the struggles fought during this period reverberated not just in Guatemala but throughout the Americas, and the selections that follow convey the scope, diversity, and importance of these events. The Guatemalan truth commission report, *Memoria del silencio* (1999), described the CIA's 1954 intervention as a "national trauma" that had a "collective political effect" on a generation of young, reform-minded Guatemalans. "So drastic was the closing of channels of participation and so extensive was the recourse to violence" by those opposed to democracy, *Memoria del silencio* argued, that this approach is "considered one of the causes of the guerrilla insurgency" that soon followed. The overthrow of Arbenz reinitiated Guatemala's "exclusivist dynamic," with the government once again doing "the bidding of a minority at the expense of the majority."

In the decades following the 1954 coup, the United States turned Guatemala into a laboratory of repression. The regime the United States installed in 1954 was corrupt and cruel, and in 1960, a good portion of the military rose in revolt, protesting corruption and the growing influence of the United States in domestic affairs. At the same time, *arbencistas*—agrarian and labor organizers active during the Arbenz presidency—regrouped, either with the now-clandestine PGT or the Partido Revolucionario, the only quasi-reform party allowed to operate after 1954. Political activism increased in the city and the country. So too did state violence, pushing many activists—some associated with the 1960 military uprising, others with civilian reform parties, including the PGT—to organize the Fuerzas Armadas Rebeldes, Guatemala's first Cold War guerrilla group, which operated mostly in the eastern lowlands. In turn, Washington stepped up its provision of equipment, training, and financing to security forces, even as repression grew ferocious. In 1966, US advisors set up and trained a death squad that kidnapped and assassinated more than thirty opposition leaders, many of them *arbencistas*. This marked the inauguration—well before Chile, Argentina, or El Salvador—of political "disappearance" as Latin America's signature act of state terror. The following year, the Guatemalan military, with significant assistance from the US military, launched its first scorched-earth campaign, killing about eight thousand civilians in order to defeat an estimated three hundred guerrillas. In an important way, these events in the 1960s—more than the 1954 overthrow of Arbenz—signaled the point of no return for Guatemala, after which the state and its henchmen, with support from the United States, committed mass terror to defend its interests.

The Best Time of My Life

Luis Cardoza y Aragón

"Poetry," Luis Cardoza y Aragón once said, "is the only concrete proof of the existence of man." Born in Guatemala in 1901, Cardoza y Aragón was a novelist, political writer, poet, art critic, democratic activist, and diplomat. After graduating from secondary school in 1920, he, like many Latin Americans of his generation (such as his fellow Guatemalan Miguel Angel Asturias and the Mexican muralist Diego Rivera), moved to Paris to join the modernist movement. Cardoza became friends with André Breton and other experimental writers, particularly those associated with surrealism.

He served a brief stint as Guatemala's consul general in New York during a short-lived reform government in the early 1930s. Then, during the dictatorship of Jorge Ubico, he lived in exile in Mexico City. He returned to Guatemala after its 1944 democratic revolution, and in 1945 he was elected to the Constituent Assembly, where he helped draft a new social-democratic charter. Through the next decade, he took an active part in the country's cultural and democratic opening; he wrote, founded magazines and artistic institutions, and held a number of diplomatic posts. After the fall of Arbenz in 1954, he once again left Guatemala for Mexico. For the rest of his life, he remained a steadfast opponent of Guatemala's successive military regimes and was one of the leading lights of Latin American modernism. He died in Mexico in 1992.

The following extract is drawn from his 1954 memoir of Guatemala's October Revolution. While Cardoza y Aragón was famous for his experimental writing style, this selection is a straightforward description of his excitement upon returning from exile to a newly democratic Guatemala, with the world—and himself— seemingly made new.

On October 20, 1944, the revolution that was transforming Guatemala reached a boiling point; I crossed the border on the twenty-second. A plane dropped us off in Tapachula, Mexico. The pilot wanted to warn us but at the same time avoid upsetting us. He was concerned, and I think he read the papers the following day fearing he would find some tragic news item about us there. On saying our goodbyes, the simplicity of his manhood found, Mexicanly, the right words. His manner was forthright but intense when he said, *"Procuren que no se los lleve la tiznada."*[1] We traveled on to Tuxtla Chico—very close to the border—to have our travel documents stamped. I had decided to make this radical change in the space of a few seconds, in the Mexican capital. Carrying very light and hastily assembled baggage, I cut ages off my life. Just a few months earlier, along with some newfound friends who had recently arrived as exiles in Mexico City, I had taken certain steps while awaiting developments in Guatemala. With those friends, and with a gun in hand, I returned to my homeland. News on the situation was garbled. The border detachment placed no obstacles in our way on entering the country. We were prepared to do anything.

We rented an automobile, distributed ourselves within it strategically, fearful of some ambush, and struck out for Malacatán. Armed groups stopped us along the way and stuck their shotguns in through the windows, pointing them at us. They checked our papers and wished us a good trip. The grassroots movement had spread throughout the country, and any of the small military garrisons that had not surrendered were in a state of expectancy. Malacatán was jubilant, armed, tense with enthusiasm and determination. They put us up for a couple of hours to give us supper. Then we would continue our journey toward San Marcos and Quetzaltenango.

The Malacatán garrison remained indecisive, and the townspeople were on the verge of attack. The garrison chief, a young officer, had quartered himself with his men; they were well-armed and had abundant ammunition. Our intervention averted bloodshed. With a small white flag in hand, we went to parley with the officer. We explained the situation to him, his duty to the people and the fact that the entire country backed the revolution. He wasn't easy to convince. He was skeptical of the news we brought, but we were able to persuade him within the agreed time limit. Otherwise, the town leaders would have attacked, inadequately armed and with little solidarity. The officer had to be dealt with, within quarters. Otherwise who knows what might have happened. We emerged from headquarters bearing the good news, and a group of volunteers formed the new garrison. The officer was given no trouble and withdrew to his home.

We returned to our lodgings, where the town had prepared supper for us. Enthusiasm was at a fever pitch. The *campesinos* hugged us, bought us drinks. A marimba started playing Guatemalan *sones*. Firecrackers, gunshots into the air, shouts of joy, pealing church bells. It was suddenly all too much for me: my land, that was in my bones, came flooding to my eyes. I began weeping and sobbing. What heart-rending joy, what anguished and jubilant tenderness. Adolescents, old people and children, women calling for the marimba to play the national anthem. I hadn't heard it in many, many years. I was deeply moved, singing it with my people on that unforgettable occasion. I don't consider myself to be either patriotic or sentimental: I simply became aware, once again, of how definitive our childhood and the power of our homeland truly are. Two hours later, it was already the dead of night and we were traveling toward the highlands of San Marcos. The garrison there belonged to us, according to what we had been told at our last stop. We took along four uniformed soldiers from Malacatán. As we were not entirely sure that they were truly on our side, we gave them the worst of the weapons and carefully distributed ourselves inside the car. Armed with another car, an escort and two officers, from San Marcos we continued to Quetzaltenango, the second-largest city in the country, also controlled by revolutionary forces. The roads were heavily guarded, and we were stopped frequently to have our papers examined.

Before dawn, we were in Quetzaltenango. We reached the capital city a day later, by night. When we passed through Patzicía, the town was still panic-stricken due to the uprising of landless *campesinos*. Some partisan of the defeated side had incited the revolt, luring supporters with promises of land. There was talk of an indigenous uprising against the Ladinos. This bloody mutiny was brutally repressed. The town was patrolled by the Red Cross of Antigua and Guatemala City, along with soldiers and armed civilians from both of these cities and from Chimaltenango.

We trundled along the dusty road, cracking jokes to distract ourselves from our worries. I was fascinated and silent; my head and my heart were overactive. I felt the impelling force of the people and rediscovered fields and towns that I had often roamed on horseback as a child. At a bend in the road, the Agua Volcano leapt into view at a distance. I had not seen it in a quarter of a century and it held my childhood, my youthful parents, Antigua. I courted the volcano with my eyes, my hands gripping the .30–.30, and I was deaf to what my companions were saying. As if I had found a young child who had been lost to me for good. The car rolled along, revealing landscapes that to me were without equal in this world, and their memories that, to me, were without equal in this world. There, at the foot of the Agua Volcano, Antigua and my parents' home, where I would have liked to have lived all my life and died all my death. My mother, a widow now, in the huge old house, listening to the eternal cantata of the fountain's dark green water in the garden, jubilant with flowers and vines. My father's ghost in the corridors, the ghosts of my brothers and sisters as children, and my own, playing and shouting. I could hear the jingling of my mother's keys hanging at her waist and see her hands working the earth under begonias and rosebushes. I would return to her, return to the womb, to my mother and to my people, the following day. For now, we were heading toward the capital city.

Because of the political violence, my mother was anxious about my return. She ached with my presence and with my absence, a very old lady now, bowed by the years, very active and with an alert head that had gone completely white. In the afternoon I caught a bus on the Guatemala City–Antigua route. I remembered the road I had traveled on foot and on horseback, by bicycle, automobile and motor coach, in every one of its bends and mountains, ravines and villages, groves of trees and tiny plants. Toward dusk, the vehicle was nearing the entrance to my town: the Matasano bridge that spans the absent Pensativo River. The first houses came into sight, washed in bright quicklime colors, the clay tile roofs spotted with fungus, the cobbled street, La Concepción fountain, the monastery and the church in ruins. Across the street, my grandparents' house, door ajar, allowing me a glimpse of the garden where as a child I went on expeditions and played circus along with unforgettable friends, while my pretty girl cousins smiled at our childish exploits.

When I got off the bus at the corner closest to home, I recognized the stones worn down by my own shoes, the silence, the stains on the cathedral walls, the gutters, the windows. I remembered the design on the cement walks in front of my house with complete accuracy. And standing before the door I had not passed through in so many years, I remembered the latchkey, short and round, and how to turn it to open the latch; the knocker's little hand, the mail slot, the wood, the cord to open the door without knocking. At the end of the street, the perfect triangle of the Agua Volcano, as vast, serene, and blue as ever, not a single gray hair on its head, a cloud adorning the peak, golden in the afternoon sun. I pulled on the cord, pushed the door open and entered with my heart in my mouth.

The little dog—so very, very old—announced my arrival and approached, tired and belligerent, to stop me. My brother Rafael appeared silently. We embraced and said nothing. Having taken two steps across the threshold of my home, I was overcome by tears. It was all too much. My mother came down the passageway, slowly, stooping, nearly blind. She already knew it had to be me. She was sobbing with joy, with worry, with who knows how many things, as I, too, was sobbing. This was the sweetest embrace of my life, and at that instant, it was worth dying, it was worth living. She was overcome, and there was no need to speak. Embracing her, I guided her a few steps further, to sit side by side on the centenary conventual bench in the passageway, facing the garden tended by her own hands. I was a young boy again, next to my mother in my old childhood home. I stretched out on the bench and put my head on her lap. She drew me close and I don't know how long we stayed like that, silent, our eyes fixed on the vines and geraniums, her hand resting on my head, slowly stroking it from time to time. I still feel her hand, as I did then, in the most intense and peaceful and infinitely tender caress. If I had not lived those indescribable moments in Antigua, in my parents' house, I would have missed the best time of my life.

Translated by Michelle Suderman

Note

1. *Translator's note*: *La tiznada* is the equivalent of *la chingada*, the source of most misfortune in Mexican popular expression; in Mexican history, according to Octavio Paz, it is the stain of original sin, the rape of Mexico by Spain. [Here the phrase could be commonly translated as "stay out of trouble down there." *Eds.*]

A New Guatemala

Juan José Arévalo

On March 15, 1945, the forty-one-year-old Juan José Arévalo became Guatemala's first democratically elected president, winning more than 80 percent of the vote. Like Luis Cardoza y Aragón, Arévalo spent the Ubico years in exile, in Argentina, where he earned a doctorate in education. During his five-year presidency, Arévalo presided over a remarkable burst of social-democratic reform: expansion of the vote; the extension of political rights, including free speech and assembly; an end to forced labor; a labor code guaranteeing the rights of workers to organize unions; health care reform; retirement pensions; and education reform. In the realm of foreign policy, Arévalo, though an anticommunist who accepted the authority of the United States, took the democratic promise offered by Allied victory in the Second World War seriously. Much to the annoyance of Washington, which had already begun to distrust Arévalo because of his support for unions, the Guatemalan president actively supported movements—most famously the Caribbean Legion—opposed to US-backed dictators in countries neighboring Guatemala: Rafael Trujillo in the Dominican Republic and Anastasio Somoza in Nicaragua.

Arévalo was an innovative educator, a critic of the rote learning that prevailed throughout much of Latin America at the time. His emphasis on education through experience foreshadowed the pedagogy of praxis later associated with Paulo Freire and Liberation Theology. His educational philosophy was part of a larger social vision that he called "spiritual socialism," a third way between Soviet communism and materialistic capitalism meant to give people an "integrity denied to them by conservativism and liberalism." Spiritual socialism was criticized as vague, but it is a good example of an insistence, prevalent throughout much of the world following the Second World War, to define democracy beyond just individual rights and freedoms to include some form of economic justice, equality, and security. The following selection is drawn from a 1945 speech given by Arévalo titled "Conservatives, Liberals, and Socialists."

Conservatism and liberalism are doctrines that in America blossomed and died in the nineteenth century. Conservatism was the political doctrine of the Guatemalans of 1821, who received their independence with little ef-

Juan José Arévalo campaigning, 1944. Anonymous photographer. From the collections of the Centro de Investigaciones Regionales de Mesoamérica, Guatemala.

fort and as a result . . . they installed a republic, or a shell of a republic, the fundamental objective of which was to conserve the Spanish way of life. . . . With the ascent to power of liberal ideas in 1871, the neocolonial system of 1821 was neutralized and a sense of national liberation began to form, an authentic Guatemalan independence with the potential for triumph, as the liberal movement counted upon men who were more morally balanced and who had firmer political convictions. But the liberalism of 1871 was just a doctrine; it was simply that doctrine we have all admired since childhood, the doctrine of national emancipation from colonial systems. But in practice, disgracefully, liberalism was from the very beginning—and continued to be until a scant few days ago—a colonial system in disguise, which with pithy words and bombastic rhetoric applied the same methods of rule as had colonialism and conservatism. . . .

Because both doctrines shared the same methods, it became . . . impossible to distinguish conservatives from liberals but for their last names. Conservatism had died a natural death, for its dimwitted goal of maintaining the systems of colonialism under the banner of the republic. Liberalism was dying a slow and tortured death by asphyxiation, asphyxiated by the mental and moral incapacity of its men to install, for once and for all, the republic. . . . During the entire twentieth century, Guatemala has been neither liberal nor conservative. It has been a people without political expression,

Passengers at Aviateca airfield in Flores, waiting for the plane, 1949. Photo by Sol Libsohn. From the collections of the Centro de Investigaciones Regionales de Meso-américa, Guatemala.

governed by men who have been ideologically empty. . . . Because of this, we were slow and suffered from blind spots in our appreciation of Guatemalans' political ideas. And this explains why Guatemala has lived the entire twentieth century, with the exception of a few fleeting interruptions, under dictatorship, isolated from the modern world. . . .

Individualistic liberalism is no longer alive in the world, and conservatism cannot be resuscitated. It has been a century now since the world has been organized according to new social concepts. . . . And it has been a century since economics, politics, and culture have been reorganized according to socialist ideas, which is to say, according to a new interpretation of history and a new valorizing of man. This socialism began as utopian, continued on as materialistic, and has come to be, in our times, spiritual. . . .

We are socialists because we live in the twentieth century. But we are not socialist materialists. We do not believe that man's essence is his stomach. We believe that man, above all else, desires dignity. To be a man with dignity or to be nothing. For this reason, our socialism is not oriented toward the naive redistribution of material goods, toward the idiotic economic equalizing of men who are economically different. Our socialism seeks to liberate men psychologically, to return to them all of the psychological and spiritual integrity that was denied them by conservatism and

"The New Sun of Liberty," a political poster from Guatemala's democratic spring.
From the Arturo Taracena Flores Collection, Broadsides, 1944–1963 at the University
of Texas, Austin. Used with permission of the Nettie Lee Benson Latin American Collection, University of Texas Libraries, the University of Texas at Austin.

liberalism. We will give each citizen not the superficial right to vote but instead the fundamental right to live in peace with his own conscience, with his family, with his possessions, with his destiny. To socialize a republic does not simply mean exploiting industry in cooperation with the workers. Rather, it begins even earlier: to turn every worker into a man who can live as a complete psychological and moral being. A worker who is well-fed and well-dressed is not our goal: the generals' horses have also been well-fed, well-harnessed, and even given hot baths and preventive medicines. Good food and good clothes are indeed needs that should be attended to. But first we must invest the worker with all of his dignities as a man, destroying at the same time the many pretexts that have been used to keep him in humiliation and servitude. Spiritual socialism is a doctrine of psychological and moral liberation. . . .

If we call this postwar socialism "spiritual," it is because in the world—as it is doing in Guatemala today—it will produce a fundamental reversal in human values. Materialistic preachings have been revealed to be a new instrument in the service of totalitarian doctrines. Communism, fascism, and Nazism have also been socialist. But they were socialist in a way that nourished with the left hand while mutilating the moral and civic essence of man with the right. National Socialism, the most modern of all these systems, could only produce a mass of mechanized workers, well-fed and well-clothed, who had lost, as the price for these advantages, their hierarchy as citizens and their authority within the family. Spiritual socialism will transcend the philosophical formula of Nazism, which only recognizes the leader, and it will begin—like liberalism—to invest its majesty in moral and civil virtue. But it will go further than liberalism by breaking the insularity of man, obliging him to integrate himself into the atmosphere of society's values, needs, and goals, simultaneously conceiving of society as an economic organism and a spiritual entity. The spiritual, however, will rule in this conception of the world and in the economic aspects of life, in order to imbue them with national sentiment.

Translated by Kirsten Weld

Pablo Neruda in Guatemala

Pablo Neruda

*In his poem "Chronicle of 1948 (America)," Chilean poet Pablo Neruda, having re-
cently fled government repression in his country, asked, from his exile in Mexico:
"How will it end . . . this bleak year? . . . This bleak year of rage and rancor, you
ask me how will it end?" It ended badly. Just two years earlier, Latin America was
awash in hope. Between 1944 and 1946, a wave of democracy had swept the continent. Dictators fell, such as Jorge Ubico in Guatemala, and countries that were
already democratic, such as Chile, extended social-welfare legislation, promoted
unionism and land reform, and enacted a slew of other policies that empowered
the disenfranchised. But in 1947, the tide turned, as local elites took advantage of
the dawning Cold War to launch a continental reaction. By 1948, a majority of
Latin American countries were once again ruled by dictators, while those that remained formal democracies, such as Chile, took a sharp turn to the right. Guatemala, though, was a notable exception to that trend, not only holding on to its
democracy but, in 1952, taking a significant step to expand it through the adoption
of an ambitious land reform. As one of the lone holdouts against the authoritarian turn, Guatemala attracted reformers, democrats, and socialists throughout the
region, including Pablo Neruda and Ernesto Guevara, soon to be known as "Che,"
who worked as a doctor in the indigenous highlands. This selection is from a talk
Neruda gave to Saker-Ti, an organization of democratic cultural activists, calling
on them to create a new democratic national culture and not to despair of Latin
America.*

I visited Guatemala in 1941, and I walked among you, hiding behind trees so
that no one would hear us talking. I came from a sonorous homeland with
a proud liberty, but here, there was a tomblike silence.

But today it is Guatemala, the tiny dark-skinned country at America's
waist, that is shining light down the path of freedom with a brilliant splen-
dor. And in contrast, it is now Chile that has joined the somber age of
America, where treason and imprisonment cast their shade over the white
southern sunlight.

But I had faith, then, in your people. In those years, the answer I was looking for beat in each breast. And I was not wrong.

Today, with every audacious assault intended to swathe your territory in shadow, once again, the same faith causes me to think that you will not shrink from the task, that you will fight for your country and for your liberty, that you will fight against the privileges that must end, and for the people who must be born; that you will fight and you will defend your independence.

And to the poets, to the writers, to the painters, to the musicians, I say: This is your path. If you do not understand that, prepare yourself to be forgotten. Intellectual enemies of the people, it is useless for you to follow the path of the Sartres, the Camus or the Bretons, of the existentialists, of the surrealists, of European tombs, of its gravediggers and death's ministers. They are the last messengers of a class in whose dying light the worms are illuminated.

We have other work to be done. We must light every snuffed-out lantern. We must bring light to all the dark corners. We must clean all the rooms of our heartbroken America. We must spark the invincible stability of liberty. We must build schools in which our painters will paint the walls, in which our musicians will give their song, in which our writers will find the new seed of new Americas. We must erase cosmopolitanism, the decadence of Paris, transplanted to our lands by reactionary forces, and we must choose as our creators those who are wholly national, those who have most deeply shown our peoples their path to the future. Only in being intensely national will we touch all the people, only by destroying the cosmopolitanism of the bourgeoisie will we arrive at the internationalism of all the workers of the world.

Women and men, friends of Guatemala, comrades, brothers: Many years ago, an exile in your country wrote the following words:

> But, is it only the haughty Guatemala City whose lands are beautiful in Guatemala? What of distinguished Antigua? And lively Quetzaltenango? And growing Cobán, the sugar bowl of Escuintla, volcanic Amatitlán, warm Salamá, scenic Huehuetenango? And while the ruins are finished, the foundations are being laid! The people lose their convent mannerisms, their apathetic tint, their sickly aspect, and they conduct their business to the sound of the centrifuges spinning around them, among the leafy tendrils, the aromas of coffee, the colors of youth and the revelations of life. Liberty opened these doors.

These were the words of love and hope left by José Martí, the Cuban liberator and writer, inscribed in your trees, in your stones, in your doorways.

It falls to me, a southern exile, to echo the same love and the same hope. Since then, dark spells and victories have shaken our America, but our people are not the same. Since then, our people have seen the two most important events in the history of humanity: the Russian Revolution and the liberation of China. Our people, despite the lies, daily see the truth; they see it through the shadows, the dawn light that awakens.

The people cannot be lied to forever. The *campesinos* know, because they read in the corn, in the wheat and in the rice, that the vast lands of China belong neither to Chiang Kai-Shek's vampires nor to Wall Street's wolves, but simply to the *campesinos* of China. The copper miners of Chuquicamata's huge, high mines in Chile—who with their chapped fingers build the wealth of foreigners, of the copper emperors—know that the land can be ours, for all men.

This is the age of truth. This is the age of actions and of deeds. I, an exile in your country which once I visited with pride for my own country's liberty, say to you: the shadow over Chile, over Santo Domingo, over Nicaragua, over Colombia, over Peru, over Venezuela—these shadows do not matter. These are the final shadows before the coming of a great dawn.

Translated by Kirsten Weld

"If That Is Communism,

Then They Are Communists"

Miguel Marmól, as recorded by Robert Alexander

Even before the Guatemalan land reform was adopted, labor activists began to organize peasant unions. Organizing in the Guatemalan countryside presented formidable cultural and linguistic obstacles because most people in the highlands didn't speak Spanish; rather, they spoke one of the country's many Maya languages. Nevertheless, rural union membership grew rapidly, first in the Confederación de Trabajadores Guatemaltecos and then in the Confederación Nacional Campesina de Guatemala. The following observations were made by Miguel Marmól, the famous Salvadoran Communist, as recorded by US historian Robert Alexander in a 1948 interview.

As a result of the reaction to the First World War, and the revolutions which followed, the governments of Central America for a time were more or less friendly to the idea of a labor movement. . . . The memory of these days and this early labor movement was kept alive in the minds and hearts of a certain number of those who had participated in them, even after the return of the ferocious dictators in the late 1920s, the 1930s, and the early 1940s. It was this memory which had a lot to do with the way in which trade unionism grew up again here and even in Salvador when the old dictators were overthrown in 1944.

With the overthrow of the dictatorship, the workers spontaneously began to organize, and they formed the Confederación de Trabajadores de Guatemala, which took a really solid form only in 1945. . . . This was for some time the only trade union central in the country, but now there are three: the CTG, the Federación Sindical de Guatemala, and the Federación Regional de Trabajadores. The differences between these organizations were not enough to really justify the split in the labor movement, and the split is due to the lack of consciousness, experience, and education on the part of the workers and their leaders here.

The Confederación de Trabajadores de Guatemala has its great strength among the *campesinos*. They have affiliated in all parts of the republic, and among the groups affiliated are many of the Indian communities, unions of agricultural laborers, and now they are organizing peasants' leagues among the sharecroppers, who are the vast majority of the *campesinos* of the country. The landlords and propertied interests generally have great fear of the CTG because it is organizing the rural workers. The CTG doesn't have much strength among the peasants around the capital city, those being in the Federación Sindical. Nor does it have the [United Fruit Company] plantations. . . . These same workers had a strike in 1945 at the time the CTG was in congress assembled, and for that reason the CTG couldn't do much for them. The strike lasted two weeks and was lost.

The living conditions of the rural workers are terrible. They eat only maize, *frijoles* [beans], they dress hardly at all, they don't wear shoes. Their housing is abominable. They earn exceedingly bad wages. However, trade unionism in the countryside has helped them a great deal. It has resulted in cutting down the work day to eight hours, with a five-and-a-half-day week. It has resulted in raising the wages from five or ten cents a day to twenty-five or even fifty cents a day. There are still many places which still pay five or ten cents, of course.

Organizing unions among the *campesinos* is very difficult. There are eighteen Indian languages spoken in Guatemala, and those who speak one cannot understand the other. Large numbers of the Indians, perhaps most of them, can't speak Spanish, or if they speak it, do so in a way that can hardly be understood. Furthermore, there is a great deal of fear and lack of confidence on the part of the Indians. They have been betrayed so often that they are very cautious and will not talk very freely. It is only when they have really decided that one is to be trusted that they will talk.

The Indians now are beginning to have confidence in the CTG. The organizers of the CTG go out from Guatemala City into the countryside, many of them practically abandoning their families and going out to do organizational work, gaining nothing from their work, and hardly knowing where their next meal is coming from. But this is all now beginning to bear fruits, though the Confederación is only three years old. The Indians now come into the capital and look up the headquarters of the Confederación. They will come in delegations, usually led by a *cacique*, and he will usually be their spokesman. He many times will not be able to talk Spanish, and the people in the office don't know the Indian languages, so Marmól has developed the technique of drawing pictures to represent what he wants to say to them. When the *cacique* understands what the idea is, he turns around and tells his *compañeros* and then turns back to continue the conversation. There are now growing up a group of leaders among the Indians in the countryside who are propagandizing the ideas of the CTG and organizing the Indians. They of course speak in the Indian languages and don't have these problems just mentioned. . . .

There is no Communist party in this country, and in any case the reactionaries, who are very stupid here, label anyone who tries to get the workers better working conditions—twenty cents a day in wages, for instance—a Communist. And this is silly because the workers are beginning to say, that if that is communism, then they are Communists. . . .

The unions are not opposed to foreign capital coming in here. However, they don't want it to dominate the country, and they want the workers to be well treated. That is not the case now, the workers have had housing, had food, had treatment. . . . But as the workers get a little better off and as they get union organization, they wake up and begin to look around them and observe, and they are no longer satisfied with what satisfied them before, and they are aware of the fact that they are being exploited, and go on to demand more and more.

—Guatemala City, August 11, 1948

Most Precious Fruit of the Revolution

Government of Guatemala

Juan José Arévalo (1945–1951) oversaw a remarkable consolidation of democratic reform. Arévalo's government abolished debt and vagrancy laws, yet in many regions planters still had an ironclad grip on local economy and society. Arévalo's successor, Jacobo Arbenz, knew that a land reform would be needed to make the promise of Guatemalan democracy real. Congressional Decree 900, the agrarian reform law that Arbenz called the "most precious fruit of the revolution," went into effect in April 1952.

The reform allowed individuals or peasant organizations to claim the uncultivated land of farms larger than two hundred acres, as well as unused municipal property and plantations nationalized from German coffee planters during the Second World War. The law also outlawed the vestiges of forced labor and gave various legal and political rights to communities of plantation workers, challenging the very core of planter power. Though largely designed by Communist Party intellectuals who had become important advisors to Arbenz, the law was designed to promote capitalist development. The reform aimed to empower peasants to demand higher salaries for their plantation work. Better wages, it was believed, would turn rural laborers into consumers and promote the growth of a national industrialist class, considered to be more "progressive" than the landed oligarchy. The reform would also force planters, who had long made their money from having absolute control over cheap (and often free) labor and land, to invest in new technologies and rationalize production. By the time of Arbenz's overthrow in June 1954, nearly 1,700,000 acres either had been expropriated or were in the process of being expropriated, including half of the more than five hundred thousand acres owned by the United Fruit Company. Much of this land was returned to large landowners after the coup.

The Agrarian Reform Law

CONSIDERING: That one of the fundamental objectives of the October Revolution is the need to realize a fundamental change in the relations of property and the methods of exploiting the earth, in order to overcome the economic backwardness of Guatemala and improve the quality of life of the majority of its people. . . .

CONSIDERING: That article 90 of the Constitution of the Republic recognizes the right of private property and guarantees it as a social function as defined by the public good or the national interest. . . .

The Following is Decreed:

ARTICLE ONE: The Agrarian Reform of the October Revolution has as its goal the liquidation of feudal property in the countryside, along with the relations of productions that gave rise to it, in order to develop capitalist methods of agricultural production and prepare the road for the industrialization of Guatemala.

ARTICLE TWO: All peonage and slavery is abolished, as are, in consequence, personal loans to peasants, peons, and agricultural workers, sharecropping, and the forced labor of Indians, in whatever form they exist. . . .

ARTICLE THREE: The essential objectives the Agrarian Reform should achieve are:

a) Develop a capitalist peasant economy and a capitalist economy in agriculture in general.

b) Provide land to landless peasants, peons, and agricultural workers.
. . .

c) Facilitate the investment of capital in agriculture. . . .

d) Introduce new crops. . . .

e) Increase agricultural credit for all peasants and agricultural capitalists in general.

ARTICLE FOUR: The National Agricultural Department will provide parcels of property to peasants, peons, and agricultural workers, up to an extension no greater than seventeen hectares. . . .

ARTICLE SIX: Indemnization [of expropriated property] will be based on the declaration [of its value] in the fiscal registry of rural propriety. . . .

National Plantation Lands

ARTICLE TWENTY-ONE: National plantation lands [owned by the government]—if the majority of its workers on each one democratically so solicit—will be divided among [the workers].

Feudal Latifundios *and Municipal Lands*

ARTICLE THIRTY-TWO: Private holdings . . . the equivalent of six *caballerías* [more than six hundred acres] that are not cultivated by their owners . . . or have been rented out in whatever form or exploited based on a

Broadsides for and against Guatemala's agrarian reform.
(*below*) The poster warns people that agrarian reform is a trick and that the government plans to steal their land. From the Arturo Taracena Flores Collection, Broadsides, 1944–1963 at the University of Texas, Austin. Used by permission of the Nettie Lee Benson Latin American Collection, University of Texas Libraries, the University of Texas at Austin.

Village leaders of San Pedro Carchá, a Q'eqchi' village in the department of Alta Verapaz, posed for this photograph the day after Guatemala's Congress passed agrarian reform. They had spent the previous night performing Maya rites in a sacred cave, and they planned to join neighboring communities to continue the ceremony in a nearby cemetery. The women are holding candles to be used in the thanksgiving ritual. Photo from the collection of Greg Grandin.

system of personal loans, either to substitute for or subsidize insufficient salaries, during any part of the three years prior to this law are to be considered *latifundios* and can be expropriated in favor of the nation or in favor of peasants and agricultural workers.

Translated by Greg Grandin

Arevalista to Counterrevolutionary

Luis Tárano, interviewed by Elizabeth Oglesby and Simone Remijnse

From 1929 to 1989, Luis Tárano was a labor contractor on the Chuacorral estate in Joyabaj, El Quiché, in the Guatemalan highlands. Chuacorral, a twenty-thousand-acre plantation owned by the wealthy Herrera family, was used nearly exclusively to house the families of workers who would seasonally migrate to the Herreras' coffee and sugar plantations on the Pacific coast. It was exactly these kind of fincas de mozos (farms that produced workers) and their debt and sharecropper arrangements—which tied workers in the highlands to particular lowland plantations—that the 1952 agrarian reform targeted for abolition.

Luis Tárano was interviewed at Chuacorral on September 21, 1999, by Elizabeth Oglesby and Simone Remijnse. In this excerpt, Tárano talks vividly about his support for the "October 20th Revolution" that brought Juan José Arévalo to power in 1944. Yet despite identifying as a political reformer, Tárano tells why he opposed Arbenz and the agrarian reform, going as far as organizing a local militia in Joyabaj and meeting secretly with coup leader Carlos Castillo Armas before the 1954 invasion. As a Ladino labor contractor, merchant, and small landowner, Tárano embodies the contradictions of the 1950s revolutionary period, when emergent middle-class reformers had multilayered ties to the countryside that complicated the reform process. With its network of agrarian committees, the agrarian reform law created the embryo of an alternate local power structure that challenged long-standing social, economic, and racial hierarchies in Guatemala's rural areas.

In Ubico's time, it was bad here. That was a true dictatorship; even in the countryside, we felt the pressure. In the important towns like Joyabaj, there was a local commander, usually some old colonel or lieutenant, and young captains who were terrible! It was enough to maintain total control over the population. In that era, they got away with all kinds of things. No one could protest, because if they did, they could be sent to jail.

The Revolution, for me, was a godsend. I felt that I had God's protection, because I became a local *arevalista* leader, a supporter of Dr. Arévalo. It was natural. After so many years of dictatorship, here comes a doctor of philosophy, a guy with a very, very good background, and politically clean, totally clean. How could Guatemalans not prefer him above the rest? This was a general feeling throughout Guatemala. All of the young people were involved. And in Joyabaj, people followed my lead; the entire *campesino* population of Joyabaj supported me in favor of Arévalo.

On October 20, my sister and I were here in Chuacorral, and we were surprised to hear explosions in the distance. We had a very good radio, and I put it on to find out what the commotion was. They were giving out the news that the government had resigned and taken refuge in the Mexican embassy. Ah! I was just about crazy with delight! Not for my own situation, but because we all longed for that change.

In those days, I didn't have a car, and there wasn't even a road between the *finca* and Joyabaj. So I saddled up my horse and rode to Joyabaj. I even brought my pistol, just in case. The silliness of youth, right? That's something a kid would do, not a mature man. But I went to Joyabaj, and when I dismounted my mother came out of the house to greet me. I grabbed her in a big hug. *"¡Ay, mamá! ¡Viva Guatemala!"* We celebrated with my mother and siblings and some friends, drinking and toasting, and my sister and I were up until two or three in the morning, glued to the radio, listening to the names of the new ministers and the first pronouncements of the government.

Look, I never again felt that kind of patriotic emotion. I felt it that time, and I have never felt it since, and I never will. Because the healthiest and most popular political movement in the history of Guatemala, even more than the Independence movement, was the October 20th movement.

Arbenz won the elections here in Joyabaj in 1950, but the agrarian reform was a disaster. The government didn't know how to carry it out. A lot of injustices were committed because the government was infiltrated by Communists. There was an agrarian inspector from Quiché who came around here. They organized agrarian committees, but with people of very low class. So the sense of the reform was lost.

The agrarian authorities wanted Chuacorral to be split into lots. The agrarian inspector was here in this house, and I explained to him, "Look, this plan of yours is not going to work. You can't just divide up the land willy-nilly. Not all of this land is farmable. What about the poor person who gets stuck with the worthless piece? It's not that I want to stick my nose into what you're doing—if you divide up this land, I will be out of here, anyway. But these poor people, what are they going to do? They will never accept your plan, and if you try to impose it, rivers of blood will be spilled, and heads will be split open like avocados."

A small band of us here who were not in agreement with the agrarian reform organized ourselves into a guerrilla group, in case they tried to come here with bloodshed in mind. I said it was better for us to die in the heat of battle than to be grabbed from behind like dogs. "You're right," they all said. This was a group of neighbors from around here, all Ladinos, no Indians. A group of Ladinos who looked up to me. We organized ourselves, and we were all armed. Of course, when it came right down to it, nothing happened, those men were all tough talkers, but their words spoke louder than their actions. These days, people would be more likely to shoot, but not in those days.

The reform law stipulated that a property bigger than two *caballerías* [about two hundred acres] could be expropriated. I had a piece of property adjacent to Chuacorral that was two *caballerías* exactly, and the agrarian committee of Joyabaj tried to take it away from me. They denounced it, and if the government had not fallen, they would have taken it.

One time I was able to meet with Castillo Armas in Tegucigalpa. I went as a courier to deliver a message from some supporters in Guatemala City. We talked awhile, and he said to me, "Look, don't you know any young officers, or friends? Tell them to be patriotic, man. Tell them to come here with me; they will get a salary, food, and a place to stay, paid for by the cause, they won't have to spend a cent. But they need to come. I need young officers to be instructors. I already have military men, but they are colonels, and they all want to be president. They don't know how to shoot, so what am I going to do? I need young officers, young men of any kind, but preferably with military training." "I'll do what I can," I answered, "but our people are very cowardly; they don't get motivated." "But motivate them yourself," he said. Well, I tried, but no one wanted to. . . .

But I did have my adventures. I was threatened with death as an *"antiagrarista."* There was a telegraph employee in Quiché we called El Conejo [the Rabbit], and luckily for me, one day El Conejo intercepted a telegram that came from Guatemala City authorizing the local authorities to capture me "dead or alive." I was returning from a trip, and when I got to Chuacorral, my wife, Alicia, handed me a suitcase and said, "You're leaving again." At first I thought I would to go to Guatemala City and maybe to the El Salvadoran embassy, but then I remembered I had a cousin who managed a government farm near Quetzaltenango, where I could hide out. I remember driving through Chichicastenango in the rain. When I got to the intersection at Los Encuentros, a police officer wanted to stop me. I remember he came out of his post eating a tortilla; he tried to shout at me to stop, but his mouth was full of food! I just put my foot to the gas pedal and floored it. Divine! I arrived at the farm in Quetzaltenango at eight in the evening. First my cousin and I hid the car, and then he took me into the house.

I spent nineteen days hiding there. Of course, I was a *"castillista,"* I supported Castillo Armas and was anxious to see the government overthrown. I, who had been a revolutionary, was now against the revolutionary government! But my cousin and his wife were *arbencistas. Ay!* That first night, we stayed up around the dinner table arguing until two in the morning! We never came to an agreement. We were both prudent, right, we knew that politics shouldn't come before family and the friendship of cousins, because really we were more like brothers. So for him, it was a pleasure to have me there. That's where I learned how to drive a tractor; while I was hiding from the government, I worked planting wheat on a government farm!

My cousin and I took turns with the tractor, and in the afternoons, while he was working, I would listen to the radio, to the radio broadcasts of the Liberation. But it drove me crazy because they never got beyond Esquipulas. Every day, Esquipulas, Esquipulas, *ay, Dios!* In the meantime, my cousin and I made a hiding place for me so that if anyone official came to the farm they wouldn't see me. I made a little cave out of hay in the back of the chicken coop, but it never came to that, since the government finally fell.

I had a friend who was the military commander in Quiché. Our wives had been in high school together in the Colegio Belén [in Guatemala City], and that sparked a friendship. They used to come here for the weekend; we'd be on the *finca* on Saturdays, and on Sundays we'd go into the town center of Joyabaj. We'd done that a thousand times. And I used to argue with the colonel; he always defended Arbenz, while I explained to him the reasons I couldn't support the government. "From the agrarian point of view, this is a disaster," I would tell him. "It's not that I am afraid of agrarian reform, but I am fearful of the way the Communists are going to implant it." "There aren't any Communists, Güicho," he would answer. "Yes, I know, Colonel, of course Arbenz isn't one, but they are manipulating him." Anyway, the two of us discussed things many times, and when he heard that I had left Joyabaj, he got angry that I hadn't turned to him. He even sent a car and driver to the *finca* to pick up my wife, Alicia, who was then pregnant with our third child, to bring her to Quiché, a gesture that I never forgot. He did that for an enemy of the government!

So, shortly after the fall of Arbenz, I went to see my friend, the colonel. "Look, Güicho," he said, "I am still an *arbencista.* He may be gone now, but I am not in favor of the *gringos* coming here to impose governments."

"Well, on the nationalist side, you're right," I told him, "but the way they were screwing us in the countryside justifies all that. They forced me to get involved; I didn't choose that, but to defend myself, I had to get involved." "Well," he said, "you're right, and you have your opinion, but to be honest, I am still an *arbencista*." You know, to say that even after the government had fallen, that was another gesture of a complete gentleman, a real man.

Later, after Castillo Armas became president, Roberto Herrera went to speak with him about Chuacorral. To get the land back, you had to present a petition to the government, and Don Roberto did that, but at the same time, he said to Castillo Armas that he didn't want the land anymore. "Because it's never been mine," he said. "It was mine by law, but these *colonos* have been living on the land their whole lives. I barely know this land. So I want to give it to them, but without it costing them a cent. I want them to have it as my gratitude for all the time they worked for me." "My pleasure," said Castillo Armas, "I am going to bring this to the attention of the Agrarian Department so that it won't cost you a cent." So that's how it was done, and in 1957, Chuacorral was turned over to the *colonos*.[1]

Well, these are histories, no? And it was all connected to the agrarian reform. That's what pushed me into all that, because, sincerely, I wasn't involved in politics and I wouldn't have wanted to do that.

Translated by Elizabeth Oglesby

Note

1. It took years to finalize the land titles for beneficiaries. See the Chuacorral case files of the Departamento Nacional Agrario, located in Guatemala City's Archivo General de Centro América, packet 16, file 10. Other *fincas de mozos* owned by the Herrera family in Cotzal, southern El Quiché, and San Martín, Chimaltenango, were not relinquished until 1982, in the midst of the counterinsurgency war.

Enemies of Christ

Archbishop Mariano Rossell y Arellano

Opposition to the October Revolution also came from the Catholic Church, led by the archconservative Archbishop Mariano Rossell y Arellano. At first, Rossell y Arellano viewed the overthrow of Ubico as an opportunity to restore the authority of the church, which had weakened under the dictatorship. But when Congress declared in 1945 that welfare should be considered a "right" and not a "humiliating charity," the archbishop began a decade-long assault on the October Revolution that culminated in an April 1954 call to insurrection. The archbishop issued a steady barrage of pastoral letters and sermons that equated Arévalo with past dictators and laid out a conception of human misery based not on class exploitation but on the secular erosion of colonial institutions and protections—including the protection of indigenous land rights—which had provided meaning, dignity, and security to Guatemalans for centuries, he said. He drew on Spanish fascism to promote a spiritual vision of "social unity" as an antidote to the fragmentation and divisiveness brought about by secular democratic politics.

At the beginning of the October Revolution, Rossell y Arellano's anticommunism was vague, and his criticisms of Arévalo and his "spiritual socialism" often missed their mark. Yet the social disruptions caused by the agrarian reform gave his criticisms some traction. He was able to tap into the growing anxiety that the reform would subvert proper relations between Ladinos and Indians, and men and women. He condemned organizers for teaching peasants "to speak in public" and for corrupting "the feminine soul among the women of the worker and peasant classes." This selection is drawn from a speech given by Rossell y Arellano to a US audience, after Arbenz's overthrow.

Guatemala is an agricultural country, the rural population of which far outnumbers the city dwellers. The peasant is the most numerous and the most important personage in our economic life. However, the distribution of the land and its riches is neither Christian nor equitable for the agricultural country which is Guatemala.

One is surprised by the admirable distribution of land which was

Coup leader Carlos Castillo Armas (*right*) honors Archbishop Mariano Rossell y Arellano, 1954. Anonymous photographer, *El Imparcial* collection. From the collections of the Centro de Investigaciones Regionales de Mesoamérica, Guatemala.

achieved under the Spanish colonial regime, in many parts of the former kingdom of Guatemala, due to the firm insistence on justice on the part of missionaries and bishops. . . . The land never had better nor more numerous owners than in the sixteenth century of our history. . . .

But human ambition knows no dikes . . . since under the banner of liberalism and its criminal economic goal of "laissez faire" and its nefarious "free competition," the powerful, the politicians, the large landowners monopolized the property of small and middle-class landowners alike, dispossessed the villages of their community property, and snatched from the church the fields and mills. . . .

The hatred of liberalism for the church was not based on opposition to its theological doctrines so much as on the role of the church as protector of the Indian. . . . The devastating storm of liberal economic rapine eliminated the small private holding which, in copious number, had been the patrimony of the sixteenth century. . . . But in spite of the fact that the prevailing social injustice was favorable to the tenets of communism, communism did not come openly and waving flags for its doctrines. No: it knew that the people of Guatemala, its peasants, above all, were profoundly religious. Liberalism had taken God from the schools, but it could not expel Him from the huts of the peasants. . . .

When the political regime, which had governed Guatemala until 1944, fell—and which, as a worthy heir of liberal ideology, had reached the point of jailing priests in the name of social justice—the Communists initiated their proselytizing campaign under the mantle of avengers of the working class and began by disguising themselves in sheepskins. They made gifts to the villages of the image of Our Lady, and they added to the name of the image the initials of their political party; for example, they would present an image of the Blessed Virgin and call her "Our Lady of Carmen of the PAR," which were the initials of the communistoid group; they proclaimed, in their campaign harangues, that they would return to the church the liberty which had been stolen from her by their predecessors in public life. Delegations of campaign leaders even reached the point of going en masse to church and taking communion at High Mass, in order to make a showing of Catholicism before the peasants and workers of the villages. . . . They offered the villages to repair their churches. . . .

While with one hand communism made good use of religion and of a show of respect for the church, in order to gain the confidence of the peasant, with the other hand it initiated a strong and well-planned strategy of building up anti-Catholic nuclei through the systematic enlistment of individuals of known immorality, to foment to the maximum in the rural communities all the vices, particularly alcoholism. . . . Well-paid prostitution was encouraged. The female adherents of communistic and leftist parties were corrupted; and in addition, when a woman of one village or another displayed gifts of proselytism or leadership, she was given a high and well-paid position in the official bureaucracy. These women were not only the leaders and the propagandists of the pacifistic movements, but also professional corrupters of the feminine soul among the women of the worker and peasant classes. . . .

Communism revived in Guatemala a racial hatred which had been nearly dead for centuries; the hatred of the Indian for the "Ladino." The peasant was told that the *conquistadores* and their descendants (the landlords) had dispossessed them from their land and that the Party would return to them the lands which had been stolen by the former. . . .

But the most attractive bait offered to the still-reluctant peasantry was the so-called agrarian reform. . . . The land-hungry peasants began systematically to take over the land; there were even acts of bloodshed, in violation of the agrarian law itself, arising out of land disputes among the peasants themselves. In localities where the peasants were reluctant to take the land, peasants from other areas were brought in who displaced the local peasants. . . .

We must not leave unmentioned that marvelous and highly effective tactic for their devilish conquest, the training of peasant leaders, locally recruited if possible and sharing the local customs. When in the villages they found a peasant gifted with facility with words and a certain ability to get along with the local people, they overwhelmed this man with money, travel, public posts, and they took steps to indoctrinate him thoroughly in their cause. They brought him to the capital, they enrolled him in training courses, they took him to international congresses, they taught him to speak in public. . . .

In the fight for social revindication the church spoke with no vacillation and condemned the crimes committed by the past political regimes—namely, conservatism and liberalism—whose blindness and hatred together with social injustice and the expelling of the farmer from his land left an open field for communism.

The church maintained a spirit of social justice, pointing out that inalienable and patrimonial ownership of the land by the peasant, a workable rural credit system, and a permanent and full-dress Christianization of the villages can save the countryside from ever falling into the hands of the Communists. The task was arduous because of the habitual blindness on all sides insisting on the concentration of land in the hands of a few. Good salaries and wages and gifts to the peasant are not enough, if he does not properly own his fair share of land. A peasant without land is half of a whole, and is unconsciously within the orbit of communist seduction.

Operation PBSUCCESS

Nick Cullather

When US president Dwight Eisenhower decided in August 1953 to overthrow Jacobo
Arbenz, the agents in charge of the operation realized that a simple military revolt
or invasion would not work. Even though social tensions had escalated in the wake
of the 1952 agrarian reform law, Arbenz still enjoyed deep popular support. The
opposition was divided, and the military was quiet. PBSUCCESS, as the CIA dubbed
its campaign to overthrow the Arbenz government, became the agency's most ambitious covert operation, a model for future actions. From Langley to Madison Avenue, the United States mobilized every facet of its power to end the October Revolution. It used the Organization of American States (OAS) to isolate Guatemala
diplomatically, worked with US businesses to create an economic crisis, and funded
and equipped an exile invasion force based in Honduras. The CIA used techniques
borrowed from social psychology, Hollywood, and the burgeoning advertising industry to erode loyalty to Arbenz within Guatemala. Radio shows incited government officials and soldiers to treason and attempted to convince Guatemalans that
a widespread underground resistance movement existed. Claiming to be transmit-
ted from "deep in the jungle" by rebel forces, the broadcasts were in fact taped in
Miami and beamed into Guatemala from Nicaragua.

By June 15, 1954, when Washington's hand-picked colonel, Carlos Castillo Armas, invaded from Honduras with a few hundred mercenaries, the CIA had softened the ground with a year-long escalating campaign of sabotage, political agitation, rumors, and propaganda designed to destabilize and demoralize government
supporters, create dissension in the military, force Arbenz to crack down on dissent, and energize the opposition. While Castillo Armas's invasion was clumsy
and could easily have been defeated by Guatemalan troops, military officers nonetheless abandoned Arbenz because they feared the power of the United States,
which they knew had organized and paid for the invasion.

The following selection gives an excellent description of the scope and intensity of the campaign, as well as the myths that surrounded it. It is from the CIA's
in-house history of its operation, written in 1992 by a scholar with access to CIA

archives, which were later declassified.[1] *The redacted parts conceal information the agency still considers too sensitive to make public.*

The Plan

The planners decided to employ simultaneously all of the tactics that had proved useful in previous covert operations. PBSUCCESS would combine psychological, economic, diplomatic, and paramilitary actions. Operations in Europe, [ ], and Iran had demonstrated the potency of propaganda—"psychological warfare"—aimed at discrediting an enemy and building support for allies. Like many Americans, US officials placed tremendous faith in the new science of advertising. Touted as the answer to underconsumption, economic recession, and social ills, advertising, many thought, could be used to cure Communism as well. In 1951, the Truman administration tripled the budget for propaganda and appointed a Psychological Strategy Board to coordinate activities. The CIA required "psywar" training for new agents, who studied Paul Linebarger's text, *Psychological Warfare*, and grifter novels like *The Big Con* for disinformation tactics. PBSUCCESS's designers planned to supplement overt diplomatic initiatives—such as an OAS conference convened to discredit Guatemala—with "black operations using contacts within the press, radio, church, army, and other organized elements susceptible to rumor, pamphleteering, poster campaigns, and other subversive action." They were particularly impressed with the potential for radio propaganda, which had turned the tide at a critical moment in the Iran operation.

The planners' faith in radio as a propaganda weapon derived from their experience in other areas of the world, and it ignored local conditions that limited the strategy's usefulness in Guatemala. Only one Guatemalan in 50 owned a radio, and the vast majority of the nation's 71,000 sets were concentrated in the vicinity of the capital, in the homes and offices of the wealthy and professional classes. Agency analysts noted that "radio does not constitute an effective means of approach to the masses of agricultural workers and apparently reaches only a small number of urban workers." Communist organizations eschewed radio and exercised influence through personal contact and persuasion. Radio, nonetheless, became a central feature of the operational plan. Although Guatemalans were "not habituated" to radio, an analyst observed, they "probably consider it an authoritative source, and they may give wide word-of-mouth circulation to interesting rumors" contained in broadcasts.

"National campaign against Communism." From the Arturo Taracena Flores Collection, Broadsides, 1944–1963 at the University of Texas, Austin. Used by permission of the Nettie Lee Benson Latin American Collection, University of Texas Libraries, the University of Texas at Austin.

[ ], Tofte, and [ ] considered Guatemala's economy vulnerable to economic pressure, and they planned to target oil supplies, shipping, and coffee exports. An "already cleared group of top-ranking American businessmen in New York City" would be assigned to put covert economic pressure on Guatemala by creating shortages of vital imports and cutting export earnings. The program would be supplemented by overt multilateral action, possibly by the OAS, against Guatemalan coffee exports. The planners believed economic pressures could be used surgically to "damage the Arbenz government and its supporters without seriously affecting anti-Communist elements."

Planners had only sketchy ideas about the potential of two crucial parts of the program: political and paramilitary action. King's aides believed that to succeed the opposition would need to win over Army leaders and key government officials. They considered the Army "the only organized element in Guatemala capable of rapidly and decisively altering the political situation." In Iran, cooperative army officers had tilted the political balance in favor of the Shah. Planners felt PBSUCCESS needed similar support, but they had few ideas on how to foment opposition. Arbenz, a former officer, remained popular among military leaders. Castillo Armas had little ap-

Carlos Castillo Armas, center, before the overthrow of Arbenz, 1954. Anonymous photographer. From the E. Taracena de la Cerda family archives. From the collections of the Centro de Investigaciones Regionales de Mesoamérica, Guatemala.

peal among his former colleagues, and his guerrillas were no match for the 5,000-man Army. Rebel forces suffered from desertion and low morale, and agents in Honduras reported that without help, the organized opposition would disintegrate by the end of 1953.

PBSUCCESS planners were disturbed by the shortage of assets around which to build a covert program. The Catholic Church opposed land reform and Arbenz, but was handicapped by its meager resources and the shortage of native priests. Foreigners were subject to deportation, and most priests avoided challenging authority. Resistance among landowners was declining "due to general discouragement" after the failure of the Salamá raid. The planners noted widespread discontent in both the capital and the countryside, but saw little prospect of stimulating disgruntled elements to take political action. The estimated 100,000 passive opponents included property owners, laborers, and *campesinos* who shared few common goals. Castillo Armas's organization, "a group of revolutionary activists, numbering a few hundred, led by an exiled Guatemalan army officer, and located in Honduras," remained the Agency's principal operational asset. In addition, some fifty Guatemalan students belonging to the Comité Estudiantes Universitarios Anti-Comunistas (CEUA) had []. The group published a newspaper, *El Rebelde*. Members who fled the country after Salamá formed an exile group and published a weekly paper, *El Combate*, which was smuggled over the border. These assets, the planners reported, did "not even remotely match the 1,500–3,000 trained Communists."

While TPAJAX [the covert operation that overthrew Iranian Premier Mohammad Mossadeq in 1953] achieved victory in less than six weeks, PB-SUCCESS planners warned that Guatemala would require more effort and patience. The Agency would have to develop from scratch assets of the sort that it had used in Iran, a process that might take a year or more. [ ] foresaw a preparation period followed by a buildup of diplomatic and economic pressure on the Arbenz regime. When pressure reached its maximum point, political agitation, sabotage, and rumor campaigns would undermine the government and encourage active opposition. During this crisis, Castillo Armas would establish a revolutionary government and invade Guatemala. The plan was silent about what would happen next.

Trusting the Agency's proven tactics to generate results, planners saw no problem in their inability to predict how the operation would play out. Reviewing their work, Deputy Director for Plans Frank Wisner remarked that "the plan is stated in such broad terms that it is not possible to know exactly what it contemplates, particularly in the latter phases." He added that he did "not regard this as a particular drawback" since adjustments could be made as the operation unfolded. King expected a long assessment phase during which specific goals and plans would be set, with periodic reassessments throughout the life of the operation. . . .

PBSUCCESS relied on the State and Defense Departments to isolate Guatemala diplomatically, militarily, and economically. In King's plan, the State Department would mount a diplomatic offensive in the OAS to declare Guatemala a pariah state and cripple its economy. State and Defense would work together to enforce an arms embargo and build up the military potential of neighboring states. The US Navy and Air Force would provide essential logistical support, maintenance, expertise, and training for paramilitary forces. Overt initiatives would create an atmosphere of fearful expectancy, which would enhance the effectiveness of covert action. PBSUCCESS would be a government-wide operation led by the CIA.

On 9 December 1953, Allen Dulles authorized $3 million for the project and placed Wisner in charge. Wisner's Directorate of Plans assumed exclusive control of PBSUCCESS, neither seeking nor receiving aid from other directorates. . . .

The State Department fulfilled its assigned duties, increasing aid to industrial and road building projects in Honduras, El Salvador, and Nicaragua, and assembling a special team of diplomats to assist PBSUCCESS from

Arbencista peasants captured after the overthrow of Arbenz, 1954. Anonymous photographer. From the E. Taracena de la Cerda family archives. From the collections of the Centro de Investigaciones Regionales de Mesoamérica, Guatemala.

Central American embassies. The group's leader, John Peurifoy, took over as Ambassador in Guatemala City in October 1953. He was in a familiar role. As ambassador to Greece during its civil war, he coordinated State [ ] activities on behalf of the royalists. An admirer of Joseph McCarthy, he shared the Senator's taste in politics. . . .

Meanwhile, [ ] established PBSUCCESS headquarters in a [ ]. The [ ] offered facilities for offices, storage, and aircraft maintenance, and two days before Christmas, the operation moved [ ], Florida, under the cover name [ ]. If asked, officers were to explain that they were part of a unit that did [ ]. . . .

PBSUCCESS was ready by the beginning of May to place maximum pressure on the Arbenz regime. [ ] had a variety of instruments at his disposal: propaganda, sabotage, aircraft, an army of insurrectionists, and the implicit threat of US military power. He used all of them to intensify the psychological distress of Arbenz and his officials. Even the paramilitary program— Castillo Armas and his *liberacionistas*—served a psychological rather than a military function. As an Agency memo prepared for Eisenhower explained, the operation relied "on psychological impact rather than actual military strength, although it is upon the ability of Castillo Armas to create and maintain the *impression* of very substantial military strength, that the success of this particular effort primarily depends." Dealing in the insubstantial stuff of impressions and degrees of intimidation, [ ] could not always measure progress, and it was difficult for even those close to PBSUCCESS to know what was happening, whether they were succeeding or failing, and why.

The Voice of Liberation

As Guatemalans turned on their short-wave radios on the morning of 1 May 1954, they found a new station weakly audible on a part of the dial that had been silent before. Calling itself *La Voz de la Liberación*, it broadcast a combination of popular recordings, bawdy humor, and antigovernment propaganda. The announcers, claiming to be speaking from "deep in the jungle," exhorted Guatemalans to resist Communism and the Arbenz regime and support the forces of liberation led by Col. Carlos Castillo Armas. The two-hour broadcast was repeated four times. For the next week the station broadcast an hour-long program at 7:00 AM and 9:00 PM daily. Although only faintly and intermittently heard in the capital, the station electrified a city where open criticism of the regime had become dangerous for journalists and private citizens alike. Government spokesmen denounced the broadcasts as a fraud, originating not in Guatemala but over the border in Mexico or Honduras. Most listeners, however, preferred to believe that brave radiomen, hidden in a remote outpost, were defying official censors and the police.

So began an operation [ ] later called the "finest example PP/Radio effort and effectiveness on the books." The voices heard in Guatemala originated not in the jungle, or even in Honduras, but in a Miami [ ] where a team of four Guatemalan men and two women mixed announcements and editorials with canned music. The broadcasts reminded soldiers of their duty to protect the country from foreign ideologies, warned women to keep their husbands away from Communist party meetings and labor unions, and threatened government officials with reprisals. Couriers carried the tapes via Pan American Airways to [ ] where they were beamed into Guatemala from a mobile transmitter. When the traffic in tapes aroused the suspicions of Panamanian customs officials, the announcers moved to [ ] and began broadcasting live from a dairy farm [ ] a site known as SHERWOOD. At about the same time, the SHERWOOD operation improved its reception in Guatemala by boosting its signal strength. By mid-May the rebel broadcasts were heard loud and clear in Guatemala City, and SHERWOOD announcers were responding quickly to developments in the enemy capital.

To direct the SHERWOOD operation, Tracy Barnes selected a clever and enterprising contract employee, David Atlee Phillips, a onetime actor and newspaper editor in Chile. When Phillips arrived in [ ] in March, one of the Guatemalan announcers explained that the target audience was mixed. "Two percent are hard-core Marxists; 13 percent are officials and others in sympathy with the Arbenz regime. . . . Two percent are militant anti-Communists, some of them in exile." The objective, the announcer continued, was to intimidate the Communists and their sympathizers and stimulate the apathetic majority to act. Initial broadcasts would establish the station's credibility, setting the state for an "Orson Welles type 'panic broadcast'" to coincide with Castillo Armas's invasion. The program would follow the lead of earlier PP efforts, combining intimidating misinformation with pithy slogans, and targeting "men of action," particularly the Army. The station's slogan became *Trabajo, Pan y Patria*, work, bread, and country.

In Phillips's account of the operation, SHERWOOD was singularly responsible for the triumph of PBSUCCESS. "When the campaign started," he observes, "the Guatemalan capital and countryside had been quiet. Within a week there was unrest everywhere." Scholars have generally given similar credit to *La Voz de la Liberación*, but were it not for a fortuitous turn of events the rebel broadcasters might have made only a muffled impact. Two weeks into the operation Guatemala's state-run radio station, TGW, disappeared from the air. Perplexed, [ ] and Phillips soon learned from Guatemala Station that TGW was scheduled to receive a new antenna and that the government's only broadcast medium would be out of commission for three weeks. Through an accident of timing SHERWOOD acquired a virtual propaganda monopoly during the most critical phase of operation PBSUCCESS. In late May, as Guatemalans witnessed a startling series of dark and portentous events, the largely illiterate populace turned to *La Voz de la Liberación* for news.

Note

1. These declassified documents can be viewed in the National Security Archive's Electronic Briefing Book No. 4; see http://www.gwu.edu/~nsarchiv/.

Sabotage for Liberty

Anonymous

The following selection is from a Spanish-language sabotage manual, one of two found in Eduardo Taracena's personal papers. Taracena was an anticommunist student leader who worked closely with the US Central Intelligence Agency, helping the agency carry out its bombing campaign, mostly against public utilities and Communist Party buildings. The manual has no author or publishing information, but its many grammatical errors—for instance, spelling sabotage with a g instead of a j, as it is spelled in Spanish—suggest that it was written in English and translated into Spanish, most likely by the CIA. Not only do the manuals provide instructive diagrams on how to make and deploy a range of explosives, such as tube bombs, remote fuses, chemical bombs, nitroglycerin, and dynamite; they morally justify terrorism and exhort Guatemalans to embrace it in order to create a "new Guatemala, free and ferocious." This celebration of purifying violence is a good example of how the United States, in the nominal defense of "liberal democracy," often resorted to promoting decidedly illiberal means.

ABSOLUTELY SECRET
SABOTAGE FOR THE LIBERATION OF GUATEMALA
PREPARATION
(30-DAY PLAN)
EXECUTION
ABSOLUTELY SECRET

SABOTAGE FOR THE LIBERATION OF GUATEMALA
The man who is not willing to die
For his liberty, deserves to live in
Slavery.

FIRST PART

I. TO THE SOLDIERS OF LIBERTY. The liberty of a people has always been won by spilling the blood of the best sons, and there will never be freedom in any country where citizens are not willing to die for it. . . .

So, the great evils of today will indirectly usher in the future well-being of Guatemala, and therefore we should accept them as something inevitable to reach our primary objective: the happiness of Guatemalans. But, will there be happiness while we live under the Communist terror that now reigns on our soil? . . .

A thousand times, no! The moment has come to put an end to this page of calamities that undermines our country's history. It's time to take our country back. It's time to make the name of Guatemala shine again, darkened by the nefarious shadow of Communism.

Guatemalans! The hour of liberation is imminent, but it is critical that all honorable citizens, those who have not been contaminated by the Communist virus, join forces and wills in the service of this noble crusade, in accordance with the instructions contained in this pamphlet, which is the only way to paralyze the nervous system of the Communist octopus that is devouring the entrails of our country. . . .

GENERALITIES

1. Introduction. Sabotage, like almost everything in life, is good or evil depending on whether it's put in the service of good or evil. It is righteous and invaluable when it is put on the side of noble causes, when it seeks the liberation of a people, when it contributes to the extermination of the oppressor forces.

Throughout time, the struggle for liberty has paralleled human development, and maintaining it has required ever-increasing sacrifices. And in this millenary struggle, sabotage has become increasingly important, to the point of being an efficient way to wage war against the enslavers of humanity. Modern history is full of innumerable and glorious pages written with the blood of the martyrs who have known how to carry out the valuable tasks that sabotage requires. . . .

The SOLDIERS OF LIBERTY must understand the sacrifices their duties imply and have the conviction that the damages they inflict on the enemy's shields are the beginning of the reconstruction of the *Patria*, and that out of the ashes of today's fires, like the sacred ibis, will arise the new Guatemala, free and ferocious. The small sacrifice of each will lead to a greater good and therefore carefully carrying out a single mission may be the foundation of final victory. . . .

A man may die, but the Cause must triumph, and the Fatherland has to be saved.

In the struggle for liberation, there are only two types of elements: friends and enemies. Anyone who doesn't understand this will not be apt for this kind of struggle.

Sentimentalism by any member of the organization is a dangerous lapse, since it must be understood that whatever the act to be carried out, it is a step toward liberty and a necessary part of the general plan, carefully studied and analyzed by the high command of the organization. . . .

3. Objective of sabotage. The objective of sabotage is to weaken the enemy with daring acts that cause major or minor material or moral damage.

Sabotage that undermines the Communist governing structure that dominates Guatemala is the weapon of liberty that conscientious citizens will wield, those who desire to provide absolute independence for their country. . . .

II. EXECUTION

The means to carry out [sabotage] are:

1. Mechanical. The mechanical procedures through which an act of sabotage can be produced are:
   1. Impurities. Sabotage through impurities is done by mixing into fuel sugar, molasses or any other ingredient that could produce partial or total destruction to the machinery, with the goal of stopping or destroying production or employment. . . .

2. Physical Acts. This system is put into practice through simple actions that could appear to be carelessness, such as loosening screws or machine parts, or tightening them too much, [or] removing pieces that impede their operation. . . .

3. Destruction. This consists of allowing raw materials to get ruined, such as taking the top off canned food or volatile liquids, etc.

4. Explosive. These are methods of sabotage in which explosive materials are used to damage or destroy a determined object . . .

   Their use in sabotage can be one of two ways: a) direct action. This is when an explosive is used in a bomb without trying to hide the nature of the article. . . . b) delayed action. This classification includes time bombs, which explode by themselves after a calculated period of time through a special incendiary device. These can be directed at people or property. . . .

   Nitroglycerin: Highly explosive, nitroglycerin is one of the best-known and most dangerous materials to handle. . . .

   Dynamite: This term is used generally to refer to explosives that have been prepared using some kind of porous or absorbent substance, such as wood pulp, flour or a similar material. . . .

BOMBAS ABIERTAS O NO DISFRAZADAS.

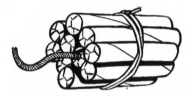

Figura número 1.- Bomba de Dinamita no disfrazada.
(10 cartuchos de Dinamita amarra
dos simplemente, un fulminante
y su mecha)

Figura número 2.- Bomba de Tubo.
(Un tubo de cañería con un extremo soldado
y con tapón de rosca en el otro, en el que
se dejará un agujero para el paso de la
mecha, en el caso de hacerse con polvora
negra, sólo es necesaria la mecha, si se
hace con pólvora blanca, dinamita o T.N.T.
colóquese un fulminante interno.)

These images—of dynamite cartridges and a tube bomb—come
from the manual from which this selection is excerpted. The manual
instructs opponents of Arbenz in the art of bomb making, including
how to construct time bombs, briefcase bombs, incendiary pens, and
improvised explosives disguised as cigars, books, and rocks. Source:
*Sabotage para la liberación de Guatemala: preparación (plan treinta dias),
ejecución*, mimeograph in Grandin's possession (n.d).

> *Tube bomb*: This bomb consists of a piece of steel or iron tubing, with
> rings at both ends to screw on a cap. It is ignited by a fuse passed
> through a small hole at one end. . . .
> *Chemical*: These are bombs that use a delayed action incendiary de-
> vice based on a chemical reaction. . . .

Translated by Elizabeth Oglesby

A Plan for Assassination

Central Intelligence Agency

As early as January 1952, the CIA *began to compile lists of Guatemalans "to elimi-nate immediately in event of [a] successful anti-Communist coup." The agency has insisted that no assassinations were actually carried out, yet it has refused to release the names of the targeted individuals to verify that none were executed. Whatever the case, in the decades that followed the coup, as the* US-*installed regime grew increasingly repressive, the compilation of such "death lists" became a routine practice. What follows is a redacted list of "Communist Personnel to be Disposed of During Military Operation of Calligeris," with Calligeris being the code name for coup leader Carlos Castillo Armas.*

TO: Chief, [   ]

FROM: [   ]

SUBJECT: Guatemalan Communist Personnel to be disposed of during
         Military Operations of Calligeris

1. Included herein is the list of Guatemalan Communist Personnel
to be disposed of during military operations to be carried out by
Calligeris.

       a. Category I – persons to be disposed of through Executive
            action (attachment # 1)

       b. Category II – persons to be disposed of through imprison-
            ment or exile (attachment # 2)

2. This list is a revision, revised by Calligeris, of an original
list prepared by Headquarters in February 1952.

Attachments: 2

Distribution: Orig. & 1, Headquarters

Orig in [   ]

243

Comunistas: Categoría #1

1.	31
2.	32
3.	33
4.	34
5.	35
6.	36
7.	37
8.	38
9.	39
10.	40
11.	41
12.	42
13.	43
14.	44
15.	45
16.	46
17.	47
18.	48
19.	49
20.	50
21.	51
22.	52
23.	53
24.	54
25.	55
26.	56
27.	57
28.	58
29.	
30.	

244

Comunistas: Categoría #2

1.
2.
3.
4.
5.
6.
7.
8.
9.
10.
11.
12.
13.
14.
15.
16.
17.
18.
19.
20.
21.
22.
23.
24.
25.
26.
27.
28.
29.
30.
31.
32.
33.
34.
35.
36.
37.

38.
39.
40.
41.
42.
43.
44.
45.
46.
47.
48.
49.
50.
51.
52.
53.
54.
55.
56.
57.
58.
59.
60.
61.
62.
63.
64.
65.
66.
67.
68.
69.
70.
71.
72.
73.
74.

245

Military Dream

César Brañas

In its immediate aftermath, the coup produced an outpouring of analysis, poetry, art, novels, and books trying to make sense of its trauma, much of which could only be published outside of Guatemala. César Brañas (1899–1976), an essayist, poet, journalist, and literary critic, wrote this poem in October 1954.

I don't think I'm wrong if more than once
I say I would have liked to be a soldier
(and a gold-braided, plumed general
in a carnival)

But a deliberate soldier, yes,
with a clean rifle in my eyes
and a rebellious air in my stride
light and sharp as a watchdog.

Attuned to the discipline of the wind
and to the profession
I would raise swallows in the barracks.

A soldier antithetical to forced
marches into the past
and anxiously inclined
to dive into an unfaithful future.

There, where you see me as a countryman
half-witted and adrift in the streets,
I carry a playful drum
soldier of an invisible army
climbing twilight's ramparts
in fierce waves
without recognizing, even in defeat, his heroism.

But my military dream ends
this side of the command and I don't know if that's good or bad
because, really, I would have been a bad soldier
for my own good
and they would have shot at my tailwind
as a deserter
because I never would have fired
on the honeysuckle, the rose, or the nightingale.

October 30, 1954.

Translated by Elizabeth Oglesby

Sueño Militar

No creo estar equivocado más de una vez
si declaro que hubiera querido ser soldado
(y general todo entorchado y emplumado
en un carnaval)

Pero soldado sí, adrede,
con un limpio fusil en los ojos
y el aire rebelde en las polainas
ligero y afilado en mastín.

Atento a la disciplina del viento
y a la carrera
cultivaría golondrinas en el cuartel.

Soldado antiejemplar para las marchas
forzadas hacia el pasado
y con paso acelerado dispuesto
a entrar a saco en el futuro infiel.

Ahí donde se me ve de paisano
torpe y a la deriva en las calles,
llevo un redoblante lleno de sol
soldado de un ejército invisible
que en vehementes mareas sube
por las rampas del crepúsculo
sin darse cuenta, ni por vencido, de su heroicidad.

Pero mi sueño militar concluye
más acá de la ordenanza y no sé si del bien y el mal
porque yo habría sido a la verdad un mal soldado
por mi bien
y me habrían fusilado por la espalda del viento
por desertor
porque yo nunca habría disparado
a la madreselva ni a la rosa ni al ruiseñor.

30 de octubre de 1954.

We Are Officers of the Guatemalan Army

November 13 Rebel Movement

On November 13, 1960, one-third of the Guatemalan military rose in revolt, led by "young officers" protesting the corruption of the government of General Miguel Ydígoras Fuentes and economic policies that ignored the needs of the majority of the population. The uprising was quickly put down with the help of the US Air Force, but a number of the rebel soldiers refused to surrender, instead reorganizing themselves in the Sierra de las Minas, in the eastern part of the country, and establishing contacts with Havana. Under the command of Lieutenant Luis Augusto Túrcios Lima, they formed the November 13 Rebel Movement, later known as the Fuerzas Armadas Rebeldes, Guatemala's first post-1954 insurgency. Below is their inaugural manifesto, broadcast throughout the country from the studio of a seized radio station.

We are officers of the Guatemalan army, who, since November 13, 1960, have been fighting to give our country a government that acts within democratic norms according to the interests of the people. . . . The young officers . . . have demonstrated their decision to definitively end with the lies and theft organized by Ydígoras Fuentes, his economic advisors, and his lackeys. As young officers, we believe that national revenues should be administered with absolute honesty and dignity. . . .

The November 13 Rebel Movement is armed and is fighting in the mountains like guerrillas, putting our young lives at the service of the people. This is who we are, youth, who were it not for the fact that we were in the military would have been insensitive to the hunger and misery of our peasants and workers, to the agony of our employees, our teachers. We are not indifferent to the hard economic time and the ruined state of our industry and commerce. . . .

We are truly dismayed when we see our children learning to write in dirt because schools do not have desks, even as Ydígoras is building a pompous showcase school for all of Central America, because he has the absurd pretension of being a leader of Central American unification. We are pained to see our sick citizens unable to be treated in our ruinous hospitals, even while Ydígoras and his buddies go from fair to fair like clowns, simulating a prosperity and economic bonanza that doesn't exist. . . .

It makes us sad, Guatemalans, to see a dreary future for our country, where one has to import even corn to make tortillas. There is no work, not in the countryside nor in the city. In the countryside, there continue to exist large, unproductive plantations. In the city, massive unemployment. Our low consumption power has paralyzed commercial activity and manufacturing.

People of Guatemala . . . Rise Up! . . . One only has to go 15 kilometers outside of the capital to see that the dogs of the wealthy eat better than our peasants. . . .

This is why the November 13 Rebel Movement is fighting. . . . We are in the mountains fighting to the death for those who are hungry, for the land that none other than John F. Kennedy is asking be given to our peasants. . . .

The hour has arrived. . . . Soon, the hour of victory will be here.

Translated by Greg Grandin

Long Live the Students!

Miguel Angel Sandoval and María del Rosario Ramírez

Students, who had been politically active during the 1944–54 reform period, remained important in the post-coup years, and some of them became leaders of the guerrilla fronts of the 1960s. In the selections below, Miguel Angel Sandoval and María del Rosario Ramírez describe the protests that broke out in Guatemala from March to May 1962, when students joined members of the railroad and other unions to take over the streets of Guatemala City to protest electoral fraud and a government that had turned its back on the urgent needs of Guatemalans. "A deluge of idealism, the spirit of liberty and equality flowed through the streets," commented one Guatemalan. The song "¡Qué vivan los estudiantes!"—"Long live the students!"—became a leitmotif. Written by Venezuelan singer Alí Primera and recorded by his band, Guaraguao, its lyrics read:

> Long live the students, garden of our happiness
> They are birds, afraid neither of animal nor police,
> Bullets nor the barks of a pack of hounds
> Damn it all, and Long live Astronomy!
> Long live the students who roar like the wind
> when they are brainwashed with religion and militarism
> They are little free birds, equal to the elements
> Damn it all, and Long Live Chemistry!
> I like the Students, because they are the yeast
> of the bread that will come from the oven, with all its flavor
> for the mouth of the poor, who eat with bitterness
> Damn it all, Long Live Literature!

March and April 1962, by Miguel Angel Sandoval

As if it were springtime, in the beginning of the 1960s student self-governance blossomed in all the high schools, the public ones, of course. The mechanism was so simple. In every school, each class elected two representatives who then formed the legislature of that school. In addition, the students organized political parties and elected a leadership council for each school. The council had a secretary of public relations, finance, culture, sports and so on. There was a student court . . . in short, it was a model of republican civics and profoundly democratic.

I remember special cultural weeks, poetry and painting contests, student journals, and sports events and dances. All this was organized by student leaders who wanted to leave their imprint on the strengthening of self-governance. In truth, it was a school within a school.

In these years, most of the schools belonged to a new student group called Frente Unido del Estudiantado Guatemalteco Organizado, better known as FUEGO [fire]. Under FUEGO's banner, students carried out demonstrations and strikes against the government. The teachers' movement and the hospital workers had FUEGO as their steady ally. . . . On March 1, 1962, many high school students joined with the university students to place a funeral wreath on the door of the Congress to protest electoral fraud and to symbolize democracy's death. And this act started the famous Weeks of March and April, which at their height had the character of a popular urban uprising to such a degree that Zone 5 was declared "liberated territory."

It was extremely impressive to see [students from] institutions such as INCA and Belén [specialized public schools] organize to paralyze traffic by laying their bodies across the streets by the hundreds; and to see men, women, and adolescents, everyone, improvising speeches in the streets and the markets, and learning in a few hours how to make a Molotov cocktail and the most flexible forms of organization in the midst of brutal repression. All this was an unforgettable school.

During these beautiful days . . . unionized workers, housewives, citizens of all ages left their marks in the Weeks of March and April. It is fair to say that for Guatemalan students the weeks of March and April 1962 anticipated the global student movement: 1968. Guatemala's March–April generation vitalized and theorized antiauthoritarianism long before others did elsewhere, and long before students in other countries mobilized. But that belongs to another history.

In our case, the [subsequent] militarization of the schools destroyed self-government. . . . Because of the closure of democratic spaces and the militarization of the country, many student leaders of these glorious weeks decided, in the most natural way, to join the guerrilla movement. . . . Because of these movements, such as those of March and April 1960, it can be said that the armed struggle in Guatemala had its base in the democratic struggles of that era, one of which was the student movement. To say that

President Miguel Ydígoras Fuentes and citizen, ca. 1960. Anonymous photographer. From the collections of the Centro de Investigaciones Regionales de Mesoamérica, Guatemala.

Student demonstrations, July 1960. Anonymous photographer from *El Imparcial* newspaper. From the collections of the Centro de Investigaciones Regionales de Mesoamérica, Guatemala.

[the armed struggle] had its origins solely in the uprising of the military officials on November 13 is to simplify and overlook the social quality of the
times, which without doubt had a profound effect on the military uprising.

Ballad of the Patriotic Young Women of the 1960s!
by María del Rosario Ramírez

Young students filled the salon. In their official white blouses, the young
women listened with great emotion to the speakers. Attentive and friendly,
young men stood shoulder to shoulder with the young women, sharing
opinions, speaking out, proposing ideas and acting upon them. All were
there as delegates of the different high schools to the most authoritative
high school organization: FUEGO.

It was a rainy afternoon. In this meeting at the Instituto para Señoritas
Belén [a prestigious women's public teacher training school], the delegates
met to debate the advantages and disadvantages of going on strike to support the schoolteachers, who were fighting against a wage freeze that had
been in effect since the North American invasion that left the teachers with
miserable wages and no protections. . . .

This was an era in which passionate Guatemalan youth, like those elsewhere in Latin America, organized and fought for a better tomorrow. The
triumph of the Cuban revolution inspired their conversations in cafes,
schools, workplaces, family gatherings. They wanted to contribute to the
consolidation of the Cuban revolution, and they built their organizations
side by side with those of workers and peasants. This helped distance them
from the limitations and demands of their petty bourgeois origins.

A flow of information came from Cuba, and we read and immediately
debated a huge number of books. There was intense social activity: roundtables, seminars about the national situation, speech contests with social
and political themes, a steady round of plastic arts, theater, music, student
newspapers, sports, fashion shows, and so many parties. Our homework
was dancing, and we danced not only to marimba but to the rock-and-roll
that filled the air. . . .

One day, looking in a drawer [at the high school], I found one of the letters that the PGT [Partido Guatemalteco del Trabajo, the Communist Party]
sent parents asking their permission for their children to join the Juventud
Comunista [the Communist youth group]. . . . [After I approached one of
the students named in the letters], she explained to me how difficult and
dangerous it was to be a member of the Juventud, but I insisted and she
brought me many documents. I read them, memorized them . . . and at-

tended my first meeting of the Juventud Comunista. Everyone was in it. I talked to my parents, who treated it as if I were joining the Girl Scouts or learning guitar. . . .

This generation of high school students had exceptional teachers, who—despite the objectives of North American advisors [the United States tried to design the public school curriculum following the coup] to give us what Paulo Freire called a "banking" education [merely depositing facts in students' brains]—taught the school program in a very different way.

Translated by Deborah T. Levenson

Denied in Full

Central Intelligence Agency

In 1963, the United States supported a second coup in Guatemala, staged to prevent the popular Juan José Arévalo from returning to the country and running for reelection. This intervention, like the 1954 one before it, only worsened the crisis. So the United States began to search for a more effective counterinsurgency response. In December 1965, Washington sent John Longan—a shadowy operator who worked many of the Cold War hot spots, from Thailand to the Dominican Republic—to Guatemala City with a mission to create a small "action unit to mastermind campaign against terrorists which would have access to all information from law enforcement agencies." Longan's goal was to centralize the operations of the police and military, training them to gather, analyze, and act on intelligence in a coordinated and rapid manner. Longan called his project "Operación Limpieza"— Operation Clean-up—and picked the notoriously ruthless military colonel Rafael Arriaga Bosque to run it.

Equipped with the most advanced telecommunications and surveillance equipment available and operating out of military headquarters, Arriaga began to carry out widespread raids. By January 1966, the American embassy was pleased with the results. "Arriaga appears to be doing a relatively good job," said one report. By the end of February, eighty operations—and a number of extrajudicial executions— had taken place. Then, between March 3 and March 5, Operación Limpieza netted its largest catch: over thirty leftists captured, interrogated, tortured, and executed, with their bodies placed in sacks and dropped into the Pacific from US-supplied helicopters. Some of their remains washed back to shore. Despite pleas from Guatemala's archbishop and more than five hundred petitions of habeas corpus filed by relatives, the government and the American embassy remained silent about the fate of the executed.

The executions took place in the three days immediately prior to presidential elections won by the civilian Julio César Méndez Montenegro, who was running as a reformer with much grass-roots support, particularly in the countryside. Among those eliminated were former Arbenz advisors, including Víctor Manuel Gutiérrez, who had been head of the labor confederation during the October Revolution,

Declassifying means never forgetting. Photo by Mauro Calanchina.
Used by permission of Ximena Morales, Prohibido Olvidar.

and Leonardo Castillo Flores, who under Arbenz was president of the peasant confederation. The execution of these arbencistas, along with other reformers, ensured that there could be no negotiated settlement to the still embryonic civil war, nor could the left return to the electoral arena. Whatever small compromise-seeking center had survived the 1954 and 1963 coups had been spectacularly eliminated, confirming the militant stance of a younger, Cuban-influenced generation of revolutionaries. The CIA itself admitted as much. After the murders, the agency wrote, an "intolerable status quo," combined with the "efficiency" of the US-created security forces, drove "usually moderate groups to violence." For his part, Méndez Montenegro, who did win the election with a large popular mandate to end the war and pursue social reforms, took Operación Limpieza's lesson to heart. The president-elect immediately signed a "secret pact" with the military, in which he agreed not to negotiate with the rebels and to pick Arriaga Bosque as his defense minister. In exchange, the army said it would allow him to be inaugurated. The pact invested awesome power in Arriaga Bosque—described by the American embassy as one of Guatemala's "most effective and enlightened leaders"—who, in 1968, would kill eight thousand civilians to defeat a few hundred guerrillas.

Operación Limpieza can be considered Latin America's first large-scale Cold War collective disappearance, previewing the application of similar tactics in Argentina, Chile, El Salvador, and elsewhere. In Guatemala, it strengthened an intelligence system that, through the course of the civil war, would be responsible for tens of thousands of disappearances, two hundred thousand deaths, and countless tortures. The complicity of the United States in this crime—along with its embassy's knowledge of the fate of the victims, despite denial of such knowledge at the time—is well documented in a series of declassified government documents, such as the heavily redacted one that follows.

PAGES 1 & 2

DENIED IN FULL

DOCUMENT DATED MARCH 1966

(b)(1)
(b)(3)
S

CIA
APPROVED FOR RELEASE
DATE FEB 1998

65-1

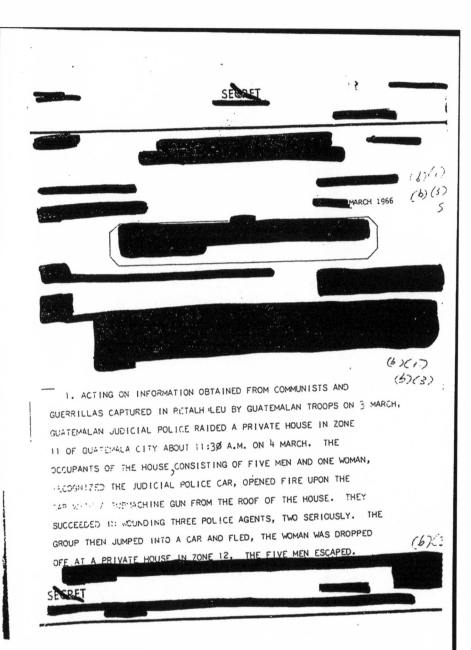

MARCH 1966

(b)(1)
(b)(3)
S

(b)(1)
(b)(3)

1. ACTING ON INFORMATION OBTAINED FROM COMMUNISTS AND GUERRILLAS CAPTURED IN PETALH ILEU BY GUATEMALAN TROOPS ON 3 MARCH, GUATEMALAN JUDICIAL POLICE RAIDED A PRIVATE HOUSE IN ZONE 11 OF GUATEMALA CITY ABOUT 11:30 A.M. ON 4 MARCH. THE OCCUPANTS OF THE HOUSE, CONSISTING OF FIVE MEN AND ONE WOMAN, RECOGNIZED THE JUDICIAL POLICE CAR, OPENED FIRE UPON THE CAR WITH A SUBMACHINE GUN FROM THE ROOF OF THE HOUSE. THEY SUCCEEDED IN WOUNDING THREE POLICE AGENTS, TWO SERIOUSLY. THE GROUP THEN JUMPED INTO A CAR AND FLED, THE WOMAN WAS DROPPED OFF AT A PRIVATE HOUSE IN ZONE 12. THE FIVE MEN ESCAPED.

(b)(3)

JUDICIAL POLICE LEARNED WHERE THE WOMAN HAD BEEN DROPPED OFF,
AND RAIDED THE HOUSE IN ZONE 12 AROUND NOON. POLICE ARRESTED
THE WOMAN AND VICTOR MANUEL GUTIERREZ GARBIN, LEADER OF THE
PARTIDO GUATEMALTECO DEL TRABAJO (PGT-GUATEMALAN COMMUNIST PARTY)
GROUP LIVING IN EXILE IN MEXICO).

    2. ▓▓▓▓▓COMMENT: GUTIERREZ HAD COME TO GUATEMALA IN
LATE FEBRUARY TO ATTEND THE NATIONAL CONFERENCE OF THE PGT. .
▓▓▓▓▓▓▓▓▓▓▓▓▓▓▓▓▓▓▓▓▓▓▓▓THE ARREST OF COMMUNISTS AND
GUERRILLAS, INCLUDING LEONARDO CASTILLO FOLORES, IN RETALHULEU
ON 3 - 4 MARCH WAS REPORTED IN ▓▓▓▓▓▓▓▓▓▓▓▓▓▓▓▓▓   (6)(1)
                                        (6)(3)
    3. ▓▓▓▓▓COMMENT: ARRESTS OF IMPORTANT COMMUNISTS, FAR
AND 13 NOV MOVEMENT MEMBERS SUCH AS GUTIERREZ, LEONARDO CASELLO   S
FLORES AND FRANCISCO JIADO GRANDOS ▓▓▓▓▓▓▓▓▓▓▓▓▓,
OF 3 MARCH) WILL UNDOUBTEDLY HAMPER GUERRILLA TERRORIST PLANS
FOR ACTION WHICH WERE SCHEDULED TO FOLLOW THE ELECTION. IT IS ALSO
POSSIBLE THAT THEY WILL BE TEMPTED TO ADVANCE THEIR TIMING FOR
SUCH ACTION IN VIEW OF STRONG LAST-MINUTE POLICE ACTION AGAINST
THEM BEFORE THE ELECTIONS.)

    4. ▓▓▓▓▓▓▓▓▓▓▓▓▓▓▓▓▓▓▓▓▓   (6)(3)

SECRET

Maybe, Just Maybe

René Leiva

Over the course of nearly three decades following Operation Clean-up (see previous selection), Guatemalan security forces "disappeared" an estimated forty thousand people, equivalent to one-third of all forced disappearances experienced in Latin America during this period. Like other Latin Americans, when Guatemalans use the word "disappear" as a verb, they do so in a way considered grammatically incorrect: in the transitive form and often in the passive voice, as in "she was disappeared." The implication of an absent actor/subject signaled that everybody knew the government was responsible, and it invested the government with unspeakable, omnipotent power. Disappeared people could be held in secret prisons for days, weeks, or months before being killed, with their bodies never recovered. For family members of the disappeared, the psychological torment was excruciating. If a body was not found, even if years went by, relatives could keep wondering if maybe, just maybe, the person was still alive. This poem, written by René Leiva, expresses the fantasy that a friend has escaped and is living his life somewhere in the world.

To Jaime Barrios Carrillo

> Maybe he's wandering through Tokyo, Quebec, or Machu Picchu
> treading the same earth
> drinking a glass of water, lemonade or wine
> but always caught in a dream.
>
> Maybe he's crossing a desert
> or a steel bridge
> or he's at the helm of an accursed whaling ship.
>
> Maybe he's sporting dark glasses
> conforming to the compass of birds
> or taking an uncertain route.

Maybe he's scratching a prison wall
or caressing a street child
or darning the pockets of his pants.

Maybe he's absorbed by an El Greco painting
or stuck in an elevator
or drinking beer in a brothel.

Maybe he's hacking down a door in a fire
or counting foreign coins on a corner
or making faces at a department store mannequin.

Maybe he's recovering from a wound
or waiting for a bus in the rain
or resting in the shade of a cypress.

Maybe he's feeding some pigeons
or tracing silhouettes in the snow
or applauding "Waiting for Godot" in a tiny theater.

Maybe he's standing at an unknown tomb
or looking sidelong into a mirror
or running after a black cat.

Maybe he's waiting for a shoe repair
or teaching a parrot to speak Guatemalan
or resetting his watch at sunset.

Maybe he's counting floor tiles in a courtyard
or jerking off on a toilet
or returning a girl's smile.

Maybe he's washing dishes in a five-star restaurant
or flying a kite on a cliff
or hurling insults with a glance.

Maybe he's speaking in signs with an obese woman
or suppressing a cough in a hospital waiting room
or tossing a ball back to some kids.

Maybe he's scaling the wall of a mansion
or exploring the library stacks
or sweating between a woman's thighs.

Maybe he's swimming toward an islet
or leaving a temple in ruins
or escaping his own execution.

Maybe he's blowing out candles on someone else's cake
or proffering forgiveness behind an opaque curtain
or closing the eyes of a corpse.

Maybe he's writing a letter
or mimicking the way a bird walks
or hearing voices.

Maybe he's bargaining for a trinket
or getting involved in a conspiracy
or vomiting bad fish.

Maybe he's buying stamps for an absurd postcard
or walking up a hill with sweets in his pockets
or planting a lemon tree in a garden.

Maybe he's knocking at an abandoned door
or whispering an Oscar Palencia poem
or following the vicissitudes of a game.

Maybe he's marking up a wall with nonsense
or succumbing to a temptation
or closing his lips against a transparent outcry.

Maybe he's borrowing money at such-and-such interest
or blowing soap bubbles in the market
or pretending to be related to the local rich guy.

Maybe he's posing for a street painter
or crying alone in a train station
or stepping out naked on a balcony with flowerpots.

Maybe he's reading in the paper that the world has died a bit
or recounting made-up adventures to an old man
or conjuring a fanciful face.

Maybe he believes deeply
or is completely deluded
or smiles at his solitude.

Maybe . . .

Translated by Elizabeth Oglesby

Acaso, tal vez

a Jaime Barrios Carrillo

Acaso vaga por Tokio, Quebec o Machu Pichu
pisando la misma tierra
bebiendo un vaso de agua, limonada o vino
pero siempre metido en un sueño.

Tal vez atraviesa un desierto
o cruza un puente de acero
o cabecea en un maldito buque ballenero.

Acaso contrata unos anteojos oscuros
o acata el consejo de las aves
o indetermina una cantidad de pasos.

Tal vez araña la pared de una prision
o acaricia un niño callejero
o zurce los bolsillos de su pantalón.

Acaso está absorto ante un cuadro de El Greco
o metido en un atestado elevador
o bebe cerveza en un burdel.

Tal vez rompe a hachazos la puerta en un incendio
o cuenta monedas extrañas en una esquina
o hace muecas al maniquí de un almacen.

Acaso se cura de alguna herida
o espera un autobús bajo la lluvia
o descansa a la sombra de un ciprés.

Tal vez alimenta a unas palomas
o traza siluetas en la nieve
o aplaude el "Esperando a Godot" en un teatrillo.

Acaso está ante una tumba cualquiera
o mira de reojo en un espejo
o corre persiguiendo a un gato negro.

Tal vez espera a que claven su zapato
o enseña guatemalteco a un loro
o compara su reloj en el ocaso.

Acaso cuenta las baldosas de una plazoleta
o puja lo infinito en un retrete
o devuelve la sonrisa a una muchacha.

Tal vez lava platos en un restorán de lujo
o vuela barrilete a la orilla de un barranco
o remite un insulto con la mirada.

Acaso habla por señas con una señora obesa
o guarda su tos muy quedo en la sala de un hospital
o devuelve la pelota a un grupo de niños.

Tal vez escala el muro de una mansión
o recorre los anaqueles de una biblioteca
o suda entre los muslos de una mujer.

Acaso nada en dirección a un islote
o abandona un templo en ruinas
o escapa a su fusilamiento.

Tal vez apaga las velas de un pastel ajeno
o perdona tras una cortina templada
o cierra los ojos de un muerto.

Acaso escribe una carta
o remeda el caminar de un pájaro
o escucha las voces sin dueño.

Tal vez regatea una baratija
o trama con otros una red de espejos
o vomita un pescado descompuesto.

Acaso compra sellos para una postal absurda
o sube una cuesta con dulces en los bolsillos
o planta en un jardín un limonero.

Tal vez llama a la puerta donde nadie
o susurra un poema de Oscar Palencia
o sigue las peripecias de un juego.

Acaso mancha una pared con esperpentos
o cede a una tentación-límite
o cierra sus labios a un grito transparente.

"Abandon all hope, ye who enter here." Installation artist Daniel Hernández-Salazar projected images of disappeared Coca-Cola union activists onto Guatemala's Congress building to denounce those elected to Congress who are responsible for human rights violations committed during the civil war in Guatemala. From the series *Fiat lux*. Photo by Daniel Hernández-Salazar. Used by permission of the photographer.

Tal vez pide dinero al tanto por ciento
o hace pompas de jabón en un mercado
o finge parentesco con el residente ricachón.

Acaso posa para un pintor callejero
o llora en un andén desierto
o sale desnudo a un balcón con maceteros.

Tal vez lee en un diario que el mundo ha muerto un poco
o narra a un viejo aventuras de nunca
o persigue un rostro que nunca tampoco.

Acaso cree hacia su profundidad
o delira por su plenitud
o sonríe a su soledad.

Tal vez . . .

Guatemala and Vietnam

James S. Corum

In May 1954, as final preparation for the CIA coup against Jacobo Arbenz was tak-
ing shape, Vietnamese liberation forces decisively beat French troops at the battle
of Dien Bien Phu, which opened the door for increased US involvement in Vietnam.
In the ensuing years, Southeast Asia and Latin America became the two primary
campuses for US counterinsurgents. Military and police advisors traveled back and
forth between the two regions, applying insights and fine-tuning tactics. In South-
east Asia, the United States progressively committed itself to directly fighting a crip-
pling, discrediting war. In Latin America, however, the United States stuck to its
strategy of working through proxy security forces. In Guatemala, in addition to the
fortification of the intelligence system described earlier in this volume, US military
advisors, including the Green Berets, worked closely with Guatemalan troops in
their attempt to root out rebels who had been operating in the Sierra de las Minas
mountain range in the eastern part of the country. The following essay by James
Corum, a scholar of military history who teaches at the US Air Force's School of
Advanced Airpower, located at Alabama's Maxwell Air Force Base, discusses the
role Washington played in training and providing equipment to Guatemala's air
force. As Corum writes, the Guatemalan pilots "demolished villages" believed to be
supporting the rebels, using bombs and napalm. Eight thousand people were killed
in a war against a few hundred rebels.

In the 1960s, the small guerrilla war in Guatemala caught the attention of
the US government, which poured considerable military aid into Guatemala
to support the rightist government. Guatemala became the focus of the
US military counterinsurgency operations in Central America in the 1960s.
Hundreds of US Special Forces soldiers were brought into the country to
train and advise the army. By the mid-1960s Guatemala's small armed forces
had been retrained as a light infantry, counterinsurgency force. The Guatemalan Air Force (Fuerza Aérea de Guatemala—FAG) was also trained and
organized to fight a counterinsurgency war. . . .

In the early 1960s, Guatemala had a small air force of a few hundred men
and a few dozen aircraft composed of World War II surplus trainers, P-51

Mustang fighters, B-26 bombers and some C-47 transports—pretty much the usual force for Central America in those days. . . . When the insurgency began in 1963, the air force supported the army with its P-51s and B-26s. At the same time, the US supplied four T-33 jet trainers as part of a comprehensive modernization program for the FAG. The P-51s of the FAG were rapidly wearing out and parts were scarce. They had become a maintenance nightmare for the air force. On the other hand, the T-33s, which were based on the F-80 fighter that had seen action as a fighter-bomber in the Korean War, were seen by the USAF as a suitable aircraft for a low-level insurgency. So, by late 1963 the new T-33s were put into service as attack aircraft. At this stage of the war, the T-33 pilots were not trained as attack pilots and had to basically learn to conduct rocket, bomb and strafing attacks literally "on the job." At the outset of the rebellion, against the advice of American advisors, the FAG acquired two more P-51s from an American dealer to serve as fighter-bombers. Despite the maintenance problems, the old propeller fighters were still excellent aircraft for counterinsurgency as they were able to carry a lot of ordnance and to loiter over a battle area for a long time. . . . In 1964, the FAG received two more T-33s from the US military aid program.

By 1965, the insurgency had expanded and now covered several departments. The US delivered another pair of T-33s as well as four armed Sikorsky UH-19B helicopters, the first military helicopters in Central America. This provided the Guatemalan forces with an air assault capability. The Sikorskys were soon equipped with two .30-caliber machine guns and two 2.7-inch rocket pods for gunship support. By 1966, a rearmed and now well-trained Guatemalan Army was ready to undertake major operations against the insurgents. Under the guidance of US advisors, the FAG reorganized its combat aircraft into a "Special Warfare Composite Squadrons" composed of 2–3 Mustangs, 1–2 T-33s, a B-26, a UH-19B and a pair of C-47 transports with their own contingent of pilots and ground crews. The Guatemalan Air Force, with considerable US assistance, initiated a large-scale bombing campaign against rebel-held areas in addition to supporting the army ground operations.

In 1967 the FAG acquired five Bell UH-1B and UH-1D helicopters from the US to reinforce its helicopter force. By this time the Guatemalan armed forces were a pretty formidable force. From 1966 to 1968 the greatly enlarged army and police forces conducted an all-out offensive against the few hundred rebels based primarily in the northeast. In addition to going after the rebels, the army attacked the rebel infrastructure and demolished villages providing support. Aerial bombing was common and napalm was used. By 1968, the rebellion had been largely stamped out at the cost of an estimated 8,000 rebels and civilians killed.

Second Thoughts

Viron Vaky

*Of the thousands of documents declassified by the US government related to its Gua-
temala policy during the Cold War, only one displays regret or doubt. In March
1968, Viron Vaky, deputy mission chief in the US embassy in Guatemala, wrote to
the secretary of state for inter-American affairs to share his thoughts about why he
thought the policy of "counter-terror" was morally and tactically wrong. "Counter-
terror" is a hard concept to define, Vaky admitted in the selection below, because
it closely mirrors the "terror" it seeks to eliminate. In the case of Guatemala, as
elsewhere, "counter-terrorism" was essentially a euphemism for the use of death
squads, torture, and disappearances in order to extract intelligence and establish
control over a targeted population through fear.*

Department of State
Policy Planning Council
Washington
~~Secret~~
UNCLASSIFIED
March 29, 1968

MEMORANDUM

To: ARA—Mr. Oliver
From: S/P—Mr. Vaky
Subject: *Guatemala and Counter-terror*

GUATEMALA AND COUNTER-TERROR

The Guatemalan Government's use of "counter-terror" to insurgency is a
serious problem in three ways:

a) The tactics are having a terribly corrosive effect on Guatemalan
society and the nation's political development;

b) they present a serious problem for the US in terms of our image in Latin America and the credibility of what we say we stand for;

c) the problem has a corrosive effect on our own judgments and conceptual values.

A. Impact on the Country.

Counter-terror is corrosive from three points of view:

1. *The counter-terror is indiscriminate,* and we cannot rationalize that fact away. Looking back on its full sweep one can cite instances in which leftist but anti-Communist labor leaders were kidnapped and beaten by the army units; the para-military groups armed by the Zacapa commander have operated in parts of the northeast in war-lord fashion and destroyed local PR [Partido Revolucionario] organizations; people are killed or disappear on the basis of simple accusations. It is argued that the "excesses" of the earlier period have been corrected and now only "collaborators" are being killed. But I question the wisdom or validity of the Guatemalan army's criteria as to who is a collaborator or how carefully they check. Moreover, the derivative violence of right-wing vigilantes and sheer criminality made possible by the atmosphere must also be laid at the door of the conceptual tactic of counter-terror. The point is that the society is being rent apart and polarized; emotions, desire for revenge and personal bitterness are being sucked in; the pure Communist issue is thus blurred; and issues of poverty and social injustice are being converted into virulent questions of outraged emotion and "tyranny." The whole cumulative impact is most unhealthy.

It is not true, in my judgment, that Guatemalans are apathetic or are not upset about the problem. Guatemalans very typically mask their feeling with outward passivity, but that does not mean they do not feel things. Guatemalans have told me they are worried, that the situation is serious and nastier than it has ever been. And I submit that we really do not know what the *campesinos* truly feel.

2. *Counter-terror is brutal.* The official squads are guilty of atrocities. Interrogations are brutal, torture is used and bodies are mutilated. Many believe that the very brutal way the ex-beauty queen was killed, obviously tortured and mutilated, provoked the FAR to murder Colonel Webber in retaliation. If true, how tragic that the tactics of "our side" would in any way be responsible for that event! But the point is that this is a serious practical political problem as well as a moral one: Because of the evidence of this brutality, the government is, in the eyes of many Guatemalans, a cruel government,

and therefore righteous outrage, emotion and viciousness have been sucked into the whole political situation. . . .

3. *Counter-terror has retarded modernization and institution building.* The tactics have just deepened and continued the proclivity of Guatemalans to operate outside the law. It says in effect to people that the law, the constitution, the institutions mean nothing, the fastest gun counts. The whole system has been degraded as a way to mobilize society and handle problems.
. . .

B. The Image Problem

We are associated with this tactic in the minds of many people, and whether it is right or wrong so to associate us is rapidly becoming irrelevant. In politics just as important as the way things are is the way people *think* things are. In the minds of many in Latin America, and, tragically, especially in the sensitive, articulate youth, we are believed to have condoned these tactics, if not actually to have encouraged them. Therefore our image is being tarnished and the credibility of our claims to want a better and more just world are increasingly placed in doubt. I need hardly add the aspect of domestic US reactions.

C. US Values

This leads to an aspect I personally find the most disturbing of all—that we have not been honest with ourselves. We *have* condoned counter-terror; we may even in effect have encouraged or blessed it. We have been so obsessed with the fear of insurgency that we have even rationalized away our qualms and uneasiness. This is not only because we have concluded we cannot do anything about it, for we never really tried. Rather we suspected that maybe it is a good tactic, and that as long as Communists are being killed it is alright. Murder, torture and mutilation are alright if our side is doing it and the victims are Communists. After all hasn't man been a savage from the beginning of time so let us not be too queasy about terror. I have literally heard these arguments from our people.

Have our values been so twisted by our adversary concept of politics in the hemisphere? Is. it conceivable that we are so obsessed with insurgency that we are prepared to rationalize murder as an acceptable counter-insurgency weapon? Is it possible that a nation which so reveres the principle of due process of law has so easily acquiesced in this sort of terror tactic? . . .

Counter-terror is, in short, very wrong—morally, ethically, politically from the standpoint of Guatemala's own interest and practically from our own foreign policy point of view.

D. What to Do?

. . . Most importantly, we should put our thinking caps on and devise policies, aid and suggestions that can make counter-terror unnecessary. It is argued that if we can remonstrate strongly to the Guatemalans, they will say we encouraged them to go ahead and now what do we suggest?

It is a good question, and we should ask ourselves that. If counter-terror is justified by Guatemalans in terms of the weakness of the legal system, is there nothing we can do to help and prod them on legal reforms? Is there nothing we can do to make them stop the brutality of torture and mutilation? Is there nothing we can do to help them develop philosophical concepts of institutions and a legal system? I know that primitive violence has gone on a long time in Guatemala and elsewhere. Do we just throw up our hands and accept all of its wrongness as long as it is also "effective" (and will history's verdict say it was "effective" in Guatemala)?

The Sweetest Songs Remain to Be Sung

Huberto Alvarado Arellano

Huberto Alvarado Arellano was seventeen years old in 1944 when he joined in the uprising led by students, middle-class professionals, and urban workers that overthrew Ubico's dictatorship. As part of a young generation of cultural and political modernists, Alvarado helped found the Partido Guatemalteco del Trabajo (Guatemalan Communist Party) and the cultural circle Saker-Ti. In 1954, after Arbenz fell and Guatemala's "civilized decade" (as Alvarado described the period) came to an end, he fled to Mexico, along with thousands of others. Many of the exiles looked to Marxist critiques of imperialism to make sense of their recent experience. Alvarado turned to Walt Whitman's Leaves of Grass.

In an essay published in Ecuador in 1955, an excerpt of which is provided here, Alvarado applauded Whitman's commitment to "democratic and progressive ideas," even as he condemned Washington's "empire of intimidation." He cautioned against letting the Cold War and the nuclear arms race generate too much pessimism: "During this shadowy and shining moment, when there are new roads to destruction and death, there is also a bright horizon; it is imperative that we go back to lessons provided by the great North American poet and remember his prediction that the 'sweetest songs remain yet to be sung.'" Alvarado's embrace of Whitman at such a low moment was not a flight into romanticism, and the 1954 coup did not diminish the Guatemalan refugee's concern for the political world. Alvarado deepened his commitment to politics, becoming general secretary of the party in exile. In turning to Leaves of Grass *to make sense of the coup, Alvarado followed earlier writers who, ever since the Cuban revolutionary José Martí introduced Whitman to Latin American readers in 1887, had invoked the poet to highlight Washington's hypocrisy and to rhetorically temper its aggression. For Alvarado, Whitman was a model for Latin America's intellectuals: as the "bard of a developing country" (nineteenth-century United States), Whitman's modernism embraced the vitality and inherently democratic and revolutionary potential of national popular cultures.*

In 1971, Alvarado returned to Guatemala and was murdered there by US-*trained security forces.*

In 1855, a North American poet wondered about the future of his work, and said: "At least a hundred years must pass before it can be definitively assessed." In reality, it took less time for the work of this questioning poet, Walt Whitman, to be recognized as the highest order of poetic inheritance.

The poet of the long walks, the builder of houses, the editor of newspapers, the teacher of children, the volunteer battlefield nurse, the paralyzed man dependent upon his wheelchair for some nineteen years, the poet with the long white beard—he is not only the first poet of the United States, but also the North American poet most representative of the aspirations and yearnings of his people. Much water has run under the bridge since then. . . . But the voice of Old Walt—the songbird of man, of nature, of machines, of life—rings true today as strongly as it did when the Puritan Yankee society of his age viciously attacked him and criticized his *Leaves of Grass*. . . . Today, facing hope and fear, confronting an empire of intimidation and the unavoidable necessity of living, the prophetic words, battle poetry, and warm, human verse of Whitman are an affirmation of humanity's glorious destinies. If any poet ever believed in man with an absolute certainty, it was Whitman. . . .

Walt Whitman's great lesson, his permanent message to our people, is enacted in the love of country, of liberty, of democracy, of progress, of man, and of life. . . .

National Poet

The economic development of the United States, the birth of a capitalist nation in search of its political and economic independence, seeking its own cultural identity, found in Walt Whitman one of its greatest defenders. . . . Whitman knew . . . perfectly well that all great poets, in order to be universal, needed to be national. In order to be universal, it is said, Dulcinea comes from somewhere, from Toboso or wherever one likes; she has an origin, she hails from a homeland. The importance and tradition of the national, for Whitman, was of the highest order; at the end of the preface of *Leaves of Grass*, he repeats the warning that "Herder taught the young Goethe that truly great poetry is always, like Homeric or Biblical tales, the result of a national spirit, which is not the privilege of a refined and select minority." . . .

Whitman had an immense love for North American man—and for man everywhere. His voice was deeply patriotic, and as such, it was also deeply worldly. He did not favor the well-being of the United States at the cost of the rest of the world's misery and oppression; he declared himself incapable of "desiring the prosperity of America at the expense of other nations." For Whitman, man was as "divine" in his own country as he was in any other of the world's regions. He was not, and never had been, a strict nationalist, with a parochial, chauvinistic vision. No, never. His voice was universal, it was the voice of one man and all men. In his poems "Salut au Monde," "Song of the Axe," and others, he sings glorious hymns to human solidarity, especially in the first poem, where he summons all beings of the earth, all the dwellers of every country, into a circle of friendship, democracy, and progress. His mass summons calls out to:

You whoever you are!
You daughter or son of England!
You of the mighty Slavic tribes and empires! You Russ in Russia!
You dim-descended, black, divine-soul'd African, large, fine-headed,
    nobly-form'd, superbly destin'd, on equal terms with me!
You Norwegian! Swede! Dane! Icelander! you Prussian!
You Spaniard of Spain! You Portuguese! . . .
You beautiful-bodied Persian at full speed in the saddle shooting
    arrows to the mark!
You Chinaman and Chinawoman of China! you Tartar of Tartary!
You women of the earth subordinated at your tasks!
You Jew journeying in your old age through every risk to stand once
    on Syrian ground!
You other Jews waiting in all lands for your Messiah!
You thoughtful Armenian pondering by some stream of the Euphrates!
    . . . .
All you continentals of Asia, Africa, Europe, Australia, indifferent of
    place!
All you on the numberless islands of the archipelagoes of the sea!
And you of centuries hence when you listen to me!
And you each and everywhere whom I specify not, but include just the
    same!
Health to you! good will to you all, from me and America sent!
Each of us inevitable,
Each of us limitless—each of us with his or her right upon the earth,
Each of us allow'd the eternal purports of the earth,
Each of us here as divinely as any is here.

Democratic Poet

Walt Whitman is a democratic poet because his ideas were fundamentally democratic and revolutionary, and he expressed those ideas so well, writing about the life of the people and the common man in order to be understood by this man of the street; he labored in order that his poetry might help human beings to live, might bring them a message of optimism, confidence, and hope. . . . The ideas of democracy, liberty, progress, and peace leap forth at every moment from the work of this North American poet. . . . He calls upon the people to not "submit themselves to the churches, old or new, Catholic or Protestant, not to this or that Saint. . . . From here onward, each must submit himself to Democracy, en masse."

This is why he urges poets to be the interpreters "before the Modern, before Democracy."

Whitman, as the bard of a developing country, in the flowering epoch of capitalism's growth in the United States, has a deep faith in the people's progress. "It is not possible to escape from the laws of progress and transformation," he will tell us. A step forward, which yesterday moved toward capitalism, today indubitably moves us along other paths of history. . . . But progress, for Whitman, had to directly bestow benefits upon man and upon all men—for the inter-American, incalculable, modern, bustling multitudes who surround us, and of whom we are an indivisible part.

Whitman is a deeply pacifistic poet. During the us Civil War, he served as a volunteer nurse. His poems about the conflict are inspired by man himself, in the human act performed in the midst of conflict, in the exaltation of humanity's virtues in the fact of the hardest test. In several of these poems, he grieves the death of the young soldiers, so much destruction and killing. . . . "The poet of the multitudes" writes for these multitudes. . . .

Realist Poet

In his poetry, Whitman tried to express the life of his age, drawing his inspiration from the men of his time. He worked to capture the ever-changing aspects of human existence; he was inspired by reality, by daily events, by the common man of his country. . . .

The "Song of Myself" must today become a "song of ourselves," a song to all the workers of the world. "Without yielding an inch," Whitman declares, "the man who works and the woman who works must be in my pages, from the first to the last." Singing to these men, to these women, and to this land and everything in it, "to this permanent miracle that is every day of light and darkness" . . . to submerge himself in the law of the "living." . . . A country on the march is a country at work. In capitalism's flowering, in its rise, it strives to multiply work and therefore to multiply exploitation. Whitman, however, always condemned exploitation. . . . The work of Whitman's songs is the work of man's creator, work that produces material benefits for all men, work that produces wealth for all.

And what of culture and national art? Like national sovereignty and the self-determination of peoples, these are concepts that have gone "out of style," protest those people who do not feel the life of their nations. Some say that with the dawning of the atomic age, it is no longer possible to speak of culture and national art. But universal culture is composed precisely of national cultures.

To be universal, one must come from somewhere. There is no human being without a mother. There is no human being without a homeland. Hailing from a country and from an epoch, art—one of humanity's highest creations—acquires its true meaning when it expresses the realities of that country and of the human beings of that epoch. . . . Walt Whitman sang to the men of his time, exalted democratic and progressive ideals, and, in keeping with his era, elevated the role of individualism and wrote for the millions of human beings in his country. Poetry is a torch, León Felipe has said, that poets pass from epoch to epoch, and which moves through the centuries. Walt Whitman carried that torch high, creating an honorable poetry for his time and his people.

Today, in this difficult and brilliant age—when on one hand new perspectives on death and destruction multiply, but on the other hand we see the horizon of a luminous future, when the atomic age can signify life or death, when men face definitive decisions—this is when poets must write of the heights of life and of men, to remember Whitman's lesson and to faithfully follow the great North American poet's prediction: "The strongest and sweetest songs remain to be sung."

Translated by Kirsten Weld

V

Roads to Revolution

Popular movements shook Guatemala between 1960 and the 1980s. The closing of political space following the 1954 coup, the history of racism and cultural oppression, lack of sufficient land, low wages, increases in the cost of living, and state violence were among the reasons why poor and middle-class Guatemalans organized. This took many forms: discussion groups, peasant leagues, indigenous electoral campaigns in local municipalities, community-development programs, cooperatives, unions, marches, fiestas, strikes, uprisings, and occupations. Only in neighboring El Salvador and Nicaragua during the same period, and Peru in the early 1960s, was there such widespread and integrated mobilization in the face of state violence in Latin America during the Cold War. Alliances formed between city and countryside, unions and peasant leagues, coastal plantations and highland communities, indigenous and nonindigenous, secular and religious activists.

Guatemala during this period was both a nominal democracy and a counterinsurgency machine. These two characteristics are central to understanding the rise and decline of the popular movements. Given the formal right to organize, speak, and protest, people did. A series of elected presidents—all but one of them military men—ruled between 1958 and 1963 and again between 1966 and 1982, and so did the death squads and torture chambers. As popular movements moved beyond voicing demands to pushing hard to win them, repression against them increased. Coups were executed in 1963 and 1982 (and serious electoral fraud was committed in 1974), suppressing popular participation until it was safe for "democracy" to return. The exhilarating vision that ordinary poor people could change the course of history in their favor was paired with a conviction that state power could be confronted successfully, whether legally or through other means. For many, politics pervaded life, in part a legacy of the previous October Revolution. Underground activists, many of whom were in the PGT, had survived the 1954 coup and found ways to continue to organize for reform. To this legacy were joined new indigenous mobilizations for cultural and economic rights, transformations within the Catholic Church, and the spread of radical Marxist ideas, all spurred on by rapid economic change.

Substantial industry developed in Guatemala for the first time in the 1960s, encouraged by the new Central American Common Market, which was supposed to create a regional middle-class market for locally made consumer goods. But us companies soon moved into the region, buying out Central American firms or opening their own, undermining the possibility of balanced development. In the countryside, export agriculture expanded, with new cotton, sugar, and coffee plantations opening along the Pacific coast. The effects of this modernization were manifold. In the countryside, the United States Agency for International Development and the Guatemalan government funded infrastructure projects, such as roads, and promoted the widespread use of new seeds and fertilizers. These developments brought new wealth for many smallholders in the highlands, but after the 1973 oil crisis led to a global spike in inflation, many farmers couldn't afford the imported seeds and fertilizers on which they had recently grown dependent. Formerly apolitical purchasing and marketing cooperatives transformed into centers of protest. On the southern coast, cotton, sugar, and cattle plantations grew at the expense of smallholders. Displaced farmers moved to Guatemala City. New, highly mechanized factories operated by Goodyear, Kern's, Max Factor, and General Mills only employed a small percentage of these migrants, paid a disgracefully low wage, and treated workers terribly. On the southern coast, plantations generally relied on seasonal workers from the Maya highlands who were forced into seasonal wage labor because they had lost land for growing subsistence crops to sustain themselves. Migrants who traveled to work on plantations were packed into the backs of cattle trucks to descend to the boiling-hot Pacific lowlands, where they lived for months at a time in open sheds called *galeras*, earning less than a dollar a day. Employers in the city and the countryside furiously fought attempts to improve conditions; workers, in turn, were radicalized by escalating violence, usually committed by death squads organized by the state or financed by employer associations.

At the same time, new forms of politics emerged. Conservative Catholic priests, nuns, and lay religious workers, both Guatemalan and foreign, entered the countryside in the 1950s as part of a campaign to instill religious orthodoxy in indigenous peasant communities. Witnessing poverty firsthand transformed many in the clergy, however, pushing them toward a perspective that throughout Latin America would take the name of Liberation Theology. This current of thought within the Catholic Church emphasized solidarity with the poor, came to see capitalism as "social sin," and worked toward building a just kingdom on earth. This social Christian movement swept across the Guatemalan highlands under various names (e.g., Catholic Action, Christian base communities, Delegates of the Word), and many of its adherents became increasingly critical of existing social relations. Members of Catholic Action in the countryside and Catholic Worker in the city promoted *protagonismo*, an understanding of poor people not as victims but as protagonists who are capable of changing the exploitative conditions of their own lives. Basic Marxist concepts of "class" and "surplus value" became common-sense categories of analysis for many urban workers, who began to esteem Christ as a revolutionary worker. In rural areas, the Church went from being a pillar of the status quo to one of the biggest threats against it.

At the same time, new indigenous organizations focusing on community and cultural identity flourished, especially in the highland areas of Chimaltenango, Quetzaltenango, and El Quiché. Cultural and class-based movements fused together in specific localities during the 1960s and 1970s. Maya-language radio programs, indigenous beauty pageants, reading groups, and a generalized indigenous-pride movement combined with struggles over land, livelihoods, and political rights. By the late 1970s, these myriad currents crystallized into electoral mobilizations that brought indigenous mayors to power in various parts of the highlands, under the banner of the reformist Christian Democrats. This was the most significant challenge to Ladino control over municipal politics since the agrarian committees of the 1950s. Increased poverty and displacement, particularly following a massive earthquake that rocked Guatemala City, Chimaltenango, and southern Quiché in 1976, brought different indigenous and popular groups together to found the Comité de Unidad Campesina, or the Committee of Campesino Unity (CUC). The importance of the CUC to modern Guatemalan history cannot be overstated. Marxism wove in and out of this tapestry of mobilization, providing compelling explanations of the root causes of poverty.

New guerrilla organizations arose out of the ashes of the 1960s defeat. Leaders of the Rebel Armed Forces (FAR) revised their ideas on *foco* theory and rethought the role of the guerrilla vanguard. Radical activists organized two new guerrilla groups—the Revolutionary Organization of the People in Arms (Organización Revolucionaria del Pueblo en Armas, or ORPA) and the Guerrilla Army of the Poor (Ejército Guerrillero de los Pobres, or EGP)—with the goal of correcting the perceived mistakes of the first FAR by combining armed resistance with mass consciousness raising, establishing a strong base of support in the western highlands and the city, and incorporating the indigenous population into their ranks. The EGP grew especially fast by fusing Marxism with radical Christian humanism and grafting its military structures onto community-based networks in Maya areas, especially in El Quiché, Huehuetenango, Chimaltenango, and the Verapaces.

No single explanation exists for why revolutionary sentiment was so widespread by the late 1970s. People traveled different roads that led them to rise up (*alzarse*) and to go to *la montaña* (to join the guerrillas). For some, taking up arms was one step in many long years of organizing and reflecting on Guatemala's social injustices. For others, *alzarse* was a survival mechanism in moments of chaos, political ferment, and terror. The revolutionary organizations influenced the popular movements, but they were not one and the same. Instead, "they were like two rivers," as Yolanda Colom, a founder of the EGP, put it. "Sometimes their currents converged, and sometimes they diverged, but they flowed in the same direction."

By the end of the 1970s, daily life in Guatemala City was a battleground. During the presidency of Romero Lucas García (1978–1982), death squads ran rampant, killing or disappearing an average of two hundred people per week. Bodies piled up in the streets and ravines of the city. Security forces singled out unionists, journalists, university professors, and progressive lawyers for execution. At the national university, hundreds of student activists were murdered. Even anticommunist political reformers were eliminated, including the popular social democrats Alberto Fuentes Mohr and Manuel Colom Argueta, a former mayor of Guatemala City. In the countryside, the massacre of dozens of protesting Q'eqchi' *campesinos* in Panzós in May 1978 sent shock waves through the highlands and was widely interpreted as a declaration of war by the government against Mayas. Violence against catechists, cooperative leaders, and the CUC, as well as the assassination of more than a dozen Maya mayors in the highlands between 1976 and 1980, signaled a closing of political space for peaceful organizing. In many places, rural activism turned revolutionary. A final break occurred on January 31, 1980, when police firebombed indigenous protesters occupying the Spanish embassy in Guatemala City; thirty-six people were killed, including several embassy employees. After the Spanish embassy massacre, Guatemala was in a state of civil war. By 1980, state repression—which wiped out the possibility of open opposition—forced Colom's "two rivers" to overflow their borders, joining in one formidable rush. During this moment of intense crisis and confusion, previously independent movements, such as the CUC, were absorbed into the clandestine structures of the insurgency.

A sense of *triunfalismo* overtook the armed movement and what was left of the civil opposition, fueled by the Sandinista revolution in Nicaragua and revolutionary advances in El Salvador. On both the left and the right, there was a widespread sense that the government was about to fall. "In 1981, the guerrillas were at the doorstep of Guatemala City, they were a day away," a prominent conservative activist recently insisted. Much of rural Guatemala was in open insurrection or on the verge of it, a scenario that masked both the weaknesses of the rebel movements and the lengths the state would go to fight back. In 1981, the Guatemala army regrouped, led by a new cohort of military strategists committed to executing a more precise counterinsurgency plan. First they went on the offensive in the city, destroying the urban guerrilla networks. Then they turned to the countryside, launching a genocidal scorched-earth campaign, the effects and legacies of which will be discussed in part 6.

A Clandestine Life

Greg Grandin

After the 1954 coup, the Guatemalan Communist Party, the Partido Guatemalteco del Trabajo (PGT), regrouped in both the countryside and the city, leading public protest and helping to rebuild a mass popular movement. The costs, though, were high, as many of its most important members were among the first to be disappeared by security forces. In Guatemala City, PGT-affiliated artisans managed to turn a pointedly anticommunist and pro-government Federación Autónoma Sindical de Guatemala, a labor federation established by the United States AFL-CIO, into a politically outspoken organization. Likewise, in the countryside, particularly in the plantation zones of the southern coast and Alta Verapaz, PGT activists helped rebuild a powerful rural union movement. One such activist, Efraín Reyes Maaz, a Maya born in the Q'eqchi' town of Lanquín in 1917, joined the Communist Party while working as a dockworker for United Fruit Company in Puerto Barrios in the early 1950s, and then helped reestablish the PGT in the Polochic Valley in the 1960s and 1970s. Known throughout his organizing life as Tono, Carranza, Marcelino, or simply, in later years, abuelo, grandfather, Reyes died on February 15, 2008, at the age of ninety-two. The below selection from Greg Grandin's Last Colonial Massacre locates his exceptional life within a larger, shared experience of the 1954 coup and its aftermath.

Efraín Reyes Maaz discovered revelation in exile. Born to a peasant family in the Q'eqchi' town of Lanquín in 1917, Reyes worked for the United Fruit Company as a dockworker throughout the October Revolution. "I should have been a *ubiquista*," Reyes says, meaning a peasant supporter of the dictator, but credits his union work, particularly his contacts with Cuban longshoremen who once sent provisions to aid a strike, with pointing him to the PGT. But he joined *"a lo ciego,"* blindly, not knowing what it meant to be a Marxist or a party member. After participating in the defense of Puerto Barrios against Castillo Armas's invaders in 1954, which he can describe with impenetrable detail, Reyes and a dozen other PGT members fled first to Belize, then with the help of a Mexican Communist Party women's support committee to Campeche and finally to Mexico City. Provided with a place to live and a small stipend, the "doubts began" and Reyes asked the PGT's legal advisor to United Fruit's dockworker union, Virgilio Guerra, "*Mire compañero*, what happened?"

Guerra gave Reyes a copy of the PGT's 1955 *Autocrítica*. "I read it, and reread it, and read it again, and suddenly I understood," says Reyes: Arbenz fell because of a "foreign intervention" allied with "Creole anticommunists" and the Catholic Church. But that initial answer pushed him to read more, not only the *Communist Manifesto* and Lenin's *Imperialism* but the Bible as well. Reyes identified with the eschatological vision of the Book of Revelation, written as it was by another persecuted exile similarly trying to find meaning in history. Yet he filled the prophecy with social content, consciously repeating Marx's adaption of Hegel's historicism. Reyes read in the darkness of his own flight Revelation's prediction of the coming of a seven-horned lamb—Christ—who would destroy the Roman Empire and install a just ultramundane kingdom. Conflating a number of the book's images, he interpreted the "seven horns as the seven empires," the last of which is the United States, which "has tried to dominate the world with a dogmatic idealist philosophy." From his studies and experiences, he developed a scorn for idealist obscurantism that he has carried with him throughout his life. He uses the distinction between the two to distance himself from, as he puts it, "ignorant peasants" easily manipulated by the army, the Church, and planters, and he prides himself on a certain scientific skepticism, a capacity to observe and learn. "I'm a bit like Santo Tomás," he says, referring to the doubting apostle, "the first materialist. I only believe what I see."

Marxism in both theory and practice opened up the world to Reyes. "Every revolutionary," he says, "carries around an entire world in his head." He returned to Guatemala in 1957 and began to rebuild the party among displaced United Fruit plantation workers in Santa Lucía Cotzumalguapa on the Pacific coast. Exhausted after three years, he went to Cuba in 1961 to recover and receive some training in guerrilla warfare. He returned at the end of 1962 and, after helping to set up a FAR guerrilla front in the Sierra de las Minas, the PGT placed him in charge of reestablishing contacts with its *arbencista* base in Alta Verapaz. Except for a brief stint in Quetzaltenango in the late 1960s, the Polochic Valley would be Reyes's principal theater of operation for the remainder of his political career. Alternately using the names Carranza, Tono, and Marcelino, he traveled with his mule through the valley's communities and plantations as an itinerant merchant. One Ladino relative of a plantation administrator in Tucurú joined the PGT because of Reyes. "After a day of selling his products," he recalls, "Reyes would return at night and preach about how we were going to make a better world, a new Cuba." "Wherever people were organized," remembers a Q'eqchi' PGT member from Panzós, "they knew Tono." In the 1970s, the PGT through the labor federation, the Federación Autónoma Sindical de Guatemala, or FASGUA, would hold weekend workshops around Cobán and Reyes would bring in small groups of Q'eqchi's to attend and act as the interpreter. An economics professor from the national university who led many of the sessions remembers "talking for two, three minutes and that Carranza would go on for ten." It was Reyes's ability to understand and translate Marxism into a Q'eqchi' cultural vernacular that made him an indispensable organizer. "We used to ask the *ancianos*," remembers Reyes, "what did the Spaniards bring when they came? God, the mirror and the cross in the sky. All idealist symbols. But what did you worship before they came? Water, earth, the sun, and corn, all material factors in the relations of production."

A life lived underground has hardened Reyes's mind. Vivian Gornick has written that the tragedy of Marxism is that in satisfying a passion to live a life with "moral meaning" it inevitably becomes dogma. And there is something of this in Reyes, for as all around him has crumbled, the war lost, the USSR gone, Cuba disenchanted, to lose his Marxism would be to lose, as he himself identifies it, his core being. Yet more than some flaw intrinsic to Marxism, it was this "ideological armour" that protected him throughout decades of clandestine life, surviving capture and torture three times, bearing the murder of countless allies: "Galileo said the world was round," Reyes responds to my question about the costs of dedicating a life to a failed revolution, "but the powerful wanted everybody to believe the world was flat, so they persecuted him. But today we know that the world is round, not flat." Rather than dissolving his identity in a larger ideological solution, as Marxism is often accused of doing, the Communist Party helped Reyes emerge from an exploitative, deeply deadening system, to develop a sharpened sense of himself as a critical being, able to observe, act in, and change the world. "If I hadn't studied Marx I wouldn't be *chicha ni limonada*," he says, "I'd be nothing. But reading nourished me and here I am. I could die today and nobody could take that from me.". . .

Reyes's rebuilding of the PGT in Alta Verapaz is all the more impressive when one considers the failure of guerrilla groups to make inroads into the area. From the 1960s onward, those groups proved unable to gain a foothold in the Polochic Valley, and their leaders complained of the "taciturnity" of Q'eqchi's, often contrasting them to the more militant Achí and Ixil. The PGT on the other hand was able to draw from second-generation commitment, working with the sons and daughters of activists from the October

Revolution. The PGT's success in eastern Alta Verapaz—at a time when in other areas the party yielded to new guerrilla groups or social movements—can partly be explained by the fact that the Catholic Church in eastern Alta Verapaz did not provide a venue through which communities could channel political demands. There existed few radical priests, such as those found among the Spanish clergy in Quiché, the Belgians on the Southern coast, or US Maryknolls in Quetzaltenango and Huehuetenango. . . . Planter power was so fierce east of Cobán that you didn't "raise your voice or your head," remembers one catechist. The clandestine structure of the PGT, absent any alternative, proved to be the only viable venue for political work in many areas of the Polochic Valley, particularly in Cahabón.

More than offering just a concealed organizational structure, PGT Marxism resonated with the lived experience of many Q'eqchi's in the lower Polochic Valley. Unlike the newer guerrilla groups, which relentlessly criticized the party not only for not incorporating "race" into its analysis and strategy but for the petit-bourgeois urban condescension of many of its leaders, the PGT never much evolved beyond its class-based understanding of revolutionary consciousness and action. Since its inception the PGT condemned discrimination, yet in the transformation to clandestine life it resisted adopting a model of "internal colonialism," that is, one that viewed Guatemalan society in specifically racial terms. By not overtheorizing ethnicity, by assigning it neither a surfeit of revolutionary virtue or counterrevolutionary vice, the PGT in effect allowed for the emergence of syncretic Q'eqchi interpretation of Marx, a kind of Maya Marxism that filled the ideological vacuum created by the overthrow of Arbenz.

It was through Reyes—who took ten minutes to say what Ladino instructors said in two—that most of this blending took place. He not only often served as the interpreter at study groups and as the primary liaison between the local party structure and the national leadership, but also ran political meetings. Such autonomy kept Ladino condescension to a minimum and allowed Reyes to preach his unique brand of Marxism. For instance, the youthful, literate intellectualism of the PGT in the 1950s had by the mid-1970s grown sclerotic, its Marxism as taught by party allies at the national university rigidified by Soviet dogma—especially its interpretation of dialectical materialism with its attendant partition of economic base from ideological superstructure. Yet it is this conceptual division between the material and the ideal which most fired Reyes's imagination, and he repeatedly refers to it in his accounts of his activism and his attempts to define himself. He often invokes Lenin's elaboration of the "unity of opposites" concept to answer questions, at times quoting the Russian revolutionary from memory to explain historical motion: "Development is a struggle of opposites, the ideal and the material," Reyes offers as an answer to why he left the PAR to join the PGT in 1950: "when a man is born, he has baby hair, but as he ages, he grows a beard. A leaf is green because of its chloroform, but then it turns. Quantitative and qualitative change."

As Marxism converted into hollow theoretics for PGT intellectuals and political leaders, for Reyes it remained a powerfully dynamic explanatory tool in his organizing work, one he used to convert the experience of nearly a decade of promissory notes into mordant aphorisms. "Idealism," he offers as a definition, "says we will be rewarded in the afterlife. Materialism says we want our pay now." Reyes explains how he would prod Q'eqchi's to stand up to plantation administrators and at the same time teach them about their surplus labor value. When a worker named Miguel voiced concern that he would be accused of being lazy for refusing to work without pay, Reyes told him to tell the administrator, "if we are not worth anything to you, then plant the money you should pay us under the coffee bush and see what happens, see if it brings you a profit." It is this capacity to elucidate, to clarify, to replace obscurant faith with critical thought that gave Marxism its value to a number of informants. For Tomás Cac to become more involved in the PGT and to become educated were one and the same, and both were driven by *necesidad*, by a need not so much for survival, although that was present too, but by a desire to understand: "No sense getting killed if you don't know why. They took many who were involved with church, with other organizations, who didn't know anything. *Mejor que sepa, me metí*—it is better to know, so I joined. The struggle of Marxism was a struggle of necessity. If we didn't, we would have continued being tricked and exploited by the landlords."

For Reyes, the ability to assess and explain was a supreme value, one that even trumped gender prejudices. Elena Chuc, a PGT organizer in the 1970s, was, according to Reyes, a *"cuadra más inteligente en charla,* she knew how to explain why there is poverty, why we are slaves, why we are subjugated, why the boss does not pay, all of these questions she was good at explaining."

National PGT leaders tended to be atheists, and doubt worked its way into the minds of regional Q'eqchi' activists. As Tomás Cac put it, "yes, the leaders who know more say that Marxism teaches that there is no god. Well, there was one, but he was persecuted for speaking the truth. His words survived, and this is what we have, but he doesn't exist any more. But in the communities, we couldn't talk about that." As part of its general indifference to the subject, the national PGT leadership neither opposed Catholicism nor took a position in regard to Maya religious practices in Alta Verapaz. "Each had their own practices, *costumbre*," says Inocente Cac of Maya and communist rituals and beliefs, "but the PGT always respected and never repressed Maya traditions, you could be part of a *cofradía* and a PGT member." Until the violence of the early 1980s made it no longer possible, PGT committees throughout the 1960s and 1970s worked with Maya folk priests who practiced a fusion of Catholic and Q'eqchi' rituals, some of whom were party members. One elderly member recalls that in the 1970s, "the elders, *los viejos*, would do their ceremony, a *mayejak*, and between 100 and 200 people showed up. We would ask for a change, for a better pueblo, a better Guatemala. We would petition the mountain, the sun, the sky. We would go pray in caves, with drums, *harpas*, *chirimías*." Such local rites put traditionalists at odds with Catholic Action "modernizers" who sought to instill a more orthodox Catholicism. In other areas of Guatemala, new insurgent organizations tended to ally with these catechists, which often put the left at odds with traditionalists. In the Polochic Valley, however, the relatively slight influence of liberation theology allowed the PGT to more directly engage Q'eqchi' spiritual beliefs and practices, accounting for the party's successful blending of the sacred and the secular.

Reyes's repeated evocation of Maya materialism is more than just a gratuitous comparison, for other less theorized informants suggest a deep resonance between Marxism and Q'eqchi' spirituality. In Alta Verapaz, as in other majority indigenous areas of Guatemala, local religious beliefs melded with Catholic doctrine to produce to different degrees an integrated and eclectic set of practices and convictions centering around the *cofradía* complex. Yet unlike other Guatemalan Maya groups, Q'eqchi's do not worship animal spirits or alter egos. Instead they conjure a sacred landscape of mountain spirits known as *tzuultaq'as*, "tellurian gods" as anthropologist Richard Wilson describes them, that bind together and influence all animate and inanimate objects. More celestial gods exist in Q'eqchi' folk religion, including the Catholic images of Christ and the saints, but they are distant, less immediately powerful than are *tzuultaq'as*. These earth gods provide Q'eqchi's with a hierarchical and interlocking set of geographic and moral coordinates. Each community is thought owned by a specific *tzuultaq'a*, while thirteen more potent mountain spirits surround the Q'eqchi' linguistic area. For traditionalists, these mountain spirits regulate the sexual and agricultural reproduction of the entirety of Q'eqchi' life and are believed to be easy to offend. They demand adherence to a set of ritualistic practices, including respect for taboos and offerings before planting, harvesting, traveling, hunting, sex, and childbirth. They also insist on a life lived in harmony with neighbors, the fulfillment of expected obligations to spouse, family and community, the granting of respect and deference to male heads of households and community elders, and the containment of individual ambitions and the excessive accumulation of wealth in an increasingly commodified and commercial world.

Within this moral polity—polity and not economy, for implicit was the notion that the world could be changed by extra-economic interventions—the PGT's vision of social justice, its hierarchical party structure and demands for discipline and unity, as well as some of Marxism's philosophical conceptions took root. Most powerful was the party's legitimate claim to be the heirs of the Agrarian Reform and the party's ongoing promotion of an ethical society centered around the just distribution and use of land, for Q'eqchi' society and culture continued to be largely linked to subsistence corn production despite the disruptions of coffee capitalism. Traditionalists hold that humans do not own the land but only have access to it as a "renewable usufruct," a belief that party activists used to frame their demand that disputed land be granted them free of charge. In 1979, an INTA surveyor, for example, complained of a "group of rebellious peasants who refused to be surveyed because they say that INTA does not have the right to give the land, because *"siendo de Dios, a ellos les pertenece"*—being of God, it belongs to them. If the PGT had gained power, its promotion of development and productive capitalism might have conflicted with anti-entrepreneurship elements of Q'eqchi' life. Yet that tension never had a chance to materialize. Rather, the two worldviews shared a certain appreciation of the "use-value" of goods. Vicente Toc reports that elders only used subsistence and local crops such as cacao, corn, and turkeys, as well as homemade candles in their offerings, as *tzuultaq'as* did not appreciate commercial products such as coffee or cardamom, for once goods are sold they lose their holiness, or *xtioxila'*.

Offerings and sacrifices were no organizing artifice, for many Q'eqchi' PGT activists shared this sacred vision of the world and structured their organizing work accordingly. They did not seek guidance directly from *tzuultaq'as*, but took, until the escalation of violence made such time-consuming routes to decision making less viable, advice from community elders who shared through dreams a more proximate relation with mountain spirits. These dream counsels helped local leaders decide not only on larger courses of actions, but on the more routine aspects of clandestine life—where to rendezvous, where to hold political meetings, what route to travel. Before performing any such tasks, they would make small offerings and say little prayers "to ensure, well, that the road was safe." And while Reyes explains his organizing strategies in Q'eqchi' communities within classic consciousness-raising terms, others remember joining the PGT through more traditional, hierarchical mechanisms of community decision making. Pedro Maquín remembers that in the late 1960s, the "elders" of the PGT came to speak to the "elders" of his village, who made a collective decision to accept their help.

As does Marxism, Q'eqchi' animism emphasized the interconnectedness of everyday life, binding the world through the inseparability of the animate and inanimate, the secular and the sacred, the material and the ideal. In trying to recall what Marxism meant to him, the son of Adelina Caal, who helped organize the Panzós protest [see "Blood in Our Throats," this volume] and is now an evangelical Christian, says that the "party taught us what we already knew, that the world was one." *Tzuultaq'as* literally means "mountain-valleys," and this duality is the essence of their power. They are both man and woman, Q'eqchi' and European, "the land as well as the spirit inhabiting it." This echo of Reyes's dialectical "unity of opposites"—a belief that everything contains within itself its own contradiction—resonates in less theorized form among many of the surviving PGT Q'eqchi' activists. In explaining the distinction between idealism and materialism, Tomás Cac says that idealism "is something that is born within you but that you haven't tried. It could turn out good or bad." For Cac, political consciousness develops through action, or, in other words, praxis. "It means not simply to wait, to not do anything to make the ideal happen," he says, "but to become organized since nothing comes on its own, from heaven."

Whose Heaven, Whose Earth?

Thomas Melville

On the eve of the 1944 Revolution, the Catholic Church had only a small presence in rural Guatemala: in the whole country, there were only 126 Catholic priests for over three million Guatemalans. In response, even before the 1954 coup, Guatemala's ultraconservative archbishop, Mariano Rossell y Arellano, launched a catechist program to broaden the church's reach, both to counter agrarian organizing and to instill orthodox Catholicism in indigenous communities, which practiced syncretic forms of popular religion that mixed pre-Hispanic and Catholic beliefs and rituals. Foreign missionaries were invited to work in Guatemala's isolated rural areas. The Maryknoll order in Huehuetenango, Spanish Jesuits and Sacred Heart clergy in El Quiché, Belgian priests in the southern coast, and Dominicans in the Verapaces were all part of a transformation within the Guatemalan Catholic Church in the 1960s and 1970s. In many communities, clergy initiated local development projects such as health clinics and cooperatives, as a way to gain converts by demonstrating the superiority of a "modernizing" Catholic ideology. This often deepened divisions with village traditionalists and with local elites such as Ladino merchants and labor contractors, creating fault lines of subsequent political conflict. At the same time, many of these missionaries were transformed by their firsthand witnessing of repression and poverty. As Catholic activism spread across the highlands, clergy and lay catechists became radicalized, and the Church went from being a pillar of the established order to one of its most threatening critics. During the late 1970s and early 1980s, eleven priests and thousands of catechists were assassinated in Guatemala.

In the following selection, former US Maryknoll priest Thomas Melville describes his first experiences in San Juan Ixcoy, in the Cuchumatán mountains of Huehuetenango. San Juan Ixcoy was one of the most intractable towns for newly arrived Catholic missionaries in that most people continued to practice Maya religious costumbre. The journey of Thomas Melville and Margarita Bradford, a nun known in Guatemala as Sister Marion Peter—whom he eventually married after he left the clergy and she left her order—is a remarkable one. Arriving to break the power of Indian costumbristas, as the first part of this selection shows, Thomas *and Margarita were transformed by their experiences in the highlands. They came to learn from those they thought they had to teach, and they chose to side with the rural poor against the local and national power structures. They helped set up cooperatives, and they introduced a generation of urban Guatemalan students to conditions in the rural areas (see "We Rose Up," this volume). Thomas and Margarita Melville were eventually accused of being guerrillas, and they fled for their lives to Mexico before going on to the United States, where they publicized the role of the United States in Guatemala and became important Christian activists in campaigns of solidarity with Guatemala and in the anti–Vietnam War movement. In 1968, the Melvilles joined Phillip Berrigan and others to burn draft files in Catonsville, Maryland, to protest the US Special Forces napalming of Guatemala and the war in Vietnam. They spent years in jail as a consequence.*

Even as my respect for the Indians deepened, I felt threatened by their approach to God. They had any number of rituals for pleasing God, for getting good crops, for warding off sickness. I tried almost desperately to stop the practices that I considered rank superstition; I wanted to teach them new rituals for reaching God, some that were not very different from their own. . . . The people of San Juan Ixcoy wanted nothing whatsoever to do with orthodox Catholicism, beyond the baptism of their children. Two priests had spent a year apiece in San Juan, but had converted no one. Four marriages had been performed, but all four couples had relapsed into paganism—if indeed they had ever given it up.

One day Father John [his religious superior] said to me: "Why don't you go over and see if you can break San Juan Ixcoy?" . . . Here was my chance to prove myself.

When I went to live and work in San Juan Ixcoy, I observed some disquieting things. In the church, 150-year-old Mass vestments were still being used by the *chimanes*, as were ancient chalices and ciboriums. I considered this sacrilegious. There were some seventy ancient statues in the church, most of which looked as if they belonged in a museum—some were missing limbs, some had no heads. I noticed that different groups of people knelt to different statues. I wondered just what their prayers meant to them, and how they related to the Catholic saints to whose statues they prayed.

Out in front of the church, there was a great wooden cross. Termites and dampness had rotted it nearly through at ground level, yet still it stood. But it was not a Christian symbol—it carried no image of the crucified Christ nor did it represent Christ's death; it was a pagan emblem, right at the very door of the church.

There was an oven in the middle of the church floor. On special occasions, the Indians would kill a chicken and burn its blood, along with incense, as a sacrificial offering.

I wondered what to do. Why was this pueblo holding out? Why did the people not come in to be married in the church?

John and I decided that the problem lay chiefly in the *brujos*, the witch doctors, whose strength was such that those who no longer believed in the old ways were afraid of reprisals by neighbors. If the rains came late, a majority of people blamed the Catholics. San Juan or San Pedro is angry, they would murmur. Someone might even kill a Catholic who was foolhardy enough to flaunt his disrespect for the ancestral ways by failing to practice the ancient *costumbres*.

How did the witch doctors terrorize the people? In this connection, it is important to understand a crucial distinction in the kinds of psychic control exercised by Indian religious leaders. . . . The *brujo* is a practitioner of evil spells and can curse the kinsmen, livestock, crops, or life of an individual who strays from the fold. The *chimán*, or medicine man, is the one who heals, who names children after washing them in the virginal spring, who helps choose the crosses and other symbols of faith and health and good fortune. The *brujo* masters the secrets of night-darkness and inner mystery; the *chimán* is a special child of the sun, of light, and openness. Nonetheless, both powers might often be joined in the same person—as, for example, in a conflict between two enemies, when one man's *chimán* might act as *brujo* to the other man. . . .

Back there in the Cuchumatán mountains, the laws reflect what the people believe and want. The central government is not represented except by a resident of the region itself. Therefore, although I was a priest, I couldn't get the keys to the front door of the church. The local Indian leaders—to whom San Juan and San Pedro were gods, not Catholic saints—held the keys, and sometimes the people would stay in the church all night, performing rites of their own. . . .

Finally, after sizing up the situation for two or three months, I told the leaders that I was *jefe* (boss) of the church and would close it around 6 PM. I felt it was time to begin to assert my authority as appointed representative of the Catholic Church. The people disagreed, but the first time I went down to Huehuetenango city for supplies, I bought a new lock. One night, after the people had closed the church and gone home, I broke off the old lock and put the new lock, to which I alone had keys, on the inside of the main door. Then I returned to the rectory through the inner door.

Next morning, when the people found the church locked from the inside, they didn't like it. But there was nothing they could do about it, as they

Thomas Melville, seated on the passenger side, writes: "This farmers' cooperative had just scraped their *quetzales* together to buy a new GMC truck. Half the town was out to meet us when we drove in. It was the first vehicle owned by a Maya in Cabricán. I cosigned for the loan, since the cooperative didn't have a credit history or sufficient down payment." Cabricán, Quetzaltenango, 1961. Photo and caption used by permission of Thomas Melville.

had no way of getting at my lock. I tried to make the new opening and closing times correspond as closely as possible to the former hours and left the church open all night on special occasions in order not to antagonize them. Nonetheless, I controlled the closings and openings of the church doors and thus began to build up my authority on religious matters.

My next action did not go as smoothly. After another month had passed, I went inside the church one night and took a sledge hammer to the adobe oven in the center of the nave. A carpenter came in and built some benches across the church to fill the space where the oven had been. . . .

The people fought back. Three women and a man accused me before the civil mayor of having deliberately kicked one of the women while she was praying in church. I was surprised that the mayor paid any attention to such a patently false accusation, making me answer the charges. I did so by demanding that the witnesses be separated; then I showed that their stories conflicted as to time, exact place, and chronology. The mayor laughed and dismissed us all. . . .

After a few weeks, the open anger over the disappearance of the oven abated, and people began greeting me again in the streets. But under the surface, there was resentment.

Next, I began removing some of the old statues, because I felt that, in their ruined condition, they played a superstitious, even fetishistic, role. The first night I took three or four of the more decrepit statues, without heads of limbs, and hid them in the attic above the rectory. I hoped no one would notice their disappearance.

However, people *did* notice. Different groups of worshippers were in charge of various statues, and even the broken ones were considered sacred. When people asked me what had happened to this saint or that saint, I said I didn't know where they were or who had taken them. They knew only I would *dare* to touch them, but what could they do? The statues were gone. . . .

I shall never know the prayers said against me, the spells placed on my name, or the people's anguish and amazement that I should continue to survive and prevail in my sacrilege against their beliefs.

. . . In the meantime, I had set up a clinic in one of the rooms of the rectory, where I gave out aspirin, administered injections of penicillin, and pulled hundreds of teeth. I distributed powdered milk to the sick, the elderly, and nursing mothers. I also established a small merchandising cooperative for sending some of the local potato crop to the capital for sale. All these things created goodwill among a sizable number of people. The couples that had been married in the church since my arrival were solidly behind me, though they sometimes worried about how far the elders would let me go. I thought that many others, though not agreeing openly with what I was doing, would be on my side or at least neutral in any showdown.

I was counting on my understanding of the Indian way of thinking to avoid any such showdown. There was much hatred toward me, and, although I greeted one and all, the majority of the people would not return my greetings, often turning their backs to me as I passed them on the trails. Still, I hoped that I could break down this attitude a little at a time.

My next undertaking was to knock over the great pagan cross in front of the church and replace it with a crucifix.

When a man from another culture and another faith interferes with the religious symbols and practices of a people in their home territory, it is as if he is trying to shift the earth on its axis. And when any man is so certain that he alone knows all the answers for a people alien to his own culture, he had better study himself and his situation and meditate on what is really before him.

There I was, in Guatemala, trying to impose ideas and practices, not merely of the Church, but also of America—which I considered superior—upon a people whose basic values, life style, and outlook I did not yet really understand in depth.

So often missionaries go out to carry the Word, forgetting that the Infinite will always, somehow, be there ahead of us. [Eventually] the Indians told me about their beliefs, and asked in turn about my God. Gradually we came to realize that our God was the same. . . . And although we could never be certain we actually understood each other's concepts, we seemed to agree that people should find themselves through relationships based on love and mutual respect. We said it in different ways, but the essential elements were the same: love and respect.

As I learned about their beliefs, I became aware of an apparent paradox: Their religion was based on fear and punishment and divine anger; yet they behaved with loving respect toward one another, My religion was one of love and charity toward others; yet in the name of my faith, there arose fear and anger and the compulsive need to placate an implacable God.

And why were these people, who had so little, so unselfish? Why were people like me, who owned so much, so careful of possessions—although Christ has promised that our sharing will be rewarded a hundredfold? The contradictions struck me more and more deeply. I began to wonder and question. . . .

For perhaps the first time in my life, I began to think for myself. And I listened to the people . . . to more than what they had to say on the surface.

Like the *quetzal*, which is said to die in captivity, the Indians of Guatemala have effectively lived in captivity since the Spanish conquest, and their spirit has long seemed dead. Yet my experience in Cabricán [a second town where Melville worked] taught me that there are levels in the human psyche in which life runs below the surface, waiting for a chance to break through. I heard the Indians' words, and I heard beneath the words the sound of the *quetzal*'s wings and I let those wings fly free in my inner valleys.

I had been taught that the sacraments of the Church should never be approached in a spirit of superstition—that these sacred rites should be experienced as joyous and enriching, not performed out of fear. Yet we told people that their babies would not go to Heaven unless they were baptized. Over a period of time I came to wonder about the actual differences in spiritual content between what we said the sacraments symbolized and accomplished and what their *costumbres* meant to the Indians. I gradually came around to the view that we were confusing differences in culture with differences in essence. For instance, I would raise my hand over a penitent's head, make the sign of the Cross, and pronounce a Latin formula—and I believed the man's sins were forgiven. For an Indian, this same spiritual miracle was accomplished by burning a fistful of tiny candles or by confessing his sicknesses to a *chimán*. I wondered if there was only a thin line between many psychological and spiritual realities. God, after all, is infinite and is not to be bound by the particulars of our Greco-Roman symbolism.

Life on the Edge

Deborah T. Levenson

New industries and rural-to-urban migration reshaped Guatemala City, turning what once was referred to during the Ubico dictatorship as a "little silver cup"—for its polished order and mix of modernist art deco and neo-Parisian architecture— into a sprawling metropolis. Yet in the process, life grew precarious for old and new residents alike. In the selection below, historian Deborah T. Levenson describes the riskiness of everyday life and how living on the edge—often literally—shaped individual consciousness and community solidarity.

Everyday life demanded that people be inventive and accept risk. Perhaps it was the trade unionists' best school. Making one's home on the slope of a ravine that could become a landslide with an earthquake tremor or in heavy rain, living with the constant sentence of the death squads, riding on over-crowded, fast-moving buses on roads made more of holes than pavement amid cars with malfunctioning brakes and no rear-view mirrors, working hard on an empty stomach, giving birth in a public hospital or at home—in short, all the ordinary demands of daily life—required the same trusting of oneself to the moment and to what was at hand that heroism does and trade unionism did.

Daily life required some measure of confidence in one's own ability to make do. Part of working-class common sense was the notion that nothing happens unless you make it happen; this was an indisputable truth in their lives, no matter how little power they had. When Joan Manuel Serrat put music to Antonio Machado's *"Caminante no hay camino; se hace el camino al andar"* (Traveler, there is no path; as you walk you make the path), it was an instant hit in the lower-class neighborhoods of Guatemala City.

In this modern city without glitter or simulacrum, no one bothered to argue that modernization was particularly positive for urban workers, no respectable identity as "worker" was ascribed to industrial workers, and there existed no imagery of the urban (or rural) population as a potential or actual "good citizenry." The elites did not hope to gain support from

Girl bathing in sink in front of her family's home. Squatter settlement in Guatemala City, 1984. Photo by Derrill Bazzy. Used by permission of the photographer.

an urban population that was neither market nor political base, and they expended almost no effort trying to do so. Instead during the period of industrial growth the state revived with new language and methods the pre-1944 tradition of dominating society through violence. Before 1944 unions were illegal and legally suppressed; after 1954 they were legal and illegally attacked by the state and by owners and managers, and matters of violence had changed qualitatively. As the industrial working class expanded in the post-1954 period, as modernization unfolded, thousands were tortured or were "disappeared" and the mangled dead body, present or absent, became the singular image of the national body politic.

This state of affairs was not accepted as natural or necessary by the urban popular classes. It was understood as barbaric and even as unbelievable. No belief system explained the death squads and disappearances, a frequent commentary was *"es una lica"* (it's a movie). . . . When industry and capitalist agriculture grew in the 1960s and 1970s without redistributing wealth in the city, there deepened a radical ideological and existential schism between rulers and ruled, rich and poor. More than an absence of hegemony existed among the city poor and working people. There was the presence of spontaneous dissent, of something approaching "inverse hegemony," the view that the state was in its essence alien and dangerous, anything it did was wrong. Although stable organization was unusual in the city, the deep fury that smoldered in the lower-class neighborhoods and within families surfaced with tremendous force from time to time. This happened with the insurrection of March–April 1962, after the 1976 earthquake . . . and in 1978 when the city exploded in reaction to an increase in the bus fare. Either as a sign of respect or as a way to win favor, no language of deference toward state officials existed in the labor movement; trade unionists publicly referred to state functionaries as "murderous psychopaths" and "barbarous, heartless, not human beings."

Hatred for the government and for the rich was part of popular urban culture. It was well expressed in the city's famous black humor, its unending supply of jokes about presidents and generals, about disasters such as disease, hunger, and earthquakes, and even about torture ("Did you know that Chupina [Germán Chupina, the police chief in Guatemala City and a reputed torturer] had a twin?" "No, what happened to his twin?" "He was born dead, with signs of torture.") Two examples illustrate the texture of a humor that divides the world between the good people and the bad state. In the first example: "Two generals are riding on an airplane over the country. The first one says, 'I'll throw down twenty *quetzals* and make twenty Guatemalans happy.' The second responds, 'Well, I'll throw down one hundred and make one hundred Guatemalans happy.' The airline stewardess, overhearing the conversation, remarks, "Why don't you both jump out of the plane and make eight million Guatemalans happy?'" In the second example: "President Lucas García [1978–1982, notorious as violent and stupid] is having his shoes shined. Wishing to pass the time and entertain his customer, whom he does not recognize, the shoeshine boy inquires, 'Have you heard the latest joke about Lucas García?' 'But I am Lucas García!' replies the president. 'In that case,' says the shoeshine boy, 'I'll tell it very, very slowly.'" Such bold jokes cast light on, and challenged the efficacy of, a political system that thrived on secrecy and invisibility. Humor sustained the monotonous daily battle with transportation, jobs, prices, water, and violence and the will to survive it. It was part of a subculture nourished in workplaces, families, and neighborhoods.

The neighborhood arenas of this subculture were the streets and open-air markets where women, men, young people, and children socialized, bars for men (usually a small back room of a corner store), and soccer matches. Played almost exclusively by men and boys, soccer was unsurpassed as a neighborhood social activity. Soccer was vital to male working-class life:

Woman parking attendant. Photo by Mitchell Denburg, ca. 1980. From the collections of the Centro de Investigaciones Regionales de Mesoamérica, Guatemala.

through teams jobs could be found, friendships were made and tested as individualism vied with collectivism on the playing field, and union meetings were sometimes convened on the field after a game.

The neighborhoods that industrial workers shared with others, such as La Parroquia in Zone 6 . . . are not well described by the word *community* insofar as this term suggests the existence of longstanding, cohesive structures and the perception of common culture or history. The waterspouts and the streets, the dust or mud, like feelings of anger, joy, grief, solidarity, envy and above all the feelings of a common destiny, were shared by a shifting population of poor people who did or did not form deep ties. For their residents, these neighborhoods were points of reference at once fragile and profound.

Cristóbal Monzón Lemus, a Guatemalan car washer in Los Angeles, captures the solid yet precarious quality of neighborhood life in his *Camino de adolescente: La vida de Ramon en el barrio El Gallito*, perhaps Guatemala's sole proletarian novel; its publication costs were covered by the dollars the author earned abroad. In Ramon's old neighborhood of El Gallito, there were always memorable local initiatives, such as soccer teams that fell apart and then were rebuilt as fast as the youngsters' homemade cloth soccer ball.

Neighbors were vital to Ramon's life, but they came and went quickly in his troubled youth, as did schooling and a series of jobs. Nothing lasted very long, but it was important anyway. Trade unionist Marco Tulio Loza recalled that on his street in La Quinta Samayoa (Zone 7), neighbors who talked to each other so rarely that they could not remember one anothers' names mobilized en masse to search hospitals, streets, ditches, ravines, and the morgue for a disappeared youth—who, it turned out, had migrated to Mexico to work (unlike most of the disappeared)—and he turned up a year later to be dubbed Lázarus, a name no one forgot.

Workers had resources. Because more than the phantasmic presence of death squads constituted their milieu, workers experienced more images of existence than torn bodies and more culture than one of terror. . . . Mexican comics were very popular in the fifties and sixties, when young people rented them to read at corner stores. . . . These comics, like other cultural commodities, celebrate the role of individual initiative, power, and imagination in history as they depicted the lives of Marco Polo, Lord Nelson, Alexander von Humboldt, Alexander Graham Bell, Sarah Bernhardt, Beethoven, and even Toussaint L'Ouverture (titled *"el Napoleón Negro"*). In the 1970s, the influence of foreign cultures grew: the number of movie houses increased; the Beatles, the Rolling Stones, and Pink Floyd were popular; *nueva canción* from Venezuela, Nicaragua, Chile, and Cuba could be heard; and television was available to the general population for the first time, broadcasting Mexican soap operas and news and US dramas and comedies. All of these media relayed their own messages of individualism, modern family life, consumer society, and, in the case of *nueva canción*, lyricism about revolution and the power of heroic individuals.

The 1954 coup and the culture of terror also did not annihilate local urban culture. Everyone in the city knew of John Wayne, Pedro Infante, Donald Duck, and Mickey Mouse, but these figures had not displaced others that were only preserved in memory and only reproduced orally. The city's popular classes kept alive, possessed, and re-elaborated complex characters: el Cadejo, the barking black animal, part dog, part goat, perhaps from medieval Iberia, who protects drunks; Tzitzimitle, of Maya origin, sometimes called El Sombrerón; Tatuana, the colonial witch condemned by the Inquisition, who stops husbands from wandering; La Siguanaba, a Nahuatl name for the strange woman who appears by water to entrap men; and La Llorona, well known throughout the region as she wanders weeping for the child whom she killed. These and dozens of stories about the devil, money, love, kindly interventions by the dead on behalf of the living, and so forth, were not only part of the popular imagination, they depended on it.

Marchers responding to police attack on the funeral procession of the assassinated labor lawyer Mario López Larrave, Guatemala City, 1977. Photo by Mauro Calanchina. Used by permission of Ximena Morales, Prohibido Olvidar.

Because the culture of terror tore apart many other social solidarities, it reinforced the impact of the most intimate cultural milieu that workers possessed, their families. . . . Absent or present, peaceful or not, family was significant. Families were often authoritarian, and they were marked by rigid conventions about what men, women, and children were supposed to think, do, and say, and by the distance between those expectations and reality. The implicit code that women tend to children and serve men, who in turn win the daily bread in the world of work outside the home and protect their obedient, dependent, silent wives and children, was subverted in many ways, whether by inclination or by poverty. Throughout the early and middle part of this century a high percentage of women were single mothers, and women worked outside the home. Poverty meant that everyone was a breadwinner, though fathers often did not provide support because they had deserted their families. . . .

To be a woman trade unionist was to struggle against an employer, a violent state, and the conventions on which much love, identity, and security depended. To be a male trade unionist was hard enough, but one important difference was that, for the most part, the personal lives of male trade unionists continued to be rote and conservative because in many respects trade unionism coincided with male gender identity. To be a "real man," a *macho*, was to protect one's family, to be brave and bold, and to not allow oneself to be abused, humiliated, or dominated. Trade unionism demanded breathtaking public heroism, and this was a male-associated character trait no matter how many publicly heroic women there were. Trade unionism was perceived by men and many women as a macho domain populated by the truly courageous and manly. . . .

Without doubt, the most important cultural idiom of families and neighborhoods was a religious one. Although the city's residents certainly did not create Christianity, one cannot escape the sense that it was the local population that breathed life into it. . . . Religious festivals became national holidays after 1954 . . . these were elaborate and heady popular productions, not commercial or state or even church affairs. The religious calendar included eating and drinking on relatives' tombs and flying kites over the dead on November 1, the burning of garbage on December 7 to rid the house of the devil, and the Christmas *posadas* and the display of handmade intricate nativity scenes on Holy Night. Holy Week was known for neighborhood-crafted carpets from colored sawdust, pine, and flower petals and the Burning of Judas, when young people made effigies of Judas and attached to them lists of his "gifts" to local neighbors ("To Don Meme, the crazy, I leave my balls, so he will have something healthy to eat. . . .) . . . On all religious holidays and especially during Holy Week, which was by far the most important holiday, no line existed between joy and suffering, camaraderie and mockery, life and death, celebration and mourning. During Holy Week Guatemalans went to the beach, drank excessively, and paid money to carry huge floats of Jesus in his life, his death throes in his death, as double penitence for a sinful, merry life. The denouement of Holy Week was the spicy soup for hangover served everywhere the Monday after the Sunday of the Resurrection.

Such popular religious culture was its own school of life, one that encouraged participation and depended on improvisation and imagination. In addition, humor energized it at the same time that death was acknowledged and given a lively presence. For better or worse, local religious culture protected its practitioners from emotional demoralization and the ethical vacuum of state discourse. It was the character armor of the poor, a way of keeping their balance while the earth shook.

Christ, Worker

Voz y Acción

Trade unionism has a long history in Guatemala, even though industrialism did not take place on a significant scale until the 1960s. From the 1920s on, railroad and banana-plantation workers, bus drivers, artisans, and especially public school teachers organized in the name of dignity, social justice, higher pay, and better working conditions. In the 1960s and 1970s, men and women who were often new to industrial work started unions in plants run by the Philip Morris tobacco company, the Japanese-owned ACRICASA textile company, and the Guatemalan CAVISA glass factory, among others. Workers also started unions in the banking and public-service sectors. Legally, worker organizing was a protected activity; in the real world, however, this formal right was often unrecognized. Security forces and employers responded with a degree of violence that made the decision to join or lead a union a life-or-death choice. The union that was organized in 1976 at Guatemala City's Coca-Cola bottling plant, for instance, won a contract only after sit-ins, marches, and the assassinations of ten labor leaders. Why risk one's life over higher wages and better treatment? The following selections from the Coca-Cola union newspaper, Voice and Action, provide an answer, illustrating how labor activism was informed by moral principles of humanism and solidarity as well as demands for basic economic rights.

Compañero Christ, Worker, today we think of you as we do every day, especially because you are one of us, those who have been persecuted for speaking the truth and for seeking a better life for your people who lived terrorized by the Romans and those traitors who supported them, and whose sole interests were money and power and not their brothers who were massacred by the military boot of Caesar's power.

Today we tell you, although you already know, we . . . have united to demand respect for workers' organizations that are suffering the worst wave of violence since 1954. We tell you that this violence is taking the lives of innocent victims that belong to your people, who are disheartened by depleted lands, the cries of the widow and the orphan, the hunger of children, the misery of youth with worms, the suffering of dishonored and imprisoned workers. . . . We are *your* people, we believe in *you*, we have found *you*, present, at our demonstrations. The Pharisees of these times would arrest you. They would not have crucified you. Instead they would take you to their cells and your name would appear on the list of those arrested along with the names of others who organize against the evils of this nation. *Compañero* Christ, observe how the Pharisees and Romans of the twentieth century violate and torture your people, who want to live in peace, in a better world. Now we don't want you to come here anymore because the first time you would be arrested and the second time who knows what would happen to you, because they would treat you as a Communist Worker.

Capitalists Cause Social Disorder

The company [Coca-Cola] often says that we will bankrupt the company by demanding our rights as workers. When there is some conflict, the company owners says that we workers and trade unionists are anarchists, disorganized lazy fools, arrogant idlers and so forth. But the capitalists and their lawyers and advisors never present the other side of the coin, which is: it is *they* who cause social disequilibrium.

How so?

Capitalists do not produce what the people need, they produce what makes them the most money. Let's look at one example: why is there a scarcity of basic grains? Simply because a handful of agricultural capitalists produce what will sell well on the world market, and that's cotton, coffee and sugar, products which yield high profits. This use of land creates shortages of basic grains and the government, to which we pay taxes, uses our taxes to import basic grains, at greater cost, and thus we all drown in inflation.

Another example?

Taking advantage of the World Cup [Argentina 1978], the company increases production and sales; they get richer, we don't get more crumbs from the table. The pace of production and sales increases, and our wages do not. We become almost blind from seeing so many bottles whirl by [on the production line] and almost deaf from the sound of the machines and almost sick with tuberculosis from so much diesel fumes. . . . Workers almost fall asleep standing up when they work extra hours at night without extra pay. *This* is disorder and anarchy.

So, *compañeros,* you can say who bankrupts society. *Compañeros:* we call on you to be ready and organized because the capitalists are ready to disorganize your lives.

Translated by Deborah T. Levenson

Campesinos in Search of a Different Future

José Manuel Fernández y Fernández

Because of its exuberance, clarity, power of convocation, and national sweep, the Comité de Unidad Campesina (Committee of Peasant Unity [CUC]) remains one of Guatemala's most important political movements. Originating among and led by Mayas in the mid-1970s, it came to include Ladino rural and urban workers. The CUC was especially strong in southern El Quiché, Chimaltenango, and parts of the southern coast. The movement drew upon diverse roots, including the remnants of the 1950s agrarian committees, and new grassroots movements of the 1960s and 1970s, such as peasant leagues, Christian base communities, Catholic Action, and Maya cultural circles. By early 1980, the CUC was strong enough to organize 150,000 Maya and Ladino workers in a strike on the large southern coast plantations, bringing cotton and sugar export production to a stop and winning wage increases even in the darkest days of the repression. The history below was written by Spanish sociologist José Manuel Fernández y Fernández in the mid-1980s, based on interviews he did when CUC was still largely underground. Published in 1988, it became a significant contribution to the reconstruction of a violently repressed history.

The CUC emerged from a long and complex economic, social, political and cultural process in the indigenous highlands. Economic changes over the preceding decades had intensified internal class divisions within indigenous communities. . . . Development projects such as those promoted by the [US-financed] Alliance for Progress, the Catholic Church, the Christian Democratic party, or the government focused on poverty as stemming from the supposed cultural "backwardness" of indigenous communities. But as indigenous peasants began to participate in these development projects, they came to see ever more clearly that their problems lay in the unequal system of land tenancy in Guatemala and the rigidity of the political system. The growing political consciousness of people in the indigenous countryside, in which CUC played a central role, combined with an alliance with other social sectors to give a revolutionary dimension to social conflict in Guatemala during this period.

The embryo of what would become CUC were the community processes in the highlands in which people came together in small groups for literacy projects and study groups. Following the popular education methods of [Brazilian educator] Paulo Freire, in the early 1970s students from the San Carlos University and some private high schools in Guatemala City started to travel to the indigenous countryside to collaborate with the Catholic Church in the literacy projects. Indigenous students who had received scholarships and training also returned to their communities to participate in this process. Pablo Ceto, a Maya-Ixil university-trained agronomist and co-founder of CUC, describes the organization's first steps:

> We had a Maya-K'iche' Cultural Association. I also met other groups of young Christians and indigenous activists. Religious leaders and students came together with indigenous peasants in search of a different future. This was the era of *concientización* [consciousness-raising] through the groups dedicated to Christian reflection, to studying human rights, studying all reasons why the peasant leagues and the cooperatives had failed. . . .

Some of the Catholic priests in El Quiché held training workshops for local catechists to study the Guatemalan Constitution. Maya leaders were especially interested in Article 1 of the Constitution that proclaims all Guatemalans to be equal regardless of race or religion. In one instance, in 1973, police stormed a parish hall in Santa Cruz del Quiché where Father Faustino Fernández was giving a mini-course on the Constitution, accusing the priest of indoctrinating the Indians.

One of the original bases of CUC was in southern El Quiché and it came out of the Christian base communities and the peasant leagues. The founders of CUC also made connections with similar processes that were developing in some communities in Chimaltenango and the southern Pacific coast. Domingo Ixcoy, a Maya-K'iche' and another CUC founder, remembers that "in 1973, especially in Santa Cruz del Quiché, in Chimaltenango and the southern coast, the people who later formed CUC took our first steps, reflecting about the Bible, literacy classes, and a lot of discussion about our major problems."

The hamlet of La Estancia, a few kilometers outside of Santa Cruz del Quiché, is one of the places where CUC was born. La Estancia was a typical village made up of small-scale farmers, weavers, and vendors. The cooperative movement of the 1960s had helped farmers increase yields on their small plots of land; it also stimulated local craft production and a general cultural renaissance in the village. But after fifteen or twenty years of prog-

In 1980, indigenous women and men formed an important contingent in the largest May Day March in Guatemalan history. For the first time, participants wore masks to hide their faces. Over forty protestors were kidnapped as the march ended; they were never seen again. Photo by Mauro Calanchina. Used by permission of Ximena Morales, Prohibido Olvidar.

ress, La Estancia fell into decline due mainly to the high price of fertilizers after the 1973 oil price shocks. The hopes generated by the cooperative movement and the reformist Catholic Action social programs evaporated.

In this context of crisis after 1973, Fernando Hoyos, a Jesuit priest, and a group of students from Guatemala City started a process of discussion in the village. One of the youths from La Estancia who took part in the meetings remembers:

> What was most important was the unity of the people there, our precise clarity about the situation of the *campesinos*, and our clarity about exploitation and about how the law discriminated against us. I remember that we never strayed from the Bible. We were always making comparisons, and that's how the darkness was swept from our eyes. We saw through to the other side of the wall.

One of the main instruments in this first phase of consciousness-raising in La Estancia was the formation of a team called Nukuj, a Maya-K'iche' word that means "preparation before a festival." This team started to make a critical analysis of the organizations in the municipality of Santa Cruz del Quiché. [According to one participant:] "We analyzed in what consisted a cooperative; a political party; the church; the peasant leagues, etc. We came to the conclusion that none of these represented our interests. Several cadres in Nukuj started a discussion group about our rights. This sped up the process of waking people up. . . ."

Soon, these discussions and literacy programs that had begun in La Estancia started to spread throughout the department [of El Quiché]. Radio Quiché (one of whose announcers, Emerterio Toj Medrano, was later a leader in CUC) facilitated this, and even remote municipalities like Nebaj and Uspantán were linked by radio. . . . Radio Quiché had religious education along the lines of liberation theology, programs in civic education about current political themes, and classes about cooperatives.

The *concienziación* that spread in rural areas in Guatemala during this decade took place in a religious context. The Church had an extensive network of communication to reach the most remote areas, and religion plays a very important role in indigenous life. As *campesinos* uncovered the connections between their concrete problems and the national economic, social and political system, they felt the need to create their own organization. Efrain, a catechist from La Estancia and one of the first CUC organizers, remembered this process:

> Many different groups worked in my village. Catholic Action was the most important, but there were also committees for community improvement and evangelical and Protestant organizations. When CUC formed, we no longer talked about religion, but about exploitation, the struggle for equality, freedom for workers, better wages. People from all the groups could relate to this. . . .

CUC started to form as a specific group after the earthquake of February 1976 that caused more than twenty-six thousand deaths and seventy thousand wounded and left a million without homes. It earned the name "class quake" because it selectively affected the marginal areas of the capital and the *indígenas* in rural areas whose fragile houses could not resist the earthquake's impact. International agencies insisted that their aid be channeled through nongovernmental, community-based institutions. This created a unique opportunity for grassroots organizations. . . .

The earthquake not only opened the door to an influx of foreign aid; it also generated a flow of cultural and human interchange between the city and the countryside and between different rural communities. Many students worked in reconstruction projects. For most of these students, it

was an eye-opening experience to see the extent of the poverty in indigenous areas and the social organization of the Maya-descendant populations.
The study groups that had formed in southern El Quiché traveled to the
hardest-hit communities in Chimaltenango, bringing food and helping
in rescue and reconstruction efforts among both indigenous and Ladino
populations. That indigenous people would help Ladinos was a new experience in Guatemala. At the same time, Ladino peasants from the southern
coast helped indigenous people in the highlands. These gestures helped
strengthen ties of solidarity between the two erstwhile antagonistic groups.
Consciousness-raising groups, peasant leagues, and some of the cooperatives built upon this climate of interchange and solidarity to join forces toward the formation of a new organization that could unite poor Indians and
Ladinos from around the country. . . .

The November 1977 march of striking miners from Ixtahuacán [Hue-
huetenango] to Guatemala City was a decisive moment for the extension
and consolidation of the organizational network that would become CUC.
The social ferment and political awareness that the march of indigenous
miners awoke throughout the highlands allowed the early members of CUC
to make contacts in new regions with individuals and groups that had a
similar outlook. One CUC member recalled:

> With the march of the miners of Ixtahuacán, we felt part of the strug-
> gle of the people of Guatemala. Even though in that moment we had
> no name, we organized our people to go out [to the Pan-American
> Highway] near Totonicapán, to wait for the miners with food, to shout
> slogans in support of their struggle. It was the same at Los Encuentros
> and Chimaltenango, giving them something to eat, being in solidarity
> with them, socializing in the evenings, and making denunciations along
> the way in every hamlet or town that they passed.

The groups that initially went about building CUC worked principally
in indigenous areas and directed their work towards indigenous people.
To analyze the structural problems that kept smallholder *campesinos* from
progressing, [CUC organizers] talked about the rich and the poor and emphasized the class nature of the problem. They insisted on the need to
unite poor Ladinos and *indígenas*. But at the same time CUC started to function very much like the customary village organizations that integrated
women, the elderly and children as participants in communitarian life. This
was truly revolutionary in the Guatemalan context, since it implied a combined consciousness of class divisions with ethnic necessities. The emphasis
on the problem of class distinguished the groups that started CUC from the

leaders of the *indigenista* movement, who thought that differences of ethnicity and culture were more decisive than those of class. . . .

CUC spread throughout the highlands by using the channels provided by existing organizations in specific contexts: peasant leagues, unions, cooperatives, Christian youth groups, sports and cultural groups, or local development committees. One of the main networks was the lay Catholic network Catholic Action, which went by various names in different parts of the country (in the Verapaces, for example, village-level Catholic social promoters were known as Delegates of the Word). The little chapels scattered among thousands of villages became meeting houses where people would gather to discuss local problems. In these apparently innocuous places, a far-reaching process of political consciousness-raising took place in these years, through a reading of the Bible that emphasized social emancipation. The leaders of these communities, catechists and Delegates of the Word, were the first to join CUC, sometimes bringing the entire community with them. In some cases, entire villages joined CUC.

The unity of Ladinos and *indígenas* became one of the principal objectives of CUC's initial founders. Yet the need for unity and cohesion was also felt *within* indigenous communities that faced the decline of their [customary] social institutions as a result of the extension of capitalist relationships throughout Guatemala. From the outset, CUC wanted to constitute itself as a new center of solidarity and community albeit explicitly political. But this was only possible in villages that were relatively homogeneous socially and ideologically. Communities where class differentiation was more pronounced tended to divide even further as CUC tried to organize. Internal divisions deepened in many communities as some of the members of Catholic Action became more politicized. Well-to-do *indígenas* and many Ladinos started to position themselves on the military's side. And many Catholic priests gravitated toward the conservative wing of Catholic Action in dismay over the growing radicalization of other Catholic Action leaders and rank and file. . . .

The emergence of CUC took place in a context of political upheaval that was created in part by the presence of armed guerrilla movements in various parts of the country. CUC's political organizing dovetailed with similar efforts on the part of the guerrilla groups, and this confluence helped CUC build up its organization from diverse local efforts into a broader strategy. From its creation, the armed Guerrilla Army of the Poor (EGP) sought to be present in and influence the popular movements; probably the closest contact between CUC and the EGP took place in the Ixil region of northern El

Quiché [for more on the relationship between CUC and the EGP, see "Indian Dawn," this volume].

On April 24, 1978, CUC made its first public statement announcing "its aim of bringing together all *campesino* organizations to advance the struggle of *campesinos* and workers." . . . CUC chose to make its presence public at the May Day march in Guatemala City that year. City residents were shocked by the boldness of this spectacle. For the first time in the nation's history, indigenous men, women, and children marched together with the popular organizations [of labor unions, slum dwellers, students and other groups], not only clearly proud of their *trajes* [traditional indigenous clothing] but with demands as members of a new organization, whose slogan was "[the] CLEAR HEAD, HEART OF SOLIDARITY, COMBATIVE FIST OF ALL THE WORKERS IN THE COUNTRYSIDE." It was clear from the onset that CUC wasn't just any organization: Indians were marching by the hundreds, including children, grandparents, entire families, with flags, signs, hoes and machetes. For the first time, indigenous speakers participated in the May Day event, and they spoke in terms even more politicized and militant than the urban labor leaders. [According to CUC leader Pablo Ceto]:

> When we started to appear publicly for the first time in May 1978, it took city residents by surprise. Never had they seen anything like it. It was not only our level of organization, because we were well organized by then. The surprise was to see comrades from the countryside in *traje*: K'iche's, Kakchiqueles, Tztuhiles, Mames, Q'eqchis, all marching together. The indigenous people had started to have a presence in the national political arena. . . .

The extension of the organization to new geographical areas [meant that] CUC became a platform linking the concrete problems and situations of different communities. In this way, a powerful and vast network of communication was established among towns and villages of different regions of Guatemala, which operated below the radar of the mainstream, government-manipulated press. For example, when dozens of Q'eqchis were massacred by army troops in Panzós in May 1978 [see "Blood in Our Throats," this volume], word spread like wildfire, and the best efforts of the government to contain the story could not prevent Mayas across the highlands from interpreting the event as a declaration of war by the government against indigenous populations.

Some indigenous organizers started to work in areas that were mainly Ladino [although] language diversity made communication difficult. Many cuc leaders had to learn Spanish as well as different indigenous languages. . . . cuc sought to unite highland *indígena* populations with the increasingly combative urban and plantation labor movement. Although cuc from its inception had to operate in a semiclandestine manner, it quickly won the support of thousands of rural workers and became the organizational backbone of the seasonal migrant labor population that alternated between lowland plantations and highland villages.

Translated by Deborah T. Levenson

Execution of a Chicken

Manuel José Arce

Poet, playwright, novelist, and newspaper columnist Manuel José Arce was born in Guatemala in 1935. Arce came of professional age just after the overthrow of Arbenz, and his work became increasingly political in reaction to the country's growing repression, in response to what he perceptively understood to be the "spectacular" function of government terror, which desensitized the population to violence and turned Guatemalans into passive spectators. He tried to break through this complacency with what he called a Theater of the Grotesque, the most important example of which was the play The Crime, Sentencing, and Execution of a Chicken, *written in the early 1970s. Arce's playwriting drew from Bertolt Brecht, European surrealists (particularly Italian playwrights from the early twentieth century), and from what in Latin America was known as the Theater of the Oppressed, associated with the Brazilian Augusto Boal, a theatrical corollary to Paulo Freire's participatory pedagogy. Deploying a Brechtian insistence on exposing the mechanics of stage production—actors move in and out of character, the audience is addressed directly as an audience, the daily news is read aloud—Arce focused on the irrational and absurd in order to unhinge bourgeois conventions, which he believed were justifying widespread slaughter, and jolt the audience alive to "reality"—an important concept to Latin America's New Left.*

The below selection contains two extracts: a reflection by Arce on writing and staging Execution of a Chicken *and an excerpt from the play itself, a ridiculous refraction of a society deformed by terror and extreme inequality. The play has many notable aspects, including its perceptive take on gender—the chicken's crimes are many, but one is being an "unnatural mother"—and its critique of technocratic solutions to what was a political crisis driven by, and benefiting, Guatemala's economic and military elites. Arce went into exile in the early 1980s, settling in Paris, France. He died of cancer in 1985.*

How and Why I Wrote The Crime, Sentencing,
and Execution of a Chicken

Newspapers published photographs of cadavers that appeared daily, washed up on shores of Río Motagua, in ravines, in streets. They all showed signs of horrendous tortures. The regime used this terror propaganda to suffocate with fear all possibility of resistance by the population; the bodies often had notes attached to them, such as "This is how we treat Reds," and signed "The White Hand" or the "Secret Anti-Communist Army." But horror, like drugs, builds tolerance in the human organism; by virtue of constant repetition, its effects become deactivated.

One day I heard someone say as he folded up the paper with disappointment, "Today there are only three deaths in the news. . . ." I felt the fury of fire in my guts, an urge to stick his head in a bucket of blood until he drowned. I knew that the urban petty bourgeois had become desensitized to the scope of the death, horror, and crime all around them because they breathed it every day. They needed to have their nose shoved in the blood. I had to explain the struggle of our people, explain who is behind the assassinations, who guides the hand of the executor of these crimes, how the petty bourgeoisie is alienated, and how the large landowning, financial, and commercial bourgeoisie is embroiled in the real struggle between an imperialism that has nothing abstract about it and the people, who are demanding the right to live.

But I had to say it in a way that it would be understood as a parable, or better put, as a fable, in the exemplary language of illusion. I had to speak in a way that didn't rely on a common political vocabulary that was ruined by overuse.

Thus I imagined a chicken.

There is nothing illegal about the death of a chicken; you can talk freely about it; it allows for a discussion about agriculture and industry. In every house in Guatemala, chickens bought alive in the markets are killed. Everyone eats eggs. Everyone eats chickens. That's what chickens are for: to be slaughtered. It's normal, habitual, as natural, normal, and habitual as the death of workers, peasants, and intellectuals who oppose tyranny. But it is not the same to see chickens killed out back, or in kitchens, as to see them killed on a stage in a theater. In the theater the chicken becomes a personality; its death becomes a symbol, a ritual. In the fictional atmosphere of the theater, a drop of real blood, even if it's a chicken's blood, acquires another dimension of meaning, and that dimension is larger than the actual chicken's death.

Secuestrados y desaparecidos | Guatemala, 31 de marzo de 1983 | PERIODICO: Prensa. Libre | 37

Desaparecido

Secuestrado

José Luis Noriega García, de 22 años, quien padece de mongolismo, desapareció desde el 22 del corriente a mediodía, cuando su mamá, señora Carmen Noriega Cabrera, lo había dejado mientras subía unas cosas, para dirigirse de la colonia Nueva Montserrat a su casa en la colonia San José las Rosas. La madre va a vender atole a dicho lugar y siempre se lleva a su hijo, porque le da pena dejarlo solo. Supone que al no verla, se bajó a buscarla y desde esa fecha no ha tenido noticias de su paradero. Ruega encarecidamente a quien sepa dónde está su hijo, se sirvan avisarle en su casa en sector 2, manzana 1, lote 25, San José las Rosas, zona 6 de Mixco. (PL)

Freddy Francisco Meda Paraão, de 24 años, desapareció desde el 16 de marzo en la aldea La Unión, del municipio de Guanagazapa. Según informó su padre, Irineo Meda Pineda, su hijo fue explorando por supuestos elementos del Ejérciles de la aldea, a bordo de una motocicleta. Cualquier información sobre su paradero será agradecida en la mencionada aldea por Rodolfo Meda Ramírez.

Adolfo Max Bac, de 25 años, fue secuestrado el 6 de septiembre de 1983 por un grupo de hombres fuertemente armados que lo sacaron de un hotel capitalino. Max Bac es pastor de la iglesia presbiteriana de El Estor, Izabal. Cualquier información sobre su paradero será agradecida en el Hotel Guatemala, ubicado en la 16a. avenida 17-46, zona 1, o en el barrio La Granja del mencionado municipio.

Asesinan a una mujer y a sus cuatro hijos

Por Eduardo Sam Aldana, corresponsal.

COBAN. — Una mujer y sus cuatro hijos fueron asesinados a tiros por un grupo de hombres armados que incursionaron la aldea Pacsupajul, situada al norte de Cobán.

Informaciones muy escuetas que se tienen sobre este hecho, indican que los desconocidos armados llegaron anteayer en horas de la tarde a la mencionada aldea, dirigiéndose hacia la vivienda de la familia masacrada.

Cuando llegaron sacaron a todos al patio y sin mediar palabra alguna dispararon sus armas sobre la indefensa mujer y sus cuatro hijos, dándoles muerte, y luego huyeron.

Posteriormente se presentaron efectivos de las fuerzas de seguridad y efectuaron un rastreo en busca de los hechores, pero el resultado del operativo no fue dado a conocer, desconociéndose si les dieron alcance y lograron la captura de algunos de ellos.

Agricultor y su hijo asesinados

El agricultor Salvador Torres Beltetón y su hijo Héctor Torres Milla, fueron asesinados a balazos, por un grupo de hombres desconocidos fuertemente armados que llegaron a sacarlos de la vivienda en la finca San Miguel, de Panzós.

Por el momento, se desconocen pormenores del hecho, por que la policía investiga los móviles y la identidad de los responsables del doble crimen.

The morning news reports a single day's toll: ten kidnappings and multiple assassinations by "armed men." *Prensa libre*, March 31, 1983.

This was quickly confirmed to me—I saw it the faces in the audience. I saw all those chicken eaters, those who read newspapers full of death while they calmly eat their breakfasts: they got upset and indignant, they even had epileptic fits. Of course, the work was prohibited, but bit by bit, in the oddest way. First, I heard that post-performance forums and public discussions were forbidden; then the projection of slides—images of Rogelia [Cruz Martínez, Miss Guatemala 1959, who was raped, tortured, and murdered in 1968 for her participation in the popular struggle and to whom Arce dedicates the play], General Ubico, and the Nicaraguan hero César Augusto Sandino, et cetera—were outlawed.

Shortly after that, the play's intermittent reading aloud of daily newspapers was prohibited.[1]

Finally, the play itself was banned. Nonetheless, we gave fourteen performances to full houses, which sparked a strong debate in the press.

Shortly thereafter "The Chicken" was staged by the Popular Theater of Bogotá (PTB) in Colombia. It was incredible. The PTB performed it five hundred times in its tour of South America. In Buenos Aires, the government permitted the play but prohibited the execution of the chicken, using some pretext related to an article in its Law for the Protection of Animals. So, the actress who had the role of Justice [the Seller of Chicken Feed, below] in the Colombian version stopped the play and explained, "We cannot execute the chicken because the law says animals should be well treated, well fed, well housed"; in sum, the chickens in the play wanted everything that striking workers who had been bestially repressed by police a few days earlier wanted. In Córdoba [then a city with a strong student and labor movement], university students shut the doors of the theater and demanded the complete version of the play, and thus voided the government's prohibition.

Years later, the Popular Theater of Bogotá came to Guatemala and performed *The Crime, Sentencing, and Execution of a Chicken* in its repertoire. The government couldn't ban the play because the PTB was part of a diplomatic government exchange [between Colombia and Guatemala] and censorship would have generated bad international press. A year later, I attended a presentation of the play that affected me more than any other: one staged by indigenous actors in Chichicastenango. My theater, the theater of a white, urban Ladino had arrived—at last—at my people's roots. Two indigenous actors, who proudly protected their cultural ancestry, had accepted me; they had accepted my version [of reality] as part of the national reality.

Translated by Deborah T. Levenson

The Crime, Sentencing, and Execution of a Chicken, or Why It Is Important to Include the Necessary Amount of Calcium in the Diet of Chickens in Order to Increase and Guarantee the Profits of the Farmer and to Ensure and Improve Poultry Production

Scene 16
Stage is empty. Fully lit. Entering stage right is the actress that has been playing the role of Gallinavada, *without makeup but still dressed as her character. In one hand she holds a stool. In the other, a live chicken. . . . She puts the bench down on the left of the stage. She now will address the audience directly, in colloquial form, while she caresses the chicken.*

GALLINAVADA: Dear spectators: until this moment I played the role that in real life corresponds to this poor thing [the chicken]. But you understand that theater has its limitations. The moment has arrived when the farce turns to reality. I am a fraud. Truth is not my stage. Now, as symbols stop being symbolic and blood begins to be real blood, I will take my exit and give the role to the real thing: this chicken now represents, in its sacrifice, what I have so far been representing in this fable. (*The actress leaves the chicken under the stool*). The symbol continues, now representing reality. It is now time for me to leave, to leave this chicken to its judgment and its sacrifice, and you to understand. (*She exits the stage, leaving the stool and the chicken*).

Scene 17

El Choco *strums his guitar, sadly singing . . . from stage right enters the* Seller of Chicken Feed *[who in the play also serves as the judge and represents Guatemala's unscrupulous commercial interests] pushing an enormous podium wrapped in chicken wire, with a seal of a fried chicken and the slogan "Justice & Co. Limited." He is dressed in a black toga and stands in the center . . . from stage right enters* Galloviejo *[a state prosecutor, representing both the military and the country's liberal professional class, who work at the service of the country's elites], pushing his prosecutor seal: a red cooler with the Coca-Cola label . . . he is also dressed in a black toga. From stage left* Farmers 1, 3, *and* 4 *enter carrying four puppets . . . which they place in front of the prosecutor's seal. . . . From stage left enters* El Verdugo *[executioner]. He is carrying in one hand a cutting block and in the other an axe. He is dressed like Superman. . . .*

GALLOVIEJO (*Talking, singing, shouting, imitating, in turn, a priest saying mass, a drill sergeant, an Italian opera soprano [and using the formal* vosotros *verb tense]*): . . . In truth, in truth, I tell you that the hour will arrive when the son rebels against his father, the soldier against his general, the lesser of the earth against their natural superiors. Order will be destroyed by disorder. Impiety will deny the face of the Lord and even the irrational beasts will not recognize man's authority. I invite you to think profoundly about Piety and Love. . . . The teacher told us: Make love and not war.

CHICKEN 5 (*From off stage*): All the roosters died in the cockfighting pit! (*His shout triggers the sounds of protest that increasingly interrupt the speech of the prosecutor*).

GALLOVIEJO: Give to Caesar what is Caesar's. Within Creation, everybody has a specific function and fate. Some are brilliant and have great responsibilities. Others are dark and humble. This is how the supreme equilibrium is established in the eternal balance. This is why there is no worse vice that subversive violence by the humble, who—forgetting love—want to use violence to upend the natural hierarchy, as it has been designated by the conservation of the equilibrium and universal concert.

CHICKEN 1 (*From off stage*): This equilibrium is unjust!

GALLOVIEJO: And what motivates the souls of those who have fallen into that error? What is the cause? The grossest appetites, the lowest passions. Gluttony! Envy! Sloth! Nothing is more hateful nor abominable before the eyes of the Lord!

CHICKEN 3 (*From off stage*): Free Gallinavada!

GALLOVIEJO: In the present case, we won't list all the many crimes of the accused. It is enough to say that in carrying out one crime, another, more monstrous one was committed. At first, it was the envy of the farmer's property . . . then it was a viscous and impure desire [leading to opposition] to a pure system of procreation, free of carnal, fleshy sin [that is, opposition to efforts to regulate the quality of reproduction through artificial insemination].

GALLINAVADA (*From off stage*): We want our roosters!

GALLOVIEJO: Followed by gluttony, a filthy urge driven by boredom!

CHICKEN 1 (*From off stage*): We are hungry!

CHORUS OF CHICKENS (Repeating rhythmically): Hungry!

GALLOVIEJO: Then came anger, when those appetites could not be sated. Then sloth, when these beings, these sinners, refused to do the work Mother Nature assigned them. . . . And then finally, crime of crimes, outrage of outrages, an aberration, insanity, apocalypse! These unnatural mothers committed the sin of the bearded Medea: They devoured their own children. Who is guilty?

CHICKEN 1: You are!

GALLOVIEJO: You are guilty!

CHORUS OF CHICKENS (Repeating rhythmically): You! . . .

CHICKEN 5: We will continue the struggle.

GALLOVIEJO: . . . For such a crime, I ask for the punishment of death. . . . I am asking society to defend itself against the putrefying cancer that corrodes, to assume its sacred duty of authority and cut from its multitudinous body the tumor. . . . I am not asking, I am demanding!

A CHORUS OF CHICKENS: Do not kill her, do not kill her!

SELLER OF CHICKEN FEED: . . . In light of the overwhelming and irrefutable evidence presented by the prosecutor, I ask the honorable jury [that is, the puppets] to give its verdict. [The puppets, their string pulled by the prosecutor, give a unanimous thumbs down.] Considering the verdict, the convicted will be submitted to decapitation. . . .

EL VERDUGO (*He advances slowly across the stage, as the chickens off stage cry. He lifts the live chicken that is below the stool and with total calm stretches its neck, raises the axe, and brings it down with one clean swing, making sure that the ax remains in the cutting block. He then carries its still writhing body and deposits it in front of the Seller of Chicken Concentrate-Judge, in total silence. . . . The scene should continue in silence until the body stops moving).*

Scene 18

GORDO 3 ([representing a technocrat, perhaps a representative from USAID] . . . *in a mellifluous voice*): Instability . . . death . . . blood. . . . The crises that afflict underdeveloped areas due to the lack of technical assistance are painful and continuous. The example we just saw of the farmers is eloquent. This is why we are obliged to continue our disinterested aid. Our analysis is that . . . if only they had modernized their primitive industry and had purchased more incubators, things would have turned out better. . . . The lack of calcium in the chicken feed forced (biologically speaking) the chickens to search for this vital element in the eggs that they themselves laid. . . . For this reason, it is important to include the necessary amount of calcium in the diet of chickens in order to increase and guarantee the profits of the farmer and to ensure and improve poultry production.

Scene 19

It seems El Gordo's speech ends the play. But, just at this moment, the stage is invaded by the actors that have played the chickens. . . .

CHICKEN 1: Just a moment. This fable hasn't adapted to reality.

CHICKEN 2: This isn't a chicken coop.

CHICKEN 5: This business about the calcium is for the chickens. But we aren't chickens.

CHICKEN 4: We are human beings!

GALLINAVADA: Okay: Here the game ends and reality begins! Turn on the lights in the hall! (*The lights are turned on*).

CHICKEN 3 (Leaving the stage and entering the seating area, she says to Choco): *Y vos*, take off those glasses. (*Choco does so; she then turns to the actors on the stage.*) Let's go, we will fight until the end!

GALLINAVADA (*Picking up the body of the dead chicken, she shouts*): We will fight until the end! (*She leaves the stage, followed by all the actors . . . shouting "We will fight until the end!" They leave the room . . . a placard descends from the ceiling with the word: "curtain." Fade to black.*)

Translated by Greg Grandin

Note

1. There is a character in the play called the Informer, whose role is to occasionally interrupt the other actors and read that day's news, making sure to include stories on local and global financial speculation, repression, and international news, particularly as it related to global anticolonial struggles. Arce gave stage instructions for the Informer to always provide exact citations, including page number and paragraph.

Blood In Our Throats

Betsy Konefal

*On May 29, 1978, the Guatemalan military massacred scores of Maya-Q'eqchi'
protesters in the Alta Verapaz town of Panzós. The killing galvanized society and
radicalized opposition to the government. But repudiation also came from an unexpected quarter: indigenous beauty queens. By the 1970s, local indigenous beauty
pageants were an important yet contested arena of cultural organizing in the highlands. Some beauty queens refused to participate in pageants after the Panzós massacre; others used the spotlight to denounce the killing. The below selection is from
the historian Betsy Konefal's research on highland indigenous organizing in the
decades after the 1954 coup.*

This photo of twenty-two young Mayas covered the front page of Guatemala's daily *El Gráfico* on July 30, 1978, accompanied by an unexpected headline:
"*Reinas Indígenas* [Indigenous Pageant Queens] Condemn This Year's Folklore Festival." As the pageant queens and supporters announced a boycott
of the state-sponsored festival, they protested intensifying army violence
against indigenous communities, referring explicitly to the recent army
massacre of Q'eqchi' Maya *campesinos* in the community of Panzós, Alta
Verapaz. While the blood of "genuine Guatemalan *indios*," as the protesters pointedly termed the Panzós victims, still soaked the ground, "all the
. . . festivals . . . in supposed homage to the *indio* of Guatemala are unjusti-
fied . . . because in daily reality the right to life is not respected, [nor] the
right to our ancestral lands, [nor the right] to our cultural practices without
paternalism."

Amid growing state violence against oppositional organizing, what was
the significance of such a protest? Who were these young people, and how
had they—coming from disparate communities and linguistic groups—
become connected to one another? Why queens and pageants to protest
state killings?

The Panzós massacre represented a turning point in Guatemala's bloody
civil war, ratcheting up tensions and giving state violence a decidedly eth-

Indigenous beauty queens and supporters protest a massacre of Mayas by the Guate-malan army in Panzós, Alta Verapaz. *El Gráfico*, July 30, 1978.

nic cast. Yet at the same time and in the same department of Alta Verapaz, the Guatemalan government maintained its *indigenista* tradition of folkloric homage to the nation's Maya "soul," most visibly in the national Folklore Festival. As symbols of authentic Maya identity, indigenous women—and especially *reinas indígenas*—played a central role in state *indigenismo* and in the annual festival. Since 1971, festival organizers had summoned lo-cal indigenous pageant queens from across Guatemala to compete in the Folklore Festival's centerpiece, a national competition for the title of Rabín Ahau. Through dress, language, and dance, contestants were called on to embody Maya authenticity for the nation. Government officials including the president typically attended the pageant. The Rabín Ahau was held up as the national representative of the indigenous race, embraced by the presi-dent himself.

Similar to other instances when repressive governments have professed to celebrate elements of the nation while in fact assaulting them, the very contradictions inherent in state actions created a means of resistance. Af-ter the massacre of Q'eqchi's, the state's own celebration of Maya folklore provided protesters with compelling language and imagery with which to denounce the crass inconsistencies in government actions. It was no acci-dent that the protesters, too, positioned the gendered symbol of indigenous identity—Maya women in community-specific dress—as the focal point of their protest. The group set out their demands in the name of the indigenous communities the women as queens represented. Drawing on but contesting ideas of Maya authenticity, they argued that the dead in Panzós were "genuine" Mayas and their "brothers." They displayed Maya identity through dress, yet protested against the state as they did so: several of the *reinas* wore Maya clothing symbolic of mourning; one young man in traditional dress raised his clenched fist in the air.

By staging their protest within the government-sanctioned space of Maya women's pageantry, could these young people get away with confronting an abusive state? Could "authentic" activists, ironically, manage to subvert the state's definition of authenticity?

The young people involved in the 1978 protest were not representative of most Mayas in Guatemala. Spanish-speaking and literate, many of them a step away from subsistence agriculture, and engaged in at least this instance of pan-community activism, they had access to schools and time to dedicate to political struggles. Although a minority, their numbers grew steadily in the 1970s, and much of the responsibility for this lay with the Catholic Church. During the previous two decades, parish priests had set up schools for Mayas in towns all over the highlands. Inspired by Liberation Theology, they simultaneously offered community leadership training and established Maya language radio schools with literacy programs run by young Maya catechists. Priests helped set up agricultural cooperatives and credit unions, again staffed by young Mayas. Indigenous *campesinos*, catechists, and students from different areas became linked to each other through church-sponsored organizing, agrarian movements, and secondary schools. Growing numbers of activists began to articulate new understandings of identity as they came to see themselves as not only rooted in their communities but part of a larger pan-Maya community, a *pueblo indígena* in Guatemala.

Local *reina indígena* pageants, begun in some places in the 1930s, became part of these broader processes of highland politicization, a means by which activists, mostly young men, could publicly convey new ideas of Maya identity, rights, and justice. Mounting military repression made pageant arenas increasingly valuable: as cultural and gendered events (and therefore deemed nonpolitical), *reina indígena* pageants were appropriated by community activists as a means to speak out and organize. When the military labeled most other forms of activism "subversive," indigenous beauty contestants like those in the 1978 protest became activists' symbolic spokeswomen.

Themes of rights and justice made their way into some queens' speeches, as leftist community groups growing at the time sponsored queen candidates. Not all contestants' speeches in the 1970s, or even a majority, could be construed as voicing resistance. But opposition groups could and did put forward contestants who protested racial discrimination, poverty and exploitation, and, increasingly, state violence. A new type of discourse took its place alongside traditional pageant speeches. The words of activist-sponsored contestants were poetic, as tradition dictated, but politically charged as well.

One K'iche' *reina* in 1977 called for pan-Maya unity in Guatemala and for indigenous people to rise up together in common political cause: "Our *pueblo* suffers so much exploitation, . . . so much violence," she told a reporter. "My *pueblo* will only move forward by unifying, because in unity is strength." Like many other *reinas* of the 1970s would do, the young woman drew on the sacred K'iche' account of origin and conquest, the *Popol Vuh*: "I exhort . . . the *pueblo indígena* . . . of Guatemala to take up the counsel of our ancestors, 'may not one, nor two be left behind, may all rise up together.'"

The idea of pan-indigenous unity in Guatemala developed as activists from different areas, queens among them, were in fact coming together. By 1974, a newly formed Coordinadora Indígena Nacional brought together activists for meetings and workshops. A devastating earthquake in 1976 connected activists to each other as young people from distant communities worked together in relief efforts. In 1977, indigenous students founded the periodical *Ixim: Notas indígenas* as a means of pan-community activism and communication. That same year, a strike by miners from Ixtahuacán, mostly Mayas, drew the attention of local organizers all along Guatemala's Pan-American Highway. Soon the nationwide *campesino* organization Comité de Unidad Campesina (CUC) was founded, linking local agrarian activists, both Mayas and Ladinos, to each other and to national opposition movements.

In these same years activist Mayas began focusing attention on community *reina indígena* pageants. Beyond sponsoring their own candidates, local organizers invited *reinas* and their supporters from other municipalities to their pageants. Queens and their sponsoring groups met in regional meetings planned by indigenous students and funded by the Catholic Church. Organizers offered workshops for the women and supporters, inviting teachers and other professionals to take part. Adrián Inés Chávez, an indigenous linguist and translator of the *Popol Vuh*, was an influential figure who traveled to communities far and wide to introduce young people to the text, which helps explain its quotation in many speeches.

As connections among pan-community activists grew, *reina indígena* pageants became a convenient place for people from different areas to get together. And with the growth of pan-community mobilization in its many forms came increasing state repression. By the late 1970s, few places remained for students or *campesino* organizers to meet. Fairs and pageants, held throughout the year on local community patron saints' days, could provide cover. At the same time, pageant candidates' speeches represented a relatively safe means by which activists could speak out in public.

Queens' politicized speeches, not surprisingly, aroused suspicion and accusations that their words were not their own. The women typically prepared speeches in consultation with their sponsors, and their speeches generally reflected sponsors' aims. Yet it is not safe to assume that the messages delivered by *reinas* were simply memorized or that the women did not take ownership of them. One *reina* in 1978 stood before a plaza filled with spectators shortly after the Panzós massacre. With an intensity that was remembered by another participant twenty-five years later, she paid tribute to the dead by both internalizing and giving voice to their suffering: *"Hermanos de Panzós, su sangre la tenemos en la garganta* [Brothers of Panzós, your blood is in our throats]." Young women like her pushed the boundaries of what the *reina indígena* stood for and conveyed to the community and the state.

Ironically, as local *reina indígena* contests became more politicized, folklorists and successive Guatemalan military governments adopted the local pageant format as their own, staging a *reina indígena* pageant at the national level for the first time in 1971. The National Folklore Festival fit perfectly into the government's symbolic efforts to forge a nation of the fragments within Guatemala's borders, a modern nation of *guatemaltecos*, but one with a glorious Maya heritage. State *indigenismo* celebrated a "Day of the Indian" and paid homage to the conquest-era K'iche' leader Tecún Umán. The selection of a national indigenous queen was a natural addition, an opportunity to personify, for Guatemalans and tourists, the "indigenous spirit" of Guatemala. State officials became enthusiastic patrons of the Rabín Ahau contest. Local *reinas indígenas* were called to the national competition from towns all over the highlands, sometimes forced to attend by local Ladino mayors. Presidents gave speeches and posed for the camera with queens.

For Guatemalan military regimes, symbolic Maya women were viewed both as essential and safe, an apolitical way to celebrate Guatemala's Maya soul and attract tourists. Yet the same officials applauding candidates for Rabín Ahau applied a very different label to Mayas in general. The familiar and ugly underside of *indigenismo* had long held the contemporary Indian (read as male) to be a dead weight on society, and, like Maya women, inherently apolitical. With the rise of the guerrilla insurgency in the highlands, though, state and military officials redefined the Indian as a potential subversive. It was this shift in thinking that paved the way for genocide.

This hypocritical state positioning on the Indian—embracing and appropriating a female Maya essence, while defining indigenous communities first as a problem and then as subversive—stood out in especially sharp relief in 1978. . . .

Many activist Mayas were involved in local *reina indígena* pageants, but bitterness toward the state-sponsored Rabín Ahau event was intense. In May 1978, shortly before the Panzós massacre, a group of Mayas published an article taking aim at the National Folklore Festival. Blasting it as a modern vestige of colonialism and exploitation, the authors charged that under the pretext of maintaining cultural authenticity, the state sought to obstruct social change, to halt the development of the Maya community at a stage of history convenient for Ladino domination. The authors asserted that because the festival required Mayas to compete with each other to be the most culturally authentic, it turned indices of exploitation into cultural elements to take pride in—bare feet, heavy loads, the alcohol abused by the *campesino* worker. "Poverty is art," they wrote, "part of the authentic indigenous culture." The Ladino contemplates the beauty of indigenous poverty, they asserted, becoming a "connoisseur" of the misery of the Indian. With biting irony that highlighted the gulf that separated *reinas indígenas* from Ladina (non-Maya) beauty queens, they wrote, "*¡Viva la belleza de la pobreza!* [Long live the beauty of poverty!]."

Already in May 1978, the authors of this piece and like-minded activists strongly opposed the National Folklore Festival. The subsequent massacre in Panzós proved their critique to be shockingly prophetic: a government that purportedly embraced Guatemala's Maya past murdered Mayas in the present.

In the aftermath of Panzós, activist Mayas devised a plan to stage a boycott of the national Folklore Festival. They convinced a significant number of *reina indígena* contestants to speak out against the massacre and denounce the festival. Women took to stages in their own communities to demand justice and joined together for the symbolic national-level denunciation featured in *El Gráfico*. The events were organized primarily by young men, and the *reinas* once again lent their services as spokeswomen. Yet the women's words and stories suggest that they too became invested in the struggle against repression. . . .

In Carchá, Alta Verapaz, the contest for local *reina indígena* took place just days after the Panzós massacre, and one woman used her presence in the pageant to condemn the killings. The *reina* candidate approached the stage walking slowly through the crowd, refusing to perform a required dance as a sign of mourning and protest. With her words she drew parallels between the lives of those in Panzós and in her community. Her speech was preserved in a church publication, which now hangs on the wall of her living room:

> *Señoras y Señores*, brothers . . . I am here with sadness. . . . I did not enter dancing because our *pueblo* is living a tragedy. Why am I sad? You know why, because of what our brothers of Panzós just experienced; you know that they were killed, and we don't know why. It could be because they are *indígenas*, or it could be because they are poor. . . .
>
> I could not dance . . . knowing that my brothers and sisters are crying for their loved ones. . . . I feel . . . what [they] are experiencing. They have not a piece of earth to live on and for this they were demanding their rights to what truly belongs to them, their lands, and for this they have been killed. You have heard the news on all the radios . . . read it in all the papers, we all know it. . . . Tomorrow it could be us, *verdad*?

After requesting a minute of silence to honor the dead, she invoked a now-famous refrain from the *Popol Vuh*, calling for all to rise up and walk forward together, leaving no one behind. She was then promptly disqualified by the (Ladino) jury of the contest for her refusal to dance. The young woman believed her message about Panzós was also unwelcome. . . .

Queens from around the highlands met to plan the Folklore Festival boycott, in a meeting that participants remember involved over one hundred people, as usual held under the auspices of a community *reina indígena* pageant. A week later, the most "valiant" of the group, as one organizer put it, assembled for the photo that would appear on the front page of *El Gráfico*. Some twenty or thirty of them—memories vary on this point—boarded a night bus and made their way from the western highlands to the capital, about six hours away, to deliver their declaration to the press.

As the queens and their supporters expressed in the declaration, the state's celebration of Maya "authenticity" a mere two months after the killings of indigenous *campesinos* in Panzós reeked of hypocrisy. "The *reinas indígenas* believe," the press article stated, "that considering the events of Panzós, in which genuine Guatemalan *indios* lost their lives, this Festival should be suspended." The queens declared:

That the recent massacre of our brother *indios* of Panzós . . . [represents] the continuation of centuries of negation, exploitation, and extermination initiated by the . . . Spanish invaders.

That the Folklore Festival of Cobán is an example of [an] . . . oppressor *indigenismo* that . . . makes the *reinas indígenas* into simple objects for tourists to look at, without respect to our authentic human or historic values.

That while the wound of Panzós still bleeds, the failure of the organizing committee of this "show" [written in English] . . . to suspend it . . . demonstrates . . . the degree of disrespect [they have] for the lives of us, *los indios*.

Government officials' comments following the Panzós killings suggest that they did not view massacred *campesinos* as "genuine Indians" deserving of rhetorical inclusion in the nation. The mayor of Panzós stated that the *campesinos* in his community were incited by "agitators" who deceived them with strange ideas about land rights. The outgoing president expressed a similar sentiment: "I know the *campesino* as peaceful, honest, and hardworking, but he has been incited . . . indoctrinated." In statements to the press, officials chose not to describe the victims in ethnic terms at all.

The protesters directly contradicted these positions. By using the very image embraced by the state, the revered indigenous queens, the protesters refuted characterizations of massacred Mayas as duped or inauthentic by insisting that they and the dead in Panzós were one and the same, genuine *indios*. The protesting queens, they claimed, and not the officially sanctioned Rabín Ahau, represented true Guatemalan Mayas—Mayas who lived and breathed, bled and died.

Guerrilla Armies of the Poor

Fuerzas Armadas Rebeldes

Ejército Guerrillero de los Pobres

Organización Revolucionaria del Pueblo en Armas

Unidad Revolucionaria Nacional Guatemalteca

In the mid-1970s, remnants from the first insurgent organization, the Rebel Armed Forces (FAR), decimated in 1968, regrouped and organized three new insurgent movements that would operate in distinct parts of the countryside throughout the next two decades. A new incarnation of the FAR built a base among urban unions and among peasant migrants in the lowland jungles of the Petén. The Revolutionary Organization of the People in Arms (ORPA) began to organize along the volcanic range that cut from Mexico to Guatemala City, giving the rebels access to both highland communities and lowland plantations. But it was the Guerrilla Army of the Poor—the EGP—that would grow the fastest.

Hoping to overcome the errors of the 1960s guerrillas, a small group of poorly armed revolutionaries—made up of both Ladinos and Maya-Achi' from Rabinal—entered Guatemala from Mexico in 1973 and began organizing in the Ixcán jungle, where Catholic activists had built a strong cooperative movement. Unlike the militaristic Cuban-style focos of the 1960s, the EGP built alliances with grassroots social organizations. The EGP theorized that building a social base within indigenous communities would prevent the kind of repression that had taken place in the 1960s. Both ORPA and the EGP organized in indigenous communities; the EGP operated mostly in the highlands, working closely with Catholic Action catechists and other political activists to organize what in many cases were entire communities. ORPA operated mainly in the communities and plantations of the Pacific coast and piedmont, building clandestine structures and recruiting people individually. Both were unique in that they recognized the indigenous population as a revolutionary force and, as did FAR, the progressive possibilities within religion.

The Guatemalan Communist Party (Partido Guatemalteco del Trabajo, PGT), continued to be influential, but it remained an ambivalent advocate for violent revolution. In the wake of the 1978 Panzós massacre (see "Blood in Our Throats," this volume) some members left the PGT to form the Nucleo de Dirección Nacional del PGT, which favored armed struggle. On February 7, 1982, this faction of the PGT joined with ORPA, EGP, and FAR in the Guatemalan National Revolutionary Unity (URNG), a united command force that aimed to coordinate military action between the four guerrilla fronts.

Below are excerpts from documents of FAR, EGP, ORPA, and—most tragic in its optimism—the URNG.

Fuerzas Armadas Rebeldes / Rebel Armed Forces (FAR), 1976

Liberation Theology and Marxism coincide on many points, not because they are the same but because they take reality as a starting point and therefore arrive at similar conclusions. It is not the confrontation between the faithful and the atheist that matters; what counts is the conflict between the oppressed and the oppressor, between the exploited and the exploiter. We see that Christians and Marxists have common objectives: the liberation of the people, the liberation of exploited and oppressed men.

The most fundamental message of the Christian faith is in the life of Christ, his message and his praxis. He called for complete liberation. . . . He came to develop a new solidarity between men. . . . He spoke of the poor and oppressed and he lived for the poor and oppressed. As revolutionaries, we affirm that Christ's importance was that he lived his own message. When he spoke of the liberation of the poor and oppressed he referred to those who were materially oppressed, with whom he lived and to whom he spoke. When he spoke of revolution, he did so by concretely fighting against the religious and political power that oppressed people; he denounced these powers and he organized until his martyrdom. He was faithful to his beliefs and to the people until death. . . . In this way he established that practice is the ultimate proof of faith.

In these times we must understand the practice of liberation as the class struggle. . . . As Marxists, we believe that class struggle is the motor force of history and that the highest expression of class struggle is the revolutionary one. We believe that it is our historical mission to advance that struggle so that the majority have political power. The social class that will lead the revolution is the urban and working class in alliance with the peasantry. . . . It is revolution that will create the conditions of liberty and fraternity that allow real freedom of consciousness. Freedom of consciousness explicitly means liberty of religion.

We support the participation of Christians in the liberation struggle of the poor and oppressed.

Ejército Guerrillero de los Pobres / Guerrilla Army of the Poor (EGP), 1978

It is impossible to speak of the existence of a united Guatemalan nation. The past and present oppressors of indigenous Guatemalans have mistakenly believed that exploitation and misery have broken the spirit of resistance of the Maya-Quiche [K'iche'] peoples, that their social and cultural traits would disappear with time and they would finally be assimilated into society. A profound and fatal error: these conditions have furthered the identity of the indigenous peoples and their rebellious spirit has increased to such a point that they can no longer be ignored. They have become decisive to the future of our nation.

The indigenous people cannot directly or freely construct their own cultural development, and they cannot legitimately participate in a society dominated by laws of exploitation that depend on the oppression of classes and of races and cultures. For this reason, no partial change in the system will end the discrimination that keeps the majority of Guatemalans subjugated. History has shown that capitalism cannot resolve these problems because the dynamics of class exploitation lead to national oppression. The real and complete liberation of national and oppressed groups is impossible within a society divided into classes; only within [socialism] will the indigenous people be able to form part of the national and cultural community without losing their identity. . . . The revolutionary struggle of our people is growing, in circumstances that have never been more favorable. The outlook for generalizing, advancing and making more profound the Popular Revolutionary War, as well as for incorporating the majority, the popular masses, into it, is good. . . .

Organización Revolucionaria del Pueblo en Armas / Revolutionary Organization of the People in Arms (ORPA), 1980

We are an organization that was born in the mountains, grew up within the difficult guerrilla life, and then spread to the cities. We are an organization that has prepared for years through secret tasks and hidden organizing in order to take up arms and fight until we are victorious over the enemies of the people. We are responsible and serious, prepared and committed . . . to the people's victory, and we will take whatever time, effort, and sacrifice is necessary to accomplish this. . . .

Guatemala is exploited and dominated by the urban and rural moneyed elite. They are the owners of our riches, they manage government, control the army, and wish to fool the people with words and promises. The army is run by generals who serve the rich. . . . The big landowners take peasants' lands and force them to go long distances to work. They increase workloads and rob people. They mistreat and disrespect workers. The life of small cultivators is very hard because the earth does not yield enough to eat. The workers in the city live without jobs or with temporary ones . . . the factory owners prohibit unions, they kill those who defend their rights.

The *gente natural* [the term ORPA used for the Maya population] has been opposed and humiliated for a long time, as their lands have been robbed and labor forced upon them. The great works of their ancestors have been destroyed, their languages and customs have been denigrated. The rich have separated them from the working class. They humiliate and mistreat them. The rich maintain division between poor people to oppress them with greater ease. . . . The people have not been fooled. The people know that the rich oppress them daily; they know about the abuse, poor treatment, and humiliation. The people are not afraid, they have faced the police, jail, and death. The people prepare to struggle until victory.

The revolution is not against religion. It respects all religions. The traditions of our ancestors are also a religion. We all have the right to practice our religions. We cannot let our religions divide us. The people has to make its own army. Our people have great force and we will be even stronger when we unite, when we have a people's army to fight the army of the rich. Our triumph is certain. . . .

We fight to end hunger and sickness. We will build houses and learn to read and write, and we will make sure that our children have a good education and a good life.

We fight to take the lands and factories away from the rich so that the peasants and workers are no longer oppressed. We fight so that the mines and the oil will serve the people. We respect the small property owners who have achieved through their hard work, without exploiting others. We fight so that there is respect and unity, to stop the degradation and humiliation of the *gente natural*. We respect the culture of our ancestors, our languages, and the customs of our natural people. . . . We fight so that everyone has work and families live well. We fight for happiness and tranquility, for the end of torture and assassinations, so that our people can live in safety. We live to fight, we fight to win.

*Guatemala National Revolutionary Unity/Unidad Revolucionaria
Nacional Guatemalteca (URNG), 1982*

Ejército Guerrillero de los Pobres, Fuerzas Armadas Rebeldes, Organización Revolucionaria del Pueblo en Armas, and the Nucleo de Direccion Nacional del Partido Guatemalteco de Trabajo render our combative and revolutionary salute to all the organizations, institutions, groups, and individuals which, with the highest spirit of solidarity, support our heroic people in the fight for their definitive liberation. . . .

Over the course of half a century, tens of thousands of Guatemalans have fallen in popular struggles against the dictatorships that have consistently served the dominant classes. . . . All this spilt blood, all this hard work and all the profound sufferings of our heroic people have not been in vain. The revolutionary process has never been stopped, it speeds forward, and we can affirm with a certainty that emanates from the daily and incessant struggles that the exploitation, repression, oppression, and discrimination against our people are coming to an end and that the revolutionary triumph of our heroic path is closer than it has ever been.

The decisive element that convinces us that the revolutionary triumph is near is this unification of the four political military and guerrilla groups into the Unidad Revolucionaria Nacional Guatemalteca, URNG. . . . The struggle of our people is advancing everywhere.

Militarily, our people have made qualitative leaps. Decades of efforts and lives spent are finally seeing fruit in the development of guerrilla warfare in almost all the national territory. In San Marcos, the Petén, Huehuetenango, Sololá, Escuintla, Quezaltenango, El Quiché, Suchitepéquez, Alta and Baja Verpaz, Chimaltenango, Guatemala City, and other places, the guerrilla actions of our people grow ceaselessly. The intensifying military advances of the recent period have caused losses for the reactionary Guatemalan military, disarticulated its systems of control and domination, and forced it to lie about the outcomes of armed confrontations and about its inability to overcome the power of the revolutionary struggle.

We, the political and military forces, are totally dedicated to the historical task to which we are assigned.

Hasta La Victoria Siempre, A Vencer o Morir, Vivimos Para Luchar-Luchamos Para Triunfar, Por Guatemala, La Revolución y el Socialismo.

Translated by Deborah T. Levenson

We Rose Up

Juan Tuyuc, Yolanda Colom, and Lucía

Those who joined the revolutionary groups did so for varied reasons. The below reflections come from three members of the Ejército Guerrillero de los Pobres (EGP), Guerrilla Army of the Poor. The first is Juan Tuyuc, who was born in 1962 in a small Kaqchikel village in the municipality of Santa Apolonia, Chimaltenango. The knowledge acquired within a family of campesinos, in his travels as an itinerant worker, and in his religious circles led him to join a Marxist-led guerrilla front in the mountains in 1980. The second is Yolanda Colom. As a high school student at Guatemala City's private Colegio Montemaria, which was run by the Maryknoll sisters, Yolanda and her schoolmates traveled to live in an indigenous community in the late 1960s. This experience in rural realities ultimately led this urbane and university-educated woman to trade a middle-class city life for almost a decade of organizing and combat in the Cuchumatán mountains. The third, Lucía, a pseudonym, is the nom de guerre of an Ixil woman who now lives in Nebaj, El Quiché. She joined the EGP as a girl in 1982 after the massacres had started and her family, or what remained of it, had been forcibly resettled into an army internment camp.

JUAN TUYUC: My parents were *campesinos,* and from the time I was four or five I worked in the countryside. This was when I started to realize, little by little, that we had to change the situation our families faced. I left home when I was around eleven years old. I couldn't afford to continue in school. It was only my third year of elementary school. When I left my home, I went to work in fairs, at the mechanical games selling lottery tickets and trinkets in different parts of the country in the east, in the west, and on the coast with other relatives. I learned Castilian [Spanish]. I had an uncle who was a vendor and sometimes I went with him. I did not know how to do much else. I learned a lot of things. I've known the situations in which children, women, and men live. I saw the *colonias* in Guatemala City. Basically I realized that the same poverty was everywhere, barefoot children, malnourished mothers, a difficult situation.

At the time of the earthquake of 1976 I went back home. Much of the country was destroyed, so I returned to my home in Chimaltenango and realized that I had to help out. I began to take a course in bricklaying, carpentry, and electricity in the town of Chimaltenango. At that time there were many opportunities because of international solidarity. There were experts from the University of San Carlos and from Germany and Spain. The Spanish Red Cross came, and they offered courses for these skills in order to build houses. We went to all the communities in the area repairing the damages; we [Juan and other Kaqchikel boys and young men from his community] came to know every hamlet in Chimaltenango. There were also courses in agriculture. We went to one every Saturday. I learned about the cultivation of fruit trees, about fertilizers and different soils and types of cultivation. In those same years—in 1976 and 1977—I became a member of a cooperative of potato farmers that empowered the farmers. Unfortunately, in 1978 the prices of potatoes dropped. There is a song called "I Die for Potatoes" that describes this. More than eight thousand kilograms of potatoes were lost. They were too cheap—about ten or twenty-five cents per kilo. It was more expensive to harvest it. Many farmers decided not to harvest the crops and they rotted completely. During that time we were looking for a market through the National Institute of Cooperatives [a government agency], but they never paid attention to us. During that time I realized that there weren't any policies that supported the farmer and agriculture. We wanted to diversify our production as *cooperativistas*. In 1978 and 1979 we were in the process of looking for alternative solutions. . . . We understood our situation and we saw how the *campesinos* of Chimaltenango who went down to the southern coast [to work on sugar, cotton, and other large-scale export crop plantations] were mistreated. There weren't decent salaries. There was no respect for the dignity of the people. There was tremendous exploitation. We decided to improve our ability to organize with the support of the Jesuits in the city.

My father was a member of the Juventud Católica [Catholic Youth] in San Juan Comalapa. Juventud Católica has it roots in the presence of the Jesuits there in the forties, fifties, and sixties. That was what my father went through. In 1976, after the earthquake, I had started participating in Catholic Action, and it gave me an entire way of life—yes, a biblical analysis of the situation, a social, political interpretation of the Bible. The Jesuits edited a magazine called *Cristo compañero*, a journal where they presented social interpretations, of the Bible, the Constitution, social conditions. In the first article of the Constitution it says the state protects life, security, and integrity. And the Bible said the same—that we have to love one another as dignified persons. So at the heart of this, we were interpreting the Bible and

Camp of the insurgent Ejército Guerrillero de los Pobres, Mazatenango, 1982. Photo by Jean-Marie Simon. Used by permission of the photographer.

making various songs like *"No basta rezar"* [Praying isn't enough]. These are songs that interpret reality and at the same time they look for a solution. CUC [Committee of Peasant Unity] and all this inspired a popular struggle. I believe that the situation made us think that there had to be change. In 1978, all the revolutionary groups were there. In 1979, that was a peak, a triumph of struggle, with many protests and huge mobilizations. We thought there would be a revolution. I remember a month after the Sandinista revolution we had a big meeting in Maria Auxiliadora [a Catholic church] in zone 11 in the capital, and our musical group sang at the mass, and we were so open, we told people what we were about. Basically there was a necessity, a conviction that we had to do something for the people. I had political conviction.

YOLANDA COLOM: Looking back, I do not know how I maintained this rhythm of activities. I guess it was our youth and the impetus that our ideals and dreams gave us. . . . In this town [Cuilco, in Huehuetenango], I washed and ironed my own clothes for the first time. I lived without electricity, TV, movies, telephone. I felt what it was like to not have medical service. . . . I broke my arm and one of the nuns and her assistant put alcohol on it, but the pain was terrible . . . my arm became inflamed and my hand swollen, and finally they took me to the hospital in Huehuetenango in the town's truck. . . . In Cuilco, I met the Maryknoll sister Rose Cordis, who was a doctor. She went throughout the department of Huehuetenango, attending to urgent and delicate cases. Nothing stopped her. A few times she traveled in a jeep, but usually she went on horseback or on foot. She operated successfully in the worst of conditions. She told us that the health problems we saw there were a result of misery and abandonment, and that the situation was not medical, but economic and social. . . .

It was in Cuilco that I felt the extreme poverty and isolation in which most Guatemalans live. I also saw the limits of the cooperatives [USAID and the Guatemalan government encouraged cooperatives to buy and sell goods in the 1960s] when they are inside dependent capitalism. I sensed how talent and will got shot down by the surrounding realities.

It was in Cuilco that I first observed—with astonishment—the human drama of forced arbitrary military recruitment. The army would stay for about twenty-four hours in town, time enough to violate human and civic rights. On fiesta or market days, the soldiers would grab youth that were not on the lookout and had not figured out how to escape during this human butchery. They took everyone, from minors to husbands who had family responsibilities, and sons who were responsible for the elderly and the sick. The army put them in a dark shack without ventilation, water, or sanitary service that was located in front of the park. There they passed the night, huddled without food. In the morning they were put in a truck to be taken to the main town. The families would come to the park anguished. They surrounded the truck; they explained, they begged, they cried, and some of them even got down on their knees in front of the military men, who were indifferent and cynical, who ignored them or made fun of them. After decades, these scenes remain intact in my memory. . . .

My stay in Cuilco was rich in learning and happiness. Laughter was daily life's principal ingredient. I don't remember a period in my life where I have laughed and enjoyed more. . . . It was also the year during which I enjoyed the most live *marimba*. . . . My leavetaking was a mix of party and funeral. We left part of ourselves there forever. The expressions of thanks and affection were deep. We left to the sounds of *marimba*, and with wild flowers, homemade candies, and thank-you notes in our hands, messages so sincere and well-intended that have always stayed in my memory. A student's mother wrote, "May you live one hundred years and have a thousand children." An elderly bricklayer and *marimbista* wrote, "Don't be content with one husband; you can get four." . . .

My stay in Cuilco made me realize that Guatemalan reality was more complicated and dramatic than I had thought. My civic responsibility could not be reduced to a year of voluntary work. From then on, my ties of work and friendship with poor people, rebellious students, social activists, Christians dedicated to social justice, and democratic people multiplied more rapidly than those of the family and social circle from which I came. In Cuilco, I discovered the limits of my Christian and civic consciousness and began the journey toward political consciousness. It was there that I took the personal and secret decision to dedicate my life to the struggle for a profound transformation in Guatemalan society.

LUCÍA: We were in a model village [Guatemalan military internment], and we had nothing to eat, and the army controlled us completely. . . . We had no resources, no means to protect ourselves, I had no *guipil* [the traditional Maya blouse], we had one *corte* [long skirt of woven cloth] between four women—[myself], my mother, my sister and my sister-in-law. We took turns wearing it. The army killed two of my sisters and two of my brothers, sickness killed my father, my other sister rose up [joined the guerrillas]. First I rose up and then she did. We went out of necessity because the army would rape us, torture us, and murder us. I asked permission to rise up. My mother authorized me because it was necessary. She was a single mother and she had worked the earth with a hoe and a machete; she had taught us how to work the cornfield when we were little.

I was twelve years old when I joined the guerrillas. Besides learning to shoot, I learned how to enter into combat, how to retreat, and what were the signals for a retreat. I had about a month of training and then it was on to combat! If we rose up it was to fight! We had to be prepared because the soldiers would come, and if we weren't prepared, that was that. All this required great determination; it was difficult, and we often suffered hunger.

When I arrived they gave me my boots, a shirt, and pants. They gave us a fistful of corn and said, "You are going to fight." I became the head of a squad when I was very young. This was in the Ixcán. Others were the heads of squadrons that had more people—a squadron was four squads, around thirty combatants. In the training, they taught me to kill soldiers, to manage my shot and to defend myself. I had good aim, and I knew how to lead. . . . I remember once we captured three AKs, which was very important [a Russian-made rifle that can be used in water]. At first I used a Mauser, which was really heavy, and then an M-16 [a US-manufactured machine gun], a Galil [an Israeli weapon] and then an AK.

I fought for eight years with the other *companeros*, and there we had friendship, with people speaking Kachiquel, Mam, K'iche', Ixil, so I had to learn to speak Spanish, and they taught us to write on leaves with chalk.

In combat who knows what happens with fear and sadness, we don't think about our families or about boyfriends, we just think about fighting the army. Even if our mouths are dry and our nervousness gives us goose bumps, when the firing starts [we don't feel that].

I remember I had a *compañera*, we were close friends, we had shared so much, we had learned so much together, we had so many experiences together. One day we were talking and enjoying ourselves and the army came like that, all of a sudden, and she died. It was International Women's Day, and every anniversary I think of her.

The combat line was not rotated because the leaders knew that we women were brave and capable, and I was always in the front line. . . . There was no difference if one was a woman, once you are there in a combat unit you had to fight. . . . In the guerrilla struggle we all ate equally; if you get hold of some bread, you break it into equal pieces for everyone. . . .

After a while I wanted to participate in another way, and they sent me to take a course in medicine. So from then on I went with a combat unit, but not as a combatant. I was on the firing line, and when there were wounded combatants, you have to practice the medicine that you learned, which makes you very nervous, but two always protected me when you go out [in front of the line] to the wounded, so you are without fear, because you are protected. . . . We rose up because the army repressed us, because the rich had put us down, for example, they did not pay enough to those who went to the coast to work. We took up arms to get rid of the rich, because they had taken our lands, they threatened us because we were poor people; they mistreated us because we were indigenous people.

Translated by Deborah T. Levenson

Communiqué

Otto René Castillo

Born in the highland city of Quetzaltenango in 1936, Otto René Castillo is one of the country's most beloved and quoted poets. Expelled for protesting the 1954 coup, Castillo studied in Leipzig, East Germany, where he worked with young filmmakers to create short film montages about armed struggle in Latin America. In 1964 he returned to Guatemala City to become director of its experimental theater, only to be forced into exile once again. Castillo's best known poem is "Vámonos patria a caminar!" ("Let's go my country, walk forward!"). Another—"Intelectuales apolíticos" ("Apolitical intellectuals"), which was translated into dozens of languages—imagines indifferent intellectuals being interrogated by the humble and untutored about "what they did when their nation died out slowly, like a sweet fire small and alone." Castillo reentered Guatemala secretly as a member of the Fuerzas Armadas Rebeldes, but, along with his compañera Nora Paiz, he was captured by security forces on March 19, 1967. Both were tortured for four days before being burned alive inside the Zacapa military base—a fate that Castillo, in his prescient last poem, thought was insignificant compared to the destruction of his country: "What a shame that I have had so small a life for a tragedy so enormous." Most of Castillo's poetry, including his political works, are love poems, as is "Communiqué," reproduced here.

no era tras la muerte
a lo que fuimos....

¡es tras la vida!

"We sought life, not death!"
Protest poster for the funeral
of student leader Robin García.
Image by Mauro Calanchina.
Used by permission of Ximena
Morales, Prohibido Olvidar.

Nothing
can
stop this avalanche
of love
This rebuilding of people
in their noblest of structures.
Nothing
can
stop the people's faith
in the singular power of their hands.
Nothing
can
stop life.
And
nothing
will stop life,
because nothing
has ever been able
to stop life.

Translated by Deborah T. Levenson

Comunicado

Nada
podrá
contra esta avalancha
del amor.
Contra este rearme del hombre
en sus más nobles estructuras.
Nada
podrá
contra la fe del pueblo
en la sola potencia de sus manos.
Nada
podrá
contra la vida.
Y nada
podrá
contra la vida,
porque nada
pudo
jamás
contra la vida.

Declaration of Iximché

Various authors

In late January 1980, a number of activists from the Comité de Unidad Campesina (Committee of Peasant Unity, or CUC), mostly K'iche's from the province of El Quiché, occupied the Spanish embassy in Guatemala City to protest mounting repression in the countryside directed at indigenous organizers. On January 31, the government responded by firebombing the building and burning thirty-six people alive, including Vicente Menchú, the father of future Nobel laureate Rigoberta Menchú. There were only two survivors, the Spanish ambassador and a badly burned protester, who later that night was abducted from the hospital by armed men and murdered, his body left at the campus of the Universidad de San Carlos. A few days later, the CUC called a meeting at the symbolically charged ruins of Iximché, capital of the precolonial Kaqchiquel kingdom. Representatives from every important indigenous organization attended, including many not allied with the guerrillas or the CUC. This unprecedented coalition produced the below declaration, linking images of a mythic pan-Maya past with the demands of an increasingly unbearable present.

In the face of all the savage deeds of the invaders, their rich descendants, and the government that is complicit with the rich of other countries like the United States; in the face of persecution, threats, torture, land evictions, deceit, and massacres committed by the army, police, and bands of killers; [in the face of] political opportunists and spies that we know are in all the towns and villages. . . .

In the face of all that, the indigenous people have never stopped struggling. History and the present are a testament to our constant struggle. Since the Spanish invasion of 1522, our Quiché [K'iche'], Tzutuíl [Tz'utujil], Pocomam, Mam, Kokchí [Kekchi or Q'eqchi'], and other ancestors fought with decision and courage to defend their lives, lands, and culture. The kakchiquels [Kaqchikels] forced the invaders to abandon the first capital of Guatemala because from the mountains they came down to wage war on them.

Among the most important rebellions after the invasion are: Chiapas in 1708. The Mams of Ixtaguacán in 1743. Santa Lucía de Utatlán in 1760. The Cakchiquel [Kaqchikel] rebellion in Tecpán in 1764. The Kokchí rebellion in Cobán in 1770. The San Martín Cuchumatanes, Santiago Momostenango, and Ixtaguacán rebellion in 1813. The Quiché rebellion led by Atancío [Anastasio] Tzul in Totonicapán in 1820. The Jumay rebellion in 1833. Another in Ixtapacan in 1839. The Canjobal [Kanjobal or Q'anjob'al] rebellion in San Juan Ixcoy in 1898. Another by the Quichés in Totonicapan in 1905. The Cakchiquel rebellion in Patricía [Patzicía]. The Xujuyu between Sololá and Suchutepéquez in 1971. And many others. This shows that our people have never stopped struggling.

In the face of this reality of suffering, such as the recent massacre in the Spanish Embassy, in which twenty-one indigenous brothers and sisters were shot and burned to death, including four women, [who are] examples of struggle as they valiantly gave their lives in this peaceful occupation, [all this] has confirmed to our people and to the people of the world their courage, dedication, will, and heroism in the struggle to liberate our lives, even though they may have to leave their parents, spouses, or children forever. This is not insignificant, since the indigenous woman is and always has been part of our struggle; she has been exploited in the cotton fields, the sugar cane fields, the coffee fields, and because of her dress and language, her customs, and as a woman she is discriminated against and abused, as in the case of the rape of women and girls, who get pregnant, by the national army and the rich, exploiters in the countryside, in the city, and in all the corners of Guatemala.

To do away with all these evils of the rich descendants of the invaders and their government, we have to struggle together with workers, *campesinos*, students, slum dwellers, and other popular and democratic sectors, and make stronger the union and solidarity of the popular movement between the indigenous and Ladinos, because the solidarity of the popular movement with the indigenous struggle has been sealed by lives in the Spanish Embassy. The sacrifice of those lives brings us closer now than ever to a new society, to the Indian dawn.

May the blood of our indigenous brothers and sisters and their example of unyielding and brave struggle fortify all the indigenous [people] to keep struggling and conquer a life of justice, struggle: FOR A SOCIETY OF EQUALITY AND RESPECT, SO THAT OUR INDIAN PEOPLE AS SUCH MAY DEVELOP THEIR CULTURE BROKEN BY THE CRIMINAL INVADERS; FOR A JUST ECONOMY WITHOUT EXPLOITERS OR EXPLOITED; SO THAT THE LAND MAY BE COMMUNAL AS IN THE TIME OF OUR ANCESTORS; FOR A PEOPLE WITH-

OUT DISCRIMINATION; FOR AN END TO THE REPRESSION, TORTURE, KID-
NAPPING, MURDER, AND MASSACRES; SO THAT FORCED CONSCRIPTION MAY
END; SO THAT WE MAY ALL HAVE THE SAME RIGHTS TO WORK; SO THAT WE
ARE NO LONGER USED AS AN OBJECT OF TOURISM; FOR A JUST DISTRIBUTION
AND USE OF OUR NATIONAL WEALTH, AS IN THE TIME WHEN LIFE AND CUL-
TURE FLOURISHED AMONG OUR ANCESTORS.

But we also have to be clear that while we struggle for all this, the rich
and their government will always accuse us of being Communists, terrorists, delinquents, subversives, guerrillas, et cetera. But in the face of fabri-
cations and lies by the rich and their government, our Indian people will
keep rising up, step by step, until we triumph, because THE BLOOD OF OUR
HEROES, MASSACRED JANUARY 31 [1980] [AND] THE LIFE, STRUGGLE AND
BLOOD OF ALL THE INDIANS AND POOR LADINOS SPILLED IN THE ROAD OF
OUR STRUGGLE HAS FERTILIZED OUR STRUGGLE.

ALL THE DISCRIMINATED AND EXPLOITED INDIANS OF THE WORLD!
ALL THE WORKERS OF THE WORLD!
ALL THE FREE AND DEMOCRATIC PEOPLES OF THE WORLD!
ALL THE AUTHENTIC CHRISTIANS OF THE WORLD!
BE IN SOLIDARITY WITH THE INDIAN PEOPLE AND
OTHER EXPLOITED PEOPLE OF GUATEMALA!
MAY ALL RISE UP, MAY ALL BE CALLED, MAY NO ONE, NOT ONE OR TWO
GROUPS, BE LEFT BEHIND!——*POPOL-VUH*

Translated by Elizabeth Oglesby

An Indian Dawn

Carlota McAllister

In the early 1980s, hundreds of thousands of indigenous Guatemalans participated in armed revolutionary struggle, mostly as members of support networks for guerrilla groups, but also in local militias, as combatants, and sometimes as leaders. In contemporary Guatemala, the question of whether this participation represented the will of Mayas themselves or that of Ladino guerrilla leaders who coerced or manipulated Mayas is a subject of ongoing debate. Given the disastrous outcome of the guerrilla struggle, it is not surprising that many people now speak negatively about their involvement with the revolutionary movement. Yet restoring a more complex picture of Maya engagement in armed struggle means understanding the potential for change that this engagement once promised.

Anthropologist Carlota McAllister explores how these dynamics played out in the Maya-K'iche' village of Chupol, which was a longstanding center of campesino activism and by 1980 was a base of support for the Guerrilla Army of the Poor (EGP). While political activism had been gestating for decades, the "insurrectional moment" from late 1980 to late 1981 was a dramatic acceleration fueled by escalating state repression and a regional context of revolutionary upsurge in Central America. Distinctions between the mass-based peasant movements and armed revolution dissolved almost overnight, as the EGP mapped out military zones in the highlands that overlay the areas of peasant organizing. EGP leader Gustavo Meoño recalls this scenario as a "vortex" whereby in some cases the EGP intensified the armed struggle, while in other cases rural populations joined the rebels so quickly that they overran the insurgents' organizational structures. McAllister's work reconstructs the chaos and intensity of this moment in one village and asks what participating in the revolutionary struggle meant for people.

The K'iche' village of Chupol, which lies astride the Pan-American Highway at the southern tip of the department of El Quiché, had been an early and enthusiastic site of organizing for the Committee of Peasant Unity, (CUC) [see "Campesinos Struggle for a Different Future" in this volume]. Under the EGP guerrilla organization's new strategic plan, it lay at the heart of the so-called Hanoi Guerrilla Zone. EGP leaders had long professed admiration for the Vietnamese anti-imperialist and anticapitalist struggle, so this name hints at the role they hoped Chupol would play in the coming revolution, as a secure center of operations and a refuge for combatants, despite its vulnerable position on one of Guatemala's most important highways. Chupolenses learned of their community's new status when the organization announced that it would henceforth be known as the EGP rather than the CUC, disregarding a subsequent vote showing the community preferred the old name.

By late 1980, therefore, Chupol had come under what was effectively EGP rule. The EGP's organizational structure of subgroups with different revolutionary tasks had come to govern most everyday community relations. The Local Clandestine Committee coordinated nonmilitary logistical support for the organization, including procuring food from the local population for combatants, finding women to cook it, securing lodging for combatants visiting the community, and similar matters. The Political Formation Team raised support for the revolutionary struggle: team members gave consciousness-raising talks but also enforced political conformity. Community defense was in the hands of the Local Irregular Forces, patrols of ten adult men trained in self-defense techniques and armed with whatever the community could provide, who took turns keeping watch for soldiers. Finally, a liaison committee, led by a Regional Director, dealt directly with the combatants operating in the area, providing them with military logistical support. Although the regional director, a K'iche' man, was not himself from Chupol, the liaison committee was made up of those Chupolense leaders who had brought the community into the CUC in the first place.

An infrastructure for military operations was also established. The EGP opened five military training camps within easy walking distance of Chupol, where young men from distant communities as well as locals could learn the art of guerrilla warfare. Clandestine Production Units—factories for making Klaymore mines and primitive 12-caliber rifles—were established, and Chupolenses began to construct a press in a neighboring village for printing EGP propaganda.

Once the support structures for revolutionary war were built, it was the job of the Political Formation Team to convince Chupolenses to man them. Sometimes the team's message was articulated in the morally persuasive idioms of Catholicism or indigenous agricultural life. But, in the final instance, anyone who refused to believe that war was coming was subjected to a taste of it. In one notorious incident, the team killed two holdouts at the height of market day, at the base of a large tree that still marks the market's entrance. Gustavo Meoño, in charge of mass organizing for the national EGP, recognized that once the EGP and communities like Chupol merged, "there were many people who, against their will, found themselves swept up in this dynamic." Participant accounts indeed suggest that the sense that revolution was imminent acquired its own life.

Meoño is among those who attribute the breathtaking swiftness of the mobilization of the area to indigenous communities' seizure of the revolutionary process: "The same massiveness and generalization that the popular organizations, principally the CUC, had achieved were now transferred to the EGP, in some communities from one day to the next." Rank-and-file Chupolense EGP supporters, in contrast, tend to describe themselves as overwhelmed by the logic of revolution, saying that they joined the organization because they believed war was coming. Even a member of the feared Political Formation Team described himself as simply acquiescing to the organization's logic at his very first political meeting: "[They said] why don't we all get together, why has everything we've done been for the army's high command, for the rich, for the government. . . . They asked me if I would join right then, and I said yes."

Whether or not they willed it, therefore—and those who willed it least and refused to heed the guerrillas' warnings about imminent war undoubtedly lived in fewer numbers to tell of their desires—Chupolenses were soon spending most of their time in war-related activities. They participated regularly in EGP acts of sabotage along the corridor of the Pan-American Highway, making blockades out of trees, digging trenches, and laying Klaymore mines. In June 1981, Chupolenses commenced construction of a series of earthworks modeled on the Viet Cong's tunnels in Cu Chi outside Saigon, earning Chupol the approving epithet of "Vietnamese village" among the urban left. An EGP member who may have visited Vietnam showed Chupolenses how to dig both *buzones*—"mailboxes" in which to store arms, supplies, clothes, and themselves in case of enemy attack—and *trampas*, three-meter-deep "traps" lined with sharpened and fire-hardened wooden stakes, to impale unwanted visitors. Also for self-defense, Chupolense women were instructed to have water boiling at all times and keep ground chili peppers handy, to throw in the faces of any soldiers who might suddenly arrive.

In the meantime, EGP actions in the area grew more aggressive: the group's communiqués reported that in June, July, and August 1981, numerous army convoys and patrols were bombed along the highway, and several military commissioners and army officers were executed. On July 19, 1981—on the second anniversary of the Sandinista Revolution in Nicaragua—the EGP further upped the ante by incorporating the four guerrilla zones of the

The top line of this leaflet, distributed by the insurgent Revolutionary Organization of People in Arms, reads: "As guerrilla triumphs increase, so do the people's hope. Many want to take up arms to get rid of these murderous governments once and for all." The dialogue represents rural people urging a rapid victory, with the guerrilla leader cautioning that the struggle will be long: "*Compañero*, we need arms to rapidly destroy the enemy," says the man on the left, to which the guerrilla representative responds: "Think about this, *compañeros*: can you destroy a thick wall with a few blows or cut down a big tree with three machete swings? No, we can't get rid of our enemy with a few blows." The bottom line reads: "We have to damage it many times in order to weaken it and prevent it from attacking us. Let's fight under intelligent leadership using guerrilla warfare." From the collection of Deborah T. Levenson.

southwestern highlands into the Augusto César Sandino Guerrilla Front (FACS). To create a "front" was to declare that insurgent activities in the area of its operations were now explicitly military.

For Chupolenses, the war began on August 15, 1981, less than a month after the establishment of the FACS. A patrol of soldiers marched into the village, undeterred by the *trampas*, and proceeded to the printing press, which was still under construction. Caught off guard, the twenty-six people who happened to be working there, including several women and children, were kidnapped. The next day, the soldiers drove their victims in a truck along the highway toward the north, killing one person every kilometer, and throwing the cadavers onto the road. The sense among organized Chupolenses that the war was inevitable meant that they had plans for what to do when it came. Now they followed these plans, fanning out in groups to other organized villages more distant from the highway. Heads of families away in the capital city or on the coast were informed by friends of the war's arrival and returned home, while many younger men, believing the war would be short, decided to wait it out away from the community. Only a few families, either because they were uninformed or because they had refused to heed the organization, remained in Chupol, only to be murdered by the army.

The soldiers established a base in Chupol's church, digging trenches in the marketplace, and ringing their compound with tanks. At first they seemed reluctant to leave the safety of the highway, but soon army patrols were making regular excursions into the hinterland to kill or kidnap Chupolenses, while planes overhead and tanks on the highway began to shell Chupolense hiding places. The army also set up roadblocks to stop and search passing cars and buses, using masked informants and lists obtained under torture to identify "subversives" and bring them into the church for interrogation, something few people survived. Chupol now became a killing center, a place where dead bodies and burning fields were always visible by the side of the road and where travelers dreaded to pass. Eventually, the military onslaught forced Chupolenses and their hosts into the high, cold mountains surrounding their villages, where they spent a year running from the army, sleeping out of doors under the rain, and eating what little food they could gather in the forest. Except for the highest-placed members of the liaison committee, they lost contact with the EGP leadership. When the Guatemalan government offered an amnesty to guerrilla supporters in 1983, the EGP finally sent a message telling Chupolenses to surrender. Using whatever scraps of white and blue plastic they could find to fashion facsimiles of the Guatemalan flag, the survivors of this long ordeal went home to find all their worldly goods burnt or stolen, and their church still occupied.

Questions about who bears responsibility for these horrors are important, and they are ones Chupolenses today themselves pose. All Chupolenses fear the army and blame it for the innumerable atrocities it committed to some degree, but many Chupolenses are also furious at the EGP. Some believe the organization provoked the army's wrath and brought the war upon them. Others accuse the guerrillas of abandoning Chupolenses in their hour of greatest need. As one man pithily argued, "They fucking left [*Se fueron a la chingada*]. What about 'Hasta la victoria siempre'?"

But perhaps more surprising than these sentiments of anger is the belief many Chupolenses sustained in the possibility of victory even after surrender. Speaking of the violence, one man told me with extraordinary equanimity, "The thing is, the struggle is like that," before revealing that he had joined up again with the EGP "as soon as I could find them" upon return. Chupolenses were also among the first rural indigenous Guatemalans to join the human-rights organizations that sprang up after the intensity of the violence lessened in the mid-1980s, a move that they describe as a continuation of their CUC-initiated struggle for indigenous rights and against the state.

How can we frame the question of what participating in revolutionary struggle meant in places like Chupol? Undeniably, August 15, 1981, marked a violent rupture with the past for Chupolenses forced to abandon not only their homes but also all the structures that had previously shaped their lives. This rupture also gave rise to further violence. In their refuge, Chupolenses answered to no governmental authority but that established by the EGP, which was not entirely sure how to begin administering entire indigenous villages. Meoño claims that in the brief months before army incursions made it impossible to do anything but run and hide, the EGP had managed to constitute a parallel state in the communities in hiding, performing weddings and registering births as well as schooling children. Chupolense recollections of this proto-state, however, emphasize its repressive functions. National EGP leaders delegated the authority to rule over the villages to the Political Formation Team, whose suspicions were strengthened by wartime exigencies, as was their perceived need to ensure total solidarity by any means necessary. When guerrilla rule became unsustainable, however, the violence grew much worse. Chupolenses describe themselves as having been reduced to the state of animals: running from the soldiers in the dark and cold, eating wild plants and roots, and taking shelter under trees or rocks, focused only on survival. Many are plagued by the horrible guilt of having failed their own children, spouses, or parents in this desperate struggle.

Mixed with the memory of the violence of displacement, however, are traces of certain "pleasures of agency," similar to those that the political scientist Elizabeth Wood encountered among former organized peasants in El Salvador. Solidarity is first among them: any occasion on which sharing is demanded elicits extensive reminiscences about how unstintingly Chupolenses' neighbors gave of their food and their homes during their time of refuge. For men, another saving grace is pride in their own ingenuity and courage in the face of the enemy. During one of many collective discussions about the extraordinary difficulties of their experiences in hiding, I asked the head of a household that had given refuge to hundreds of Chupolenses how he had managed to get food to feed them all. "I'm so glad you asked that!" he exclaimed, animatedly describing the footpaths and bypasses, known only to local indigenous residents, that he and others would take to get to the market in Chichicastenango and bring back their purchases. Other men told me about escaping from patrols of soldiers by lying to them, scolding them for their bad behavior, confusing them with clever arguments, or even by relieving themselves by the side of the road as the soldiers passed in order to appear unafraid. Stories in this heroic register are so common that it is hard to believe revolutionary mobilization was entirely imposed on Chupolenses.

But Chupolense nostalgia about their intellectual and political exchanges with Ladino guerrilla leaders perhaps speaks most directly to the question of whether Mayas possessed a "revolutionary will." After July 1981, when an army operation uncovered many of the guerrilla safe houses in the capital city, urban insurgents from the EGP as well as other guerrilla groups tried to escape repression by fleeing to rural strongholds. Visiting Chupol's hinterland, imagined as liberated territory but with the added attraction of proximity to the capital, became a kind of rite of passage for urbanites seeking to join the struggle in the mountains, according to one former EGP member. At a mental health workshop in Chupol where a group of survivors was asked to draw a mural representing their history, they recalled this period by depicting the guerrillas as giants surrounded by the smaller stick figures of Chupolenses themselves, dutifully spelling out the acronyms of all the organizations to which these giants had belonged. Those who had greater contact with the visitors proudly recite their names, which include those of many leaders still prominent in the political party the former insurgency has become. These memories, like those of the man who asked "What about *hasta la victoria siempre*," are sometimes tinged with a sense of betrayal, but the poignancy of these accusations shows the value Chupolenses placed on these relationships and the fellowship they provided in a struggle that was understood as shared.

Given this understanding, it is significant that even Chupolenses who now revile the insurgents ultimately affirm the opportunity the war gave them to fight back. Despite their anger, many refuse to count their time with the EGP as an entirely failed endeavor, arguing that "at least Ladinos learned that we have to be respected, *que no nos vamos a dejar* [that we won't be pushed around]." The modest gain of reformulating their relationships with Ladinos is not all that Chupolenses desired from revolutionary war. But if Guatemalan history is a long story of Ladino oppression of indigenous people, these new relationships provide a glimpse of the Indian dawn the Declaration of Iximché had hailed.

Lithograph from Carlos Mérida's *Estampas del Popol Vuh*, 1943. It illustrates how Hunahpú and Xbalanque, the hero twins of the sacred book of the Maya, descend fearlessly into Xibalbá, the place of terror and death. Mérida (1891–1984) was familiar with avant-garde art in Mexico and Europe, and he developed a subtle and stirring style and color scheme that defy easy categorization. From the collection of Deborah T. Levenson.

Cofradía member, by Juan Sisay, ca. 1970s. Perhaps the country's most important Maya painter, Juan Sisay was born into a *campesino* family near Lake Atitlán. The self-taught Sisay (born 1921–assassinated 1989) painted his subjects with clarity and respect. Image used by permission of Arte Maya Tz'utuhil.

Community mural in San Juan Comalapa, Chimaltenango. Stretching for two blocks along the town's entrance, this multipanel mural depicts the history of Comalapa's Kaqchikel-Mayas from the pre-Conquest era and Spanish colonialism through the nineteenth and twentieth centuries, including graphic renderings of the trauma of the 1980s. This panel recognizes the militant community activism of the 1970s, a bold testament to an often-silenced history. Photo by Emma Maasch, 2010. Used by permission of the photographer.

Born in 1959 in the Kaqchikel town of San Juan Comalapa, Chimaltenango, María Elena Curruchiche paints everyday scenes with humor and a keen eye for the often-ignored role of women in rural village life. Curruchiche's father and grandfather were recognized oil painters, and she puts her own imprint on their tradition, captioning her miniature paintings with sly narrative titles. Paintings by María Elena Curruchiche, 1999. From the collection of Greg Grandin.

(*opposite top*) "Las dos mujeres son hermanas; van a repartir el sitio; cada una tiene su licenciado." (The two women are sisters; they are dividing a property lot; each has a lawyer.)

(*opposite bottom*) "El muchacho solo; la gente hisiero una mujer de escoba su compañera." (The young man is single; the townspeople have made him a broomstick woman to be his companion.)

(*top*) "Las mujeres vendiendo güipuiles y guaro escondido." (The women are selling *huipiles* [tunics] and hidden moonshine.)

(*bottom*) "Están pesando maize; el señor pesa un quintal." (They are weighing corn; the man weighs one *quintal*.)

Sin título (Untitled) by Moises Barrios (b. 1946). From the series *Nuestro futuro no es como antes* (Our future is not what it was), 2000. Used by permission of the artist.

Isabel Ruiz (b. 1945) performs *Matemática sustractiva* (Subtractive math), 2008, by drawing forty-five thousand lines in reference to the number of people "disappeared" during Guatemala's thirty-six-year armed conflict. A man followed behind, erasing the chalk marks, after which Ruiz would start the drawing again. The performance, dedicated to the disappeared Guatemalan writer Luis de León, took place in Antigua at an international exhibition of twenty-five Latin American artists on *The Disappeared*. Photo by Francisco Morales Santos. Used by permission of Isabel Ruiz.

San Manuel exilio mártir (San Manuel martyred exile). Sculpture by Colectivo La
Torana (Marlov Barrios, Plinio Villagrán, Erick Menchú, and Norman Morales y Josué
Romero). Exhibited in the Bienal de Arte Paiz in Guatemala City, 2010. La Torana is
one of Guatemala's most creative collectives of young artists. In the group's words,
this sculpture is a saint who "does the contrary of 'good,' an inverted saint who helps
delinquents, whose life is devoted to crime, getting easy money, passing undetected
under the nose of the law, and vanishing into the air." Photo by Andrés Asturias. Used
by permission of La Torana.

VI

Intent to Destroy

By 1980, open political dissent in Guatemala was tantamount to a death sentence. The government's incineration of protesters inside the Spanish embassy in January of that year signaled a declaration of war. Death squads roamed the streets of Guatemala City, and kidnappings and killings of community activists continued unabated in the countryside, propelling further radicalization. In February 1980, a strike organized by the Committee for Peasant Unity shut down Pacific coast plantations in the middle of the harvest season. The strike represented a new alliance between highland seasonal migrants, mostly indigenous, and full-time plantation workers, mostly Ladinos—a nightmare scenario for a landed elite that had long relied on racism to forestall union organizing. In the face of escalating repression, including the collective kidnapping of twenty-seven union leaders in June 1980 and the murder of dozens of university professors, popular organizations went underground. By 1981, armed revolutionaries had stepped up actions in the capital and in sixteen of the country's twenty-two provinces. In the halls of the National Palace there were whispers of an imminent insurgent victory.

On the international scene, 1980 saw the election of US president Ronald Reagan, who immediately signaled an escalation of the Cold War. The triumph of the Sandinista revolution in Nicaragua and the worsening civil war in El Salvador pushed Central America to the front and center of US foreign policy. Reagan and his advisors envisioned Guatemala as a strategic bulwark against the region's revolutionary upsurge, but the US government had limited options there: military aid had been cut off under President Jimmy Carter in 1977 because of human-rights concerns, and the brutal news coming out of Guatemala in the early 1980s made a resumption of aid seem unlikely. Advisors to Reagan began crafting alternatives, including working through international proxies, such as Argentina's military government, to provide covert assistance and training to the Guatemalan army. "Soft" aid was channeled to Guatemala through a network of us-based private organizations; these included conservative evangelical churches, whose presence in Guatemala grew rapidly during the 1980s.

With business elites growing alarmed at the incompetency of their army and capital flight paralyzing the economy, it was becoming increasingly clear to ranking military officers that the army needed a new strategy to defeat the guerrillas. The first stage of the new plan—implemented by a rising cohort of counterinsurgent theorists in late 1981 under president General Romeo Lucas García—was the annihilation of the urban insurgency. This step was necessary to prevent the guerrilla organizations from consolidating a political presence in Guatemala City. The second stage, which also began under Lucas García and continued with even greater ferocity after a coup installed the evangelical General Efraín Ríos Montt as head of state, moved thousands of government troops into the mountains for rural pacification.

The army used massive systematic violence to drive a wedge between the guerrillas and their rural support base. In its 1999 report, *Memoria del silencio*, the un-administered Guatemalan truth commission, known as the Commission for Historical Clarification (CEH, for its Spanish acronym), documented more than six hundred massacres committed by government forces against civilians in predominately Maya areas between 1981 and 1983. The violence was extreme. Soldiers burned hundreds of villages to the ground and depopulated entire regions. By 1983, the army had brought the countryside under its effective control, forcing the guerrilla groups into a retreat from which they never fully rebounded. Army operations wrenched away the rebels' social base of support, profoundly altering Guatemalan rural life in the process. The Catholic Church estimated that more than one million people were displaced from their homes during this period, and at least 150,000 fled to Mexico as refugees. This "scorched earth" counterinsurgency shattered families and broke the agricultural cycle, leading to hunger and widespread deprivation, as refugees hiding in the mountains and lowland jungle scavenged roots and wild plants to survive. Not since the Spanish invasion had Guatemala's indigenous populations seen anything so devastating.

One question that confronted the CEH was whether the Guatemalan state had committed genocide. Were Mayas killed because they were Maya, or were they killed because the army believed they were the support base of the insurgency? The international Genocide Convention defines genocide as the "intent to destroy, in whole or in part, a national, ethnic, racial or religious group, as such." The difficulty of establishing an "intent to destroy" led some observers to argue that the massacres in Guatemala between 1981 and 1983 were not genocide. The army was not motivated by hatred of Mayas, this reasoning goes, but by the goal of defeating the insurgency. In areas of the country where there was little or no rebel presence, the army did not inflict the same terror on indigenous communities, and government-allied forces did torture, execute, and disappear nonindigenous activists. But the CEH, by treating "motive" and "intent" as separate categories of analysis, ruled that acts of genocide had indeed been committed. In other words, the army's overarching *motive* was to defeat the guerrillas, but to do this, it *intentionally* targeted entire indigenous communities. The truth commission argued that Guatemalan military strategists drew on long-held racial assumptions regarding indigenous culture to single out Mayas *as such* as the internal enemy, using brutal, unrelenting savagery to cut off indigenous communities from the insurgency and break down communal organizations identified as seedbeds of guerrilla support.

The most centralized, coordinated phase of the counterinsurgency was executed with a racist frenzy, which included the murder of children—often by beating them against a wall or crushing them with the bodies of dead adults—as well as amputations, impalings, eviscerations, abortions by bayonets, and burning victims alive. In some areas, indigenous language and dress were effectively outlawed, and sacred Catholic and Maya sites were profaned. In villages that remained united in opposition to the military and government, the army forced intracommunal violence. It was a common tactic to make members of a community commit violence against their neighbors. Often the army encouraged their civilian allies to avail themselves of their victims' property and their surviving wives and daughters. At times, children were forced to murder their parents. Such terror not only fractured local solidarity; it also achieved the objective of the pacification campaign by binding the perpetrators in a blood ritual to the state, as represented by the army.

Military strategy was not limited to a scorched-earth war, however. Adhering to the common counterinsurgent assumption that development is security's handmaiden, the army followed up its "Victory '82" offensive with "Firmness '83" and "Institutional Renewal '84," designed to create conditions for a militarized reconstruction of the devastated regions. Army strategists studied the successes and failures of counterinsurgencies elsewhere in the world, particularly in neighboring El Salvador, where only a massive infusion of US money had saved the Salvadoran army from defeat. Guatemalan strategists concluded that the Salvadoran military had failed to consolidate long-term dominance over the countryside, thus allowing rebels to establish local sovereignty. Guatemalan officials came to believe that their war of extermination had to be followed up with a massive and permanent "war of reconstruction."

This war had three components: First, internally displaced refugees were rounded up and resettled into army-controlled "model villages" and "development poles." Second, the military set up "interinstitutional coordinating councils" to tightly control food aid and other governmental and nongovernmental assistance to the resettled populations. Last, the army established a network of village-level civil-defense patrols to invert the guerrillas' social support base and bring the civilian population into the war on the side of the army. By the mid-1980s, nearly one million Guatemalan teenagers and adult men participated in the civil patrols, and the patrols operated throughout wide areas of the countryside, especially in the Maya regions. Civil patrollers accompanied soldiers on search-and-destroy missions to ferret out isolated rebel columns, and patrollers were ordered to kill suspected guerrilla collaborators in their own villages or in neighboring communities. Most importantly, the civil patrols functioned as a vast intelligence-gathering arm for the military. Patrol commanders closely monitored the movement of people and goods in and out of their communities, and they were obliged to give regular reports to the army. Through the civil-patrol network, the Guatemalan army inserted itself into the fabric of everyday village life, and this local-level militarization became one of the most pernicious legacies of the counterinsurgency.

In August 1983, a coup replaced Ríos Montt with General Óscar Humberto Mejía Victores, who continued the high command's phased plan for political transition. This plan included the promulgation of a new constitution and national elections in 1985. Violence continued, but wholesale massacres subsided. In January 1986, Christian Democrat Vinicio Cerezo was inaugurated as Guatemala's first civilian president in two decades. Winning by an ample margin in fraud-free elections, Cerezo seemed to hold out the promise of a better future for Guatemala's majority; but having a civilian in the National Palace did not signal a break with the past. Cerezo reminded Guatemalans during his inauguration speech that he had "received the government but not the power." The army had sponsored the civilian transition; the army would dictate its limits. One long-range aspect of the military-brokered transition to democracy, as advocated by Cerezo's minister of defense, General Héctor Gramajo, was the creation of national stability through increased government expenditures in education, health, and infrastructure, in order to dampen social radicalism and ensure the long-term survival of the state. But even this strategy proved too ambitious when it ran into the intransigence of economic elites; in 1988, a bid to reform Guatemala's regressive tax code nearly brought Cerezo down. In the wake of the tax debacle, the government abandoned state developmentalism, privatized public utilities, and opened up the economy to increased foreign investment and imports.

Popular movements in Guatemala began a cautious, brave revival after the mid-1980s. Relatives of people disappeared by state security forces held weekly vigils in front of the National Palace. The economic crisis spurred the tentative emergence of a small urban labor movement as well as protests by students and shantytown dwellers. On May Day, 1986, thousands of rural peasants marched from Guatemala's Pacific coast to the capital in a dramatic appeal for land. By the end of the 1980s, the army's grip on rural village life loosened somewhat, and communities began to protest the onerous civil patrols and the persecution of civilians in the conflict zones. The end of the decade brought prospects for peace talks between the government and the rebels. This spurred a renewed wave of violence against activists, however, as the army sought to prevent the armed Left from using the peace process to rebuild its political alliances.

Thunder in the City

Mario Payeras

By 1981, the army's counterinsurgency offensive in Guatemala City was in full force. Mario Payeras, a founder of the Guerrilla Army of the Poor (Ejército Guerrillero de los Pobres, or EGP) writes of the demolition of urban safe houses belonging to a sister rebel group. For the army, destroying the guerrillas' strategic rearguard in the capital was the first stage in an all-out counterinsurgent offensive, preventing the insurgents from developing the sort of urban political presence that rebels in neighboring El Salvador achieved. The extensive intelligence system the United States helped put into place, starting in the mid-1960s, was key to this operation, as was the support given by Israeli and Argentine security advisors, who provided sophisticated technology and training that helped the army monitor electricity and water use to detect guerrilla safe houses. For their part, the guerrillas, unable to grasp the full extent of the army's intelligence capabilities, desperately tried to plug their own security breaches and maintain a chain of command. By late 1981, the rebels were, as Payeras notes, "fish swimming above a net that had not yet closed." The net soon closed, forcing urban cadres into a chaotic retreat to the countryside or into exile.

On July 8, 1981, the spectacular phase of the urban antiguerrilla campaign had begun. Midmorning on that Wednesday, one of the radio stations in the capital began reporting that in Vista Hermosa, an elegant suburb to the east of the city, a violent combat was taking place between soldiers and guerrillas trapped inside a private residence. [The military] was not letting the press or private citizens through. Fire trucks and police patrol cars were heading to the area with sirens on and lights flashing. . . . Something quite serious was going on. Subsequent news bulletins indicated that the army was firing a cannon at the besieged residence. Around midday, a strong explosion heard all over the city put an end to the resistance of the guerrillas holed up inside. . . .

Newspaper accounts the next day gave ample details on the operation. The security forces had destroyed a safe house of the Revolutionary Organization of the People in Arms (ORPA), with around seventeen combatants inside, in the largest antiguerrilla operation in recent years. Surrounded since dawn inside the residence, the guerrillas had resisted until midday. . . . After the combat ended, seventeen bodies supposedly were discovered inside the ruins of the house. They were all young, both men and women, most of them armed with automatic rifles. From the available information it could be deduced that the house was used as a place to make explosives, since a large quantity of fabricated mines was discovered, as well as instruments and raw materials for their manufacture. A foreign professional had rented the house with false papers. . . .

The [ORPA] *compañeros* had observed a strict regime of clandestinity with apparently no cracks for casual detection by third parties. The combatants stationed there on their way to other fronts did not know the location of the house. They were brought in with their eyes blindfolded in vehicles with polarized windows, and they kept up a rigorous discipline inside the house. Neighbors probably heard a large number of different voices coming from the house, which could have been a breach in security. But that alone couldn't have explained the raid. Perhaps someone informed about the house. But we discounted this, since those who knew the house had either died in the combat or were under the control of the organization at that moment. . . . Twelve days before the raid, the army . . . had presented on television two captured combatants from the affected organization. Both were indigenous *campesinos*, very young . . . and it is possible that these prisoners could have described the inside of the house where they had stayed . . . and thus the enemy could have deduced the kind of infrastructure used by the organization in these maneuvers. It wouldn't have been difficult to make a list of these kinds of buildings that were rented in the city and undertake a detailed and secret investigation of each one. . . . Yet even with all that, we concluded that the margin of security was still wide enough in our case, and if the enemy had hit our sister organization it was because of errors committed by the *compañeros*. With respect to the rest, we thought that the quantity of rented dwellings in the city numbered in the thousands and the enemy's apparatus couldn't investigate all of them. . . .

All of these theories came crashing down the next day. On Friday the tenth, two days after the first attack, the afternoon papers gave more details of a large-scale military operation. A new residence, this time . . . on the city's south side, had been surrounded by troops, this time starting at midday. In the entire urban sector, prolonged gunfire and cannon blasts were heard. Subsequent information reported an even higher number of deaths for the sister organization this time. A large arsenal of explosives, ammunitions, military equipment, and loads of propaganda had been seized. Among

the dead there were once again women and some university professionals.
. . . According to press reports, the house had been detected through a denunciation by neighbors, who had noticed unusual or suspicious activity
inside. . . . As long as we didn't commit similar mistakes, we would be okay.
Once again, this was a mansion, rented by people using false documents,
vehicles with polarized windows; a large number of combatants bunked
there clandestinely. Cots, oversized cooking pots, large quantities of stored
food supplies—in other words, obvious guerrilla barracks that in the event
of an attack would turn into terrible rat traps.

The analysis of the new raid and additional information on the first gave
us more concrete explanations. For starters, it was clear that the enemy had
sufficient prior information and that the second attack was part of an entire
military campaign plan. . . .

Over the next few days, from the most diverse sources, we began to
receive all kinds of "explanations." . . . In February, if we remembered correctly, there had been a general housing census. Students, public employees,
statisticians, as is typical in these cases, had gone from house to house with
forms to count the urban population. They asked the number of people in
each dwelling and the name and occupation of each one. The basic information on the tenants was registered on these forms. All this information
had been computerized. Later . . . new census takers, this time from private
agencies, registered age, income, and even opinions on social issues. . . .
Using this data set, it wouldn't be that difficult for investigators to locate
family nuclei made up of young couples whose jobs didn't exist or whose
names didn't coincide with those originally given. Houses rented by young
couples without verifiable jobs, or by someone whose data didn't match the
original census, were investigated secretly and in detail. Others argued that
the purpose of the survey was to establish how long a family had lived in a
given house. Since the enemy surmised that guerrillas changed houses frequently, as their cover was blown, any house rented in the last six months
was going to be investigated. . . . Later on, a new variant was added to this
theory. The key to the enemy's investigations was studying the lease itself.
A rental contract is supposed to be drawn up before a notary public. The
document registers information on the renter as well as a cosigner. The enemy, it was argued, was investigating all rental and real estate sale contracts
by examining notary records. An order had gone out to lawyers and nota-
ries to present this confidential documentation to the Supreme Court. . . .
All this information was passed along to the army's computer centers. . . .

The military's operational saturation of the city was becoming obvious. . . . In the streets, meanwhile, the traditional mechanisms of control

were unchanged. Vehicles with a certain type of license plate, already well known by us, continued to be used by security patrols. These were the usual "armed men," dressed as civilians, nasty looking, in vehicles that easily gave away the mission of their passengers. Roadblocks also continued at certain points throughout the city. Discretely, however, new enemy agents began operating, breaking completely with the known characteristics. For instance, these were men who looked like "new rich" businessmen riding in luxury cars. Their clothes and manners corresponded perfectly to the sector of the city in which they operated. Their weapons could not be seen, although what *was* visible was the long radio antenna on their vehicles. . . .

.   The raids on the guerrilla safe houses had several immediate implications. The first and biggest was that the scheme of renting properties with shaky documentation could no longer be maintained. We needed to vacate those properties as fast as possible, before the enemy hit them, one by one. This basic conclusion led to other consequences. In each house, captured prisoners and documents created new complications and potential risks. Even if the renter's identification papers were false, often the cosigner's documents were real, and that person from then on would face obvious risks. This situation was made worse by the fact that, in general, the people who offered these kinds of services were not militants, and the organization could not order them to go underground. They were citizens with a legal life, with wives, children, regular jobs and commitments that the organization could not just annul by decree. The enemy's blade did not distinguish degrees or hierarchies of commitment but summarily captured or assassinated all involved. Two brothers of one *compañero*, one a leaseholder of one of our safe houses, were kidnapped and immediately killed. That was based on their last names, and the enemy had no scruples about killing both, even though only one had signed the lease. The enemy's interest in personal documents or legal vehicles had the same implications. After every new attack, the number of legal assets we had to dispose of and contracts we had to cancel grew. . . .

Landlords, fearing that the military could demolish their property in a raid—the stories of which were being sensationalized by the press—began to question tenants. . . . Very soon we realized that many of our precautions were falling short. We realized, for example, that not all of the deaths reported by the military were real. The *compañeros* could also have been captured alive. If no one saw the body, they could not be presumed dead. . . .

One of the characteristics of the clandestine urban struggle was the high degree of operational compartmentalization. Although the method of conspiratorial art wasn't always followed to the letter, as a general policy it was often enough to protect the militants and resources from the enemy. Yet, during an offensive, this method could backfire. Allowing each militant to know only a piece of the picture meant the organization could protect the rest of its members and keep functioning. . . . But the parceling of information, during particular moments, also hindered the leadership from dispatching word of a threat to the structure or establishing quickly the key information needed to make life-and-death decisions. During critical moments, it often meant that people would have to wait for the next day's contact with the militant who knew someone else's name, and address, or a crucial piece of information, before sending the alert back through the chain to those whose lives could depend on a crucial piece of information. Many lives were saved or lost depending on whether the warning arrived in time or too late.

As a consequence of all this, the clandestine structures that had been set up artificially in the city collapsed. After the army assaulted the first residences with a great show of force and publicity, the clandestine functioning of the urban guerrilla war quickly came undone. . . . The cannon blasts from one raid had barely subsided when a new safe house would be attacked. At first, the endangered houses would be evacuated by their tenants in secret, in an orderly way, taking out people, weapons, documents, furniture, clothes, provisions. The rapidity of the raids, however, accelerated our preventive maneuvers. The entire urban front entered a period of disorienting last-minute evacuations. Some houses were abandoned with breakfast still on the table or the lights left on, depending on when its occupants received the order to leave. One house was abandoned just two days after the tenants had moved in. It had been evacuated preventively a couple of weeks prior by another clandestine cell, and the new *compañeros* received information that the house would be attacked the next morning. We were closing the mortal circle of a war that rested on weak foundations. . . .

In reality, the use of military intelligence involving prisoners was just one of the enemy's sources of information. The military's analysis of our propaganda, of our tactics, the study of seized documents . . . gave the adversary a torrent of crucial intelligence to act on. . . . No piece of information, as minuscule as it might seem, was unimportant in this death struggle. The army's intelligence priorities were to establish the organizational structure and composition of the guerrilla groups, as well as their conceptual underpinnings, their methods of recruitment and operation. . . . The army accumulated, processed, and systematized all available information. It drew on techniques drawn from science, sociology, psychology, psychiatry, computer science, film, radio, photography. It concentrated on both short- and long-term goals. . . . Special teams were dedicated to studying each revolutionary organization, as well as popular and democratic groups. These teams then proceeded to attack each of these organizations in turn. . . .

By the beginning of August [1981], the urban guerrillas were like fish swimming above a net that had not yet closed. What happened to the urban front was only part of the counteroffensive launched by the enemy against the revolutionary movement. The insurgency, which had spread guerrilla warfare to the whole country, was preparing for the final stages of the military struggle. . . . But the insurgency had an Achilles' heel: its strategic rearguard continued to be located in the capital, a center of services and also an important battleground. What happened in the city had great resonance for the guerrillas' ability to act nationally and internationally. For the enemy command, meanwhile, the primary objective was the strategic dislocation of the revolutionary war, forcing the guerrillas to change their plans and lose their key flank in the city. . . . The key weapon was intelligence, complemented by psychological warfare and propaganda. In short, that is what happened. Over the next weeks, after destroying the guerrillas' strategic urban rearguard, the anti-insurgent campaign moved into its rural counterinsurgency phases, exploiting its early success and maintaining the initiative. We were learning the rigorous logic of the laws of warfare. We paid for that lesson in blood.

Translated by Elizabeth Oglesby

The San Francisco Massacre, July 1982

Ricardo Falla

By the end of 1981, the Guatemalan army had successfully dislodged the urban guerrilla forces from the capital city. The next phase of the counterinsurgency war focused on asserting military control in the countryside, especially in the highlands
and northern lowlands, where the Guerrilla Army of the Poor had been organizing
among Maya communities for several years.

    Anthropologist and Jesuit priest Ricardo Falla documents one of the largest mas-
sacres at the San Francisco farm in northern Huehuetenango, where an estimated
three hundred people were killed. In its wake, thousands of people fled nearby villages, causing the depopulation of a large swath of territory along the Guatemala–
Mexico border. This case exhibits many patterns also present in other massacres,
such as the physical concentration of the population and the methodical separation
of women and men, all of which indicate a level of premeditation on the part of the
army. In the early 1980s, no human-rights organizations functioned openly in Guatemala, and testimony came from a lone survivor who made his way into Mexico.
His words upon his arrival in Mexico capture a shock so sharp that he struggles
to grasp his own existence: "Eleven in the morning it must be, and I come here to
Santa Marta, but I'm like an idiot. I don't see anything clearly. I'm not even sad.
I don't think anything. I haven't eaten, I haven't eaten. I have no coat, I have no
clothes. This is what I see. Nothing, nobody! I have no hat, nobody."

Several things prompt me to present the documentation and analysis of the
massacre which took place on the rural estate of San Francisco in the area
of Nentón in the department of Huehuetenango in Guatemala.

    The scale and intensity of repression in Guatemala have made it impos-
sible to document any of the massacres in depth as was done in 1978 in the
case of Panzós in Alta Verapaz. . . . The public is numbed by so many figures and names of unknown places. An in-depth study of one massacre will
enable readers to imagine what the others might have been like, and enable
them to deeply feel the horror of such an event.

    Another reason for examining the San Francisco massacre is that it caused the flight of some 9,000 refugees from northern Huehuetenango to Mexico at the end of July and the beginning of August 1982. Following the path of the news of the massacre from the village itself to the sister village of San José Yulaurel, to neighboring villages like Yalambojoch, Yalanhuitz and Yalcastán and later, to the refugee camps and the major newspapers, allows us to see how the news alters as it passes from mouth to mouth. Though variations occur, the basic truth remains. Some testimonies pass through second and third hand sources, but they should not be dismissed because some data is mistaken or numbers changed.

A Summary of the Facts

The broad outline of facts as they are already known [*New York Times* October 12, 1982] is that on July 17, about 11 AM, 600 foot soldiers arrived from Barillas frustrated at their failure to find a guerrilla camp previously located in the nearby mountains and apparently ready to wipe out the village-estate of San Francisco. Simultaneously, an army helicopter—the unmistakable sign that the actors were not guerrillas—arrived and landed on the soccer field with supplies for the soldiers. The colonel in charge of the operation ordered the resident Chuj Indians to congregate in the center of the village for a meeting. Even though the villagers noted that the faces of the officials were disturbed, they were not afraid because on June 24, the army had passed through with friendly words and without causing any damage. The soldiers scattered to call the women from their houses. Then they gathered the men and closed them in the courthouse and put the women in the small church. The two structures were about 20 meters apart and even though the people were for all practical purposes jailed they could hear what was happening in one place or the other.

The soldiers cut up the meat from one of the bulls they made the villagers give them upon arrival. Then they began to shoot the women in the church. Those who were not killed that way were taken to their houses where they were killed with machetes. While in the houses, the soldiers stole cassette recorders, radios, clothes and money. With that and funds robbed from the cooperative, they took about 20,000 *quetzales* [one *quetzal* equaled one dollar in 1982]. Next, they returned to the church to kill the children who, separated from their others, had been left crying and screaming. They killed them by slitting open their stomachs and smashing them against hard wooden poles. Witnesses saw the horrifying spectacle through holes in the courthouse window and for a moment when the soldier standing guard opened the courthouse door.

The Buried/Los sepultados. Photographic interpretation of a clandestine grave at San Francisco Nenton, Huehuetenango, Guatemala. Photo by Daniel Hernández-Salazar. Used by permission of the photographer.

After killing the children, they began with the men—first old men, then the working men and youths. They took them outside in groups and killed most of them. Inside the courthouse, they killed the local authorities—the sheriff, the auxiliary mayor and the police. The estate administrator was not sacrificed at San Francisco, but was tied up during the massacre and killed several days later on the road between Yalambojoch and Bulej when the army was pulling out of the area. About 5:30 PM, seven men managed to escape through the window of the courthouse, but the army noticed them and opened fire. Four lived and made it to refuge in Mexico the following day. One was fatally wounded and died in the hospital in Comitán, Mexico. Of the three remaining survivors, one was interviewed in August by the Christian Solidarity Committee of the San Cristóbal de las Casas diocese and near the end of September in Colonia Santa María, an *ejido* near the border in Chiapas, by the Guatemalan Justice and Peace Committee.

Six other men were still alive in the courthouse and it was getting late. Grenades were thrown into the building. Two men survived, but were completely covered with blood. When the soldiers piled the corpses inside the courthouse, they dragged the two onto the heap. Later, about 7 PM, these two managed to escape through the window, but one was heard because of the noise of his boots and was riddled with bullets. The other had removed his boots and hid in the bush. He arrived in Mexico the next day together with one of the men who had escaped at 5:30. This 57-year-old man told us the story of the massacre on the evening of September 4, 1982, in the Mexican *ejido* of Santa Marta. His account was given in the presence of some 20 men from San Francisco who had escaped the massacre either because they were in the fields or, in one case, because the individual was a member of the civil patrol and fled when he went to look for bulls to feed the army.

Most of the 20 men were from San José Yulaurel, a 90-hectare extension which was given to the villagers of San Francisco by the National Institute for Agrarian Transformation about five years ago. Although all belonged to the larger family of San Francisco, some survived because they lived in Yulaurel or, if they had a house in each place, happened to be in the fields. San Francisco itself is a 180-hectare rural estate owned by Colonel Victor Manuel Bolaños. It was nearly abandoned by the owner because about a year ago, the guerrillas were moving freely in the area feeding on his livestock (400 head in 1980) and there was at least one period when thievery was rampant. . . . From this we conclude that for the army the necessity of wiping out San Francisco lay in its role as a source of supply for the guerrillas. . . . In the massacre described, some of the army's counterinsurgency tactics are obvious:

a) The isolation of men from women and women from children seems ordered to facilitate the giving of information about the whereabouts of the guerrillas or about their collaborators or the location of arms, etc. . . .

b) The premeditated scorching of an entire village forces the remaining population to flee. This established a border strip which is vacant and/or mixed with a population which the army controls in strategic hamlets. In this way, guerrillas are impeded from being supplied, hiding, or receiving information or support from the civilian population.

c) In interior areas the army has a new weapon—hunger. Mountain and cliff areas to where the civilian population has fled in terror are surrounded, and the flow of goods such as food from the market—salt, sugar, beans—is cut off. There have been cases of peasants killed just for carrying a 50-pound bag of sugar over their shoulders. When the peasants surrender to the army, their leaders are eliminated. Others are presented as converts or even as victims dominated by the force or the fear of the guerrillas.

d) In the controlled villages, the army forms civil patrols to help dominate the population, keep watch at night, look for guerrillas, serve as parapets and cannon fodder for the army, kill suspicious parties even though they are brothers, etc. . . .

e) The use of Indian soldiers of different languages and municipalities to repress the indigenous population is a way to take the bite out of a class struggle which might be supported by an ethnic contradiction. With this, the government sidesteps the accusation of genocide.

We Cannot Confirm nor Deny

US Department of State
US Embassy in Guatemala

The three declassified US government documents presented below give a sense of debates among diplomats about how to respond to mounting state terror in Guatemala, as well as the strategies they deployed in denying such terror was taking place. In the first memo, dated October 5, 1981, an official from the US Department of State's Bureau of Human Rights and Humanitarian Affairs assesses the US government's options for dealing with repression in Guatemala. The memo notes cases where similar repression has "succeeded," such as the dirty wars in Argentina and Uruguay, and also cases where such repression has exacerbated support for the insurgency. The memo recommends the State Department adopt a wait-and-see approach to Guatemala: "If the repression does work and the guerrillas, their supporters and sympathizers are neutralized, we can in the aftermath of the repression work to restore normal relations. . . "

The next two cables, dated October 21, 1982, are related to the San Francisco massacre described by Ricardo Falla in the previous selection in this volume. One describes an aborted embassy mission to the department of Huehuetenango to investigate accusations that the army had massacred villagers. Bad weather prevents the mission from reaching the massacre sites, and the cable notes that the attempt has exhausted the embassy's travel money, precluding further attempts to verify the situation. The next cable, issued a day later, is a systematic attempt to discredit the work of international human rights organizations such as Amnesty International. These groups, the cable asserts, are being used as part of a "disinformation campaign" to blame the Guatemalan army for the violence and prevent the United States Congress from authorizing military aid to Guatemala.

Guatemala: What Next?

UNCLASSIFIED

~~SECRET~~

MEMORANDUM

TO: APR/PPC—Mr. Einaudi

FROM: HA/HR—Robert J. Jacobs

SUBJECT: Guatemala: What Next?

I read with keen interest Ambassador Chapin's assessment of General Walter's recent visit to Guatemala. In essence Ambassador Chapin concludes that President Lucas is not going to address our human rights concerns, that we must recognize this fact, and that we must now decide whether "national security considerations" require that we nevertheless go ahead with security assistance.

The following observations and conclusions are predicated upon the implicit assumption that those around General Lucas—if not General Lucas himself—are at least "amorally rational"—that is, their fundamental objective is their survival and they will do nothing which they *know* will result in their self-destruction.

In conversation with General Walters, President Lucas made clear that his government will continue as before—that the repression will continue. He reiterated his belief that the repression is working and that the guerrilla threat will be successfully routed. He prefers US assistance in this effort but believes that he can succeed with or without US help.

General Walters' efforts to persuade President Lucas that the repression will only spread the guerrilla contagion were evidently unsuccessful.

Historically, of course, we cannot argue that repression always "fails" nor can Lucas argue that it always "succeeds." Recent history is replete with examples where repression has been "successful" in exorcising guerrilla threats to a regime's survival. Argentina and Uruguay are both recent examples which come to mind. Indeed, in Guatemala during the late 1960s and early 1970s, a policy of repression succeeded in routing the guerrilla threat to the then existing regime. However, there are also contemporary examples where repression "failed"—Greece under Col. Papadopalous, Iran under the Shah, Nicaragua under Somoza, and Venezuela under Pérez-Jiménez.

The point is the rather obvious one that only in time will we and the Guatemalans know whether President Lucas is correct in his conviction that repression will work once again in Guatemala. If he is right and the policy of repression is succeeding and will result in the extermination of the guerrillas, their supporters, and their sympathizers there is no need for the US to implicate itself in the repression by supplying the GOG [Government of Guatemala] with security assistance. We did not provide such assistance to Argentina in waging its "dirty war" against the guerrillas in that country. Now that that "war" has been concluded, we are endeavoring to re-establish more normal relations with Argentina. It would seem that the Argentina experience is relevant to Guatemala. Having failed in our efforts to dissuade the GOG from its policy of repression we ought to distance ourselves from the GOG and not involve ourselves in Guatemala's "dirty war." If the repression does work and the guerrillas, their supporters and sympathizers are neutralized, we can in the aftermath of the repression work to restore normal relations with the successors to President Lucas.

Our conviction that repression will not contain the guerrilla threat but only exacerbate and compound it, will likewise only become evident over time. At such time as the failure of repression to contain and eradicate the guerrilla threat becomes evident, demands for a change in policy *within* the GOG—and the army in particular—should emerge. At such a juncture the crisis in relations between Guatemala and ourselves will have politically "matured" in the sense that it will then be ripe for a successful US diplomatic initiative. The GOG under internal pressure will have no choice but to seek political and military assistance from the US more or less on our terms.

Whether President Lucas is right or wrong in his conviction that repression will succeed in neutralizing the guerrillas, their supporters and sympathizers, the US posture ought remain one of distancing itself from the GOG. If Lucas is right and the GOG can successfully "go it alone" in its policy of repression, there is no need for the US to provide the GOG with redundant political and military support. The provisioning of such assistance would needlessly render us a complicit party in the repression. If we are correct in our conviction that the repression will not succeed and will only exacerbate and compound the guerrilla threat, then we ought to distance ourselves from the GOG until such time as it arrives at this realization and is prepared to address our human rights concerns in return for renewed US political and military support.

The remaining question is whether we indeed have the time to await either the success or failure of the GOG's present repressive policies. The answer to that question depends upon an assessment of whether the guerrillas represent a proximate, intermediate, or long-range threat to the GOG. If there is no proximate threat—that is, the guerrillas do not represent a military threat to the survival of the present Guatemalan regime over the next 12 months—then it would seem that we can await either the success or failure of the GOG's repressive policies. The nature of military threat posed by the guerrillas can best be assessed by the intelligence community. Before deciding upon any next step in Guatemala we ought, therefore, undertake such an intelligence assessment.

We Cannot Confirm nor Deny

UNCLASSIFIED

~~CONFIDENTIAL~~

OCTOBER 21, 1982

FM: AMEMBASSY GUATEMALA

TO: SECSTATE WASHDC IMMEDIATE

SUBJECT: EMBASSY ATTEMPT TO VERIFY ALLEGED MASSACRES
        IN HUEHUETENANGO

Summary: Three Mission officers visited the department of Huehuetenango by air on October 20 in an attempt to check the villages of San Francisco and Petanac, sites of alleged large-scale massacres purportedly carried out by the Guatemalan army. Bad weather forced us to turn back from the highest elevations of northern Huehuetenango; we were unable to reach either village. EMBOFF did, however, reach the conclusion that the army is completely up front about allowing us to check alleged massacre sites and to speak with whomever we wish. End summary.

The purpose of this visit was to check first-hand two sites of alleged GOG massacres . . . Petanac, where the army is supposed to have killed 89 people on July 14; and Finca San Francisco (actually a small village), where the army allegedly slaughtered some 300 people on July 18. Both villages are located in the municipality of San Mateo Ixtatan. The army has denied that either incident took place.

We flew to the army base at Huehuetenango proper on October 20. . . . We were again informed that the military situation in Huehuetenango is fairly well in hand. Nevertheless, there are areas that the GOG does not control, mostly the fringe areas of the department that border Mexico. Guerrillas apparently cross the border with some frequency, spreading mayhem, propaganda and terror. San Francisco and Petanac are in such an area, far north from central Huehuetenango. We were told that San Francisco and neighboring Yalambojoch had been abandoned because of guerrilla activity in the area. Petanac was said to have few people still living there, but no civil defense patrol. We were invited by the military authorities in

Huehuetenango to travel wherever we might wish, with the caveat that we were on our own if we touched down outside of the area secured by the army. Suitably advised, we left for San Francisco. The weather was bad when we left and worse when we attempted to rise yet higher in northern Huehuetenango. The pilot advised us he could not reach the area in such weather. We returned to the army base in Huehuetenango proper.

Comment: Although we were unable to reach San Francisco and Petanac, there are several points worth noting about the attitude of the army. EMBOFF knows that the ranking officials at the Huehuetenango base were perfectly aware of the purpose of our visit. Yet, the commanding, civic action, operations and intelligence officers all offered us the run of the department, and this without an army escort. If these officers have something to hide, they do not seem overly concerned about us finding it. Then again, if San Francisco is now abandoned—and EMBOFF believes that it is—we would have found nothing to confirm or deny the massacre reports. Petanac, however, is apparently still inhabited. If the weather was clear, we could have easily reached either village. In sum, we cannot at this time confirm or deny the reports of massacres in this area; we can, however, affirm that the army has no objection to our crisscrossing their combat zones in search of information we deem necessary to possess.

This trip, at a cost of approximately $1,600, has exhausted Embassy travel money. We should like to attempt to check these sites again in better weather. We will need, however, additional funding. End comment. [Frederic] Chapin [US ambassador to Guatemala]

UNCLASSIFIED

~~CONFIDENTIAL~~

OCTOBER 22, 1982

FROM: AMEMBASSY GUATEMALA

TO: SECSTATE WASHDC IMMEDIATE

SUBJECT: ANALYSIS OF HUMAN RIGHTS REPORTS ON GUATEMALA
          BY AMNESTY INTERNATIONAL, WOLA/NISGUA, AND
          GUATEMALAN HUMAN RIGHTS COMMISSION

Summary. The Embassy has analyzed reports made in the US by Amnesty International, WOLA/NISGUA [the Washington Office on Latin America and the Network in Solidarity with the People of Guatemala] and the Guatemalan Human Rights Commission. We conclude that a concerted disinformation campaign is being waged in the US against the Guatemalan government by groups supporting the Communist insurgency in Guatemala. This has enlisted the support of conscientious human rights and church organizations which may not fully appreciate that they are being utilized. This is a campaign in which guerrilla mayhem and violations of human rights are ignored; a campaign in which responsibility for atrocities is assigned to the GOG [Government of Guatemala] without verifiable evidence; a campaign in which GOG responsibility for atrocities is alleged when evidence shows guerrilla responsibility; a campaign in which atrocities are cited that never occurred. The campaign's object is simple: to deny the Guatemalan army the weapons and equipment needed from the US to defeat the guerrillas. Thus, the groups backing the guerrillas intend to win the war against the GOG by making the US Congress the battlefield. It is the old but effective strategy of "divide and conquer." As Solzhenitsyn pointed out in his Nobel lecture, "Anyone who has once proclaimed violence as his method must inexorably choose the lie as his principle." If those promoting such disinformation can convince the Congress, through the usual opinion-makers—the media, church and human rights groups—that the present GOG is guilty of gross human rights violations, they know that the Congress will refuse Guatemala the military assistance it needs. Those backing the Communist insurgency are betting on an application, or rather misapplication of human rights policy so as to damage the GOG and assist themselves. In the fight to win Central America, the Communists know full well the importance of Guatemala: the largest and most economically potent country in CA, strategically located next to Mexico. The Embassy notes that the three human rights groups whose reports are analyzed in this cable, whatever their nominal allegiance, use many of the same incidents of alleged atrocities in their reports; nor do the reports ever cite alleged guerrilla atrocities or assassinations of police and government officials with the exception of four or five incidents in the AI report. It seems beyond question that the three reports are drawing on many of the same sources, sources specified in the WOLA/NISGUA report—sources most of which are well-known Communist front groups in Central America and in the US. Although Embassy believes it likely that the Guatemalan army has indeed committed some atrocities, the assertion that they committed all the massacres attributed to them is not credible, especially since analysis indicates the guerrillas are responsible in many cases. If the GOG were indeed engaged in massive extrajudicial executions—a "mad, genocidal campaign"—in the highlands, one must wonder why Indians are joining the civil defense patrols in great numbers, and why thousands of Indians are coming to the army for refuge in such places as Nebaj, Choatulum, and San Martín Jilotepeque. In sum, Embassy believes that what is being planned, and successfully carried out, is the Communist-backed disinformation plan mentioned above. End summary.

What follows is a selection of comparisons of what each human rights report says about a particular incident, what Guatemalan press or other Embassy sources say about that incident, and a conclusion. The list is selective merely to conserve time and space; Embassy has analyzed and compared every one of the 145 incidents in WOLA/NISGUA, 47 in CDHG, and 68 in AI, and selects those below to illustrate the five principal characteristics that became apparent in the analysis: common source, "double reporting" (one incident reported twice or three times as separate incidents), responsibility undeterminable, distortion or press reports, and incident unverifiable. . . .

WOLA/NISGUA: March 24. Alta Verapaz. Villages of Sacatalji, Cruxmax, San Isidro Samuc, Pacayas Cisiram, El Rancho Zuixal, Chiyuc, in Coban township. 100 peasants killed by army. Villages burned and bombed. Source: CUC [Committee for Peasant Unity].

CDHG: Reported for March 24: names first three villages, no victims, burned all houses. For March 24–27: names Las Pacayas, Quixal, Chiyuc. 100 victims. Bombed from helicopters. Source: (for all CDHG citations) "Guatemalan press."

AI: As in CDHG, reports as two incidents of same dates as in CDHG, adding the village of Samuc de Coban for March 24, saying the villages were all reportedly burned to the ground; casualty figures are "not clear" for March 24–27; AI gives Las Pacayas, Cistram (or Cisirau), El Rancho Quixal, and Chiyuc, saying the villages were bombed, leaving 100 people dead. No source.

Newspapers: No such report, contrary to CDHG claim.

Conclusion: Note CUC source, shared language, double-reporting in CDHG and AI, and lack of any Guatemalan newspaper report. Incident unverifiable, possible fabrication.

WOLA/NISGUA: March 30. Quiche. Chinique. 55 peasants murdered by army. Source: CUC.

CDHG: Reported for April 13. Same place, same number. Source: "Guatemalan press."

AI: Reported for March 30–April 3. Same place, same number. Authorities claim encounter between guerrillas and civil defense patrol.

Newspapers: Army reported terrorists killed over 40 persons.

Conclusion: CDHG distortion of press (CDHG implies GOG responsibility; press stated army attributes to terrorists). AI even-handed, actual responsibility undeterminable.

AI: March 31. Chimaltenango. Estancia de la Virgen, in San Martín Jilote-peque township. 29 peasants killed (15 shot, 4 burned to death) by heav-ily armed men. Most huts burned. Peasant groups blame army.

WOLA/NISGUA: Not cited for that date, but see April 14. 20 peasants mur-dered by army. Source: *El Dia* (Mexican).

CDHG: Not cited for that date, but see March 23 for Estancia de la Virgin (*sic*), Chicocon, Chuatalun (actually, Choatulum) and Chipila, 250 vic-tims, houses burned, corn taken (or burned?); see also CDHG April 15, Estancia de la Virgen, San Martín Jilotepeque, 250 victims (again?), "cal-culate that since December, 1500 killed, 175 houses burned." Apparent double reporting.

See also AI at April 26–27, "32 peasants murdered in different communities in Quiche and Chimaltenango, during the latter half of April, 27 stran-gled in Estancia de la Virgen, Tioxia, Chuatatlun (*sic*), and Chicocon, township of San Martín Jilotepeque."

Newspapers: No such report for March 31. For April 14, newspapers re-ported survivors said armed men burned about 150 homes.

Conclusion: There is no newspaper report about March 23 (CDHG), or March 31 (AI), or April 26–27 (AI). If the newspapers' April 14 report is backdated to AI's March 31 incident, survivors blamed armed men, not army. At best, responsibility undeterminable, and confusion of dates and numbers makes any clear picture impossible. . . .

WOLA/NISGUA: April 23. Suchitepequez, Mazatenango. 2 prisoners mur-dered, 2 kidnapped by death squad. Source: *El Dia* (Mexican). Compare WOLA/NISGUA same date, same place, same source, 3 men (two named) kidnapped by death squad.

CDHG: Nothing cited.

AI: Nothing cited.

Newspapers: Police reported 2 prisoners killed, 2 kidnapped from police car.

Conclusion: The first part of the WOLA/NISGUA incident cited above is pos-sible. Responsibility undeterminable; it could have been a death squad, or it could have been leftists. The second incident appears to be double-reporting; incident unverifiable. It bears saying that this is one of only two incidents on the entire comparative rundown that Embassy con-cluded was possibly true as set forth, which is why it was selected for inclusion here. The other appears at May 16.

Acts of Genocide

Commission for Historical Clarification

The Commission for Historical Clarification (Comisión para el Esclarecimiento Histórico, CEH) was established as part of the peace negotiations between the rebels and the government that finally brought Guatemala's internal armed conflict to an end in 1996. The CEH's mandate was to investigate human-rights violations and acts of violence and to write a report detailing the causes, methods, and consequences of the violence. The CEH and its three-hundred-person staff worked for nearly two years, receiving more than eight thousand testimonies in closed sessions around the country, interviewing key witnesses and analyzing hundreds of primary and secondary sources, including declassified US government documents. Its twelve-volume report, Memory of Silence, *estimated that two hundred thousand people were killed or disappeared during the span of the conflict and documented 669 cases of massacres. Ninety-three percent of these crimes were committed by forces linked to the Guatemalan state, three percent were committed by guerrilla groups, and four percent were of other or unknown origin. Eighty-three percent of identified victims were Maya. The selection below focuses on the legal and historical reasoning the commission used to conclude that the Guatemalan government committed "acts of genocide" against Mayas in 1981–1983. The CEH describes how the army came to define entire Maya communities as "internal enemies"; thus, the annihilation of Maya populations was intentional, even though the military's overarching motivation was to defeat the insurgency.*

In the wake of the Second World War and the Nazi atrocities committed against European Jews, the international community recognized the need for a global guarantee to safeguard the right to existence for ethnic, racial, or religious nationalities or communities. As a result, under the rubric of the United Nations, the Convention for the Prevention and Punishment of the Crime of Genocide was elaborated. Adopted by the General Assembly through Resolution 260 (III) on December 9, 1948, the Convention took effect on January 12, 1951. . . . Guatemala ratified the Convention on January 13, 1950. Therefore, the Convention was in effect during the entire time of the armed conflict. . . .

"Never again this savagery." A mural in a chapel depicts a massacre in the village of Plan de Sánchez, Rabinal, Baja Verapaz, on July 18, 1982, in which Guatemalan army troops killed 268 people. Photo by James Rodríguez, 2007. Used by permission of the photographer.

Article II of the Convention defines the crime of genocide and its requirements in the following terms:

> Genocide means any of the following acts committed with intent to destroy, in whole or in part, a national, ethnic, racial or religious group, as such:
>   (a) killing members of the group;
>   (b) causing serious bodily or mental harm to members of the group;
>   (c) deliberately inflicting on the group conditions of life intended to bring about its physical destruction in whole or in part;
>   (d) imposing measures intended to prevent births within the group;
>   (e) forcibly transferring children of the group to another group. . . .

The subjective element, or the intent to destroy the group, has been interpreted in international jurisprudence in the following way: "The intentionality specific to the crime of genocide does not need to be expressed clearly; it can be inferred from a certain number of facts, such as the 'general political doctrine' from which the actions arise . . . and the repetition of destructive and discriminatory acts." [The CEH is quoting from, and basing its arguments on, proceedings of the International Criminal Tribunal for the former Yugoslavia (ICTY)—*Eds.*]

It is very important to distinguish between the "intent to destroy the group, in whole or in part," that is, the positive determination to do this, and the motives for this intent. In order to determine genocide, it is enough to intend to destroy the group, whatever the motive may be. For example, if the motive for destroying an ethnic group is not racist, but strictly military, this is still a basis to determine the crime of genocide.

An act fulfills the requirements of a genocidal crime as defined by the Convention even if it forms part of a broader policy that is not directed at physical extermination as such. In this sense, it is relevant to distinguish between genocidal policy and acts of genocide. A genocidal policy exists when the final objective of the actions is the extermination of a group, in whole or in part. Genocidal acts exist when the final objective is not the extermination of the group, but other political, economic or military ends, in which the means that are utilized to achieve this goal contemplate the extermination of the group in whole or in part. . . .

Methodology

The period of analysis was 1981 through 1983, when the highest levels of violence were registered. The analysis centered on particular regions, and specifically on certain ethnic groups, where the CEH had evidence that the brunt of human rights violations took place: 1) Maya-q'anjob'al and Maya-chuj, in Barillas, Nentón, and San Mateo Ixtatán, northern Huehuetenango; 2) Maya-ixil, in Nebaj, Cotzal and Chajul, department of Quiché; 3) Maya-k'iche' in Zacualpa, department of Quiché; and 4) Maya-achí, in Rabinal, Baja Verapaz. . . .

The CEH sources were analyzed exhaustively. In each region, regular and "illustrative" cases were examined, as were individual and collective testimonies, declarations from key witnesses, including agents or ex-agents of the state, and regional context reports. This data was compared with other sources, such as the army's military campaign plans, communiqués from the guerrillas, press reports, declassified documents from the United States, and field investigations. . . .

General Policy

The human-rights violations described in this section occurred within the framework of the counterinsurgency or "counter-subversive" war, which was guided by the National Security Doctrine. . . . In accordance with the National Security Doctrine, the army defined the "annihilation of the internal enemy" as a strategic objective of the counterinsurgency war. The army understood the internal enemy to include two categories of individuals, groups, and organizations: those who tried to undo the established order through illegal actions and who were represented by "Communist revolutionaries," and those who, without being Communists, tried to undo the established order.

This doctrine also affirmed that the "counter-subversive" war should take as its "object" the population, since the "subversive" war (the guerrillas) sought to achieve its ends through the active participation of the population. . . . It would therefore be necessary to maintain or regain the population's loyalty and make people participate actively in the war, on the side of the government.

As early as the 1970s, when the guerrillas operated in the eastern region of the country, with a majority Ladino [nonindigenous] population, the army was already identifying the highland population (primarily Maya) with the enemy. The Military Intelligence (G-2) Manual of 1972 expresses this clearly: "The enemy has the same sociological characteristics as the inhabitants of our highlands."

In the 1980s, the army outright identified the Indian with the internal enemy. [According to its "Victoria '82" military plan] the army considered that the guerrillas had been able to tap into the historical problems of the primarily indigenous populations in the highlands, [such as] land scarcity and poverty, appropriating their demands:

> The great Indian masses of the nation's highlands have heard themselves in the subversion's proclamations, with their banners of land scarcity and immense poverty, and due to the long years of consciousness raising, [these populations] see the Army as an invading enemy.
> . . .

The army considered that the "great Indian masses" of the highlands made up the social base of the guerrilla movement:

> Strong points . . . of the enemy . . . its social base, resting on the Indian peasant. . . .

The perception of the armed forces was shared by civilian government functionaries. Francisco Bianchi, secretary of then de facto president Efraín Ríos Montt, not only identified the Indian with the guerrillas, but also affirmed that the consequence of this identification was elimination: "The guerrillas won over many Indian collaborators, therefore the Indians were subversives, right? And how do you fight subversion? Clearly, you had to kill Indians because they were collaborating with subversion." . . .

Racism has polarized Guatemalan society, dividing it into two main groups, Indians and Ladinos. Racism has occupied a central position in the thinking and practice of dominant sectors of Guatemala society toward "*los indios.*" Racism is also present among members of the armed forces. The consideration of the "other" as separate, inferior, is expressed in the following statement from the former de facto president Efraín Ríos Montt: "Naturally, if a subversive operation exists in which the Indians are involved with the guerrilla, the Indians are also going to die. However, the army's philosophy is not to kill Indians, but to win them back, to help them."

In the imagination of a sizable Ladino sector, racism feeds the belief that "the *indios* are going to come down from the mountains and kill Ladinos." This fear exists because some Ladinos think that the indigenous populations feel an historic rancor toward them, for the hardships faced since the Conquest. The ideological context of racism thus favored the army's equation of the indigenous populations, a sort of ancestral enemy, with the insurgents. At the same time, racism nourished an attitude toward Indians as different, separate, inferior, almost less than human and outside of the universe of moral obligations, making their elimination less problematic.

Final Conclusions

In the four regions examined, the violence was massive and overwhelmingly affected the Maya population. In the Ixil and Rabinal areas, the percentage of the population killed was 14.5% and 14.6%, while in northern Huehuetenango and Zacualpa, the percentage of the population killed was 3.6% and 8.6%. Likewise, the victims of massacres and other human-rights violations documented by the CEH were mainly Maya, in a much greater proportion than the ethnic distribution between Mayas and Ladinos. In the Ixil area, 97.8% of the human rights violations were against the Maya population; in northern Huehuetenango 99.3%; in Rabinal 98.8%; and in Zacualpa 98.4%.

These overwhelming proportions indicate that the Maya populations of these regions were the target of human-rights violations, in an objective and discriminating way. . . . Within this general discrimination in the selection of victims, in which Maya groups were affected most of all, those responsible for the killings made no distinction by age, sex, or condition of the victims. For example, in the four regions, in the period from February to October 1982, killings of children, women, and elderly people, as well as men, were carried out. The army acted against the community, rather than

Mr. Nicolás Chen, a survivor of a 1982 massacre in the village of Río Negro, visits a community memory museum in Rabinal. Here he touches a photograph of his daughter, Marta Julia Chen Osorio. The photograph's caption reads: "She was murdered when her gestation period was about to be completed. The soldiers, acting as medics, induced a forced cesarean with machetes. The assailants, who wanted to see how a child grows inside a mother's womb, accomplished their feat. How is it possible that someone can take the life of defenseless human beings so unjustly?!" Photo by James Rodríguez, 2007. Used by permission of the photographer.

making accusations—founded or unfounded—against individual community members. . . .

First Conclusion

. . . . The CEH concludes that the repetition of destructive acts directed systematically against Maya population groups, including the elimination of leaders and criminal acts against minors who could not have been military targets, makes clear that the victims' only common factor was belonging to specific ethnic groups, and that such acts were committed with intent to destroy, in whole or in part, those groups. . . .

Among the most significant actions directed at the destruction of Maya groups, identified by the army as the enemy, were killings. . . . According to testimonies and other compiled evidence, the CEH has established that in these killings, which had characteristics of massacres, both regular and special military forces participated, as did members of the civil-defense patrols and military commissioners. In many cases, survivors identified the heads of the nearby military detachments as the leaders who commanded these operations.

Second Conclusion

The analysis of these acts has allowed the CEH to form the conviction that in nearly all these cases, the perpetrators' purpose was to kill the maximum number of members of the group.

In nearly all these killings, the army carried out some of the following preparatory acts: either diligently rounding up all villagers before killing them; or surrounding the entire community; or taking advantage of situations where the population was gathered already, such as celebrations or market days, to carry out the killings.

In its study of the four regions, the CEH establishes that, together with the killings, which by themselves were enough to eliminate the groups defined as enemies, members of the army or patrollers systematically committed acts of extreme cruelty, including torture and other cruel, inhuman, and degrading treatment, whose effect was to terrorize the population and destroy the foundations for social cohesion, especially when people were forced to watch or carry out these acts themselves. Especially frequent were collective rapes of women, done publicly to leave an indelible impact on social reproduction in the community.

Third Conclusion

The CEH concludes that among the acts perpetrated with intent to destroy numerous Maya groups, in whole or in part, multiple actions were also committed that constituted grave injuries to the physical or mental integrity of the affected Maya groups. . . . The investigation also showed that killings, especially those that took the form of indiscriminate massacres, were accompanied by the razing of villages. The most notable case is the Ixil region, where between 70% and 90% of the villages were razed. Also, in northern Huehuetenango, Rabinal and Zacualpa, entire villages were burned to the ground, goods were destroyed, and crops were burned, leaving these populations without food.

Moreover, in the four regions studied, people were persecuted as they fled. . . .

Fourth Conclusion

The CEH concludes that, among the aforementioned acts perpetrated with intent to destroy numerous Maya groups in whole or in part, some [actions] meant deliberately inflicting on the group conditions of life that could bring about, and in many cases did bring about, its physical destruction, in whole or in part. . . . The analysis of the CEH demonstrates that coordination of military structures occurred at the national level, which permitted an "efficient" deployment of soldiers and patrollers in the four regions studied. For example, operations that included aerial support required high-level authorization and coordination with ground actions. . . . For example, the "Victory 82" plan establishes that "the mission is to annihilate the guerrillas and the parallel organizations," and the "Firmness 83" plan resolves that the army should support "its operations with the greatest number of civil defense patrols, to be able to raze all of the collective cultivations that the subversion possesses in determinate areas, where it is plainly proven that there is an active participation and collaboration of compromised villages that sympathize with and are organized by the subversion."

All of this has convinced the CEH that the acts perpetrated with intent to destroy numerous Maya groups, in whole or in part, were not isolated acts, nor excesses committed by out-of-control troops, nor were they the result of improvisation by low-ranking officers. With great consternation, the CEH concludes that many of the massacres and other human-rights violations committed against [Mayas] responded to a broader, strategically planned policy, whose actions followed a sequential and coherent logic.

In addition, the CEH has evidence that similar things occurred repeatedly in other Maya regions. Given all the options for combating the insurgency, the state opted for the one with the highest toll on human life among the civilian, noncombatant population. Refusing other options, such as a political rapprochement with the civilian, noncombatant population it considered disaffected, the state opted for the annihilation of those it deemed enemies.
. . .

Fifth Conclusion

Therefore, the CEH concludes that agents of the Guatemalan state, in the framework of counterinsurgent operations conducted in 1981 and 1982, carried out acts of genocide against the Maya people in the Ixil, Zacualpa, northern Huehuetenango, and Rabinal regions. . . .

Sixth Conclusion

The Guatemalan state did not take any action to investigate and punish those responsible, even though many of the responsible parties were publicly known. . . .

Seventh Conclusion

The CEH concludes that the Guatemalan state failed to comply with its obligations to investigate and punish the acts of genocide committed in its territory, violating Articles IV and VI of the Convention for the Prevention and Punishment of the Crime of Genocide.

Translated by Elizabeth Oglesby

Exodus

Victor Montejo

The military's counterinsurgency caused a massive population displacement in much of rural Guatemala, especially the central and western highlands and the northern lowland jungles, primarily Maya areas where guerrilla forces were most active. In many places, the escaping populations were pursued and killed as they fled. By the end of 1982, the Guatemalan Catholic Church estimated that more than one million people—15 percent of the population—had been displaced at least temporarily. The army's "Firmness '83" battle plan called for crops to be razed throughout the countryside in order to deny the guerrillas a food supply and ensure that the displaced populations would be dependent on government aid as they were resettled by the army into newly reorganized villages under military control. Some 150,000 Guatemalan refugees fled north into Mexico, where eventually more than forty thousand settled into camps organized by the United Nations.

Victor Montejo, a Maya-Jakaltek anthropologist, traveled to the refugee camps in the late 1980s. In this selection, he recounts the refugees' desperate flight into Mexico, where they hid from Mexican immigration officials and the Guatemalan army that pursued them across the border. The refugees' testimonies are replete with details of horror, loss, and trauma, yet their stories also illustrate a remarkable perseverance. As time went on, Guatemalan refugees found ways to survive and even flourish in the new camps. Free from the militarization of daily life prevalent in Guatemala, they organized popular education and health projects. For many, however, the desire to return to their lands and communities in Guatemala was never far from their minds.

There was great pain among the people who were the first refugees. Some did not bring anything, not even blankets to sleep on. But what was more painful were the cries and lamentations of the many who were widows. With their now fatherless children, they cried and cried inconsolably. All the pain was shared, for everybody had suffered intensely. Almost everybody there, reunited in exile, had lost one or more of their relatives and loved ones, and an immense sadness settled over all the people. On seeing such suffering, some good Mexican families passed the information to other Mexican communities that there were thousands of poor Guatemalan families starving near the Mexican border. Some Mexicans of the region started to bring some corn, beans, and clothes for the Guatemalan refugees.

Although the refugees knew they were in Mexican territory, fear prevented them from sleeping. . . . The violence and death had penetrated deep into the consciousness of even these little children. Everybody was frightened because the noise of the Guatemalan helicopters searching the Mexico-Guatemala border could be heard all night.

Word of the presence of thousands of refugees along the southwestern Mexican border attracted many people from nearby and distant Mexican villages who wanted to see for themselves. Others had different objectives; they sought to gain from the suffering of the people. Many from Paso Hondo, Comalapa, Comitán, Tuxtla, and other places came with the intention of taking the fatherless children from their mothers. Families with a number of children were asked to give up some of them to the Mexican people, who were eager to adopt them. . . .

Others who had come to ask for children showed new clothes to the parents, and said, "Listen, we will dress them well. Here are the clothes, and don't worry." Others offered to buy the children. Because they had nothing to give to their children and because they did not want them to die, some parents gave up their children to these people, who were very aggressive, even pulling the babies from the arms of their mothers. Some children went to caring Mexican families, perhaps without children of their own. Other children, particularly older girls, were pressed into household or workshop labor. It was discovered later that some of these girls were forced into prostitution, even though their parents were told they would be household help. This did not seem to be an organized activity but rather an attempt by nearby urban Mexicans, particularly those from Comitán, to take advantage of a desperate situation.

Since Jakaltek families do not give children away even under conditions of extreme poverty, the refugees reacted almost immediately to what they had done and began to mobilize at once to recover the children who were given up for adoption. The refugees found out that some people had not acted in good faith and had given false addresses. Others who had acted in good faith and were moved by compassion returned the children immediately when they heard the pleas of their mothers or their relatives. For others, the situation was more difficult. It was only later, with the help of the Mexican authorities, that many parents found the addresses of those who took the children and were able to retrieve them. . . .

Afraid of the immigration officers and of the Mexican army, which had supposedly come to force the refugees to go back to Guatemala, thousands of refugees gathered at the edge of the hammock bridge on the Río Dolores and split into small groups. Each group continued to penetrate farther inside Mexican territory, trying to avoid the Guatemalan army, the immigration officials, and the Mexican army. And constantly they heard the Guatemalan helicopters, searching and firing their machine guns in the mountains near the Mexican border.

The refugees lived this way from January until March 23, 1982, when the same Guatemalan army overthrew the president, General Lucas García, and put into place General Ríos Montt, the leader of the military coup. The refugees who had gone back to their villages in Guatemala returned to the refugee settlements in Mexico to tell their relatives the great news, that the genocidal government of Lucas García had been overthrown and now, according to radio broadcasts, there was peace.

Thousands of families received the news with great happiness. They were suffering from hunger and wanted to go back home and start their lives again. Also, as it was March, they could at least clean a piece of land and plant their cornfield to secure food for the next year. This was the time when the fields should be burned for planting corn, to be ready for the first rains of May. . . . [But] the news from more distant places, which came by radio and by word of mouth from travelers, was that the new military government was even more terrible than the one that had been deposed.

The Flight

In June 1982, the counterinsurgency war returned to the Cuchumatán highlands, especially to northwestern Huehuetenango. The helicopters began to bomb the communities again, and people fled toward the border. . . .

In July 1982, when refugees crossed the Mexican border in great numbers, thousands of families were deeply affected. Thus, traditional family life was again disrupted, as it had been during the Spanish invasion of 1524. . . . Entire families had to hide in the mountains, so the children had to learn to be quiet to avoid the soldiers who were searching for them. These incredible escapes from death traumatized the children at a very early age. . . .

During the first months of the arrival of the refugees in southern Mexico, Mexican families living close to the Guatemala-Mexico border were very helpful. They were hospitable to the Guatemalan refugees because, being poor *campesinos* themselves, they understood the urgency of the refugees' situation. . . .

In early 1982, Mexican authorities granted some refugees asylum and provided documents for them to work and live in Mexico legally, but many other refugees were harassed or deported. By November 1982, the policy of deportation had stopped, but refugees were given only F-8 visas, which substantially restricted their ability to work and permitted them to live only in official camps within fifty kilometers of the border. . . .

By 1983–1984, the possibility of returning to their homeland seemed distant for the refugees, and they began to look for a more secure place to reconstruct their lives in exile. . . .

Some refugee families moved to Mexican towns and cities close to coffee plantations, as they preferred to struggle for their subsistence on the plantations, as they had done in Guatemala, rather than live at the mercy of Mexican authorities and camp organizations. Other refugees divided themselves into families and groups of relatives and tried to enter Mexican communities as laborers. These groups tried to assimilate immediately to hide themselves from Mexican immigration authorities. . . .

Relocation of the Guatemalan Refugee Camps

[The Mexican government] devised a plan for the relocation of the refugees from Chiapas and the Guatemalan border to the states of Campeche and Quintana Roo in the Yucatán peninsula. Relocation was to begin in June 1984. . . .

The prospect of being moved caused dread among the refugees. Added to their usual burden of insecurity about shelter, work, and daily food, they now worried about how they would manage their lives in a distant place where no Guatemalan Maya had ever gone before. The refugees resisted the move also because in the previous few years, they had been moved forcibly from place to place like nomads. Many people, including those with large families, women, and elders, wanted to remain close to the Guatemalan border, hoping to return to their homeland. The reasons refugees gave for opposing relocation centered on geographic and cultural concerns. For them, proximity to the border meant being close to home communities, which kept alive the dream of returning and helped to maintain kinship and communal ties.

The camps in southern Mexico were built where the refugees could see the mountains of Guatemala. Their exile was softened by their hopes and their constant view of the Cuchumatán highlands, the homeland to which they wished to return. But by the end of 1984, COMAR [Mexican Commission to Aid Refugees] had already relocated several camps to Campeche and Quintana Roo against the will of the refugees. . . .

The refugees felt more physical security in the Yucatán settlements, but they did not achieve self-sufficiency. And because the refugee camps were located far from major population centers, job opportunities outside the camps were limited, and it was difficult for the refugees to become integrated into the workforce of nearby Mexican communities.

Villa Cocalito

The refugee community of Villa Cocalito [in Chiapas] was composed of approximately two hundred families or about six hundred people, mostly Jakalteks and Ladinoized Mayas from the town of Buena Vista in the municipio of Santa Ana Huista in the Cuchumatán highlands. . . .

Housing in Villa Cocalito was organized in a circle around an open space at whose center stood a large tree. The tree and its surrounding area provided a common plaza and meeting place for the community. Houses were constructed of wooden pilings and sticks and roofed with thatch. The floors were dirt. All family activities—cooking, eating, and sleeping—were carried out in this basic shelter. Each dwelling housed an extended family consisting of grandparents, sons and their wives, their children, and two or three related families. The short streets and paths between the houses and around the community were dirt, muddy during the rainy season and dusty when it was dry. There was no electricity in the camp. People arose when the roosters crowed at the earliest light of dawn, and the sounds of machetes chopping firewood and the slap, slap, slap of hands forming tortillas greeted the sunrise. Soon after sunset, activities for the day ceased. Kerosene lanterns and flashlights provided the only illumination after dark.

The residents of Villa Cocalito had built a small, one-room schoolhouse and a building that served as the community clinic and as a guest house for overnight visitors. These were constructed of the same wooden walls as the houses but were roofed with tin donated by the Catholic diocese. There was no building constructed for use as a church, and the refugees walked to services at the Catholic church in La Colonia.

Almost every family owned a dog, a pig, and some chickens. The dogs roamed freely around the camp, as did the chickens. Pigs were tied to trees or kept in small huts constructed for them. Eggs improved the basic diet of the refugees, but for the most part chickens ready to be killed for consumption were sold to the Mexicans for cash income. A few families had donkeys, and their owners had to cut a supply of grass for them when the workday was over. They were then tied to trees on the outskirts of the camp.

The refugees traveled mainly on foot, carrying whatever needed to be transported. Those who had donkeys would ride, but most walked wherever they needed to go. Donkeys were also useful in hauling firewood and other carrying chores. When the refugees worked for Mexican *campesinos*, they were sometimes transported to the fields in trucks. Unlike their home communities in Guatemala, the flatter terrain in Mexico and the presence of dirt roads made bicycles a more common form of transportation in Villa Cocalito. After the first bicycles arrived in the camp, most of the young people became proficient riders and traveled around the area and between the refugee camps. A few refugees even rode their bicycles from the camps to cross the border on dirt roads away from the main border crossings and visit their home communities in Guatemala, a trip of twelve hours each way.

The major local market was held in Comalapa on Saturdays and Sundays, and refugee households tried to send one person to buy whatever items—soap, medicines, or extra foods—they needed. . . .

There was no telephone in the camp, the nearest one being a pay phone in La Colonia a mile away. It was used only when absolutely needed by the camp spokesperson, schoolteachers, or the representative of the CCPP [Permanent Commissions, a refugee organization] to communicate with headquarters in Comitán. . . .

COMAR provided the refugees' food; it brought supplies of dry fish, rice, vegetable oil, bananas, canned pork, onions, corn, and beans every fifteen days, distributed according to the official list of members of registered families. Not everyone liked all the foods that COMAR distributed, and families occasionally traded with other families, exchanging those things they disliked for items that suited them better. Some foods were universally disliked. Canned pork, which was donated by the governments of Canada and Holland, was very unfamiliar, and at first it was often sold or exchanged for something else. And the constant occurrence of infections and sore throats among the children was blamed on chemicals in the dry foods supplied by COMAR. In general, the later years in exile saw better diets and healthier children. Children usually had three meals a day, with tortillas, beans, and canned pork for breakfast and lunch and rice, tortillas, or *pozol* for dinner.

When the refugees had money it was often used to buy supplemental foodstuffs. Some refugees rented larger plots of land from Mexicans and grew an acre or more of corn and beans, the sale of which would pay their rent and make a small profit. But for the most part only small plots of land

Guatemalan refugees in Camp Puerto Rico, Chiapas, Mexico, December 21, 1982. Attendees of this meeting are discussing international aid. Photo by Antonio Turok. Used by permission of the photographer.

were available to only some of the refugee farmers, who grew small quantities of corn and beans for their families. . . .

Women came to the rescue of their devastated family economies with their traditional art of weaving. They wove hair ribbons, belts, napkins, tablecloths, and wall hangings in all their free time, receiving help from their daughters (and sometimes husbands and sons) with the household tasks that took away from their weaving time. The woven items were sold by the church groups of southern Mexico, especially by the nuns of the seminary in the Diocese of San Cristóbal, who formed the backbone of the movement to aid refugee women by reselling their craft work in a store in San Cristóbal and through international outlets. In good months the women's work could contribute the equivalent of $50 to $60 a month to the family income. Because of their early fears of being identified as Guatemalan refugees by Mexican authorities, none of the Jakaltek people wore their traditional *traje* (clothing). And because they needed to produce weavings for cash income, women preferred to sell *cintas*, belts and ribbons, rather than wear them. Men, women, and children wore Ladino clothing that was relatively cheap and could be purchased in a local market. Almost all of the adult women had their *traje* stored away in their houses, but among the Jakatek women it was never worn in Mexico, even for special occasions.

Outside the camps but within the larger *mestizo* Mexican community, *traje* marked people as refugees, as Mayas, and as people to be looked down on, abused, and disrespected. It was better to avoid this humiliation by leaving the *traje* unworn. . . .

In addition to participating in the celebration of the patron saint's day of the local Mexican community, the refugees of Villa Cocalito also celebrated the saint's day of their village in Guatemala, the Virgin of the Nativity. Following a religious celebration in the morning, the catechists would remind the refugees of the causes and the history of their exile. In the afternoon there were soccer tournaments against local Mexican teams, the *marimba* was played, and there was dancing until eight o'clock in the evening. The Maya artistic group in the camp would sing its songs in Pop'al Ti' and people would remember their origins and the reasons for their exile. On the festival of their patron saint they remembered with sadness the time when the army first arrived in El Limonar. And refugees from other camps came to visit relatives and friends in Villa Cocalito on this day. . . .

The pattern of life in other refugee camps was similar, but in other camps there were different ethnic groups, different struggles over resource allocations, and different economic opportunities for the refugees. In some, work on the coffee or sugar plantations replaced communal labor for the local Mexican community and supplied alternative sources of income. The geographic location of a camp also meant important differences in people's lives. Those camps far from roads or high in the mountains received fewer services, and, perhaps, less official interference, and those camps close to Mexican towns offered other opportunities for work.

The Oil Lamp

Antonio L. Cota García

Jakaltek-Maya poet Antonio L. Cota García was a refugee in Chiapas, Mexico, during the 1980s. In this poem, he writes of the refugees' splintered identity as they wait to return to Guatemala, the small hope that still flickers, and the importance of remembering their history.

It is ten o'clock at night
Saturday, May 14, 1988.
Barely, an oil lamp, blackened
by its long use, gives me its light,
and it is similar to my age and the pains
that consume my weakened body,
tied to the history
of refuge in Mexico.

Arrow without rest
wind without destiny.
My desk?
Just an old flat-bottomed wooden washtub
cracked at the bottom
like the history of my country,
split in two, split in two,
where the voice
is only a voice which nobody hears,
and the ears deaf to voices,
hearing as weak as the same oil lamp
that hardly gives me its light.

The palace where we live?
Everybody fits in it,
and makes us laugh.
Its size, four square meters

and inside everybody fits
and we still welcome everyone.
It is incredible! Someone would say:
How can so many live with so little
and so few with too much?

The oil lamp has survived seven years
while the history is split in two
but its halves move in tandem
attending with loyalty its mission
to walk always with you.
How many would dislike its presence?
How many arms would raise against its innocence
as if in reality, the oil lamp
would be responsible for the impertinence
of illuminating even the one that dislikes its light.

But, if they would know
that its light is the nested future,
if they would know that its heat
is love that overflows,
Then, my oil lamp and my old age
Would be well accepted.
. . . But no!

We are intruders who do not take anything,
we are strangers who invade them by fear,
we are old threads of an ancient glory
that cause shame to those who don't know our history
and admiration for those that value our culture.

And this is how our lives are consumed
within the livelihood of our experience,
and even if so many condemn our presence
the oil lamp will continue with its dim light
and on the cracked bottom of the old wooden washtub
we will continue night after night, our duty
of writing down the history of our people in exile.

Arbitrary Power and Sexual Violence

Matilde González Izás

Rape was widespread during the worst years of the armed conflict, although there is little documentation, because many women are reluctant to talk openly about it. Guatemalan sociologist Matilde González Izás spent several years conducting an oral history of San Bartolomé Jocotenango, a town in the conflictive province of El Quiché. Here, during the 1980s, sexual violence against women was both an individual and a collective practice. González Izás' work shows how local authority figures such as military commissioners and civil-patrol commanders were granted arbitrary power over life and death. Part of the way this power was exercised was through the conquest of women's bodies. In many cases, victim and perpetrator continue to live in close proximity, and the social stigma of rape helps maintain a veil of silence around these crimes.

In the war zones, "taking," "using," or "appropriating the enemy's women" constituted a central part of the repressive actions of the army and the civil patrol. . . . In San Bartolo, the rape of women was so serious and systematic that the majority of these women will not even talk about, much less denounce, these incidents. . . . Shame and social stigma prevent them from denouncing what happened. Some women erase the experience from their conscious memory because the pain of remembering the trauma is unbearable. . . .

In this municipality, women were raped by members of the army, as well as by the men who for years had ruled their town—such as ex-military commissioners, ex-commanders of the civil patrol, and mayors. These authority figures ordered other men in the community to commit the mass rapes. Here, as in many other places affected by the war, women were seen as "booty" and also as "bait" to trap the *hombres del monte* (their husbands who had joined the guerrillas or were hiding in the mountains). . . .

Through rape, the army and civil-patrol commanders also sought to denigrate the women and destroy them physically and mentally. In this way, they assured the silence of these women in the face of what was going on. Raping the women meant not only taking control of their bodies but of their wills. The men needed to convert them into accomplices, into their property. . . . Raping her was a way to conquer her, a way to break her will and force her to keep quiet; raping her meant making her "betray" her murdered, kidnapped, or persecuted male relatives, as in this testimony by Carmelina:

> After they killed my husband, they raped me. My husband was al-ready dead when they raped me. Juan Ordoñez killed my husband and wanted to force me. He said, "Your husband's already dead, so you're going to live with me. . . . If you don't want to come with me, I will kill you! We'll shoot you. You're here with us, you see what we're doing, maybe one day you'll speak about it, we'd better kill you, so you won't say anything. If you don't want to come with me, I'll send the soldiers here to your house, so they'll rape you in the house."

Taking Women: The Violation of the Home

In military sweep operations, the rape of women—those who didn't flee to the mountains—constituted a threat, if not torture, to force them to talk. . . . This threat, or the rape itself, took place at the same time that soldiers or patrollers defiled their house, hit their children or brothers and sisters, sacked their granaries, killed their animals, and broke their dishes and cooking utensils. . . .

The rape of the mother was also a psychological torture for the chil-dren, the majority of whom did not understand what was happening. It was common that while the mother was being raped, the children were taken somewhere a slight distance away from the scene, so they could not see the violation. But they could hear it, which increased their level of confusion and anxiety. . . . At the same time, soldiers and patrol commanders took advantage of the anguish of the children to torture them psychologically. The recurrent message children remember being told is: "It's your father's fault! Your father is a thief, a bad person, a guerrilla. It's his fault that we're going to kill your mother! You have to tell us where your father is, where the bad people are. If you don't tell us, we're going to set fire to everybody. We're going to burn you alive!"

Women as Bait

Another goal of keeping women captive was to capture the men hidden in the mountains. The majority of men who took refuge in the mountains did so because their names were on target lists to be killed. They thought the persecution would be temporary and that in a few days they would be able to return home, to the normality of their job and family life. They never imagined that their exodus would be permanent, much less that it would put their wives and children in jeopardy. . . . The patrol would stand guard inside or near these men's houses, knowing that they would return to see or pick up their families. Several men were ambushed as they were "talking to their wives or eating a hot tortilla." In some cases, the women were able to warn the men of the danger; in others, the women were forced to collaborate with the army and civil patrol to capture their own husbands. . . .

Ritual Rape

After the first rapes that were carried out in the family space and in the presence of children, the women from all the outlying areas of San Bartolo were forced to come into town. Then, inside the Catholic Church building, a group of between 100 and 150 women were concentrated, including the adults, children, and the aged. The military commissioners and civil patrol commanders ordered the women to be raped. The women were forced to undress in front of everyone. They were tied to the ground, raped by soldiers and then by their own community members, neighbors or relatives. This happened repeatedly in the final weeks of December 1981, and January and February 1982. One of the women who saw and lived through this experience relates:

> That mayor forced the patrollers to bring the women. . . . They brought them into the salon and then the soldiers came in and made the women undress. They took the women's clothes off and raped them. First the soldiers, and then the patrollers. . . . The women are forced, forced. The soldiers said, the ones that don't take off their clothes, we'll kill right here and now. So the women thought, maybe we'll live a few more days, and they had to do it. There, in the salon that's in the convent, right there, they tied the women to the ground. Like that, tied up, right on the ground. . . . There were about 100 women there. . . .

For the army and its allies, the mass rape represented the dance of the victors, the spectacle of shame through which the entire community became accomplices to war crimes. . . . No one remained untouched, no one would have the moral solvency to judge, much less denounce what had happened. . . .

It's important to point out that in all the testimonies of mass rape in San

Bartolo, the ones who gave the orders were authority figures—the mayor and military commissioners—who were responsible for carrying out the laws, norms, and customs of the municipality. Yet, against their mandate, it was these men who "let everything loose." They were the ones who forced the other men in the community to "commit their crime, to rape and take possession of as many women as they wanted [whether they were relatives or not]." They were the ones who imposed an order based on abuse and impunity. . . .

During these mass rapes, many men who were already on patrol duty were forced to be present as soldiers and other patrollers raped their mother, sister, wife, or daughter with impunity. Finally, these aberrant acts provoked rebellion on the part of some patrol members who demanded an end to the abuses against their women. . . .

The Houses of Women: Sexual Slavery

If the men who were serving in the patrol were able to prevent their women from being raped after a long conflict with "the bosses," the widows and women whose men had taken refuge in the mountains were not as lucky. They were obliged to "do service" in the military base. Doing service meant staying in town, "making tortillas for the soldiers and the patrols and letting these men do whatever they wanted with them." In other words, the women remained confined in the military base [the Catholic Church's convent building, which was occupied by the military] or in one of the "houses of women" where they would live under threat and constant surveillance, subject to the whims of the soldiers and patrollers who could decide when and how they wanted to "occupy" them. "Doing service" meant suffering in silence all the abuses and offenses of the "enemies" of their husbands and/or fathers.

The commissioners and patrol commanders set up these "houses of women" in vacant buildings in town. There, young women between the ages of 11 and 20 were kept captive. The argument used to establish this system of sexual slavery was that "the soldiers were far away from home, so they needed women." . . .

One women who was a witness relates:

For around two years, the women were there, for about two years they were raping the women. Every day they raped them. Until things calmed down, and then they let them go. A few women left, little by little. They escaped. . . . The ones who were trapped there couldn't even go home. They told them, if you go home, we'll kill you! . . . That's what they did [in the convent]. They said, if you're in the convent, you'll be okay . . . but you can't leave. Okay, but at any moment, they could rape them. They're abusing them any time they want, that's why they make them stay there.

A variant of the system of sexual slavery was private slavery, or the appropriation of the women of community leaders on the part of the military commissioners and civil-patrol bosses. There are several cases in this municipality of women who had to agree to live with a boss to save themselves from the abuses committed by the troops. To force the women to live with them, the mechanism utilized was terror and intimidation. The women were terrorized regularly by men who described the atrocities inflicted on their murdered husbands. They were warned they would face the same atrocities—dismemberment with a knife, being burned alive, or being thrown over a cliff—or that they would be "thrown to the soldiers" to be gang-raped, as in the following case:

One day another guy and I heard that our wives had other husbands. That other men had made them live with them. They say that they locked them in a room at night, and ten soldiers would come in, and the patrollers. These men came in and [one of them] said to my wife: "Look, you, first of all, we left your husband dead. We left him tied to a stake. By now his eyes are being eaten by buzzards. Why are you waiting for him? Second, should we tell the soldiers to have a go at you, or do you want to come just with me? I'll go with you. What do you think?"

So, the women, I think, went with them. Our husbands are dead, they must have thought. Why go with a crowd of soldiers? So they said okay. And that's how it happened. She still lives with that man. I haven't spoken to her since then. I never could speak with her. Now, if I go to town, I feel a huge sorrow. . . . I know that she suffered, too. What could she do if they were threatening her? It's not her fault. . . .

During my fieldwork, I confirmed that several women from San Bartolo were still living with their rapists and that the relationship these women had with the men had the appearance of normalcy. In the intimacy of the house, and in silence, the women live the violence and repeated abuse inflicted by the men.

Confronting Military Power

From the moment when the civil defense patrols were created, and the military base was installed, all of the town's entrances and exits were under surveillance. No one could walk around inside or outside the town without being watched and intercepted by the patrol. . . . Evading the military blockade was not easy. Yet, at various moments, different groups of women attempted to flee. As a first step, they would hide in the abandoned houses at the edge of town; then, at night, with their children in tow, and with the kids' mouths covered with cloth (so that the soldiers and the patrol would not hear them cry), they would walk in the ditches until they reached their family members hiding in the mountains. Some groups were discovered in their attempt to flee and suffered severe punishment at the hands of the army and patrol bosses. . . .

In 1983, once the civil patrol had achieved absolute control over the municipality, the vigilance was relaxed. That was when the largest flight of women took place. Many of the women [left the region and] went to the southern coast. . . .

Either fleeing or staying required an extraordinary bravery on the part of the women in San Bartolo, just to continue living after the atrocities to which they had been subjected. The majority of these women kept going in silence; yet, when one of them breaks her silence, her words reveal the incredible struggles that each and every one must have faced as they were trapped in the convent, forced to undress in public, gang-raped, or forced to live with one of the town's assassins.

The following quote is an example of this daily, silent struggle, in which many of the women challenged the authoritarian power, demanding "that they kill us!"

> They didn't rape me, I was with my sisters, we were walking in a group and we held our ground. We are not going to give service in the convent, we said to the patrol. How dare you tell us to give service in the convent. If . . . you already killed our husbands . . . how are you going to make us? If you want to kill us . . . then kill us already! We'll all die, and not just our husbands. I stood my ground. The soldiers didn't rape me. . . .

Translated by Elizabeth Oglesby

Surviving

Recovery of Historical Memory Project

The Recovery of Historical Memory Project was run by the Human Rights Office of the Guatemalan Catholic Archdiocese during the mid-1990s as an alternative truth commission. It worked at the community level with locally trained "animators" who encouraged people to speak about their experiences during the worst years of political violence. This selection from its final report, Guatemala: Never Again, *describes how people dealt with the violence and fear that tore their lives apart. Coping mechanisms could be individual or collective, including self-censorship, acts of solidarity, and organizing for survival and for justice.*

Social Solidarity

Family members and neighbors were the main sources of support. These kinds of support were given in moments of great danger and social isolation for the victims, and they are remembered with significant gratitude:

> A woman named Apolinaria, she didn't have a husband, she had four daughters and a baby son, she didn't have a house, and my father said to another member of the village council, "We're going to help this woman because she doesn't have a house." And the other one said: "If you donate the land, I'll put in the wood and the roof, and we'll do it this week." They got people together and then they made a little house for Apolinaria, and she lived there a while. (Case 3880, Choaxán, Quiché, 1982.) . . .

> I didn't stay at home; I went to his family's house, they treated me very well, they did all they could for me, and I'll always be grateful. (Case 5042, El Naranjo, Santa Lucía Cotzulmalguapa, Escuintla, 1984.)

> For us it was very meaningful and very sad. Some relatives and friends avoided us in the street, like we had leprosy. And some really stuck their necks out during the state of siege, the state of emergency, the state of martial law, and all those states. They visited us at night, risking their

lives. People offered us houses to hide in. We never hid because we never had a reason to; we never did anything that wasn't legal, like any human being, like any clean and sincere Guatemalan. (Case 5444 [assassinated university professor], Guatemala City, 1979.) . . .

In the search for the disappeared, which took place in a context of extreme danger and lack of recognition on the part of military authorities, sometimes people who had been witnesses informed family members of what they had seen or even accompanied the family in the official inquiries.

. . . Thanks to the people of Concepción, who would imagine that at the bottom of those gullies people were living, but it was thanks to them, otherwise we wouldn't have known about the bodies that were being thrown in there. (Case 0141, kidnapping and assassination, Quetzaltenango, 1994.)

Even though people tended to flee in the midst of great confusion and urgency, most times the exodus was a collective movement in which acts of solidarity took place in the midst of the emergency, preventing people from being left behind or captured by the army. For torture survivors, the support of neighbors and family members aided the person's physical and psychological recovery by providing a safe refuge, help in caring for wounds and assistance for basic needs.

My husband carried me, he put me on his back and carried me that way, we came to a riverbed and he told me to drink a little water. I could barely go on, but I had to endure that suffering. (Case 8352, Mayalán, Ixcán, Quiché, 1981.)

The neighbors gave me a hat and food and water. I went home. My family came; "Thank God you came back," they told me. Later, they heated water and bathed me. They dug a hole and buried my clothes that were all stained with blood. Also, I still have the scars where they tied us with wire and nylon rope. (Case 3017, Chiticoy (and military base), Rabinal, Baja Verapaz, 1983.)

In other cases, solidarity was less about offering concrete things and more about accompanying the affected people. This sense of accompaniment was very important in reducing people's feelings of isolation and helping the victims' ability to function in daily life.

I went over to my brother's, and he got up and came back with me and stayed with me, because I was afraid, because the doors didn't have bolts because they'd been knocked down. (Case 1505 [Kidnapping], Dolores, Petén.)

The Disappeared. Members of the Mutual Support Group demonstrate outside the National Cathedral in Guatemala City in 1985 to demand information about their disappeared loved ones. Photo by Daniel Hernández-Salazar. Used by permission of the photographer.

Trying to Change Things

A lot of testimonies refer to the ways people tried to do something to respond to the situation in spite of the difficulties, from looking for relatives who were captured or disappeared to direct confrontation with the army. This contrasts with the common image of victims as passive.

In the cases of kidnappings, in spite of fear and harassment, family members tried to obtain information about loved ones. They looked in hospitals and made multiple visits to the morgue to try to identify their kidnapped relatives amid the many bodies there. But they also made official inquiries and explicit demands to the military base responsible for the capture or military authorities in charge of the situation.

> We never heard from him again. His family, when they found out about the kidnapping, they starting looking for him. They went to the army with a photo, but the soldiers told them they didn't know anything. They spent hours like that and they didn't find him [the victim's body appeared in a ditch several days later]. (Case 0045, Quetzaltenango, 1981.)

Even though inquiries usually met with indolence, obfuscation, or direct threats, these efforts are an indication of how far many people were willing to commit themselves to attempting to find their loved ones alive.

> Five days after giving birth, I went to Xela [Quetzaltenango] to see him, but they told me, "Why are you looking for your husband? If he's here, he's on the list, look, look at his name. He's okay, and you've just given birth, you're going to die." So I told them, "Show him to me, show him to me. I want to talk to him." They said, "Why do you want to talk to him, or do you want to end up like him?" So I came home. (Case 0059 [temporary disappearance], La Victoria, Quetzaltenango, 1983.) . . .

Learning Experiences and Struggles for Change

Any form of social organization not controlled by the army was criminalized during the worst years of the political repression. This meant that many people were afraid to organize, afraid even of the word "organization" given its past connotations. Yet, in spite of this demobilizing effect, some people came together as a consequence of having suffered the violence.

> The family fell apart. My sister disappeared in 1985. My nieces and nephews went to live with my mother. Later, they came looking for us and we couldn't go back. My mother got sick. My brother's oldest daughter was raped by her stepfather. We lost the store, the animals. Later, my mother and I joined GAM [Grupo de Apoyo Mutuo, Mutual Support Group] and Famdegua [Families of Guatemala's Disappeared]. Acting as a group gives us courage. (Case 417, Nuevo Progreso, San Marcos.)

At first, these organizational steps were focused on practical things and mutual support in the face of fear. The need for information about disappeared family members was one factor that brought people together and gave them the courage necessary to make demands. Women were often the ones who carried out these actions, because a large number of survivors were women, and at times it was more difficult for the army to persecute women. . . . In the beginning, these were small steps, but as time went on, the groups developed important organizational experience and political projection. Initially, their actions were local, such as going together to a military base. Later, by the mid-1980s, the demands took on a more public character directed at the government. Yet, at least at the beginning, rather than a well-defined public platform, the heart of these experiences was community survival. . . .

> When my husband died, he left us with a lot of needs, and we suffered. But then we started thinking, two or three women, we started thinking about our suffering and what we could do about it. And we started thinking that we had to do this, to save the men, to save the young people. . . . We should raise our heads, we said, and we did, and it started when my husband died, and two or three of us came together and others raised themselves up as well, and that's how this organization came about [CONAVIGUA, Guatemalan National Widows Committee]. (Case 2793, Chuicaca, Patzité, Quiché, 1984.) . . .

Suffering Converted into Action

> It's important that I survived to be able to denounce everything I saw, including the names of those responsible. Maybe if I hadn't survived, the remains would never have been exhumed. . . . Without my testimony, there wouldn't be three people in prison now for that massacre. I want to denounce all this in court, but it takes a long time, and many judges don't believe it, even the judges threaten you. (Key informant, Rabinal massacre, Baja Verapaz, 1982.) . . .

> A few months later, a human-rights organization was created. I went right away to sign up, and I started a pretty hard struggle, because my hope was to find [the person] alive, to not have that doubt. Because if they're in prison, at least you know they're there, and even if they're sentenced to a hundred years, you still have the hope of being able to see them. But unfortunately, it didn't happen like that. We started that really, really hard struggle, and I think that it strengthened our own consciousness, because it's not just the struggle for my family, in my case six people, but the struggle for all the disappeared in Guatemala, all the kidnapped people, because you realize you're not alone. In the moment of the kidnapping you think you're alone, right? Sometimes you speak blasphemy against God: if I'm struggling for a better society, why does the Lord allow these things to happen? (Case 5449, Guatemala City, 1984.) . . .

> Well, what were we going to do? The fear itself showed us how to resist, the pain and the suffering showed us how to think, because, look, we

hadn't really thought like that before. (Case 4071 [extrajudicial execution and flight into the mountains], Nebaj, Quiché, 1983.) . . .

Collective educational activities to share experiences, analyze current conditions, and learn about rights have been in many cases the only social spaces available to people to speak about what happened, create meaning out of that experience, and recover the dignity of the dead. This highlights the significance of these spaces and the importance of work to recover historical memory.

Translated by Elizabeth Oglesby

Inverting Clausewitz

Guatemalan Army High Command

On August 12, 1987—about a year after Guatemala returned to nominal constitutional rule—members of the army high command gathered in a luxury hotel in Guatemala City to hold a public forum called "Twenty-Seven Years Fighting For Liberty." The forum's purpose was to explain the strategy behind the military's counterinsurgency programs and how success in the war had led, step by step, to the present "democracy" in Guatemala. Speaking to high-level business leaders and government functionaries, army officers stressed that consolidating a long-term counterinsurgency project meant building a strong state to bring about national stability. That would cost money, and the military officers admonished the elites that they owed a "security debt" to the country. The army supported a tax reform proposed by the Christian Democratic civilian government, a reform vehemently opposed by many in the elite.

In this selection, Colonel Mario René Enríquez Morales, director of civilian affairs, and General Héctor Alejandro Gramajo Morales, minister of defense, discuss how the Guatemalan army studied and expanded upon classic counterinsurgency doctrines. Enríquez Morales describes the army's efforts to construct a permanent presence in rural communities by replacing "paternalistic" and ineffectual civic-action programs with a more integrated application of psychological warfare and the formation of a cadre of local leaders linked to the military. Gramajo Morales explains that the army high command has an integrated conception of the Guatemalan state, which requires concerted action on the political, economic, and social fronts, as well as the military. Far from abandoning the anti-insurgent war, Gramajo notes that his conception of peace is an inversion of the famous phrase by the Prussian military theorist Carl von Clausewitz: "War is a continuation of politics by other means." For the Guatemalan army, Gramajo asserts, the country's transition to formal democracy was a "continuation of war by other means." Gramajo warns the oligarchy not to waste the historic opportunity to ensure national stability by building a strong developmentalist state as an integral part of the effort to neutralize the guerrillas.

Opposition to the high command's national-stability project came from disgruntled sectors of the military as well as some members of the oligarchy. In May 1988, these groups came together in an aborted coup against the Christian Democratic government of Vinicio Cerezo. Although the coup failed, it led to political realignments that ended the vision of a developmentalist state as neoliberal economic reforms took hold.

Colonel Mario René Enríquez Morales, director of civilian affairs: The degree of pacification we've attained is a product of the army's study and analysis of the tactical operations of the enemy, its general strategy and strong and weak points. But the greatest achievement has been in the area of our own capacities, building the ideological and philosophical bases of our own military doctrines, which, I can assure you, are a product of the effort and initiative of the officials of the army. . . . In the revision of the program of Civic Action and its substitution by Civilian Affairs, we came to the conclusion that the doctrine of Civic Action was no longer applicable to our environment because of its tendency toward paternalism. As the new programs took effect, based on the thesis of developmentalism and integrated participation, a new situation unfolded in which our people became the architect of their own development and expressed their needs in a real and direct way to their army.

We still need to gain the full understanding of all levels of society, so that they can unite in this effort, because terrorism is fed above all by underdevelopment, misery, and poverty. To the extent that salaries continue to be manipulated in the countryside, and *campesinos* continue to be sacrificed with jobs and workdays that are impossible to carry out without the utmost human effort, all the more distant will be the hour in which we consolidate peace. . . .

The work of the Civilian Affairs units is based on scientific and doctrinal principles of anthropology and sociology, turning to the social sciences to be able to comprehend the large discrepancies from one village to another within our great nation, from one indigenous community to another, and which together make up an intertwined mosaic of passions, interests, goals, and procedures, which had been adroitly exploited by the terrorist leaders to hide the true purposes and goals of their aggression. For these reasons, the army units have to add to their military capabilities and virtues a knowledge of the social reality of the community. . . .

The army does not actively take part in the political parties, but it wants the political process to go forward. This should not polarize Guatemalan society; on the contrary, it helps strengthen a national consciousness in the psychosocial arena, which up to now has been so divided. In this political moment, we need to count on the efforts of all those who have the ability to form or orient public opinion, and to plan, direct, finance and organize in Guatemala. We need to come together to repair the damages suffered because of the terrorist action, so that we can give to the most needy sectors the opportunities to incorporate themselves into the rest of the economically active population, so that the end result of these years of calamity, pain, and mourning will not be just another futile journey.

General Héctor Alejandro Gramajo Morales, minister of national defense: The army is participating actively in the strengthening of the democratic system. The army is dedicated to maintaining all military action as a function of national stability, and we are determined to maintain the constitutional order as a principal factor to achieve national stability, stability that should serve to generate well-being for Guatemalans. We have an integrated strategy. . . . We are plunging into the educational system with a new participatory philosophy, in which academic freedom coexists with disciplined military training, so that all officers can gain a broad exposure and develop analytical skills. . . .

We believe that the current political moment offers us a third opportunity we must grasp. The first opportunity of modern times was the presidency of Arévalo, which the radicals, or the inexperienced or ebullient groups, wasted. Later, the opportunity of 1966 we did not see as an opportunity. The army in that period was not up to the task; neither was the existing political system, and we lost a second opportunity. Now we are faced with a third opportunity in which the civilian leadership is sharing responsibility with the army. I can assure you that the institution I represent, honorably and temporarily, is doing everything it can to contribute its grain of sand in this third opportunity, the proof of which is that we are here with you, objectively and honestly. . . .

Of course, it is necessary to create political initiatives, and in this vein, we have achieved our objective of inverting the philosopher of warfare, Clausewitz, in saying that in Guatemala, politics should be the continuation of war. . . .

But this does not mean that we are abandoning the struggle; neither does it mean that we are betraying those who spilled their blood or those who left behind their family, nor that we are not following the policy contours laid out by our predecessors. We are still on battle footing, renovating the method of fighting, but not forgoing it.

In the current moment, we believe—with much modesty, of course, and hopefully that's how you see us—that we are the stabilizing institution of this transition. We are the institution that strengthens democracy and the democratic system that the people of Guatemala have chosen.

We visualize the interests of the nation as a whole . . . in which military action has to be linked to economic, political, and social action. We believe everything is inter-connected. The army can't do everything, nor can politicians, the private sector, or the popular organizations. We have to do things within an integrated conception of the Guatemalan state. This is a challenge for the military leadership and we are committed to it. So we exhort other sectors to make their calculus and take advantage of this third opportunity.

Translated by Elizabeth Oglesby

Assistance and Control

Myrna Mack

Guatemalan anthropologist Myrna Mack was one of the first researchers to investigate conditions in rural Guatemala in the aftermath of the scorched-earth campaign, documenting how large parts of the countryside were still highly militarized even after Guatemala's 1986 return to nominal democracy. Much of Mack's work focused on the Ixil region of northern El Quiché, where the army applied its counterinsurgency policies with the greatest ferocity. Believing that the majority of the Ixil population supported the guerrillas, the army destroyed nearly all of the Ixil villages during 1981 and 1982, displacing more than 90 percent of the population. The army rebuilt these villages as "model villages" or "strategic hamlets," and the military tightly controlled disbursement of aid to any displaced people who returned. Mack also studied Alta Verapaz, although the intensity of the conflict had subsided by the time Mack carried out her research in the late 1980s, and the Catholic Church maintained an important presence there, providing aid to the displaced populations.

Myrna Mack published her research on the displaced in Guatemala in early 1990. On September 11, 1990, she was stabbed to death outside her office by an army death squad. It is widely believed that her assassination was in reprisal for her pioneering work documenting conditions in rural Guatemala in the wake of the counterinsurgency campaigns.

The first families who returned from the mountains or jungles had been constantly hounded and were in miserable conditions. Many were placed in camps under military control and were taught the new organizational structures that would prevail in the communities where they were to settle. These included the concentrated layout of villages, civil defense patrols, improvement committees, the authority structure of the patrols, and monthly reporting in person at military bases. During this period the army monopolized contact with the internally displaced and oversaw their treatment. . . .

Since it was believed that this population had to be wrenched from the guerrillas, their treatment was marked by re-education programs, a policy spelled out in the National Plan for Security and Development. . . . The army, in applying the general concept of "security and development" during this period, constructed development poles . . . in Quiché, Alta Verapaz, Huehuetenango, Chimaltenango and Petén. . . . These communities, whose physical layout follows a nucleated pattern, are also called "model villages" or, in the international media, "strategic hamlets," echoing the term used in Vietnam. . . . Residents complain that they must live "all piled up on top of each other . . . like chickens in a coop." Freedom of movement was eliminated—and often still is—in favor of a system of passes which the bearers can only obtain by providing their destination and length of absence.

The development poles in the Ixil Triangle and Alta Verapaz began as reception camps for the displaced who returned in 1982 and 1983. One army official estimates that the military regime attended 42,000 people in the Ixil Triangle alone. This figure represents the entirety of the population in the affected area; in other words, virtually 100 percent of the population there was relocated into the reconstructed villages. . . .

The following account reflects one displaced returnee's experience with the military sweeps that areas such as the Ixil Triangle have undergone in the last decade:

> In 1981, 2,000 soldiers came to carry out the offensive. Then more came later on. By then I couldn't tell how many. But they always came, they always came, every two, every three, or every five weeks. One year they ceased operations in 1986, they didn't come . . . Toward the end of September 1987 it was very difficult because of all the patrols and soldiers, and you couldn't stay. Let me tell you, as a grown-up you can put up with a lot, but the little ones? And many women were giving birth on the riverbanks, or bearing children in the mountain brush. Sometimes they were born in the rain. And the children always crying from hunger.

This last offensive involved 4,500 Guatemalan soldiers and lasted from the latter part of 1987 into the first few months of 1988; it had two objectives—to retake the population that had hidden in the mountains over the years, and to reestablish military control of the region in order to resettle the returned population. . . .

Whether directly or through civil patrols, the military is the first authority to have contact with the displaced the moment they return or are captured. Their first days back, the returnees are placed under watch and required to give diverse kinds of information. . . .

The level of military intervention also depends on the level of conflict in

Watched over by two soldiers and armed with a rope and a gun, a "volunteer" member of the civil patrol stands guard in front of the military outpost in Panajxit, Quiché, 1983. Photo by Jean-Marie Simon. Used by permission of the photographer.

the area of return. El Quiché is considered the "red zone" of the country; in the words of a resident of the Ixil Triangle, "Here, you simply don't see, feel, or notice that there exists in Guatemala a civilian government. . . ." On the other hand, the level of armed conflict in Alta Verapaz, where fewer displaced have returned, is appreciably lower. In Alta Verapaz there was a considerable decrease in armed conflict since 1984. The Catholic Church, considered to be one of the most credible institutions in the country, has fostered protection and support for several groups of returnees in this area since 1986. Therefore, those contemplating a return first sought out the local ecclesiastical authorities. . . . Unlike in El Quiché, where the Church was effectively forced to close down following the assassination of two of its priests, the Alta Verapaz Diocese was able to preserve its infrastructure, in spite of assassinations and kidnappings suffered by several of its catechists. . . .

Despite the broad efforts of the Church to afford haven and welcome in Alta Verapaz and elsewhere, there is scant buffer between the military and the returnees. In February 1987, when 100 returnees came on their own initiative to Church authorities in search of protection, the local military zone commander, several armed soldiers, and others in civilian dress showed up unannounced, and sowed great fear among the group whom they began to interrogate on the spot. . . . The first tragic experience [among the Alta Verapaz returnees] took place in mid-1986 when two persons, from a group of 37 internally displaced returnees under Church protection, were "mysteriously" removed from the parish building where they were sleeping. . . .

The first stage [of the return of the displaced in the Ixil region] consists of recording information of importance in security matters, providing medical assistance, clothing, and food, and "democratic or civic education." This last activity consists of political talks and video recordings intended to "bring the displaced up to date regarding their country." The displaced are lectured on the "trickery of the subversives," the risks they would run by returning to the mountains, and the peace they currently enjoy.

In the second stage, the families of returnees decide where they will resettle, usually it is in their original community, now to be reconstructed as a "new" community. . . . The returnees who are still housed in [civilian government–run] facilities must first obtain authorization from the local military detachment in order to go and set up temporarily in nearby communities while they work on reconstructing the village and establishing the new forms of organization under which they will live. In the third stage, the community is reconstructed according to a "nuclear" or "concentrated" plan, in contrast to the traditional dispersal of the agrarian communities. . . . The fourth stage contemplates, at some future time, production programs with technical assistance for crop diversification. . . . In the majority of the communities, there simply do not exist the minimal conditions necessary for economic reactivation. . . .

A significant gap exists between development policy as conceived, and its actual implementation. . . . The Ixil region is a "security zone," so the residents must often interrupt their work from a day up to an entire week to serve in civilian defense patrols, military sweeps or other spontaneously announced tasks. . . . In the areas where the greatest displacement occurred, one can observe the effects of the ideological efforts of the Army and the fundamentalist churches that have cultivated the notion that the displaced and the repatriated refugees are "subversives." The notion gets expressed in different ways, but the effect is the same—to proscribe and stigmatize this sector. . . .

The return of the families has brought about conflicts in the heart of the communities. Many returnees are the object of resentment, particularly if they have received land and work because of their status. Much more often, however, they must begin to reintegrate themselves into the commu-

On December 2, 1990, soldiers fired on a crowd of protesters in the town of Santiago Atitlán, Sololá, killing 13 people. After the killing, residents organized a successful campaign to evict the army from the town. Here, Santiago Atitlán citizens sign a petition calling for the removal of the local military base. Photo by Juan Rolando González Díaz. From the collections of the Centro de Investigaciones Regionales de Mesoamérica, Guatemala.

nity and take up work under less favorable circumstances. "Now I'm even poorer than before," was the refrain that summed up the situation.

There are religious and secular as well as national and international entities among the nongovernmental institutions (NGOs). Several of them had focused on "development assistance" many years before beginning to assist the displaced and the repatriates. . . . It was during this period that a great number of evangelical churches and fundamentalist sects sprung up in Guatemala, with strong backing from the regime of general Ríos Montt (1982–1983). Unlike the traditional Protestant churches—Presbyterian, Episcopalian, Lutheran, and Methodist—that had been in the country for many years, the churches that have cropped up over the last 10 years actively promote a conservative political agenda and are very well funded by their coreligionists in the United States. That these churches received the active support of the same elements in the army and ruling regime who had made no effort to disguise their distrust of the Catholic Church or regarded its social services as subversive has not been lost on the NGOs. . . . There are three clear tendencies among the NGOs. Some work closely with the army and the government in key areas of programs for the displaced. Others, in accepting the challenge of assisting the displaced wherever they are found, struggle to maintain their autonomy without contravening the conditions laid down by the army and the government. Finally, there are those whose disagreement with the thrust of the counterinsurgency programs and aversion to being co-opted by the army is so strong that they avoid direct work with the displaced. . . .

One of the clearest ways in which the country's political conditions complicate aid to the displaced is the continual military vigilance over the assistance provided to the displaced in El Quiché and Alta Verapaz. This makes it impossible for the NGOs to carry out their activities in a tension-free environment. . . . The investigative team learned of several instances in which army personnel have harassed communities working with NGO and Catholic Church projects. These incidents are consistent with the frequent warnings and innuendos that patrol commanders and military commissioners express to workers in development programs. As a result, some NGOs have to rule out the possibility of providing assistance in given areas. Until the military loosens control, these humanitarian organizations will continue to feel caught between the needs of a population in desperate straits and the security requirements of the army. . . .

The concern of many NGOs is that the prevailing pattern of emergency assistance will undermine positive ethno-cultural values. According to one NGO official who expressed his frustration at attempting to promote independent, integrated development and self-sufficiency, "our only job is to attend to misery."

We Are Civilians

Communities of Population in Resistance of the Sierra

In 1987, with the start of regional peace talks in Central America, the army started a new offensive in northern El Quiché. This offensive was intended to "recover" the displaced populations still hiding in the mountains outside military control. Military analysts viewed these populations as strategically important in the peace process; strategists were fearful that the remnants of the guerrilla groups might declare a "liberated zone" in northern El Quiché, where approximately fifteen thousand people were living in the so-called Communities of Population in Resistance of the Sierra. The army was worried that international agencies such as the International Red Cross could be called in, amid calls for the application of the Geneva Conventions regarding treatment of noncombatant populations, giving the rebels political leverage in future peace talks.

The Communities of Population in Resistance of the Sierra were struggling to survive in the midst of war. Even as they were living clandestinely under the dense forest cover of the mountains, constantly harassed by aerial bombing campaigns, they organized impressive communal farming, education, and health programs. On September 7, 1990, the CPR published the following statement in the Guatemalan press. This was the first time that the existence of the CPR became publicly known in Guatemala, and it was the beginning of a process of "coming out of the shadows" for these populations.

The representatives and delegates from all the Communities of Population in Resistance of the Sierra, gathered in our First General Assembly, declare to the government and people of Guatemala and to the governments and peoples of the world: The Communities of Population in Resistance of the Sierra are composed of Guatemalan civilian *campesino* populations . . . who have been displaced from our places of origin, families, ethnic groups and the rest of the Guatemalan population due to army repression against our people.

Since 1981 and 1982, when our people demanded their rights, the army unleashed a heavy wave of repression, massacres, human rights violations, destruction of crops and bombings against us, which continues at present. Since this time, the army has invaded and occupied our lands, villages and towns. They pursue us, destroy our belongings and trample on all of our rights. We are resisting because we feel and live in our own flesh, the pain caused by the injustice of past and present governments which pursue, assassinate and bombard us with sophisticated weapons which are unfit for humanity. . . . The army . . . alone or accompanied by civil patrols, continues to destroy our crops and houses and to capture or kill our families. Our communities suffer human rights violations daily as they are bombarded by the Air Force or by army artillery. . . . Therefore, we are resisting in order to defend our rights, families, and the lives of our communities.

We declare that the reasons for our resistance are: the struggle for our lives and rights and against army invasion and occupation of our lands, villages and towns; in order not to be subjected to the organization of civil patrols and model villages which the army has imposed on our people by force; so that army repression against our population be ceased; so that the government and the army respect the human rights of our people.

Just as other Guatemalan brothers and sisters have defended their lives and rights by fleeing and hiding in the cities, forming new organizations or taking refuge in other countries, we have decided to defend ourselves by resisting in our mountains, organized in community, without abandoning our lands and peoples.

The Communities of Population in Resistance—CPR—are part of the popular organization in Guatemala which resists and struggles against injustice, the violation of human rights, and army and government repression against our peoples. After conducting an extensive popular forum with our entire population, we declare our most urgent thoughts, needs and demands to the Guatemalan government with the people of Guatemala, democratic governments and peoples of the world as our witnesses:

1. That the government recognize our demands as a civilian *campesino* population in resistance and part of the Guatemalan population. . . .

2. That the government acknowledge our right to return freely to our places of origin from which we fled. . . . Our return must be: voluntary, free, organized, collective, with accompaniment and support from national and international humanitarian and human rights organizations. In order to achieve this, the Communities of Population in Resistance demand that the government demilitarize our lands, villages and towns because we want peace and the freedom to return to our lands of birth

A school organized by the Communities of Population in Resistance, northern El Quiché, late 1980s. Photo by Derrill Bazzy. Used by permission of the photographer.

and to work them freely. [We demand] that . . . the government withdraw [the soldiers] and lock them in their barracks because our people are so tired of their persecution, killing and bombardment that we never want to see them again.

3. The government must remove the military, social, political and economic cordon it has maintained around our communities for eight years through civil patrols, military bases and posts, prohibiting the entrance of people, international organizations and commerce. In other words, full freedom of movement. . . .

4. That the army and the government permit the free entrance of national and international human rights and humanitarian organizations, as well as our churches, to our communities. . . . The government must also return to us our family members who have been forcibly resettled in model villages. . . .

No law or government which is authentically democratic, can deny our right to exist. . . . No law or government which is authentically democratic, can deny the right of just and respectable organizations to testify to our situation and life before the Guatemalan people and the world. . . . No law or government in the world which claims to respect human rights can deny us the right to receive pastoral and humanitarian assistance from our churches. These are not just rights belonging to a few people but to all of humanity. As long as the government and the army do not permit a new life, a new time, a new demilitarized situation, liberty, peace, security, authentic democracy, and respect for human rights in our lands, we will continue to resist. We are struggling and resisting in order to live in a society where there is peace and liberty for all.

Time to Get Up

Francisco Goldman

A prizewinning novelist and journalist, Francisco Goldman is the author of a number of intricately composed books, including the novel The Divine Husband *and the nonfiction work* The Art of Political Murder. *Goldman was born in Boston, Massachusetts, to a Guatemalan mother and Jewish American father, similar to the protagonist of his first novel,* The Long Night of White Chickens, *excerpted here.* Long Night *is a murder mystery that follows Roger's attempt—with the help of a close friend, the honest yet cynical journalist Moya—to uncover the facts behind the killing of his childhood nanny, Flor de Mayo Puac. Moya's refrain, repeated throughout the novel, that "Guatemala no existe"—Guatemala doesn't exist—captures the sense that state terror had so broken the country that it could never be put back together. In the passages below, Goldman lovingly renders scenes—early-morning military jogging in Guatemala City's central plaza, and the lethal chaos that ensues from a government order that suddenly reversed traffic flow in the capital—that capture the militarization of public space and the switchback capriciousness of life under jackboot rule that marked Guatemala in the 1980s. As an appropriate finale for a part of the* Reader *focused on the nightmare of Guatemala's counterinsurgency, the selection ends with the line: "Time to get up."*

It's raining outside, though not heavily. Half an hour ago it was torrential, a delicious reverberation that seemed to come from the earth instead of the sky, going right through me. I'm drinking coffee, smoking filterless Payasos (a white-faced clown with the smile of a lighthearted idiot waving from every poinsettia red, thirty-five-*centavo* square little pack); I have a copy of yesterday's *New York Times*, purchased this morning for the equivalent of two bucks at Palacio de las Revistas, the Palace of Magazines, just down the block, and this notebook in which I am trying to commence this chronicling of the investigation into Flor's life and death that Moya and I have agreed to collaborate on. Moya already refers to this place as my *oficina*, though I sit nearly as often in the Picadilly on *La Sexta*—Sixth Avenue—or at the table closest to the sidewalk in the Fo Lu Shu. Moya and I met here in the *pastelería* this morning. Just a touch patronizingly, he warned me about government informers, who are everywhere, including, of course, his own newspaper office, too many of them eager and ignorant enough to misunderstand any kind of conversation. *Orejas*, they're called—*ears*. I'm supposed to act from now on as if even the old women sitting at the next table—one of them plaintively monologuing, ". . . he's a good son, a good son, he adores his mother, *la adora*, he puts his mother above everything"—might be *orejas* too. I'm to be a *tumba*: our secrets sealed inside me as if inside a tomb.

I yawn like crazy. This constant fact of paranoia, no matter how abstractly abided, tires me, I think. Every afternoon I feel just sapped. But it must be the altitude, too, and all the unfiltered motor fumes in the air and probably gastrointestinal germs working as silently inside me as this blend of excitement and fear and other more familiar emotions, which I try not to let my expression betray. (Yawn, drink coffee, smoke, read newspaper, scribble in notebook, keep a quietly watchful eye and a tuned ear. . . .) And the rain, and the afternoon light that looks washed through ashes. Guatemala City is a mountain city, and during the rainy season especially the sky couldn't feel closer or heavier. . . .

That day five years ago, when the government changed the direction of one-way traffic on the city's major avenues, Moya was right here in Pastelería Hemmings, sitting at a table with three other students, two guys and a girl, they were huddled over a copy of the afternoon daily (the very same afternoon paper, *El Minuto*, that in less than two years Moya would find himself working for) that had just hit the streets, its headline announcing that so far that day ten people had died, either in traffic accidents or from getting run over. I hadn't realized he was Moya yet—he would recognize me first—but I could hear them talking about it as I stared out the window, heard a bitterly deadpan voice (his) from their table saying in Spanish, *Permit me to say that as a way of relieving traffic congestion I find this not bad. Eliminate the drivers, eliminate the pedestrians.* And then the girl's voice petulantly saying, *Permíteme decir que no es cosa para chistes, vos*, it isn't anything to joke about. . . .

About a week later my favorite cousin, Catalina, Catty to all of us, then a senior at the Colegio Anne Hunt, would tell how a teacher who had been particularly affected by the chaos of the traffic change that day, one of the perpetually young Señorita Something teachers, said, "This proves the government doesn't care about people." Anne Hunt might have fired her for getting political in class that way, if it had gotten back to her. But what made Catty's story funny was that this teacher was practically obsessed with her car, a brand-new red Toyota she'd won in a raffle only months before. Catty said this teacher couldn't have been more *exagerada* in her pride over this car if she'd tried, always telling her class things like "Imagine how it improves the psychology to drive a car with all the windows down in the morning instead of riding the bus, to breathe fresh morning air instead of bus exhaust and the smells of all the people pressed against you, so many of them, let's face it, very poor and unhygienic people." Or she'd leave books and papers behind in the car just so she could make a show of saying, "Will someone volunteer to go out to my car and get them? It's a red Toyota, and today it is parked just down the block, on the left side, right under that jasmine tree. If it rains today my car will be covered with jasmine blossoms, and if I drive home with the windows down, I'll smell jasmine all the way!"

But this teacher had been so traumatized by the chaotic traffic that day that she'd started leaving her car at home and riding the bus, and in the days since had turned into a real *melancólica* in class, listless and distracted and constantly sipping hot lettuce tea from a thermos for her nerves. All of which culminated in the scene out in front of the school just after the siesta break one afternoon when a young lower-class man accosted this teacher as she came walking down the sidewalk from the bus stop. Through eaves-dropped snatches of his tormented shouting and the teacher's pleading whispers, Catty and her friends were able to piece together a puzzle revealing that for months her teacher and this man had been meeting in her parked Toyota during the siesta, but only when it rained and rained hard, which at the height of the rainy season was just about every afternoon, to kiss and maybe even to make love with the rain closing them off from all the world in their cozy, black vinyl, made-in-Japan love nest. But this love affair was over now that the *señorita* felt too afraid to drive in her car anymore. And how could it ever be resumed now that her lover's outraged and indiscreet tantrum had let the students in on their secret? "*Pobrecita,*" poor thing, lamented my cousin Catty, while she sat facing me on the piano stool in her Uncle Jorge's study, where she was waiting with placid impatience for her boyfriend's daily evening visit and telling me this story. "Why couldn't he have waited? calmed her? helped her to feel confident about taking her *carrito* out in traffic again? But that's how men are, *verdad*? They take everything personally! *Pues sí.*"

And later that same evening of the day they changed the direction of the traffic, when I went back to the furnished apartment in Zona 10 that Flor was already renting, carrying my own copy of *El Minuto* and its TEN DEAD headline, Flor had just washed her hair, had it turbaned in a towel, and was sitting on the couch, doing absolutely nothing apparently, which was not characteristic. ("You won't believe who I ran onto in Pastelería Hemmings. Moya! Remember Moya?"—it didn't mean much to her, no reason that it should have then.) But it's amazing how easy it is just to sit around doing nothing in Guatemala, or anywhere in the tropics perhaps—it isn't the heat, because Guatemala City isn't especially hot and in November, December it gets cold. But day after day you can just sit around doing nothing and it doesn't feel particularly wrong or even tedious. Back then I thought several times that maybe this was the reason Flor had returned here and seemed interested in staying a while: that after so many years of balancing heroic overachieving with the more banal but just as constant demands of house-work and, more recently, earning a living, not to mention what seemed to me years of unbroken and rather obsessive socializing, that Flor was finding it pleasurable to sit around being lazy and anonymous: that she even felt a perverse and paradoxically self-negating attraction to a place—her native country!—where everywhere you look hard work seemed only one more aspect of a general futility it was easiest to escape by just not doing any-thing, but only if you could afford to, and she could. (But then, within two months, she would throw herself into her new job running Los Quetzalitos, and for the next three years plus work harder than she ever had before.) Anyway, I handed Flor the newspaper and she snapped it open like it was what she'd been waiting for all day. And then seconds later tossed it aside, "Oh well. Let them eat cake."

Because what were ten more dead people that summer? . . .

That afternoon in Pastelería Hemmings, at a table of ten people from the States, a man was waving a copy of that *El Minuto* with its TEN DEAD head-line and was yelling, in English, "I don't believe it! The monkeys! What a bunch of monkeys! Does this say it all or what? I'm going to take this home and have it framed!"

People heard him, and some were offended. Heads turned. Guatemalans take offense easily and viscerally—you can feel it in a room, sense their breathing quickening, their tempers rising, sense a blackening rage even, when it's really bad, when they're about to lose it, utterly.

That's when I noticed the guy who turned out to be Moya staring at me.

I looked away, out the window. Honest to god, chaos was as tangible as if the whole city had just been flipped upside down and back over again. Guatemalan traffic can terrify me even on slow Sundays, but that day, all

over the place, people were turning the wrong way down one-way avenues. People were looking the wrong way as they stepped off the curbs.
Truckers were trying to bash their way through directionless traffic jams
anyway. Bus drivers were slipping confusedly back into routes they'd been
following for years. People were being injured and killed. Guatemala City,
a flat plateau city in the Valley of the Virgin, was echoing with bleating car
horns. Not even the birds could have felt safe; they must have stayed up in
the air. And the usual traffic sounds, ranging from the high beady spitting
of mufflerless motorbikes to the wall-shaking thunder of mufflerless buses,
from the iron gnashing of ancient gearboxes to the smooth-shifting hum
of expensive imports, the clanging of so many flimsy body parts as shock-
less '59 Pontiacs and trucks that are nothing more than loose piles of junk
go banging over potholes and bumps, the artillery of so many backfires far
away and nearby—all these sounds were accelerated and amplified that day;
it sounded as if everybody was trying to get out, to flee the city all at once.

One thing I know about Guatemala now is that little of this sort happens here, no matter how shocking or outrageous, without reason, without
actual people sitting down somewhere and deciding that it should happen.
Though sometimes their reasoning can seem just as outrageous or bewil-
dering as the thing done. The new traffic ordinance was meant to improve
the traffic flow, and in that way was even linked to promised improvement in the economy. Because the perpetually jammed up traffic at certain
transit points in the city's layout was responsible for making people late
for work, for wasting gasoline and diesel, and that affected, among other
things, the profitability of buses, as did the slow traffic, which also hindered
truckers passing through downtown on their way to the highways leading to the coastal ports, and time is money. It was especially supposed to
improve the traffic flow through the crucial maze of rotaries, underpasses,
and switchbacks down at one end of Zona 1, suturing together downtown's
old, dense grid of straight, narrow streets and the wide boulevards and ex-
pressways of the newer residential and industrial zones beyond. This area,
during the rush hours, was usually impassable. My other uncle, Dr. Nelson
Arrau, warned ahead of time that the whole thing might be a scam anyway, a contract awarded by government or city officials to some self-made
urban planner in return for a payoff, resulting in an essentially berserk and
thoughtless recommendation. And though the government had announced
the new ordinance days ahead, Uncle Jorge predicted the disaster, and he
is an *ultra* patriot. It's not like everybody reads the papers, he said. And of
course they don't, not in a country of rampant illiteracy where much of the
Indian population, at least half the national population, doesn't even speak

(*above and facing*) From the series *Tarzán López*, which depicts the Rey Gitano travel-ing circus. The circus has crisscrossed Guatemala since the 1930s, including during the years of the armed conflict. Photos by Jaime Permuth. Used by permission of the photographer.

Spanish. And it's not like *everybody* listens to the radio, paying special attention to every government public service announcement or motivational message, of which there are many. And of course people are going to get confused, or just forget. It wouldn't even take that many to screw it all up.

In the end traffic flow *was* actually improved a little (though now, five years later, it's as bad as it ever was). By that night the number of fatalities reached thirteen. It's the kind of thing that could happen in any small, poor country, you were supposed to say.

Or else, "*Guatemala no existe . . .*" et cetera—So claimed Moya that afternoon in Pastelería Hemmings, reciting the speech that was in fact the opening paragraph of a French thriller he'd read in translation—something about a philosophical Gallic trucker and his hair-raising drive across Guatemala transporting a dangerous cargo, various native and foreign malevolents in pursuit—which ended with the line "Guatemala doesn't exist, and I know, because I have been there." . . .

Payaso cigarettes, Gallo beer, windows open and my sound box turned down low, Wilfredo Vargas lewdly, robustly growling, "*Miiii medicina eres túúúúú . . .*"

This is the bedroom I chose for myself, an addition Abuelita had built over the rear part of the house, completed only a few years before the night she sat down in an armchair downstairs, let her head droop to the side, and went to sleep forever. "She passed away just like that, without any warning, just like a little bird," that's how my mother tells it. I'm sitting at the unevenly carpentered, untreated pine desk I bought the other day from an Indian vendor who was carrying it down the street on his back with four crude chairs stacked and roped between the upturned legs. "Just the desk," I said. Moya, when he saw it, he said it reminded him of what the dictator Estrada Cadrera said long ago when after more than two decades in power he was deposed and imprisoned: "I have been like the Indian carpenters of Totonicapán, up at dawn and working hard every day of my life, forever making bad furniture."

Maybe it's just the absence of the motor fumes and traffic uproar that makes breathing actually pleasant at night, that lets the mountains flow invisibly into the quiet of the city at night, into all its earthquake cracks. You imagine you can smell the infiltrated histories of soaked forests where the sun never penetrates, where a dead tree can remain standing perfectly mummified in the wet dark air for centuries, until someone comes along and just pushes on it with their hand or kicks or leans against it and *poof!*: it collapses into a pile of fine peat power and drunken ants at their feet ("Sixty million years of constant photosynthesis!" I read that in a magazine article on the Guatemalan cloud forests). Every night smells quite a bit like leaf-burning season in New England, as if the damp smoke of faraway slash-and-burn farming mixes with the smoke from a million charcoal cooking and garbage fires lingering over the city's peripheral slums-ravines.

Usually, at night, at this time of year, it rains for at least a little while. You don't actually find Caribbean crabs scampering around the patio in the morning but from the rain's clatter—heavy drops gradually quickening and suddenly subsiding, unlike the afternoon downpours, which come all at once—you almost expect to. What I do find in the central patio sometimes is the small antique fountain filled to the brim and moths or butterflies floating, their wings washed absolutely translucent, antennae twitching like tiny oars. And once sunk to the bottom and looking like a tiny medieval samurai buried in a limpid green tomb, a drowned hummingbird.

It's three in the morning and I'm nearly exhausted enough for sleep, though there's something about my night here, this constant and more or less unfocused impatience and agitation I've been feeling, that keeps an echoing din going inside me, one that seems to grow louder the quieter it gets outside. Though this neighborhood, in Zona 1, with streets dark and deserted at night like a labyrinth of canals, is never completely quiet. Sounds wake you in and out of sleep. The sudden squeal of faraway tires, backfires that sound like gunshots; the police who walk their beats in pairs, communicating with each other across the empty blocks in the warbled code of a Maya whistling language, sounding like commando owls on secret missions into the night air behind enemy lines. This is the precise hour when the invisible city, as wide as the actual one, of crowing roosters starts coming to life, inciting the invisible city of howling, barking, yapping dogs. And when the light is deepest phosphorescent blue, that's when the soldiers of the Presidential Guard—the National Palace is only blocks away—come out of their predawn jog through the glowing mists, hundreds of rhythmically stomping boots against wet pavement and the occasional warrior druids' cry of some militant slogan being sounded off (Moya says his grandfather could remember when all military parades or processions were silent: "Because back then soldiers went barefoot, *vos!*"). Every 6:00 AM but Sunday I'm jolted back awake by the screeching transmission and thunderous idling of my neighbor's messed-up car in the echo box of his tiny garage, just over the wall on the other side of the narrow courtyard beneath my window. . . .

And one dozing spell later, from nearby or from farther away but always because it's always *somebody's* birthday, dawn's staccato explosions, strings of birthday firecrackers being set off, often accompanied by the fainter celebrations of mariachi bands singing *"Mañanitas."* . . . Then the uproar of the morning's first mufflerless buses, and ambulant street vendors crying out like professional mourners: *"Avocaaaaados"*—as if every avocado in Guatemala died yesterday. Ever hear a man pour all his plaint and grief into the word for eggplant? *"Berenjeeeeenas."* They pass in the street, stop by barred, shuttered windows or kitchen service doors to ring and ring, bleating out a name for whatever they're selling: *"Zapaaaatos"*—the ambulant cobbler. It's such an Indian sound: deep, resonant, ancient, the sound, somehow, that an immense, gnarled, and knotty old hardwood oak, ripped open by lightning, might make. But Indians have worked as street vendors in cities since Spanish colonial times, haven't they? Pitching their products as if embodiments of the Indian soul to people living behind high walls and barred windows ever since? The Spaniards could have forbidden it if they didn't like it, decreed a thousand lashes for smuggling of excessive complaint or pagan anguish into the word for eggplant. Instead they must have encouraged this bathetic bleating as the key to good salesmanship! But why? (must ask Moya) . . . And then the *Bandas de Guerra*, the War Bands, public school kids practicing year-round for Independence Day parade, marching through the street in school uniforms, boys and girls playing rudimentary martial music on snare and bass drum, a few xylophones, a few trumpets. Also the daily Pan Am flight to Miami, taking off and shattering the morning in its thundering, straining, protracted reach over the mountains and volcanoes, rattling windows and walls. Time to get up.

VII

An Unsettled Peace

On December 29, 1996, the Guatemalan government and the Guatemalan National Revolutionary Unity (URNG), the coalition representing the four guerrilla groups, signed the peace agreement that ended more than three decades of armed conflict. Intermittent negotiations had gone on over the previous ten years, a period punctuated by heightened danger for activists, leftist politicians, and intellectuals as the military sought to circumscribe the left's political influence in the peace process. This long prelude to peace also sharpened divisions within the army and the Guatemalan upper class: conservative elites and hard-line army officers, united in part by their opposition to these negotiations, threatened to overthrow Guatemala's civilian government in 1988 and again in 1993.

Most of the military high command supported peace talks, however, because they wanted to demonstrate that the army had won the war. The accords did not broker peace between two powerful armies; the guerrillas were weak, scattered, and without a military future, and popular support had diminished sharply. Even so, the signing of the cease-fire brought a sigh of relief to Guatemalans throughout the country. At least the war would end.

But three decades of violent political conflict and a brutal counterinsurgency campaign in the early 1980s had left two hundred thousand dead. There were tens of thousands of widows, orphans, and refugees. The country's social fabric had been ripped apart, especially in the rural communities that had suffered massacres, forced displacement, and abuse by aggressive military commissioners and civil-patrol commanders. In the cities, at least one entire generation of trade-union activists, community leaders, and intellectuals had been killed, disappeared, or forced into exile.

Most of the peace agreements dealt with the immediate concerns of ending the war. They provided for demobilizing the guerrilla forces and integrating the URNG into the political system, dismantling the army-run civil patrols, resettling the displaced populations, establishing a Truth Commission to investigate human-rights abuses and crimes committed during the war, and reducing the size of the military. Two accords addressed the longer-term goals of confronting Guatemala's history of racism and social inequality. An agreement on indigenous peoples committed the Guatemalan state to recognize the identity and rights of the Maya, Garífuna, and Xinca populations and to undertake a series of reforms to support multiculturalism (see part 8 of this volume). A socioeconomic accord affirmed that Guatemala's "historical social imbalances must be corrected" and called for increased government spending on health and education and a reform of Guatemala's regressive tax code. This accord also advocated for a national land registry and land market, although it stopped short of calling for a redistributive agrarian reform.

Taken together, Guatemala's peace agreements are a broad condemnation of the country's structural inequities, and they offer the promise—if not the reality—of far-reaching change on issues such as civilian-military relations, justice reform, ethnic relations, women's rights, and rural development. The Guatemalan peace process created an opening for civil-society groups to organize and make demands on the state. Multiple commissions were formed before and after the accords, bringing together government representatives, nongovernmental organizations, private-sector leaders, and social movements to discuss national themes. Although these consensus-building exercises become frustrating without substantive progress, they would not even have been possible in Guatemala a generation ago.

Even before the final accord was signed, the peace process helped foster a climate of greater political freedom in Guatemala. The refugees came back from Mexico, exiles returned, and a new category of "victims" movements began the work of uncovering the violent past. Communities demanded exhumations of massacre sites and set up memorials of different types. Artistic production bloomed. Political violence waned for a short time, until the 1998 murder of Catholic Bishop Juan Gerardi reminded Guatemalans that the structures of repression were still intact.

The peace accords held out the promise of a more inclusive democracy in Guatemala. Yet progressive forces have remained fractured and unable to consolidate an effective political alternative. And even though it might be possible now for reformers to assume governmental authority via elections, the processes of privatization and trade liberalization that were implemented in Guatemala beginning in the 1980s make the state seem less relevant as a transformative agent. Indeed, the winners of the Guatemalan peace appear to be the country's business elites. As the army has withdrawn from overt political rule and the radical mass movement is contained, new elite sectors have stepped in with their own political projects. Two of Guatemala's postwar presidents, Alvaro Arzú (1996–2000) and Oscar Berger (2004–2008), came from upper-class families and represented elite interests. Modernizing elites have a prodemocracy tenor, but their economic grip is as strong as ever.

In its final report in 2004, the United Nations verification mission (MINU-GUA) noted both achievements and barriers in Guatemala's postwar transformation.[1] Concrete advances were made in the political realm: the cease-fire held; the rebels disarmed; the size of the army shrank; a new police force was created; and the civil-defense patrols were disbanded. A small but vocal human-rights community actively presses for accountability and justice, and there have been important steps forward in the struggle against impunity, with several landmark trials against military officers in recent years.

Yet Guatemala has largely failed to live up to the promise of the peace accords with respect to deeper structural reforms and consolidation of the rule of law. The root causes of the armed conflict are largely unchanged, including extreme poverty, highly inequitable land distribution, and government abandonment. Guatemala remains one of the most unequal countries in the world. More than half of Guatemalans live in chronic poverty, and one-fifth live in extreme poverty. Economic elites refuse to pay even minimally higher taxes to finance an expansion of government services to the poor. Modest changes in land tenure have occurred in recent years, as large landholders sold off unprofitable plantations, but the skewed agrarian structure is intact, and land conflicts still often turn violent.

The legacy of the war is still present in the chilling influence of the so-called "hidden powers": clandestine networks of active and retired military officers now reconstituted as organized-crime rings. Guatemala has been turned into a major drug corridor between North and South America, with a corresponding corrosion of public safety and threats to democratic governance. In 2006, the Guatemalan government signed an agreement with the United Nations to create a new International Commission Against Impunity to identify clandestine security groups and organized-crime networks and help dismantle and prosecute them. This is a potentially important step toward combating the ongoing violence and systemic impunity that has crippled the Guatemalan judicial and political system.

No one predicts that Guatemala will return to armed struggle. But the demands that led to the armed struggle—especially for fair wages, land rights, and respect for human life—have not been met. The atrocities of the past have now been documented amply, but as MINUGUA's report noted, Guatemala has had "truth without justice," and a deeper national healing is still an unrealized aspiration.

Note

1. United Nations Mission for Guatemala (MINUGUA). *Ninth and Final Report on Fulfillment of the Peace Accords in Guatemala*. Guatemala City: MINUGUA, 2004.

Right to Return

María García Hernández and Mama Maquín

Between 1981 and 1983, an estimated 150,000 Guatemalan villagers fled across the border into southern Mexico to escape army massacres. More than forty thousand refugees settled into camps run by the United Nations (see part 6 of this volume). Although the refugees yearned for their homeland, most were reluctant to return to Guatemala during the 1980s out of fear or because the army had given away their land parcels to other land-starved families. The refugees began to make their voices heard, however, and in 1992 the Guatemalan government signed an agreement with refugee organizations in the camps in Mexico (known as the "Permanent Commissions of Guatemalan Refugees"). The agreement affirmed the refugees' right to return to Guatemala and offered government assistance in acquiring land to resettle. Thousands of refugees returned collectively to Guatemala over the next few years, even though the war was still going on. The refugees' demands for rural demilitarization and the right to return to their lands helped pave the way for broader peace negotiations between the Guatemalan government and the URNG after 1994.[1]

Refugee leader María García Hernández is a founder of Mama Maquín, an organization of Guatemalan refugee women named after an elderly rural activist killed in the 1978 Panzós massacre (see "Blood in Our Throats" in part 5). In this selection, she discusses how women refugees struggled for equal rights within the camps and during the arduous return to Guatemala.

As refugees, we never forgot the pain that we suffered in the war. . . . We organized ourselves, electing representatives to run the refugee camps, all of whom were men. As time went on, we were able to continue to shape our organization, in regard to health and education. Women began to organize in small groups with vegetable gardening, handicraft and bread-making projects. . . .

In 1987, we began the struggle to return to our country by electing our representatives, the Permanent Commissions of Guatemalan Refugees, to negotiate with the government the conditions of security and dignity under which we would return as organized collective groups. This process of negotiation took five years and resulted in the signing of a seven-point accord on October 8, 1992. Among the points was the right to own land to live on and work, via a revolving credit scheme for land purchase [wherein the cost of the land is to be repaid by the community to its own internal organization or association for future projects, not to the government].

The return to Guatemala has been difficult for those who decided to return home: the accords are not complied with as we would have wished, receiving credits for the purchase of land is a very slow process, and often the land for sale has many legal problems. Many studies have to be carried out to determine if the price set by the owner is appropriate, and if it is not, then the negotiation is over and the groups have to start from the very beginning again by looking for other lands.

In 1990, we created our own organization of Guatemalan refugee women, called Mama Maquín, to create awareness of the discrimination and marginalization that women face, a situation that is even worse in our case as indigenous women and poor *campesinas*. In the return process and reinsertion phase, an especially important goal is to promote and strengthen our participation in decision-making within our family and our community.

After the October 8, 1992 Accords were signed, we held various meetings and workshops with the leaders and members of Mama Maquín in order to analyze the content of the accords, and we realized that women who are married or in common-law unions were not taken into account in terms of the right to land. Only men, widows, and single mothers were, the latter two groups being considered as vulnerable groups and as female heads-of-households respectively. That is when we decided to fight for the right to be co-owners of the land for our own security and that of our daughters and sons, so that the woman will not be left out in the street if the man sells the land or abandons his partner. This also means recognizing the value of the work that we carry out in the house and the fields.

To have co-ownership of the land, we have to sign the legal document used to solicit the credit for land purchase. We also have to participate in the whole process, which means making visits to look for possible lands for settlement and participating in the negotiation of the land purchase and the return movements. It also means becoming members of the co-operatives that are being formed in our communities because lands are being transferred into the name of the co-operative, and by definition they belong to its members. We have the right to be members, with voice, voting rights and the right to elect people and be elected to leadership positions in the co-operative and community structures. . . .

The Guatemalan refugee and returnee women are clear about the fact

Children participate in the annual village fair at Primavera del Ixcán in El Quiché. Primavera del Ixcán is a community of internally displaced refugees established in 1996. Photo by James Rodríguez, 2007. Used by permission of the photographer.

that land is the most important family possession that we can have. Land is an integral space for the development of *campesino* and indigenous women and men, a space where we can live and work, defend our rights and pass on our culture, customs and languages to our daughters and sons.

The task we have set ourselves is not easy because even with our consciousness and determination there are situations that limit or complicate our participation, among them the fact that we are responsible for childcare, for our families, for housework; we lack experience in traveling outside our communities and taking part in negotiations. Many of us cannot read or write. But in spite of all this, bit by bit, we have been opening up new opportunities for participation in order to achieve a society where women and men truly live harmoniously between themselves and with nature—as held in our worldview that has been passed down to us from our Maya ancestors. . . .

Achievements

We have formed our own organization as a basis for gaining respect for our rights. . . . We have an awareness of our rights to be co-owners of the land and thus participate on equal terms with men in decision-making and in problem solving. We are aware that our domestic work, our reproductive role and our productive work—all of which are all fundamental to achieving community development and our own development—are to be valued.

Obstacles

The responsibility for childcare and domestic work, which is neither valued nor recognized, is still a major obstacle to our participation in improving our situation. Much work remains to be done in order to sensitize and train men and institutions to value and assist in these tasks. There is a lack of legal assistance with a gender focus and a lack of funding for follow-up organizational work, so that women can successfully negotiate their inclusion in the co-operative and defend their joint land ownership.

Leaders with experience gained as refugees are now dispersed throughout the various returnee communities and are also concerned with their own survival, with less energy and time for the organization. Members of Mama Maquín in general, once back in Guatemala, have faced many difficulties in their organized work given the post-conflict economic, political, social and cultural situation of the country, and often have to give priority to their own survival. . . .

In conclusion, we call upon all women of the world to fight together for a world with equality and justice. As refugee women we have experienced, firsthand, the horrors of war and exile. We face, with our families, the challenges of coping with the losses and sufferings of war and exile. But we encourage everyone not to be overcome by anguish and other setbacks. All women and men can help search for ways great and small to lead us to a resolution of our most urgent needs and the wish of all humanity to have a world of justice and peace. Of the international organizations, governments and institutions and the world at large, we ask that they not abandon us in our goals that would benefit all women. We value the participation of these institutions and governments in achieving the peace accords recently signed in Guatemala. We ask that they continue to give their support in the follow-up and verification of these accords so as to truly construct peace from within the family, the community and the society as a whole. For the equality and dignity of women, the return to our country is our right; the participation of women is an absolute necessity in the construction of peace.

Note

1. The collective refugee returns ended in 1999. By that time, twenty-two thousand Guatemalan refugees had opted to stay in Mexico and pursue legal integration there; many of these were young people who had grown up in Mexico. See Paula Worby, "Refugee Return and Reintegration in Guatemala: Lessons Learned by UNCHR, 1987–1999" (Geneva, Switzerland: UNCHR, 2000).

What Is Reconciliation?

Helen Mack

Helen Mack is one of Guatemala's most prominent human-rights activists. In 1990, an army death squad assassinated her sister, the Guatemalan anthropologist Myrna Mack. For more than a decade, Helen Mack confronted Guatemala's political and military establishment in an effort to prosecute her sister's murder. In 1992, she won Sweden's Right Livelihood Award, known as the "Alternative Nobel Peace Prize," and she created the Myrna Mack Foundation in her sister's memory. The Myrna Mack Foundation is now a leading voice in Guatemala on issues of human rights, justice, and accountability. In this essay, Helen Mack argues that Guatemala's peace accords in and of themselves are not enough to bring about long-term societal reconciliation. Indeed, there is no broad consensus as to what reconciliation might mean.

The peace accords in Guatemala do not treat the topic of reconciliation specifically. In general terms, the accords mention national unity, harmony, and solidarity, but they don't delve deeply into these concepts. A national reconciliation law was part of the accord for guerrilla disarmament, but this law was limited to precluding prosecution for crimes committed during the armed conflict. This omission was clearly deliberate, because the concept of "reconciliation" requires broad social, political, and institutional transformations, something for which Guatemalan society is not prepared, especially those who still hold power. . . .

Reconciliation, then, as a concept does not form part of the consciousness of the ruling bloc. . . . The topic is given a restricted meaning from the perspective of victims; for example, in common use, reconciliation means bringing the military to justice for human-rights violations or giving attention to the memory of the victims or to the mental health of survivors. The burden of "reconciling themselves" therefore falls on the victims.

Other essential components of reconciliation are left out, such as institutional transformation, economic improvement, the reconstruction of the social fabric after so many years of war, the restoration of trust and personal relations, the recovery of dignity for survivors, and the search for social justice.

In Guatemala's postwar context, some individuals and institutions have tried to put the topic of reconciliation on the national agenda, but these efforts have stalled for lack of concrete, integrated proposals. On the opposing side, various governments, high-level judicial authorities, political leaders, the business class, and other power brokers have put forward ideas such as "a fresh start," "look toward the future, not back at the past," and "don't seek revenge" as being synonymous with reconciliation.

Conveniently for the active and retired members of the military, a stigma has been attached to the quest for justice, truth, and moral reparation. Social leaders, civil-society organizations, and victims have not been able to forge a broad consensus in support of a true reconciliation process. . . . This process should focus on what we mean by reconciliation and what mechanisms or tools might help achieve it. We have to go back to square one to correct the erroneous and stigmatizing concepts, and we have to consider new commitments that weren't part of the peace negotiations.

This process could begin with the consensuses that already exist within the peace accords, combined with the doubts that numerous social organizations have expressed. Crucially, however, this effort should not be the sole responsibility of social sectors; the government must also assume its responsibility by guaranteeing compliance and encouraging ongoing reconciliation processes.

Given the specific history and effects of the armed conflict, reconciliation should not be thought of as a linear process. . . . Reconciliation is painful, because on an individual level people confront their fears, emptiness, mistrust, and insecurities. On a collective level, it's a process that demands a high degree of political will and responsibility because it implies concrete, measurable, deep changes to combat social injustice, guarantee that the painful past will not be repeated, repair damages, and, above all, establish the truth about what happened.

On a collective level, the changes involve a real shift in the relationship between the state and society, a redistribution of power, and a transformation in the historically adverse conditions that maintain the population in a permanent state of confrontation: in short, the peace commitments. On a personal level, it means the work of each person to tap into their internal strength to heal the effects of suffering and rupture produced by Guatemala's cruel conflict. . . .

Guatemala is a clear example of how structural issues can impede a society's advancement toward reconciliation, because the country has yet to

"Memory, truth, justice." Photo by James Rodríguez.
Used by permission of the photographer.

overcome its centuries-old legacy of racism, sexism, poverty and destitution, malnutrition, illiteracy, unemployment and semifeudal employment, citizen insecurity, ideological confrontation and social conflict, political violence, impunity and arbitrary persecution, and much more. These types of contradictions have persisted since the colonial era.

Another problem is the weakness of the political system, which continues to protect elite interests, as well as the dysfunctional mechanisms for mediation and representation of citizen interests. There is, therefore, a functional distancing between the governing elites and the people they govern, a situation that is sharpened by the lack of real spaces for participation and by the recurrent practices of political exclusion. . . .

Yet, even given all these obstacles, there are some reasons to be hopeful for the possibility of a reconciliation process in Guatemala. There is more opening now to begin to talk about problems and topics that until recently were considered taboo, which demonstrates that the population is less and less afraid to speak out. Also, civil-society organizations are stronger and better able to organize and actively participate in the search for solutions to move the country forward in new ways.

Translated by Elizabeth Oglesby

Promised the Earth

Gustavo Palma Murga

Fights over land—among rural dwellers, between communities, but especially be-
tween large landowners and smallholders—have long characterized Guatemalan
history. By the 1970s, two-thirds of Guatemala's farmland was controlled by just 2
percent of the largest landholdings. Rural land demands had reached a crisis point,
and a violent backlash by the government and large landowners set much of the
countryside aflame. In the early 1990s, with the war winding down, agrarian activ-
ists hoped that peace negotiations between the military and the guerrillas would
resolve Guatemala's "land problem." Yet, as Guatemalan historian Gustavo Palma
Murga points out, the 1996 peace accords failed to include provisions for redistrib-
uting land, essentially locking the country's dramatically skewed land-tenure sys-
tem into place.

December 19, 2006; Barrio La Revolución, El Estor, Izabal. Maya Q'eqchi' com-
munity members build homes on land whose ownership is disputed by the
Guatemala Nickel Company, a subsidiary of Canadian mining company Skye
Resources. Photo by James Rodríguez. Used by permission of the photographer.

(top) January 8, 2007; Barrio La Unión, El Estor, Izabal. Jesusa Ixtecoc Juarez pleads for her home as it is taken apart during the violent evictions of Maya Q'eqchi' communities by Skye Resources: "I am alone. If I die tonight, it will be because they took my home made from sticks, which cost me 25 *quetzales* [roughly US$3]." Photo by James Rodríguez. Used by permission of the photographer.

(bottom) January 9, 2007; Barrio La Revolución, El Estor, Izabal. The next day, employees of the Guatemala Nickel Company burn the huts of Maya Q'eqchi' community members. Photo by James Rodríguez. Used by permission of the photographer.

The 1996 Agreement on Socio-Economic Issues and the Agrarian Situation does not contain a strategic, long-term vision of rural development. The accord's overly technical, market-driven proposals do not begin to address economic injustice and inefficiency nor the deep historical grievances that are the root causes of past and ongoing rural conflict.

During talks over the socio-economic accord, various organizations within Guatemala presented their own proposals to peace negotiators. Among the more radical of these was submitted by the National Coordination of Campesino Organizations (CNOC). CNOC's central proposals were land tenure reform and greater rights for *campesinos* in natural resource management. The most radical element was the clause calling for a redefinition of land ownership and use based on the idea of the "social function" of property. This directly challenged definitions of private property upheld by every Guatemalan government since 1954 and enshrined in the 1985 constitution. The CNOC proposal contained several sets of demands:

> 1. *campesino rights*, including demilitarization of rural areas, the speeding-up of the legal paperwork to register *campesino* organizations, and a fair wage;
> 2. *democratization of land use*, including recovery of communal and other lands illegally taken from *campesinos* during the previous 40 years, state expropriation of idle lands, the creation of a high-level commission to verify the peace accords on agrarian matters, and distribution of state lands to *campesinos* in the form of collective titles;
> 3. *technical and financial support*, based on clearly defined policies respectful of Maya worldviews and responsive to the collective interests of *campesinos* with regard to production, distribution, and commercialization.

The CNOC proposals were debated within the Civil Society Assembly (ASC) [a consortium of social organizations formed to discuss the peace accords], but they were significantly diluted in the final ASC submission to the peace talks. The ASC proposals made tacit concessions to the neoliberal preoccupations of the private sector, recognizing the "historical grievances" of Guatemala's land problem, while recommending a more "rational and efficient use of land" . . . to reflect the "comparative advantage" of Guatemala in the new global economy.

In December 1994, the private sector umbrella organization, the Coordinating Committee of Agricultural, Commercial, Industrial and Financial Associations (CACIF), which had boycotted the Assembly, produced its own set of recommendations. In contrast to the CNOC and ASC proposals, CACIF argued against the idea of social property. CACIF decried past attempts at redistributive land reform and called for the privatization of the few remaining communal or municipal lands, on the grounds of "technical efficiency."

After more than a year of acrimonious debate, the Agreement on Socio-Economic Aspects and the Agrarian Situation was finally signed on May 6, 1996. The accord clearly recognizes the complexity of the land problem in Guatemala. It acknowledges that concentration of land ownership is not a technical necessity but the result of political and historical processes. While arguing that private investment has a fundamental role to play in securing an "efficient and equitable agricultural sector," the accord proposes that the government play a central role in coordinating the efforts of a wide range of institutions.

The accord commits the government to a "global strategy" with ten core objectives:

1. social participation;
2. improving access to land ownership;
3. a more equitable distribution of credit, technology, training and information;
4. organization of the rural population;
5. legal reforms;
6. prompt settlement of land conflicts;
7. the creation of a land registry to clarify land ownership;
8. measures to ensure labor protection;
9. measures to ensure environmental protection;
10. tax reform.

Within this broad strategy, key government commitments included:

1. Strengthening local and national agricultural development councils to enhance the decision-making role of rural organizations, such as cooperatives, small farmers' associations, family businesses and trade unions.

2. The creation of a new, properly financed National Trust Fund for Lands to promote access of tenant farmers to land ownership. Land allocated by this fund would be state-owned (including state-owned farms and illegally settled public land) . . . or land purchased by the government on the open market. . . .

3. Legal reform to simplify procedures for registering land ownership and to protect and regulate community-owned land.

4. A land registry developed through a new land survey.

5. A land tax on underused and undeveloped lands.

The Socio-Economic Accord partially reflects the various positions of the interested parties. Yet [it emphasizes] reallocating resources within a marginally reformed institutional context based on private ownership and the market. There are no provisions for structural changes in land tenure or for expropriating unused or underutilized lands, while the notion of social property is entirely absent. In terms of underlying philosophy, therefore, the private sector's vision predominates. Most analysts explain this by pointing to the weakness of the insurgent Guatemalan National Revolutionary Unity (URNG) and the powerful influence of landowners on government negotiators. It is also widely believed that the guerrilla leadership opted to make strategic concessions on the land issue in order to conclude the peace process as quickly as possible and facilitate their own future participation as a legal political party.

The reaction of the Guatemalan business sector to the accord was generally positive. CACIF president Humberto Preti hailed it as an important step toward ensuring agricultural productivity while providing "legal certainty" for landowners. The National Farmers' and Ranchers' Council (CONAGRO) saw the agreement as a basis for national development within the framework of economic globalization. Government negotiator Gustavo Porras Castejón argued optimistically that the land registry and taxes on idle land would solve land conflicts, while Rodrigo Asturias (Commander "Gaspar Ilom" of the URNG) hailed the accord as the first significant agreement on land reform for many years. . . .

In marked contrast to these positive interpretations, many popular organizations, along with the URNG rank and file, were less enthusiastic. CNOC, the Committee for Campesino Unity (CUC) and the National Indigenous and Campesino Coordination (CONIC) called the accord "insufficient" for resolving land conflicts. CONIC was the harshest in its criticism, stating that "these are minimum accords that do not satisfy Maya and *campesino* demands, because our positions were not taken into consideration and because [the accord was signed] behind our back."

In a personal interview in August 1997, CONIC leader Juan Tiney argued that the retention of Article 39 of the Guatemalan Constitution, which enshrines the principle of private landed property as an inherent human right and gives extensive state guarantees for landowners to use and enjoy their property, consolidates the present unequal system of land ownership. He also questioned the capacity of the land fund and land tax to provide economic opportunities for *campesinos*, emphasizing the lack of state-owned or fallow lands available for redistribution, and the difficulties inherent in defining what is taxable idle land, especially given landowners' tremendous lobbying power. With regard to the land registry, Tiney criticized the lack of clarity over the definition of property rights. It appears that lands illegally seized from poor *campesinos* throughout history can now be registered as legal holdings. There is no questioning of how a title came to be held, although many were undoubtedly obtained through bribery, fraud and coercion. Neither is there any mention of what is to be done in cases where the legitimacy of land titles is contested, and overlapping claims exist. In some cases, community claims to land stretch back a century, but titles recently granted tend to legitimize the claims of new owners.

Negative reactions also came from sectors of the civic opposition not specifically involved in land issues. For Rigoberto Quemé, indigenous mayor of the city of Quetzaltenango, the accord proposes non-distributive land reform, putting *campesinos* at the mercy of market forces and the pressures of the credit and banking system, while downplaying the importance of social issues. According to the Coordination of Organizations of Maya People of Guatemala (COPMAGUA), the accord breathes fresh life into structures inherited from the colonial period, and fails to challenge the overriding interests of large landowners. Writing for the Latin American Faculty of Social Science (FLACSO), Leopoldo Sandoval Villeda highlighted how the new National Trust Fund for Lands is likely to make a significant impact in only two areas: the recovery of some illegally occupied public lands in the northern department of Petén and in the Northern Transversal Strip (an area which was illegally settled by large landowners and military officers during the 1970s) and the commercial purchase of lands with limited official finances. As such, it represents an unsatisfactory, piecemeal and minimalist approach to land reform.

The institutions set up for implementation of the Socio-Economic Accord are supposed to mediate between landowners, the government and *campesinos*. Remarkably few verification mechanisms were specified, however, and so far, the interests of the powerful landowning sector have prevailed within these institutions. In June 1997, the government announced that it lacked the resources to carry out the land registry promised in the accord, and that it intended to contract the service to private firms. CONIC and other organizations opposed this idea, convinced that the land registry is primarily a state responsibility and that private firms would favor large landowners.

To understand the prospects of the Socio-Economic Accord for addressing Guatemala's land problem, it is essential to examine the political and economic agendas that have influenced its design and implementation. Broadly speaking, two agendas have dominated Guatemalan politics in recent years. The first of these, the so-called "peace agenda," was concerned with bringing about a negotiated solution to the armed conflict and satisfying the international community. This agenda was reflected in the text of the accords, which struck a fine balance between reformist rhetoric and a pragmatic consolidation of established interests. The second agenda was the overriding concern of the government to "do the right thing" in the face of pressure from the international financial institutions, particularly the International Monetary Fund. Now clearly paramount in government thinking, this agenda comprises two main priorities: "managing" macro-economic imbalances and "modernizing" the state via privatization. Both these agendas overlook the multifaceted problems and aspirations of the majority of rural Guatemalans. They do not alter the historic favoring of agro-exports over domestic production, nor do they address the historical grievances that underpinned the war, such as centuries of displacement and socio-economic exclusion.

The Socio-Economic Accord recognizes previously neglected issues such as access to credit and technology and land titling, but it does not articulate a broad, national and long-term vision of development, and it avoids any direct challenge to the inequitable status quo. Its appeals to a "transparent land market" may bring about a partial alleviation of rural poverty, but more substantial dimensions of the land problem have been postponed for future generations. As a consequence, low-level conflict is likely to continue, as expressed in *campesino* land invasions, strikes by rural workers and clashes between smallholders and armed agents of wealthy landowners. In all probability, simmering agrarian unrest will not lead to a full-scale rekindling of the war, yet it may well preclude a substantive and stable peace in the Guatemalan countryside.

Disagreement

Ana María Rodas

Ana María Rodas, a Guatemalan poet and journalist, was the winner of the 2000 Guatemalan National Prize in Literature. In this poem, she expresses the frustration felt by many people in Guatemala because the peace agreements cannot erase the legacy of mass killing during Guatemala's long civil war.

Don't talk to me about anything.
Tonight I'm not in the mood for words
or speeches
about peace accords anywhere.
What peace did they broker in my name?
Who gave them permission to do it?
No one on this interminable list
I hold in my hands
said
go ahead, sign that deal.
They didn't ask my permission when the powers that be
decided that a war
that was growing cold
would be better played out in another's patio.
They let loose their poison,
sat and counted profits
competing to carve up the Moon.
While
here, as if nothing, the dead piled up
and the disappeared
and exiles and hatreds.
Forty years the game went on.
It didn't go badly for me; I'm still alive.
But this list, this list that makes me weep when I read it,
is the debt for that deal.

Don't come to me to stamp it paid.
Our feelings won't be written off
nor our grief nor the spilled blood
nor the memory of the dead.

Translated by Elizabeth Oglesby

Desacuerdo

No me hablen de nada.
Esta noche no estoy para palabras
Ni discursos
Sobre los acuerdos de paz en ningún lado.
Qué paz acordaron en mi nombre?
Quién les dio permiso para hacerlo?
Ninguno de esta lista interminable
Que llevo entre mis manos
Dijo
Adelante, firmen ese convenio.
A mí no me pidieron opinion cuando los grandes
Decidieron que una Guerra
si se enfriaba
podia jgarse major en patio ajeno.
Saltaron su veneno
se sentaron a contra ganancias
a competir por esculpir la Luna.
Mientras tanto
aquí, como si nada, se acumularon muertos
y desaparecidos
y exiliados y odios.
Cuarenta años duró el juego.
A mí no me fue mal, aún estoy viva.
Pero esta lista, esta lista que me hace llorar cuando la leo
es la factura final de aquel convenio.
No me vengan con sellos a estampar un cancelado.
Aquí no se cancelan los afectos
ni los llantos, ni la sange derramada
ni la memoria de los muertos.

The Atrocity Files

Kate Doyle

In the late 1990s, when both the Catholic Church and the United Nations were carrying out their respective investigations into Guatemala's history of political terror, Guatemalan security forces repeatedly insisted that they had destroyed all bureaucratic records concerning the war, thus greatly limiting the scope of the inquiries. Then, on July 5, 2005, two officials from the Guatemalan office of the Human Rights Prosecutor (Procuraduría de Derechos Humanos—PDH), investigating a complaint about improperly stored explosives in a police compound in a working-class neighborhood in the capital, stumbled upon what is estimated to be seventy-five million pages of documents pertaining to the operations of Guatemala's National Police. A major internationally funded program began to catalogue the documents, most of which were in disarray and in an advanced stage of decomposition. It is believed that the results of this archival project will yield insight not only into urban political repression during the civil war, but also into repressive police activities going back to the late nineteenth century, when the National Police was founded as part of the consolidation of the liberal coffee state. The description below was written by Kate Doyle, an analyst who works for the National Security Archive, a nongovernmental research institute in Washington, DC. Her efforts to push the United States to declassify information related to its activities in Guatemala has been critical in supporting a number of human-rights projects, including the United Nations Comisión para el Esclaracimiento Histórico and the Spanish government's prosecution of Guatemalan military officers on charges of genocide.

I arrived in Guatemala three weeks after the archive was discovered. Traffic being what it is in Guatemala City, it was midmorning by the time we pulled up to the gates of the police base. The van from the prosecutor's office had inched its way across town from the city's historic center to the teeming residential zone through outdoor markets, past herds of live goats and around diesel-belching buses to make a journey of three kilometers in about forty minutes. Now we idled before the walls of a vast local outpost of the *Policía Nacional Civil,* until a guard waved us through with an indifferent flap of his hand.

Carla [Villagrán, a senior staff member in the prosecutor's office] weaved expertly around the rusted shells of abandoned vehicles stacked two stories high with one hand on the wheel, holding her cell phone against her ear with the other. Our car heaved over the broken ground until we reached the paved entrance to a cluster of low buildings at the edge of the compound. As we unsnapped seat belts and gathered our bags we could hear the agitated barking of police dogs trapped in their cages nearby. We opened the doors and tumbled out into a cool, gray morning, staring up at the narrow windows facing the courtyard. We could see the paper already through the cracked glass. Carla grinned as she handed me a pair of rubber gloves. "Are you ready?"

I entered a maze of pitch black rabbit holes, corridors that led nowhere, dripping ceilings, broken lights hanging by frayed wires and ominous stains underfoot. Women employees of the police who worked as records administrators greeted us in a small antechamber and then led us into the first room. On every available centimeter of the cement floor there were towers of mildewed paper and file folders, tied in twine and entombed in grit. The paper was decomposing before our eyes—wet paper and rotting paper, charred paper, paper brown with mold, paper becoming compost with small seedlings growing through it. We stumbled from one damp cavern to the next, skirting rusted file cabinets and the sharp edges of old license plates littering the floors. The stench of decay was strong; all around us were insect carcasses and bat droppings, feathers, bird shit, and the nibbling of rats. We breathed the dead air through our flimsy paper masks.

There were five buildings in all. Each building harbored its peculiar secrets. In one, metal file cabinets lined the walls with improvised labels scrawled in black marker across the drawers: "assassinations," "homicides," "kidnappings." In another, we stepped gingerly over haphazard trash heaps, which on closer inspection included thousands of black-and-white ID photos. The staff was sweeping them into piles and transferring them into clear plastic bags. A multitude of tiny faces stared at the invisible camera.

I chose a record off the floor at random. It was a 1979 report on three unidentified cadavers found in the gullies at the edge of Guatemala City. Finding bodies and failing to identify them was evidently a central preoccupation for the National Police; there were scores of photographed corpses, men and women memorialized as battered faces black with blood or swarming with maggots, each labeled with the same name: "*desconocido*," unknown. There was a picture of an amputated left hand, "owner unknown," a bloated corpse stuffed in the trunk of a car. Then there were the snapshots of a few soon-to-be-unknown bodies, such as the young man seated with his back to a rough concrete wall in button-down shirt and jeans, looking at the photographer hopelessly through dark eyes, his hands tied behind his back with a piece of rope.

As we moved from room to room, the police ladies accompanied us, obligingly yanking open drawers when requested or slipping pages out of bound folders to show us. They balked only once, when we came upon a pile of records from the old Detective Corps, a greatly feared special operations squad that existed in the 1970s and early 1980s, notorious for its role in the kidnapping, torture and execution of suspected subversives. We asked the woman in charge to hand us some file folders but she began shaking her head no and then her finger, shaking it at us, no, no, "*No se puede, no se puede*," that can't be done. It took us a few minutes to understand that we weren't prohibited from looking at them; she, however, still had strict orders, almost ten years after the abolition of the National Police, not to touch.

Carla and I tiptoed up some concrete steps to the second floor of one building. A rooftop terrace looked over the junkyard that inhabited this corner of the base, weeds twisting through what was left of the pavement below. The air was intensely revivifying, though it hung as densely as ever over the cityscape. Back inside, we found a series of tiny windowless spaces, most no wider than a pig pen, with heavy wire netting wedged over the tops to create a kind of cage. There were old, torn mattresses, some with brownish stains dried hard into the fabric, the detritus of an ancient occupancy.

Along one wall was a shelf of books, including selected works of Lenin and a biography of Stalin, seized from their owners for their dangerous content. Internal police employee files were jammed into drawers rusted shut by time, including ID cards for thousands of "*orejas*"—"ears," the civilians who worked for the police as informants, ratting out their neighbors. Years of personnel lists, or "*nóminas*," lay scattered on tabletops, identifying individual police agents and their superiors, where they served and in what capacity. There were hundreds of rolls of undeveloped film, huge outdated computer floppy disks; enormous leather-bound ledgers listed "captured Communists" in the faded spidery ink of long ago.

For human rights investigators the archive was the discovery of a lifetime, the long-abandoned scene of a terrible crime. The effort required to salvage the records and recover the evidence buried in them, however, seemed beyond human power. Even more challenging, how could the countless pages be rendered meaningful to the rest of society? Would their opening lead to another symbolic acknowledgment of the brutal past or a transformation of the country's history? . . .

Pile of identification cards waiting to be processed in the Historic Archive of the National Police in Guatemala. Photo by Daniel Hernández-Salazar. Used by permission of the photographer.

Lupita oversees the team analyzing records of the Second Corps. When I visited she was looking at the files of the unit's Police Hospital, where political prisoners were hidden in a clandestine section called the *cuartito* or the *cuarto especial* (the little room or the special room). The internal records of the hospital list the names and age of detainees held secretly; Lupita was matching them against lists of the disappeared distributed by organizations during the same period. For example, the Association of University Students published a list that included Dr. Carlos Padilla Gálvez, a surgeon attending the needs of the poor, who was kidnapped on August 26, 1982, from his hospital in Sololá by unidentified armed men. But in one of the Police Hospital's internal records Dr. Padilla appears as a prisoner to be transferred to the "special room" on September 12. (Padilla was one of the lucky ones. Two months after his abduction, the government ordered his release from the Second Corps.) . . .

Like many of the older investigators at the archive, Lupita—whose husband was disappeared in 1983—has spotted the names of people she knew as she trolls the police records for the PDH. In one of the registries listing "subversives" seized in anticommunist sweeps in the days after the 1954 coup, she even found her grandfather, "which is so strange, because he always said 'screw the Communists!' " she told me with a smile. Lupita considers her work among the police documents *"un regalo de vida"*: the chance of a lifetime. I heard that phrase a lot from former militants-turned-archivists. They are people whose fates were turned completely upside down by the conflict—men and women, now middle-aged, who gave up every semblance of normal life to join the movement.

Gustavo Meoño, the archive director, was 17 when he left his family in 1966 to join a radical group of American Maryknollers helping peasants settle an uninhabited jungle region in central Guatemala. He threw his lot in with the guerrillas after the missionaries were recalled from the country by their order in 1967. As a result, Gustavo never attended university; he operated underground as an organizer, "talking to labor leaders, to students, to Christians," slipping in and out of Guatemala secretly until he returned for good in the mid-1990s. "I came from a poor family," he tells me, "and it was a shock for them, who worked so hard to get us into school." Gustavo is a tall, mournful-looking man whose heartfelt style inspires many of the younger archive employees—just as he inspired a generation of young Guatemalans to join the movement during the 1970s and 80s. He is the first to admit that the clandestine life robbed him of any hope for a vocation—"I have no training except for what life has taught me"—but sees the archive work as a natural extension of the fight for justice that he says consumed him during the armed conflict. Gustavo's background is by no means unique within the PDH project; most of the senior personnel overseeing the effort to rescue the files come directly out of the *militancia*—former leaders, guerrilla combatants, fund-raisers or organizers, now enjoying the chance of a lifetime to make sense of their struggle through documents that explain, in part, why it was doomed from the start. . . .

The survival of the National Police archive may seem difficult to comprehend. But its destruction would have contradicted the force that drives bureaucracy itself. "I record, therefore I am": the files are the proof of a government's power. They shelter the history of its officers, of their importance, achievements, and investigations. During times of state terror, even the most incriminating documents may not be discarded, because the agents responsible for them believe that their institutions will survive forever. And afterwards, it is often too late. Enduring regimes like Guatemala's produce a massive paper trail, which cannot be disappeared overnight.

But the citizen also needs the files. The archive does more than simply confirm his status as victim; it preserves and restores his history. For contained within the records of repression in countries around the world is evidence not only of brutal human rights abuse, but also of defiance and social protest—a rejection, even during the most intense periods of state violence, of a regime's economic and political project, and a reimagining of what the country might become.

Today, the Guatemalan police archive hums with purpose. The ruined cars that cluttered its entrance have been pushed aside. The little patio in front has been swept and a fence has gone up around the buildings. Inside, more than 200 people labor over the records: some cleaning them, some boxing, others reading or typing into computers bought with the help of the European donors. There are eight state-of-the-art scanners that operate 16 hours a day; more than two million pages have been digitized so far.

"We've made a complete inventory of everything we have now, and we update it every day," Gustavo told me. "I want an archive that is ordered, organized and accessible. That is my dream. I think about it all the time— with the shelves lined up and everything in its place. I want the research to continue indefinitely, where nothing can happen to destroy it or interrupt the work." He pauses. He is lost in his reverie. The years of struggle, the lost youth, the scattered hopes, the dead companions have come to this. "I want to create a museum, a memory center. It's another dream. This place should be cleaned up of all the garbage so we can build a park and plant trees with the names of the disappeared. It will be a forest of memory."

Memory of an Angel

Daniel Hernández-Salazar

Since the 1980s, Guatemalan photographer Daniel Hernández-Salazar has created both documentary and aesthetic works exploring state terrorism and historical memory in Guatemala. His four-panel series, Clarification, *was published on the cover of the report of the Catholic Church's Recovery of Historical Memory Project (*REMHI*), titled* Guatemala: nunca más *(Guatemala: Never Again) and released in April 1998. The final photograph of this series, the shouting angel titled* So That All Shall Know, *became an iconic image in Guatemala, representing the struggle against silence and impunity. Hernández-Salazar's Street Angel project, described by the artist below, began in 1999 as a public art initiative in Guatemala City to commemorate the first anniversary of the assassination of Bishop Juan Gerardi Conedera, coordinator of the* REMHI *project, who was bludgeoned to death with a concrete slab in front of his rectory home in Guatemala City, two days after the report's public presentation.*

As detailed in Francisco Goldman's painstaking investigation, The Art of Political Murder, *responsibility for Gerardi's killing reached into the highest ranks of the military and government. Bishop Gerardi presided over the Catholic diocese in El Quiché during some of the worst years of political repression, prior to the church's decision to evacuate the diocese in 1980. As the peace process moved forward in the mid-1990s, Bishop Gerardi's advocacy on behalf of indigenous communities and human rights led to the launching of the* REMHI *project, which was understood to be a parallel "truth commission," carrying out its work in advance of and supporting the officially recognized* UN-*run Commission of Historical Clarification.*

The idea of hanging photos in the streets has been with me long before I started my project Street Angel; to be exact, ever since a friend gave me a photography book that included photos by Ernest Pignon. Ernest Pignon installed a series of lithographs with the image of the poet Rimbaud around the streets of Charleville, France. A few years later, I saw the work of Cuban artist Félix González-Torres in Mexico, which cemented my interest in expressing myself in public spaces.

My original project was to install a photo of the work *Para que todos lo sepan* [*So that all shall know*] on a wall near the central plaza in Guatemala City.

This work is dedicated to the memory of Bishop Juan Gerardi Conedera, assassinated in this city on April 26, 1998. Bishop Gerardi was bludgeoned to death two days after the publication of the report of the Recovery of Historical Memory project (REMHI), a report that described two hundred thousand cases of human rights violations in Guatemala during thirty-six years of civil war. In February 1999, I decided to combine my desire to remember and denounce the lack of progress on the case, with the idea of "appropriating" public spaces. From there, the urban intervention project Street Angel was born.

The first thing to do was to convince a bunch of people to collaborate with me on the intervention itself, installing the murals, which were copies of the original work. Then, we had to select the places where they would be installed, according to three criteria: a) that the place be symbolic in relation to the crime and the lack of clarification; b) that the site be a place where many passersby would see the mural; and c) that the place have its own particular "magic." This phase took me a couple of weeks until I decided on thirty-five sites.

The next step was to find the fastest and most clandestine way to install the murals at the selected points, in the shortest amount of time and with minimal risk for the participants. The installation would be done at night so that the images would surprise the public on the morning of April 26, the first anniversary of the murder of Bishop Gerardi. The images would not have any accompanying text, since the image itself was associated with the REMHI report, for which Bishop Gerardi was killed. Also, installing the image without text would produce a more questioning, ambiguous, and unsettling effect on the observer.

The installation was done as planned and without much delay on the night of April 25. The next morning, I followed up with a series of photos of the angels. I made an exception this time to work in color (my work is always in black and white) in order to create a distance between the murals,

So That All Shall Know/Para que todos lo sepan. This image of an angel was created to illustrate the cover of the Catholic Church's truth report. The piece combines an image of a naked man with an image of a pair of scapula bones from a victim assassinated during the Guatemalan civil war. The bones had been exhumed from a clandestine grave, and the artist photographed them at the Guatemalan Forensic Anthropology Foundation laboratory. Photo by Daniel Hernández-Salazar. Used by permission of the photographer.

the metaphors, and the reality that remained in color. In this way, a dialogue was created between the two dimensions.

A few days later began what I called the "hunt for the angels" on the part of people or institutions who felt exposed or attacked by the presence of the murals in certain places. As an anecdote, in one case, a stone similar to the one that supposedly was used to kill Bishop Gerardi appeared below the image that was installed in front of the obelisk monument on Próceres de la Independencia Boulevard. In other cases, as the significance of the angels became apparent, they were "eliminated" by "unknown people." I think it's important to mention that some of the images that disappeared were located in the Army Stadium, the Campo de Marte [a military complex], the former [Military] Polytechnic School, and the headquarters of the National Police.

The rest of the murals disappeared over time, especially after the rains started. It was very interesting to watch the life of these images pass quickly, remembering the lives of the many people who were disappeared. In the pieces that came unglued, I saw the pages of reports or lists that were slowly spilling out over time.

Over the years, I have felt the need to continue and expand this installation in order to establish parallelisms between the "Guatemalan holocaust" and other atrocities elsewhere in the world. The atrocities committed against Guatemalan people have been made invisible by powerful interests and remain something difficult to explain to locals and foreigners. For that reason, I decided to continue the Street Angel project but in a wider scenario and with broader scope and meaning. I want to compare what happened in Guatemala with similar tragedies in different geographies, such as Auschwitz in Poland, Hiroshima in Japan, or Tlatelolco in Mexico, as well as other places where civilian populations have paid the toll of armed conflicts. That way, I hope that my work helps call attention to the atrocities committed in Guatemala and puts Guatemala's history on the world map.

Journalist Maurice Echeverría wrote about this intervention: "You realize that art isn't or shouldn't be just a complement to social, political or individual reality, but a symptom, sign, symbol, representation and truth. From now on, *Nunca más* [the title of the REMHI report] will have this quality of an angel that slices through reality, in dark hues with a tint of red. Art redeems us from the crime. Eyes look at us from every corner."

Translated by Elizabeth Oglesby

A Good Place to Commit Murder

Philip Alston, United Nations Special Rapporteur

The end of Guatemala's civil war in 1996 did not mean an end to violence in the country. Violence in contemporary Guatemala encompasses a number of phenomena, including social cleansing, rural lynchings, killing members of the judiciary and human-rights defenders, and the rapidly rising murders of working-class women. In 2006, the United Nations special rapporteur on extrajudicial, summary or arbitrary executions issued a sharply worded report on violence in Guatemala, urging the government and society of Guatemala to "take control of its future." There are five thousand or more killings a year in Guatemala, the report noted, yet Guatemala has a single-digit conviction rate for murder. The weakness of the judicial system is due to a "distinct lack of political will," the report concludes. Guatemala faces a choice: implement a working criminal justice system or "fall back on the brutal tactics of the past."

Guatemala has a single-digit conviction rate for murder. The implication is obvious and disturbing: Guatemala is a good place to commit a murder, because you will almost certainly get away with it. . . .

If Guatemala is to stop being a good place to commit murder, its criminal justice system institutions must be reformed so that more crimes are effectively investigated, more suspects are successfully apprehended, and more cases effectively prosecuted. This will require major budget increases, the implementation of long overdue reforms, a relentless campaign against corruption, and serious inter-institutional cooperation. More simply, it will require a society-wide focus on the bottom line: The state must meet its obligation to apprehend and convict criminals. . . .

One approach to crime control that meets considerable support is that of the *mano dura*: cracking down on undesirable elements with an iron fist. In its more respectable forms, *mano dura* policy prioritizes harsh punishment and heavily militarized sweeps over prevention, prosecution, and rehabilitation. In its more extreme forms—what one interlocutor termed "super *mano dura*"—it prioritizes force over legal process. There is a sense that a swift and brutal response to crime is more likely to be effective than the inherently more lengthy process of investigation, arrest, prosecution, trial, and punishment. Indeed, given the failings of the criminal justice system, turning to on-the-spot executions of suspected criminals appears to some as the only available option.

However, not only does the summary execution of criminal suspects and other "undesirables" violate international law, but Guatemala's own recent history demonstrates the concrete danger of this approach to crime control. To the outside observer, the rhetoric of *mano dura* bears an uncanny resemblance to that of the "national security" doctrine that was implemented in many Latin American states in the 1970s and early 1980s and brought unqualified disaster. In concrete terms, moreover, the methods are difficult to distinguish from the tactics of counterinsurgency. The "selective killing" that swept Guatemala throughout the 1980s and early 1990s is notably similar to the "social cleansing" plaguing Guatemala today. Similarly, the lynchings taking place throughout the country today are strongly reminiscent of the counterinsurgency practices of the PACS [army-organized civil defense patrols] during the armed confrontation. To the outside observer, it is difficult to understand why the continuing use of these practices is not a matter of universal concern. Unfortunately, however, it appears that even for many who suffered greatly during the armed confrontation, the methods of counterinsurgency remain the most obvious means of maintaining "order." It would be prudent for all Guatemalans to carefully consider whether they want Guatemala to move fully beyond its legacy of armed confrontation or for it to, instead, remain in a permanent state of low-intensity lawless violence.

The other approach to crime control that Guatemala might choose is that pursued by other countries in the region to good effect and reflected in the peace accords and international human rights law: Guatemala can develop a working criminal justice system aimed at ensuring the rule of law. Almost all of the formal rhetoric of the political parties endorses this approach. The tragic reality, however, is that almost every component of the current system is radically under-funded, dysfunctional, or both. Congress bears an enormous responsibility for this state of affairs, but those in government, civil society, and the private sector could also do far more.

Many in government are genuinely committed to a system of criminal justice based on prevention, prosecution, and rehabilitation. Partly due to Congress's failure to provide adequate resources and to enact necessary legislation, this commitment does not always bear fruit. In the domain in which government officials would appear to have the most potential to create change—the reform of institutional structures, policies, and working methods—their efforts often appear tangential to the root problems. There are many institutions, roundtables, and commissions developing plans, policies, studies, and frameworks, but too often these remain just words. Many of the concrete steps taken, such as establishing specialized units to deal with particular high-profile problems, are too often small projects that do more to assuage criticism than create results. In government and in civil society there is a worrying tendency to avoid confronting vested interests that would impede the reform of existing institutions by conjuring up new institutions that are not (yet) occupied by vested interests. Those who reject the counterproductive brutality of the *mano dura* and believe in the rule of law must think more strategically and build the coalitions necessary to make that vision a reality.

There is, however, little political will to end impunity and implement a working justice system capable of ensuring the rule of law. There is diffidence among the elite and in Congress regarding the commitments made in the peace accords related to security and the criminal justice system. For the wealthy, effective policing and criminal justice is a low priority in part due to their reliance on private security guards. (There are roughly 100,000 private security guards in Guatemala, more than five times the number of police.) The lack of political will to establish a functioning criminal justice system in part reflects a sense that the state has very limited responsibilities to society, and that it is wholly appropriate for even security and justice to be private rather than public goods. There is a sense that the state has fulfilled its responsibilities so long as it protects the borders and refrains from killing innocent people. This understanding of state responsibility is incompatible with the content of that concept under international law.

The Congress has demonstrated little political will to establish a functioning criminal justice system, often allowing key legislation to linger for years. In addition, the inadequacy of the resources allocated to the institutions constituting the criminal justice system is a justified complaint of nearly every interlocutor in and out of government. This complaint is widely articulated by comparing the resources available in Guatemala to those available in other countries, especially El Salvador, a neighboring country that also emerged from a devastating civil war in the recent past. Guatemala has, even after accounting for the difference in population, far fewer police officers, criminal investigators, prosecutors and judges than El Salvador. When government officials complain about a lack of resources, it serves in part as a convenient excuse: Yes, people get away with murder, but you cannot expect more when I have so few employees, such poor

In memoriam by Jessica Lagunas, 2007. The 572 bullet shells in the jewelry box represent the number of women murdered in Guatemala during 2006. © Jessica Lagunas. Photo by Roni Mocán. Courtesy of the artist and Rollo Contemporary Art. Used with permission.

equipment, etc. As an excuse, it is indeed somewhat self-serving: one would imagine that Guatemala could do better than a single-digit conviction rate for murder without spending an additional dollar. Nevertheless, the resources provided to the national police, the Public Ministry, and the courts are woefully inadequate and place a harsh upper limit on how effective the criminal justice system will be.

It is important to emphasize that, while limited resources may provide some excuse for particular government agencies, it provides no excuse at all for the state as a whole. Guatemala is not an exceptionally poor country, and it could readily afford a criminal justice system on par with that provided in other Central American countries. While Guatemala's per capita gross domestic product is significantly less than those of Belize, Costa Rica, and Panama, it is roughly equal to that of El Salvador, twice that of Honduras, and nearly three times that of Nicaragua.

The reason the executive branch of the Guatemalan state has so little money to spend on the criminal justice system is that the legislative branch, the Congress, imposes exceptionally low taxes. Again, to put this in perspective, as a percentage of gross domestic product (GDP), Guatemala's total tax revenue has hovered on the high side of 10 percent of GDP, and according to the latest estimates, tax revenue amounted to 9.6 percent of GDP in 2005. In regional comparison, its tax revenue is a lower percentage of GDP than that of Belize, Costa Rica, El Salvador, Honduras, or Nicaragua, and radically lower than that of the countries of South America. Neither would higher taxation need to impose any greater burden on the poorer segments of the population given that Guatemala has higher income inequality than every other country in the region, including Costa Rica, El Salvador, Honduras, Nicaragua and Panama.

It is precisely because Guatemala could so readily afford a far better criminal justice system that it is impossible to fully distinguish the issue of resources from the issue of political will. The lack of resources is due to a lack of political will: rather than funding a high-quality criminal justice system, Congress has decided to impose very low levels of taxation and, thus, to starve the criminal justice system and other parts of government. Insofar as impunity is due to a lack of resources, it is also due to a lack of political will.

Guatemalans are not ignorant of the problems confronting their country and are aware of the policies that could be pursued to ameliorate those problems. First, Guatemala has the detailed plan for social transformation provided in the peace accords. Moreover, Guatemala has received copious recommendations from the international community on how to realize the commitment made in the peace accords and its obligations under international human rights law. . . . The question today is less what should be done than whether Guatemala has the will to do so. Thus, with the understanding that other reports have already provided sound and widely understood recommendations regarding nearly every facet of the problem of extrajudicial executions facing Guatemala today, I will be sparing in my recommendations and succinct in my conclusions:

Many kinds of violence afflicting Guatemala are poorly understood, impeding efforts to craft solutions and mobilize coalitions for change.

Continuities between current violations and those from the period of armed confrontation are surprisingly widespread and should be the cause of great concern among both the national and international community.

The resort to executions of suspects and other persons considered socially undesirable as a strategy for ensuring order and reducing crime should be absolutely and categorically rejected at every level of government.

While there is insufficient information to reliably determine how many killings are committed by state agents versus private individuals, both appear to be widespread. Any strategy to confront these killings must have two prongs: a) relentlessly root out the practice of social cleansing by government bodies; b) reform and expand the criminal justice system to effectively investigate and prosecute murders.

A lack of political will and of resources allocated to criminal justice has made effective crime control impossible. Guatemala must fully accept the scope of state responsibility under international law and take the necessary measures—including costly measures—to bring crime under control in a manner that is effective and just. . . .

Congress should greatly increase the funds allocated to the institutions of the criminal justice system.

A witness-protection program adequate to address the needs and fears of witnesses, including victims, to human rights violations in which the State or other powerful actors are implicated. . . .

Foreign donors are playing a complex, and in some ways problematic, role: rather than funding projects that the state cannot afford, they are funding projects that the state has simply opted not to be able to afford. Insofar as these projects benefit those with the least power over the legislative agenda, such foreign assistance is commendable. Moreover, foreign assistance makes up a relatively small proportion of the government's budget, and its withdrawal would not necessarily stimulate more responsible fiscal policies. Nevertheless, the donor community should carefully consider whether its assistance is doing as much as possible to push the state to assume its own responsibilities.

At the end of the day, even the crisis in relation to extrajudicial executions can be attributed in good part to the government's failure to behave in a fiscally responsible manner. The refusal of the elites to raise the overall level of income derived from taxation to a level at which an honest and effective police force and system of justice can be afforded, along with a system which respects core economic, social and cultural rights, has produced predictable and sometimes disastrous results. After all, even governments get what they pay for.

The Untouchable Narco-State

Frank Smyth

The UN-brokered peace accords did not dismantle Guatemala's anticommunist se-
curity apparatus. And with the Cold War over and the threat of a democratic left
quashed, the individuals and institutional factions affiliated with that apparatus
could turn to more lucrative, yet no less deadly, pursuits. Military and parami-
litary agents have grown out of their death-squad roots, grafting themselves onto the
highest levels of government and society, making alliances with sectors of the tra-
ditional oligarchy, arrivist entrepreneurs, and common criminals. Amnesty Inter-
national says this "unholy alliance"—in addition to presiding over narcotics and
arms trafficking, money laundering, kidnapping, car theft, and illegal logging—in
effect runs the country, which best can be described as a "corporate mafia state."
Though nominally a constitutional democracy, most major political parties are
deeply implicated in this crime network, and they represent competing factions of
this alliance. The following selection is by Frank Smyth, a freelance investigative
journalist who started reporting on Guatemalan death squads in the 1980s.

The alert went out across the state this past July. A McAllen-based FBI analyst wrote a classified report that the Department of Homeland Security
sent to US Border Patrol agents throughout Texas. About 30 suspects who
were once part of an elite unit of the Guatemalan special forces were training drug traffickers in paramilitary tactics just over the border from Mc-
Allen. The unit, called the Kaibiles after the Maya prince Kaibil Balam,
is one of the most fearsome military forces in Latin America, blamed for
many of the massacres that occurred in Guatemala during its 36-year civil
war. By September, Mexican authorities announced that they had arrested
seven Guatemalan Kaibiles, including four "deserters" who were still listed
by the Guatemalan Army as being on active duty.

Mexican authorities say the Kaibiles were meant to augment *los Zetas*,
a drug gang of soldiers-turned-hitmen drawn from Mexico's own special
forces. It's logical that the Zetas would turn to their Guatemalan counter-
parts. In addition to being a neighbor, "Guatemala is the preferred transit

point in Central America for onward shipment of cocaine to the United States," the State Department has consistently reported to Congress since 1999. In early November, anti-drug authorities at the US Embassy in Guatemala told the Associated Press that 75 percent of the cocaine that reaches American soil passes through the Central American nation.

More importantly, perhaps, the dominant institution in the country— the military—is linked to this illicit trade. Over the past two decades, the US Drug Enforcement Administration (DEA) has quietly accused Guatemalan military officers of all ranks in every branch of service of trafficking drugs to the United States, according to government documents obtained by the *Texas Observer*. More recently, the Bush administration has alleged that two retired Guatemalan Army generals, at the top of the country's military hierarchy, are involved in drug trafficking and has revoked their US visas based on these allegations.

The retired generals, Manuel Antonio Callejas y Callejas and Francisco Ortega Menaldo, are Guatemala's former top two intelligence chiefs. They are also among the founders of an elite, shadowy club within Guatemala's intelligence command that calls itself "*la cofradía*" or "the brotherhood," according to US intelligence reports. The US reports, recently de-classified, credit *la cofradía* with "engineering" tactics that roundly defeated Guatemala's Marxist guerrillas.

Guatemala's military intelligence commands developed a code of silence during these bloody operations, which is one reason why no officer was ever prosecuted for any Cold War–era human rights abuses. Since then, the same intelligence commands have turned their clandestine structures to organized crimes, according to DEA and other US intelligence reports, from importing stolen US cars to running drugs to the United States. Yet not one officer has ever been prosecuted for any international crime in either Guatemala or the United States. . . .

Guatemala is hardly the first military tainted by drugs; senior intelligence and law enforcement officers in many Latin American nations have been found colluding with organized crime. But what distinguishes Guatemala from most other nations is that some of its military suspects are accused not only of protecting large criminal syndicates but of being the ringleaders behind them. . . . Guatemala, alone in this hemisphere, has failed to either prosecute or extradite any of its own alleged drug kingpins for at least 10 years. . . .

Guatemala has long been sluggish in efforts to take legal action against its military officers for human rights violations. That impunity has since spread to organized criminal acts as well. The turning point came in 1994, when Guatemala's extraditions of its drug suspects came to a dead stop over a case involving an active duty army officer. The case highlights both the terrible price for those who seek justice in Guatemala and the timidity of the United States in demanding accountability.

A military intelligence officer back in the early 1980s, Lt. Col. Carlos Ochoa briefly trained at the US Army Command and General Staff College in 1988. Two years later, the DEA accused him of smuggling drugs to locations including Florida, where DEA special agents seized a small plane with half a metric ton of cocaine, allegedly sent by the colonel.

State Department attorneys worked for more than three years to keep Guatemala's military tribunals from dismissing the charges, and finally brought Ochoa's extradition case all the way to Guatemala's highest civilian court. The nation's chief justice, Epaminondas González Dubón, was already well respected for his integrity. On March 23, 1994, Guatemala's Constitutional Court, led by González Dubón, quietly ruled in a closed session (which is common in Guatemala) four-to-three in favor of extraditing Ochoa.

Nine days later, on April 1, gunmen shot and killed González Dubón behind the wheel of his own car in the capital, near his middle-class home, in front of his wife and youngest son. On April 12, the same Constitutional Court, with a new chief justice, quietly ruled seven-to-one not to extradite Ochoa. The surviving judges used the same line in the official Constitutional Court register—changing the verdict and date, but not the original case number—to literally copy over the original ruling, as was only reported years later by the Costa Rican daily, *La Nación*.

The Clinton administration never said one word in protest. The US ambassador in Guatemala City at the time, Marilyn McAfee, by her own admission had other concerns, including ongoing peace talks with the Guatemalan military. "I am concerned over the potential decline in our relationship with the military," she wrote to her superiors only months before the assassination. "The bottom line is we must carefully consider each of our actions toward the Guatemalan military, not only for how it plays in Washington, but for how it impacts here." . . .

Ochoa may not have been working alone. "In addition to his narcotics trafficking activities, Ochoa was involved in bringing stolen cars from the US to Guatemala," reads a "SECRET" US intelligence report obtained by US lawyer Jennifer Harbury. "Another military officer involved with Ochoa in narcotics trafficking is Colonel Julio Roberto Alpírez de Leon."

Alpírez, who briefly trained at the US School of the Americas in 1970, served "in special intelligence operations," according to a US Defense Intelligence Agency (DIA) report. A White House Oversight Board investigation later implicated him in the torture and murder of a Marxist guerrilla leader who was married to the Harvard-trained lawyer Harbury, and in the torture and mysterious decapitation of an American hotelier named Michael Devine. Col. Alpírez, since retired, has denied any wrongdoing and he was never charged with any crime.

But Ochoa, his former subordinate, is in jail today. Ochoa was arrested—again—for local cocaine dealing in Guatemala City. . . . Ochoa was later sentenced to 14 years in prison, and he remains the most important drug criminal ever convicted in Guatemala to date. . . .

The impunity that shields Guatemalan military officers from justice for criminal offenses started during the Cold War. . . . It was also during this Cold War–era carnage that the army's *la cofradía* came into its own.

"The mere mention of the word '*cofradía*' inside the institution conjures up the idea of the 'intelligence club,' the term '*cofradía*' being the name given to the powerful organizations of village-church elders that exist today in the Indian highlands of Guatemala," reads a once-classified 1991 US Defense Intelligence Agency cable. "Many of the 'best and the brightest' of the officers of the Guatemalan army were brought into intelligence work and into tactical operations planning," it continues. Like all documents not otherwise attributed in this report, the cable was obtained by the nonprofit National Security Archives in Washington, D.C.

According to the 1991 cable, "well-known members of this unofficial *cofradía* include" then army colonels "Manuel Antonio Callejas y Callejas" and "Ortega Menaldo." (Each officer had briefly trained at the US School of the Americas, in 1970 and 1976, respectively.)

The intelligence report goes on: "Under directors of intelligence such as then-Col. Manuel Antonio Callejas y Callejas back in the early 1980s, the intelligence directorate made dramatic gains in its capabilities, so much so that today it must be given the credit for engineering the military decline of the guerrillas from 1982 to the present. But while doing so, the intelligence directorate became an elite 'club' within the officer corps." . . .

The violence left the military firmly in control of Guatemala, and it did not take long for this stability to catch the attention of Colombian drug syndicates. First the Medellín and then the Cali cartels, according to Andean drug experts, began searching for new smuggling routes to the United States after their more traditional routes closed down by the mid-1980s due to greater US radar surveillance over the Caribbean, especially the Bahamas.

"They chose Guatemala because it is near Mexico, which is an obvious entrance point to the US, and because the Mexicans have a long-established mafia," explained one Andean law enforcement expert. "It is also a better transit and storage country than El Salvador because it offers more stability and was easier to control."

DEA special agents began detecting Guatemalan military officers running drugs as early as 1986, according to DEA documents obtained through the US Freedom of Information Act. That's when Ortega Menaldo took over from Callejas y Callejas as Guatemala's military intelligence chief. Over the next nine years, according to the same US documents, DEA special agents detected no less than 31 active duty officers running drugs.

"All roads lead to Ortega," a US drug enforcement expert said recently. "Even current active-duty officers may have other ties with retired officers. They have a mentor relationship."

US intelligence reports reveal the strong ties that *cofradía* high-level officers cultivated with many subordinates, who are dubbed "the operators." "This vertical column of intelligence officers, from captains to generals, represents the strongest internal network of loyalties within the institution," reads the 1991 US DIA cable. "Other capable officers were being handpicked at all levels to serve in key operations and troop command," this US report goes on. "Although not as tight-knit as the *cofradía*, the 'operators' all the same developed their own vertical leader-subordinate network of recognition, relationships and loyalties, and are today considered a separate and distinct vertical column of officer loyalties."

Cofradía officers extended their reach even further, according to another US intelligence cable, as the mid-level officer "operators" whom they chose in turn handpicked local civilians to serve as "military commissioners [to be] the 'eyes and ears' of the military" at the grassroots.

Few criminal cases better demonstrate the integration between the Guatemalan intelligence commands and drug trafficking than one pursued in 1990 by DEA special agents in the hot, sticky plains of eastern Guatemala, near the nation's Caribbean coast. This 15-year-old case is also the last time that any Guatemalans wanted on drug charges were extradited to the United States. Arnoldo Vargas Estrada, a.k.a. "Archie," was a long-time local "military commissioner," and the elected mayor of the large town of Zacapa. US embassy officials informed (as is still required according to diplomatic protocol between the two nations) Guatemalan military intelligence, then led by Ortega Menaldo, that DEA special agents had the town mayor under surveillance.

Vargas and two other civilian suspects were then arrested in Guatemala with the help of the DEA. Not long after, all three men were extradited to New York, where they were tried and convicted on DEA evidence. But the

DEA did nothing back in Guatemala when, shortly after the arrests, the military merely moved the same smuggling operation to a rural area outside town, according to family farmers in a petition delivered to the US Embassy in Guatemala City in 1992 and addressed simply "Señores D.E.A."

"[B]efore sunrise, one of the planes that transports cocaine crashed when it couldn't reach the runway on the Rancho Maya," reads the document which the peasants either signed or inked with their thumbprints. The document names the military commissioners along with seven local officers, including four local army colonels whom the farmers said supervised them.

One of the civilian military commissioners the peasants named was Rancho Maya owner Byron Berganza. More than a decade later, in 2004, DEA special agents finally arrested Berganza, along with another Guatemalan civilian, on federal "narcotics importation conspiracy" charges in New York City. Last year, the DEA in Mexico City also helped arrest another Guatemalan, Otto Herrera, who ran a vast trucking fleet from the Zacapa area. Then–Attorney General John Ashcroft described Herrera as one of "the most significant international drug traffickers and money launderers in the world."

Yet, not long after his arrest, Herrera somehow managed to escape from jail in Mexico City. Not one of the Guatemalan military officers the farmers mentioned in their 1992 petition has ever been charged. As the DEA's Senior Special Agent Glaspy explained, "There is a difference between receiving information and being able to prosecute somebody."

In 2002, then-Chairman Ballenger forced the Bush administration to take limited action to penalize top Guatemalan military officials thought to be involved in drug trafficking. "The visa of former Guatemalan intelligence chief Francisco Ortega Menaldo was revoked," confirmed State Department spokesman Richard A. Boucher in March 2002, "under a section of the Immigration and Nationality Act related to narco-trafficking, and that's about as far as I can go into the details of the decision."

By then, Ret. Gen. Ortega Menaldo had already denied the US drug charges, while reminding reporters in Guatemala City that he had previously collaborated with both the CIA and the DEA dating back to the 1980s. Indeed, a White House Intelligence Oversight Board has already confirmed that both the CIA and the DEA maintained at least a liaison relationship with Guatemalan military intelligence in the late 1980s and early 1990s when it was run by Col. Ortega Menaldo.

The CIA, through spokesman Mark Mansfield, declined all comment for this article. . . .

Today the shadowy structures of Guatemala's intelligence commands are so embedded with organized crime that the Bush administration, for one, is already calling in the United Nations. Putting aside its usual criticisms of the international body, the administration supports a proposal to form a UN-led task force explicitly called the "Commission for the Investigation of Illegal Armed Groups and Clandestine Security Apparatus" in Guatemala. So far the only nation to yield its sovereignty to allow the United Nations a similar role is Lebanon, where UN investigators are digging into the murder of a former prime minister. . . .

So what are US officials and Guatemalan authorities doing to stop the military officers involved in drug trafficking?

"In terms of public corruption against both the army and others, [Guatemalan authorities] have a number of investigations underway, right now," then-Assistant Secretary Robert B. Charles said earlier this year at a State Department press conference. But, in keeping with past practices, not one of these suspected officers has been charged in either Guatemala or the United States.

More troubling still is a recent case involving those Mexican soldiers-turned-hitmen, the Zetas. This past October 22, seven members of the Zetas were arrested in a Guatemalan border town with weapons and cocaine. The Associated Press reported that, according to Guatemalan authorities, the Zetas came to avenge one of their members who had been killed in Guatemala. Despite the evidence against the men, a little more than a week after their arrests, Guatemalan authorities inexplicably set them free.

Filóchofo

José Manuel Chacón

Filóchofo is the alter ego of cartoonist José Manuel Chacón. An everyman philoso-pher who lives in a shack perched precariously on the side of a barranco, one of the shantytown ravines that crisscross Guatemala City, Filóchofo has offered mordant commentary on the corruptions and comforts of Guatemala's rulers since the mid-1990s, revealing the limits of the country's return to constitutional rule. In a country where the press is often timid in its reporting, Chacón can be cutting in his exposé, peppering populist jokes with facts embarrassing to politicians, chafas (military officers), and oligarchs. Fired from one newspaper after another, today no venue carries Chacón's one-panel cartoon on a regular basis. Working in the tradition of cartoonists such as the Argentine Joaquín Salvador Lavado (aka Quino), creator of Malfada, and the Mexican Eduardo del Río (aka Rius), Chacón, with quick, simple lines, embodies in Filóchofo a simultaneous sense of resignation, outrage, and wry humor needed to survive life on the edge.

LA FIRMA DE LA PAZ... NO DEBE SER
SÓLO EL SILENCIO DE LOS FUSILES:
SE REQUIERE SALUD, EDUCACIÓN, TRABAJO,
JUSTICIA SOCIAL... Y SOBRE TODO
DEMOCRATIZAR LA CANASTA BÁSICA,
DE LO CONTRARIO...

© HOY A LAS 15:00 HRS. FRENTE A LA PLACA DE OLIVERIO CASTAÑEDA
DE LEÓN – CON UN CLAVEL ROJO – TODOS LOS AMANTES DE LA PAZ.

"Peace . . . should not be just silencing the guns. It requires
health, education, employment, social justice . . . and above
all, democratizing the consumer basket. Otherwise . . ." Cartoon by José Manuel Chacón. Originally published in *La otra
historia: de los Mayas al informe de la comision de la verdad* by José
Manuel Chacón, 1999, 185. Used by permission of the artist.

¿ EN QUÉ DEPORTES OLÍMPICOS
PODRÍAMOS PARTICIPAR...

SALTO ALTO

"In which Olympic sport could we compete? High jump-
ing . . ." Cartoon by José Manuel Chacón. Originally published
in *En el año de la paz, no firme, pero bien firmada* by José Manuel
Chacón, 1997, 84. Used by permission of the artist.

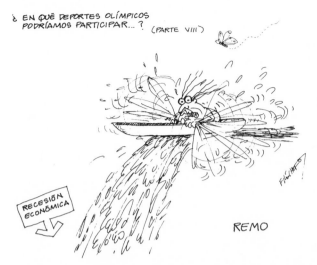

¿ EN QUÉ DEPORTES OLÍMPICOS PODRÍAMOS PARTICIPAR... ? (PARTE VIII)

REMO

"In which Olympic sport could we compete? Rowing . . ." Cartoon by José Manuel Chacón. Originally published in *En el año de la paz, no firme, pero bien firmada* by José Manuel Chacón, 1997, 85. Used by permission of the artist.

EN QUÉ DEPORTES OLÍMPICOS PODRÍAMOS PARTICIPAR... ? (PARTE VII)

MARATÓN

"In which Olympic sport could we compete? Marathon . . ." Cartoon by José Manuel Chacón. Originally published in *En el año de la paz, no firme, pero bien firmada* by José Manuel Chacón, 1997, 85. Used by permission of the artist.

Art and the Postwar Generation

Anabella Acevedo

Young artists have developed new spaces, collectives, and themes in the aftermath of the war. As in other Latin American countries that experienced extreme political repression, historical memory has become a recurring subject. Perhaps not surprisingly, despair, emptiness, and even boredom are other themes among young artists who nonetheless still maintain Guatemala's rich tradition of artistic nerve and social critique, capturing both the beauty and the tragicomedy of the everyday. In the following excerpt, art critic Anabella Acevedo focuses her attention on how the creation of a "center of sociability" called Casa Bizarra helped young artists exchange ideas, produce new work, organize events and protests, and even work with the municipal government to restore the city's beautiful colonial core and turn a number of its buildings into airy public spaces. Sometimes criticized for their iconoclasm and autodidacticism, these young artists in postwar Guatemala are nonetheless admired for their rejection of traditionalism and for their barrier-breaking performance art.

When twenty-something José Osorio returned to Guatemala from Mexico, where he had just graduated as an engineer from the Monterrey Technological Institute, he met up with some old friends who had rented a large house in the old section of Guatemala City for a sort of cultural commune. In Mexico, José had decided that what he really wanted to do was dedicate himself to contemporary art, and so one of the first things he did back in Guatemala was look up his friend Giovanni Pinzón, whom he had known since the days when both had been expelled from the prestigious Catholic high school Liceo Javier. Giovanni was leading a group called Suburban Bohemia, and he had just started to paint. José returned to Guatemala in December 1996 (the month that Guatemala's peace accords were signed), and by January, he was living in what would become known as Casa Bizarra (Bizarre House) in the center of Guatemala City.

Because they were, in their own words, "offered only a culture of violence," José and his friends opened the downtown cultural center as an artistic association in which young people could support each other in their various aesthetic pursuits. Barely beyond adolescence, they wanted nothing to do with formal politics, adults, or the university; their interest was to create, learn on their own, and, of course, have a good time. For them, the term "politics" was linked to violence, the state, and political parties, all of which they wished to avoid. They preferred the margins.

When Casa Bizarra was created, recreational spaces in the city were rigidly separated. On one hand, there was the so-called Zona Viva [Zone 10], a nightlife hot spot for upper-middle-class and upper-class youth. On the other hand, there was *el centro*—downtown—where everybody else went. Well-to-do young people saw *el centro* as dangerous and uninteresting, and that was precisely the spot chosen for Casa Bizarra, perhaps in order to be less visible in those moments, since "down here they don't see us," in the words of the project's creators. The project's organizers preferred to use the open street as their space for art, a space where they experimented with street theater, painting in the parks and looking for ways to relate to the people around them.

Few of the young artists actually lived in Casa Bizarra, but they spent all their time there, in a space where the son of a president and a drug addict from the streets were equal as artistic autodidacts; where the only edict was, in the words of Casa Bizarra leader José Osorio, "go mad," that is, see reality in another way, show something new without the judgment of any intellectual or academic discourse. "We were bad painters and bad writers, but we were doing something that belonged to us," a kind of "exercise in freedom," in Osorio's words. Casa Bizarra was important artistically because it provided a space in the absence of others for exhibitions and education. These youths organized their own workshops, exhibits, publications, everything that the previous generation could not do during the armed conflict. There was also space for other experiences, including drugs, something that separated the young *bizarros* even further from "correct" and "acceptable" society.

José Osorio speaks of the group as a "generation of the new criticism," searching for identity in an "intolerant and mean city," an identity later called "urban" as in "the tortilla-and-Coca-Cola generation," part of a new national consumerism of goods and postures. "They judged us because we didn't like *marimba* and folklore," said poet Simón Pedroza. The *bizarros* sought to go beyond the traditional markers of national identity, criticizing both state paternalism and the notion that Guatemalan artists had to "die of hunger." The successful rock group Bohemia Suburbano provided a good model because it could be both artistic and make money.

Limpieza social (Social cleansing), 2006, by the performance
artist Regina José Galindo for *The Power of Women*, Galleria
Cívica, Trento, Italy. Used by permission of the artist and Pro-
meteo Gallery di Ida Pisani (Milan).

Casa Bizarra as an actual physical space lasted only a year, and it later
reopened as a bar called Giraluna, where these young people held concerts
to earn enough money to sustain themselves. This didn't last, though, and
the bar closed in early 1998. According to [art critic] Rosina Cazali, "perhaps
the most interesting thing, and what gives honor to the name Casa Bizarra,
was their use of performance as a spontaneous act with an eclectic quality
that united literary expression with scenic large-scale production."

Around this time, the municipal government appointed Javier Payeras
[Casa Bizarra poet and nephew of EGP leader Mario Payeras] to head a new

historical restoration project of the city center, the *centro histórico*. Javier called together a group of *bizarros*, and they thought up the idea of setting up a kind of Casa Bizarra in the streets, based on the notion of democratic culture that had initially guided them. This work soon turned José Osorio into a cultural promoter, because he took it upon himself to create an "urban culture," what the Ministry of Culture and other government institutions considered "informal art." Osorio's method was to invade public spaces and take art into the streets, from rock concerts and clowns to experimental art and publications from the Casa Bizarra publishing house. That is how the Equipo de Arte Urbano [Urban Art Team] was born. . . .

The first *centro histórico* festival in which the Urban Art Team collaborated was seen as a way to bring people together during the transition of the peace accords. During this time, the work of particular artists and writers, such as Regina José Gallindo, Sandra Monterroso, and Alejando Marré, became more established. Yet in 1999 the festival was marred by a violent encounter between the police and a group of youths attending a rock concert: police attacked the concert, confusing youthful euphoria with a gang threat, because the authorities thought anyone wearing a black t-shirt and sporting body piercings must be a *marero*, a gang member. The result was disheartening: the media blamed the youth, and the city hall organizers of the official festival didn't come to their defense. In many minds, this was confirmation that the peace process in Guatemala was far from being consolidated, and moreover that the general attitude toward alternative expression by young people remained traditionalist and recriminatory.

Although most of the the *bizarros* broke with the official *centro histórico* festival after the incident with the police, they kept on promoting public and performance art in the old city center. Two events from 2000 are noteworthy: a performance protest during Army Day that year, and the Octubre Azul (Blue October) public art festival. Octubre Azul marks the close of this first stage of the youth-created, public art movement of the 1990s.

June 30, 2000

June 30 is Army Day in Guatemala, or Day of the Martyrs, in the words of a protest sign hung across the National Cathedral, in whose towers several soldiers stand guard. People have gathered in Guatemala City's central park to watch the parade, because the day is a national holiday and any change in the normal routine is welcomed. For others, the park is their only space for recreation. Still others have come to celebrate the shameful idea of a glorious and defending army, as the government's master of ceremonies repeats over and over again throughout the morning, in a voice as artificial as the event itself. Two small groups are protesting the violence of Guatemala's past and present, its ongoing impunity, and everything the army has come to signify in Guatemala. Javier del Cid and a friend of his known simply as "Pérez" have organized a performative act and have invited one of these groups to participate.

At 9:30 AM, a voice over the loudspeaker announces the start of the parade. The announcer's voice is drowned by the roar of overflying planes and helicopters, a sound that may strike fear in anyone who remembers what those sounds meant in other times. Nevertheless, everything seems festive: there are street vendors, photo booths, lots of kids, and a large crowd gathering. At one end of the park is an oversized pine table put up by installation artist Francisco Aullón [this table, as tall as a small house, was made in the rustic style common in rural Guatemala].

At 10:00 the parade passes in front of the National Palace—now called the Palace of Culture—and on the other side of the street is a group of people dressed in black, holding red carnations (symbolizing Guatemala's repressive past) and shouting slogans against violence. Meanwhile, Javier del Cid and Pérez have climbed on top of Aullón's huge table and covered it with plastic.

At 10:30, more people are around the table, and the protest group in front of the place has grown large enough to make their voices heard. As soldiers pass by, some are hit by red carnations.

At 11:00 Javier del Cid gives the sign to begin. People form a circle, holding hands, some dressed in white (Javier's group) and others in black (the other group). Javier's group starts to roughly bind and gag the volunteers who agreed to participate in the performance, dragging some of them to the table, where the "captors" climb onto the table and start throwing black paint down upon the prisoners. No one moves except Javier and Pérez, who take the paint in their hands and are soon half covered in black. By this time, many spectators have forgotten the parade and have encircled the table, looking on with surprise. No one laughs or interrupts; all are fixated on the black paint raining down. Suddenly, the artists stop, stand to attention and offer a military salute. Behind them can be seen the cathedral and the sky. Someone begins to untie the "prisoners" while Javier and Pérez take down the paint-splotched plastic sheet, which the liberated prisoners carry over to a spot where a giant skull has been placed. They fold the sheet as if it were a flag and leave it hanging over a small monument to the victims of the violence that stands at one end of the central park. Meanwhile, Javier and Pérez have climbed back onto the giant table and have covered it this time with a multicolored plastic tablecloth. Have they redressed history? Have they remembered it only to whitewash it?

Octubre Azul (Blue October), 2000

From October 1 to October 30, 2000, a month-long street festival, conceived as "open to creation and debate," took place in the downtown historic center. The event was proposed by the Urban Art Team and announced in the following way:

> The month of October is connected to the Guatemalan social imaginary. To say October evokes a breath, a ballad to our national history. October is a synonym of the 1944 Revolution and the utopian democracy that persists in our memory. October is the month when the sky turns an intense blue. This color is a metaphor for our different states of consciousness, for our nostalgias. As an effort to reevaluate and rescue the intellectual and artistic spirit that the 1944 October Revolution promoted, we propose that the younger generation partake of Octubre Azul as a space for their expositions, creations, and debates.

What is interesting about this evocation of the 1944 Revolution is that it references a political event as an intellectual and artistic revolution. In addition to "giving a platform to emerging artistic work," the most important goal of Octubre Azul was "to enrich theoretical and critical knowledge within the Guatemalan artistic milieu," inviting "all those artists who open spaces for creation on the experimental level with an emphasis on public intervention, literature, dance, and unconventional events." The festival included a broad array of art expositions and public performances, in an attempt to "democratize" art and make it available to diverse audiences. Chosen spaces included markets, parks, public buildings, and church atriums; the important thing was to show that art doesn't belong to the elite. In this sense, the connection with the October Revolution of 1944 was evident. Yet Octubre Azul sought another kind of revolution that was not explicitly political. The festival ocurred only once, but it was a watershed event in its approach toward art and public dialogue. Blue October was the launching pad for many artists and art collectives; for instance, the Caja Lúdica (Playful Drum) collective came out of this festival. Caja Lúdica is one of the most important artistic and social projects in recent years: the collective organzies public art events and workshops in Guatemala City's slums and in some of the most war-torn communities in the highlands.

Postwar Generation, Fast Food Generation, Generation@.com

> We are the bloodstained knife . . .
> a syllable, dot
> spider
> minute
> Spain's mistake . . .
> We are the debris
> the legacy
> the postwar.

This excerpt from a poem by Javier Payeras is a preamble to a deeper understanding of this group of young people. Not all the artists of this generation belonged to an alternative group like Casa Bizarra; for some of the more "intellectualized" artists and writers, the *bizarros* were seen as simple exhibitionists with little or no connection to "real" art. Writer Alexander Sequén Mónchez makes this point:

> Christened pompously as the "postwar generation," they focus vacuously on a parade of theatricality, without conviction or passion for what they believe or dream. The search for instant fame is the extension of their stupidity. They don't say anything because they have nothing to say; their purpose—seizing space—achieves only a temporary luminosity. . . . It's a kind of chest-beating science fiction that says "look at me, applaud me" . . . a striptease unconvincing to even the densest observer. . . .

Maybe most of these young people, especially with their early work, do not bring anything new to international art. But what is certain is that the artists of Casa Bizarra have initiated a new stage in spontaneous expression. . . . In this sense, Rosina Cazali's remarks are insightful:

> With this generation we see something that goes beyond playing with public space, even though here, this in itself is an artistic awakening. On one hand, this generation reflects a fragment of the complex weave of realities that reinforce and project the cultural, psycho-political, social, and economic changes through which we are passing. On the other hand, this generation has provocative proposals that challenge our conventional and traditional milieu, and does so in plain view. . . .

Finally, the *bizarros* have been criticized by other young people who point to the social distance between the artists and the spaces they claim to represent. While the *bizarros* want to speak with a "subaltern" voice,

Building community through art: the youth arts collective Caja Lúdica (Playful
Drum) organizes art workshops and *comparsas* (carnival parades) in working-class
neighborhoods in Guatemala City and in villages in Baja Verapaz affected by the war.

theirs nevertheless remains the voice of those who can choose to assume a
proletarian posture.

Why give so much attention to the artists and writers linked to Casa
Bizarra? There are several reasons. This group brought together artists,
writers, and fellow travelers interested in an alternative culture, freely ad-
mitting people from diverse social classes, educational backgrounds, and
professional trajectories. These young people are interested in multidisciplinary artistic experimentation, inspired by contemporary artistic practices uncommon in Guatemala until recently, such as interventions, performance art, installations, video installations, and direct action. Finally, this
group of artists is proactive about bringing forth their ideas and projects.

Of course, not all the attention paid to this group has been positive. While
they are praised for their dynamism and spontaneity, they are criticized for
the lack of rigor in many of their proposals, because much of what they do
has an element of "show" (intentionally, of course), and because they have
received a lot of attention without really consolidating the spaces they occupy experientially. Despite criticizing the existing system, they don't have
any fixed ideological stance. Finally, they are criticized (justly or unjustly)
for not accepting as models the established artistic and literary figures of

Guatemala, such as Nobel laureate Miguel Angel Asturias, preferring to identify with lesser-known artists and writers such as Roberto Monzón and Isabel de los Angeles Ruano.

At the same time, most of these young people are self-taught artists, and few of those who write have studied literature formally. Many only realized after the fact that their kind of performance art was also being practiced in other places outside Guatemala.

Many terms have been used to describe this group. "Postwar generation" refers to the fact that chronologically their work becomes known around the time of the peace accords in 1996, but it also alludes to the disenchantment within Guatemalan society after thirty-six years of armed conflict that left the country shattered and marked the end of the revolutionary utopias. The writers and artists who produced during the years of the war were more explicit about the political context of their work, and many were recognized as "committed artists" who were involved in some way in the armed conflict. The generation that began to produce just before and after the signing of the peace accords addressed the effects of the war on a wounded and despairing country. On one hand, they were conscious of having inherited a fragmented and violent society. On the other hand, they wanted to assume the mantle of modernity with all that this implies, but without an explicitly political commitment. They supported the general values of justice and equality, but not a specific message; one only has to see many of the performances of Regina José Galindo to understand this. Perhaps this is why earlier generations of artists and writers have had a hard time accepting this new generation and their unorthodox art, which seems to scorn everything. Many of the "emerging artists," for their part, dislike the label "postwar generation," even though the expression is inevitable. Another term is "Generation X" (in Guatemala, a publishing house called Editorial X specializes in publishing alternative works by young authors). Still another term is "urban art" or "emerging artists of the city," as Sergio Valdés Pedroni has said, arguing that it's still too early for a rigorous analysis of postwar urban youth art.

Perhaps it is too early to speak of an artistic and cultural "Guatemalan vanguard," or maybe it's unnecessary given all the spaces and absences we have to decipher in the here and now in Guatemala. But at the same time, behind these alternative spaces and efforts, these journeys, there might be a way to survive our history, to tell it and above all to question it. "Guatemalan vanguard?" Terms mean little if behind them are works that don't need to be defended or praised to understand their significance.

Translated by Deborah T. Levenson and Elizabeth Oglesby

I Walk Backwards

Humberto Ak'abal

*Humberto Ak'abal is a renowned Maya poet from the K'iche' town of Momoste-
nango, in the highland department of Totonicapán. His poem below was originally
published in K'iche' in 2001.*

Now and then
I walk backwards.
It is my way of remembering.
If I only walked forward,
I could tell you
about forgetting

Tz'olq'omin b'e
K'o kuriqa'
kintz'olq'omij ri nub'e:
xa jewa' kinna'tisaj jun jasuch.
Weta xata nutukel kinb'in chonuwach
kin kwin nek'uri kinb'ij chawe ri', ri
ucholaj ri sachib'al

Translated from Spanish by Deborah T. Levenson

VIII

Maya Movements

One of the consequences of the military's genocidal war against indigenous populations has been a campaign by those who survived it to reclaim and nourish Maya cultural identity and life. What has called itself the Pan-Maya Movement arose from the ashes of fires lit by the state, to make claims based on a renewed and deepened sense of ethnic pride that perhaps was catalyzed by the shutting down of other venues for political action. Much of the writing on the Pan-Maya Movement that emerged in the last years of the war tended to present Pan-Maya activism as a new thing, springing from the ruins of a failed—or crushed—national project. Its roots, however, are old and diverse. They trace back to the social processes of state formation and class transformation that gave rise to the modern Guatemalan nation.

From its inception in the mid-nineteenth century, the extension of coffee capitalism took place through collective exploitation defined along ethnic lines, including forced labor, vagrancy laws, and debt peonage targeted primarily at indigenous peasants. In response, rural leaders throughout the nineteenth and twentieth centuries often drew on the language of liberal nationalism to contest such abuses. "We are knocking on the door of our political emancipation," wrote 122 Q'eqchi's in 1920, to demand the "indisputable rights of the Indian." After 1944, this indigenous engagement with liberal nationalism combined with other secular and religious left political traditions and was catalyzed by the increasing government repression. The October Revolution detailed in part 4 of this volume had an explosive effect on indigenous political activism, allowing community leaders to retake local political power, which Ladinos had increasingly monopolized since independence. By 1948, twenty-seven of the forty-five municipalities with the highest indigenous population had Maya mayors. Agrarian activists likewise took advantage of Arbenz's land reform to establish local-level organizations.

In the 1970s, much of the ethnic content of the armed struggle found expression, as we saw in part 5 of this volume, in the language and action of the Committee for Peasant Unity (CUC), a peasant movement that came to be allied with the rebel Guerrilla Army of the Poor (EGP). Following the worst of the slaughter in the early 1980s, a number of indigenous insurgents broke ranks with the EGP and its sister organization ORPA, mostly due to the racism they experienced within these revolutionary organizations. These militants formed specifically Maya armed insurgencies, taking names such as Nuestro Movimiento (Our Movement), Movimiento Indígena Revolucionario (Revolutionary Indigenous Movement), and Movimiento Revolucionario del Pueblo Ixim (Ixim Peoples' Revolutionary Movement). One such organization, the Movimiento Indio Tojil (Tojil Indian Movement), circulated a manifesto that called for the establishment of an independent Maya socialist nation. After the genocide, new organizations that were allied with specific guerrilla groups, such as Consejo de Comunidades Etnicas Runujel Junam (Council of Ethnic Communities Runujel Junam—We Are All Equal) and the Coordinadora Nacional de Viudas de Guatemala (National Coordinating Committee of Widows), deployed the language of indigenous rights to demand a restoration of the rule of law. And in 1992, a group of indigenous peasant activists broke with the CUC to form the Coordinadora Nacional Indígena y Campesina (CONIC), which continued fighting for land and labor rights but with greater emphasis on the cultural content of their demands.

Despite the dense, plural, multilayered history of the origins of the indigenous-rights movement, even before the war ended there existed a tendency—both among foreign observers and Pan-Maya activists themselves—to draw a sharp divide between "culturalists," on the one hand, and "popular movement" groups like CONIC on the other, which were still associated with the left. The same divide that led to the formation of short-lived Maya guerrilla movements in the early 1980s reemerged at the 1991 Encuentro Continental 500 Años de Resistencia Indígena, Negra y Popular, a continental social forum held in the city of Quetzaltenango. By this point, a growing number of Maya activists present at the meeting were no longer willing to subordinate their demands to the cause of a defeated insurgency. After the war, many indigenous intellectuals, some themselves politicized in left political circles, began to offer histories of the Pan-Maya Movement that downplayed the contribution of indigenous activists and communities to the formation of revolutionary organizations. In an influential account, Demetrio Cojtí Cuxil describes the Movimiento Indio Tojil, whose vision for the armed establishment of an autonomous Maya nation was avowedly socialist, as an apolitical cultural-rights organization. "The members of the movement," he wrote, "were between two fires, that of the guerrilla and the army."[1]

More than ten years after the end of the war, much of the political agenda of the postwar Pan-Maya Movement has stalled. As political scientist Rachel Sieder notes, the demands of the movement were moderate to begin with, compared to similar activism in other Latin American countries, particularly in Bolivia and Ecuador, where indigenous movements have recently waged successful campaigns demanding land reform and opposing transnational corporations over environmental issues and control of resources. In contrast, in Guatemala—notwithstanding the ongoing militancy of groups like the CUC and CONIC—the Pan-Maya Movement focused its demands mostly on vague calls to respect indigenous language, culture, and spirituality. In Guatemala's peace accords, government negotiators agreed to incorporate indigenous customary law into the national legal system. But when the matter was put to a national vote in May 1999, as required by the constitution, business elites financed a scare campaign that helped defeat the initiative, stoking fears that the recognition of customary law would serve as a stalking horse for challenges to private-property rights. The government did ratify the International Labour Organization's Convention 169, guaranteeing a wide range of social and cultural rights to indigenous peoples. These include the right of communities to be consulted about the use of natural resources within their territories; as can be expected, these rights haven't been enforced, yet they have given indigenous activists rhetorical backing in their confrontations with multinational corporations, as illustrated by the Sololá conflict over mining (see "Solidarity Is a Characteristic of the Maya People," this section).

Despite setbacks, the "Mayanization of everyday life" has continued apace. In the countryside, the political and economic empowerment of indigenous peoples that began with the work of peasant leagues, cooperatives, Catholic Action, and the Christian Democratic Party has advanced considerably. Small cliques of Ladinos no longer control municipal politics, markets, credit, and labor contracting. Many schools throughout the highlands offer bilingual education, and there is a general revival of indigenous language and spiritual practices. Migration from one's home community, either to Guatemala City or the United States, no longer necessarily means a loss of ethnic identity. There is an increased—though still contested, as Irma Alicia Nimatuj's essay below suggests—acceptance of indigenous language and dress in spaces previously thought of as the province of Ladinos. At the same time, there is also an important recognition that Maya identity is not reducible to language and clothing; many professionals, including professional women, can adopt western dress and still consider themselves Maya. Political protest—for land, for unions, against mining and genetically modified corn, for decent jobs, in defense of the environment, for all the things that make life tolerable and dignified—is commonly done in the name of past ancestors and Maya deities. In fact, with much of the culturalist agenda either defeated or frozen, the most vocal advocates for indigenous rights are those groups fighting for social justice, which are often linked to a broader transnational anticorporate globalization movement that includes demands for immigrant rights.

In March 2007, after a visit by us president George W. Bush to Iximché, an archaeological site that many consider sacred, Maya priests conducted a cleansing ceremony. "We will burn incense, place flowers and water in the area where Mr. Bush has walked to clean out the bad energy," said Morales Toj, head of the Maya Youth Movement. "That a person like [Bush]—with the persecution of our migrant brothers in the United States, with the wars he has provoked—is going to walk in our sacred lands is an offense for the Maya people and their culture," said Juan Tiney, a conic leader.

Note

1. See Betsy Ogburn Konefal, *For Every Indio Who Falls: A History of Maya Activism in Guatemala, 1960–1990* (Albuquerque: University of New Mexico Press, 2010).

The Kí-chè Language

Adrián Inés Chavéz

Adrián Inés Chavéz was a provincial schoolteacher from the Western Highland town of San Francisco El Alto. He was well known for developing an innovative K'iche' orthography, founding the Academia de la Lengua Maya-K'iche', and publishing a new edition of the Popul Vuh. For this work, he has been embraced by postwar cultural activists as the father of modern Pan-Mayanism. But Chavéz also represents the new political and cultural possibilities opened up by the 1944 democratic spring: active in the teachers union in the 1940s and a supporter of Juan José Arévalo, he served as the secretary of culture in Quetzaltenango's labor federation during the October Revolution. In the 1970s, Chavéz began to travel the country, giving workshops on indigenous language, culture, and history, helping to shape an interpretation of repression through the prism of racism and ethnic discrimination. Below is a selection from one of his earliest efforts to standardize the K'iche' (or, as Chavéz spelled it, Kí-chè) language.

Why Is Kí-chè a Language?

The word "language" [*idioma* in Spanish] is formed from two Greek etymological elements; *idios*, which means own, special, characteristic, typical; and *phonema*, which means the sound of a language. As a result, that which is called "language" is the language of a people, an expression that is not taken from another people. One who speaks Kí-chè is of the same Kí-chè people; it is a language that hasn't taken its fundamental characteristics from another people . . . and that is why it is called Kí-chè. But there is something more; it has rules that govern its sentence structure, its conjugation, and its pronoun declination. . . . Kí-chè is not a dialect, a form of speaking derived from decadence. It is a language.

Notwithstanding four centuries of neglect, Kí-chè preserves much of its precepts of pronunciation, above all in the areas where there the Kí-chè population is concentrated, such as in Totonicapán and Quiché.

Why Is It Called Kí-chè?

The capital of the Kingdom of Kí-chè during the time of the conquest was called Óumar Kaj, whose ruins today are more than a kilometer from the department capital of Santa Cruz del Quiché; its topography and physical layout give the impression that it was a royal house or a city temple. The metropolis Óumar Kaj (or, Utatlán, as it was called by the *indígenas* that came from Mexico with Alvarado) was in a region where maguey [agave] was extensively cultivated, a plant with many industrial and medicinal uses. . . . And since the Kí-chè name given to the membrane of its leaves is *wuj ki,* translated as "maguey paper," one can infer that it was used for writing. This totally contradicts the opinions of many historians who believe that the Kí-chè people didn't have their own writing system, an opinion that is also proven false by a correct interpretation of the *Pop wuj* (not *Popol buh* as the book is often erroneously called). . . .

Corruptions of the Kí-chè Language

Because there was no alphabet at the time of the Conquest that could transmit the vanishing indigenous writing system, no grammar to maintain the correct form of writing and pronunciation, with a dictionary to preserve the old words, and no schools to teach the Kí-chè language, many words have slowly changed their structure until they have totally lost their true meaning, even to the point where *indígenas* use words without knowing their exact lexicographic content. . . .

People who speak the Kí-chè language well will not know the meaning of the following words, which haven't been written correctly since the use of roman letters: *Parrashaj, Chirrenox, Tacajalvé, Palá, Calel* . . . But if you would spell these words like this: *P Rash Aj, Che Re Nôj, P Toajal, P la, Oalel* . . . any *indígena* would know that they mean "Where is the green cane?" "That which belongs to Renoj," "By way of the coast road," "By the bushes," "Hauler." . . . The general law of evolution affects languages . . . and many Kí-chè words have changed as a result. The influence of Spanish, as well as the languages of the indigenous Mexican allies of the *conquistadores,* has contributed to this change, especially those Kí-chè words whose phoneme is impossible to represent by roman letters. It is important to revive them with scientific precision. A poorly written word lends itself to multiple interpretations, and it loses its legitimate meaning. Here is an example:

POPOL BUH: Starting with the title of the notable book of the Kí-chè people, in the text of the document appears the following passage: *rumal mahabi*

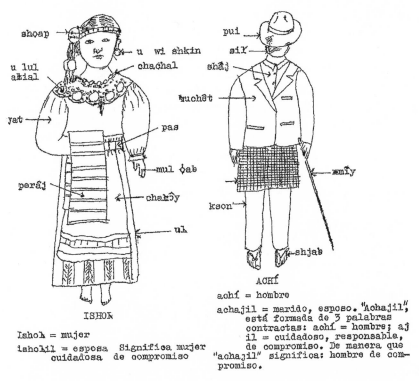

shoap — u wi shkin — chachal — u lul akial — yat — pas — peráj — mul ĉab — chakôy — uk

pui — siℓ — shâj — kuchêt — emℓy — kson' — shjab

ISHOK

Ishok = mujer

isholil = esposa Significa mujer
    cuidadosa de compromiso

ACHÍ

achí = hombre

achajil = marido, esposo. "Achajil"
    está formada de 3 palabras
    contractas: achí = hombre; aj
    il = cuidadoso, responsable,
    de compromiso. De manera que
    "achajil" significa: hombre de com-
    promiso.

Adrián Chávez used illustrations from daily indigenous life, such as this drawing of the traditional dress of a Ki-chè couple, to help revive and standardize the Maya language. From *El idioma Ki-chè y su ortografía* (second edition), Quetzaltenango, Guatemala, 1966.

chic ilbal re pop buh. This is the only mention in the whole of the document of the phrase *popo voh.* But it turns out that in using the word *popo* there is an error due to the Spanish influence, because in the Ki-chè language there are no *palabras graves* [words with the stress on the last syllable]. . . . The correct word is *Pop.* . . . But when used as *Pop Vuh,* a person who was not an *indígena* would hear an *o* between the two monosyllabic words . . .

Upon reading the book, one has the impression that this is a narrative of events, of natural occurrences, of gods, and of the history of the Ki-chè people, which confirms the understanding of the word *Pop* as meaning *events,* or what we understand to be *history. Vuh* is nothing more than the consequence of the anarchy of writing during the colonial period. . . . In the case of *Vuh,* the letter *V* is used as a *U (Vniversidad, vna, lvz, conqvista,* etc.) and the letter *H* is pronounced as a *J.* . . . But in practice, the first letter of *Vuh* is a real consonant, which is why some translators like to change the letter *B* for a *V*, without taking into account the paleographic aspect of the matter. From this, the word often appears as *Buh*, *Buj*, or *Bu*, which, as has already been mentioned, has no meaning in the Kí-chè language.

The word *Wuj* means book, paper, letter, public writing, according to its function in a sentence. Thus we know that in the indigenous text, it means book. In conclusion, *Pop wuj* means *Book of events. Popol buh*, from the Kí-chè point of view, has no meaning.

Translated by Greg Grandin

Our History Is a Living History

Rigoberta Menchú

Perhaps no figure bridges the indigenous mobilization associated with the left and the cultural politics associated with the Pan-Maya Movement as completely as Nobel Laureate Rigoberta Menchú. A Maya-K'iche' born in the village of Chimel in the municipality of Uspantán in 1959, Menchú's family became involved first in Catholic Action and then in the Committee of Peasant Unity (CUC) and the Guerrilla Army of the Poor. Security forces killed most of her family, including two brothers, a sister-in-law, three nieces and nephews, and two parents. Her father, a prominent CUC activist, was killed in the 1980 firebombing of the Spanish embassy. Menchú became famous when she recounted her story of activism and repression in her first-person testimony, published in Spanish under the title (translated here into English) My name is Rigoberta Menchú and this is how my consciousness was raised. *The English-language version of Menchú's book was published under a different title:* I, Rigoberta Menchú: An Indian Woman in Guatemala. *The book was a worldwide phenomenon, taught in universities not only to illustrate Guatemalan history but also as an example of the Latin American "testimonial" genre. Menchú won the Nobel Peace Prize in 1992 for her efforts to raise awareness about indigenous rights. Many interpreted her award, in the five hundredth anniversary year of the Spanish arrival in the Americas, as a symbolic compensation for the destruction wrought on indigenous peoples by European colonialism in the Americas and throughout the world. Below is her Nobel Lecture.*

Your Majesties, the king and queen of Norway,
the honorable members of the Nobel Peace Committee,
Your Excellency, the prime minister,
Your Excellencies, members of the government and the diplomatic corps,
dear Guatemalan countrymen and women,
ladies and gentlemen,

I feel deep pride for the honor of having been awarded the Nobel Peace Prize, a deep personal feeling and pride for my country and its very ancient culture, for the value of my community and people, for the love of my country and of Mother Nature. . . . I consider this Prize, not as a reward to me personally, but rather as one of the greatest conquests in the struggle for peace, for human rights and for the rights of the indigenous people, who, for five hundred years, have been split, fragmented, victim to genocide, repression and discrimination. Please allow me to convey to you all what this Prize means to me. . . .

The Nobel Prize is a symbol of peace, and of efforts to build up a real democracy. It will stimulate the civil sectors so that through a solid national unity, these may contribute to the process of negotiations that seek peace, reflecting the general feeling—although at times not possible to express because of fear—of Guatemalan society: to establish political and legal grounds that will give irreversible impulses to a solution to what initiated the internal armed conflict.

There is no doubt that it provides hope to the struggle of the indigenous people in the entire continent. It is also a tribute to Central Americans who still search for stability, for their future, for the path of development and integration. . . . Paradoxically, it was actually in my own country where I faced, on the part of some, the strongest criticism, reserve and indifference, to the fact that the Nobel Peace Prize has been awarded to this Quiché Indian. Perhaps because in all of Latin America, it is precisely in Guatemala where the discrimination towards the indigenous, towards women, and the repression of the longing for justice and peace, is most deep. . . .

With profound pain, on one side, but with satisfaction on the other, I have to inform you that the Nobel Peace Prize 1992 will have to remain temporarily in Mexico City, in watchful waiting for peace in Guatemala. . . .

Please allow me, ladies and gentlemen, to say some words about my country and the civilization of the Mayas. The Maya people developed and spread geographically through some three hundred thousand square kilometers. They occupied parts of the south of Mexico, Belize, Guatemala, as well as Honduras and El Salvador and developed a very rich civilization. . . . They were great scientists in the fields of mathematics, astronomy, agriculture, architecture, and engineering; they were great artists, sculptors, painters, and weavers. . . . The Mayas discovered the value of zero in mathematics, at around the same time that it was discovered in India and later passed on to the Arabs. Their astronomic forecasts based on mathematical calculations and scientific observations were amazing. They still are. They prepared a calendar more accurate than the Gregorian, and in the field of medicine they performed intracranial surgical operations.

One of the Maya books, which escaped destruction by the *conquistadores*, known as the *Codex of Dresden*, contains the results of an investigation on eclipses, predicting sixty-nine solar eclipses that occurred on a thirty-three year cycle. . . . Who can predict what other great scientific conquests and developments these people could have achieved, if they had not been conquered by blood and fire, and subjected to an ethnocide that affected nearly fifty million people in the course of five hundred years?

I would describe the meaning of this Nobel Peace Prize in the first place as a tribute to the Indian people who have been sacrificed and have disappeared because they aimed at a more dignified and just life. . . . This growing concern is comforting, even though it comes five hundred years late. . . .

To us Mother Earth is not only a source of . . . the corn that is our life, but of so many other things that the privileged ones of today strive to possess. The Earth is the root and the source of our culture. She keeps our memories, she receives our ancestors and she demands that we honor her and return to her. . . . From these basic features derive behavior, rights and obligations in the American continent, for the indigenous people as well as for the nonindigenous, whether they be racially mixed, blacks, whites or Asian. . . .

If the indigenous civilization and the European civilizations could have made exchanges in a peaceful and harmonious manner, without destruction, exploitation, discrimination, and poverty, they could, no doubt, have achieved greater and more valuable achievements for humanity. Do not forget that when the Europeans came to America, there was already a flourishing and strong civilization there. One cannot talk about a "discovery of America," because one only discovers what is lost, or what is hidden. . . . We, the indigenous, are willing to combine tradition with modernism, but not at any cost; we will not permit our future be reduced to ethnotourism.
. . .

It is known throughout the world that the Guatemalan people, in struggle, achieved in October 1944 a democracy, defined by institutional stability and human rights. Guatemala at the time was an exception in the American continent. . . . But in 1954 a conspiracy associated the traditional national power blocs—those inheritors of colonialism—with powerful foreign interests and overthrew the democratic regime. . . . The economic, social, and political subjection that derived from the Cold War was what initiated the internal armed conflict. . . . In the attempt to crush rebellion, dictatorships committed the greatest atrocities. They leveled villages and murdered thousands of peasants, particularly Indians, hundreds of trade union work-

ers and students, outstanding intellectuals and politicians, priests and nuns.
. . . The practice of "disappearance" was invented in Guatemala, as a government policy.

As you know, I am myself a survivor of a massacred family. . . .

No less characteristic of a democracy is social justice—a solution to the horrifying statistics of infant mortality, of malnutrition, lack of education, of illiteracy, of unsustainable wages. . . . Today, we must fight for a better world, without poverty, without racism, with peace in the Middle East and in Southeast Asia. . . . For a just and peaceful solution in the Balkans; for the end of apartheid in South Africa; for the stability in Nicaragua, that the peace agreement in El Salvador be observed; for the reestablishment of democracy in Haiti; for the complete sovereignty of Panama. . . .

Our history is a living history. It has pulsated, withstood and survived centuries of sacrifice. It now comes forth again with strength. The seeds, dormant for such a long time, sprout today with some uncertainty, since they germinate in a world plagued by confusion and uncertainty. There is no doubt that this process will be long and complex, but it is no utopia. . . .

By combining all the shades and nuances of its people—the Ladinos, the Garífunas, and Indians—in the Guatemalan ethnic mosaic, we can interweave diverse colors without introducing contradictions, without becoming grotesque or antagonistic. But we must make the cloth vivid and of a superior quality, just the way our weavers weave a *huipil* blouse, brilliantly harmonized, a gift to humanity.

Thank you very much.

Translated by Greg Grandin

The Pan-Maya Movement

Demetrio Cojtí Cuxil

Demetrio Cojtí Cuxil is one of Guatemala's most prolific scholars and activists. Born in the Kaqchikel town of Tecpán, Cojtí became politically involved in the 1970s, when he participated in national-level indigenous conferences, or seminars, organized by the Coordinadora Indígena Nacional, and wrote under a pseudonym for Ixim, an important monthly magazine published from 1977 to 1979 focusing on indigenous issues. In the early 1980s, he traveled to Belgium to complete a doctorate in communications, and he returned to teach at the University of San Carlos and Rafael Landívar University. He served as vice-minister of education during the administration of Alfonso Portillo (2000–2004). Below is an excerpt from his history of the Pan-Maya Movement, whose goal is to unite disparate Maya groups in a cultural revival.

The Maya movement seeks to defend the Maya in their quality as a people, in which they are the principal actor. . . . The Maya movement is holistic and generalized, and cannot be reduced to its political, social, cultural, or religious elements. . . . The Maya movement has the following characteristics:

It is Guatemalan. Considering that the Maya are a people without a state, made up of nationalities or ethnic groups without self-determination, the movement seeks to achieve degrees of autonomy for each nationality, and the highest grade of autonomy for all Maya, equal to the sovereignty that the Ladino enjoys. . . .

It is Mayanist. The essence of the movement in Guatemala is the Maya people or nation. It is a Mayanist movement because it is initiated in and for the self-affirmation and liberation of the Maya. . . .

It is anticolonial. The Maya movement opposes the theory and practice of the invasion and domination of one people over another. In that sense, it opposes the colonial oppression of all peoples of the world, and, in particular, opposes the oppression of indigenous *pueblos* of America. . . .

It is emancipating and liberating. The Maya movement opposes the doctrine and practice of the oppression and assimilation of the Maya peoples and nationalities, which comprise the two faces of current internal colonialism in Guatemala. . . .

It is defensive and protective. The Maya movement seeks to defend the Maya people and contests an existing state [that is] predicated on the elimination of Maya culture and a standardization of Ladino or mestizo culture. . . .

It is egalitarian. The movement's struggle for Maya rights, which do not contradict the national rights that Ladinos today enjoy, considers that both groups can coexist in equality. . . .

It is secular and democratic. The Maya movement is based on a loyalty to the nation or the ethnic group and not to any religious belief. It recognizes that Maya spirituality is part of its culture and a source of resistance. . . .

It is legalistic and respectful of human rights. The movement struggles for the national rights of the Maya people using legal and pacific means, within the framework of the laws and possibilities of the liberal state. . . .

It is multiclass and antiracist. The Maya movement seeks collaboration among different social sectors and strata; it ignores racial differences. The idea of social class or race is not a basis of the Maya movement. . . . Furthermore, the movement recognizes that pure races and biological differences do not exist. The movement is not class-based; it defends the interests of a people and not a socially determined class. . . .

With the exception of assimilated Mayas, the Maya people are Mayanist and anticolonialist, yet with different degrees of consciousness and forms of action. The illiterate Maya peasantry has much more cultural authenticity, and has the consciousness of a people *for itself.* . . . The Maya peasantry and proletariat incorporated into popular organizations (unions, peasant leagues, etc.) has a more developed consciousness as a class *for itself,* often combined with an indigenous consciousness *in itself.* This is because their organizations privilege social struggles over ethnic struggles. . . . Lower- and middle-class educated indigenous people, having passed through the Ladino school system, have less cultural authenticity [but] sustain a Mayanist or anticolonial discourse and want to have a more authentic Maya praxis. This group has progressively developed a consciousness of a people *for itself*—that is to say, it has become aware of its situation as a colonized community and a people, and it is beginning to organize in the cultural or political sphere in order to defend its national interests. . . .

The current Maya movement seeks to transform Guatemalan society into a multinational society and to construct mechanisms for the lasting coexistence of all the ethnic communities that make up the country and its two majority groups (Maya and Ladino). Guatemala should at least be

"500 years of indigenous, black, and popular resistance," Nahualá, Sololá, 1992. Photo by Juan Rolando González Díaz. From the collections of the Centro de Investigaciones Regionales de Mesoamérica, Guatemala.

a multinational state, binational in the sphere of Maya and Ladino peoples, and multiethnic in the sphere of ethnic communities and nationalities. This goal of a free and just ethnic order should reflect the combined interests of the Maya and Ladino people, which include the improvement of the social situation of the Maya people, the cultural autonomy of the various ethnic communities, and the relative political autonomy of the entire Maya people.

As such, the state needs to stop personifying Ladino nationhood and promoting only Ladino culture and values. The state should be both emotionally and formally neutral. . . .

Ethnic pluralism and political equality can be achieved by implementing a framework of shared power, with the following characteristics: participation of representatives of all the significant ethnic groups in the national government, along with a high degree of autonomy for each ethnic group; proportional distribution of the national budget; . . . and the right of veto granted to ethnic minorities. Pluralism and equality can be achieved with cultural autonomy for each ethnic community.

Translated by Greg Grandin

The Authorized Indian

Charles R. Hale

The ethics of "multiculturalism" can contest historically exclusive ideologies and institutions and can advance both political and cultural democratization. Yet the multicultural discourse can also be used to co-opt and divide indigenous movements, with institutional space ceded and some rights granted while other demands are ignored, silenced, or actively repressed. In Guatemala, this dichotomy is strikingly captured by the government's 2005 announcement that the Casa Crema—the building that formerly housed the Ministry of Defense—would be the new offices of the Maya Language Academy and would be the site of a new television studio to broadcast "programs on Maya culture, interculturalidad, *and spirituality." As anthropologist Charles R. Hale points out, this announcement was made even as the military had begun a violent eviction of rural Mayas from farms they had been occupying for three years.*

The dichotomy is also evident in a country where indigenous cultural rights are officially sanctioned while actual Indians starve. In some rural areas, children don't have enough food to prevent malnourishment, yet they have access to bilingual textbooks. World Bank reports documenting the ongoing economic misery of the Maya are now translated into indigenous languages (see, for example, the 2005 World Bank study Indigenous Peoples, Poverty and Human Development in Latin America, *which was made available in K'iche'). In the following essay, Hale discusses a new binary that defines indigenous identity in Guatemala—permitted/ proscribed—even as Maya activism has rendered the old Ladino/Indian divide no longer viable.*

During the 1990s, Dr. Demetrio Cojtí Cuxil gained a well-earned reputation as "Dean" of Maya studies in Guatemala. A prolific scholar and public intellectual, Cojtí deeply influenced the debate on Maya cultural and political rights. Many dominant culture Ladinos associated him with the most assertive of Maya demands that directly challenge their long-standing racial privilege. To express their anxieties about these challenges, they often distinguished between principles they endorsed, like the idea of cultural equality, and "extreme" Maya demands that they associated with violence and conflict. When asked to elaborate, they would often turn personal: "Ah, Demetrio Cojtí, for example—he is 100% radical."

In 1998, I talked with Cojtí about the contradictory mix of opportunity and refusal in the policies of the Arzú administration (1996–2000) toward the Maya, which he summarized succinctly: "Before, they just told us 'no.' Now, their response is '*sí, pero*' ['yes, but']." When Cojtí later accepted the post of Vice Minister of Education in the newly elected Portillo government, speculation reigned. Had he "sold out"? Was he out to test the limits of "*sí, pero*"? Gaining experience for a time when Mayas would control the state? Three years into the Portillo administration (2000–2004), I lunched with some Ladino schoolteachers, participants in the teachers' strike of 2003 against neoliberal downsizing. They scoffed when I remarked that, a few years earlier, they had described Cojtí as a radical: "He's part of the government now, even worse than the others."

Like Guatemala, nearly every other country in Latin America has recently been transformed by the rise of collective indigenous voices in national politics and by shifts in state ideology toward "multiculturalism." The latter, combined with aggressive neoliberal policies, forms part of an emergent mode of governance in the region. Far from opening spaces for generalized empowerment of indigenous peoples, these reforms tend to empower some while marginalizing the majority. . . .

In its mid- to late-20th-century heyday, the state ideology of *mestizaje* had the same dual quality of today's multiculturalism: in some respects egalitarian and in others regressive. . . . Although seeking assimilation, state ideologies of *mestizaje* also drew strength from the continued existence of the Indian Other. Sometimes temporal distance separated this Other from the ideal *mestizo* citizen, as with the celebrated Aztec past in Mexico. Elsewhere, this distance was spatial, as with the people of the Amazonian jungle lowlands, portrayed as inhabiting a world apart. Most often, these two dimensions merged, creating a powerful composite image of the racialized Other against which the *mestizo* ideal was defined. . . .

While this *mestizo* project remains strong, its power as an ideology of governance is slipping. For good reason, it has been the first object of indigenous resistance across the region. Policies of assimilation threaten ethnocide. Unitary citizenship precludes culturally specific collective rights. . ... Yet the decline of the *mestizo* ideology of governance results from other forces as well. Neoliberal democratization contradicts key precepts of the *mestizo* ideal. Downsizing the state devolves limited agency to civil society, the font of indigenous organization. The return to democracy—even the "guardian" or "low-intensity" variants predominant in the region—provides these organizations space for maneuver. Even aggressive economic reforms, which favor the interests of capital and sanctify the market, are compatible with some facets of indigenous cultural rights. The core of neoliberalism's cultural project is not radical individualism, but the creation of subjects who govern themselves in accordance with the logic of globalized capitalism. The pluralism implicit in this principle—subjects can be individuals, communities or ethnic groups—cuts against the grain of *mestizo* nationalism, and defuses the once-powerful distinction between the forward-looking *mestizo* and the backward Indian. Governance now takes place instead through the distinction—to echo a World Bank dictum—between good ethnicity, which builds social capital, and "dysfunctional" ethnicity, which incites conflict.

Explanations for the shift toward a "multicultural" public sphere in Latin America take two principal tacks. The first highlights the creative and audacious political agency of indigenous peoples. The second . . . emphasizes structural or institutional dimensions. . . . Although both explanatory tacks are valid, they miss the way neoliberalism also entails a cultural project, which contributes both to the rising prominence of indigenous voices and to the frustrating limits on their transformative aspirations. The essence of this cultural project, the desired outcome of the government's *"sí, pero,"* is captured in the figure of what Rosamel Millaman and I have called the *"indio permitido"* ("authorized Indian").

The phrase *"indio permitido"* names a sociopolitical category, not the characteristics of anyone in particular. We borrow the phrase from Bolivian sociologist Silvia Rivera Cusicanqui, who uttered it spontaneously, in exasperation, during a workshop on cultural rights and democratization in Latin America. We need a way, Rivera noted, to talk about how governments are using cultural rights to divide and domesticate indigenous movements. . . .

A reasonable starting point for exploring this new form of governance is the distinction between cultural rights and political-economic empowerment. Throughout Latin America, first-round concessions of newly christened "multicultural" states cluster in the area of cultural rights, the further removed from the core concerns of neoliberal capitalism the better. In Guatemala, government endorsement of the Academy of Maya Languages signaled the beginning of the multicultural era. Soon thereafter, the Minister of Culture and Sports has become known as the "Indian" cabinet post, filled by a Maya in the last two administrations. . . .

At times, the contrast between cultural and political-economic opportunity turns blatant and brutal. Newly inaugurated Guatemalan president Oscar Berger held a ceremony upon naming Rigoberta Menchú "Goodwill Ambassador," and turning over the Casa Crema (a building formerly assigned to the Ministry of Defense) to the Academy of Maya Languages. He announced that the Casa Crema would also house a new television show, " . . . to carry programs on Maya culture, *interculturalidad*, and spirituality." Simultaneously, Berger stood by as the Armed Forces began the violent eviction of landless indigenous *campesinos* that had occupied over 100 farms in the prior three years. . . .

Neoliberal multiculturalism is more inclined to draw conflicting parties into dialogue and negotiation than to preemptively slam the door. Civil society organizations have gained a seat at the table, and if well connected and well behaved, they are invited to an endless flow of workshops, spaces of political participation, and training sessions on conflict resolution. In Guatemala, the great wave of such government initiatives came just after the signing of the Peace Accords in December 1996. The country was soon awash in international aid, with Maya civil society as the privileged recipient. This example helps explain why the pattern is so widespread: indigenous rights are, in bureaucratic jargon, a "donor driven" priority. Web sites of the World Bank and Inter-American Development Bank are awash with glowing articles about indigenous and Afro-descendant empowerment. . . .

Once the cultural project of neoliberalism is specified, these limits become more evident. As a first principle, indigenous rights cannot violate the integrity of the productive regime, especially those sectors most closely linked to the globalized economy. If an indigenous community gains land rights and pulls these lands out of production, this poses no such threat, especially given the likelihood of the community's return to the fold through a newly negotiated relationship with the market. All the contrary if, for example, indigenous movements were to challenge the free-trade zones that shelter *maquila*-type production, declare a moratorium on international tourism or create their own banks to serve as the "first stop" for remittances from indigenous peoples working abroad. These latter demands would be sure to evoke the wrath of the neoliberal state. . . .

A second principle, also limiting the scope for possible change, has to do with the accumulation of political power. Neoliberal multiculturalism permits indigenous organization, as long as it does not amass enough power to call basic state prerogatives into question. These prerogatives are not about the state as the primary locus of social and economic policies, which now generally derive from the global arena. Nor do they revolve around the state's role as legitimate representative of the people, a dubious proposition for many. Rather, at issue is the inviolability of the state as the last stop guarantor of political order. . . .

With the *indio permitido* comes, inevitably, the construction of its undeserving, dysfunctional, Other—two very different ways to be Indian. The *indio permitido* has passed the test of modernity, substituted "protest" with "proposal," and learned to be both authentic and fully conversant with the dominant milieu. Its Other is unruly, vindictive and conflict prone. These latter traits trouble elites who have pledged allegiance to cultural equality, seeding fears about what empowerment of these Other Indians would portend. Governance proactively creates and rewards the *indio permitido*, while condemning its Other to the racialized spaces of poverty and social exclusion. Those who occupy the category of the *indio permitido* must prove they have risen above the racialized traits of their brethren by endorsing and reinforcing the divide. . . .

The point is not to lionize radicals or to place them beyond critique, but to challenge the dichotomy altogether, and thereby redefine the terms of indigenous struggle. A crucial facet of resistance, then, is re-articulation, which creates bridges between authorized and condemned ways of being Indian. . . . As globalized economic change continues, strategies of re-articulation can only become more difficult to achieve. Growing numbers of indigenous peoples are leaving rural communities for urban areas, where education, jobs and some hope of upward mobility can be found. Many continue northward to the United States. With few exceptions, the locus of economic dynamism has shifted from agriculture to activities such as *maquila* production, remittance-driven financial services, tourism and commerce. Rural Indian households are most likely to remain stuck in a cycle of critical poverty. Despite these rapidly changing demographic and economic conditions, indigenous leaders—increasingly urban and urbane—still draw heavily on the Utopian discourse of indigenous autonomy, exercised in quintessentially rural, culturally bounded spaces. This discourse can reinforce the ideology of the *indio permitido*, creating authorized spokespeople, increasingly out of touch with those whose interests they evoke. Re-articulation, in contrast, would build bridges among indigenous peoples in diverse structural locations: from rural dwellers, to workers in the new economies, to those who struggle from within the neoliberal establishment. To be effective, re-articulation will also need to draw on reconfigured political imaginaries, and on Utopian discourses of a different hue. . . .

Perhaps, then, Dr. Cojtí's strategy requires a second look and a more subtle reading. During the same visit to Guatemala in which I spoke with my teacher friends about their strike, I asked Cojtí about the inner workings of the Ministry of Education. He divided the overwhelmingly Ladino bureaucracy into three groups: hard-core racists and race progressives, both minorities; and an ambivalent majority that implemented the new "multi-cultural" mandate without conviction, as the path of least resistance. With ironic humor and characteristic cogency, he offered his own explanation for having taken the job: to carry out a critical ethnography of the "Ladino" state!

Transnationalism and Maya Dress

Irma Alicia Velásquez Nimatuj

Neoliberalism may allow for the acceptance of some forms of multiculturalism, as the preceding selection suggests. Yet in the essay below, anthropologist Irma Alicia Velásquez Nimatuj argues that the "transnationalization of capital" has actually deepened racism. The liberalization of economic relations has led to an intensification of poverty in some rural areas, driving peasants—many of them indigenous—off their land and into the city, where a good number of them become indigent. Yet the same liberalized economy has led to increased foreign investment in the tourist industry. Mayans, particularly Maya women, become esteemed objects of folklore—"Guatemala's biggest tourist attraction," Velásquez writes—even as real Maya suffer increasing poverty, which both reinforces and generates racism. Velásquez Nimatuj holds a doctorate in anthropology, writes a newspaper column, and is one of the country's most respected intellectuals, yet in 2002 she was refused entrance into a bar in a prosperous area of Guatemala City because she was wearing traje *(indigenous dress), an experience that prompted these reflections.*

June 5, 2002, promised to be like any other normal day, consisting of another round of work and meetings. At five in the morning I left home in Quetzaltenango for the capital with several Ladino and Maya friends to attend a meeting of the Agrarian Platform (Plataforma Agraria), which brings together farming and civil organizations and university institutions in support of farm workers' demands. Their aims include the drawing up of a state agricultural policy, something totally lacking in this essentially agricultural country. I had been working with them since returning to Guatemala in December 2001. . . .

After this presentation, a group of us decided to go to a restaurant to talk over the day's work. We were from different academic disciplines and different parts of the country. With the idea of having a beer together, we chose the popular El Tarro Dorado (The Golden Mug) tavern chain. We went to this tavern in the affluent neighborhood known as Zone 13. When I reached the door with four other women, a security guard in civilian

Mi segunda piel (My second skin) by Paula Nicho Cuméz, ca. 2004. Used by permission of the National Museum of the American Indian, Washington, DC, and Arte Maya Tz'utuhil.

clothes said politely to the other women: "This way, please." To me he said loudly: "But not you: women in *traje típico* [folkloric dress] aren't allowed in." As the only Maya woman there, I couldn't believe my ears. I asked the guard to repeat what he had said, and again looking straight at me he said: "The management refuses entry to women wearing *traje típico*, so I can't let you in." At this repetition of the racial discrimination directed at me for wearing K'iche' dress, a shiver ran through me from head to toe. I remember taking hold of my *perraje* (shawl) and wrapping it round my bosom, as if looking for strength to resist such racial discrimination in the 21st century. My eyes filled with tears; a wave of indignation but also anger and courage swept through me.

My four companions (two of them were lawyers) intervened, explaining that to refuse me entry because of my regional dress would be a violation of my human rights under domestic legislation and under international conventions ratified by Guatemala. These legal arguments aroused the attention of the second security guard, this one in uniform and carrying a heavy caliber automatic firearm. Both guards listened to the statement of the constitutional and international violations that were being committed. Both replied that the others, who were not wearing regional *traje* and therefore were not indigenous, could go in, but that management policy did not allow me in the restaurant [since wearing K'iche' *traje* identified me publicly as a Maya woman in a high-class district of the capital].

I interpreted this act of racial aggression as a violation of my human rights committed firstly by the restaurant owners, who form part of the small oligarchy that has controlled our country economically, politically and culturally for centuries. The racist and classist rules enforced by low-level employees like those security guards come from a pyramidal power structure at whose base are such employees, who simply obey orders from above.

And secondly, my rights were violated by the State of Guatemala itself for letting the Government Ministry allow the running of restaurants and shops where racial discrimination is part of a management policy implemented on a daily basis in leisure spaces of that kind.

The Wearing of Regional Dress as a Political Act: Part I

The particular act of racism that I had personally experienced made me reflect on what it means culturally, racially, socially and politically for the Maya women of Guatemala to wear our regional *traje* on a daily basis in the different parts of the country. Starting from this particular case—which reflects the everyday experience of racial discrimination that most Maya women in Guatemala face whenever we risk leaving our homes and towns to work, study or carry on any other activity—my own experience has enabled me to grasp the political dimensions of wearing different dress in a country that was founded on the basis of social exclusion enforced by racist structures. Whenever we are seen in regional *traje*, the ruling classes are reminded of the failure of their efforts to make us disappear, which have ranged from genocide to ideological coercion. Five centuries of humiliation have not succeeded in bringing the Maya people to their knees.

For the Maya, leaving our own communities means losing the cultural shield that protects us when we live and work in the towns or villages where we are usually in the majority and where we understand the logic of how life operates. But when, owing to economic necessity or for some other reason, we decide to leave our communities, we come up against the other Guatemala, "imaginary Guatemala," urban and capital-city Guatemala, where we are rejected by almost all the Ladinos who wield political and economic power.

The everyday racism faced by Maya women—those that refuse to give up regional dress—has invaded every area of our lives. We live it and feel it through discriminatory words and acts on city and rural buses, in public and private offices, in the streets, in restaurants, on university campuses, in public and private schools and colleges, in leisure areas and even in places of worship. So common are these human rights violations that many Maya women act as if they barely notice them: they take them as a normal part of the burden of contempt that goes with being an indigenous woman, and so they do not challenge them.

So I must stress that wearing our *trajes*—whether they be K'iche', Mam, Kaqchiquel, Tz'utujil, Pocomchí, Jakalteca or others—is not simply a matter of standing up for our cultural rights. For postwar Guatemala it has become a political challenge: that of breaking the various ideological, legal, colonial and contemporary racist structures that exist in all spheres of the Guatemalan State. Though they have evolved somewhat since 1997, these structures have not disappeared. Furthermore, the transnationalization of capital has in many respects strengthened these structures. They still reign supreme in the exclusive circles of the Guatemalan oligarchy and are present in all sections of the Ladino (non-Maya) and *mestizo* ("mixed-race") population, both middle-class and poor. It is they who maintain and often reinforce the various racial stereotypes, including the racist and sexist jokes about what Maya women have under their *corte* (skirt) or *huipil* (blouse), with reference to their sexual organs and the presence or absence of underwear. The investment of transnational capital in the tourism industry has led to a more extensive folklorization of Maya cultures and images of Maya women, and here too the Guatemalan state has played a key role in accommodating the needs of the tourism industry.

This particular violation made me think about the various forms of historical resistance that our ancestors, our grandmothers and mothers, have been putting up since 1524 A.D. . . . Associated with this historical resistance is the everyday resistance that we contemporary Maya women carry on in different forms and with a variety of instruments to challenge and face up to the constant acts of racial discrimination that we refuse to accept in spite of the constant but subtle pressures of "modernity" to give up our regional dress. Individual and collective acts of everyday resistance, such as legal battles in national and international courts, public denunciations made through the mass media, and the formation of political organizations of Maya women are some examples of how we challenge the system in which we live.

Transnational Capital and Folklorization versus
Social Reality of Maya People

The racial exclusion faced by Maya women who wear regional *traje* bears no relation to the "folkloric" use made of our diverse regional dresses and fabrics by the government and the Ladino elite to promote the tourism industry of our country abroad. Guatemalan embassies and consulates all over the world commonly display photographs, posters or paintings of indigenous girls and women in regional dress, all smiles and perfect silhouettes: native people are presented as Guatemala's biggest tourist attraction, belonging to the past yet living in the so-called modern world.

People from "Western" countries are supposed to be fascinated by places where "natives," "exotic savages" or "Indians" of past centuries can still be seen today. The policy is to show visitors a static and unchanging native culture, as if the indigenous peoples of Guatemala and elsewhere did not have an evolving culture that is constantly being renewed.

While the government collects taxes and the tourism industry profits from the display and sale of garments—such as the *huipil, corte, perraje* and the hair ribbon called *cinta*—woven by Maya men and women from different regions of Guatemala, Maya people never get any credit for their art and still less the fair price for creative work that artists obtain in "core" countries. Many Guatemalan restaurants and hotels of the exclusive districts of Guatemala City that serve visiting tourists and businessmen commonly have a display of textiles and also photos, posters, etc., that combine Maya faces (mostly female), regional costumes and landscapes with ancient pyramids. These images are important marketing tools for the tourism industry. While Maya culture is commodified in these images, they bear no relation whatsoever to the Maya men, women, children and elders who eke out a living in these exclusive districts, working as labourers or servants, selling woven fabrics, furniture or sweetmeats, or even begging. (Lately a sizeable number of indigenous people have taken up begging because Guatemala's complex realities forced them to leave their villages and go to the capital, where life operates differently and there is no place for them.)

In other words, Maya textiles are "folklorized," meaning that they are presented as something totally separate from the social, political and economic context in which they were made. As if economic pressure had no impact on the making of regional dress. As if the political effects or pressures on the regions concerned were not reflected in these garments. As if the civil war endured by the Maya people for 36 years did not modify, alter and even eliminate some elements of weaving in Maya communities, especially in areas where the war raged most fiercely. This folkloristic separation between the Maya weaver's art and the social context of the people who design and make the textiles has always been part of the policies of both the government and the dominant economic and political elite. However, new political economic pressures linked to neoliberal changes in the world economic system have aggravated this problem by making Guatemala more dependent on the investment of transnational capital in the tourism industry. Thus official state and economic elite policy at home and abroad has been to exploit Maya people through the "unequal exchange" of textiles that are bought cheap from local Maya producers and sold at high prices to tourists, and to folklorize Maya cultures through cultural representations of Maya cultures that ignore the complex economic, social and racial realities endured daily by some eight million Maya men and women that live in this small Central American country. . . .

The Wearing of Regional Dress as a Political Act: Part II

Also ignored is the struggle of an ever-increasing number of Maya women from different parts of Guatemala who have emigrated to the capital for various reasons and who in spite of all the racial pressures survive without giving up their regional *traje*. On the contrary, in the context of the Beauty Pageant, Maya women are simply seen to be proudly wearing a *huipil* from

their own community (or some other region). Many Maya women emigrated to the capital in the 1980s as the only way to escape the atrocities of
the Guatemalan army. Thousands had even been kidnapped by the army
to be used as sexual slaves or forced to prepare meals, wash clothes and
perform other tasks. In this way, thousands of Maya women once again
became displaced persons within their own country, often when still young
girls. These Maya women and their families took refuge in poor, working-
class areas of the capital, but typically did not give up regional dress, though
their *traje* underwent considerable changes because the women could no
longer weave as they had done in their own community.

Another reason for this migration was the extreme poverty of their communities, which forced them to emigrate in search of jobs. Most were employed as domestics in the houses of Ladino or mestizo city-dwellers and
many found work in assembly plants (*maquilas*) built at the end of the 1980s.
Today, hundreds of the workers in these assembly plants are Maya women
who come to work in regional *traje*, though a significant proportion have
been forced to adopt Western clothing.

Final Remarks

Maya textiles and regional dress carry many meanings: cultural symbolism, centuries of history, a changing and sometimes contradictory indigenous culture, respect for nature, and so on. But it is time to start recognizing that these same textiles also carry a history of racial, cultural, social
and economic exclusion that we Maya of Guatemala have endured but have
resisted for over 479 years. The textiles and regional dress are also a sign of
the historical and day-to-day resistance that Maya women have put up to
maintain and pass on their culture.

The Maya textiles of Guatemala cannot be understood if we do not realize that for Maya women, whether they are professionals or factory workers, wearing a *traje* in contemporary Guatemala means to challenge the
"imaginary Guatemala" that has been socially constructed by a small economic elite with power and control over the State. Within this imaginary
nation the only space for Maya people, textiles, and dress is as a folkloric
cultural representation, a marketing tool and a source of profit for local
and transnational capital. Here Maya cultures are reduced to a decoration
in public or private areas or as museum pieces, where they have some ambiguous historical value but are ultimately presented as static objects, their
main contribution to the country being to enrich the tourist industry. To-

day more than ever, many Maya women are aware that wearing regional *traje* in our country is not just a cultural right but also a bold political act that asserts the right of the Maya to self-determination.

Investment in the tourist industry can be practiced in ways that may benefit indigenous communities of Guatemala or other peripheral countries. For example, small-scale foreign or local investment in the tourism industry can be regulated by indigenous communities so that the profits made from tourism can benefit the communities where such tourism is located and in ways where the tourism industry does not harm the dignity of the Maya people or harm or privatize the biosphere. So far I have discussed how the indigenous communities of Guatemala have been negatively affected by the tourism industry, especially that controlled by national and transnational capital. However, many indigenous communities do not oppose the tourism industry entirely and some have in fact been able to secure a modest living as small business owners that cater to foreign tourists. Thus, the role of national and transnational capital in the tourist industry is complex and may have both negative and positive consequences. Oftentimes, however, the negative consequences are ignored. Furthermore, there are substantial differences between small and large-scale investment in the tourism industry and community or capitalist control of this industry.

The transnationalization of culture and capital is complex. On the one hand, it permits indigenous people to work in solidarity with other people and cultures around the world against racism, discrimination and exploitation. On the other hand, the transnationalization of culture and capital permits the folklorization of, and hence racial discrimination against, indigenous people. The forms that the political resistance of indigenous people assumes are also very complex and constantly changing. Maya people resist the folklorization of our culture at the same time that we assert our right to cultural difference.

The fight to be recognized as Maya people with full historical, cultural, political, legal, economic and social rights within our own country and abroad continues to be one of the principal challenges. Our fight as Maya women to bring down and transform the racist structures that prevent us from being accepted with our regional dress in various places continues to be a daily struggle. We need to resist the forces of the transnationalization of culture and capital at the same time that we need to take advantage of the new spaces of resistance that these forces create.

Just as I finished this article, I saw that on December 15, 2002, a Mam woman, Olimpia López, was refused entry by a discotheque in the city of Quetzaltenango because she was wearing the red *huipil* and black *corte* that identifies her as a Mam woman from San Marcos department. This is another violation of human rights and an insult to the dignity of Maya women and to the entire Maya people of Guatemala. It shows we still have a long way to go in achieving racial equality for our mothers, for ourselves and for our daughters. Let us hope for solidarity from other indigenous and non-indigenous women in the world who understand our complex reality and give real support to our fight for equality in the areas of race, class and gender inequalities.

Mayanization and Everyday Life

Santiago Bastos, Aura Cumes, and Leslie Lemus

For more than one hundred years, from the late nineteenth century to the late twentieth century, most political and intellectual leaders in Guatemala viewed the country's Maya majority through the lens of "Ladinization," a desired integration of indigenous populations into the dominant, nonindigenous culture. That vision of homogenization broke apart after the 1980s. State and international discourses of multiculturalism and the emergence of a Mayanist intellectual movement helped define a new national terrain for Guatemala as a pluri-ethnic country. Throughout the country, a confluence of changes brought new visibility to Maya political, economic, and cultural participation. These processes of "Mayanization" are perceived and experienced in varying ways. In 2008, a team of Guatemalan and international researchers completed a multiyear study on Mayanization and everyday life in Guatemala, studying how multiculturalism is received and reinterpreted by people who are not necessarily part of the formal Pan-Maya Movement. The case studies summarized here present a broad range of the lived experiences of "Mayanization" in contemporary Guatemala.

> Saying "Indian" is just a soft way of saying "*indio*," that one isn't anything. Really, this term is an insult . . . we are Mayas.—Leader of Grupo Bonampak, San Juan Sacatapéquez

> "We won't be known anymore as Indians, or poor people, or dark-skinned people; now we'll be known as Ch'orti'-speaking people."—Ch'orti' leader

San Juan Sacatapéquez, just outside of Guatemala City, has a history of direct ties to the development of the national Maya movement, and the national movement, in turn, has influenced politics and local organization in the municipality. A number of local organizations promote Maya culture, including Kaqchikel language education, Maya cosmovision, and political-religious organization. . . . Leaders demonstrate a strong degree of ethnic identification in line with the national Maya movement, although this identification is not univocal.

One of these local organizations is the Indigenous Association of San Juan Sacatapéquez, formed in 1965. During the 1960s and 1970s, this organization was part of a broad "indigenous pride" movement dedicated to promoting folkloric events such as theater, dances, music, and the election of indigenous beauty queens, especially in the town center, where urbanized indigenous families lived. Another organization is the San Juan Bautista Ecumenical Cooperative, a credit union started in the 1970s by a Catholic priest and a group of indigenous catechists from the town center. It originated as part of the cooperative movement of that period, with direct ties to the indigenous movement. The cooperative supports local Maya cultural events and donates funds to local Maya organizations. Its director and board of directors are Mayas from the urban town center, and the institution requires that its employees speak Kaqchikel and wear the *traje típico* [indigenous clothing] of the locality.

In 1980, Grupo Bonampak was born in San Juan Sacatapéquez ["Bonampak" refers to the ancient Maya temples and murals of southern Mexico; see part 1 of this volume]. Grupo Bonampak organizes Maya cultural events in the town center and surrounding villages, focusing on the election of the indigenous beauty queens. The group's leaders consider these activities a counterweight to the education system and media that emphasize Ladino culture; they also reject criticism of these activities as mere "folklore," countering that they are familiarizing young people with a more authentic vision of the culture of their ancestors. . . .

In Patzún, Chimaltenango, the work of Maya professionals to encourage Kaqchikel language education has come together in a community radio station called Sinakan Stereo. Sinakan Stereo proposes the recovery and promotion of Maya culture and identity. Radio programs include broadcasts on Maya mathematics, cultural values, oral history, and natural medicine; a program directed by local *ajq'ija'* [day-keepers] on Maya spirituality; live broadcasts of Maya ceremonies; and political themes such as indigenous rights, women's rights, municipal laws, and citizen responsibility.

In some of the poorest regions of the country, or areas where prior forms of community organization were crushed by military repression, the multicultural discourse has enabled indigenous communities to challenge local power relations, recover a sense of individual and collective self-esteem, and make specific demands for rights.

For instance, during the 1990s the Maya organization Majawil Q'ij and the Academy of Maya Languages went to work in the Ch'orti' region of eastern Guatemala (Caomotán, Jocotán, and Olopa in Chiquimula and La Unión in Zacapa). Ethnic shame was palatable among the inhabitants of the region. . . . The Ch'orti's were called (and they called themselves) "village people," or "peasants," in contrast to Ladinos, who called themselves "civilized," or "town people." The Ch'orti's felt vulnerable to the coercive presence of Ladinos in their towns, and discrimination ran the gamut from being humiliated by being called "*indio*" to having to sell their products below cost, all of which eroded their individual and collective self-confidence.

Majawil and the ALMG held seminars and training sessions to introduce the Pan-Maya Movement's proposals to local leaders. Later, an intensive campaign began to promote the learning of the Ch'orti' language in the region. Language recovery was popular, and it was a key ingredient in the process to gain confidence and ethnic self-esteem. For the first time in a long while, Ch'orti's from different villages came together, people who had not been in direct contact for many years. A revitalized Ch'orti' ethnic identity spilled over into new expressions of community organization that eventually helped local communities obtain economic aid for community development projects. Key to the Ch'orti's efforts was linking practical concerns over subsistence struggles with expressions of ethnic reaffirmation, all of which helped local Ch'orti's defend themselves publicly against the historic Ladino dominance in their region.

The village of Choatalúm, San Martín Jilotepeque, was one of the hardest hit by military repression during the armed conflict. In 2000, a few years after the signing of the peace accords, people from Choatalúm made contact with organizations that were working on the exhumation of mass graves, where massacre victims are buried. The exhumations became important symbolic spaces: they helped vindicate the dead and gave people a small bit of humanity and dignity back. Victims' committees were formed in Choatalúm, and a mental health project was started, mixed in with cultural programs based on Maya cosmovision. These programs accompanied the groups of victims and helped strengthen their organization. Until recently, the Choatalúm committees were self-identified merely as "indigenous" groups, and only village elders spoke Kaqchikel. But the work that was done around the exhumations, including the demand for psychological and social reparation, encouraged people to take up the idea of being "Maya." This helped make ethnic identity a source of pride and strength, and this, in turn, has helped strengthen other kinds of community organization.

In the municipality of Chisec, Alta Verapaz, another area hard hit by the repression, the Cancuén archaeological project began in 1999 in the lowland zone between Alta Verapaz and the Petén jungle. Archaeologists directing this project repeatedly used the term "Maya" to explain the goals of the excavation. Learning about the archaeological discoveries led residents from surrounding communities to reaffirm their own Maya ancestry, declaring, "we are the grandchildren of the Maya." They began to perform Maya ceremonies. Some of these ceremonies were of a religious or spiritual character, and others were more politicized. This activity encouraged local leaders to begin to demand that the organizers of the archaeology project pay more attention to local development needs, for example, by hiring local workers, helping to build roads and schools, and investing in projects of economic diversification.

Other expressions of ethnic pride are not necessarily linked to specific political demands but are taken up as part of everyday life, often leading to various forms of syncretism. In Comalapa, Chimaltenango, the town's patron saint festival combines elements of Catholic ritual with popular culture and Mayanist symbols and discourses. As part of the festival, during the election of the Rumi'al Q'a Tinamit [literally, "the daughter of our *pueblo*," or indigenous beauty queen], the contestants wear the robes of the local *cofradías* [Catholic-inspired religious brotherhoods] while espousing slogans such as: "Many years ago, they cut off our branches, but they could not destroy our roots, and we are still here practicing our culture" [this is an adaptation of a slogan used by the leftist Committee of Peasant Unity during the 1970s and 1980s; see part 5 of this volume]. Contestants then lip-sync popular music songs from the radio, on a stage set up in front of the atrium of the town's Catholic church. . . .

Syncretism also shapes how a younger generation experiences ethnic identity, as articulated by Marcos, a young Comalapa man. Marcos graduated from high school in Comalapa, but because of his family's precarious economic situation he migrated to Guatemala City to work. Marcos is a great fan of rock music, which he doesn't think runs counter to his evangelical faith. He even joined a fledgling rock band in the city made up of other indigenous youth. He says that for this group music is a way to get to know other cultures, to feel free, and to demonstrate the dynamism of the younger generation, even as they continue to self-identify as indigenous. Although he's not familiar with the Mayanist movement or organizations, Marcos thinks it's important for indigenous people to know their history and language. For his cohort, rocker attire such as bracelets and distinctive caps gives them a sense of national identity, but Marcos doesn't see any contradiction between being a rocker and being indigenous.

The Mayanist cultural movement is not without its critics. In San Juan Sacatapéquez, many indigenous merchants claim to be "proudly indigenous," yet at the same time they want to "overcome backwardness." Based on their own experience with racism and discrimination, these merchants express concern over being labeled as *"indio,"* "illiterate," "poor," "peasant," or "someone without education, intelligence or possibilities." Their children generally pursue technical or professional careers, and they worry about having a good job and economic security. Espousing a modernizing ideology is a way to break with the past, yet they are not trying to become Ladinos. They do not deny their indigenous culture and identity, but neither do they support the demands of the Mayanist movement, since, for them, *"lo maya"* (everything Maya) means glorifying the past and going back to a traumatic history of being *"indios atrasados"* or "backward Indians," something they want to leave firmly behind. For this group, discussions about ethnic relations are an obstacle, insofar as they detract from what they see as the more important issues of overcoming poverty and social inequality, and achieving "progress." Although, on one hand, they support the struggle against racism and discrimination, on the other hand they are not interested in "all this Maya stuff," by which they mean the recovery of a Maya cosmovision and specific cultural demands.

In other cases, indigenous identity has been strengthened in recent years on the margins of the Pan-Maya Movement. In San Bartolo Aguas Calientes, Totonicapán, a long-standing boundary dispute with neighboring Momostenango has fortified a sense of local identity that people express in terms of being *sanbartolenses* (residents of San Bartolo), or simply K'iche's, without necessarily identifying with Pan-Mayanism. In Jacaltenango, Huehuetenango, migration to the United States has risen exponentially in recent years. This has been accompanied by cultural programs of music and dance in both sending communities in Jacaltenango and receiving communities in Florida and elsewhere, reaffirming a particular Popti' identity that is now transnational.

Translated by Elizabeth Oglesby

Solidarity Is a Characteristic
of the Maya People

Dominga Vásquez, interviewed by

Simona Violetta Yagenova

In Sipacapa, a municipality in the department of San Marcos, residents have been carrying out a long campaign to prevent Vancouver, British Columbia–based Goldcorp from expanding an open-pit gold mine into their town's territory. Since beginning operations in the late 1990s with a $45 million loan from the World Bank, the mine has brought few jobs—two hundred among a local population of forty thousand—and much contamination, including high levels of cyanide (used to extract gold from rock) and heavy metals such as copper, aluminum, and manganese in water supplies. In response to the opening and operation of this mine, as well as others that foreign corporations have opened in recent years, indigenous communities have held a number of unofficial consultas, or community-based referendums, in which voters overwhelmingly have called for an end to mining operations. In all cases, the votes were declared illegal by Guatemala's Constitutional Court, but they indicate why much of the business community mobilized against the 1999 indigenous-rights constitutional referendum, which would have recognized local customary law—the basis on which many communities are mobilizing against outside corporations.

In December 2004, a protest took place in the municipality of Sololá, near Lake Atitlán, in response to rumors that the government had granted concessions to corporations to begin mining within the town's jurisdiction. Over the previous year, community activists, working in conjunction with national-level organizations such as Defensoría Indígena, had been in touch with indigenous activists elsewhere, including sipakapenses, who shared with them stories of violence and environmental contamination that accompanied mining operations in their communities. So when a truck loaded with heavy mining equipment on its way to Sipacapa passed through Sololá along the Pan-American Highway, community members impeded its passing, embargoing the vehicle and cargo for more than thirty days.

The protest took place through community organizations traditionally identified with local indigenous politics. Sololá is unique in that it still retains from colonial times an autonomous Municipalidad Indígena, an indigenous authority distinct from the "official" municipal office. It was this institution, through the leadership of the Alcaldesa Indígena (indigenous mayor), Dominga Vásquez, that mobilized opposition, holding multiple meetings to build consensus throughout Sololá's many villages. And the community framed its opposition to mining by invoking a number of articles from the International Labor Organization's Convention 169, which calls for the protection of indigenous rights and which Guatemala, as part of the peace process, ratified in the 1990s. The standoff, recounted by Vásquez below, ended when the government sent in two thousand police and three hundred heavily armed soldiers. In the ensuing confrontation, one protester was killed, and fourteen were injured.

In February 2004, the United Nations peace accord monitoring mission was still in Sololá, and they asked us about the mining licenses. We didn't know anything about it . . . so we began to look for more information. . . . Most of our information came from Q'eqchi' indigenous defense organizations in Izabal [a region of eastern Guatemala where mining conflicts have flared in recent years]. The Q'eqchi's came to give us a training session and told us about all the destruction caused by mining. They also had information from the Ministry of Energy and Mines about all the mining licenses granted nationally. So we sent a commission to the ministry. The human-rights office investigated, and Congress gave us a copy of the information, which said that mining exploration licenses had been granted for Sololá. . . .

This was our fear, and the truth is that it caused us a lot of fear because we realized that mining brought destruction, not benefits. So then we told people in the community. We also knew that several articles of Convention 169 of the International Labor Organization stipulate that we have the right to be consulted, and the government is obligated to consult us regarding how our resources are managed. People said: they haven't respected us, they have to respect us because we are the ones who live in these lands. We need our natural resources to be respected and protected since we live from these resources. We organized community meetings and drew up documents to ratify our opposition to mining exploration and exploitation.

People showed that they want to be present and that they are not afraid, and they're not going to tire out. We have to keep going, people said. . . .

With the problem of the cylinder [a piece of heavy equipment being trucked to San Marcos along the Pan-American Highway, which passes Sololá], we consulted with the communities, by way of the local develop-

Community members in Nentón, Huehuetenango, reject mining activities in their region during a local consultation, 2007. Photo by James Rodríguez. Used by permission of the photographer.

ment councils and the village mayors, to see what people thought about letting the cylinder pass through Sololá or not. A majority of people said they would not let it pass until the government granted a meeting or set up a dialogue, because we know perfectly well that here in Sololá there are mineral exploration licenses. People thought that if the cylinder were blocked, the government might give us an opportunity to negotiate and to ask what is going to happen with the mining licenses in Sololá. That's what people said in the town meetings. . . .

The government claims that we had planned the January 11 action, but nobody knew that the cylinder would pass by on that day. How did the population come together? The truth is, I can't say for sure, but in the communities there are ways to communicate quickly: calls go out on community radio stations or by phone or by using a loudspeaker. That's how the announcement went out that the cylinder was going to pass by. I think that's what happened.

Solidarity is a characteristic of the Maya people. Our cosmovision enables us to be in solidarity with another department [region], another people who are suffering or who face unfortunate circumstances. So, since solidarity is a special characteristic of the Maya people, well, no way did we want the cylinder to get to San Marcos. It was like we were living that situation [the war] again. I saw women crying bitterly because of what was happening. People had no arms to defend themselves against a combined government force. Many people started crying as we saw the wounded taken from La Cuchilla to the hospital. It was something so terrible, deplorable, twelve people gravely wounded, one young man who lost his index finger after a tear gas canister was thrown at him. . . .

We think that the peace accords, especially the accords on socioeconomic and agrarian conditions, establish that we have the right to organize, the right to petition, and to feel as if we are being taken into account. The peace accords are fundamental for us, but for the government it's as if they no longer matter, they're out of fashion. Convention 169 is an international treaty; it's been ratified by Guatemala. We think this law is far greater than the Constitution. The government should base its decisions on the Convention. Not consulting us is a complete violation of the Convention; they are not protecting, but destroying Mother Nature.

Since last year, the local indigenous mayor, the Defensoría Indígena [a nongovernmental organization that protects indigenous rights], the Departmental Council on Indigenous Peoples, and the Association for Communal Development and Environmental Clean-up have taken on the work of informing people, and currently there is a new council against mining, called Oxlajuk Ak'abal. . . . Our strategy is to join forces, and together with other indigenous authorities from other municipalities we are planning activities and actions.

We've never been protected against delinquency here. But a cylinder on its way to San Marcos was protected. That makes us feel really bad, really sad. We've never seen such a gigantic, monstrous thing. Our little children realize this—the image is seared into them—that a steel thing was protected and given more value than a life, as don Raúl Castro Bocel was gunned down by the police.

On behalf of the indigenous authorities, we roundly reject the intervention of transnational corporations in our territory. They have no business exploiting minerals that belong to the people of Guatemala. As this movement is strengthened, maybe we will be strong enough to put pressure on Congress. They should think about their people, the ones who voted for them and who put them in Congress. Laws should be discussed before they're passed, to make sure a majority of people approve, instead of just a small group deciding for everybody. I think this movement is going to get strong enough to increase pressure to respect our rights.

Translated by Elizabeth Oglesby

Back to Iximché

Third Continental Summit of Indigenous Nations and Pueblos of Abya Yala

With much of the agenda of the cultural Pan-Maya Movement unrealized, organizing energy has passed to more combative organizations, such as those fighting the Sipacapa mining project, discussed in the previous selection, or demanding land and labor rights. Many of these organizations have established important ties to indigenous movements in Bolivia and Ecuador, which have a longer history of fighting transnational capital. In March 2007, a number of Maya groups joined with indigenous peoples from throughout the Americas to hold a week-long Continental Summit of Indigenous Nations and Peoples of Abya Yala. Abya Yala, a Kuna term meaning "land in its full maturity," is often used by indigenous groups to refer to the entire hemisphere of the Americas. The 2007 summit was held in Iximché, Guatemala, the precolonial Kaqchikel capital and a symbolic site of past indigenous protest meetings (see part 5 of this volume). The gathering issued a declaration, reproduced below. The declaration fuses a language of ethnic and cultural rights with an invocation of social and economic struggles, including a struggle against neoliberalism and for food sovereignty, and it calls for an alliance with nonindigenous popular movements throughout the Americas.

We the children of the Indigenous Nations and Pueblos of the continent, self convened and gathered at the III Continental Summit of Indigenous Nations and Pueblos of Abya Yala realized in Iximché, Guatemala the days of Oxlajuj Aq'abal, thirteen powers of the Spirit of the Dawn (26th of March) to Kají Kej, four powers of the Spirit of the Deer (30th of March, 2007):

We hereby affirm the Declaration of Teotihuacán (Mexico, 2000), the Declaration of Kito (Ecuador, 2004) and ratify our millennial principles of complementarity, reciprocity and duality, as well as the struggle for our territories in order to preserve our Mother Nature and the autonomy and self-determination of our Indigenous Peoples. We announce the continental resurgence of the Pachacutic (the return) along with the closure of Oxlajuj

Baq'tun (long count of 5,200 years) and as we approach the door of the new Baq'tun, we journey together to make of Abya Yala a "land full of life."

We have survived centuries of colonization and now face the imposition of the policies of neoliberalism that perpetuates the dispossession and sacking of our territories, the domination of all of social space and ways of life of the Indigenous Peoples, causing the degradation of our Mother Nature as well as poverty and migration by way of the systematic intervention in the sovereignty of our Nations by transnational companies in complicity with the government states. In preparation to face and confront the challenges of the new times upon us, we now determine:

To commit to the process of alliance among our indigenous nations, and among our indigenous nations and the movements for social justice of the continent that would allow us to collectively confront the policies of neoliberalism and all forms of oppression.

To make accountable the government states for the ongoing dispossession of our territories and the extinction of the indigenous peoples of the continent, due to impunity for the transnational corporations and their genocidal practices. . . .

To ratify the ancestral and historical rights to our territories and the common resources of Mother Nature, reaffirming the inalienable character of these rights as being non-negotiable, unquantifiable, without impediment, and unrenounceable even to the cost of our lives. . . .

To consolidate the processes now in effect to strengthen the re-foundation of the government states and the construction of pluri-national states and pluri-cultural societies via Constituent Assemblies with direct representation of the Indigenous Pueblos and Nations.

To advance in the exercise of our right of autonomy and self-determination as Indigenous Peoples. . . . .

To ratify our rejection of the Free Trade Agreements that make vulnerable the sovereignty of our Pueblos. . . . .

To reaffirm our decision to defend the nutritional sovereignty and struggle against the transgenetic invasion. . . .

To ratify the struggle for the democratization of communication and the implementation of public policies. . . .

To alert the indigenous peoples regarding the policies of the Inter-American Development Bank, the World Bank and organizations of the like that penetrate our communities. . . .

For the well-being of the Indigenous Peoples, we now decide:

To demand of the international financial institutions and the government states the cancellation of policies that promote concessions for the

Maya priests perform a purifying ceremony at the archaeological site of Iximché to clean out "bad energy" following a visit by US president George W. Bush in March 2007. Photo by Moisés Castillo. Used by permission of the photographer.

extractive industries (mining, oil, forestry, natural gas and water) from our indigenous territories.

To condemn the policies of exclusion of President Bush and the government of the United States demonstrated in the act of construction of the wall along the border with Mexico while at the same time attempting to expropriate the common resources of our Mother Nature of all the peoples of Abya Yala by implementing expansionist plans and acts of war.

To condemn the intolerant attitude of the government states that do not recognize the rights of indigenous peoples. . . .

To condemn the imposter and terrorist democracies implemented by the neoliberal governments, which results in the militarization of our indigenous territories and the criminalization of our legitimate indigenous struggle and social justice movements. . . .

In order to enact these words and realize our dreams, from resistance to power:

We constitute ourselves as the Continental Coordinator of Indigenous Pueblos and Nations of Abya Yala, creating a permanent vehicle of linkage and interchange. . . .

In this process we delineated the following actions:

To fortify the organizational processes and struggle of the Indigenous

Peoples with the full participation of our women, children and young people.

To convene a Continental Summit of Indigenous Women of Abya Yala and a Continental Summit of the Children, Adolescents and Youth of the Indigenous Nations and Pueblos of Abya Yala.

To convoke a continental mobilization of Indigenous Peoples to save Mother Nature from the disasters caused by capitalism, manifested by global warming. . . .

To endorse the candidacy for the Nobel Peace Prize of our brother Evo Morales Ayma, President of Bolivia.

To demand the decriminalization of the coca leaf.

"We have dreamt our past and we remember our future."

Iximché, Guatemala, March 30, 2007.

IX

The Sixth Century

The Guatemalan artist Moisés Barrios greeted the year 2000 with a pictorial series called *The Future Will Not Be What It Was*. One sequence of painted images included a clock face riddled with bullet holes, a shirt stained with blood, a gun, and a grotesque Superman, surrounded by questions and statements such as: "Are guns basic necessities?" "Somber reflection: the future is the past's garbage" and "We have proof of progress: the progressive increase of violence." Clearly, Barrios is not optimistic.

As Guatemala enters the sixth century since the Spanish invasion, many things have changed. The defining dream of a socially just country—achieved through either reformist national capitalism, as represented by the 1944–1954 era, or a popular socialist revolution—has been, it seems, definitively laid to rest. There are Guatemalans today who have never heard of Jacobo Arbenz, much less his land reform. For many, the ensuing civil war has become a receding memory. The underfunded national San Carlos University, once a center of critical humanist thought, has become staid and conformist, supplanted by private universities promoting either neoliberal economics or technical careers. Robust calls for class solidarity and an end to exploitation have given way to more acceptable demands for "citizenship rights" and "inclusion"—though in a country as hierarchical as Guatemala remains, even these more modest claims can still be deemed a threat. Generally dismal electoral campaigns have replaced popular protest.

Policies promoting industrial development have given way to a desperate race to attract low-wage *maquila* factories, which assemble textiles or electronics primarily for the external market. Under the auspices of the Central American Free Trade Agreement, the rapid spread of mining, hydroelectric, biofuel, and petroleum operations wreak havoc on local ecosystems, poisoning land and water, while the opening of national markets to us agroindustry destroys local economies, wiping out many smallholding farmers. Coffee at least provided some employment, however seasonal and low-paying. But the cultivation of African palm—Guatemala's new boom crop, used to make ethanol—needs little labor. It has also become a prime agent of tropical deforestation, pushing deep into the Petén and Ixcán.

Violence has changed, as Barrios suggests: it has gotten worse. Crime permeates every nook of life, and murder has become commonplace. In a population of about fifteen million, about six thousand people are murdered every year. Yet Guatemala has only a single-digit prosecution rate for murder, reflecting impunity's grip. Repression is a central part of the drug and arms trafficking that have joined export agriculture and *maquila* work as mainstays of the economy. The main achievement of Plan Colombia, Washington's counterinsurgent and antinarcotics initiative in the Andes— which has lasted nearly twenty years and has cost billions of dollars—is the disruption of aerial smuggling networks. But this effort has done nothing to limit either Colombian supply of cocaine or US demand for it, thus creating an opportunity for Central American and Mexican organizations to step in and assume control of the overland transport of the product. As a result, violence associated with the drug trade has skyrocketed, completely reversing whatever fragile gains the peace process had made in strengthening Guatemala's political institutions. In 2010, for example, large parts of the department of Alta Verapaz, including the once-sleepy town of Cobán, were taken over by the Zetas, a Mexican criminal organization famous for beheading its enemies. The Zetas were founded, in part, by ex-members of the Kaibiles, a ruthless Guatemalan special forces military unit trained by the United States during the Cold War. Squeezed by Plan Colombia to the south and Mexico's equally disastrous war on drugs to the north, other regions in Guatemala and in neighboring Honduras have likewise been either overrun by narcos or militarized by security forces, which are themselves deeply involved in criminal activity.

The Guatemalan state remains the property of a wealthy minority. The dream of counterinsurgent theorists such as General Héctor Gramajo (see "Inverting Clausewitz," part 6)—that the army would manage a postwar national project—has given way to a state described by social scientists as "captive" to organized crime syndicates, which include scions of the established oligarchy, *arriviste* economic elites, members of the military, and corrupt political parties. (Gramajo himself is gone, killed in 2004 by a swarm of bees on his southern coast plantation.) Without the unifying power of anticommunism, what used to be a centralized paramilitary apparatus has fragmented into competing minicartels involved in car thefts, bus robberies, illegal logging, and arms and drug running. The presence of youth organized in the transregional gangs Mara Salvatrucha and Mara 18 is real and disturbing, but these juvenile delinquents from impoverished neighborhoods have become the scapegoat for the adult violence and corruption that proceed on a vast scale.

Many rural areas are witnessing a revival of death-squad repression, now carried out by private (and legal) security firms targeting community activists who are protesting the intensification of mining operations and the creation of biofuels plantations. In March 2011, for instance, in the Q'eqchi' town of Panzós—where a 1978 massacre marked a turning point in the country's civil war (see part 5)—security forces violently evicted thousands of Maya peasant families opposing the efforts of Carlos Widmann, brother-in-law of recent Guatemalan president Oscar Berger, to plant sugar and African palm on corn land. The evicted peasants futilely begged to be allowed to harvest some of their crops. During the eviction, at least one person was killed, many were wounded, and others were arrested; and as of this writing, thousands are still living in makeshift shelters on the side of the road. Widmann's enterprise is capitalized by the Central American Bank for Economic Integration as part of the larger multilateral lending that supports the production of biofuels to be sold in the United States. A month prior to the eviction, the bullet-ridden bodies of four Q'eqchi' Maya community leaders—Catalina Muca Maas, Alberto Coc Cal, Amilcar Choc, and Sebastian Xuc Coc—were found in a nearby river.

What options do Guatemalans have for something better? Many have become evangelical Christians—not all of them to escape the corruption of politics, as some have argued, but to redeem politics, as pastor Harold Caballeros of Shaddai Church believes possible. A minority of young men and women join gangs; others migrate. Trying to get to the United States has become the new dream—which, for some, turns into a nightmare of death in the deserts of the US borderlands. Human-rights organizations estimate that eight out of ten women migrants are raped at some point in the journey. Many migrants survive the trip, of course; they find jobs and send money home to support families and sometimes whole communities. Remittances increased dramatically starting around 2001, hitting $4 billion annually in 2007. This is more than any other source of foreign-exchange revenue for Guatemala and far more than any source of foreign aid; in fact, the Inter-American Development Bank calls remittances "Central America's most important poverty alleviation program." But since the 2008 economic crisis, the amount of money sent back to Guatemala fell by about 10 percent, with UNICEF reporting that some families have had to take their children out of school as a result.

Throughout the United States, from San Diego and Tucson to Milwaukee, Wisconsin, Indiantown, Florida, and Lynn, Massachusetts, Guatemalans and other Latin Americans are changing the demographics and politics of the country. By 2025, nearly one in three children in the United States will be Latino, many of them first-generation children of migrants. Although the small numbers who join gangs receive publicity, other immigrants breathe new life into the labor movement, in places like Las Vegas, Los Angeles, and, as one selection in this part describes, North Carolina. Many of these new-comers try to keep alive the traditions they valued back home. In 2008, in New Bedford, Massachusetts, the Organization Maya K'iche' held a prayer ceremony around a fire pit on the Mashpee Wampanoag Tribal Council grounds, burning incense and offering chocolate and alcohol in gratitude for the year's blessings, which included free legal counsel following an im-migration raid. As do other undocumented workers, all Guatemalans in the United States without a proper visa live in fear of being caught up in the cogs of the increasingly punitive security state—hostile local governments, aggressive Immigration and Customs Enforcement Agents, privatized de-tention centers, and intimidating courts—of the post-9/11 United States.

Much has not changed in Guatemala. The vast majority of Guatema-lans are still poor, and the land-tenure system remains extremely unequal, even though many Guatemalans depend on land in one way or another. Foreign capitalists still seek Guatemalan resources. But hope perseveres. In the sixth century, neighbors continue to join together to make life a bit more bearable. Indigenous activists, feminists, gay-rights advocates, envi-ronmentalists, peasants, and trade unionists organize as best they can. Pro-gressive human-rights activists try to bring those responsible for the terror of the 1980s to justice. Rural peoples continue to claim land and demand control over natural resources. However isolated and constricted their room to maneuver, committed intellectuals and students strive to provide trenchant analysis and offer alternative programs of humane, sustainable development.

In this sixth century, all that is certain about Guatemala's future is that it is Guatemalans who will live it out; one only hopes that it is they who decide how.

A Modern Faith

Julio Zadik

The following photographs were taken by Julio Zadik (1916–2002). He received some renown in the middle of the twentieth century—he was invited to exhibit at the Pan American Union in Washington in 1949, and through his work with his family's lithograph business he became friends with some of Guatemala's most distinguished artists and writers—but his work largely had been forgotten by the time of his death. Yet through all the turmoil and tragedy documented in the preceding chapters, he continued to produce a remarkable corpus, capturing everyday life with a profound sympathy and grace. He left a legacy of tens of thousands of images, whose "rediscovery" upon his death is leading to a revision in the way scholars think about Latin American modernism.

Zadik practiced photography—his "hobby," as he called it—quietly and meticulously, day after day, month after month, decade after decade. The art historian most responsible for Zadik's current renaissance, Valia Garzón, writes that Zadik used a "systematic method in an artistic-visual world quest, anchored in a modern faith that an efficient survey of the 'appearance' of things—such as that provided by art—yields possible access to their 'essence.'" Zadik's "concern for form, for the fragment and the detail, brings him, in one direction, to photographic abstraction, and, to another, to the study of small natural elements, and even to the miniscule: leaves, flowers, and insects."

Sin título (Untitled),
1937. Photo by Julio
Zadik. Used by permis-
sion of the Julio Zadik
Estate.

(left) Michatoya 3 Mayo,
1958. Photo by Julio
Zadik. Used by permis-
sion of the Julio Zadik
Estate.

Social Campaign,
c. 1944. Photo by Julio
Zadik. Used by permis-
sion of the Julio Zadik
Estate.

(left) Izote, 1950. Photo
by Julio Zadik. Used
by permission of the
Julio Zadik Estate.

Spiritual Warfare

Harold Caballeros

In Guatemala, the catastrophe of the 1976 earthquake in the context of a civil war spurred a rapid spread of Protestantism, particularly Pentecostalism, a charismatic renewal movement that believes in the active involvement of the Holy Spirit in everyday life. Perhaps more than in any other Latin American country, the spread of evangelical Protestantism in Guatemala was closely linked to counterinsurgency. After losing Nicaragua to a revolution infused by radical Christian ideals of social justice, an emerging transnational religious right decided to draw a line in the sand in Guatemala. In this new crusade, politics trumped theological differences. Evangelicals would still think of Catholics as heathens—Pastor Hector Caballero's speech below discusses Christians as distinct from Catholics—but they would join in common cause with ultraconservative Catholic organizations, such as Opus Dei, to launch a religious counterrevolution against the kind of Christian humanism that drove much of the Guatemalan left.

The country's most infamous evangelical was General José Efraín Ríos Montt, a former Christian Democrat Catholic turned Pentecostal, who seized power in 1982 and executed the worst phase of the genocide described in part 6 of this volume. Ríos Montt was closely allied with evangelicals in the United States who supported Ronald Reagan's agenda to roll back the left in Central America. US televangelist Pat Robertson used his vast media empire to defend Ríos Montt against charges of crimes against humanity and organized "Operation Love Lift," raising much of the "humanitarian aid" that the Guatemalan army used to pacify the countryside. Evangelicalism continues to attract new converts. In a world shattered by political terror, with the Catholic Church's political project—both Christian-democratic reformism and liberation-theological militancy—defeated, an increasing number of the country's poor find solace in a church that emphasizes moral certainty and personal responsibility.

Many of Guatemala's Pentecostal leaders are self-consciously political; they see themselves as redeemers not just of souls but of nations. Harold Caballeros is pastor of the popular El Shaddai Ministries and a recent presidential candidate in Guatemala. Caballeros has emerged as a major international figure in the "New

Apostolic" evangelical movement, comfortably combining End Times millenarianism with the optimistic modernism of self-help talk. Caballeros was ordained in the ministry by Houston preacher John Osteen, father of bestselling preacher Joel Osteen, whose "prosperity gospel" is criticized by more conservative evangelicals for emphasizing self-affirmation at the expense of scripture. Despite this eclecticism, Caballeros, like many Pentecostal leaders, reveals a coherent worldview, one that provides a moral justification for free-market capitalism. Whereas Liberation Theology drew on Karl Marx to reveal the social and political causes of poverty, evangelicals like Caballeros update Max Weber to argue that culture, values, and religion are central to instilling the self-discipline and restraint needed to propel both individuals and nations out of misery.

Weber's rationalism is only one pillar of the New Apostolic movement, however. For many New Apostolics, the evangelization of the world takes place on multiple levels, beginning with the supernatural: "spiritual warfare" can save individuals, communities, and nations from the demons that cause social ills. Once these malignant "territorial spirits" are expunged, "delivered" Christians can complete the merger of church and state and the fulfillment of God's kingdom. As an example of spiritual warfare, Caballeros describes the redemption of the K'iche' town of Almolonga. After Pentecostals drove out the town's demons—in the form of a Catholic cult of Maximón, or San Simón—Almolonga was transformed from a community afflicted by "poverty, alcoholism, violence, ignorance, witchcraft, occultism, and idolatry" (as Transformaciones, *an evangelical documentary, described the community) into one of the richest agricultural towns in Guatemala, producing "God's vegetables," as they are known because of their enormous size. In this selection, Caballeros discusses the history of his church and his vision for Guatemala.*

In 1976, February 4, Guatemala experienced a terrible tragedy, an earthquake that killed 27,000 people in three minutes. It was a terrible situation, and our conclusion today is that the eyes and the hearts of the people went up to the Lord in that terrible day. Because Pentecostalism had been present for 95 years in Guatemala, and the percentage had not gone higher than 1.2 percent of the population. But then right after that earthquake something happened, and now in 30 years Guatemala has gone from 1.2 percent Christians in the population to 40 percent today, an amazing growth curve that now puts Guatemala along the line of South Korea in the number of conversions. . . .

In 1979, the first day of December in 1979, a Saturday, I received the Lord Jesus Christ in my heart. I had finished my law degree; graduation was two or three days ahead of me when I met [my wife] Cecilia, and Cecilia introduced me to the Lord, and that's how I got my experience, my personal experience with Jesus Christ, and that's how I was born again. After being raised in a Catholic family, having attended a Jesuit school, I was born again in 1979. The next Saturday I was baptized in water, and two Saturdays afterwards I received the baptism of the Holy Spirit, becoming a Pentecostal. A tongue-speaking, born-again believer. . . .

My born-again experience was marked by those words of prophecy. We started the ministry, we came to Houston, and we were ordained in the wonderful Lakewood Church by Pastor John Osteen and we came back to Guatemala to start our church called El Shaddai. . . . We started this church with very little experience, very little understanding, but with a lot of enthusiasm, and a vision, a very strong vision. . . .

I took hold of that vision and went back home and understood in my heart that prayer was the key to victory. Prayer was the key to revival. Prayer was the key to obtaining this trilogy: revival, reform, restoration of society. I wanted that. I wanted it so bad for my country. I thought prayer was the end, prayer was the objective. Prayer is it, I used to say. Along with prayer I learned about intercession. We became very sophisticated, we learned about prophetic intercession. We learned about spiritual warfare. We learned about spiritual mapping, and so on and so forth. It was very exciting. The decade of the 90s was like an open veil for us. We expected to achieve victory because we had gotten hold of the key, prayer. . . . In 1998, we celebrated a congress, a world congress in Guatemala where 6,000 or 7,000 people attended; 1,200 of them came from more than 110 nations. It was very exciting. . . .

At the very same time, we were promoting a laboratory case, an amazing case, a supernatural case called Almolonga. Almolonga is a very small city in Guatemala, 16,000–17,000 people. It was a very poor city with two main problems, poverty and alcoholism. Not only those, but idolatry and the temple of a particular entity called Maximón located in the center of town. This Maximón entity was an idol that was worshipped since nobody can remember. But then one day, the Holy Spirit comes, Pentecostalism shows up in Almolonga, and the pastors start to pray. One of them receives two cassette tapes and hears for the very first time about the ministry of deliverance. Casting out devils, he says? What is that?

Two, three, four nights afterwards, a woman comes to church and says, pastor, look at me. She was all bruised. Her husband had hit her again. And she says, can you come and pray for my husband? The pastor says, I will not go and pray for your husband because he's very dangerous. She says, my husband is totally drunk and asleep. Asleep? I will go and pray, he says. He comes to pray for the man, and at the very second of laying hands and praying, the man wakes up, and with a very strange voice says "I am Maximón." The pastor had about two seconds to rewind the two cassette tapes, and started to deal with the demon in the name of Jesus. Half an hour later, this man was totally delivered, and the faith of this pastor had grown tremendously, and the man was absolutely saved. He received the Lord Jesus Christ. The next Saturday he came for baptism, and very soon he came to the pastor's house and said, can you tell me what happened to me? The pastor explained the best he could, because he really didn't know much. He explains the best he can, and the man says, you know why I'm asking? Because I have many friends who are now like I was a week ago. Can I bring them? One by one, they started to be delivered, saved.

In a town of 16,000 or 17,000, news traveled really fast. The other pastors came and asked, what's happening? He didn't know much. He couldn't explain the theology behind it. He really didn't know how to explain. So he says, I guess the best thing we can do is to invite the preacher who preached in these two tapes. So they brought these preachers from El Calvario, the church I told you about. This happened in 1972. They invited these preachers, and between 600 and 700 people were delivered that weekend. After that, a revival started in Almolonga. The priests of the temple of Maximón noticed and said, what's happening? We are losing power. Eventually, they left town. They left the territory, and Almolonga passed from being one of the very poorest cities in Guatemala to become today one of the most fertile valleys in the country, producing these amazing carrots that you might have seen [holds his hands up about 18 inches apart to demonstrate the purported size of the carrots]. I should have brought a couple because nobody believes until they see them. And Almolonga became a model of transformation. What prayer can do for a city is more than what we used to think in terms of only conversion.

Transformation is more than converts. Transformation means something else. At the very same time we were facing problems that we are still facing today, with violence and crime and poverty and other social maladies that made us think. And we came to a conclusion. And we said, conversion is not enough. This is where we learned the principle of numbers are not enough. We are missing something. We use a word to understand this, and the word of course is discipleship. God never called us to make converts; he called us to make disciples. . . .

In 2000, the Apostolic Council was established in Guatemala with some apostles, and it has certainly marked a change, a difference in our society. Then we came to 1 Thessalonians 5:13 and understood that spirit, soul and body does not apply only to a person but also to a society, or a commu-

San Pedro Sacatepéquez, San Marcos. Evangelical Christians praying in the home of a woman whose house collapsed and who lost several of her children in a mudslide.

nity, or a city, or a nation. Spirit, soul and body led us to understand that the powers in the spirit realm influence or develop a particular culture, an idiosyncrasy that then determines the state of society, in the form of a worldview, in the form of a mindset, in the form of a mentality or in the form of a culture. That's when we came to the point of starting to understand Matthew 28 and the concept of discipling nations. A concept like culture matters, and I'm thinking of course about Larry Harrison and the Anglo-Protestant culture and now I'm thinking about Samuel Huntington [see Lawrence E. Harrison and Samuel P. Huntington, *Culture Matters: How Values Shape Human Progress* (2001)]. . . . Wonderful people I have had the privilege of meeting and working with. And then the hero: Max Weber. And the idea that Protestantism can make a difference in a country that is so hurt by social maladies, like my country has been for the last forty or fifty years, 36 years of civil war.

If we start to think about the city of sin, I can call it like that, and we start to think about Cain and then Nero, we will eventually see that the Bible speaks about the Great Babylon. But then there's a second city that I call the City of God, as St. Augustine did, and we think about the city of Abel or you can call it the one of Abraham or Moses, or David or Jesus Christ. And we will end up having a wonderful city called the New Jerusalem. When we think about those two cities, when we think about a city, we think about a structure that is created or consists of systems. We cannot think about a city and only think about buildings, and bridges and rivers and highways. We have to think about systems, economic systems, financial systems, legal systems, and so on and so forth. . . . Isn't it a paradox that Brazil and Argentina and Mexico are probably the richest countries in the world but at the very same time they have some of the poorest people in the world? Isn't it amazing that Guatemala has such a fertile soil that can actually feed the whole of Central America, but our people are dying because of hunger? I mean there is something that is not working right.

When we think about systems, we have to think about righteous and non-righteous systems, distorted situations, distorted by sin. Then we come to understand a little more about the new wineskin versus the old, and I come to realize that it is basically a difference in the emphasis on scripture. The old wineskin in Guatemala, I'm talking about the 1970s and the 1980s, probably the early 1990s. The emphasis was made on the leaven of the world, leaven understood as it has been in the Bible always as something which is dirty because it pollutes, because it ferments, because it is something that is mundane and worldly. Society was not Christian and was identified with the world and the world is under the Evil One. It's dirty, it's worldly, it's mundane. What was the church's answer to that? The church's answer was to build up walls of separation to prevent pollution, to prevent, and this was the most widely used word, contamination. Do not hear the music of the world or you will be contaminated. Do not watch the movies of the world, do not go to the university of the world, do not visit people who are worldly and so on and so forth. . . . So we became something totally separate from society and we became totally self-centered, very liturgic, experts in all facets of liturgy, wonderful praise, wonderful worship, wonderful preaching, wonderful ministry inside the walls of the church. That happened in my nation. The walls of separation were higher and higher, thicker and thicker. The church became self-centered and liturgy-oriented. . . . Our eschatology determined our social theory, and the result was a separation. We abdicated our responsibility to society.

In the new wineskin, the concept of leaven is redeemed by Jesus Christ in Matthew 13:33 when he says, "The Kingdom of Heaven is like leaven." . . . All of a sudden we began to emphasize a different scripture. We are the salt of the earth and the light of the world. We have to go out to society. . . . In those days we were afraid of them contaminating us. All of a sudden now we are not afraid anymore; we want what we have inside to come unto them. We stop being only salt, preserving, preventing corruption, and we become light, invading fearlessly the darkness. This brings us to a level of engagement with society, and engaging society demands answers. What we call just, fair or righteous systems must come from God's wisdom, from his word, or words, like a prophetic word. . . . there is not a single square inch in the universe over which Jesus Christ does not claim sovereignty, saying mine, mine, mine. The whole world is awaiting this engagement.

Now, the Guatemalan church faces a challenge: to go back and reconquer lost spaces, in education, in schools and universities, in the media, TV, radio, the newspapers, social action, and, of course, politics. Taking the normativity that we find in the Old Testament, enriched by the experience of the New Testament, to create those principles and values that must dictate morals and eventually be translated into public policy. An articulation of these principles is the challenge that Guatemala faces today.

I want to finish by asking a question. What is the future challenge of Pentecostalism in Guatemala? As I understand it, the challenge is the articulation of a national vision. To have a national identity . . . for this great nation of America. A Manifest Destiny, a City Upon a Hill. Pentecostalism in Guatemala has now the challenge of discipling the nation through a Christian biblical worldview. . . . In order to permeate society, to reach that point expressed in Jeremiah 29:11, where he says, "'For I know the plans I have for you,' says the Lord. 'They are plans for good and not for disaster, to give you a future and a hope.'"

God's Pristine Sound

Meyer Sound Laboratories

The spread of evangelicalism has transformed the Guatemalan landscape. Every small town now has numerous evangelical churches, while its capital and provincial cities are home to megachurches, along with more modest Pentecostal halls. Evangelicalism's rise has also changed the country's soundscape. Not too long ago, the quiet of early Sunday mornings, both in the countryside and in urban barrios, was interrupted by the persistent yet gentle ringing of Catholic parish church bells. Today, one is likely to be rousted out of bed by raucous evangelical sermons and amplified religious music. The following selection—a press release issued by the Meyer Sound Laboratories corporation—documents the installation of a cutting-edge sound system in Guatemala City's MegaFráter—the largest building in Central America and the biggest Christian church in all of Latin America.

Guatemala's Fraternidad Cristiana de Guatemala (also known as Mega-Fráter) is the largest Christian church in Latin America. Measuring a stunning 1.217 million square feet, this massive structure includes a school, restaurant, swimming pool, full television and radio production facilities, a heliport atop an eight-story parking garage, a 12,500-seat theater in their main sanctuary, a stage larger than most major concert venues, and much more.

To find a powerful sound system capable of delivering even coverage for spoken word and live music material in the expansive room, MegaFráter turned to Guatemala City–based Pro Sound. After thorough considerations by a committee which included the church's senior pastor, Jorge Lopez, a self-powered system based on Meyer Sound's MILO® line array loudspeaker was chosen. "For me, the biggest priority for our sound system is intelligibility," says Lopez. "It's not just about the volume or output of the music. People come here to be moved by the word of God. We need the best audio solution which allows our audience to enjoy every facet of our services."

The installed system is comprised of four clusters of nine MILO line array loudspeakers and one MILO 120, along with eight M3D-Sub directional subwoofers flown for low frequency content. Six MID line array loudspeakers and 12 UPM-IP loudspeakers provide fill at the front and under the balcony. The Meyer Sound Galileo loudspeaker management system with two Galileo 616 units handles drive and processing. "Given the size and layout of the main theater, we knew that four clusters would be the best design to reach all points in the auditorium evenly," explains Melvin Chuy, President of Pro Sound, who handled the sound system design with the company's Pablo Hernandez "El Chino" and Miguel Chuy. "When we played around with MAPP Online ProT [acoustical prediction program], we tested several different cabinets, and found the MILO to be the best option. Its response, power, coverage area, and especially its intelligibility were all astounding."

Melvin Chuy is delighted with the customer service and technical assistance from Meyer Sound staff in Berkeley and Mexico throughout the installation process. "We had amazing support from Meyer," adds Melvin Chuy. "Its engineers came and helped us with measurements and various details. They also provided training to the in-house engineers to help them learn the new system."

The end result is pristine sound for MegaFráter's services and a reliable audio system that the crew can depend on. "As a church, we couldn't be more satisfied with MegaFráter's level of audio," says Lopez. "And for the musicians on stage, it's like a dream come true." Already the largest church in all of Latin America, the congregation continues to grow and set new standards for technology in houses of worship around the world.

The New Face of Labor and Capital

Corey Mattson and Marie Ayer

Guatemalan industrial development, based on the production of consumer goods for the domestic market, boomed from the 1950s until the middle of the 1970s. Things changed in the 1980s, when many of these old factories shut down and new ones that produced exclusively for the external market opened. Known as maquilas, *or assembly plants, they were owned by foreigners, most often South Koreans, and were staffed by primarily young single women and teenagers who received extremely low pay to sew together cut-to-pattern cloth into blue jeans and shirts for brand-name companies such as Liz Claiborne and Van Heusen. By 2004, the* maquila *sector employed 108,000 workers in 225 textile factories on the outskirts of Guatemala City and in nearby towns such as San Juan Sacatepéquez, Villa Nueva, and Chimaltenango. Protected by barbed-wire fences and guard posts,* maquilas *seem more like penitentiaries than factories. For young people entering the labor market who do not want to work in agriculture, a job at a* maquila *is one of the few options available to them, short of emigration. The work is hard, and organizing efforts have met with resistance, as the following article by Corey Mattson and Marie Ayer reveals. The authors are volunteers at the* US-based organization STITCH, *a labor-rights organization active in uniting Central American and* US *women to exchange strategies on how to confront workplace injustices.*

The use of the word *maquila* in Central America originates from the Arabic word *makila*, which referred to the amount of flour retained by the miller in compensation for grinding a farmer's corn in colonial times. Today the term retains some of its original meaning. In current usage, a *maquila* is a factory contracted by corporations to perform the last stages of a production process—the final assembly and packaging of products for export. Transnational corporations (TNCs) supply *maquilas* with the preassembled material, such as cloth and electronic components, and *maquilas* employ workers to assemble the material into finished or semi-finished products. The *maquilas* then export 100% of their products back to the TNCs.

The *maquilas* of Guatemala and other developing countries are one consequence of economic globalization and the "global factory" system. In some industries, entire production processes once housed under the roof of one factory have been dispersed to numerous production centers around the world. But, as has been the reality for centuries, the production processes have not been split equally between industrialized and developing countries. In the industrialized countries of the "North," the TNCs design and engineer the products, plan production processes, supply the raw material, and sell the finished products. In developing countries of the "South," the workers in *maquilas* assemble the saleable product, working for extremely low wages and without basic rights. In this developing "global factory" system, the *maquila* is a new center of production, where low-paid workers cheaply provide a significant share of the world's industrial labor. . . .

Beginning in the early 1970s, corporations faced a severe crisis of profitability. As profit rates fell to dangerously low levels, TNCs looked into increasing productivity and lowering production costs to restore profitability. One such way to restore and maintain the profit margins in their firms was to attack the gains of industrial, oftentimes unionized, workers. Companies started to slash their wages and destroy their unions. . . . Rather than risk a protracted fight with unions in these richer countries, corporations decided to move their easily transferable, labor-intensive production processes completely overseas. They began to contract with independent *maquilas* to do the work for them. Whether by reducing wages in the North or moving their factories to the South, the TNCs stood to benefit tremendously with windfall profits, gained at the expense of workers in both the industrialized countries and developing countries. . . .

The development of the *maquila* arrived late in Guatemala in comparison to other countries in Central America and the Caribbean Basin. From 1966 to 1982, three laws were passed to attract *maquila* investment to Guatemala, yet substantial *maquila* growth did not materialize. In fact, the US Agency for International Development (USAID) spent millions of dollars to foster *maquila* development, but these US-backed efforts produced no results in the 1970s. Many potential investors, foreign and domestic, were scared away by the political insecurity caused by the guerrilla insurgency in the countryside and the military's counterinsurgency war. . . .

In the 1980s the conditions for *maquila* investment improved significantly, setting Guatemala upon a course that USAID promoters and entrepreneurs describe as "*maquila*-led industrialization." The single most important factor was the revival of US foreign assistance. USAID revived its *maquila* promotion program as part of its economic aid package to Guatemala in 1986, led by experienced personnel of the *maquila* industry. Within three years, general US official assistance totaled more than $800 million, doubling the US assistance given to Guatemala in the preceding 40 years. As its primary goal, USAID sought to cultivate in Guatemala a new class of *maquila* entrepreneurs, a class that would eventually lead and manage the "neoliberal revolution" in Guatemala. The newly established Nontraditional Products Exporters Association (AGEXPRONT) began promoting and assisting companies to export non-traditional products, like raspberries, flowers and clothing. The organization of this trade association, funded by millions of US taxpayer dollars, increased the strength of both domestic entrepreneurs and US corporate interests, further helping facilitate changes in favor of *maquila* expansion in Guatemala. . . .

The impact of increased *maquila* activity is visible throughout peripheral areas of Guatemala City, where large, new factories dot the rugged landscape and shantytowns of tin and cardboard amble up precariously steep hills. Despite the tremendous growth of *maquilas* in Guatemala, some argue that *maquilas* and "free trade," by themselves, have not provided the country with a sensible and humane path to industrial development. As the industry has functioned thus far, the *maquila* sector operates as a foreign "enclave" within Guatemala, an export platform for multinational corporations without significant connections to other branches of the Guatemalan economy. Two points should be made concerning the "enclave" nature of the industry. First, *maquila* owners (both foreign and Guatemalan) take advantage of the low cost of labor within the country, as well as the incentives offered by the Guatemalan government and international trade rules, to cheaply and conveniently access the gigantic United States apparel market. Secondly, it has been argued, much of the increased growth of *maquilas* does not greatly benefit local economies through increased overall investment. Assembling imported inputs into low-value goods contributes very little value to the country's economy. In fact most of the *maquila* profits are repatriated to the United States or Asia. Like the small amount of corn paid to the miller for his or her service, the meager wages paid to workers are the main economic benefit to the country.

The *maquila* has been the birth of a new working class in Guatemala, comprised of tens of thousands of workers, many of whom have left their landless poverty in the countryside to seek their fortune in the city. According to AGEXPRONT, today over 100,000 persons work in approximately 250 *maquilas* in Guatemala. Another 15,000 persons work in *maquila*-related jobs such as factory security and transportation of workers. Approximately 80% of *maquila* workers are women, a significant fact given that men have historically constituted the vast majority of manufacturing workers. . . .

. . . The working conditions inside *maquilas* are often appalling. Unventilated workrooms, unsafe workshops, verbal abuse, sexual harassment and abuse, firings for pregnancy, arbitrary dismissals and forced overtime are just some of the issues workers face in Guatemalan *maquilas*. Given this grim reality and the fact that conditions vary from factory to factory, most *maquila* workers do not work in the same plant for very long. In fact, somewhere between 10% and 30% of the *maquila* workforce resigns or is fired every month. Most *maquila* workers move from job to job, seeking the best rate for their time. Many work only long enough to save money to start their treacherous trek to the United States.

Currently, the industry minimum wage is $3.70 (Q29) per day plus a variety of production bonuses arbitrarily calculated and inconsistently awarded by the owners of the *maquila*. With production bonuses and overtime, a good machine operator in a large *maquila* earns about $170 (Q1300) per month. Minimum living expenses for an average family (5.38 members) calculated by the national institute of statistics for April 2000 was $284 (Q2185) per month. . . .

In addition to the stress of supporting a family on a *maquila* wage, many workers incur health problems due to factory conditions. Bathroom access is restricted, causing kidney infections. Permission to see a doctor is usually denied, allowing illness to reach a critical stage before it is treated. Respiratory problems are common due to poor ventilation. The legal workweek is 44 hours long; nevertheless, it is not uncommon to work 70 to 80 hour weeks in the *maquila*. This increases the number of industrial accidents and causes repetitive motion injuries. All told, many workers do not work more than a few years in the *maquila* before health problems force them back into the informal economy. . . .

In an effort to change these conditions, *maquila* workers have repeatedly attempted to organize unions in Guatemala. However, this has proved to be extremely difficult. There are currently only two independent *maquila* unions in Guatemala, and neither have collectively bargained contracts yet. Although both the Guatemalan Constitution and Labor Code guarantee workers' freedom of association, hardly any of these laws are enforced. This leaves workers extremely vulnerable to employer attacks. Unionization campaigns by workers are routinely met with retaliatory firings, psychological intimidation, the relocation of factories, and even attempted murder. The history of the union campaign at the Camisas Modernas plants, owned by Phillips Van Heusen, reveals the obstacles to union organizing in Guatemala. After ten years of brave union struggle and a well-organized US solidarity campaign, workers won their union and the first union contract on the industry. However, one year after the victory, Phillips Van Heusen shut down the factory and shifted production to five different non-union plants in the area.

With changes in international trade rules in store, the *maquila* in Guatemala will be facing serious restructuring . . . [as] China becomes fully integrated into the world market, unleashing onto the market a huge productive capacity for both high- and low-value products, and approximately 1 billion extremely poorly paid workers.

Pollo Campero Takes Wing

Nation's Restaurant News

Flights from Guatemala City to Los Angeles California no longer smell like fried chicken: Pollo Campero, a fast-food chicken chain so popular among Guatemalans that travelers regularly bring boxes of its product when they visit relatives outside the country, has gone global. Founded in Guatemala City in 1971, the chain moved first into El Salvador and later into Mexico. In 2002, Pollo Campero opened its first franchise in the United States, following Central American immigration routes into such cities as Los Angeles, Houston, and Miami. By 2007, the chicken chain had expanded to nearly three hundred restaurants in eleven countries, including China and Indonesia, and inked a deal to open its chicken outlets inside Walmart stores across the United States. Now the chain is planning to open a franchise in Florida's Walt Disney World.

In 2005, Newsweek highlighted Pollo Campero president Juan José Gutiérrez as one of its "10 Biggest Thinkers for Big Business." Indeed, Pollo Campero sits at the pinnacle of one of Central America's most expansive business empires; its parent company, the Bosch-Gutiérrez family-run Corporación Multi-Inversiones, controls more than three hundred businesses in Central America, the Caribbean, and South America, including poultry and food processing, construction and real estate, financial services, and hydroelectricity production. The article below, which appeared in the trade journal Nation's Restaurant News, *describes the opening of the first Pollo Campero restaurants in Los Angeles.*

Los Angeles. As American restaurant brands strive to plant their banners around the globe, Pollo Campero, a 170-unit chicken chain based in Guatemala, has turned the tables and established a strong US beachhead here.

Propelled by sales that reached $1 million in the first seven weeks at its initial Los Angeles unit, Pollo Campero has opened two more counter-service branches in the area since April. . . .

Immigrants from the eight Central American countries where Pollo Campero units enjoy strong customer loyalty have been credited with the unusually robust initial sales in Los Angeles following the concept's debut there. The first LA location, near downtown, was going through 17.5 tons of chicken a week and cutting off block-long lines of customers at 6 PM in order to close by midnight. . . .

The chain, which specializes in fried and rotisserie-cooked marinated chicken, anticipates opening a store in Houston in November and is on the verge of signing a franchise deal for Washington, DC; Maryland; and Virginia. Plans also call for the opening of franchised outlets in Atlanta, Chicago, Miami and New York.

In a phone interview from the chain's headquarters in Guatemala City, Pollo Campero vice president Roberto Denegri said: "Within the next five years, we hope to have close to 200 units in the US. We have had all kinds of proposals from people who want to franchise. But we want to go carefully—we want to manage the growth."

Denegri said Pollo Campero's primary target is the Central American community living in the US, followed by the more general Hispanic population and then all consumers. "The Latino population in the US is growing fast," Denegri said. "There's been an explosion of Latino culture there— movies, music, writers."

In fact, Hispanic consumers in the United States will spend about $580 billion in 2002, according to a study by the University of Georgia's Selig Center for Economic Growth. The report forecasts that the figure will rise to $926 billion by 2007. . . .

Furthermore, the Hispanic population appears to be growing at a faster rate than the general population. The number of Hispanics living in the United States increased by 58 percent between 1990 and 2000, compared with an overall 13-percent growth rate. . . . The early success of the inaugural Pollo Campero outlet in La Curacao department store in the Pico-Union district of Los Angeles surprised even company officials. Members of the city's Latino immigrant community began lining up outside the restaurant as early as 6 AM . . .

"Sales were well above expectations," [Denegri] explained. "They were huge numbers."

He said the long lines in the initial weeks were a result of pent-up customer demand for the product, which over the years has achieved something of a cult status in cities with large Latino populations. US residents from Central America often carry Pollo Campero chicken back to the United States when they return from visits to their homelands.

"You would get on a plane from Guatemala City to Los Angeles, and the whole plane would smell like Campero," Denegri said.

To help meet that demand, the company opened branches at the Aurora

International Airport in Guatemala City and at San Salvador International Airport in El Salvador. . . . Jerry Azarkman, who co-owns [the US franchise] and four La Curacao department stores with his brother Ron, said he couldn't believe the response to Pollo Campero. "People waited in line for nine and a half hours," he said.

Los Angeles' Central American residents "had pride that [a restaurant chain] from their country broke the barriers and came to the United States," Azarkman added. "They saw McDonald's and KFC open in Central America. Now they're seeing someone from their country coming here. . . ."

Pollo Campero was founded in 1971 in Guatemala City. Soon afterward its founders exported the concept to El Salvador, where it also flourished. Company executives opened branches in those two countries exclusively until 1991, when the concept debuted in Honduras. In 1994 a decision was made to franchise the chain, and three years later the first licensed unit opened in Panama. Over time franchises opened in Ecuador, Costa Rica, Nicaragua and Mexico.

Today the chain generates sales of about $300 million annually with its three basic types of chicken—original fried recipe, extra crispy and rotisserie-cooked—all flavored with a spice-herb blend. Other lunch and dinner selections include chicken nuggets and strips, chicken burgers and sandwiches, and sides of french fries, mashed potatoes, fresh and prepared salads, and desserts.

Unlike the US stores, Pollo Camperos in Latin America are open for breakfast, lunch and dinner and feature a full-service format.

The New Men of Maize

James Klepek

*In Jacaltenango, a Mayan-Mam community in the highland department of Huehue-
tenango, there are nearly fifty different words to identify distinct varieties of corn.
Ok k'ej wah is grown in the cold highlands and has yellow kernels. Kĕx sat means
"black eyes" and is planted in the temperate piedmont. Ockal tsaiik translates as
"sixty days," and it grows best in the hot lowlands. Horrific violence was visited
on this community (see Víctor Montejo's "Exodus," part 6 of this volume), including
the widespread destruction of subsistence agriculture during the "scorthed earth"
campaigns of the early 1980s. Yet a recent study found that there are more varieties
of corn in Guatemala today than there were eighty years ago. Most of the newer
strains, like the* super enano *(super dwarf), tend to be for commercial cultivation
in hot lands, with a quick growing cycle, white kernels, and higher yield. Still,
local farmers continue to take care to maintain the genetic purity needed to reproduce this diversity, and they are keenly aware of when certain strains of corn were
introduced into the community and where the strains came from. Corn, in other
words, continues to serve as the foundation of life for many Jacaltecos, despite the
rapid economic and political changes that their community has experienced over
the last half century.*

*But their ability to deploy their local knowledge and maintain community con-
trol over corn cultivation is under threat. In the essay below, the geographer James
Klepek documents the intense campaign, waged by both Monsanto Corporation and
the* US *Department of Agriculture, to introduce genetically modified corn in Guatemala, which many fear will lead to a loss of genetic diversity and increased dependency on Monsanto-patented seeds. Klepek also discusses the ways in which opposition to genetically modified or "transgenic" seeds (which have been engineered
with traits from other plant or animal species, mostly to be herbicide tolerant and
insect resistant) has united indigenous and environmental activists, who have so
far managed to forestall the legalization of transgenic corn.*

Corn or maize, now the most widely produced crop in the world, originated in Mesoamerica and became a staple food source around 3000 BC for

an emerging Maya civilization. The *Popol Vuh* describes the Guatemalan K'iche' Maya as the "people of maize," their very flesh and bones created from yellow and white corn. Yet, as illustrated by Nobel Prize laureate Miguel Angel Asturias in *Men of Maize,* the expansion of commercial corn production in the early twentieth century created growing tensions between the plant as a commodity and as the foundation of subsistence-based agriculture. "Sown to be eaten, it is the sacred sustenance of the men who were made of maize," Asturias wrote. But "sown to make money it means famine for the men who were made of maize."

Current controversy over genetically modified (GM) agriculture in Guatemala is particularly emblematic of escalating conflict between subsistence-based corn production and elite-oriented commercial agriculture.

The country is home to thirteen landrace corn varieties and nine subraces; along with southern Mexico, it is the center of global corn biodiversity. The concentration of corn diversity reflects the importance of locally adapted seed varieties developed through centuries of farmer breeding and innovation. For the rural Maya, *criolla* corn seed represents a vital source of sustenance and a reproducible means of production. Even with the availability of high-yielding hybrids, 91 percent of corn planted is grown from *criollas*. In addition, small farmers have incorporated characteristics from hybrid varieties such as shorter stalks and faster growing times into saved seeds. With limited economic resources as well as diverse and often marginal growing environments, farmer seeds offer stable yields with little or no application of expensive chemical inputs. In total, small-scale farmers account for 96 percent of the total agricultural population. They are responsible for the majority of corn production, more than half of which is dedicated to subsistence use.

Guatemala has one of the highest degrees of economic inequality in Latin America, with poverty and food insecurity disproportionately concentrated in Maya communities. Small-scale corn producers face numerous structural challenges, including extreme land inequality (2 percent of the population controls 57 percent of the arable land); competition from US corn imports, which now make up one-third of domestic corn consumption; and the dismantling of government credit and subsidies. During an escalating food crisis, official institutions have nonetheless been unwilling to address these structural issues. In 2007, rising US demand for corn-based ethanol triggered a 78 percent increase in Guatemalan corn prices. Despite stated goals of encouraging domestic production, the official response to the crisis has been limited to food aid, with efforts to support small-scale corn production in the Maya highlands still virtually nonexistent.

Within this context, Monsanto—the largest seed company in the world,

"The rescue of Maya culture and land is the struggle for life and peace." Community mural, depicting a wide yellow road of corn leading to the national palace, created by the National Network for the Defense of Food Sovereignty, located near the Pacific port city of Champerico. Photo by James Klepek. Used by permisson.

estimated to control up to 97 percent of the market share for GM corn—and its new Guatemalan subsidiary are portraying GM agriculture as key to the modernization of domestic corn production. The acquisition of the Central American seed company, Semillas Cristiani-Burkard (SCB), by Monsanto in June of 2008 for $135 million marked a solidification of US agricultural biotechnology interests in Central America. With SCB now continuing as a subsidiary of Monsanto, the companies are poised to exert tremendous control over seed production throughout the region. The acquisition built on a long history between Monsanto and SCB in Guatemala. Monsanto established its first Guatemalan operations in 1965, and a year later, corn seed company Semillas Cristiani was founded in neighboring El Salvador. With the onset of political turmoil, SCB transferred its headquarters and production farms to Guatemala in 1980, benefiting from a partnership to market hybrid corn for Pioneer Hi-Bred in exchange for technology transfer. Most importantly, SCB's research and development department utilized a pool of local seeds and publicly developed corn varieties to create tropically suited commercial hybrids.

In the 1990s, SCB emerged as one of the largest grain seed producers in

Latin America, operating in twelve countries in Central America and the Caribbean, as well as in Mexico, Colombia, and Venezuela. With the commercialization of GM agriculture in the United States, the company began working with Monsanto, carrying out field investigations of GM corn in 1998, 2000, and 2005. In 2007, SCB was developing GM corn varieties utilizing Monsanto's traits and its own tropical corn hybrids, with plans to release them for commercial sale by 2012.

In addition to patent protection currently being implemented under the Central American Free Trade Agreement (CAFTA), the companies have focused on shaping regulations to allow the commercialization of GM corn with support from US trade interests. In 2005, the US Department of Agriculture's Foreign Agricultural Service (USDA-FAS) hosted a technical workshop, with the participation of SCB and Monsanto, in support of efforts to halt a legislative proposal for the regulation of GM agriculture based on a United Nations–sponsored biosafety program. What biotechnology proponents found most troubling about the initiative, which was drafted by the National Council of Protected Areas (CONAP), was that it proposed a lengthy review process to assess and prevent the environmental risks of GM corn cross-pollination to local corn biodiversity. Furthermore, the incorporation of socioeconomic considerations—including the impacts of the technology on small-scale farmers and the consultation of popular organizations opposed to GM agriculture in decision-making—was viewed as a threat to the commercialization of GM corn.

In response to this legislation, biotechnology proponents supported the Ministry of Agriculture and Livestock (MAGA) in drafting Accord 386–2006, which approved the production of GM seeds for export in 2006. In 2007, these groups were focused on revising existing regulations to further allow sale of biotech seeds within the country. Nonetheless, the Ministry of the Environment and Natural Resources (MARN), responsible for final approval of new GM crops, had not yet developed a stance on the technology. Throughout 2007, the USDA-FAS channeled efforts through a technical commission on biotechnology to sway CONAP and MARN. The technical commission prominently featured private-sector participants from SCB, the sugar sector, and the food industry. Commission participants from the government and academia expresssed concern over the role of agricultural elites in shaping the trajectory of biotechnology commercialization. According to one government member of the technical commission, "private-sector representatives from big industry are mainly interested in having little regulation. . . . I am not expressing frustration towards Monsanto," he said, "but I believe it should be the government's role to develop seed varieties like this. The issue

I struggle most with is biodiversity and cross-pollination. Is it responsible to make transgenics of food that Guatemalans grow?"

This question reflects concerns over protecting local biodiversity, controlling the corn seed, and assessing the extent to which GM corn would help alleviate or exacerbate tensions between elite and small-scale agriculture. Despite these concerns, the technical commission, with USDA-FAS support, has since promoted a more singular narrative de-emphasizing risks to biodiversity and subsistence livelihoods.

This was evident during the nation's first National Seed Fair, in 2007, coordinated by MAGA, SCB, and Monsanto. SCB's director made a presentation likening the spread of GM traits in the environment to the exchange of genes in traditional farmer seed selection, arguing that new biotech genes would enhance biodiversity. Particularly troubling was a simultaneous recognition of the importance of preserving agrodiversity while asserting an inevitable displacement of local seeds through industrialization: "It is necessary," he said, "to have adequate seed banks to be able to conserve our biodiversity. In the long term, it is not sustainable to continue growing *criollas*. If producers wish to continue forward and have higher productivity to be profitable, they cannot keep growing *criollas*."

If predictions of the widespread adoption of GM agriculture prove correct, germplasm banks would preserve local seeds necessary for public research and development while exerting greater private control over the production and provision of the seed supply. The company further believes that rising corn prices will trigger a return of large-scale agricultural producers to basic grains in Guatemala and throughout Latin America. In this sense, the increased marginalization of small farmers is portrayed as a natural if not desirable component of agricultural modernization.

So far the commercialization of GM corn in Guatemala remains uncertain. In a 2007 interview, the director of SCB told me that "once our GM corn varieties are ready for public release, Guatemala will have to decide whether it wants to remain the center of commercial corn seed production in Latin America." If not, the company is considering transferring operations to neighboring Honduras, the only country in Mesoamerica currently growing GM corn commercially. Despite being essentially excluded from official biotechnology regulatory discussions, popular opposition has played a significant role in explaining the uncertain political climate of GM corn discussions.

Concerns over agricultural biotechnology are bringing together popular organizations, each deploying its own narratives of the technology, to try to block attempts to legalize GM corn. In Guatemala, alliances between broadly defined Maya and environmentalist organizations are most clearly evident under the National Network for the Defense of Food Sovereignty (REDSAG). REDSAG's membership includes more than two hundred groups organized around indigenous and nonindigenous rural *campesino* rights, agrarian reform, sustainable agriculture, and environmental protection. Their focus is emblematic of a broader international food sovereignty movement that links access to food (food security) to questions of control over food production and seed resources. REDSAG is particularly focused on promoting local agriculture through "revitalizing appropriate technologies that liberate agricultural producers from dependency on agricultural chemicals and conventional technological packets."

Concerns over the impacts of GM corn on food sovereignty brought together rural leaders and environmental activists in a series of public food aid denouncements in 2002, 2005, and 2007, when REDSAG analysts found that US corn distributed to Maya communities contained GM traits not approved for human consumption in the United States or Europe. Besides health risks, there was fear that unmilled GM corn was being planted and cross-pollinating with local varieties, threatening biodiversity and subsistence livelihoods. REDSAG also strengthened knowledge alliances in opposition to GM corn through a series of native seed fairs focused on mobilizing rural communities and fomenting alternative agricultural production. The largest of these events, held in Sololá in 2007, included the participation of thousands of agricultural producers and community leaders from around the country and Central America. A major component involved linking scientific concerns about the potential health and environmental risks of GM corn to wider discussions about the implications of free trade, corporate seed control, and the expansion of industrialized corn production for small-scale farmers.

REDSAG organizers also focused on disseminating a view that differed from the seed sector's emphasis on the inevitable disappearance of *criolla* seeds, instead emphasizing the viability of local agricultural production. A central focus of the event was providing a forum to exchange local corn seeds as well as seeds from other essential Maya crops like beans, squashes, and peppers. Many of the participating farmers were also beneficiaries of programs to establish local seed banks through providing materials like silos and technical assistance. At the same time, seed fair participants visited nearby farm projects as a means for producers to share knowledge about agricultural diversification, seed selection and planting, and the use of nonchemical plant fertilization and pest control.

Opposition continues. In August of 2008, around thirty thousand Maya and *campesino* activists stopped traffic in the capital of Guatemala City to protest US corn imports under CAFTA and the expansion of agro-export farming, while demanding subsidies for the production of nontransgenic basic grains. These protests were significant for linking the food crisis to fundamental issues of free trade, land reform, and a revitalization of corn production that leaves room for small-scale producers. This breadth of mobilization has not been seen since the late 1970s.

For Sale

Real estate advertisement,
El Periódico, *June 23, 2007*

Over the last decade, Guatemala, along with other Central American countries, has passed legislation that has led to a rapid expansion of extractive and energy industries, such as mining, logging, petroleum, hydroelectricity, and cultivation of African palm and sugar for ethanol production. Sugar has long been planted on Guatemala's southern coast, but the cultivation of African palm for biofuels is relatively new, and its rapid spread is having a disruptive effect on rural life. As more and more land is devoted to biofuels, there is less room to plant corn, beans, and other basic food stuff, raising the cost of living for the rural poor. African palm does not require much labor, so the industry generates few jobs and nearly no decent-salaried ones. The daily wage for a palm cutter in 2008 was about six dollars.

Biofuel production is highly controlled by a few companies. Guatemalan sugar magnates, such as the Herrera, Botrán, and Molina families, control ethanol production, while African palm production is centered around half a dozen companies, including Palmas del Ixcán, a subsidiary of Houston-based Green Earth Fuels, owned by Riverstone Holdings, the Carlyle Group, and Goldman Sachs.[1]

Small landowners, some of them working with historic peasant organizations such as the Comité de Unidad Campesina, have fought to stem the environmental threat represented by large-scale corporate monoculture. Landowners have resorted to intimidating and killing peasant activists, suggesting that biofuels have revitalized the old planter–death squad alliance that held sway throughout Guatemala through much of the Cold War. In the Q'eqchi' community of Panzós, the site of an infamous 1978 massacre, paramilitaries have terrorized families fighting the spread of ethanol corporations.

African palm has spread most rapidly in the department of Izabal, as well as the lowland jungle regions of the Petén and the Ixcán. For example, more than one hundred thousand acres in the municipality of Sayaxché, in the southeast corner of Petén, have been sold to biofuel and hydroelectric projects, displacing almost two thousand families. In some cases, entire communities have sold their lands to corporations, decamping elsewhere to start anew, pushing deeper into the jungle and accelerating the cycle of deforestation. The advertisement, which appeared in a major Guatemala newspaper in 2007, announcing the sale of ten plantations, many of them in the Petén, gives a good sense of the gold-rush-like frenzy—African palm, sugar, and other biofuel crops are priced on the international market as an energy commodity, and are thus subject to futures speculation—that marks this latest cycle of land dispossession and concentration. (Note: One caballería *equals a little more than one hundred acres.)*

Ten African Palm Fincas *for Sale*

The appeal of a new generation of fuels, along with a growth in demand, has provoked a massive extension of African palm cultivation throughout the entire national territory.

Both businesses and governments see in African palm an economic and energy alternative. They say it also generates clean electricity. The introduction of this plant will provide new opportunities for employment, the building of infrastructure, education, and health.

"It is possible that in five years, we will have more than a million acres planted in all of Central America, mainly in Costa Rica, Honduras, and Guatemala. The next few years will see a strong growth in African palm cultivation, along with the expansion of the sugar sector, because both crops are positioned in the commodities markets as ideal for the production of biodiesel and ethanol," said Bernardo López, the Minister of Agriculture, Livestock, and Food.

THIS IS YOUR OPPORTUNITY TO ACQUIRE PLANTATIONS IN:

1. Sayaxché: 30 beautiful caballerías
2. Right next to this lot is another 200 more caballerías
3. Petén: 105 caballerías
4. Chisec: 90 caballerías
5. Petén: 70 caballerías
6. Abutting the Usumacinta River: 70 to 100 caballerías
7. Izabal: 30 caballerías
8. Izabal: 90 caballerías
9. Izabal: 80 caballerías
10. Izabal: 50 caballerías

AND THERE IS MORE

For more information call the cell phone number . . .

Translated by Greg Grandin

Note

1. Luis Solano, *Estudio del destino de la producción de caña de azúcar y palma africana y la situación de la producción y el mercado de agrocombustibles en Guatemala* (Guatemala City: ActionAid Guatemala, 2009).

The Vast, Breathing Rainforest Is Changing

By Mary Jo McConahay

The large lowland Petén rainforest gives Guatemala a unique geography. On a map, it looks like a stovepipe jutting into Mexico's Yucatán peninsula. The Petén has long held a special place in Guatemalan nationalism, similar to the role the Amazon rainforest plays in Brazilian culture. This vast forest, home to Maya ruins and spectacular ecological diversity, has also served as a refuge for settlers and criminals; today it is a major drug corridor. In recent years, the pace of deforestation has accelerated rapidly, and soon, it seems, the Petén forest will no longer exist. Below, Mary Jo McConahay, author of Maya Roads: One Woman's Journey among the People of the Rainforest, *describes the many threats facing the region.*

I first came to Petén in the 1970s, reading a found paperback of *The Exorcist* to pass a long, dreary bus ride on pocked roads from Belize. Stepping off at Tikal, breathing the jungle air, I immediately felt the rainforest's richness, its promise of discoveries to come. Later, the night called mysteriously with cries of birds and unseen animals. "There is no place like this on earth," I thought. Archaeologists and workmen outnumbered tourists like me, who had come to see remains of ancient Maya civilization.

The Petén of those days is gone. Since the 1990s I have reported on the region, drawn by its persistent frontier character, the beauty of still-extant jungle, and most recently, the sensation of being a witness to history in a key corner of the continent. Petén is the center of the largest tropical lowland forest north of the Amazon, a continental lung stretching from Mexican Chiapas to western Belize. It is one of the earth's remaining safeguards against radical temperature variation. What becomes of its verdant carpet, the concentration of trees that absorb heat-trapping carbon dioxide, links Petén directly to global concern about climate change.

When I arrived more than thirty years ago, tomb-robbing and animal poaching worried Petén. Today it faces challenges so much more fundamental that failing to meet them means Petén is likely to disappear in the near future as the unique jungle outland of Guatemalan history.

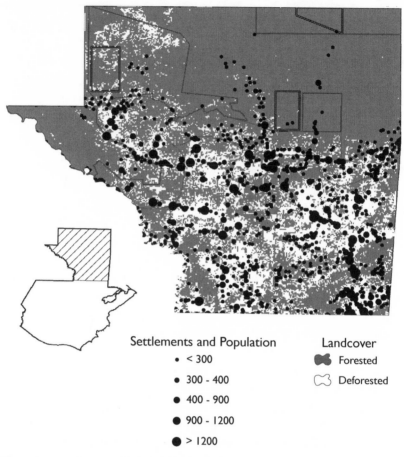

Settlements and Population
- • < 300
- • 300 - 400
- • 400 - 900
- ● 900 - 1200
- ● > 1200

Landcover
- Forested
- Deforested

In recent years, the rate of deforestation in Petén has quickened, even in nominally protected reserves, such as the Maya Biosphere. Map by Jason Arnold and Daniel Irwin, NASA/SERVIR 2010.

Since 1998, according to the US Drug Enforcement Agency (DEA), Petén's geography and lack of law enforcement have made it a key transit corridor in the international drug trade. Always a pioneer destination, it continues to draw so many peasant farmers, pushed out by Guatemala's dramatic imbalance in land ownership elsewhere, that forest goes up in smoke at an increasing rate, and precious species, some unique to Petén, face extinction. Ranchers destroy forest for pasture. In addition, likely unintended consequences of proposed tourist megaprojects disenfranchise the community and threaten to further upset ecological balance. Official corruption and traditional impunity mean more of Petén each year is sold to the highest bidders or crooks who trade in serious threats. Drug-trafficking families are rooted in patches of land they call their own. Petén is presenting a challenge to governability and rule of law.

For all its strategic importance and place in the Guatemalan imagination, the Petén region has been the most hidden in the country's history. Petén covers a full third of national territory, 23,000 square miles, but for the first century and a half of independence, it was the Wild North, the ultimate unknown. Roadless tropical forest infested with deadly vipers, ruled by the kingly jaguar. Better to stay home.

Novels by Virgilio Macal Rodriguez, for instance, still taught in Guatemalan schools, portray the northern jungles as lands of mystery and raging beauty, their inhabitants wise with forest knowledge and instinct, but not always trustworthy. As a young boy, Guatemalan-born writer Victor Perera recalled seeing Lacandón Maya, who once lived from Petén to Chiapas, exhibited in a cage at a fair in the capital. . . .

During the 1960s and 1970s, Petén's military governors regarded the Petén's largely unpopulated tracts as an ideal social safety valve. Landless peasants nationwide had been left with little hope after the 1954 US-orchestrated coup. . . . Encouraged by the military, peasant farmers in cooperatives, or individually, moved to the North, where they were given titles to parcels but little or no support. Nevertheless, along the Pasión and Usumacinta Rivers, and inland at places like Dos Erres, some cooperatives and communities grew and thrived, despite the jungle soil's shortcomings for agriculture. . . . . .

Tropical rainforests cover only five percent of the earth, but nurture half of all animal and plant species. Petén is home to endangered species, some found nowhere else. . . . In 1989, the Law of Protected Areas aimed to prevent timber companies, cattle ranchers and farmers from destroying trees. The following year's creation of the four million acre Maya Biosphere Reserve aimed to protect jungle, stop new settlements, and provide development assistance to already-resident communities, giving them a stake in conservation. A new entity, the National Council of Protected Areas (CONAP), was created to keep watch over Guatemala's reserve of global genetic patrimony.

Those were heady days. International journalists, including myself, reported on a new kind of no-go territory, at least for migrants. The northernmost third of the Petén became devoted to parks, biotopes, and multiple-use zones. We watched an influx of environmentalists, scholars, and scientists. I visited communities where artisan families, supported in business methods by outsiders, learned to live for a year from products of a single tree, instead of slashing and burning dozens to plant corn. I met women trained to use solar ovens and easily made, low-smoke stoves that replaced open cook-fires, saving not only the forest, but the women's eyesight as well. In multiple-use zones, communities received concessions for sustainable forestry projects.

In the wake of all the investment and hopes, Petén's twenty-first century began with the unexpected—the bolder presence of a global drug trade feeding the us market. Petén has also become clearly marked by the inevitable consequence of Guatemala's own irrepressible history of violence and historic imbalance in land ownership: struggles for land are taking place, mostly on the part of poor farm families. . . .

In [the Maya Biosphere's] Laguna del Tigre [National Park], ranchers abound, and drug families use the cattle spreads as a screen for runways to transport drugs. The small planes may be damaged on landing or simply abandoned once a drop is made, leading Drug Enforcement Agency operations chief Michael Brun to characterize northern Guatemala as "an aircraft graveyard." A vast majority of the cocaine destined for the United States now transits Central America, reports a 2010 us Army Strategic Studies Institute monograph. . . .

One conap administrator confessed that a drug lord offered him a deal: goons would police the rainforest against destruction, if conap would ignore drug drops. "I told him no," said the official, shrugging his shoulders ruefully.

conap, unarmed, has little effective authority and often not even enough gas for its vehicles, although it does manage to capture ill-gotten timber, often from trucks. Police authority remains unrespected. To hunt down a farmer suspected of cutting trees, for instance, it is the army that goes in, accompanied by conap and police. The sense of 1980s-style militarization returns. Drug traffickers appear to remain unaffected.

When I arrived to live in Guatemala in 1989, many new acquaintances told me the political violence of the 1980s unfolded in the capital and the highlands, and in the Ixcán, not Petén, honestly seeming to believe it was so. . . . Traveling in the north, however, I soon realized the war hit communities once invited to make a new life on the land. Hundreds had died, the majority at army hands. The region's displaced, and many others uprooted when hundreds of villages disappeared elsewhere in the country, sought survival in Petén's remote jungle, where they have lived as farmers, some for more than twenty years, without electricity or medical clinics. In 1990, eleven "illegal" communities existed in Laguna del Tigre. Today they number thirty-seven, with a total population of about 45,000.

Even Peteneros with legal land titles do not always rest easy. Parcel holders outside the protected areas, in a block of communities south of Las Pozas, battled the bureaucracy's famous *trámites* (paperwork) for twelve years until receiving proper documentation for their land. Now many say they are under pressure to sell, including threats of violence. The sold land becomes part of the growing African palm oil industry, held by private companies.

Petén is not only Guatemala's largest department, but also the fastest growing in terms of population, from just 25,000 in the 1960s to an estimated 614,000 residents today. The Cuatro Balam initiative, announced with much fanfare in 2008, plans to meet job and development needs for (Peteneros by expanding tourism, granting rights to private companies for business in the rainforest area, and aiming to bring up to a million tourists to Petén each year. (Tikal, the best-known ancient Petén Maya site, currently draws between 140,000 and 180,000 visitors yearly.) Cuatro Balam plans include a university specializing in environment studies, a belt of hotels and resorts, and an agricultural sector to keep farmers out of the core area.

Critics say such development by private companies will destroy much of what is left of the Petén rainforest. Local residents complain they are not consulted about plans that may change their lives considerably. It remains a question whether Peteneros, traditionally farmers, cattlemen, and others who work with the land and forest, will easily become a tourism workforce or even be interested in the jobs.

Cuatro Balam is set to be anchored by the sprawling El Mirador archaeological site, with the Maya world's largest pyramid, Danta, and many smaller sites. Deep in thick rainforest seven miles south of the Mexican border, El Mirador is reached by three-day trek from the nearest town, or by helicopter. By 2023, however, Cuatro Balam expects to run a train at ten miles per hour on jungle tracks, with "imperceptible" noise, to El Mirador, Piedras Negras, Tikal, and Uaxactun. Critics suggest tracks may interrupt some animal trails and maintenance access roads will destroy more forest, and they question to whom the train's noise will be "imperceptible. . . ."

The Global Heritage Fund has named the Mirador project area as one of the most important endangered world cultural heritage sites. It is indisputably the country's highest-profile archaeological enterprise. An executive director of the foundation that sponsors the project is actor and director Mel Gibson, who produced the 2006 film *Apocalypto*, controversial among Maya scholars. Archaeologist Richard Hansen, the project director who has worked in Mirador for thirty years, emphasizes the need to preserve Mirador's rainforest environment, not simply structures. He has said he envisions a five-star eco-lodge developed by Guatemalan entrepreneurs as an example of the kind of tourism that could draw in funds to help preserve the Biosphere.

"This is the last gasp," Hansen told the Guatemala magazine *The Revue*. "If we fail, we lose the whole basin. I want to preserve it for the future."

Cuatro Balam itself, however, can arguably be seen as a development project and investment opportunity rather than a conservation effort. The idea behind it is that poor countries cannot afford to rope off sensitive land, that it must produce some economic gain for a nation and its people. Colom has emphasized partnership with private enterprise; already supporting the El Mirador "centerpiece" are major partners such as Wal-Mart Central America, construction material giant Cementos Progreso, and several banks, with the Inter-American Development Bank matching private funds.

Residents of Laguna del Tigre worry. "Cuatro Balam is the biggest monster," said one long-time area farmer. He was attending a meeting with twenty-five men and women in La Libertad, to discuss challenges to their vulnerable situation. "What they want is to eliminate our communities, but we will defend life." . . .

On the feast of St. Amelia, patron of one Laguna del Tigre community, a Catholic priest baptized babies, asked a blessing for wild forest animals, and addressed the congregation's concerns in a homily. "First before all is the human being," he said, "and then companies. We can join with other groups in the *monte* to make our situation known."

Petén will continue to be a promised land for Guatemalans looking for work and land. It will be a proving ground for commitment to the Peace Accords, a test of will and capacity to fight drug traffic and corruption. Guatemalan and international visitors, meanwhile, will come as I once did, for the love of sites of ancient Maya civilization, the adventure found on Petén's rivers and in its wildlands, and the chance to know Central America's own enchanting rainforest, vast stretches of jungle that exist much as they did at the time of creation.

Death by Deportation

Greg Campbell

For many young people, the dream of a better Guatemala has been replaced by the struggle to get out of Guatemala. Most who come to the United States are looking for jobs, but increasingly youth have arrived fleeing the gangs called maras *that threaten them with death for refusing to join the gang or for trying to leave it. One young man's attempt to avoid a life of crime ended when he was returned to Guatemala, where he was murdered by the gang, just as he told the* US *immigration judge he would be. One horrid irony of this is that the* maras *began in Los Angeles; they arrived in Guatemala and elsewhere in Central America after United States immigration authorities deported Central Americans to their countries of origin.*

They say you don't hear the shot that kills you. Bullets always outrun the reports that announce them, and if the aim is good, death comes before the whip-crack of the shot can catch up. There's no telling whether or not this was the case with 16-year-old Edgar Chocoy, who was gunned down March 27 [2004] in the streets of Villa Nueva, a town overrun by street gangs on the outskirts of Guatemala City. The day he was killed, he'd come out of hiding at his aunt's house to buy juice and lingered in the littered intersections of the crime-ridden city to watch a Roman Catholic procession of saints through the streets. He never returned. By the time his family was told of his murder four days later, he'd already been buried in an unmarked grave in a cemetery for the homeless. . . . Chocoy's death came as a surprise to no one, least of all him. In spite of all of his efforts to avoid this fate, his life ended much as he'd predicted it would—in a flare of violence that's all too familiar in Guatemala's cities. Years earlier, at an age when most children are more concerned with their grades than their imminent murders, Chocoy sought every avenue of escape. Knowing that he'd been "green lighted"—marked for death—by members of a notorious gang he was trying to untangle himself from, he hid out with relatives until that became too dangerous for them, bused alone to Mexico, then illegally entered the United States in search of his mother who'd left him when he was 6 months old. Two years after he left, however, he was deported back to Guatemala by a Denver immigration judge who either didn't believe his testimony that he would be killed there or didn't care. By denying his application for asylum in the United States, Judge James Vandello effectively sentenced him to death.

Two and a half weeks after being returned to Villa Nueva, street executioners carried out that sentence, just as Chocoy said they would.

He'd heard those bullets coming for years. . . .

Born to an impoverished Guatemalan family, when he was six months old, his mother left him in the care of her father so that she could work in the United States. Chocoy lived with his grandfather—who was always either at work or at church . . . As solace for his loneliness, Chocoy made friends of the kids he met in the street and at school. Many of the older children came to be like the family he'd never had. The trouble was that they were all members of a street gang . . . Mara Salvatrucha [MS-13] . . . [that] he suddenly found himself a member of in the summer of 2000. All he knew is that his new "friends" taught him how to rob chains and watches from pedestrians. They gave him a sense of belonging and purpose, however misguided it may have been.

As he explained it to the judge during the January 4 hearing on his asylum application, "They were the only friends I had, and I only knew them. . . . I thought they were the only family I had."

It's unlikely that he could have known what he was really getting into; after all, he was only 12 years old at the time. . . .

[W]hen he was 14 he visited a different neighborhood and met kids who weren't in a gang. . . . By distancing himself from Mara Salvatrucha, Edgar took his life in his hands. One of the rules learned quickly as a member of Mara Salvatrucha is that you do not leave the gang. He was beaten and robbed for dropping out of sight, and finally he was told that he would be killed unless he paid the gang 3,000 quetzales—the equivalent of $375—in a week. . . . At 14 years old, Chocoy left Guatemala in fear for his life. . . .

There's nothing unique about Chocoy's flight north in an attempt to escape the violence that is synonymous with Mara Salvatrucha. In the past six months, thousands have done so, a wave of tattooed refugees who see the United States as a safe haven from the persecution they know will befall them for trying to escape Mara Salvatrucha's clutches. . . . The US response to this wave . . . has been simple: round them up and deport them. In October, local and federal law enforcement conducted "Operation Fed Up" which resulted in more than 60 arrests of Mara Salvatrucha members in Charlotte, N.C., who were immediately processed for deportation. . . .

"I am certain that if I had stayed in Guatemala the members of the gang MS would have killed me," Chocoy wrote in an affidavit. "I have seen them beat people up with baseball bats and rocks and shoot at them. I know they kill people. I know they torture people with rocks and baseball bats. I know that if I am returned to Guatemala I will be tortured by them. I know that they will kill me if I am returned to Guatemala. They will kill me because I left their gang. They will kill me because I fled and did not pay them the money that they demanded." . . .

At his January 4 hearing, Chocoy pleaded with the judge for his life. His testimony is punctuated by numerous statements that he would be killed if he were returned. As [lawyer Kim] Salinas put it in her closing arguments, Chocoy made a number of bad decisions in his young life, "but he also made a very good decision, that is, to leave the gang," she testified. "But when he made that decision, he was punished by persecution. . . . Edgar made a choice to . . . escape from the life he'd known and to escape from the Mara Salvatrucha." . . . He was denied that chance because the gang Mara Salvatrucha controls through force and fear because it doesn't serve their interest to have children leave them to play soccer and video games. Edgar made a decision to better his life and for that decision he was beaten, his life was threatened and he was forced out of his home, out of his school and out of his country. "Edgar's now before you for his final chance to save his life," she continued. "He's asking you not to send him back to a country where he's been identified as one who must be killed. He's asking you not to send him back into the arms of his persecutors. He's asking you for one final chance to escape the gangs and become a child, a child who's safe from fear and danger, a child who's free to attend school, to pursue a career, to live in a home [with] a family. . . . He's asking for the opportunity to become a productive adult. He's asking that you not deny him his ultimate chance."

In giving his verbal decision about Chocoy's application for asylum, Judge Vandello recapped Chocoy's case and considered a slew of supporting documents, including an affidavit from Bruce Harris, the director of Casa Alianza, a Central American children's advocacy group, which said that sending Chocoy back to Guatemala would be a death sentence for him. . . . He read a letter from Santiago Sanchez, a counselor at Homeboy Industries, who said Chocoy had support and a suitable home with an aunt in Virginia who offered to raise him, an offer that was initially approved by the Office of Refugee Resettlement. . . . The judge acknowledged several reports on gang violence in Guatemala, including one that said an average of 30 to 40 children are murdered every month in Guatemala in gang-related violence. Finally, he said he found Chocoy's testimony to be credible.

"He appears to have told his story honestly and directly," Vandello said. "I have no reason to doubt his credibility."

Nevertheless, Vandello denied the asylum application, effectively sentencing Chocoy to death. Vandello declined to comment for this article, but in the transcript from the hearing he based his decision on his belief that Chocoy could safely return to Guatemala and live an anonymous life, in spite of all the testimony to the contrary. . . .

The 16-year-old was too tired to fight Vandello's decision. Salinas says he ultimately decided not to appeal because he couldn't stand being locked up until a new hearing could get under way.

Chocoy was returned to Guatemala on March 10.

On March 27, he was shot dead.

I Feel Enraged

Robin Christine Reineke

Robin Christine Reineke, a doctoral student in anthropology at the University of Arizona, Tucson, sent the following e-mail to friends in July 2010. The drowned woman to whom Reineke refers in her correspondence is, at this writing, likely to be identified as a twenty-five-year-old Guatemalan, one of thousands to transverse the inhospitable Sonora Desert that month, attempting to cross into the United States for the simplest of all things: work. Reineke volunteers as a researcher with the Office of the Medical Examiner in southern Arizona's Pima County, where she collects missing persons reports on migrants and attempts to match them to unidentified bodies found in the desert. The office has handled 1,700 such bodies over the past decade. As do other Arizonans who volunteer at the Office of the Medical Examinar or who belong to border humanitarian groups such as No More Deaths/No Más Muertes, Reineke works to alleviate the suffering of undocumented migrants crossing the border. What Reineke describes is a horror that speaks for itself; her empathy and outrage give hope that people on the US side of the border, who can cross over to Mexico on a whim to have a good Mexican lunch or buy crafts, can stand in support of those who might die trying to cross it.

Hello Team,

It has been a long week at the OME [Office of the Medical Examiner]. Today is the 15th of July, and the office has records for 40 deceased border crossers since the 1st of the month. This brings the total for the year to more than 130, and may surpass the numbers for the worst month on record at the office, July 2005. The office already had to retrieve the old refrigerated truck that was used in past years. Dr. Parks [the chief medical examiner] expects we may have to get another before the summer is over, as we only have 20 spaces left.

I spent much of the morning trying to compare records for unidentified decedents to missing persons reports. After hours, I still have made no headway, which could mean that the missing persons reports we have will be for another 15–20 dead.

Cruzando fronteras (Crossing borders) by Paula Nicho Cuméz. Used by permission of Arte Maya Tz'utuhil.

The pages and pages of unidentified people I am flipping through are daunting. They are being found left and right. TOPD [the Tohono O'odham Police Department] goes out to find one body, and they come back with three. Border Patrol goes on a chase, and they literally drive over a body. A Picture Rocks family found a decomposing body in their front yard.

There have been 5 or 6 unidentified women since the beginning of the month. One of them jumped into a canal after border patrol pursued the group. She drowned and was found the next morning. Autopsy revealed that she was 10 weeks pregnant. I saw her this morning when I looked at her teeth. She is young, beautiful.

I can't identify any of them so far. Many have ID cards with them, many don't. Nothing is conclusive. There are so many families calling, and none of the names match. Everything leads me to doubt myself—maybe, even though he was Mexican, he was using a false name, maybe he got deported and tried to cross again later, maybe they forgot to tell me about the gold on her upper front teeth. While I want to have something to tell the families, I don't want to hope that they are dead. I feel apologetic either way.

Most of all, I feel enraged. We all knew that the anti-immigrant sentiment was going to explode with the economic downturn. I guess I just didn't expect it to impact me so much. In every vicious statement, it's like there is an acceptance of this. And it is what you don't hear just as much as what you do hear. Yesterday there was a report on [National Public Radio] about a search continuing after three days for three hikers lost in Arizona after they went in search of some lost treasure. Three hikers, and they have helicopter teams, cadaver dogs, several police departments, a citizen search crew, national news coverage. . . . I had a very specific report a few weeks ago, with a highway number and mile markers, a 300 meter radius, a good triangulated map, and a description stating that the body was left between two large crosses built with rocks. [The guy] at BORSTAR [Border Patrol Search, Rescue and Trauma] told me, "well Robin, we can't waste our resources looking for the dead while we can focus our energy on apprehending people and saving their lives." So I guess search and rescue is about apprehending people "and saving their lives."

A distraught husband of a missing Guatemalan woman showed up at the OME yesterday and angrily demanded that we lay out all the bodies on the street so that he could go through them to find her. I think I would feel enraged too, if I did not understand why the office wouldn't let me try to find my family member. It must just seem like we are arbitrarily denying him the opportunity to find her, especially given the reluctance of so many officials to do something to help.

I cringe to think what the next 15 July days will bring.

Thanks for letting me vent.

R

Prayer for a Migrant

Petrona

In many parts of the Guatemalan countryside, nearly everyone has at least one family member who has emigrated to look for work in the United States. Those left behind must depend on money sent back to Guatemala. In the selection below, a mother from Soloma, high in the Cuchumatán mountains of Huehuetenango, asks Petrona, a Maya-Q'anjob'al prayersayer's wife, to pray for her migrant sons.

> . . . God Jesus Christ . . .
> At the edge of the mat the sides are not joined . . .
> But here are flowers and candles
> From your daughter, Lord.
> Your sons are there,
> The hands and feet of Enrique are there,
> The hands and feet of Gervasio.
> A few flowers, candles
> For the hands and feet of Enrique,
> The hands and feet of Gervasio;
> Here are their flowers and candles, Lord.
> Oh God, it is said there is no money,
> It is said there are no quarters [money].
> Let something reach her hands, reach her feet, Lord. . . .
>
> Now then, Lord, open the hands of work,
> Open work for Enrique,
> For the hands and feet of Gervasio.
> Here are some flowers, here are some candles, Lord,
> For their health, their life,
> Wherever they are seated,
> Wherever they are resting, Lord.
> No money is arriving from them!
> A little has arrived, a little money from him;

Five months ago a little money arrived for his mother.
Go, Lord, come Lord,
It is five months since his cassette arrived, Lord;
Five words from him, that was his letter, Lord.

Why doesn't a half-quarter arrive
For his mother, for your María, Lord?
For what reason, Lord?
Is he indulging in worldly things [vices]?
Is it because of beer, because of *aguardiente*,
Is it because of cigars?
It is a fact that unprotected girls have arrived there,
That a multitude of young men have arrived
In that far land, in that far town;
Perhaps they are indulging in worldly things [vices]. . . .

Make him remember his mother at midnight,
At dawn, in the afternoon,
At dusk, at midnight, at midday then.
Enter into his head, enter into his ear,
Sit him on your lap,
Embrace him. . . .

Why oh why does the money not arrive?
Because he cannot get employment, work?
May his hands, his feet be appreciated
By the gringo, by the gringa.
Find, reveal, and release
Cash and work for him, Lord.
Let him look, let him observe,
Let his head think, let his ear think,
Let his body think,
At midday, in the afternoon, at dusk, Lord. . . .

Dyos Jesucristo . . .
Xam pop, manjunejoq spakiloq . . .
Pax ay jun flores, kandelas
yet xala hakutz'in unimal mamin.
Tom aytoq heb' naq unetu',
aytoq heb'naq sq'ab yaqan naq Enrique,
Sq'ab' yaqan naq Gervasio.

Ch'an jun flores, kandelas.
sq'ab' yaqan naq Enrique,
sq'ab' yaqan naq Gervasio;
tixab' flores kandelas heb' naq ti' mamin.
Ay Dyos k'amab' stumin,
k'amab' smedio,
k'amab' skwartiyo.
Chi jayli sq'ab', chi jayli yaqan mamin . . .

Ani xin mamin, jaqti sq'ab' smulnajil,
jaqteq strabajo naq Enrique,
sq'ab' yaqan naq Gervasio.
Tix flores tix kandelas, mamin,
skawiloq yikisaloq,
b'ay wixan,
b'ay chotan mamin.
Ka k'am ch'en timin chi jayi!
Chi jayta jab', jab'en ch'en yet naq;
toxa chi ajol cinco mes xa sjayi a la madre.
Elaneq mamin, titaneq mamin,
ayxab' cinco meses sjay skaset naq mamin;
cinco palabras naq, skarta naq mamin.

Tzet yuj xam k'am chi jay jun medio kwartiyo
b'ay stxutx, b'ay María mamin?
Tzet yin tzet yuj mamin?
Matol kosa del mundo chi sjatne,
matol kerb'esa, tol awariente,
matol sigarro?
Axkaytu b'eqan oktoq ix unin
winaq unin latz'an oktoq,
snajatil tx'otx' snajatil konob';
matol kosa del mundo chi sjatne' . . .

Aq' pax sna' stxutx chuman aq'wal,
tz'eyan aq'wal, yayk'u,
sq'eqb'I, chuman aq'walti chuman k'un ti' xin.
Tol ch'ok yul sjolom, tol ch'ok yul xikin,
cheleq eloq,
laq'eq eloq . . .

Tzet yin, tzet yuj xan manoq jay tumin?
Tzet yuj xan manoq elteq mulnajil, strabajo?
Ocheb'eloq sq'ab' yaqan
yui naq gab'acho, yuj ix gab'acho.
Sayeq elteq, jaqeq elteq stijon elteq
tuminti, medioti, trabajoti, mamin.
Tol chi ok tukanoq, chi ok t'ananoq,
tol chi sna sjolom, tol chi sna xikin,
tol chi sna smimanil,
chuman k'u, yayk'u, sq'eb'entaqil, mamin.

Architecture of Remittances

Photographs by Andrea Aragón and Andrés Asturias

Huehuetenango is Guatemala's far northwest province, bordering Mexico, where the Sierra de los Cuchumatanes soars to over twelve thousand feet. Home to some of Guatemala's largest Maya groups, including the Mam, Chuj, and Q'anjob'al, Huehuetenango was one of the hardest-hit areas during the armed conflict in the 1980s, and tens of thousands of huehuetecos *fled as refugees (see part 6, "Exodus"). The exodus of* huehuetecos *to the United States has accelerated since the 1980s. Today, transnational movements of all kinds, including migration and drug trafficking, mark everyday life in Huehuetenango, as in much of the Guatemalan highlands, even while structural poverty persists. The migration of* huehuetecos *to the United States, and the money they send back, has created an intense housing boom in towns and villages. Family space has changed, but even more noticeably, the new dwellings arise as symbols of social prestige, "modernity," and development. Yet, while the illicit economy creates new wealth for some, such as local "coyotes" who charge large sums of money to move people across borders, for each success story there are many invisible failures. This economy of risk creates new class divisions within communities, as many people go into debt to local moneylenders to finance migration journeys that may or may not be successful.*

In 2009 and 2010, the Architecture of Remittances project, curated under the auspices of the Centro Cultural de España in Guatemala City, brought Guatemalan anthropologists together with photographers to document these contemporary social processes. The photos and text presented below capture the dramatic changes to the built landscape in regions of Huehuetenango affected by transnational flows.

> "There was a *'coyota'* [a female 'coyote']
> named doña Corina
> who charged $1,000
> to take people across the border without problems.
> This town should build a monument
> to her."

Photo by Andrés Asturias. Used by permission of the Centro Cultural de España, Guatemala City.

Photo by Andrea Aragón. Used by permission of the Centro Cultural de España, Guatemala City.

"Family reunifications
don't turn out the way people hope
for the simple reason that
neither mother nor son know each other anymore.
They are strangers
who only know each other through photographs."

Photo by Andrés Asturias. Used by permission of the Centro Cultural de España, Guatemala City.

"He comes to visit the house only twice a year.
The rest of the year it's closed . . .
the furniture is covered to keep it nice.
He comes for three or four days
just to see the house, clean it, and then he's gone again."

"He thinks about coming back when
he retires.
Look, I think it's important to always
keep the family together,
although we may be spread out,
to come back one day to a common point.
This house can be that point.
That's what they think, and that's what I think."

"The house was built with a plan
that the son sent
based on the layout of space in the apartment
where he lives in the United States."

" . . . if she had not gone,
we wouldn't be able to study,
we wouldn't have a house,
or a vehicle for working."

Photo by Andrés Asturias. Used by permission of the Centro
Cultural de España, Guatemala City.

Photo by Andrés Asturias. Used by permission of the
Centro Cultural de España, Guatemala City.

"The son left eight years ago
for the United States.
Later, he sent for his wife.
They bought fields and a little piece of land with trees,
land for planting,
and a fresh-water spring.
Along the way he was kidnapped,
and the local coyote abandoned him.
His father had to sell the house
to pay $3,000."

"The house first. The car and business come later.
Those who like living in the countryside can buy land.
The house is the greatest need and it brings prestige,
the picture of success."

Translated by Elizabeth Oglesby

Visits to Chacash

As told to Yolanda Edelmira Figueroa Granados, Cecilia Lilian Alonso Granados, and Antonio Ariel Herrera Alvarado

Guatemala's northwestern province of Huehuetenango is changing rapidly as a result of international migration. Yet in this heavily Maya region, oral traditions still connect people to the striking landscape of the Sierra de los Cuchumatanes. In 2005, a team of Guatemalan researchers collected legends, folk tales, and stories from Huehuetenango. Many of these oral histories describe the social and spiritual meaning of specific places in the Cuchumatán mountains. The selection below describes Chacash Hill, a sacred site for Maya religious practices.

One of the highest spots in the Cuchumatán mountains is Chacash Hill, near Villa de Chiantla, which some say has the shape of a mango pit. This hill can be seen from any point and is visible from far off.

Don Eulalio Fabián was born near this hill and still lives in its shadow. Over his lifetime he has heard many stories about Chacash Hill. People go to Chacash hill to *hacer una costumbre* [hold a Maya ceremony], making offerings or promises to a "Supreme Being," either at the hill's summit or in one of the caves at its base. People come to ask for whatever they want, not only for their own personal gain but also in the name of humanity. They bring firecrackers, candles, and food to share. Chacash is a sacred spot where people come who know how to say prayers, and, if their faith is alive and strong, they can pray for all humanity.

Don Eulalio says he has visited this place many times with don Eusebio Mártir Morales, a wise person in these matters. He has seen how people come from as far away as Xela [Quetzaltenango], Almolonga, San Francisco el Alto and other places. They come to do *costumbre* and make promises, religious and holy things. It is a spiritual act, full of faith, an age-old ritual, although at the moment few people keep alive this tradition of going to

Chacash Hill. . . . The Catholic Church doesn't protest this *costumbre*, since it's been going on for such a long time, but the evangelical sects are opposed to it.

Don Eulalio says, "In this invocation, people pray for the harvest, for the animals, for the health of the family, for humanity, for all the positive things that mark their faith. It can be done any time of the year, in summer or winter, whenever a person feels a need to pray they can visit Chacash. This might be during Holy Week, at New Year's, or during a saint's day festival; the important thing is to show faith."

The visits to Chacash Hill are part of the spiritual needs of the people, who ask for blessings for their families, animals, crops, and for all humanity.

Translated by Elizabeth Oglesby

Maya Pyramids

Diane M. Nelson

In rural Guatemala in the early 1990s, it was hard to buy a soda with a five-quetzal bill, because a general shortage of money often made it difficult for owners of small tiendas to make change. But after the war ended, cash flowed in from Europe- and US-funded development projects, remittances, and increased local commerce, reshaping the countryside. With the influx of money came new opportunities for speculation and get-rich-quick schemes, including the episode described below by anthropologist Diane Nelson.

I heard about the strange case of El Millonario (the Millionaire) from Natalia, a Maya friend from Joyabaj in southern Quiché. One day at her kitchen table she told me the details, and we laughed at the total preposterousness of it. They said he had four wives up in his hilltop mansion. He also had a Hummer. He was known to whip open his fanny pack full of cash and donate to any cause. He was going to help people get half a million *quetzales* each. Some had already taken home huge baskets of money.

"It's like a *telenovela*," I said.

She agreed with a giggle: "The story is impossible!" But, moments later, she was shaking and grief stricken. "My people! My people! How could they have done this? If you were me, what would you do? People want to believe. They think you can get rich without struggle, without sacrifice."

In the early 2000s, as far as people could remember, El Millonario—a Maya man from nearby Zacualpa—had launched a "development project," one meant to help the neediest victims of the war. Only indigenous people were invited to participate, because Ladinos already had plenty. In accordance with the "moral hazard" philosophy of many international aid projects, people who wanted to participate needed to put in a few *quetzales* of their own, to show they were serious and not just looking for a handout. Those who did would reap great rewards.

"People were pressuring me to join," said a man who transports people and livestock in an old truck. "They said, 'What's wrong with you? We're going to have new cars, new trucks, so many animals we'll have to buy land to pasture them all. You'll be sorry then!'"

The candidate for mayor from the URNG—the former insurgent coalition turned political party—explained that El Millonario's organization was "Maya, all Maya, at all levels. He started with the traditional authorities in outlying hamlets, the *sacerdotes mayas*, the *aj'q'ij* [Maya priests], and then the Catholic catechists and even some evangelicals. Local leaders went door to door, drawing on the esteem people had for them. They organized through the *cofrades*," the brotherhoods that care for saints and organize dances and festivals. He said, "They are organized and credible, and people are used to *aportando*, contributing for the greater good, to sharing money and resources through them. This is our *estilo cooperativo*; you give something and then you get." Later he explained that El Millonario had "*promotores, enganchadores, contratistas, habilitadores, adelantados*"; these were all different terms that described the labor contractors who have used money, force, or debt to recruit workers for southern coast plantations since the nineteenth century. "They helped get to people," he explained. "It became like a company."

Whole hamlets got involved. One man said, "People got mad and said anyone who says it's a lie is someone who already has money, who is just envious and jealous because poor people and indigenous people want to have some too. People were drowning in their hopes for salvation. People put all their money in, every little bit to contribute. It was contagious." Another man said, "It was an insanity of riches."

The gentleman who drove an old truck and was pressured to join for a new one claims he never did. But now he has a new vehicle anyway, bought with the proceeds from ferrying believers up the Cerro Kumatz, or Snake Mountain, where El Millonario began to hold nighttime ceremonies. He wasn't just giving talks anymore; he began holding ceremonies because at some point the story had changed. It was no longer an earthly donor but the Ajau itself, the world spirit, that would provide the half a million *quetzales*. Obtaining this bounty required an undivided heart and unquestioning faith, demonstrated in ritual actions such as crawling over gravel. People spoke of spending seventeen hours kneeling in "sacrificial ceremonies." One woman recalled: "It was all so strange. There were tons of people up there as the day [for distribution] got close. There were huge candles everywhere. They were calling on the Seven Powers [local folk deities]. They said if you have gold in your mouth, you have to take it out, because if they see it, they won't help you; it's wealth. So people pulled out their own teeth. It was like a horror film."

But just as the great distribution was about to occur, El Millonario's mansion went up in flames, destroying all the money (although some say the stacks and piles of currency were cut newspapers with a single bill on the top and bottom). As with any Ponzi scheme, whatever was sustaining people's faith collapsed, and in its place an equally widespread, enthusiastic intention emerged: get that *hijo de la gran puta*. Word spread quickly through the villages, and a lynch mob formed to hunt down El Millonario, with the crowd growing along the way to his burnt-out home. Unable to find him there, they burned his Hummer, his gasoline station, and his hotel. On the remains of the buildings they painted *prohibido negociar, propiedad de la gente* (people's property, sale prohibited). Some remember a marimba accompanying this festival of destruction.

No police report was ever filed about this *gran estafa* (big con), this Maya pyramid scheme; nor has any formal process been opened against El Millonario, who remains missing. The only media coverage of an event that affected an entire province, bankrupted tens of thousands of people, and "disappeared" close to one million dollars was in a small-circulation newspaper. When a Ladino economist friend showed me the article, he said, "When I first read it, it seemed like a rumor, or a myth. Like a dream. It was impossible. What makes people believe this?"

My friend Natalia's anguish was for "her" Maya people being so shatteringly deceived, subject to another economic devastation so soon after the human and material losses of the war. She is also keenly aware of the racist stereotypes of indigenous people as easily *engañado* (duped). But she also wonders, "How could they have done this?" A preliminary answer might be that the dream logic of El Millonario's scam amalgamated many old and new forms of social organization and understandings of human relations with that perennial nonhuman actant: money. For example, everyone in Joyabaj knows that on Cerro Kumatz you can make deals with the devil. They tell of a great three-headed horned snake the size of a bus with baskets of money dangling from its horns. The snake appears to people who've made the right offerings and have the *cojones* to approach it. Such stories intermingle with religious and *cofrade* structures and traditions of *aportando* (helping) and sharing, with century-old labor migration strategies, and now with the new magic of postwar development aid, that river of money flowing freely through the highlands after the 1996 peace accords. These combine with the mysterious emerging logics of the remittance and drug economies, where suddenly people do seem to get rich without sacrifice. In this milieu, El Millonario's promises didn't look so impossible.

And, of course, it's not only gullible highland Indians who believe such fictions. At Natalia's table I told her about Bear Stearns's recent collapse, and I reassured her that people in the United States also put all their money into worthless pyramid schemes sometimes. At the time, she seemed unconvinced, but since then the whole shebang has crashed. The United States's own Millonario (Bernard Madoff), the world's largest banks, the organizations that rated and insured them, and the governments entrusted with regulating them have failed, devastating the global economy. Along with El Millonario's victims, most of us now live in the terrible dystopian aftermath of a planetary and intergenerational Ponzi scheme of looting, mayhem, and dispossessed losers.

I tell the story of El Millonario to make the strange familiar (Maya people praying on a mountaintop for magical baskets of money) and the familiar strange (is global finance really so different?), but also to connect it to other "impossible" projects. It seems impossible that so much money was extracted from such poor people, but Guatemala's plantation economy is based precisely on making enormous fortunes from the labor of indigenous peons, some of the poorest people on earth. Joyabaj and Zacualpa are *fincas de mozos*; literally, labor reserves for the lowland sugar growers. The modern economic order of financial markets is similarly rooted in extraction from just these people. Wall Streeters may claim that their only role was to make all that money, and that it was profligate spenders misunderstanding risk who caused the crash; but the truth is that the bubble's trillions of dollars in profits were extracted from poor people via subprime loans at very high interest rates, and the "derivative" bets placed on them. So some people do get rich without struggle, because the sacrifice is borne by others.

I'd like to connect the story of El Millonario to another "impossible" project: the revolution. El Millonario's home, Zacualpa, is one of the four genocide cases in the CEH [Guatemalan Truth Commission] report because support for the URNG was very strong there. People fought against being the site of extraction, based on the fundamental principle that no one should get rich at the expense of others. I mourn, with Natalia, the losses caused by the war and by El Millonario's Maya pyramid, but I am encouraged by the survival of something the genocidal state tried to make "impossible": an *estilo cooperativo*, people contributing toward the greater good.

Maya of Morganton

Leon Fink

Fear of la migra *is a routine part of daily life for undocumented workers. Yet some migrants choose not to live in the shadows but to fight. Over the last two decades, Central Americans have revitalized US labor movements, helping to turn cities like Las Vegas and Los Angeles into union towns. Many bring to the struggle their experiences in social-justice movements back home in unions, progressive church organizations, literacy programs, peasant movements, and sometimes even the armed insurgency. Others with less direct organizing experience nonetheless often share the sense of mutual support common to peasant or indigenous life, which contributes to labor solidarity. In the selection below, labor historian Leon Fink describes the traditions and experiences that propelled a remarkable fight led by Maya migrants, mostly from the K'iche' town of Aguacatán, in the department of Huehuetenango, to bring a union to Case Farms poultry processing plant in Morganton, North Carolina. After years of struggle, which included building an impressive church–community coalition, the union won an election. But Case Farms, which has plants scattered throughout the South and the Ohio valley and relies heavily on cheap, undocumented Latino workers, refused to negotiate, and eventually the union lost its certification.*

How the pre-migration experience of the Aguacatecos may have contributed to their reactions once in Morganton requires a closer look at individual cases. Paulino López Castro, a *campesino* with only two years of schooling, had fled Guatemala in 1987. . . . It took him eighteen days to reach Aguacateco friends in Oregon and Washington, where for several months he picked fruit. Several years of agricultural labor followed, with Paulino seasonally cycling between the Northwest and the West Palm Beach, Florida, area, while also working in occasional forays to visit family back in Aguacatán. In early 1993, word of indoor work in a more temperate climate drew Paulino to Case Farms, where a cousin and a few friends already worked.

That [the Case Farm activists] invoked the term *"huelga"* [strike] in 1993 and again in 1995, Paulino attributes to a general awareness of strikes on coffee plantations [in Guatemala], recurrent teachers' strikes, as well as the famous Guatemala City Coca-Cola strikes which stretched across a decade from 1975 to 1985. Paulino himself speaks repeatedly of the strike as a matter of "reclaiming our rights" and of the workers' appeal to "our human rights." . . .

Abstract notions of justice and injustice, of course, did not determine who would stand up to authority in a showdown. Here, for example, the connection between Paulino López and his nephew José Samuel Solís López suggests the significance of distinctive family ties and influence within a larger field of social action. Samuel, in fact, was just twenty-six years old when he followed his uncle from Guatemala to Morganton via Indiantown, Florida, some months after the 1993 strike. An avid reader and informal student of politics, he quickly identified with what he calls the "uprising" of 1993 and instinctively linked himself to the events leading to the 1995 strike and its unionizing aftermath. "That day the *compañeros* in live chicken [weren't allowed] to go to the bathroom. They said we will stop working. [Three] Aguacatecos started the work stoppage. . . . From that day to this we have been in a struggle. . . . We [Aguacatecos] are all united, no one is left behind."

The López Castro clan had an eclectic, live-and-let-live religious identity. Paulino, for example, had converted to the Protestant church of his mother-in-law in Aguacatán, but he had found no formal church to his liking in the United States. Both for him and for José Samuel, religion had since become more of a private than public force. "I feel," he says, "that the word of God protects us in this world. I feel that this help from God protects us from *las cosas malas* (the bad things). I am not a proper [Christian], I am not perfect, but I feel part of that [Protestant] church." Back home in Aguacatán, Paulino's successful political nephew, Marcelino Perez Castro, allows that his family has equally journeyed over the religious as well as the political map. Marcelino's grandmother was *evangelica* [Protestant], his father Catholic, and his mother Protestant. In recent years, Marcelino himself has inclined towards the ancient Maya spiritualism of *costumbre*. Following the Maya calendar, he anticipates another "great turning" in the world in 2012; in the meantime, however, he insists that religious differences do not matter in local political decision-making. . . .

For some, educational training seems to have served as a crucial formative experience. . . . Beginning in 1965, after a constitutional revision allowed for using the native languages within a larger Castillianization process, *promotores bilingües* [bilingual promoters, or native Maya speakers who had completed the sixth grade of primary school] were assigned to schools across the country. . . . Aguacatán was fortunate to be in the front rank of such bilingual initiatives, with schools reaching out to the aldeas with both youth and adult literacy programs as early as 1966. . . . Félix Rodríguez, who threw himself into the Case Farms strike of 1995, became a union committee member, and later served as one of three protagonists in a union-led hunger strike a year later, was a direct product of the chain of Awakateco bilingual education. Born into a "puro Awakateco" family of *campesinos* in the aldea of Cantón in 1973, he had begun school at age eight, spending half the day studying, the other half working with his father in their fields. At age twelve, he was able to attend the newly-opened Instituto Mayense from which he graduated in 1991. Forced by economic reasons to suspend plans for a higher degree, Miguel, then twenty-one, arrived in Morganton in 1995 nurtured by reports he had received from an older brother. . . .

Félix entered Case Farms just as the simmering grievances there had reached a boiling point. "The situation in the plant was hard," he remembers, "if someone got sick, they [the company] didn't care." On the "whole bird" line where he was working, "there had been two persons, they now put only one. The people started to realize what was happening. . . . Everything started when some of our people who had been working there for some time said that we must change that, and we started to support them. When they stopped the line, everybody stopped work, then [the leaders] said we should leave. When we got outside the only person there to help us was Daniel Gutiérrez, he must have talked to the *padre* [Father Ken]. From there we walked to the Church. For three days or so we met in the Church." Quickly, Félix involved himself in the daily meetings which developed out of the strike into an organizing committee for the union. Previously, Félix had known "practically nothing" of unions, "I had no idea and no interest until this problem arrived at Case Farms." What he does acknowledge, however, were prior beliefs in "social justice," which came "in part from the family and from the Instituto [Mayense], because there they taught us, they trained us, there they helped us to know what is good for our people. We [Aguacatecos] were formed by our indigenous ancestors so that we must give of ourselves for the good of those who come after us. . . ."

Other forms of political learning were also evident among the worker-émigrés. For Marta Olivia Gálves, for example, a native of Guatemala City . . . who emerged as a union pioneer at Case Farms, practical political knowledge initially derived from events very much "on the ground." Raised by her mother and an uncle in a wood and plastic lean-to shelter, sometimes going without even the daily ration of tortillas and beans, forced to repeat first grade and then having to quit school altogether to work in the market at age twelve, Marta nevertheless nurtures memories of freedom and invention within her urban girlhood. A "big talker" who liked to "run in the streets" with her friends after school, Marta captained her girls' basketball team. Among her prize possessions was a school uniform she bought to wear for parades on the national *día de la libertad* (independence day—September 15); she wisely bought it "big" to last, taking down the hem a little each year and occasionally refurbishing the dress's colors with store-bought paint. But Marta Gálves's biggest learning experience arrived in the aftermath of the Guatemalan earthquake of 1976 that left 22,000 dead, 77,000 injured, and over a million homeless. Among the survivors, cooperative local efforts made up for absent or utterly corrupt governmental rebuilding programs. As Marta remembers, "Many people died and our neighborhood became a ravine and we took a football field, we occupied it. We organized ourselves to keep this land. . . . We struggled with the government. We lived there four years. We improved that land with the help of the government. . . . Later, when the football players returned the government told us we had to leave. . . . We asked the government for other land. They sold us new land. We won. They built us facilities. I have this [property] there today."

Drawing on long-established community survival skills and the leadership of those with a variety of pre-migration experiences, the Morganton workers had already made important organizational gains in the period leading up to the 1995 strike. The advances were registered on a variety of levels. Local Guatemalans enrolled by town of origin in a vigorous, all-Hispanic soccer league. Similarly, Guatemalan religious life proliferated with the establishment of two local Hispanic evangelical churches, in addition to the growing constituency at St. Charles Catholic Church, where Guatemalans monopolized a weekly Sunday mass, launched a vigorous charismatic meeting on Saturdays, and established distinctive Maya choir groups which practiced at all hours of the weekend.

A sophisticated sign of community organization emerged weeks prior to the unionizing strike of 1995 with the formation of a local Aguacatán burial society. Common among other hometown associations of Central American migrants, the specific idea of sending bodies home to Aguacatán for burial sprang directly from Paulino López. When his own 21-year-old son Remigio died of illness in Indiantown in 1989, "friends, countrymen, Aguacatecos . . . gathered the money to send his remains to Guatemala . . . there began the idea to organize." Following the death of Roberto Vicente Rodríguez in an automobile accident in Morganton in April 1995, Paulino drew on his earlier experience to institutionalize the self-help network through a *directiva* [leadership committee] on which he served as treasurer. From this experiment came the beginning of a nation-wide network of *directivas*, which regularly respond to local appeals for help: "Here in Morganton we [Aguacatecos] have maybe one hundred apartments. The *directiva* decides how much we ask from each person. It is an obligation. All the people are in agreement. Twenty-five dollars or twenty dollars from everyone. The money is collected and we telephone other *directivas* in places like Missouri, and other states, from these places come a list with twenty or thirty Aguacatecos, and it comes with all the money in a money order." The money is sent home to the widow, mother, or closest of kin. If there is more than is needed for the transportation and funeral expenses it is expected to be applied to the family's welfare. . . .

Back in Aguacatán the burial society created by the émigrés also has a presence in the life of the community. Marcelino Mendoza Velásquez, for example, is one of five people from the town district El Calvario, who attends to messages, sent through Paulino López, from the Aguacateco network in the US. In case of a death abroad, Marcelino, who has a laboring job with the town (among other tasks, he helps to organize the weekly market day), receives a phone message, collects a wired monetary commission, then goes to the Guatemala City airport to pick up the body.

As the contact center between the home and diasporic community, the *directiva* of *aguacatecos* clearly carried an emotional and symbolic significance beyond its practical functions. As such, the fact that the "secretary" of the *directiva* in 1995, José Samuel Solís López, was also on the strike committee and subsequent union organizing committee suggested the seamless connection between the Case Farms struggle and the "official" interests of the community.

On the one hand, therefore, the gathering mobilization among immigrant workers clearly drew on older sources of allegiance. . . . The adversity of outward circumstances, the challenge of finding a toehold in a new land, perhaps acted to reinforce communal ties, creating a hedge against an individualism heedless of its affects on one's closest neighbors. In most cases, after all, the migrant individual's welfare in the United States—finding a job, a place to live, transportation to work, acquiring a work permit or green card—depended on an interlocking community network. Cemented by a common language, family and old friendship ties, or merely common memories of home—this sense of groupness derived from an identity constructed across generations, an identity which conjured up the dead and made it important for the dead in North Carolina to return to Aguacatán for a final reconnection with the ancestors.

If the Morganton *aguacatecos* clearly drew on ties forged in their home country, then the migration experience seems also to have affected the definitions and boundaries of *aguacateco* fellowship. In particular, the traditional separation between "pure Awakatecos" and "Chalchitecos" all but vanished in the new land. An older view of ethnic character differences, to be sure, still surfaced in the memory of Paulino López, a local "westerner" or "puro Awakateco":

> [Awakatecos] have a calm character. For example, if I have a problem with you, between our sons, or between animals, we say, "Friend, I have a problem with you" [or] "how much can I pay you for the damages?" This is the calm way. On the other hand the Chalchitecos, are full of rancor. "You did something bad to me. I am going to take revenge on you". . . . They like to argue, they are organized, and they easily joined the guerrillas.

Yet, Old Country divisions, according to Paulino, possessed decreasing significance: "They [the Chalchitecos] are another race [in origin], but they have become Awakatecos." Whatever fine distinctions remain in the homeland simply no longer operate abroad. In Morganton, avows Paulino, "we respect that we are all *aguacatecos*, we are united." The Morganton *directiva*, moreover, made no distinction by ethnic (as opposed to linguistic) origin. "We are in a country that is not ours," José Samuel explains.

Full Moon

Jessica Masaya

Journalist, story writer, and essayist Jessica Masaya was born in 1972 in Guatemala City, where she studied drama at the Universidad de San Carlos. She has won numerous awards for her short stories, including first prize in the 1999 Concurso del Cuento Corto de la Fundación Myrna Mack. The publication here of the following story, "Luna llena" or "Full moon," from her collection Club de los Aburridos, *marks the first time her work has appeared in English. Writing about youth in Guatemala City, Masaya conveys closures and openings within the city's overlapping worlds.*

Yeah, it's strange and out of the ordinary that I have this CD in my collection.

You know; it was one of those promising nights and we all got together on the late side, ready for who knows what.

There wasn't anything special to do, so first we went to our dealer's to buy the necessary little bags of cocaine. The girls stayed in the car—as usual—on the corner, but this time we saw a patrol car full of cops park in front of that whore house so I quickly got into the driver's seat, put on music, turned on the interior lights and we started to act like we were putting on make-up. By the time the patrol car came we were smearing on rouge for the third time and we looked like clowns.

A cop with a face full of lust told us that we should get out of there; there was going to be a raid because vice-ridden, malicious youth had come to buy drugs in that house of ill repute. "No way!"—I said with my eyes as round as huge saucers. I started the car and parked around the corner to figure out what to do just when Cindy's cell rang and it was Luis saying that Fideo, our dealer, had disappeared like magic and that they were trapped inside so they'd have to pretend to be clients until the raid was over. "Sure thing," Cindy replied jealously. Luis told us we should get a drink at one of those dives in this prostitute-infested area and wait until they came. The idea of going into some shabby *cantina* surrounded by whorehouses drove us into hysterics.

The only place where there weren't many people and we could park was that old xxx discotheque, the one that used to be good but had gone down-hill. I think my parents went there when they were first a couple. It was so ancient, we didn't think that it still existed but since it was only a block from where Fideo was, we decided to go in. When we went in I was immediately hit by a shut-in smell of worn carpet, the odor of a gross motel, a stale smell like old smoke and cheap perfume. Definitely, we thought, this place had become a hideaway for married men and their lovers, ugly and poor solitary guys and whores. But honestly we really fit in since we were super made up, with a lot of blush. Accustomed to having someone else pay, we didn't have enough for a bottle of nothing. Whatever; we acted like those women who go out looking for company, sitting there the entire time with one sad beer.

And the music was so *cholero*. For sure, if I had sniffed my quota and drunk a little vodka, I could have gotten into it, ended up dancing and wig-gling my butt. But with nothing in the nose and not enough alcohol, noth-ing was happening. Right off these creepy single guys gave us the eye, wait-ing for us, with our mini-shirts, padded bras and boots. Just one of Karla's glares, with her famous arched eyebrow, was enough to stop them from hitting on us. Better that no one bother us because we were just waiting for our own true studs.

My friends were so full of stupid loud talk—"*guácala*" [gross] "shit" "what music!" "what time will my sweetheart get here?"—that conversation was impossible. So, I had time to think. It bothered me that I couldn't be happy without my dose even through for some time I had claimed I wasn't an ad-dict. But that night, I started to doubt it. I looked around. All these people were simple. They weren't all dressed up for partying. They were just there, so guileless and they seemed happy. I guessed that there was no gang head-ing into the toilet to snort. My new boots were killing me, the wax depila-tion still stung (including in my noble parts), and my latest piercing made me feel uncomfortable and all swollen. Suddenly I envied those middle-aged ladies with their low heels, hairy legs all pale and faces blotted by sun.

Then I fixed my eyes on those two. A couple, I guess he was forty and some and she was thirty and a bit. Both were dark skinned, short, curly haired and flat nosed; she was sort of overweight, her big arms showed, and her tummy threatened to slip out of her cheap blouse. But none of this mattered. When he went for the drinks, she stared at him, captivated. Then they whispered things and kissed like in a Hollywood movie. It was like nobody was around them.

The dj was into his *merengue* bit, and lively dancers swept up the old dirty floor. The man in the couple I'm telling you about went to have a word with the dj and after he returned to her, they waited, happily. Then their song started. It's not a bad song, it's not that tacky. And the lyrics are good: "In the starry night, under the full moon I want to tell you, my love, a thousand beautiful things, and steal a kiss from you to seal the pact of our love that starts today." And they went to dance. I have never seen two bodies dancing together as if they were one, moving exactly as if each knew the moves of the other. They touched as if caressing each other and their light feet seemed to be in the air. But the most spectacular was that they sang the song as if their lives depended on it, they looked into each other's eyes that seemed about to cry, then they hugged like the pleasure was too much. With all my heart I wanted to be her in that moment, get back my simple hopes and not have to put anything in me to not be bored.

Finally our guys found us and they had to pull me by my arms to get me out of that place since I couldn't stop watching that strange and marvelous spectacle. My crowd teases me to this day saying that night transformed me and the abstinence of that moment had damaged my brain, just because I am learning to dance *merengue* and I've forced Miguel to learn as well (I threatened I wouldn't give any zoom-zoom). And I could not rest until I found out who sang that song and I bought Elvis Crespo's CD.

Sometimes, on Sundays when we are alone at my place, when I'm not all dolled up and Miguel hasn't shaved, we buy a bottle of cheap rum. He makes *cubas* with Coke and lime while I flirt with him. Next, in our private discotheque we put on "Full Moon" to make us happy and he pulls me out to dance and we sweep the floor, while we look in each other's eyes and sing. "I want to tell you I love you since that day when your look met mine." And even though we always end making love in the sweetest way, I feel something missing, but maybe we are going in the right direction.

Translated by Deborah T. Levenson

Keep On Keeping On

Yolanda Colom, interviewed by Isabel Recinos Arenas

Middle-class, city-born and -raised, Yolanda Colom spent twenty-one years in the guerrilla group Ejército Guerrillero de los Pobres (EGP), and six of these fighting in the mountains (see "We Rose Up," part 5 of this volume). After the war, she returned to civilian life with only the revolutionary movement on her "résumé." Re-integrating into postwar Guatemala was not easy for an older woman still revolutionary in outlook. Eventually, she found her métier at an all-girls' school where she is employed as a grounds worker. She continues her work of social transformation by educating young women, staff, and parents about collective gardening, recycling, and rescuing waste from urban ravines. The following interview was conducted by Isabel Recinos Arenas, a graduate of the school.

YOLANDA COLOM: In 2004, the directors of the school decided it was the right time to turn the institution's attention to the natural environment in a more direct manner. The institution already taught about environmental problems in classes and many teachers had built pedagogical activities around these, and I was hired in grounds and maintenance with an eye to literally resolving the environmental questions on the school's extensive lands, over seventy hectares, most of which wasn't used. A green area in the middle had been planted with samplings but it had been abandoned and became overgrown. It's one thing to do a bit of re-forestation here and there, and another to undertake taking on the question of ecological development in an integrated manner, which means cleaning up the whole area, enriching the soil, cultivating the vegetation, and educating adults and youth about how to approach and interact with the natural environment.

ISABEL RECINOS ARENAS: *You mean during the planting season?*

YC: What had been done was to put boxes for little gardens near the classes; the students planted, waited for the plants to germinate and that was that. So, a few years ago, as part of this new curriculum, I planned and built a greenhouse with the students, and we cultivated a vegetable garden in there. Now it has reached the point where kindergarteners and children from primary grades permanently care for the garden as part of their required curriculum. It is part of their schoolwork; it's way beyond some minimal assignment! Now we have permanent beds marked off by tempered planks all year round. The children don't just plant seeds and then transplant them to beds when these germinate, but they regularly come to weed, rake, water, and eventually harvest. Everything is handled through natural methods, and the children do it. They eat the fruits of their labor. It's completely organic, we got all the chemicals out of here. And if the production is abundant, the children take home produce, radishes, carrots, beets, lettuce . . . and *chile* peppers. We tried planting *chile* peppers and it was so successful, we harvested so much.

It means so much that the children do this work here on the school grounds. It gives them the idea of the process of life—in this case of plants, vegetables, the idea is that children and adults as well all understand that life is made of processes, not just of single acts or statistics, but that these are part of processes. The child accompanies the little plant, and realizes its necessities and the risks it confronts on the road to fruition.

IRA: *When you started working here, what was your impression of the school?*

YC: Well, like any other, this educational institution does not escape the more general social situation. The school has been a microcosm of a system of thinking and of organization with roots in the history of our country, in a ton of factors. Like all others, this institution has personified consumerism, the production of waste, the tendency to never recycle, or repair or search for creative means of giving more life—or many lives—to material resources. . . . It's classic Western civilization and capitalist production.

There was no encouragement for creativity in restoring or repairing material things or finding new uses for them: a bottle can be a flower vase; later, it can hold paint brushes; it can become a piece of art; it can be primary material to sell or recycle. So the idea now is to repair, care for, store, classify, recreate. This means changing habits and deep customs, which is never easy, but I think the school is now moving forward in some areas faster than I could have imagined, like the collaboration of the children in not creating garbage.

Last year we in maintenance evaluated our work, and we see progress. It is not like Superman or Spider-Man comes to perform miracles; it's collective work, and the whole collective has to understand it, enjoy it, and be disciplined. The [grounds] workers here are of peasant origin and I encourage and teach them, so that they value their work. There isn't anyone who can't make marvels. Before, either problems weren't solved or specialists were called; now the workers in maintenance do it. This is stimulating and they become more interested. . . . There is mutual respect. We create tools here. We don't go buy them, we make them out of what metal we find in the ravine [the school property edges down into a deep ravine]. We make hoes out of discarded pipes, we use sheet metal that has been left, we use all kinds of things that are thrown into the ravines—faucets, hoses, doors, glass, scraps of metal.

IRA: *Yolanda, in relation to your past, how do you see this project? Does it have a relation to the past, or is this completely another chapter in your life?*

YC: Of course it's another chapter, but you continue to be the same person. Look, I'm working here because I need to work to survive, I need a wage, I need to work as long as I live because it's my only income. When I returned from exile, from the first I wanted to do political work, organizational work to develop political consciousness, and organize the popular sectors, youth, women, the majority that isn't in power. At first I worked with other *companeros* to try to build institutions dedicated to creating political and civic popular leadership within the middle classes. We did that for a number of years but we couldn't keep it going for financial reasons. . . . For a while I worked part time at Landívar [Universidad Rafael Landívar, Guatemala's prestigious private Jesuit university]. I have never completed university studies, I never had a career, I never wanted to follow a career, either before or after [going into the mountains], but I was very interested in research, and I went to Landívar to work in a project about ethnicity and culture, a topic I had experienced, in practice, for years. This was the only time I ever worked within the heart of a university. I worked there for two years, and it was a marvelous experience for me, I had absolute support for and freedom in my research.

But I realized that this wasn't my world. Even through the university opened its doors to me, I saw from inside students, faculty, university councils—the anxieties, the contradictions. Well, that is not my world. I also did research for other foundations, including on the [Guatemalan] military, another field with which I am familiar! But being who I am—I am very independent in my way of thinking, and I am a practical person, a person of actions—I need more challenge. I like being inside the process, I like to take responsibility, to delegate, to form teams, cultivate leadership. Here at the school I can do some of that. I feel more satisfied. At my age I learn new things, even though I don't have academic preparation in environmental studies. I was not starting from zero in these questions. I saw farms as a child; I was around adults who loved the outdoors and who taught me to enjoy nature. When I went into the mountains, nature was entirely foreign to me. And the [armed] struggle taught me how to survive in the mountains, in nature. I know how to make rustic constructions and clear undergrowth. I know these things because I had to learn them to survive, to exist.

I have always sought my own path. I read theory and I study and I reflect, but I am practical, and I learn best in practice. I read books about trees and plants, but I go around and look at greenhouses elsewhere, I look at how the seedlings are arranged, how scrap is collected and materials organized and warehoused. I look at the people working—I observe. Observing is an attitude of permanent learning.

Translated by Deborah T. Levenson

Orgullo Gay

Photographs and essay by José Manuel Mayorga

Gays and lesbians face terrible risks in Guatemala. As many have come out of the closet, they have been subject to increased violence. More than forty openly gay, lesbian, and transgender people have been murdered in the last few years, and many of the most prominent rights activists, such as Claudia Acevedo, an activist in Colectiva de Lesbianas Liberadas, have received death threats. Gay spaces nevertheless continue to appear, and the now annual Orgullo Gay (Gay Pride Parade), captured below by the Guatemalan photographer José Manuel Mayorga, proceeds without incident through Guatemala's busy downtown and into the central plaza. In July 2008, several of Mayorga's photos were enlarged and exhibited in the plaza, where they remained for one month without being vandalized. Mayorga, in his forties, is part of a generation of courageous and cosmopolitan intellectuals. Here is a selection of his work, along with a caption he composed in reference to the gay movement and to accompany the photograph titled Belles de Jour.

The name of this piece—*Belles de Jour*—alludes to the Luis Buñuel film, which opened in Guatemala in May 1968; any other resemblance is purely coincidental. The girls in the portrait are exercising their free will in the name of "I imagine, therefore I exist"—what Claude Cahun [Cahun, 1894–1954, was an avant-garde left-wing French photographer and artist who challenged notions of gender] felt in her day when she did her self-portraits. Today, they are visual testimonies of a transgression of the established order. The idea here references gender as an image of identity; this portrait of women is of people living their lives. They are who they are, and they feel comfortable dressing in a manner appropriate for a Saturday afternoon in the tropics. Is this a simulated reality? Whatever the case, a symbolic femininity openly defining the masculine in a conservative and macho country requires guts.

This is the first decade of the twenty-first century. In Central America new winds seem to stir, and for moments we feel that in these lands we can

La hada buena (The good fairy). Gay pride parade, Guatemala City, 2007.
Photo by José Manuel Mayorga. Used by permission of the photographer.

Belles du jour. Gay pride parade, Guatemala City, 2007. Photo by José Manuel Mayorga. Used by permission of the photographer.

exercise respect for difference. However, uncontrolled violence and every-day intolerance contradict this claim, and the wave of femicides makes us remember the title of Carmen Rico-Godoy's novel, *Como ser mujer y no morir en el intento* [How to be a woman and not die trying]. History shows us that each of us does as we must, as did Joan of Arc.

Translated by Deborah T. Levenson

Word Play

Isabel de los Angeles Ruano, with photos
by Fotokids/Fundación de Niños Artistas

Life goes on . . . Isabel de los Angeles Ruano, author of the poem below, "Word Play,"
is a noted poet in her sixties who lives itinerantly on the streets of Guatemala City.
The accompanying photographs come from Fotokids/Fundación de Niños Artistas,
a project started in 1991 by US photographer Nancy McGirr to teach photography to
children in Guatemala City's slums (www.fotokids.org).

I have a secret violin,
with no strings or notes,
no scores or symphonies,
a little violin,
dark, sweet
that I carry inside.
It makes no sounds,
and nobody hears
its melody
that sometimes is tenderness
I stole from silence.

Translated by Dina Bursztyn and
Deborah T. Levenson

Angelito (Little angel). Photo by Jessica Aguilar,
age 13. © copyright Jessica Aguilar 1999/Fotokids.
Used by permission of Fotokids/Fundación de
Niños Artistas.

Saltando la cuerda (Skipping rope). Photo by Marta Loarca, age 9. © copyright Marta Loarca 1995/Fotokids. Used by permission of Fotokids/Fundación de Niños Artistas.

Juego de palabras

Yo tengo un violín escondido,
sin cuerdas y sin notas.
sin partituras ni sinfonias,
es un pequeño violín,
oscuro, dulce
el que yo llevo adentro,
sin que suene,
sin que nadie oiga
aquella melodía
que a veces es ternura
que le robé al silencio.

Suggestions for Further Reading

General Suggestions

Adams, Richard N., and Santiago Bastos. *Las relaciones étnicas en Guatemala, 1944–2000.*
   Antigua, Guatemala: Centro de Investigaciones Regionales de Mesoamérica, 2003.
Cambranes, J. C., ed. *500 años de lucha por la tierra: Estudios sobre propiedad rural y re-*
   forma agraria en Guatemala. Guatemala City: FLACSO, 1992.
Camus, Manuela. *Las ideas detrás de la etnicidad: Una selección de textos para el debate.*
   Antigua, Guatemala: Centro de Investigaciones Regionales de Mesoamérica, 2006.
Comisión para el Esclarecimiento Histórico. *Guatemala: Memoria del silencio.* 12 vols.
   Guatemala City: United Nations Operating Projects Services, 1999. The commis-
   sion's twelve-volume report is available in Spanish (along with an English-language
   summary of the report's conclusions and recommendations) at http://shr.aaas.org/
   guatemala/ceh/mds/spanish.
Filóchofo. *La otra historia: (de los mayas al informe de la "Comisión de la Verdad")/contada*
   por Filóchofo. Guatemala City, 1999.
Fried, Jonathan L., Marvin Gentleman, Deborah Levenson, and Nancy Peckenham.
   Guatemala in Rebellion: Unfinished History. New York: Grove Press, 1983.
Gellert, Gisela, and Julio Pinto Soria. *Ciudad de Guatemala: Dos estudios sobre su evlucion*
   urbana (1524–1950). Guatemala City: Editorial de la Universidad de San Carlos, 1992.
Handy, Jim. *Gift of the Devil: A History of Guatemala.* Boston: South End Press, 1984.
Human Rights Office of the Archdiocese of Guatemala. *Guatemala: Never Again!* Gua-
   temala City: Proyecto Interdiocesano de Recuperación de la Memoria Histórica,
   1998.
Levenson, Deborah. *Hacer la juventud: Jóvenes de tres generaciones de una familia trabaja-*
   dora en la ciudad de Guatemala. Guatemala City: AVANCSO, 2005.
Luján Muñoz, Jorge, ed. *Historia general de Guatemala.* 6 vols. Guatemala City: Asociación de Amigos del País, Fundación para la Cultura y el Desarrollo, 1993–1999.
Menchú, Rigoberta. *I, Rigoberta Menchú: An Indian Woman in Guatemala.* Edited and introduced by Elisabeth Burgos-Debray. Translated by Ann Wright. London: Verso,
   1984.
Morales Santos, Francisco. *Los nombres que nos nombran: Panorama de la poesia guate-*
   malteca (1782–2007). Guatemala City: Magna Terra, 2010.
Smith, Carol, ed., with the assistance of Marilyn M. Moors. *Guatemalan Indians and the*
   State: 1540 to 1988. Austin: University of Texas Press, 1990.

Taracena Arriola, Arturo. *Etnicidad, estado y nación en Guatemala.* 2 vols. Antigua,
Guatemala: Centro de Investigaciones Regionales de Mesoamérica, 2002.

Witzel de Ciudad, Renate. *Más de 100 años del movimiento obrero urbano en Guatemala.*
3 vols. Guatemala City: Asociación de Investigación y Estudios Sociales,
1991–1993.

Wolf, Eric. *Sons of the Shaking Earth.* Chicago: University of Chicago Press, 1959.

Part I. The Maya: Before the Europeans

Carmack, Robert M. *Quichean Civilization: The Ethnohistoric, Ethnographic, and Archaeological Sources.* Berkeley: University of California Press, 1973.

———. *The Quiché Mayas of Utatlán: The Evolution of a Highland Guatemala Kingdom.*
Norman: University of Oklahoma Press, 1981.

Gustafson, Lowell S., and Amelia M. Trevelyan, eds. *Ancient Maya Gender Identity and
Relations.* Westport: Bergin & Garvey, 2002.

Inomata, Takeshi, Daniela Triadan, Erick Ponciano, and Kazuo Ayama, eds. *La política
de lugares y comunidades en la antigua sociedad maya de Petexbatun: Las investigaciones
del Proyecto Arqueológico Aguateca, segunda fase.* Guatemala City: Ministerio de Cultura y Deportes, Dirección General del Patrimonio Cultural y Natural, and Instituto de Antropología e Historia, 2009.

Lohse, Jon C., and Fred Valdez Jr. *Ancient Maya Commoners.* Austin: University of Texas
Press, 2004.

Schele, Linda, and Mary Ellen Miller. *The Blood of Kings: Dynasty and Ritual in Maya
Art.* Fort Worth: Kimbell Art Museum, 1986.

Sharer, Robert J., with Loa P. Traxler. *The Ancient Maya.* Palo Alto: Stanford University
Press, 2005.

Tedlock, Barbara. *Time and the Highland Maya.* Albuquerque: University of New Mexico Press, 1982.

Part II. Invasion and Colonialism

Akkeren, Ruud van. *La visión indígena de la conquista.* Antigua, Guatemala: Centro de
Investigaciones sobre Mesoamérica, 2007.

Asselbergs, Florine G. L. *Conquered Conquistadors: The Lienzo de Quauhquechollan:
A Nahua Vision of the Conquest of Guatemala.* Leiden: CNWS Publications, 2008.

Bode, Barbara. *The Dance of the Conquest of Guatemala.* New Orleans: Middle American
Research Institute, Tulane University, 1961.

Carmack, Robert. *Rebels of Highland Guatemala: The Quiché-Mayas of Momostenango.*
Norman: University of Oklahoma Press, 1995.

Contreras, Daniel. *Una rebelión indígena en el partido de Totonicapán en 1820.* Guatemala
City: Imprenta Universitaria, 1951.

Few, Martha. *Women Who Lead Evil Lives: Gender, Religion and the Politics of Power in
Colonial Guatemala.* Austin: University of Texas Press, 2002.

Gosner, Kevin. *Soldiers of the Virgin: The Moral Economy of a Colonial Maya Rebellion.*
Tucson: University of Arizona Press, 1992.

Herrera, Robinson A. *Natives, Europeans, and Africans in Sixteenth-Century Santiago de Guatemala*. Austin: University of Texas Press, 2003.

Jones, Grant D. *The Conquest of the Last Maya Kingdom*. Palo Alto: Stanford University Press, 1998.

Kramer, Wendy. *Encomienda Politics in Early Colonial Guatemala, 1524–1544: Dividing the Spoils*. Boulder: Westview Press, 1994.

Lovell, W. George, and Christopher Lutz. *Demography and Empire: A Guide to the Population History of Spanish Central America, 1500–1821*. Boulder: Westview Press, 1995.

Lutz, Christopher. *Santiago de Guatemala, 1541–1773: City, Caste, and the Colonial Experience*. Norman: University of Oklahoma Press, 1994.

MacLeod, Murdo J. *Spanish Central America; A Socioeconomic History, 1520–1720*. Berkeley: University of California Press, 1973.

Martínez Peláez, Severo. *La patria del criollo: Ensayo de interpretación de la realidad colonial guatemalteca*. Guatemala City: Editorial Universitaria, 1970. Translated into English under the same title; translated by Susan M. Neve and W. George Lowell. Durham: Duke University Press, 2009.

Maxwell, Judith. *Kaqchikel Chronicles: The Definitive Edition*. Austin: University of Texas Press, 2006.

Patch, Robert W. *Maya Revolt and Revolution in the Eighteenth Century*. Armonk: M. E. Sharpe, 2002.

Piel, Jean. *Sajcabajá: Muerte y resurrección de un pueblo de Guatemala, 1500–1970*. Translated by Eliana Castro Ponlsen. Mexico City and Guatemala City: Centre d'études mexicaines et centraméricaines and Seminario de Integración Social, 1989.

Recinos, Adrián, ed. *Crónicas indígenas de Guatemala*. Guatemala City: Editorial Universitaria, 1957.

Rodríguez, Ileana. *Transnational Topographies: Island, Highlands, Jungles*. Minneapolis: University of Minnesota Press, 2004.

Saint-Lu, André. *La vera paz: Esprit évangelique et colonization*. Paris: Centre de recherches hispaniques, Institut d'estudes hispaniques, 1968.

van Oss, Adriaan. *Catholic Colonialism: A Parish History of Guatemala, 1524–1821*. Cambridge: Cambridge University Press, 1986.

Ximénez, Fray Francisco. *Historia de la provincia de San Vicente de Chiapa y Guatemala de la Orden de Predicadores*. 3 vols. Guatemala City: Tipografía Nacional, 1929–1931.

Part III. A Caffeinated Modernism

Arévalo Martínez, Rafael. *Ecce Pericles! La tiranía de Manuel Estrada Cabrera en Guatemala*. 3rd ed. San José, Costa Rica: Editorial Universitaria Centroamericana, 1983.

Bunzel, Ruth Leah. *Chichicastenango: A Guatemalan Village*. Locust Valley: J. J. Augustin, 1952.

Casaús Arzú, Marta Elena. *Guatemala: Linaje y racismo*. Guatemala City: F&G Editores, 2007.

———, and Oscar Guillermo Peláez Almengor, eds. *Historia intelectual de Guatemala*. Guatemala City: Centro de Estudios Urbanos y Regionales, Universidad de San Carlos de Guatemala, 2001.

Castellanos Cambranes, Julio. *Café y campesinos en Guatemala, 1853–1897.* Guatemala City: University of San Carlos, 1985.

Dosal, Paul. *Doing Business with the Dictators: A Political History of United Fruit in Guatemala, 1899–1944.* Wilmington, DE: SR Books, 1993.

———. *Power in Transition: The Rise of Guatemala's Industrial Oligarchy, 1871–1994.* Westport: Praeger, 1995.

Grandin, Greg, *The Blood of Guatemala: A History of Race and Nation.* Durham: Duke University Press, 2000.

Grieb, Kenneth J. *Guatemalan Caudillo: The Regime of Jorge Ubico, Guatemala 1931–1944.* Athens: Ohio University Press, 1979.

Gudmunson, Lowell, and Hector Lindo-Fuentes. *Central America, 1821–1871: Liberalism Before Liberals.* Tuscaloosa: University of Alabama Press, 1995.

Guzmán Böckler, Carlos, and Jean-Loup Herbert. *Guatemala: Una interpretación histórico-social.* Mexico City: Siglo Veintiuno Editores, 1970.

Ingersoll, Hazel. "The War of the Mountain: A Study in Reactionary Peasant Insurgency in Guatemala, 1837–1873." PhD dissertation, George Washington University, 1972.

King, Arden. *Coban and the Verapaz: History and Cultural Process in Northern Guatemala.* New Orleans: Middle American Research Institute, Tulane University, 1974.

Reeves, René. *Ladinos with Ladinos, Indians with Indians: Land, Labor and Regional Ethnic Conflict in the Making of Guatemala.* Palo Alto: Stanford University Press, 2006.

Sullivan-González, Douglass. *Piety, Power, and Politics: Religion and Nation Formation in Guatemala, 1821–1871.* Pittsburgh: University of Pittsburgh Press, 1998.

Taracena Arriola, Arturo. *Invención criolla, sueño ladino, pesadilla indígena: Los Altos de Guatemala: De región a estado, 1740–1850.* Antigua, Guatemala, and San José, Costa Rica: Centro de Investigaciones Regionales de Mesoamérica and Porvenir, 1997.

Tax, Sol. *Penny Capitalism: A Guatemalan Indian Economy.* Washington: Institute of Social Anthropology, Smithsonian Institution, 1953.

Torras, Rosa. *Así vivimos el yugo: La conflictiva conformación de Colotenango como municipio de mozos.* Guatemala City: AVANCSO, 2007.

Wagner, Regina. *Los alemanes en Guatemala, 1828–1944.* Guatemala City: Afanes, 1996.

Woodward, Ralph Lee. *Rafael Carrera and the Emergence of the Republic of Guatemala.* Athens: University of Georgia Press, 1993.

Part IV. Ten Years of Spring and Beyond

Adams, Richard Newbold. *Crucifixion by Power: Essays on Guatemalan National Social Structure, 1944–1966.* Austin: University of Texas Press, 1970.

Arias, Arturo. *After the Bombs.* Willimantic: Curbstone Press, 1995.

Asturias, Miguel Angel. *Week-end en Guatemala.* Buenos Aires: Editorial Goyanarte, 1956.

Bauer Paiz, Alfonso. *Como opera el capital yanqui en Centroamérica (El caso de Guatemala).* Mexico City: Editorial Iberoamericana, 1956.

Cambranes, J. C. *La presencia viva del Che Guevara en Guatemala.* San José, Costa Rica: Editorial Cultural de Centroamérica, 2004.

Cardoza y Aragón, Luis. *La revolución guatemalteca*. Guatemala City: Editorial Pensativo, 1995. Reprint: 1994.

Cullather, Nick. *Secret History: The CIA's Classified Account of Its Operations in Guatemala, 1952–1954*. Palo Alto: Stanford University Press, 1999.

Flores, Marco Antonio. *Fortuny: Un comunista guatemalteco*. Guatemala City: Universidad de San Carlos, 1994.

Forster, Cindy. *The Time of Freedom: Campesino Workers in Guatemala's October Revolution*. Pittsburgh: University of Pittsburgh Press, 2001.

Galeano, Eduardo. *Guatemala: País ocupado*. Mexico City: Nuestro Tiempo, 1967.

Gleijeses, Piero. *Shattered Hope: The Guatemalan Revolution and the United States, 1944–1954*. Princeton: Princeton University Press, 1991.

Grandin, Greg. *The Last Colonial Massacre: Latin America in the Cold War*. Chicago: University of Chicago Press, 2004.

———, ed. *Denegado en su totalidad: Documentos estadounidenses liberados*. Guatemala City: AVANCSO, 2001.

Handy, Jim. *Revolution in the Countryside: Rural Conflict and Agrarian Reform in Guatemala, 1944–1954*. Chapel Hill: UNC Press, 1994.

Immerman, Richard. *The CIA in Guatemala: The Foreign Policy of Intervention*. Austin: University of Texas Press, 1982.

Jonas, Susanne Bodenheimer. *Guatemala, plan piloto para el continente*. San José, Costa Rica: EDUCA, 1981.

Pellecer, Carlos Manuel. *Arbenz y yo*. Guatemala City: Editorial Artemis-Edinter, 1997.

Pinto Soria, Julio César. *El estado y la violencia en Guatemala (1944–1970)*. Guatemala City: Universidad de San Carlos de Guatemala, Centro de Estudios Urbanos y Regionales, 2004.

Rolando Morán [Ricardo Ramírez]. *Turcios Lima*. Havana: Instituto del Libro, 1969.

Schlesinger, Stephen, and Stephen Kinzer. *Bitter Fruit: The Untold Story of the American Coup in Guatemala*. New York: Doubleday, 1982.

Streeter, Stephen. *Managing the Counterrevolution: The United States and Guatemala, 1954–1961*. Athens: Ohio University Press, 2000.

Toriello Garrido, Guillermo. *La batalla de Guatemala*. Guatemala City: Editorial Universitaria, Universidad de San Carlos de Guatemala, 1955. Reprint: 1997.

Vilanova de Arbenz, María. *Mi esposo, el presidente Arbenz*. Guatemala City: Editorial Universitaria, 2000.

Yagenova, Simona Violetta. *Los maestros y la Revolución de Octubre (1944–1954)*. Guatemala City: Editorial de Ciencias Sociales, 2006.

Yashar, Deborah J. *Demanding Democracy: Reform and Reaction in Costa Rica and Guatemala, 1870s–1950s*. Palo Alto: Stanford University Press, 1997.

Part V. Roads to Revolution

Adams, Richard Newbold. *Joaquín Noval como indigenista, antropólogo y revolucionario*. Guatemala City: Editorial Universitaria, Universidad de San Carlos de Guatemala, 2000.

Aguilera Peralta, Gabriel. *Dialéctica del terror en Guatemala*. San José, Costa Rica: Editorial Universitaria Centroamericana, 1981.

Albizures, Miguel Angel. *Tiempo de sudor y lucha*. Mexico City: Praxis, 1987.

Berger, Susan A. *Political and Agrarian Development in Guatemala*. Boulder: Westview Press, 1992.

Bizarro Ujpán, Ignacio. *Campesino: The Diary of a Guatemalan Indian*. Translated and edited by James D. Sexton. Tucson: University of Arizona Press, 1985.

Black, George. *Garrison Guatemala*. New York: Monthly Review Press, 1984.

Brintnall, Douglas E. *Revolt against the Dead: The Modernization of a Mayan Community in the Highlands of Guatemala*. New York: Gordon and Breach, 1979.

Colom, Yolanda. *Mujeres en la alborada*. Guatemala City: Artemis, 1998.

Davis, Sheldon, and Julie Hodson. *Witness to Political Violence in Guatemala*. Boston: Oxfam America, 1982.

Falla, Ricardo. *Quiché rebelde: Religious Conversion, Politics, and Ethnic Identity in Guatemala*. Translated by Phillip Berryman. Austin: University of Texas Press 1978. Reprint: 2001.

Figueroa Ibarra, Carlos. *El proletariado rural en el agro*. San José, Costa Rica: Piedrasanta, 1979.

Guzman Bockler, Carlos, and Jean-Loup Herbert. *Guatemala: Una interpretación histórica-social*. Mexico City: Siglo XXI, 1971.

Harbury, Jennifer. *Bridge of Courage: Life Stories of the Guatemalan Compañeros and Compañeras*. Monroe: Common Courage Press, 1994.

Hernández Alarcón, Rosalinda, Andrea Carrillo Samayoa, Jacqueline Torres Urízar, Ana López Molina, and Ligia Z. Peláez Aldana, eds. *Memorias rebeldes contra el olvido*. Guatemala City: Ediciones la Cuerda, AVANCSO, Plataforma Agraria, 2008.

Jonas, Susanne, and David Tobis. *Guatemala*. New York: North American Congress on Latin America, 1981.

Kobrak, Paul. *Organizing and Repression in the University of San Carlos, Guatemala, 1944 to 1996*. Washington: American Association for the Advancement of Science, 1999.

Levenson, Deborah. *Trade Unionists against Terror: Guatemala City, 1954–1985*. Chapel Hill: UNC Press, 1994.

Lopez Larrave, Mario. *Breve historia del movimiento sindical guatemalteco*. Guatemala City: Editorial Universitaria, 1979.

Macías, Julio César. *La guerrilla fue mi camino: Epitafio para César Montes*. Guatemala City: Piedra Santa, 1997.

May, Rachel A. *Terror in the Countryside: Campesino Responses to Political Violence in Guatemala, 1954–1985*. Athens: Ohio University Press, 2001.

McClintock, Michael. *The American Connection: State Terror and Popular Resistance in Guatemala*. London: Zed Books, 1985.

Melville, Thomas, and Marjorie Melville. *Guatemala: Another Vietnam?* New York: Penguin, 1971.

Melville, Thomas, and Marjorie Melville. *Guatemala: The Politics of Land Ownership*. New York: Free Press, 1972.

Murga Armas, Jorge. *Iglesia católica, movimiento indígena y lucha revolucionaria*. Santiago Atitlán, Guatemala: Impresiones Palacios, 2006.

Payeras, Mario. *Days of the Jungle: The Testimony of a Guatemalan Guerrillero 1972–1976.* New York: Monthly Review Press, 1983.

Plant, Roger. *Guatemala: Unnatural Disaster.* London: Latin America Bureau, 1978.

Porras Castejón, Gustavo. *Las huellas de Guatemala.* Guatemala City: F&G Editores, 2009.

Ramírez, Chiqui. *Guerra de los 36 años: Vista con ojos de mujer de izquierda.* Guatemala City: Editorial O. de León Palacios, 2000.

Renato Barillas, Byron, Carlos Alberto Enríquez Prado, and Luis Pedro Taracena Arriola. *Tres décadas, dos generaciones: El movimiento estudiantil universitario, una perspectiva desde sus protagonistas.* Guatemala City: Helvetas Guatemala, 2000.

Toriello Garrido, Guillermo. *Guatemala: Más de 20 años de traición, 1954–1979.* Guatemala City: Editorial Universitaria, 1979.

Torres Rivas, Edelberto. *Interpretación del desarrollo social centroamericano.* San José, Costa Rica: EDUCA, 1977.

Van Den Berghe, Pierre L., and Benjamin N. Colby. *Ixil Country: A Plural Society in Highland Guatemala.* Berkeley: University of California Press, 1969.

Warren, Kay. *The Symbolism of Subordination: Indian Identiy in a Guatemalan Town.* Austin: University of Texas Press, 1989.

Part VI. Intent to Destroy

AVANCSO. *Donde está el futuro? Procesos de reintegración en comunidades de retornados.* Guatemala City: AVANCSO, 1992.

————. *Glosas nuevas sobre la misma guerra: Rebelión campesina, poder pastoral y genocidio en Guatemala.* Guatemala City: AVANCSO, 2010.

————. *La política de desarrollo del estado guatemalteco 1986–1987.* Guatemala City: AVANCSO, 1987.

Ball, Patrick, Paul Kobrak, and Herbert Spirer. *State Violence in Guatemala, 1960–1996: A Quantitative Reflection.* Washington: American Association for the Advancement of Science, 1999.

Burns, Allan F. *Mayans in Exile: Guatemalans in Florida.* Philadelphia: Temple University Press, 1993.

Carmack, Robert, ed. *Harvest of Violence: The Maya Indians and the Guatemalan Crisis.* Norman: University of Oklahoma Press, 1988.

Equipo de Antropología Forense de Guatemala. *Las masacres en Rabinal, estudio histórico antropológico de las masacres de Plan de Sánchez, Chicupac y Río Negro.* Guatemala City: Equipo de Antropología Forense de Guatemala, 1997.

Falla, Ricardo. *Massacres in the Jungle: Ixcán, Guatemala, 1975–1982.* Translated by Julia Howland. Boulder: Westview Press, 1994.

————. *Negreaba de Zopilotes: Masacre y sobrevivencia finca San Francisco, Nentón.* Guatemala City: AVANCSO, 2011.

Figueroa Ibarra, Carlos. *El recurso del miedo: Ensayo sobre el estado y el terror en Guatemala.* San José, Costa Rica: Editorial Universitaria Centroamericana, 1991.

Garrard-Burnett, Virginia. *Terror in the Land of the Holy Spirit: Guatemala under General Efraín Ríos Montt, 1982–1983.* Oxford: Oxford University Press, 2009.

Gramajo Morales, Héctor Alejandro. *De la guerra—a la guerra: La difícil transición política en Guatemala*. Guatemala City: Fondo de Cultura Editorial, 1995.

Green, Linda. *Fear as a Way of Life: Mayan Widows in Rural Guatemala*. New York: Columbia University Press, 1999.

Inforpress Centroamericana. *Guatemala: Elecciones 1985*. Guatemala City: Inforpress Centroamericana, 1985.

———. *Guatemala: A Year of Promises*. Guatemala City: Inforpress Centroamericana, 1987.

Jonas, Susanne. *The Battle for Guatemala: Rebels, Death Squads, and US Power*. Boulder: Westview Press, 1991.

Manz, Beatriz. *Paradise in Ashes: A Guatemalan Journey of Courage, Terror and Hope*. Berkeley: University of California Press, 2004.

———. *Refugees of a Hidden War: The Aftermath of Counterinsurgency in Guatemala*. Albany: State University of New York Press, 1988.

Melville, Thomas. *Through a Glass Darkly: The US Holocaust in Central America*. Philadelphia: Xlibris Corporation, 2005.

Méndez de la Vega, Luz. *Toque de queda: Poesía bajo el terror, 1969–1999*. Guatemala City: Artemis Edinter, 1999.

Montejo, Victor. *Testimony: Death of a Guatemalan Village*. Translated by Victor Perera. Willimantic: Curbstone Press, 1987.

Nolin, Catherine. *Transnational Ruptures: Gender and Forced Migration*. Hampshire, UK: Ashgate Publishing, 2006.

Painter, James. *Guatemala, False Hope, False Freedom: The Rich, the Poor and the Christian Democrats*. London: Latin America Bureau, 1987.

Perera, Victor. *Unfinished Conquest: The Guatemalan Tragedy*. Berkeley: University of California Press, 1995.

Salvadó, Luis Raúl, and Julia González. *La ciudad y los desplazados por la violencia*. Guatemala City: AVANCSO, 1997.

Saxon, Dan. *To Save Her Life: Disappearance, Deliverance, and the United States in Guatemala*. Berkeley: University of California Press, 2007.

Schirmer, Jennifer. *The Guatemalan Military Project: A Violence Called Democracy*. Philadelphia: University of Pennsylvania Press, 1998.

Simon, Jean-Marie. *Guatemala: Eternal Spring, Eternal Tyranny*. New York: Norton, 1987.

Torres-Rivas, Edelberto. *Crisis del poder en Centroamérica*. San José, Costa Rica: Editorial Universitaria Centroamericana, 1981.

Zimmerman, Marc and Raúl Rojas, eds. *Voices from the Silence: Guatemalan Literature of Resistance*. Athens: Ohio University Press, 1998.

Zur, Judith N. *Violent Memories: Mayan War Widows in Guatemala*. Boulder: Westview Press, 1998.

Part VII. An Unsettled Peace

Archivo Histórico de la Policia Nacional. *Del Silencio a la Memoria: Revelaciones del Archivo Histórico de la Policia Nacional,* Guatemala City: Archivo Histórico de la Policia Nacional, 2011.

Cabrera Pérez-Armiñan, María Luisa. *Violencia e impunidad en comunidades mayas de Guatemala: La masacre de Xamán desde una perspectiva psicosocial.* Guatemala City: Equipo de Estudios Comunitarios y Accion Psicosocial, 2006.

Carlsen, Robert S. *The War for the Heart and Soul of a Highland Maya Town.* Austin: University of Texas Press, 1997.

Chase-Dunn, Christopher, Susanne Jonas, and Nelson Amaro, eds. *Globalization on the Ground: Postbellum Guatemalan Democracy and Development.* Lanham: Rowman & Littlefield, 2001.

Estrada Búcaro, Rossana Moguel Estrada, and Romeo Moguel Estrada, eds. *Voces de posguerra: Antología de poética de Guatemala.* Guatemala City: Fundación Guatemalteca para el Desarrollo del Arte, 2001.

García Noval, José. *Para entender la violencia: Falsas rutas y caminos truncados.* Guatemala City: Editorial Universitaria, 2008.

Goldman, Francisco. *The Art of Political Murder: Who Killed the Bishop?* New York: Grove Press, 2007.

Gómez Dupuis, Nieves. *Peritaje psicosocial por violaciones a los derechos humanos.* Guatemala City: ECAP, 2009.

González Palma, Luis. *Poems of Sorrow.* Santa Fe: Arena Editions, 1999.

Hernández Pico, Juan. *Terminar la guerra, traicionar la paz, Guatemala en las dos presidencias de la paz: Arzú y Portillo (1996–2004).* Guatemala City: FLACSO, 2005.

Hernández-Salazar, Daniel. *So That All Shall Know/Para que todos lo sepan.* Photographs by Daniel Hernández-Salazar. Edited by Oscar Iván Maldonado. Austin: University of Texas Press, 2007.

Jonas, Susanne. *Of Centaurs and Doves: Guatemala's Peace Process.* Boulder: Westview Press, 2000.

Manz, Beatriz, Elizabeth Oglesby, and José García Noval. *De la memoria a la reconstrucción histórica.* Guatemala City: AVANCSO, 1999.

McCleary, Rachel M. *Dictating Democracy: Guatemala and the End of Violent Revolution.* Gainesville: University Press of Florida, 1999.

Moller, Jonathan. *Our Culture Is Our Resistance: Repression, Refuge, and Healing in Guatemala.* Photographs by Jonathan Moller. Foreword by Rigoberta Menchú. New York: PowerHouse Books, 2004.

———, and Derrill Bazzy. *Rescatando nuestra memoria: Represión, refugio y recuperación de las poblaciones desarraigadas por la violencia en Guatemala.* Guatemala City: F&G Editores, 2009.

Nelson, Diane M. *Reckoning: The Ends of War in Guatemala.* Durham: Duke University Press, 2009.

North, Liisa L., and Alan B. Simmons, eds. *Journeys of Fear: Refugee Return and National Transformation in Guatemala.* Montreal: McGill-Queen's University Press, 2000.

Popkin, Margaret. *Civil Patrols and Their Legacy: Overcoming Militarization and Polarization in the Guatemalan Countryside.* Washington: Robert F. Kennedy Memorial Center for Human Rights, 1996.

Remijnse, Simone. *Memories of Violence: Civil Patrols and the Legacy of Conflict in Joyabaj, Guatemala.* Amsterdam: Rozenberg Publishers, 2002.

Rosada-Granados, Héctor. *El lado oculto de las negociaciones de paz: Transición de la guerra a la paz en Guatemala.* Guatemala City: Fundación Friedrich Ebert, 1998.

Sandoval, Miguel Angel, and Augusto Ríos. *La izquierda y la transición democrática.* Guatemala City: Editorial Oscar de León Palacios, 1997.

Sanford, Victoria. *Buried Secrets: Truth and Human Rights in Guatemala.* New York: Palgrave Macmillan, 2003.

Segovia, Alexander. *Modernización empresarial en Guatemala: Cambio real o nuevo discurso?* Guatemala City: F&G Editores, 2004.

Shillington, John. *Grappling with Atrocity: Guatemalan Theater in the 1990s.* Madison: Fairleigh Dickinson University Press, 2002.

Sieder, Rachel, ed. *Guatemala After the Peace Accords.* London: Institute of Latin American Studies, University of London, 1999.

Snodgrass, Angelina Godoy. *Popular Injustice: Violence, Community and Law in Latin America.* Palo Alto: Stanford University Press, 2006.

Taylor, Clark. *Return of Guatemala's Refugees: Reweaving the Torn.* Philadelphia: Temple University Press, 1998.

Trudeau, Robert. *Guatemalan Politics: The Popular Struggle for Democracy.* Boulder: Lynne Rienner, 1993.

Valdez, J. Fernando. *El ocaso de un liderazgo: Las élites empresariales tras un nuevo protagonismo.* Guatemala City: FLACSO, 2003.

———, and Myra Palencia Prado. *Los dominios del poder: La encrucijada tributaria.* Guatemala City: FLACSO, 1998.

Washington Office on Latin America. *Hidden Powers in Post-Conflict Guatemala.* Washington: Washington Office on Latin America, 2006.

Part VIII. Maya Movements

Arenas Bianchi, Clara, Charles R. Hale, and Gustavo Palma, eds. *Racismo en Guatemala? Abriendo debate sobre un tema tabú.* Guatemala City: AVANCSO, 1999.

Asociación de la Mujer Maya Ixil. *Voces e imágenes: Mujeres mayas ixiles de Chajul/Voices and Images: Mayan Ixil Women of Chajul.* Guatemala City: Magna Terra, 2000.

Barrios, Lina E. *Tras la huellas del poder local: La alcaldía indígena en Guatemala del siglo XVI al siglo XX.* Guatemala City: Universidad Rafael Landívar, Instituto de Investigaciones Económicas y Sociales, 2001.

Bastos, Santiago, and Manuela Camus. *Quebrando el silencio: Organizaciones del pueblo maya y sus demandas (1986–1992).* Guatemala City: FLACSO, 1993.

———. *Abriendo caminos: Las organizaciones mayas desde el Nobel hasta el acuerdo de derechos indígenas.* Guatemala City: FLACSO, 1995.

———. *Entre el mecapal y el cielo: Desarrollo del movimiento maya en Guatemala.* Guatemala City: FLACSO, 2003.

Camus, Manuela. *Ser indígena en ciudad de Guatemala.* Guatemala City: FLACSO, 2002.

Chirix García, Emma Delfina. *Alas y raíces: Afectividad de las mujeres mayas = Rik'in ruxik' y ruxe'il: ronojel kajoqab'al ri mayab' taq ixoqi'.* Guatemala City: Grupo de Mujeres Mayas Kaqla, 2003.

Fischer, Edward F. *Cultural Logics and Global Economics: Maya Identity in Thought and Practice.* Austin: University of Texas Press, 2001.

————, and R. McKenna Brown, eds. *Maya Cultural Activism in Guatemala*. Austin: University of Texas Press, 1996.

Gálvez, Víctor, Claudia Dary, Edgar Esquit, and Isabel Rodas. *Qué sociedad queremos? Una mirada desde el movimiento y las organizaciones mayas*. Guatemala City: FLACSO, 1997.

Grupo de Mujeres Mayas Kaqlá. *La palabra y el sentir de las mujeres mayas de Kaqlá*. Guatemala City: Grupo de Mujeres Mayas Kaqlá, 2006.

Hale, Charles R. *Más que un indio, More Than an Indian: Racial Ambivalence and Neoliberal Multiculturalism in Guatemala*. Santa Fe: School of American Research Press, 2006.

Hendrickson, Carol. *Weaving Identities: Construction of Dress and Self in a Highland Guatemala Town*. Austin: University of Texas Press, 1995.

Little, Walter E. *Mayas in the Marketplace: Tourism, Globalization and Cultural Identity*. Austin: University of Texas Press, 2004.

López Batzín, Marta Juana. *Enfoques teóricos políticos en el reconocimiento del sistema jurídico maya en Guatemala*. Guatemala City: Asociación Oxlajuj Ajpop, 2008.

Metz, Brent E. *Ch'orti'-Maya Survival in Eastern Guatemala: Indigeneity in Transition*. Albuquerque: University of New Mexico Press, 2006.

Montejo, Victor. *Maya Intellectual Renaissance: Identity, Representation and Leadership*. Austin: University of Texas Press, 2005.

Nelson, Diane M. *A Finger in the Wound: Body Politics in Quincentennial Guatemala*. Berkeley: University of California Press, 1999.

Ochoa García, Carlos. *Derecho consuetudinario y pluralismo jurídico*. Guatemala City: Cholsamaj, 2001.

Pedro Pitarch, Shannon Speed, and Xochitl Leyva Solano (editors), *Human Rights in the Maya Region*, Durham: Duke University Press, 2008.

Sacalxot, Martín. *Derecho maya como sistema jurídico (Maya' Ch'ojib'al)*. Guatemala City: Fundación CEDIM, 2008.

Sandoval, Miguel Ángel. *De Iximché a Iximché: El recorrido reciente de las luchas indígenas*. Cuadernos del Presente Imperfecto 7. Guatemala City: F&G Editores, 2008.

Sieder, Rachel, ed. *Multiculturalism in Latin America: Indigenous Rights, Diversity and Democracy*. New York: Palgrave Macmillan, 2002.

Turqui, Juliana Edith. *Trabajadores indígenas en la ciudad de Guatemala y el movimiento maya: Explorando la representación de demandas étnicas y laborales*. Guatemala City: University of San Carlos, 2006.

Velásquez Nimatuj, Irma Alicia. *Pueblos indígenas, estado y lucha por tierra en Guatemala: Estrategias de sobrevivencia y negociación ante la desigualdad globalizada*. Guatemala City: AVANCSO, 2008.

Warren, Kay B. *Indigenous Movements and Their Critics: Pan-Maya Activism in Guatemala*. Princeton: Princeton University Press, 1998.

Watanabe, John. *Maya Saints and Souls in a Changing World*. Austin: University of Texas Press, 1992.

Wilson, Richard. *Maya Resurgence in Guatemala: Q'eqchi' Experiences*. Norman: University of Oklahoma Press, 1995.

Part IX. The Sixth Century

Arenas, Clara, ed. *En el umbral: Explorando Guatemala en el inicio del siglo veintiuno*. Guatemala City: AVANCSO, 2007.

Bastos, Santiago, and Manuela Camus. *CONIC: 11 años de lucha por la madre tierra, la vida y la paz*. Guatemala City: Coordinadora Nacional Indígena y Campesina, 2003.

Berger, Susan A. *Guatemaltecas: The Women's Movement, 1986–2003*. Austin: University of Texas Press, 2006.

Camus, Manuela. *La sorpresita del norte: Migración internacional y comunidad en Huehuetenango*. Guatemala City: Centro de documentación de la Frontera Occidental de Guatemala, 2008.

Falla, Ricardo. *Alicia: Explorando la identidad de una joven maya*. Guatemala City: AVANCSO, 2005.

———. *Juventud de una comunidad maya: Ixcán, Guatemala*. Guatemala City: AVANCSO, 2006.

———. *Migración transnacional retornada: Juventud indígena de Zacualpa*. Guatemala City: AVANCSO, 2008.

Fischer, Edward F., and Peter Bensen. *Broccoli and Desire: Global Connections and Maya Struggles in Postwar Guatemala*. Palo Alto: Stanford University Press, 2006.

Foxen, Patricia. *In Search of Providence: Transnational Mayan Identities*. Nashville: Vanderbilt University Press, 2008.

García Noval, José. *Tras el sentido perdido de la medicina: Un ensayo a la luz de la ética sobre la desaparición del sujeto en el trabajo en salud*. Autores invitados 10. Guatemala City: AVANCSO, 2003.

Garrard-Burnett, Virginia. *Protestantism in Guatemala: Living in the New Jerusalem*. Austin: University of Texas Press, 1998.

Gellert, Gisela, and Silvia Irene Palma. *Precariedad urbana, desarrollo comunitario y mujeres en el area metropolitana de Guatemala*. Guatemala City: FLACSO, 1999.

Goldín, Liliana R. *Global Maya: Work and Ideology in Rural Guatemala*. Tucson: University of Arizona Press, 2008.

Grandia, Liza. *Tz'aptzooqeb': El despojo recurrente del pueblo Q'eqchi'*. Guatemala City: AVANCSO, 2009.

Hamilton, Nora, and Norma Stoltz Chinchilla. *Seeking Community in a Global City: Guatemalans and Salvadorans in Los Angeles*. Philadelphia: Temple University Press, 2001.

Hurtado Paz y Paz, Laura. *Dinámicas agrarias y reproducción campesina en la globalización: El caso de Alta Verapaz, 1970–2007*. Guatemala City: F&G Editores, 2008.

Levenson, Deborah T. *Por si mismos: Un estudio preliminar de las maras en la Ciudad de Guatemala*. 2nd ed. Guatemala City: AVANCSO, 2003.

Loucky, James, and Marilyn M. Moore. *The Maya Diaspora: Guatemalan Roots, New American Lives*. Philadelphia: Temple University Press, 2000.

Medina Lopez, Jorge Alberto. *La insoportable levedad del empleo: Informalidad y precariedad laboral: El caso del parque "la parroquia."* Guatemala City: FLACSO, 2007.

O'Neill, Kevin Lewis, and Kedron Thomas, eds. *Securing the City, Neoliberalism, Space
and Insecurity in Postwar Guatemala.* Durham: Duke University Press, 2011.

Piedrasanta Herrera, Ruth. *Los chuj: Unidad y rupturas en su espacio.* Guatemala City:
Armar Editores, 2009.

Solano, Luis. *Guatemala: Petróleo y minería en las entrañas del poder.* Guatemala City:
Inforpress Centroamericana, 2005.

Tierney, Nancy Leigh. *Robbed of Humanity: Lives of Guatemalan Street Children.* Saint
Paul: Pangaea, 1997.

Tobar Estrada, Anneliza. *Entre mundos ajenos: Encuentro de percepciones de jóvenes ex-
pandileros y acompañantes sobre la sociedad guatemalteca.* Guatemala City: FLACSO,
2007.

Films

AbUSed: The Postville Raid. Directed by Luis Argueta (United States). A documentary
about the arrest and deportation of more than one hundred Central Americans
from a meatpacking plant in Iowa. 2010 (English and Spanish).

Dark Light of Dawn. Directed by Edgardo Reyes (United States–Guatemala). This
documentary, commissioned by the Guatemalan Human Rights Comission, gives
an overview of the years of conflict and shows how the manipulation of political
power allowed repression to continue after civilians returned to power in 1986.
1987 (English and Spanish).

Dirty Secrets: Jennifer, Everardo and the CIA in Guatemala. Directed by Pat Goudvis
(United States). This documentnary illustrates the CIA's decades-long complicity in
Guatemalan state violence and human-rights violations through the story of one
woman's search for her husband. 1998 (English and Spanish).

Discovering Dominga. Directed by Patricia Flynn and Mary Jo McConahay (United
States). This startling documentary chronicles the extraordinary journey of
an Iowa housewife named Denese who finds her roots as Dominga in the war-
torn Maya village from which she was adopted as a child. 2003 (English and
Spanish).

El norte. Directed by Gregory Navas (United States). This Oscar-nominated classic
deals with both genocide and immigration as it tells of a Maya sister and brother
who leave war in Guatemala and travel with great difficulty—and without
documents—into an unwelcoming United States, where they make their lives. 1983
(English).

El silencio de Neto. Directed by Luis Argueta (Guatemala). This award-winning film
was Guatemala's first submission to the Academy Awards and the first Guatemala-
produced film to be distributed internationally. *El silencio de Neto* brilliantly captures Cold War politics within Guatemala through the lyric vision of a young boy
as he strives to fulfill his dreams. 1994 (Spanish).

Father Roy: Inside the School of the Assassins. Directed by Robert Richter (United States).
In telling the story of one priest's efforts to close the US Army's School of the

Americas in Georgia, this documentary shows how the United States has been involved in training repressive Latin American militaries, including Guatemala's. 1997 (English).

Goodbye Baby. Directed by Pat Goudvis (United States). Based on interviews, this documentary explores the many controversies around adoption in Guatemala. 2005 (Spanish and English).

If the Mango Tree Could Speak. Directed by Pat Goudvis (United States). This award-winning documentary intimately portrays ten boys and girls talking about war, peace, justice, identity, and friendship as they grew up in the midst of war in Guatemala and El Salvador. 1993 (Spanish and English).

La bodega. Directed by Ray Figueroa (Guatemala). A film about a brother's quest for retribution for the rape of his sister. 2009 (Spanish).

La isla. directed by Uli Stelzner (Guatemala). A hard-hitting documentary about the records of the "disappeared" in the archives of the national police. 2010 (Spanish).

Las cruces, poblado próximo. Directed by Rafael Rosal (Guatemala). An award-winning film that dramatizes the story of guerrillas and villagers confronting the military in the Guatemalan highlands. 2006 (Spanish).

Sacred Soil. Directed by Olivia Carrescia (United States). This short documentary follows Guatemalan forensic anthropologists as they recover bodies from mass graves and face state repression for their brave and invaluable work. 2009 (English and Spanish).

Todos Santos Cuchumatán: Report from a Guatemalan Village and *Todos Santos: The Survivors*. Both directed by Olivia Carrescia (United States). The first (1979) of these two documentaries describes the vibrant prewar life in the Mam village of Todos Santos. The second (1989) shows the village's wartime devastation as community members struggle to defend their lives and their culture. English, Spanish, and Mam.

When the Mountains Tremble. Directed by Tom Sigel and Pamela Yates (United States). This courageous, award-winning documentary tells of the war in the highlands and the history that led up to it. It includes an interview with the then-unknown Rigoberta Menchú. 1983 (English and Spanish).

Internet Resources

Archivo Histórico de la Policia Nacional (http://archivohistoricopn.org). This massive human rights documentation project is making available to the public the records of Guatemala's National Police, including material related to death squads and forced disappearances during the period of the armed conflict.

Arte y literatura de Guatemala (http://www.literaturaguatemalteca.org). This award-winning website has links to major Guatemalan literary and artistic works.

Arte maya (http://www.artemaya.com). This website provides an excellent introduction to major Maya painters.

Documigrante (http://documigrante.wordpress.com). This blog documents a Guatemalan migrant's journey north.

Guatemala page of the Latin American Network Information Center (http://lanic .utexas.edu/la/ca/guatemala), part of the Virtual Library of Latin American Studies, hosted by the University of Texas. The largest collection of Internet links to Guatemalan resources and organizations.

Guatemala Scholars Network (http://www.vanderbilt.edu/gsn), an organization of academics and professionals whose major research field is Guatemala. The Guatemala Scholars Network maintains resource lists and organizes panels and conferences on Guatemala.

Inforpress Centroamericana (http://www.inforpressca.com), a respected weekly bulletin of news and analysis on Guatemalan and Central American politics and economics. Inforpress also publishes an English-language edition, *Central America Report*.

Network in Solidarity with the People of Guatemala (http://www.nisgua.org/home .asp). This website's resource page (http://www.nisgua.org/resources/links.asp) has links to an extensive network of social-justice organizations both in Guatemala and abroad.

Research Centers and Libraries

Asociación para el Avance de las Ciencias Sociales (AVANCSO) (http://www.avancso .org.gt). AVANCSO, based in Guatemala City, is a respected research institute and publisher. AVANCSO is renowned for its multidisciplinary, collaborative investigations, and it works closely with social movements to offer holistic analysis and policy proposals related to political power, poverty, inequality, land tenure, violence, the environment, racism, and other pressing problems. As part of its original intellectual work, AVANCSO also investigates questions of subjectivities and social imaginaries.

Biblioteca César Brañas (http://bibliotecacesarbranas.blogspot.com). The César Brañas library, located in Guatemala City, contains a wide variety of books and ephemera related to Guatemala's literary history.

Centro de Investigaciones Regionales de Mesoamérica (CIRMA) (http://www.ama.edu .gt/cirma). Located in Antigua, Guatemala, CIRMA has Central America's largest library and photographic archive. It has an ever-growing historical archive, containing a diverse collection of holdings related to all aspects of Guatemalan history, particularly the armed conflict. CIRMA also runs undergraduate and graduate study-abroad programs focused on Central American history, anthropology, and social-justice issues.

Facultad Latinoamericana de Ciencias Sociales (FLACSO) (http://www.flacso.edu.gt). FLACSO Guatemala, in Guatemala City, is the Guatemala affiliate of the established Latin American social science research network.

Acknowledgment of Copyrights and Sources

Epigraph

"El Dinosaurio," by Augusto Monterroso, from *Obras completas (y otros cuentos)* (Mexico City: Imprenta Universitaria, 1959).

Part I. The Maya: Before the Europeans

"Popol vuh," by Anonymous, from *Popol Vuh: The Definitive Edition of the Mayan Book of the Dawn of Life and the Glories of Gods and Kings*, translated by Dennis Tedlock (New York: Simon & Schuster, 1996), 98–104. Translation © 1985, 1996 by Dennis Tedlock. Reprinted by permission of Simon & Schuster, Inc. All rights reserved.

"Breaking the Maya Code," by Michael D. Coe, previously published as "A Triumph of the Spirit," in *Archaeology*, September/October 1991, 39–44. Reprinted by permission of the author.

"Gendered Nobility," by Rosemary A. Joyce, from *Ancient Bodies, Ancient Lives* (New York: Thames & Hudson, 2008), 96–99, 103–106. Copyright 2008 by Rosemary A. Joyce. Reprinted by kind permission of Thames & Hudson Ltd., London.

"Rabinal Achí," by Anonymous, from *Rabinal Achí: A Mayan Drama of War and Sacrifice*, translated by Dennis Tedlock (New York: Oxford University Press, 2003), 119–24. Translation © 2003 by Dennis Tedlock. Reprinted by permission of Oxford University Press.

"Apocalypto," by Bruno Waterfield, previously published as "Dutch Prepare for Maya Apocalypse," in *The Telegraph* (London), June 25, 2008. Copyright Telegraph Media Group Limited 2008.

Part II. Invasion and Colonialism

"Invading Guatemala," by various authors, from *Invading Guatemala: Spanish, Nahua and Maya Accounts of the Conquest Wars*, edited by Matthew Restall and Florine Asselbergs (University Park: Penn State Press, 2007), 27–35, 104–110.

"Tecún Umán and the Conquest Dance," by Irma Otzoy, adapted from "'Tekum Umam: From Nationalism to Maya Resistance," PhD dissertation, University of California, Davis, 1999. Used by permission of Irma Otzoy.

"Great Was the Stench of the Dead," by W. George Lovell, from *Conquest and Survival in Colonial Guatemala: A Historical Geography of the Cuchumatán Highlands, 1500–1821,*

Part III. A Caffeinated Modernism

"The Saddest Day in Cantel," by Anonymous, from the unpublished and undated manuscripts "El día más triste de la historia de Cantel" and "Narración del fusilamiento de los cinco mártires del día 4 de septiembre de 1884," found in the Municipal Office of Cantel. Translation © 2011 Kirsten Weld. Mimeograph in Greg Grandin's possession.

"The Ladino," by Severo Martínez Peláez, from *Guatemala, seminario estado, clases sociales y cuestión etnico-nacional* (Mexico City: Centro de Estudios Integrados de Desarrollo Comunal, 1992), 122–28. Translation © 2011 Deborah T. Levenson.

"Accustomed to Be Obedient," by Richard N. Adams, adapted from *Etnicidad en el ejército de la Guatemala liberal (1870–1915)* (Guatemala City: Facultad Latinoamericana de Ciencias Sociales [FLACSO], 1995). Used by permission of the author.

"Conquest of the Tropics," by Frederick U. Adams, from *The Conquest of the Tropics.* Vol. 1 of *The Romance of Big Business* (Garden City: Doubleday, Page and Co., 1914), 194–219.

"Marimba," by Arturo Taracena Arriola, previously published as "La marimba: un instrumento nacional," in *Tradiciones de Guatemala: Revista del Centro de Estudios Folkóricos* (Guatemala City: Universidad de San Carlos, 1980), no. 13, 1–15. Translation © 2011 Kirsten Weld. Used by permission of the author.

"¿Vos sos de Guatemala?" by the Proyecto Lingüístico Quetzalteco de Español, originally published as *El voseo en América Central* (Quetzaltenango, Guatemala: Proyecto Lingüístico Quetzalteco de Español, 2007), 14–18; 29–43. Translation © 2011 Kirsten Weld. Used by permission of Carlos Sánchez/Proyecto Lingüístico Quetzalteco de Español.

"A Taste of History," popular Guatemalan recipes. Collected by the editors.

"Magical Modernism," by Catherine Rendón, previously published as "Temples of Tribute and Illusion," in *Américas*, July–August 2002, 16–23. Reprinted with permission by *Américas*.

"El señor presidente," by Miguel Angel Asturias, from *El Señor Presidente*, translated by Frances Partridge (New York: Atheneum, 1983), 7–11. Used by permission of Victor Gollancz, an imprint of The Orion Publishing Group, London.

"La chalana," by Miguel Angel Asturias, Alfredo Valle Calvo, David Vela, and José Luis Barcárcel, first published in *No nos tientes*, April 7, 1922. Text and facsimile published in *Viernes de dolores: Edición crítica de las obras completas de Miguel Angel Asturias*, by Miguel Angel Asturias, edited by Claude Couffon and Iber H. Verdugo (Paris: Editions Klincksieck, 1978), 13:81–83. Translation © 2011 Greg Grandin.

"A Mexican Bolshevik in Central America," by Carlos Figueroa Ibarra, previously published as "El 'bolchevique mexicano' de la Centroamérica de los veinte," in *Memoria*, September–October 1990, 213–25. Translation © 2011 Kirsten Weld. Used by permission of *Memoria*.

"Anthropology Discovers the Maya," by Carol A. Smith, adapted and expanded by the author from her essay, "Interpretaciones Norteamericanas sobre la raza y el racismo en Guatemala: Una genealogía crítica," in *Racismo en Guatemala? Abriendo el debate sobre un tema tabú*, edited by Clara Arenas Bianchi, Charles R. Hale, and Gustavo Palma Murga (Guatemala City: Asociación para el Avance de las Ciencias Sociales [AVANCSO], 1999), 93–126. Used by permission of Clara Arenas.

Part V. Roads to Revolution

"Campesinos in Search of a Different Future," by José Manuel Fernández y Fernández, from *El Comité de Unidad Campesina: Orígen y desarrollo* (Guatemala City: Centro de Estudios Rurales Centroamericanos, 1988), 3–20. Translation © 2011 Deborah T. Levenson. Reprinted by permission of José Manuel Fernández y Fernández.

"Execution of a Chicken," by Manuel José Arce, from the introduction to *De una ciudad y otros asuntos: Crónica fidigna* (Guatemala City: Ministerio de Cultura y Deportes, 1992), n.p., and from *Delito, condena y ejecución de una gallina y otras piezas de teatro grotesco* (Guatemala City: Ministerio de Cultura y Deportes, 2004), 1:88–101. Translation © 2011 Deborah T. Levenson and Greg Grandin.

"Blood in Our Throats," by Betsy Konefal, adapted from "'May All Rise Up': Highland Mobilization in Post-1954 Guatemala," PhD dissertation, University of Pittsburgh, 2005. Used by permission of Betsy Konefal.

"Guerrilla Armies of the Poor," by various authors, originally published in *Opinión Comunista*, December 1976, 9–16. The selection includes excerpts from the following sources: "Internal Document," by the Ejército Guerrillero de los Pobres, from "Materiales de formación política, línea de masa del EGP durante la guerra popular revolucionaria," 1978, in the Colección Payeras-Colom at CIRMA; *La siembra*, by the Organización Revolucionaria del Pueblo en Armas, 1980, mimeograph in Deborah Levenson's possesion; "Saludos de las organizaciones revolucionarias," by the Unidad Revolucionaria Nacional Guatemalteca, 1982, mimeograph in Deborah T. Levenson's possession. Translation © 2011 Deborah T. Levenson.

"We Rose Up," by Juan Tuyuc, Yolanda Colom, and Lucia. "Juan Tuyuc," from an interview with Juan Tuyuc by Deborah T. Levenson, October 3, 2005, transcript in Levenson's possession; "Yolanda Colom," from *Nuestras utopías: Mujeres guatemaltecas del siglo XX*, by Norma Stoltz Chincilla (Guatemala City: Terra Viva, 1998), 233–66, used by permission of Norma Stoltz Chincilla; "Lucia," from *Memorias rebeldes contra el olvido*, eds. Rosalinda Hernández Alarcón, Andrea Carrillo Samayoa, Jacqueline Torres Urízar, Ana López Molina, and Ligia Z. Peláez Aldana (Guatemala City: Ediciones la Cuerda, AVANCSO, and Plataforma Agraria, 2008), 73–102. Used by permission of AVANCSO. All translations © 2011 Deborah T. Levenson.

"Communiqué," by Otto René Castillo, originally published as "Comunicado," in *Poemas* (Havana: Casa de Las Américas, 1971), 34. Translation © 2011 Deborah T. Levenson.

"Declaration of Iximché," by various authors, originally titled "Declaración de Iximché," February 1980. Mimeograph in Elizabeth Oglesby's possession. Translation © 2011 Elizabeth Oglesby.

"An Indian Dawn," by Carlota McAllister, written exclusively for *The Guatemala Reader*.

Part VI. Intent to Destroy

"Thunder in the City," by Mario Payeras, from *El trueno en la ciudad: Episodios de la lucha armada urbana de 1981 en Guatemala* (Mexico City: Juan Pablos Editor, S.A., 1987), 65–90. Translation © 2011 Elizabeth Oglesby. Used by permission of Juan Pablos Editor, S.A.

"The San Francisco Massacre, July 1982," by Ricardo Falla, originally published as "The Massacre at the Rural Estate of San Francisco, July 1982," in *Cultural Survival Quarterly* (Spring 1983), 43–44. Reprinted by permission of *Cultural Survival Quarterly*.

"Guatemala: What Next?" by Robert L. Jacobs, US Department of State, Bureau of Humanitarian Affairs and Human Rights, from a memo dated October 5, 1981, titled "Guatemala: What Next?" "We Cannot Confirm Nor Deny," by anonymous US Department of State officials, from confidential cables titled "Embassy Attempt to Verify Alleged Massacres in Huehuetenango," October 21, 1982, and "Analysis of Human Rights Reports on Guatemala by Amnesty International, WOLA/NISGUA, and Guatemala Human Rights Commission," October 22, 1982. Declassified documents from the National Security Archive Guatemala Documentation Project. Available at http://www.gwu.edu/~nsarchiv/latin_america/guatemala.html. Accessed December 27, 2009.

"Acts of Genocide," by the Comisión para el Esclarecimiento Histórico, from *Memoria del silencio* (Guatemala City: United Nations Office of Project Services, 1999), 3:314–423, paragraphs 3198–3215 and 3581–3606. Translation © 2011 Elizabeth Oglesby. The entire Comisión para el Esclarecimiento Histórico report is available in Spanish at http://shr.aaas.org/guatemala/ceh/mds/spanish/. Accessed December 27, 2009.

"The Refugee Exodus," by Victor Montejo, from *Voices from Exile: Violence and Survival in Modern Maya History* (Norman: University of Oklahoma Press, 1999), 108–118, 125–31, 133–43. Copyright © 1999 by the University of Oklahoma Press, Norman. Reprinted by permission of University of Oklahoma Press.

"The Oil Lamp," by Antonio L. Cota García, from *Voices from Exile: Violence and Survival in Modern Mayan History*, edited by Victor Montejo (Norman: University of Oklahoma Press, 1999), 214–15. Copyright © 1999 by the University of Oklahoma Press, Norman. Reprinted by permission of University of Oklahoma Press.

"Arbitrary Power and Sexual Violence," by Matilde González Izás, from *Se cambió el tiempo: Conflicto y poder en territorio k'iche'* (Guatemala City: AVANCSO, 2002), 405–24. Translation © 2011 Elizabeth Oglesby. Used by permission of AVANCSO.

"Surviving," by the Human Rights Office of the Archbishop of Guatemala, from *Guatemala: Nunca más* (Guatemala City: Oficina de Derechos Humanos del Arzobispado de Guatemala, Proyecto Interdiocesano de Recuperación de la Memoria Histórica, 1998), 1:169–98. Translation © 2011 Elizabeth Oglesby. Used by permission of the Human Rights Office of the Archbishop of Guatemala.

"Inverting Clausewitz," speeches by Colonel Mario René Enríquez Morales and General Héctor Alejandro Gramajo Morales, from the forum Twenty-Seven Years Fighting for Liberty, Guatemala City, August 12, 1987. Reprinted from *Guatemala 1986–1994: Compendio del proceso de paz, cronologías, análisis, documentos, acuerdos* (Guatemala City: Inforpress Centroamericana, 1995), 327–29. Translation © 2011 Elizabeth Oglesby. Used by permission of Inforpress.

"Assistance and Control," by Myrna Mack, from *Assistance and Control: Policies toward Internally Displaced Populations in Guatemala*, translated by the author and the Hemispheric Migration Project (Washington: Center for Immigration Policy and Refugee Assistance, Georgetown University, 1990), 11–27.

Part VII. An Unsettled Peace

"Filochofo," by José Manuel Chacón, from *La otra historia: de los Mayas al informe de la comision de la verdad* (Guatemala City: published by author, 1999), 185; *En el año de la paz, no firme, pero bien firmada* (Guatemala City: published by author, 1997), 84–85. Reproduced by permission of José Manuel Chacón.

"Art and the Postwar Generation," by Anabella Acevedo, from "Marginalidades, transgresiones, y negocaciones: La violencia en Guatemala através de las prácticas culturales de los jovenes" (unpublished manuscript in Elizabeth Oglesby's possession). Translation © 2011 Deborah T. Levenson and Elizabeth Oglesby. Used by permission of Anabella Acevedo.

"I Walk Backwards," by Humberto Ak'abal, originally published as "Tz'olq'omin b'e," in *Tejedor de palabras* (Guatemala City: Cholsamaj Fundacion, 2001), 21. Translation © 2011 Deborah T. Levenson. Used by permission of Humberto Ak'abal.

Part VIII. Maya Movements

"The Kí-chè Language," by Adrián Inés Chávez, from *El idioma Kí-chè y su ortografía,* 2nd ed. (Quetzaltenango, Guatemala, 1966), 1–4, 15, 27. Translation © 2011 Greg Grandin.

"Our History Is a Living History," by Rigoberta Menchú, from her untitled Nobel Peace Prize acceptance speech. Published in *Les Prix Nobel: The Nobel Prizes 1992,* edited by Tore Frängsmyr (Stockholm: Nobel Foundation, 1993), 157–87. Translated by Greg Grandin. English and Spanish versions available at: http://nobelprize.org/nobel_prizes/peace/laureates/1992/tum-lecture.html © The Nobel Foundation 1992. Used by permission.

"The Pan-Maya Movement," by Demetrio Cojtí Cuxil, from *El movimiento Maya* (Guatemala City: Cholsamaj Fundación, 1997), 67–72. Translation © 2011 Greg Grandin. Used by permission of Demetrio Cojtí Cuxil.

"The Authorized Indian," by Charles R. Hale, originally published as "Rethinking Indigenous Politics in the Era of the 'Indio Permitido,'" in *NACLA Report on the Americas* 38, no. 2 (September/October 2004), 16–21. Reprinted by permission of Charles R. Hale and the *NACLA Report on the Americas;* copyright 2004 by the North American Congress on Latin America, 38 Greene St., 4th Floor, New York 10013.

"Transnationalism and Maya Dress," by Irma Alicia Velásquez Nimatuj, originally published in *Global Security and Cooperation Quarterly Newsletter,* Spring 2003. Reprinted by permission of the Social Science Research Council.

"Mayanization and Everyday Life," by Santiago Bastos, Aura Cumes, and Leslie Lemus, from *Mayanización y vida cotidiana: Textos para el debate,* edited by Santiago Bastos, Aura Cumes, and Leslie Lemus (Guatemala City: FLACSO, CIRMA, Cholsamaj Fundación, 2007), 32–53. Translation © 2011 Elizabeth Oglesby. Used by permission of Santiago Bastos, Aura Cumes, and Leslie Lemus.

"Solidarity Is a Characteristic of the Maya People," from an interview with Dominga Vásquez by Simona Violetta Yagenova, from "Los pueblos indígenas frente a la minería de cielo abierto: El caso de Sololá," by Simona Violetta Yagenova, in *Guatemala: Aproximación a los movimientos del año 2005: Observatorio de movimientos, demandas y acción colectiva,* edited by Simona Violetta Yagenova (Guatemala City:

Part IX. The Sixth Century

Index